Beyond Labels

Navigating Gender, Sexuality, Identity, and Belonging in the LGBTQ+ Community

By

Bernadette Horn

Disclaimer: This book is a work of nonfiction. Every reasonable effort has been made to ensure the accuracy of the information provided. However, the author is not responsible for any errors, omissions, or outcomes resulting from the use of this material. Throughout this book, various organizations, services and resources are mentioned for informational purposes only. Their inclusion does not constitute an endorsement by the author, nor does it imply any formal relationship, affiliation, or sponsorship. Readers are encouraged to independently research these organizations, verify their services and consult qualified professionals when seeking advice or support. This work is intended as a resource for personal, educational and community use. It aims to inform, provoke thought and inspire compassionate reflection. It is not a substitute for professional legal, medical, psychological, or financial guidance. The views expressed are those of the author and do not necessarily reflect those of any individuals or organizations mentioned.

Trigger Warning: Some chapters address sensitive topics, including trauma, discrimination, abuse and mental health struggles. Reader discretion is advised.

For permissions or inquiries, contact the author at: admin@bernadettehorn.com

Published by: Bernadette Horn
(Self-Published)

ISBN: 978-1-0370-7712-8

First Edition: 2025

Cover design by: Marthie de Wet

Printed in the United Kingdom

Dedication

To my life partner, your unwavering love, your quiet strength and your fierce support, have been my compass and my calm. This book would not exist without your steadfast presence. You are my home.

To those who refuse to be defined by labels, who navigate love, identity and existence on their own terms and to the countless LGBTQ+ voices, past, present and future, whose courage, resilience and authenticity inspire change.

May this book stand as a tribute to your strength, your journey and the transformative power of living beyond society's expectations.

You are seen. You are heard. You are never alone.

Let this be a beacon, like the Lambda (λ), a symbol once reclaimed in defiance and pride, reminding us that the future is not just something we inherit, but something we create. Free from limitations. Full of boundless possibilities. λ For liberation, for love, for all of us.

About the Author

Bernadette Horn writes to spark the conversations that are too often left in the margins. With Beyond Labels, she offers readers a deeply reflective and wide-ranging exploration of LGBTQ+ life, not a memoir, but a textured, multi-dimensional journey through the lived realities, questions and complexities that define queer existence today.

Across thirty chapters, Bernadette weaves together cultural critique, emotional truth and community insight. She navigates the evolution of queer love and relationship structures, the nuances of gender identity, the emotional impact of hormone therapy and the enduring power of intergenerational storytelling. Her work moves from the personal to the political, from the science of attraction to the philosophy of drag and from grief and ghosting to climate change and artificial intelligence, always with an eye on what it means to belong, resist and reimagine in a heteronormative world.

Rather than offering definitive answers, Bernadette creates space, for contradiction, for curiosity and for quiet truths. Whether unpacking the role of chosen family, exploring the intersection of queerness and disability, or considering the psychological toll of exile and erasure, her voice remains empathetic, probing and accessible. Each chapter reflects her commitment to honouring nuance and holding space for lived experience without flattening it into simplicity.

Bernadette doesn't write from a place of authority, she writes from a place of invitation. She asks us not only to listen, but to feel and reflect. Her approach celebrates queer identity as fluid, relational and resilient, something that defies reduction and instead demands deeper understanding.

Beyond Labels is not just a book, it's a conversation, a mirror, and a call to reimagine how we see one another and ourselves.

A Note on Terminology:

In this book, the term Queer is used as an inclusive and expansive umbrella term. It is a label that many individuals in the LGBTQ+ community embrace to describe a broad spectrum of sexual orientations, gender identities and lived experiences that fall outside cisnormative and heteronormative expectations.

While Queer has a complex and sometimes painful history, it has also been reclaimed by many as a term of empowerment, defiance and connection. That said, not everyone is comfortable with, or chooses to use this label, and that choice is deeply personal and valid.

Language evolves, and so do the ways we name ourselves. This book acknowledges and respects the diversity of identities within the LGBTQ+ community and it uses Queer as a unifying term while honouring the individuality and self-determination of all people. Everyone's journey of identity, love and belonging is unique, and each deserves to be seen, heard and valued.

Contents

Introduction – Breaking Free from Labels

1. Why LGBTQ+ Narratives Need More Depth

In recent years, the visibility of LGBTQ+ identities in media and public discourse has undeniably grown. From mainstream TV and books to global campaigns, queer characters and storylines are no longer rare. On the surface, this seems like progress, representation where there was once erasure. But beneath the surface lies a deeper question: What kind of representation are we really getting?

Representation only becomes meaningful when it reflects the complexity of real lives. A gay best friend in a sitcom or a trans side character isn't the same as a fully realized queer narrative. Visibility without depth risks caricature, tokenism, or repetition. When media recycles the same coming-out storylines or trauma arcs, LGBTQ+ identities get flattened into single-note narratives.

Many queer individuals are tired of seeing themselves portrayed only through struggle. While hardship exists, it's not the whole story. LGBTQ+ life is vast, it includes joy, boredom, family, work, curiosity, contradictions and the ordinary. Yet many mainstream portrayals fall short, preferring safe, familiar narratives over fresh, complex ones.

Often, queer characters are defined only by their queerness. Identity becomes a plot twist, a challenge, or a reveal, rather than a natural aspect of a full life. Rarely do we see queer characters allowed the same emotional range, personal growth, or everyday reality as cisgender, straight characters. Where are the scenes of making dinner, dealing with aging parents, or navigating a mid-career slump?

When depth is present, it's often in indie films, web series, or lesser-known books, works by LGBTQ+ creators who bring authenticity and a lived perspective. These storytellers explore unscripted relationships, fluid identities, and the tension between visibility and privacy. These quieter stories matter. They don't shout, but they stay with you.

Intersectionality adds another layer. LGBTQ+ stories aren't just about gender or sexuality, they intersect with race, disability, class, religion, neurodivergence, and location. A Black lesbian in a rural town doesn't live the same reality as a white gay man in a big city, yet both might be filed under the same umbrella. Without showing these layers, we lose the rich texture of queer life.

It's not just about adding more characters, it's about complicating them. Queer people, like all people, contain contradictions. They change their minds, hold messy opinions, and make mistakes. Some long for marriage, others reject it. Some want children, others don't. Some crave community, others solitude. Real depth embraces imperfection and complexity.

We also need stories beyond the formative years. Coming out is powerful, but it's only a chapter. What happens after? After the first protest, the first kiss, the first heartbreak? Our narratives must expand to reflect the full spectrum of queer existence, not just its beginnings.

Where are the stories about aging, caretaking, midlife crises, retirement, or long-term queer love? LGBTQ+ lives are long and layered and our stories should be too.

Joy is often overlooked. Queer joy isn't a cute counter to queer pain, it's a force. It's the joy of chosen family, drag shows, safety, and love. Too many stories lean on trauma to gain legitimacy. But joy is just as honest, just as necessary. Its absence leaves an incomplete picture.

To deepen LGBTQ+ narratives, we must also shift who tells them. Authorship matters. When queer stories are filtered through a straight lens, they lose resonance. Elevating LGBTQ+ writers, filmmakers, and creators isn't just about equity, it's about truth. A story hits differently when it's told by someone who has lived it.

There's a growing hunger, not just for visibility, but for resonance. People want to see themselves reflected in their contradictions, softness, humour, fears, and quiet truths. They want to feel seen, not simply acknowledged.

This is about moving from recognition to understanding. Representation isn't a checkbox, it's a bridge between lives and empathy. Depth invites us to cross that bridge, to see queer lives not as novelty or exception, but as wholly human stories.

To do this, we must go beyond labels. We must ask better questions. Make room for silence, ambiguity, growth. We must capture the private, the in-between, the small moments that make up real lives. Because when we do, we don't just change the story. We change what it means to be fully seen.

2. The Limitations of Representation in Media within the LGBTQ+ Community

Representation matters, but not all representation is created equal. Over the years, the visibility of LGBTQ+ characters and narratives in mainstream media has increased, a shift that many hail as progress. And it is. But visibility alone does not guarantee justice. As the LGBTQ+ community continues to navigate a rapidly evolving media landscape, one truth becomes clear, representation without depth can often be just as damaging as invisibility.

For decades, media portrayals of queer people were either non-existent or overwhelmingly negative, villains, punchlines, or tragedies. The queer-coded villain, the predatory queer trope, the lonely, doomed gay man or the hypersexualized lesbian, all served to reinforce societal discomfort with queerness. Today, those depictions are slowly giving way to more palatable images, the gay best friend, the quirky trans sidekick, the bi character who's perpetually "figuring things out." But even these seemingly positive shifts often fall short. Why? Because they tend to flatten queer identity into a handful of digestible archetypes.

Representation, when reduced to tired stereotypes or shallow tokenistic inclusion, does more to comfort mainstream audiences than it does to reflect the lives of LGBTQ+ people.

The presence of a single queer character in an ensemble cast is often considered a win, even if that character is poorly written, lacks agency, or exists only in relation to others. Tokenism is not representation. It is a form of narrative check-boxing, one that allows creators to appear inclusive without doing the work of crafting fully realized queer stories.

This limitation stems, in part, from who gets to tell these stories. Historically, media production has been dominated by cisgender, heterosexual creators. When queer stories are filtered through lenses that are not intimately familiar with queer experiences, the result is often a reliance on clichés, assumptions and overgeneralization. Even well-meaning allies can fall into the trap of centering narratives around struggle, coming out, or trauma, important elements, yes, but not the entirety of queer life.

This "trauma-centric" approach to LGBTQ+ storytelling, while rooted in reality, has become overrepresented. Coming out narratives, while once revolutionary, are now ubiquitous. They often present queerness as a challenge to be overcome, a deviation from the norm that requires justification. What gets lost in this singular framing is the joy, humour, complexity and mundanity of queer lives. Where are the stories about queer people simply existing? Where are the narratives about queer friendship, elderly queer love, queer ambition, or queer mediocrity?

Furthermore, media representations often exclude or misrepresent the most marginalized within the LGBTQ+ umbrella. Trans, non-binary, intersex, disabled, Black, Indigenous and other queer people of colour are routinely sidelined. Their stories, when told, are frequently distorted by cultural misunderstanding or reduced to their trauma. There is a deep need for intersectional narratives that acknowledge how race, gender, class and ability, shape queer experiences.

And yet, there is hope. Independent creators, particularly those from within the LGBTQ+ community, are reshaping what representation can look like. Web series, indie films, podcasts and literature are offering a broader spectrum of queer identity, messy, joyful, complicated and real. Shows like Pose, with its predominantly trans and Black cast, challenge the industry to do better. Creators like Janet Mock, Angelica Ross, and others, are pushing for not just inclusion, but creative control.

Social media has also provided a platform for queer voices long excluded from mainstream spaces. TikTok, YouTube and Instagram have become hubs of queer creativity and self-expression, often fostering more authentic portrayals than television ever could. Here, representation is not bound by gatekeepers, but driven by community.

Still, these victories are often on the margins, and they highlight just how much work remains. We need more queer writers in writers' rooms, more queer directors behind the camera, more queer producers at the helm of studios. We need to move beyond diversity as an aesthetic and embrace it as a value. Representation must be rooted in the reality of lived experiences, not constructed to appeal to market trends or corporate branding opportunities. Rainbow capitalism, the corporate appropriation of LGBTQ+ symbols during Pride Month, is another dimension of shallow representation. It reduces identity to a seasonal aesthetic rather than a lived reality.

Companies that paint their logos in rainbow colours while contributing to anti-LGBTQ+ legislation or ignoring the voices of queer employees offer a veneer of inclusion without substance. Visibility in marketing cannot replace structural support or honest storytelling.

It's not just about being seen, it's about being seen truthfully. A well-rounded queer character doesn't need to be flawless or inspirational. They need to be human. Flawed, funny, confused, certain, awkward, brilliant, queer people are all of this and more. The goal is not perfection but authenticity. Representation should reflect the community in all its contradictions and colour.

As audiences, we have a role to play too. We must seek out and support queer creators. We must critique what's lacking while celebrating what's done right. We must hold media accountable, not just for including us, but for representing us well.

In the end, true representation is not a trend or a milestone, it's an ongoing process. It evolves as communities evolve, as understanding deepens, as new voices emerge. And while media alone cannot fix systemic injustice, it can shape the way we see each other and ourselves. It can offer a mirror where there was once only a void.

So let this be a call, not just for more representation, but for better representation. Let us demand stories that honour the full spectrum of LGBTQ+ life, stories that do not reduce but reveal, that do not tokenize but humanize. In telling richer, truer queer stories, we move closer to a world where everyone can find themselves reflected, beautifully and without compromise.

3. The Impact of Language on LGBTQ+ Identity

Language is more than a tool of communication, it is a vessel of culture, a mirror of power structures, and an architect of identity. Within the LGBTQ+ community, language has long played a dual role, it has been both a means of empowerment and a mechanism of limitation. As society continues to evolve, so too does the language we use to describe ourselves and each other.

However, the complexity of this evolution underscores a central truth, language does not simply reflect identity, it actively shapes it. Understanding the impact of language on LGBTQ+ identity requires an examination of its power to affirm, its tendency to constrain, and its potential to transform.

At its most empowering, language gives name to experiences that might otherwise remain invisible. The coining and popularization of terms like "non-binary," "genderqueer," "asexual," and "pansexual" have offered individuals the tools to articulate parts of themselves that mainstream language often failed to capture.

This act of naming is not trivial, it is foundational. To name an identity is to validate it, to assert its existence and to claim space within a world that often denies or erases queer experiences. For many, discovering the right words can feel like finding a mirror for the first time, an encounter with self-recognition and belonging.

Language also fosters community. Shared terms and expressions create a sense of collective identity and solidarity. Phrases like "chosen family" or "coming out" carry weight not just because of their definitions, but because of the emotional and historical resonance they hold within the LGBTQ+ experience.

Slang and coded language, such as Polari in mid-20th century Britain or ballroom vernacular in Black and Latinx queer communities, have historically served as lifelines, ways to communicate safely, to bond and to resist oppression. These linguistic cultures are acts of resilience, carving out space in hostile environments.

Yet, as much as language can liberate, it can also confine. Identity labels, while useful, often come with rigid definitions and social expectations. A person who identifies as bisexual, for instance, may encounter scepticism or be pressured to "prove" their attraction to multiple genders. Similarly, transgender individuals might find their identities flattened by reductive understandings of gender that language has not yet evolved to fully express. The act of labelling can inadvertently enforce binaries, foster gatekeeping, and exclude those who do not fit neatly into predefined categories.

The limitations of language are particularly apparent when it comes to gender. Most languages are built upon binary grammatical structures, reinforcing the notion that gender exists only in two fixed forms. For non-binary, genderfluid, and agender individuals, this creates a daily struggle for recognition. In English, the singular "they" has gained traction as a gender-neutral pronoun, but resistance remains, both grammatically and ideologically. In languages with gendered nouns and pronouns, such as Spanish or French, the challenge of inclusivity is even more pronounced. While activists have proposed inclusive alternatives (e.g., "Latinx,"), these innovations often meet with institutional resistance or linguistic purism.

Furthermore, the language of legal and medical institutions continues to lag behind lived experiences. Official forms, identification documents, and healthcare systems frequently rely on outdated or binary gender classifications, forcing individuals to choose between misrepresentation and erasure. This disconnect between institutional language and personal identity has tangible consequences, from denied services to invalidated personhood. The impact is not just semantic, it is material and psychological.

Despite these constraints, there is undeniable power in linguistic innovation. Queer communities have consistently and creatively reimagined language to better reflect the nuances of their lived realities. The rise of neopronouns, the reclamation of formerly derogatory terms, and the creation of entirely new vocabularies, signal a dynamic relationship between language and identity. These evolutions are often grassroots and community-led, highlighting the role of lived experience in shaping linguistic change.

The personal nature of language cannot be overstated. The words we use to describe ourselves are deeply tied to our sense of self. They are intimate declarations, political assertions and emotional lifelines. When someone finds a term that fits, whether it's "genderqueer," "demisexual," or simply "queer", it can be transformative.

Conversely, when language fails us, when it misgenders, erases, or boxes us in, it wounds. It is in these moments that we see most clearly the stakes of linguistic representation. The internet and social media have accelerated the evolution of queer language.

Online spaces provide platforms for marginalized voices to share, adapt, and challenge language in real time. Hashtags, memes, and discussion threads, have become tools of both education and identity formation.

This democratization of language allows for greater nuance and diversity, but also surfaces tensions around appropriation, exclusion, and authenticity. The pace of change can be overwhelming, but it also speaks to the vitality of language as a living, breathing force.

Ultimately, the impact of language on LGBTQ+ identity lies in its dual capacity, to both liberate and limit. It offers visibility, community, and self-expression, while also reflecting societal biases and institutional inertia. Navigating this terrain requires a constant balancing act, between clarity and complexity, between naming and openness, between standardization and fluidity.

As we move forward, it is crucial to remain critically engaged with the words we use and the systems that shape them. Language must be treated as a tool that evolves alongside our understanding, not a static structure that dictates who we are. This means making space for new expressions, challenging outdated norms, and listening to those whose experiences language still fails to capture.

In the end, language is not the final word on identity, but it is often the first. And in the LGBTQ+ community, where visibility and voice have long been hard-won, every word counts.

4. Moving Beyond Stereotypes in the Queer Experience

Stereotypes are seductive in their simplicity. They offer digestible narratives about identity, suggesting that a few overused tropes can explain the breadth of a community's existence. For the LGBTQ+ community, these tropes, whether it’s the flamboyant gay best friend, the tragic trans figure, or the hypersexualized bisexual, have long shaped public perception.

While some of these depictions might arise from fragments of lived realities, they flatten rather than deepen our understanding. In moving beyond stereotypes, we must reframe how we think about queer lives, not as caricatures, but as rich, diverse and deeply human.

At the heart of this problem is the tension between visibility and accuracy. Representation has improved, but many of the images that circulate in mainstream media and public discourse remain limited. The very act of being “seen” can be a double-edged sword when the lens through which we are viewed distorts us. Visibility that centres on stereotypes often does more harm than good, it keeps people locked in expectations that feel alien to their true selves.

Stereotypes, by definition, rely on repetition and familiarity. They are cognitive shortcuts, easy ways for society to “know” a group without actually engaging with its complexity.

In the queer context, they range from the benign to the deeply damaging. Lesbian women are often portrayed as either hypermasculine or fetishized. Gay men are expected to be fashionable, effeminate, and comic relief. Trans and nonbinary people are frequently tokenized, misunderstood, or framed through the lens of transition alone.

These portrayals become both cultural artifacts and social pressures, templates individuals feel they must adhere to in order to be recognized as valid or "authentically" queer.

The impact of this is both internal and external. Internally, queer individuals may find themselves policing their own identities, feeling as though they are "not queer enough" if they don't match popular images.

For those still coming to terms with their identity, this can create confusion and shame. Externally, society treats LGBTQ+ people through these assumptions, expecting behaviour, appearance, or language that aligns with preconceived notions rather than personal truth. It affects relationships, employment, healthcare, and broader participation in public life.

Stereotypes also disproportionately affect those at the intersections of multiple identities. Queer people of colour, queer people with disabilities, older queer individuals and those from rural or religious backgrounds, are often left entirely out of the dominant narrative. Their stories don't fit the mold, so they are erased or misunderstood. This marginalization within an already marginalized community deepens social exclusion and reinforces narrow ideas about what queerness looks like.

So how do we move beyond these limitations? The answer begins with storytelling, authentic, diverse, and expansive storytelling. When queer people are allowed to tell their own stories, on their own terms, the result is a mosaic rather than a monolith. A single experience cannot represent a community, but a tapestry of stories can begin to show the scope of queer life. Literature, film, podcasts, art, and digital media created by LGBTQ+ voices, offer a counter-narrative, one rooted in nuance rather than stereotype.

We also need to ask better questions. Instead of seeking the "typical" queer experience, we must explore what queerness means across different contexts. How does it look in a small rural town versus a major city? What does it mean to be queer and also neurodivergent, or devoutly religious, or an immigrant? Empowerment lies not in fitting a mold, but in being free to exist outside of it. By inviting complexity, we make room for everyone at the table.

Education is another vital tool. From school curriculums to workplace training, understanding the harm of stereotypes must be part of broader conversations about diversity and inclusion. This is not about censorship, it's about context. It's about teaching critical media literacy so people can recognize when a character is a stereotype and understand what's missing from that portrayal. It's about ensuring LGBTQ+ history and culture are taught in ways that reflect both struggle and joy. Because when people are equipped with knowledge, they're more likely to engage with others, especially those different from themselves, with empathy, respect, and openness.

And perhaps most importantly, we need to actively foster inclusive and compassionate environments, online, in our families, in our communities, where people feel genuinely safe being themselves, even when that self doesn't align with traditional norms or expectations. Encouraging curiosity, listening without judgment, and allowing people to self-define, are acts of profound respect and solidarity.

This work is not only for queer people, it's for everyone. Challenging stereotypes benefits society at large. It helps build empathy, dismantle prejudice, and foster genuine connection. Queer liberation is not about creating a new set of rigid ideals, it's about undoing the idea that anyone must be defined by a fixed identity at all.

To move beyond stereotypes in the queer experience is to embrace the unknown, the unexpected, the beautifully contradictory. It is to recognize that queerness is not a singular narrative, but a chorus of stories, each adding something vital to the whole. It is to refuse to let media, politics, or public opinion reduce a vibrant community to a set of clichés.

The goal is not to erase the flamboyant gay man, the butch lesbian, or any identity that has found power in a previously maligned stereotype. Rather, it is to ensure that those identities are understood as parts of a broader spectrum, not its totality. Everyone should have the right to live outside the expectations others impose on them.

In celebrating that freedom, we honour the true spirit of queerness, not just as a sexual or gender identity, but as a way of being that challenges norms, expands possibilities, and affirms the humanity in all of us.

Chapter 1

Love Without Boundaries

---

1. The Erasure of Asexual and Aromantic Narratives

In the broader conversation around LGBTQ+ identities, asexual and aromantic individuals are often pushed to the margins, if they are acknowledged at all. These identities, which challenge deeply ingrained cultural narratives around love, sex, and relationships, are frequently misunderstood, minimized, or erased entirely. This chapter seeks to highlight the persistent invisibility of asexual and aromantic people, explore the roots and consequences of that erasure and offer a compassionate perspective, through which these experiences can be more fully recognized and included within both the queer community and society at large.

1.1 Understanding Asexuality and Aromanticism:

A foundational step in addressing erasure is clarity. Asexuality, broadly defined, refers to individuals who experience little to no sexual attraction. Aromanticism describes those who experience little to no romantic attraction. Both exist on spectrums, some people identify as gray asexual or demiromantic, reflecting experiences that don't fit neatly into binaries. Importantly, neither identity is synonymous with celibacy or emotional disconnection, rather, they offer alternative ways of experiencing intimacy and connection.

Yet despite this complexity, mainstream media, educational systems, and even LGBTQ+ spaces, often conflate these identities with stereotypes of coldness, repression, or incompleteness. The lack of accurate representation contributes to their invisibility and, in many cases, to internalized doubt or shame among those who identify this way.

1.2 Cultural and Social Factors Contributing to Erasure:

One of the most powerful forces behind the erasure of asexual and aromantic people is society's deep entrenchment in allonormativity and amatonormativity, the assumptions that all people experience sexual and romantic attraction and that such attractions are essential to a meaningful life. These norms are everywhere, in films that centre romantic love as the ultimate goal, in social scripts that treat partnership as a rite of passage, and in institutions that prioritize coupledom, often at the exclusion of other forms of connection.

Even within LGBTQ+ advocacy, there's a tendency to focus on reclaiming the right to sexual expression, understandable, given the long history of queer sexuality being policed and pathologized.

However, this can inadvertently sideline those for whom sex or romance are not central to identity or fulfilment. When sexual liberation becomes the only narrative of queer freedom, those who don't share that framework can be made to feel like outsiders in their own community.

1.3 Media Representation and the Problem of Absence:

Representation in media plays a pivotal role in shaping societal understanding. When it comes to asexual and aromantic identities, however, the landscape is sparse. Characters who are explicitly ace or aro, are rare, and when they do appear, they are often subtly "corrected" over time, eventually given romantic or sexual arcs to conform to audience expectations.

This lack of visibility has real consequences. For many, media serves as an early mirror, something that can validate their experience or at least spark questions. The absence of relatable narratives reinforces the idea that asexuality and aromanticism are anomalies, too rare or "niche" to warrant attention. It also limits the public's vocabulary and empathy, making it harder for allies to understand and support these identities.

1.4 Internalized Invisibility and Mental Health:

Being unseen can be deeply isolating. Many asexual and aromantic individuals report feeling broken or out of step with their peers, especially during adolescence when societal emphasis on dating and sexual exploration intensifies. The result can be internalized erasure, not just the experience of being excluded, but the belief that one doesn't deserve inclusion.

Mental health challenges such as anxiety, depression, and identity confusion, can be compounded by this invisibility. Without language or community to validate their feelings, many suffer in silence or suppress their identities altogether. This erasure isn't just social, it's emotional, psychological, and deeply personal.

1.5 Resistance and Community Building:

Despite the challenges, asexual and aromantic communities have been carving out space, online, in academic discourse, and within activist movements. These efforts often emphasize self-definition, intersectionality, and the importance of diverse relationships that go beyond romance and sex.

Online platforms have played a critical role in this movement, offering visibility, validation, and a sense of belonging. Hashtags like #AceVisibility and #AroSpec have helped foster solidarity, while blogs, zines, and forums, allow for the sharing of lived experience and nuanced discussion. These communities push back against the dominant narratives and advocate for broader understandings of love, fulfilment, and connection.

By reclaiming their stories, asexual and aromantic communities challenge narrow ideas of love and intimacy, offering broader, more inclusive ways of connecting and belonging.

1.6 Intersectionality – The Overlapping Margins:

It's also essential to recognize that asexual and aromantic identities do not exist in a vacuum. People of colour, disabled individuals, neurodivergent people, and those from religious or culturally conservative backgrounds, often experience multiple layers of invisibility or misunderstanding. For example, some disabled individuals are presumed asexual without agency, while others struggle to have their asexual identity recognized as legitimate rather than "a symptom."

This intersectionality demands a more holistic approach to representation, one that acknowledges how different forms of marginalization can compound and how inclusion must be intentionally expansive.

1.7 Toward Inclusive Queer Futures:

Creating space for asexual and aromantic voices within the broader LGBTQ+ community is not just an act of justice, it's an expansion of possibility. It allows for a queerness that is not defined solely by who we love or desire, but by how we relate, resist, and redefine.

Inclusion means more than adding letters to an acronym. It means reshaping cultural narratives, questioning default assumptions, and embracing the full spectrum of human experience. It means making room for identities that don't conform to dominant expectations, even within queer spaces.

As we work toward a future that is more inclusive and affirming, we must ask, whose stories are being told and whose are still waiting to be heard? In answering that question, we begin the work of not just recognizing, but truly valuing, the rich diversity of queer identities, including those that have long been erased.

1.8 Rethinking Love and Fulfilment – Broadening the Queer Narrative:

Mainstream LGBTQ+ narratives often prioritize romantic or sexual attraction as the ultimate form of fulfilment, which leaves little space for asexual and aromantic experiences. These identities challenge the widespread assumption that love and connection are always tied to romantic or sexual relationships.

However, fulfilment and meaningful connections can manifest in various ways. Platonic relationships, chosen families, personal accomplishments, and intellectual or emotional ties all play a vital role in shaping a rich, balanced, and fully realized sense of self.

Broadening our understanding of what it means to be fulfilled opens up the possibility of a more inclusive queer community, one where asexual and aromantic identities are not just recognized, but valued. Moving beyond the conventional focus on romance and sex allows for a more expansive view of intimacy and belonging. By doing so, we create room for all identities to thrive, reshaping the narrative of love and fulfilment within the LGBTQ+ community.

*What We're Told vs. What's True – Asexual and Aromantic Realities:

What We're Told (Misconceptions & Media Tropes):	What's True (Lived Ace & Aro Experiences):
Asexuality is just a phase or a sign of trauma	Asexuality is a valid, enduring identity. It's not a phase or trauma-related. Many ace people have known this from a young age
Aromantic people are cold or emotionally stunted	Aromantic people form deep emotional connections. They have rich friendships and are capable of love, just not romantically
Asexual people just haven't met the right person yet	Asexual people can have fulfilling relationships without sexual attraction. Their connections are often based on emotional intimacy or shared experiences
Aromantic people are isolated or lonely	Many aro people lead fulfilling social lives, forming connections based on friendship, family, and community
Asexual and aromantic identities are caused by trauma or lack of sexual experience	These identities are intrinsic. They are not a result of trauma or lack of experience, but part of human diversity
Aromantic people are "waiting" for romance	Aromantic people are not waiting for romantic love. They don't prioritize romance in their lives
Ace and aro people can't have fulfilling relationships	Ace and aro people form strong, meaningful Relationships, platonic, familial or emotional
Asexuality means no interest in intimacy	Asexual people often engage in non-sexual intimacy, such as cuddling or emotional connection
Demisexuality is just "waiting for the right person"	Demisexuality involves experiencing sexual attraction only after a strong emotional bond is formed. It's a distinct identity
Aromantic people are just too picky to find love	Aromantic people don't desire romantic love. It's not about being picky, it's about not experiencing romantic attraction
Asexuality is just a phase or a sign of trauma	Asexuality is a valid, enduring identity. It's not a phase or trauma-related. Many ace people have known this from a young age
Ace and aro people aren't oppressed Enough to need visibility	Ace and aro people deserve visibility, not because of oppression, but because every identity matters
Aromantic people are just too emotional and need to "tone it down"	Aromantic people have emotional depth and experience affection, but their emotions are not centred on romance
Asexual or Aromantic people are broken or missing something essential	Asexual and aromantic identities are natural variations of human attraction and are whole in themselves

2. Love Beyond Traditional Relationship Models – Queer-platonic and Companionate Love

Love is often framed through the lens of romantic and sexual partnerships, a narrow cultural script that excludes many valid, meaningful forms of connection. For members of the LGBTQ+ community, especially those who are asexual, aromantic, or disinterested in conventional relationship structures, this script can feel alienating. Reimagining love through a broader lens helps us recognize that intimacy and connection can thrive outside romantic and sexual confines.

Queerplatonic and companionate relationships offer alternative models of deep connection. These forms of love defy heteronormative expectations yet remain grounded in care, commitment, and emotional closeness. They challenge traditional ideas of bonding and invite us to think more expansively about how people support one another and build lives together. Embracing these models means honouring diverse, meaningful ways of loving, ones that are equally valuable, even if they don't fit within conventional norms.

2.1 The Dominance of the Romantic Ideal:

Society often upholds romantic love as the ultimate goal of human connection, a narrative deeply embedded in media, literature, religion, and social customs. This romantic ideal tends to be exclusive, prioritizing monogamous, sexual and often heteronormative pairings.

While some find comfort in this model, it marginalizes those whose relationships don't conform, friendships seen as "less than," single people viewed as incomplete, or asexual and aromantic individuals erased altogether. For queer individuals, whose lives often already challenge traditional structures, romantic expectations can feel doubly restrictive. Redefining what counts as love opens space for broader, more authentic expressions of connection.

2.2 Queer-Platonic Relationships – Redefining Intimacy:

Queer-platonic relationships (QPRs) emerged from a need to describe a bond that exists outside traditional romantic or platonic definitions. These relationships are often deeply intimate, emotionally committed, and may include cohabitation, life planning, or raising children, without the romantic or sexual component usually assumed in such bonds. For many, especially within the aromantic and asexual communities, QPRs offer a framework to express love, commitment, and partnership in ways that reflect their lived experience.

QPRs are not about rejecting love but redefining its terms. They reject the societal hierarchy that elevates romantic partnerships above all else, instead prioritizing emotional intimacy, mutual care, and intentional connection. These relationships highlight how arbitrary our lines around "friend" and "partner" can be. The language surrounding QPRs, terms like "zucchini" (a common in-joke name for a queer-platonic partner), demonstrates a need for new vocabulary, to reflect new understandings of love and intimacy.

2.3 Companionate Love – A Radical Return:

Companionate love has existed long before the rise of modern romantic ideals. Rooted in mutual respect, shared values, and emotional support, companionate love often emerges in long-term friendships, chosen families, and non-romantic cohabitation.

While historically overshadowed by romantic narratives, it's gaining visibility as more people choose alternative lifestyles, living with friends, raising children in co-parenting arrangements, or forming long-term households with no sexual or romantic basis. In queer communities, where survival often depended on chosen families and support systems outside blood ties, companionate love has long been a cornerstone. This model of love allows for sustained connection that is not dependent on sexual or romantic chemistry.

It is powerful in its quietness, radical in its stability, and often more enduring than many romantic entanglements. By recognizing companionate love as equally valuable, we move toward a more inclusive understanding of relational fulfilment.

2.4 Breaking the Hierarchy of Relationships:

A key issue in mainstream narratives is the "relationship escalator", the assumption that intimacy progresses through a specific series of steps, dating, monogamy, sex, cohabitation, marriage and so on. This hierarchy devalues friendships, community bonds, and non-traditional relationships, reducing them to secondary roles in a person's life.

In queer contexts, this model can be even more limiting, especially for those who cannot, or choose not to, fit within it. People in QPRs, long-term friendships, or alternative family structures often find themselves explaining or defending their relationships.

To move beyond this, we must dismantle the idea that one kind of love is superior to others. Instead, we can view relationships as constellations, diverse, fluid, and grounded in mutual respect. By honouring all forms of love equally, we empower people to create lives that reflect their true needs and desires, rather than conforming to prescribed norms.

2.5 Cultural and Social Resistance:

Despite growing awareness, non-romantic and non-sexual relationships still face cultural pushback. Legal structures, media portrayals, and even casual conversations are geared toward romantic coupling. There's little legal recognition for QPRs or companionate partnerships, no spousal benefits, no default next-of-kin status, and minimal visibility in policy or media.

Friends are often dismissed as temporary or secondary, despite many people relying on them for emotional survival. This resistance reflects a deep discomfort with forms of love that cannot be easily categorized or monetized.

But it is within these "in-between" spaces that queer communities have long flourished. By continuing to live and love on their own terms, people in these relationships are already creating the future they want to see.

2.6 Conclusion – Expanding Love's Lexicon:

The world doesn't suffer from too much love, it suffers from too narrow a definition of it. Queerplatonic and companionate relationships challenge us to think more expansively, more compassionately, and more authentically about how we connect. They remind us that love is not a one-size-fits-all experience. It can be tender without being romantic, committed without being sexual and deeply fulfilling without following a predefined script. In embracing these forms of love, we not only affirm those who have been pushed to the margins, we also free ourselves to seek out the relationships that truly nourish us. This is not about discarding romance, but decentering it from its unchallenged pedestal.

3. Exploring Relationship Anarchy – Rewriting the Rules of Love

In a society where love is often confined by rigid rules, monogamy, hierarchy and exclusivity, Relationship Anarchy (RA) invites a radical rethinking of how we approach love and relationships. At its core, RA believes that relationships should be defined by mutual consent, autonomy and intentionality, rather than adhering to societal expectations. For the LGBTQ+ community, RA offers the opportunity to redefine love and intimacy on their own terms, free from traditional constraints. This introduction sets the stage by contrasting restrictive norms with the boundless possibilities RA presents.

3.1 The Origins and Ethos of Relationship Anarchy:

Relationship Anarchy (RA), a concept introduced by Swedish activist Andie Nordgren, emerged as a direct challenge to traditional relationship constructs. Rooted in feminist and queer theory, RA questions hierarchical models that prioritize romantic and sexual relationships over others, like platonic bonds or chosen families. Central to RA is the idea of transparency, self-awareness, and the freedom to define relationships on one's own terms, rather than following inherited societal scripts. This philosophy strongly resonates with queer communities, who have long resisted and redefined conventional norms of love and connection.

3.2 Deconstructing Normative Scripts:

The dominant relationship model follows a rigid, predictable path: dating, exclusivity, marriage, cohabitation, and potentially children. These normative scripts are deeply embedded in culture and further solidified by legal and economic structures. For LGBTQ+ individuals, these expectations can feel especially restrictive, as their identities often disrupt the foundations of these norms. Relationship anarchy challenges these traditional relational hierarchies, affirming that intimacy can take countless forms, none inherently more valuable than another.

3.3 Why Queer Communities Gravitate Toward RA:

Queer lives have historically resisted categorization. From chosen families to fluid identities, many in the LGBTQ+ community already live outside heteronormative templates. Relationship anarchy not only validates this resistance but also equips individuals with a language and framework for it. It can be particularly empowering for queer folks, offering flexibility, inclusivity and autonomy in how relationships are defined and nurtured. RA provides a space for queer individuals to honour their unique relational needs, allowing them to shape connections free from societal constraints. Relationship anarchy challenges traditional relationship hierarchies, allowing queer individuals to define connections on their own terms, fostering authenticity and mutual respect without imposed labels.

3.4 Love Without Hierarchies – Flattening the Relational Field:

Relationship Anarchy (RA) rejects the traditional "relationship escalator," which prioritizes romantic and sexual relationships. Instead, RA values all types of connections, romantic, platonic, familial and even financial, as equally important. By flattening relationship hierarchies, RA allows individuals to define their connections based on mutual consent and personal needs, rather than societal expectations. This approach offers a more inclusive, customized way of forming relationships.

3.5 Commitment, Not Control:

Critics often misunderstand Relationship Anarchy (RA) as a rejection of commitment or emotional connection. In fact, RA promotes a kind of commitment based on openness, honesty, and mutual choice, rather than following societal expectations. Instead of assuming that relationships must follow a set path, like exclusivity or long-term partnership, RA allows individuals to define and continually reevaluate the terms of their connections. The misconception that RA leads to shallow or disconnected relationships is challenged here, as it actually fosters deeper, more intentional bonds.

3.6 Communication as a Foundation:

Clear, compassionate communication is central to RA. Without predefined roles or expectations, every aspect of a relationship, from boundaries to desires, requires ongoing, explicit discussion and renegotiation. For LGBTQ+ individuals, who often face identity-based microaggressions or systemic erasure, this focus on open dialogue is deeply validating. RA nurtures connection through honest communication, creating a space where relationships can evolve based on mutual respect and shared values. This emphasis on transparency fosters a more flexible approach to relationships, enhancing emotional connections and deepening mutual understanding of each other's shifting needs and boundaries.

3.7 Autonomy and Interdependence:

Relationship Anarchy (RA) encourages individuals to embrace their autonomy while still fostering meaningful, shared connections with others.

It challenges the common belief that fulfilment requires a romantic partner, promoting the idea that people can be whole on their own. For many in the queer community, particularly those facing additional challenges related to race, disability, or class, RA offers both freedom and a sense of solidarity. It allows people to define relationships on their own terms, balancing independence with the intentional connections they choose to create. RA fosters a space where individuals can cultivate self-sufficiency while still forming supportive, non-hierarchical relationships that prioritize mutual care and respect.

3.8 Challenges of Practicing Relationship Anarchy:

While Relationship Anarchy (RA) offers an empowering framework, it is not without its challenges. Cultural conditioning, jealousy, time constraints, and internalized societal norms, can make it difficult to fully embrace a non-hierarchical approach to relationships. Additionally, societal systems are rigidly structured to support traditional, monogamous relationships, with legal protections and societal recognition often favouring coupled dynamics.

These practical and emotional obstacles can complicate the journey towards living non-traditionally, making it essential to acknowledge the real-world difficulties individuals may encounter. Navigating these barriers requires ongoing self-reflection, intentional communication and strong community support, to sustain authentic, non-normative relationship choices.

3.9 The Role of Community in RA:

Because RA can be isolating in a world that privileges coupledom, building intentional communities becomes essential. Chosen families, queer collectives and friend-based support systems, provide the social and emotional scaffolding that RA often requires. The power of community plays a vital role in sustaining unconventional relationship models, offering connection, affirmation and shared values in place of traditional societal structures. These communities provide a sense of belonging and solidarity, ensuring individuals can thrive in relationships that prioritize personal choice. They offer connection, affirmation and shared values, creating a strong foundation in place of traditional societal structures.

3.10 RA and Intersectionality:

RA is not practiced in a vacuum. Race, class, disability, and cultural background all shape how people experience and implement it. Recognizing these intersecting factors is crucial, as not everyone has equal access to the freedoms RA promotes. By applying an intersectional lens, we can better understand how RA might evolve to be more inclusive and reflective of the diverse lived experiences within the LGBTQ+ community. An intersectional approach ensures that RA is accessible and meaningful for all individuals, regardless of their background or identity.

3.11 Imagining New Futures for Love:

At its heart, RA is an invitation to imagine more expansive, liberating, and honest ways of loving. It's not a formula but a mindset, one that prioritizes respect, consent, and creativity.

For queer individuals, it's a way to reclaim narratives around love and belonging. Rather than offering rigid answers, RA encourages individuals to embrace possibility over prescription and to co-create relational futures rooted in authenticity. RA opens up the possibility for love that exists outside of societal expectations, where individuals can define their own needs and desires. It encourages a continuous exploration of what connection can look like, offering the freedom to reshape love on one's own terms, without conforming to traditional norms.

3.12 Conclusion – Choosing Connection on Our Own Terms:

Relationship anarchy offers a bold rethinking of love and connection, one that resonates deeply with queer communities tired of being confined by outdated norms. It encourages all of us to pause, reflect, and ask, What do we truly want from our relationships? And what would it look like to build them with intention, courage, and care? Rather than following a script, RA hands us a blank page and the pen. By embracing RA, queer individuals have the opportunity to redefine their relational needs and desires, fostering authentic connections that reflect their true selves. It empowers us to create bonds that prioritize respect and consent, while breaking free from the constraints of traditional relationship models.

4. Intimacy vs. Romance – Are They Mutually Exclusive?

In mainstream discourse, intimacy and romance are often treated as interchangeable. Pop culture tends to portray deep connection through the lens of romantic or sexual love, making it difficult to imagine intimacy that doesn't culminate in romance. For members of the LGBTQ+ community, many of whom live outside traditional relationship structures, this conflation can feel limiting. This introduction sets the stage for a deeper exploration of how intimacy and romance intersect, diverge and inform one another, especially within queer lives. Challenging these assumptions allows for a broader, more inclusive understanding of connection, where intimacy and romance are not confined to traditional frameworks, but are instead redefined to honour the diverse experiences within queer relationships.

4.1 Defining Terms – What Do We Mean by Intimacy and Romance?

To understand whether intimacy and romance are mutually exclusive, we first need to define them. Intimacy often refers to closeness, vulnerability, trust, and deep emotional connection. It can exist in friendships, family bonds, chosen kin, and even brief, impactful interactions. Romance, by contrast, is socially coded, it tends to involve desire, flirtation, exclusivity, and is often presumed to lead to sex or long-term coupling. Historically, these concepts have been framed through a heteronormative lens, but within queer contexts, such definitions are increasingly being challenged and redefined.

4.2 Cultural Conditioning and the Romantic Ideal:

Much of society is shaped by the "romantic ideal," a culturally dominant narrative that places romantic love at the pinnacle of human connection. We are taught that to be truly fulfilled, one must find a romantic partner. This belief permeates movies, books, music, and even family expectations.

For queer individuals, this model can be doubly restrictive, as it often excludes or distorts non-heteronormative relationships. Exploring how cultural conditioning impacts our perception of intimacy reveals the ways queer lives often push against and subvert this romantic hierarchy. By questioning these norms, queer communities create space for diverse forms of connection that are equally meaningful and valid.

4.3 Queer Friendships and the Power of Non-Romantic Intimacy:

Friendship, especially in LGBTQ+ spaces, is often a life-saving, life-affirming form of intimacy. Queer friendships tend to blur the boundaries between platonic and romantic affection, creating bonds that are emotionally intense and deeply committed. Throughout history, queer communities have relied on friendships not just for support, but as primary sources of love and connection. This challenges the idea that intimacy must be romantic to be meaningful, and instead highlights how non-romantic relationships can be rich, nourishing, and foundational. Queer friendships often transcend traditional boundaries, offering a profound form of emotional connection that is both validating and healing. These relationships stand as proof that intimacy is not confined to romantic love, but can thrive in deep, platonic bonds rooted in trust, care, and shared experiences.

4.4 The Aro/Ace Perspective – Decentering Romance and Sex:

Aromantic and asexual individuals provide crucial insight into the false equivalence between intimacy and romance. Many aro and ace people experience deep emotional intimacy without romantic or sexual attraction, proving that these experiences can be distinct. By centering the ace/aro spectrum, we can examine how their experiences challenge dominant cultural scripts and broaden our understanding of human connection. Intimacy, in this light, can be felt and expressed in a multitude of non-normative ways, from sensory closeness to intellectual vulnerability, reminding us that connection isn't one-size-fits-all.

4.5 Queer-platonic Relationships and Companionate Bonds:

Queer-platonic relationships (QPRs) exist in a liminal space, more than friendship, but not quite romance. They resist easy categorization and, in doing so, question the very boundaries between intimacy and romance. QPRs often include shared life commitments, cohabitation, and emotional exclusivity, yet they are not romantic in the traditional sense. In LGBTQ+ communities, these relationships reflect an innovative approach to connection, one that honours emotional depth without relying on romantic coding. Companionate partnerships and QPRs challenge conventional structures and offer expansive, affirming alternatives to how intimacy can be lived and understood.

4.6 Touch, Affection, and Physical Closeness Beyond Romance:

Physical touch, hugging, cuddling, and holding hands, is often framed as inherently romantic or sexual. However, within queer spaces, these actions frequently serve as expressions of solidarity, care and deep emotional closeness that exist outside the bounds of romance.

LGBTQ+ individuals often navigate physical intimacy in ways that challenge conventional expectations, embracing touch as a vital, affirming form of connection. By redefining what physical affection can mean, queer communities offer a more liberated and inclusive understanding of intimacy. This also opens up conversations around the cultural taboos surrounding non-sexual touch and how those norms might be reimagined.

4.7 The Role of Language in Shaping Expectations:

Language both reflects and reinforces our relationship frameworks. Terms like "just friends" or "more than friends" imply a hierarchy that places romantic love at the top, often minimizing the depth of other connections. In queer communities, there has been a deliberate effort to invent or reclaim terms, such as queer-platonic, entangled, or life partner, that more accurately capture relationships outside traditional categories. By expanding the vocabulary used to describe intimacy, people can better validate diverse, fluid bonds and challenge the idea that only romance deserves recognition and depth. This evolving language helps dismantle societal norms, creating a more inclusive understanding of what meaningful connection can look like.

4.8 Societal Implications – Legal and Social Recognition:

Even when intimacy exists outside the bounds of romance, society often fails to recognize or validate it. Legal and institutional systems, such as those governing marriage, inheritance, immigration, and hospital visitation, are designed to prioritize romantic and legally sanctioned partnerships. As a result, deeply intimate connections that don't fit within these frameworks are frequently overlooked or dismissed. For queer individuals, whose most significant relationships may be platonic, communal, or otherwise non-normative, this lack of recognition can lead to emotional and material vulnerability, underscoring the need to rethink how intimacy is acknowledged and protected.

4.9 Personal Liberation and Reimagining Love:

Rethinking the boundaries between intimacy and romance can be deeply liberating. For LGBTQ+ individuals, whose identities are often shaped by self-inquiry and resistance to normativity, this kind of reflection opens the door to more authentic and expansive expressions of love. Questioning inherited narratives allows for emotional and philosophical freedom, creating space to define intimacy on one's own terms, rooted not in convention, but in honesty, care, and intentional choice. This process of reimagining love fosters personal growth and strengthens the ability to form connections that truly reflect one's values and desires. Challenging norms empowers individuals to embrace diverse, and fulfilling expressions of love, unbound by societal expectations.

5. The Role of Friendship as a Core Component of LGBTQ+ Love

In dominant cultural narratives, love is often equated with romantic or sexual partnerships. While friendship is valued, it is rarely portrayed as the central form of deep emotional connection. However, for many in the LGBTQ+ community, friendship is not just important, it is often the most enduring and affirming expression of love.

Queer friendships challenge narrow cultural definitions of love, offering a more expansive and resilient vision of intimacy rooted in mutual care, trust and solidarity. By emphasizing the importance of chosen families and friendships, these connections demonstrate how love can thrive in many forms beyond romance, fostering a deep sense of belonging and emotional support.

5.1 The Historical Significance of Friendship in Queer Lives:

Throughout history, queer people have relied on friendship as a survival strategy in the face of rejection, discrimination and invisibility. In times when coming out could mean exile from family or community, friendships often became chosen families. These bonds, built through shared experiences and collective resilience, served as lifelines in hostile environments. The historical roots of queer friendship reveal how these relationships have long provided emotional sanctuary and embodied radical forms of kinship. These friendships not only offered emotional support, but also helped foster a sense of community, solidarity and shared identity, making them vital to the survival and thriving of queer people throughout history.

5.2 Chosen Families and Emotional Kinship:

The concept of chosen family has become central to LGBTQ+ culture. Unlike traditional family structures based on blood ties, chosen families are forged through mutual support, shared values, and deep emotional intimacy. These networks of care often serve as primary sources of love, stability and belonging, particularly for queer individuals who may be estranged from biological relatives. Friendships often grow into chosen families, reflecting how queer people build enduring bonds that meet emotional and practical needs outside conventional familial norms. Chosen families offer a space where queer individuals can define their own sense of belonging, free from societal expectations and cultivate relationships that prioritize mutual respect, care and authenticity.

5.3 Friendship as Resistance to Romantic Hierarchies:

Mainstream society tends to elevate romantic love as the pinnacle of human connection. This hierarchy diminishes the significance of platonic bonds, often relegating them to the background. Queer friendships actively resist this narrative by centering non-romantic intimacy as equally, if not more, fulfilling. By subverting normative relational scripts, these friendships challenge the assumption that only romantic love can offer depth, devotion, or lifelong commitment. Queer friendships challenge the notion that only romantic love can offer depth, proving that non-romantic bonds can be just as fulfilling.

5.4 Friendship and Queer Emotional Intimacy:

Queer friendships are often characterized by deep emotional transparency, vulnerability and interdependence. These relationships create space for individuals to be seen and accepted in their full complexity, without the pressures of romantic expectations. Emotional intimacy in queer friendships is not "less than" romantic love, rather, it's a different and equally profound expression of love.

This type of emotional closeness is essential to queer wellbeing, offering a safe and nurturing space for connection, growth and support. These bonds allow queer individuals to express parts of themselves that may be marginalized, creating a strong sense of belonging and acceptance that extends beyond traditional relationship norms.

5.5 The Blurring of Platonic and Romantic Boundaries:

In many LGBTQ+ lives, the line between friendship and romance is not always clear-cut. Some friendships involve physical affection, cohabitation, or long-term commitment without fitting into conventional definitions of romance. These liminal relationships, often called queer-platonic or companionate partnerships, highlight the fluid and evolving nature of queer connections. They show how the boundaries between love and friendship can blur in liberating and deeply personal ways, creating spaces where emotional intimacy thrives without the constraints of traditional labels. These relationships challenge the traditional dichotomy between platonic and romantic love, offering a more nuanced and inclusive understanding of emotional bonds.

5.6 Friendship as a Source of Queer Joy and Celebration:

Beyond survival, friendship in queer communities is also a source of joy, playfulness and celebration. Queer friendships often create affirming spaces where identities are not just accepted but celebrated. Whether through mutual creativity, activism, or simple companionship, these relationships are marked by a profound sense of shared meaning. They bring joy, spark imagination, and offer emotional nourishment, enriching the lives of those who participate in them. Queer friendships are a source of joy and celebration, offering creative connection and mutual support. These bonds foster self-expression and shared experiences.

5.7 Physical Intimacy in Friendship:

Touch and physical closeness are often reserved for romantic or sexual relationships in mainstream narratives. However, in queer friendships, cuddling, hand-holding, or sleeping next to one another can be expressions of love and comfort, without romantic implication. These friendships challenge restrictive norms around physical intimacy and offer new ways to understand embodied care between friends, expanding the definition of love and connection beyond traditional boundaries. These forms of physical intimacy provide emotional reassurance and deepen the bond between friends. They offer a sense of belonging and security, expanding the definition of love and connection beyond traditional boundaries.

5.8 Friendship in Queer Aging and Longevity:

As LGBTQ+ individuals age, friendship remains a sustaining force, particularly for those who do not follow traditional life paths involving marriage or children. Queer elders often rely on long-term friendships for caregiving, emotional support and community. In these connections, love transcends traditional norms, creating chosen families that offer deep emotional fulfilment.

These friendships provide continuity, shared history, and enduring love, offering a vital source of strength and connection as individuals navigate the challenges of aging outside conventional relational frameworks. For queer elders, friendships often become primary sources of support and care, replacing the traditional familial structures. These relationships offer a sense of belonging, helping to preserve a rich tapestry of shared experiences while fostering resilience through the aging process.

5.9 Language, Legitimacy and the Recognition of Queer Friendships:

Despite their importance, queer friendships often lack the recognition given to romantic relationships. Legal, social, and cultural systems rarely acknowledge the depth of non-romantic partnerships. Language and societal structures frequently fail to capture the legitimacy of these bonds, reinforcing the idea that only romantic connections are valuable or legitimate. Rethinking these frameworks is crucial, as it opens space for a more inclusive understanding of love. This includes the need for terminology that better reflects non-romantic relationships, such as "life partner," and the push for legal recognition of such connections.

5.10 Friendship as Healing and Transformation:

For many LGBTQ+ individuals who have experienced trauma, rejection, or marginalization, friendship becomes a powerful site of healing. Queer friendships provide unconditional support, validation and shared resilience, offering a space to rebuild trust and reclaim self-worth. These connections are not just sources of emotional refuge, but also transformative forces, helping individuals navigate and overcome past hurts. Queer friendships act as sanctuaries for healing, where individuals can process pain and grow stronger together. Through mutual care and understanding, these relationships help to restore a sense of belonging, enabling transformation and personal empowerment.

5.11 Conclusion – Centering Friendship as Love:

Reimagining friendship as a central form of love challenges the romantic ideal and broadens the scope of how we understand intimacy, commitment, and care. For queer individuals, friendship is not secondary, it is sacred. By centering friendship in narratives of love, we validate the richness and diversity of human connection. The final reflection calls for honouring, prioritizing, and celebrating friendship as a core component of LGBTQ+ love, advocating for its equal recognition, investment and reverence. Centering friendship as a form of love invites a broader, more inclusive view of connection, one that goes beyond traditional romantic frameworks. For queer people, this shift reaffirms that friendship is just as meaningful, transformative and necessary as any romantic bond.

Chapter 2

Gender and Sexuality – More Than Just Two Choices

---

1. Navigating the Fluidity of Gender – Beyond the Binary and Non-Binary Spectrum

Gender has long been viewed through a rigid binary lens: male or female, man or woman. This framework, ingrained in language, culture, and institutions, shapes how society views identity and behaviour. Yet it fails to capture the richness of lived experiences. Gender is not fixed or absolute, it is expansive, evolving, and deeply personal. Questioning the binary invites a deeper, more compassionate understanding of who we are.

1.1 The Binary Model and Its Limitations:

The gender binary is not a universal truth, but a social construct reinforced over centuries by culture, religion, and systems of power. It assumes everyone fits neatly into one of two categories, determined at birth. But this model excludes countless people, trans, non-binary, genderqueer, gender fluid, whose experiences defy these confines. Even those who identify within the binary are pressured to conform to restrictive norms. These limitations hinder authenticity for all of us. This binary framework not only erases the existence of diverse gender identities but also upholds rigid societal expectations that severely stifle individual expression and self-discovery.

1.2 Beyond Non-Binary – Understanding the Gender Spectrum:

Non-binary identities have gained visibility, providing language and validation for those alienated by traditional categories. Yet non-binary is not a singular or static identity. Some people feel aligned with multiple genders, others with none. Some experience gender as fluid, shifting over time. These identities are not trends or phases, they are authentic expressions of self. Gender is best understood as a wide and dynamic spectrum, not a set of fixed points. Recognizing this spectrum means embracing the complexity and fluidity of gender identity.

1.3 Cultural Histories and the Impact of Colonization:

To understand gender fully, we must also look beyond Western narratives. Around the world, many cultures have long recognized more than two genders. Indigenous North American nations honour Two-Spirit people. South Asia has Hijras, and Samoa embraces Fa'afafine. These identities have deep spiritual and cultural significance. Colonialism violently suppressed these traditions, replacing them with binary gender norms. Reclaiming these histories is essential to understanding gender diversity as an ancient, enduring aspect of human existence, not a modern invention. In doing so, we honour resilient identities and resist the colonial norms that still shape gender today.

1.4 Language, Labels and the Power to Self-Define:

Language plays a crucial role in gender identity. Pronouns and labels help people communicate their truth. For many, finding the right words is liberating. But language is also evolving, just like gender. No label can perfectly capture someone's full identity. That's okay. What matters is choice and agency. A respectful approach to language, learning, listening, adapting, creates space for people to feel seen and affirmed. Mistakes are part of the process, what matters is care and growth. Honouring self-definition means valuing language as a tool for connection, not confinement.

1.5 Gender Fluidity in Daily Life and Embodiment:

Gender fluidity shows up in many ways. Some people change their names, voices, or appearance. Others express their gender internally without external shifts. Every journey is unique, and no path is more valid than another. There is no singular way to be gender fluid, non-binary, or trans. Rejecting rigid norms allows people to live with greater authenticity. It's not about fitting into another box, it's about honouring who we truly are.

1.6 Intersectionality – How Gender Interacts with Other Identities:

Gender doesn't exist in a vacuum. It intersects with race, culture, disability, class, and sexuality. A Black trans person's experience differs from that of a white non-binary person. Cultural and systemic factors shape how freely people can express their gender. This is why intersectionality matters. We cannot work toward gender liberation without also addressing racism, ableism, and economic inequality. Justice requires a holistic, inclusive approach.

1.7 Creating Supportive and Inclusive Spaces:

Exploring gender can be joyful, painful, freeing, or confusing, often all at once. Support matters. Self-compassion is key, there's no right timeline or way to define yourself. Community can offer affirmation and belonging. For allies, the work begins with listening. Use people's chosen names and pronouns. Speak up when others are disrespected. Create spaces that don't assume gender. These acts may seem small, but they can be life-saving. Building supportive and inclusive spaces requires continuous effort, empathy, and a commitment to creating environments, where all gender identities are honoured and respected.

1.8 Conclusion – Embracing the Infinite Possibilities of Gender:

Embracing gender fluidity is about reimagining the world. What if no one had to choose between two boxes? What if gender were seen as a canvas for creativity, connection, and truth? When we release the idea of fixed roles, we allow everyone the freedom to be themselves. Gender is not a checklist or a performance. It's a journey, personal, evolving, and worthy of respect. By honouring the spectrum of gender, we honour the fullness of humanity, who we are and who we are still becoming. In embracing the infinite possibilities of gender, we move closer to a world where authenticity is not just accepted but celebrated. This celebration is not only personal, it's deeply political, shaping a future rooted in freedom and truth.

2. The Unspoken Struggles of Gender-Nonconforming People in Non-Western Cultures

Gender diversity is not unique to the Western world. Long before the rise of Western LGBTQ+ discourse, countless cultures recognized and honoured individuals who defied conventional gender norms in ways that were nuanced and often deeply spiritual. And yet, the global narrative around gender variance remains largely Western in its definitions, visibility, and language. This oversight leaves many people outside the gender binary in non-Western cultures unspoken for, caught between local silences and global frameworks that don't quite fit. Rather than speaking over those who live these truths, it is essential to advocate for their recognition, dignity, and the space to exist fully and freely, without erasure or simplification. These stories deserve to be seen and heard on their own terms.

2.1 Historical Recognition of Gender Diversity:

Contrary to the notion that gender-nonconforming identities are a modern invention, many cultures have long embraced gender diversity. In South Asia, Hijras have existed for centuries and are mentioned in ancient Hindu texts. Indigenous North American nations have recognized Two-Spirit people as carriers of both masculine and feminine energies, often holding roles of spiritual importance. The Fa'afafine of Samoa and the Bakla in the Philippines represent culturally embedded third-gender identities that predate colonial contact. These examples are not exceptions, they are evidence of a broader human reality. Yet colonization, religious imperialism, and the export of Western gender binaries have often erased or criminalized these roles, transforming respected identities into sites of stigma.

2.2 Cultural Silencing and Internal Conflict:

In many non-Western societies, gender-nonconforming people live in the shadows, not because they are rare, but because visibility can be dangerous. Cultural emphasis on honour, tradition, and familial duty, often compels individuals to suppress their authentic selves for fear of bringing shame. The silence that surrounds them is not just societal but internal. The absence of language, role models, or supportive community makes self-recognition difficult. People may know that they are "different," yet lack a culturally safe way to express that knowing. The result is a painful form of internal exile, where identity becomes a source of both intimacy and isolation.

2.3 Legal and Social Marginalization:

Beyond personal and cultural silence lies the stark reality of legal discrimination. In many countries, gender-nonconforming individuals face criminalization, denial of legal gender recognition, and exclusion from healthcare or employment. Laws may explicitly target expressions of non-binary identity, or they may fail to acknowledge such identities at all, rendering individuals invisible in policy and unprotected by rights. Even when legal protections exist on paper, social enforcement is rare, and violence remains a constant threat. State institutions often work in tandem with cultural attitudes to suppress gender variance, punishing those who live outside prescribed norms.

2.4 Between Resistance and Erasure – The Role of Modern Globalization:

Globalization has brought both opportunities and challenges for gender-nonconforming people in non-Western societies. On one hand, increased access to the internet, international media, and global LGBTQ+ movements has helped many discover language and community. On the other hand, Western-centric narratives of gender identity can sometimes overwrite or devalue local frameworks. A Hijra might be told she is "transgender," a term that may not fully align with her lived experience. A Two-Spirit person might find themselves forced to choose between "male" or "female" when applying for a visa. Advocacy must recognize that while shared solidarity is powerful, it must not come at the expense of cultural specificity.

2.5 Family, Faith and the Personal Cost of Survival:

The intersections of gender, family and faith, often create some of the most intimate struggles for gender-nonconforming individuals. In cultures where family bonds are paramount, rejection can lead to emotional exile, homelessness, or disinheritance. For those embedded in deeply religious communities, gender variance is often met with spiritual condemnation. This creates profound internal conflict, the yearning to belong collides with the need to be whole. Survival may mean hiding, code-switching, or leading double lives. And yet, in these difficult spaces, people still find ways to persist, seeking love, affirmation, and meaning where they can. These quiet acts of resilience are powerful testaments to the strength it takes to live one's truth in the face of loss.

2.6 Acts of Quiet Resistance and Resilience:

Despite the challenges, gender-nonconforming people continue to resist invisibility in both quiet and powerful ways. Through underground art, grassroots organizing, ancestral storytelling, and the creation of chosen families, they carve out space for themselves and others. In some cases, communities have begun to reclaim suppressed traditions, breathing new life into cultural roles once deemed obsolete or taboo. These acts of resistance may not always make headlines, but they are the foundation of change. Resilience is not always loud, it often resides in small, everyday decisions to live truthfully, even when the world refuses to see you. These everyday acts of courage quietly reshape culture and expand what's possible for future generations.

2.7 The Need for Inclusive Advocacy and Global Listening:

As global conversations around gender expand, it is crucial that non-Western voices are not only included but centred. Advocacy must move beyond importing Western models and instead ask, what does justice look like in this context? What language, values, and cultural meanings matter here? Supporting gender-nonconforming people in non-Western cultures means resourcing local efforts, protecting cultural autonomy and creating platforms for those, who live these realities to speak for themselves. Listening is not passive, it is a radical act of solidarity. True inclusivity means shifting power, centering lived experiences, and trusting that liberation must be locally defined and led.

2.8 Conclusion – Honouring the Unspoken:

The struggles of gender-nonconforming people in non-Western cultures are not new. What is new is the global willingness, still emerging, still uneven, to listen, to witness, and to honour these lives. Their stories are not merely tales of hardship, but of endurance, beauty, and transformation. The silence they live with is not emptiness, but a call, to open our eyes, expand our frameworks, and make room for truths that are as old as humanity itself. To honour the unspoken is to remember that the margins are not empty. They are filled with lives that matter, and it is long past time we made space for them to be heard.

3. The Impact of Colonialism on Indigenous Gender Identities

Gender diversity is not a new or Western phenomenon, it has existed for centuries across many Indigenous cultures around the world. These communities have long recognized and celebrated gender-nonconforming individuals in ways that were deeply integral to both social and spiritual life. In cultures from Native American to Samoan to Zapotec traditions, gender diversity was an essential part of the fabric that made up these societies. Individuals who embodied both genders or existed beyond the male/female binary were not merely tolerated, but respected and revered. However, with the advent of colonialism, these gender systems were systematically dismantled, erased, or vilified, with colonial powers imposing their binary understanding of gender. The long-term and far-reaching effects of these colonial actions continue to resonate today, as Indigenous gender-nonconforming people remain marginalized, often silenced, and face a constant struggle for both recognition and survival within both their communities and the broader society.

3.1 Pre-Colonial Indigenous Gender Systems:

Before colonialism, many Indigenous cultures had complex and nuanced understandings of gender that extended beyond a binary framework. In many Native American communities, for example, the concept of "Two-Spirit" people existed. Two-Spirit individuals embodied both masculine and feminine energies and were often seen as possessing special spiritual power. These people were valued as healers, leaders, and community guides. Similarly, in Samoa, the Fa'afafine, individuals assigned male at birth who adopt a feminine gender identity, have been an integral part of Samoan culture for centuries. The Muxe community of the Zapotec people in Oaxaca, Mexico, also embraces individuals who are assigned male at birth but live their lives as women, playing important social and cultural roles. These individuals were not simply anomalies but essential parts of their respective communities, revered for their spiritual and cultural contributions.

3.2 The Colonial Imposition of Binary Gender Norms:

Colonialism brought with it the imposition of rigid Western gender norms, based on the binary understanding of male and female roles. European colonizers, often driven by their Christian moral values, viewed gender diversity as unnatural and immoral. They considered non-binary gender identities a threat to their patriarchal structure, which was central to the colonial project.

Under colonial rule, Indigenous ways of understanding and expressing gender were not just suppressed, they were criminalized. Laws were passed to outlaw gender variance, and religious missionaries played an active role in dismantling the spiritual and cultural recognition of gender-nonconforming people. Colonizers often attempted to impose their Christian views of gender, where only male and female roles were accepted, and anything outside of this binary was considered a violation of social norms.

3.3 Erasure of Indigenous Gender Identities:

The erasure of Indigenous gender identities was not just a matter of cultural change, it was an act of violence. Gender-nonconforming individuals were forced into conformity, often through violence, religious indoctrination, and legal oppression. The existence of gender-diverse people was erased under the weight of imposed colonial laws. For example, the Indian Act of 1876 in Canada was used to eliminate the recognition of Two-Spirit people, suppressing Indigenous cultural identities and enforcing Western gender norms. Similarly, in residential schools, Indigenous children were stripped of their cultural identities, forbidden from speaking their languages, and forced to adhere to Western gender roles. This systematic oppression had long-lasting consequences, creating a legacy of trauma and disconnection from cultural roots that continues to affect Indigenous gender-nonconforming people today.

3.4 The Continuing Legacy of Colonialism:

The violent history of colonialism does not remain in the past. The legacy of colonial rule continues to impact Indigenous gender-diverse people in the present. These individuals still face exclusion from both mainstream society and even their own communities, where traditional gender roles have often been reclaimed in the wake of colonialism. Gender-nonconforming Indigenous people often experience a double marginalization, they are excluded by the larger colonial society that still clings to binary gender norms, and they are sometimes rejected by their own communities, which struggle to balance the resurgence of traditional cultural values with the continued pressures of colonial influence. The persistence of these challenges today is a reminder of the enduring effects of colonial violence on gender diversity and the ongoing struggle for recognition and rights.

3.5 Internalized Colonialism and Its Effects:

Alongside the external oppression faced by gender-nonconforming Indigenous people, colonialism also caused deep internalized trauma. Through generations of colonial violence, many Indigenous communities were taught to reject their non-binary identities. Gender-diverse individuals were forced to deny their authentic selves, resulting in feelings of shame and displacement. This internalized colonialism led to the loss of important cultural knowledge and practices surrounding gender diversity, contributing to the erasure of identities and a disconnection from pre-colonial traditions. For many Indigenous gender-nonconforming people, this internalized shame has created a barrier to self-acceptance and pride, making it difficult to reconnect with the cultural and spiritual practices that once honoured their identities.

3.6 Reclaiming Indigenous Gender Identities – A Path Toward Healing:

Despite centuries of colonial violence and erasure, Indigenous gender-diverse people are resisting these legacies. A resurgence of Two-Spirit movements, which seek to reclaim the visibility and importance of gender-nonconforming people in Indigenous communities, has emerged in recent years. These movements are not only about restoring the traditional roles of Two-Spirit individuals, but also about creating space for new generations to express their gender identities freely. Indigenous activists are playing an important role in challenging the rigid gender binaries imposed by colonialism and advocating for the rights and dignity of gender-diverse people.

By reconnecting with their cultural roots and revitalizing traditional practices, these movements are helping Indigenous communities reclaim the diversity of gender identities that existed before colonialism. Efforts to restore the status of Two-Spirit people and other gender-nonconforming identities in these communities are crucial for the survival and healing of Indigenous cultures. These movements reflect a growing awareness of the need to decolonize not only gender but also culture, spirituality, and community life.

3.7 Conclusion – The Struggle for Recognition and Healing:

The impact of colonialism on Indigenous gender identities has been profound, leading to the erasure and criminalization of gender diversity in many Indigenous communities. The struggle for the recognition of Indigenous gender-nonconforming people is rooted in the need to heal from centuries of oppression and violence. However, there is hope. The ongoing efforts to revitalize and reclaim Indigenous gender identities reflect a powerful resistance to colonial erasure.

By supporting these efforts and listening to Indigenous gender-diverse voices, we can help ensure that their identities are recognized, respected and celebrated in ways, that honour their cultural and spiritual contributions. The journey toward healing, self-determination and justice for Indigenous gender-diverse people is ongoing, but it is a crucial part of the broader movement toward equality and respect for all marginalized identities.

4. Hormone Therapy and Its Emotional Effects on Relationships

Hormone therapy is a deeply personal and often life-affirming part of many transgender and gender-diverse individuals' transitions. For many, it brings a profound sense of alignment between inner identity and outward appearance, a crucial piece of self-actualization.

But as physical and emotional changes unfold, relationships with partners, family, friends, and even the self can shift in ways that are complex, sometimes painful, but often revealing. Recognizing these emotional dimensions is essential to understanding the full impact of hormone therapy, not only as a medical process, but as a deeply relational and human journey. Supporting someone through hormone therapy means embracing change with compassion, patience, and a commitment to evolving together.

4.1 The Internal Landscape – Emotional Changes During Hormone Therapy:

Hormone therapy, involving testosterone or estrogen, introduces significant emotional shifts. Many people describe feeling more emotionally present, sensitive, or even expressive in new ways. For trans women and trans-feminine individuals, estrogen may gradually soften emotional responses, heighten emotional vulnerability, and meaningfully change how stress, connection, or intimacy is processed. For trans men and transmasculine individuals, testosterone might boost confidence, alter energy levels, or shift the way emotions are felt and expressed.

These shifts can be empowering, offering relief from dysphoria and unlocking emotional expression previously suppressed. But they can also be disorienting. Some individuals may struggle to navigate new emotional experiences, questioning whether they are still "themselves." The internal changes often ripple outward, affecting how one communicates, bonds, and relates to others. Understanding these experiences requires emotional awareness and support, not only from the individual, but also from those around them. Emotional transformation is not isolated, it weaves into every connection a person holds.

4.2 Romantic Relationships – Intimacy, Change and Growth:

Romantic relationships are often deeply affected by hormone therapy. Partners may witness both visible changes and evolving emotional or sexual dynamics. For some couples, these shifts bring deeper intimacy. One partner's increased self-confidence or emotional openness can enrich connection. A previously distant person might become more affectionate, and a couple might discover new shared experiences as one transitions. Yet, for others, these changes introduce challenges. Hormonal effects may shift libido, sexual orientation, or how affection is expressed. One partner may struggle to understand their loved one's new emotional patterns, and established relationship dynamics might no longer feel aligned. What's essential is communication. Transitioning doesn't mean discarding a relationship, it invites a transformation of it. Both partners need room to express emotions, fears and hopes. Honesty, patience, and compassion, can help love adapt and even grow stronger during a time of great change.

4.3 Familial Bonds – Relearning and Reconnecting:

Family dynamics also shift as hormone therapy progresses. Parents, siblings, and extended relatives, may feel unsure how to relate to someone undergoing emotional and physical transformation. There may be confusion, grief, or even resistance, especially in families where rigid gender roles were once accepted without question. These reactions are understandable, but they must never outweigh the importance of respect and support. As hormone therapy helps someone live more authentically, families have a chance to meet the real person behind the expectations. A child might become more open-hearted. A sibling might rediscover their sense of humour or voice. These are not losses, they are revelations. For families willing to grow, hormone therapy offers a chance to build deeper, more honest bonds rooted in truth rather than assumption. The journey may be emotional, but it can also be healing.

4.4 Friendships and Social Circles – Shifting Dynamics:

Friendships, too, are impacted by the emotional effects of hormone therapy. Some friends rise to the occasion, becoming steadfast allies and chosen family. They learn, grow, and adapt alongside their trans loved one. Others may drift away, confused or uncomfortable with changes they don't understand. Hormone therapy can reveal which connections are rooted in authenticity and which were dependent on a past version of the individual. This clarity can be painful, especially if old friends withdraw. But it also creates space for deeper, more meaningful relationships to form. Those who remain, who listen, support, and evolve, often become cherished companions on the transition journey. The emotional shifts involved in hormone therapy not only challenge existing relationships in unexpected ways, they also have the potential to strengthen and deepen the bonds that matter most.

4.5 Self-Relationship – Coming Home to Oneself:

Perhaps the most profound emotional effect of hormone therapy is the transformation in one's relationship with themselves. Many describe a sense of finally coming home, of seeing themselves reflected in the mirror in a way that feels right. Hormones don't just change the body, they often bring forward long-suppressed emotions, identity clarity, and the ability to feel joy and peace in one's own skin. That said, self-relationship is not always easy. Emotional wounds may reopen. Old coping mechanisms might no longer work. There may be mourning for time lost to dysphoria or societal pressure. But these challenges are part of the healing. Hormone therapy, for many, is about becoming whole. Learning to trust, love, and care for oneself amid change is not a linear path. It's filled with highs, lows, and everything in between. But it is always worth walking.

4.6 Conclusion – Embracing Emotional Transformation:

Hormone therapy is more than a medical process, it is an emotional and relational evolution. It affects not only the person transitioning, but everyone connected to them. Navigating this change takes courage, empathy, and commitment from individuals and their communities alike.

Whether in romantic partnerships, family dynamics, or friendships, the emotional effects of hormone therapy offer an opportunity to deepen love and expand understanding. Relationships may be tested, but they can also be transformed. At its core, hormone therapy offers a gift, the chance to live truthfully. And when that truth is embraced, with compassion and care, it can reshape every connection for the better. Love, after all, is not diminished by change. It grows in its presence.

For loved ones, hormone therapy may challenge old dynamics or assumptions. The person they thought they knew is still there, but transforming in ways that can feel unfamiliar or unpredictable. Navigating this shift requires openness and humility. Some relationships may stretch and grow in surprising directions; others may fracture under the weight of change. Both outcomes are real, and both deserve acknowledgment without shame. When met with empathy and curiosity, hormone therapy invites deeper love, new intimacy, and mutual understanding.

*Navigating Hormone Replacement Therapy:

PRE-THERAPY ASSESSMENT

- This is the initial stage where medical professionals assess your health, review potential risks, and discuss goals for hormone therapy
- It serves as a key decision-making stage in the transition process

INITIATION OF HRT

- Hormone replacement therapy begins.
- This may involve injections, patches, or oral medications, depending on personal goals

EARLY EMOTIONAL EFFECTS (0-3 MONTHS)

- **Emotional shifts:** Mood swings, higher sensitivity, feelings of anticipation or anxiety, confusion or relief in body changes
- **Heightened self-awareness:** learning new emotions tied to gender

EARLY PHYSICAL EFFECTS (0-3 MONTHS)

- **Skin and hair changes**: Acne or smoother skin, hair thinning or growth in new places
- **Energy shifts**: Some people feel more energized or fatigued

ONGOING PHYSICAL EFFECTS (3-12 MONTHS)

- **Physical changes:** Body composition shifts, growth of secondary sex characteristics like facial hair, deeper voice, breast growth
- **Continued development:** Changes stabilize and some individuals may feel more aligned with their identity

ONGOING EMOTIONAL EFFECTS (3-12 MONTHS)

- **Euphoria:** Body aligning with gender identity
- **Self-image:** Fluctuating self-image as body changes occur

ADJUSTMENT & SUPPORT

- Regular dose tweaks, managing side effects
- Peer support, counselling and holistic well-being

FUTURE: LONG-TERM WELL-BEING

- **Stable physical goals:** Aligned body & mind
- **Emotional resilience:** confidence, comfort and truth
- **Holistic care:** Mental health and social support integrated

*How Gender, Culture & Religion Intersect:

CULTURAL NORMS & TRADITIONS

- Societal expectations and roles often define gender within specific cultural frameworks (e.g. How gender roles are learned in childhood, what roles are culturally accepted
- Gender roles in rites of passage, family roles

RELIGIOUS BELIEFS & PRACTICES

- Religion doctrines and teachings influence how gender is perceived, both spiritually and socially
- Some religions include gender-diverse identities, others may challenge them

PERSONAL BELIEFS & PRACTICES

- Gender identity is a deeply personal journey. It's shaped by the intersection of culture, religion and personal experiences

POINTS OF TENSION & HARMONY

- Cultures and religions may clash or coexist with individual gender identities. Some tensions exist in reconciling personal beliefs with societal or religious norms
- However, there are also inclusive spaces where new traditions emerge

DIALOGUE & RESISTANCE

- Communities challenge outdated norms, creating safe spaces for gender-diverse people
- Cultural movements, faith groups and activists work together to form progressive, inclusive spaces for marginalized identities

FUTURE: INCLUSIVE, DECOLONIZED PRACTICES

- A future where sacred practices affirm gender diversity
- De-colonized spirituality embraces tradition
- Evolving faith spaces foster inclusion and belonging

5. Intersection of Religion, Culture, and Gender Identity

Gender identity does not exist in a vacuum. It is shaped, expressed, and understood within layered systems of meaning, among them, religion and culture are two of the most powerful. For LGBTQ+ individuals, particularly those who are transgender, nonbinary, or gender nonconforming, navigating gender identity often means negotiating these deeply rooted belief systems. The intersection of religion, culture, and gender identity can be a powerful source of affirmation, deep conflict, or profound personal transformation.

It is within this intersection that some of the most nuanced and challenging conversations about selfhood, belonging, and authenticity emerge. Exploring these tensions is not about dismantling faith or erasing cultural traditions, but about recognizing the full humanity of those whose lives span multiple worlds.

5.1 Historical Harmony – Gender Diversity in Religious and Cultural Traditions:

Long before modern discussions of LGBTQ+ rights or visibility, gender diversity was present in many religious and cultural contexts across the world. In Hinduism, deities like Ardhanarishvara reflect a divine embodiment of both masculine and feminine energies. Indigenous spiritualities across the Americas often included Two-Spirit individuals, people who held sacred roles precisely, because of their gender variance. In pre-colonial Africa, gender fluidity was not uncommon, communities held space for individuals who defied rigid gender roles, often with great respect.

These histories reveal that the clash between religion, culture, and gender identity is not inevitable. Many traditions once held more expansive views of gender, grounded in spirituality, ancestry, and community. The narrative that religion and gender diversity are incompatible is, in part, a byproduct of colonial imposition and Western religious norms. Uncovering these lost or silenced stories is a vital act of reclamation for many LGBTQ+ individuals seeking to honour both their identities and their heritage.

5.2 Colonization and the Narrowing of Gender Belief Systems:

Colonialism not only redrew borders and imposed political systems, it also transformed spiritual and cultural landscapes. With colonization came the enforcement of binary gender roles and heteronormative expectations, often justified through missionary Christianity and European legal frameworks. Sacred gender roles were criminalized, erased, or labelled as sinful. Indigenous and local spiritual leaders who embodied or affirmed gender diversity were often persecuted, and traditional understandings of gender were replaced with rigid Western models.

This history helps explain why many contemporary religious and cultural institutions remain hostile to gender diversity. The dissonance that LGBTQ+ individuals feel in these spaces is not the result of their identities being incompatible with faith or culture, but rather the outcome of historical erasure.

To move forward, there must be a reckoning with this legacy and an effort to distinguish between cultural authenticity and colonial residue.

5.3 Personal Struggles – Faith, Identity and Belonging:

For many gender-diverse individuals, religion is not something to be discarded, it is a core part of their identity, upbringing, and community. But reconciling gender identity with religious teachings can be emotionally taxing and isolating. Many face rejection from their faith communities, struggle with internalized shame, or are forced to choose between spiritual life and authentic self-expression.

This tension often goes unspoken, hidden beneath layers of fear and silence. A trans person in a conservative mosque, a non-binary youth in an evangelical church, or a genderqueer Hindu navigating familial expectations, each carries a private burden that is both spiritual and social. Yet within these struggles, resilience emerges. Some individuals reinterpret sacred texts, seek out affirming religious communities, or create new rituals that affirm both their faith and gender identity.

The journey is not about perfect alignment, but about creating space for spiritual and gender truths to coexist, even if that coexistence is messy, evolving, and deeply personal.

5.4 Cultural Pressures and Gender Norms:

Beyond religious institutions, cultural expectations around gender roles can be deeply entrenched and difficult to challenge. In many communities, gender is not just about identity, it is linked to family honour, social roles, and intergenerational continuity. A deviation from these roles can be seen as a betrayal or even a threat to communal cohesion.

Gender-diverse individuals often face not only personal rejection but systemic barriers, denial of inheritance, exclusion from rituals, or forced conformity. The pressure to perform traditional gender roles can be especially intense in diasporic communities, where cultural preservation is seen as a form of survival in foreign environments.

At the same time, culture is not static. Around the world, LGBTQ+ individuals are redefining cultural traditions to be more inclusive. New ceremonies, language adaptations, and storytelling practices are emerging, honouring both heritage and queerness without compromise.

5.5 Bridging the Divide – Emerging Spaces of Inclusion:

Across faiths and cultures, efforts are growing to build more inclusive spaces. Queer imams, rabbis, priests, shamans and spiritual leaders are stepping forward to affirm the sacredness of gender-diverse identities. Community groups are hosting interfaith dialogues on gender and sexuality. Scholars are reinterpreting ancient texts through queer and trans lenses. These movements are not marginal, they are vital acts of spiritual and cultural renewal. In these spaces, LGBTQ+ individuals are not merely accommodated, they are celebrated.

Their experiences are seen as offering unique insights into the divine, the communal and the human condition. Inclusion is not about compromise, it is about embracing the full spectrum of creation, culture and identity.

5.6 Toward Wholeness – A Vision of Intersectional Liberation:

At the intersection of religion, culture, and gender identity lies not only struggle, but the possibility of wholeness. When people are forced to deny parts of themselves to belong, they are denied the fullness of life. But when all aspects of identity are honoured, spiritual, cultural, gendered, a more honest and liberated existence becomes possible.

To reach this vision, empathy is essential. Religious leaders, cultural elder, and communities must listen deeply to the stories of gender-diverse people, not to judge or fix, but to witness. Likewise, LGBTQ+ individuals must be supported in their right to claim both faith and identity, to challenge dogma, without discarding what gives them strength.

This work is slow, tender, and ongoing. But it is work worth doing. Because every person deserves to live in truth, and to be embraced fully in the places they call sacred and home.

Chapter 3

The Role of Community in LGBTQ+ Relationships

---

1. The Hidden Hierarchies Within LGBTQ+ Spaces

LGBTQ+ communities are often celebrated for their inclusivity, diversity, and resistance to societal norms. However, within these spaces, complex power dynamics persist that often go unspoken. These hierarchies, based on race, gender, class, ability, and other factors, can marginalize certain groups within the very communities that are meant to be spaces of refuge and equality.

Recognizing these hidden hierarchies is essential for fostering true inclusivity and solidarity within LGBTQ+ spaces. By critically exploring these power dynamics, we can better understand how they manifest and identify pathways for empowering marginalized groups, ensuring that all individuals within LGBTQ+ communities have an equal chance to thrive and contribute.

1.1 The Intersection of Identity – Understanding Layers of Privilege:

LGBTQ+ communities are incredibly diverse, but not all members experience the same level of privilege or oppression. The intersections of race, gender, class, and ability deeply influence how individuals are treated within these spaces. For example, white, cisgender, gay men may experience privilege over transgender, non-binary, or Black LGBTQ+ individuals. This often leads to the marginalization of those at the intersections of multiple marginalized identities, such as queer people of colour or disabled LGBTQ+ individuals.

Understanding how different aspects of identity intersect to create layered experiences of privilege and marginalization is crucial in identifying the power imbalances within LGBTQ+ spaces. Rather than a monolithic experience of queerness, LGBTQ+ identities are multifaceted, and those who hold intersecting identities may face unique challenges that are overlooked or dismissed in mainstream LGBTQ+ spaces.

1.2 Hierarchies Based on Gender and Sexuality:

Despite the broad definition of "queer" identity, gender and sexuality-based hierarchies often emerge in LGBTQ+ spaces. For instance, cisgender gay men can sometimes hold more power within LGBTQ+ organizations and spaces, overshadowing the voices and needs of transgender, non-binary, and gender non-conforming individuals. Additionally, bisexual individuals, especially bisexual women, may face invalidation or marginalization from both heterosexual and gay communities. In LGBTQ+ spaces, the prioritization of certain identities, often the most visible or socially accepted (e.g. gay, cisgender, white) over others, creates a form of internal hierarchy.

This dynamic often leads to a lack of support for those whose experiences do not fit neatly into the dominant narratives about queerness, and they may find themselves excluded from conversations, decision-making processes, or leadership roles within LGBTQ+ organizations.

1.3 Race and Ethnicity – The Marginalization of LGBTQ+ People of Colour:

LGBTQ+ spaces are often criticized for being disproportionately white, with queer people of colour (QPOC) frequently feeling alienated within predominantly white LGBTQ+ communities. This racial divide highlights the intersection of race and queerness, where people of colour are not only marginalized for their sexual or gender identity, but also face racism within LGBTQ+ spaces. The dominance of white, cisgender, gay narratives within LGBTQ+ organizations, can contribute to the erasure of the specific struggles faced by LGBTQ+ people of colour.

Racism within LGBTQ+ communities is a persistent issue that must be addressed if the community is to live up to its ideals of equality and justice. It requires not only acknowledging the existence of these racial divides, but also intentionally creating space for QPOC voices, experiences, and leadership. These efforts should go beyond surface-level or tokenistic inclusion and actively work toward dismantling deeply entrenched racial hierarchies within LGBTQ+ spaces.

1.4 Classism and Accessibility – The Exclusion of Low-Income LGBTQ+ Individuals:

Another hidden hierarchy within LGBTQ+ spaces is classism, which often disproportionately affects low-income individuals. LGBTQ+ communities, particularly in urban centres, can sometimes operate within a culture of affluence, where expensive venues, exclusive events, and inaccessible resources create barriers for people who cannot afford to participate in these spaces. This class divide within LGBTQ+ circles, excludes individuals from lower socio-economic backgrounds, preventing them from fully engaging with the community or receiving the support they need.

This hierarchy also extends to issues of accessibility, particularly for disabled LGBTQ+ individuals. Many LGBTQ+ events and spaces are not designed with accessibility in mind, further isolating those with disabilities. To truly achieve inclusivity, LGBTQ+ spaces must prioritize accessibility, ensuring that everyone, regardless of income or ability, can engage meaningfully within the community.

1.5 The Role of Allies and the Challenge of Privilege:

Allies, those who do not identify as LGBTQ+ but support the community, also play a role in reinforcing or challenging power dynamics within LGBTQ+ spaces. While allies are essential in advocating for LGBTQ+ rights, their presence can sometimes lead to the marginalization of LGBTQ+ voices, particularly when allies take up too much space or do not listen to the specific needs of the community.

Allies must be conscious of their privilege and recognize when their involvement in LGBTQ+ spaces becomes performative or counterproductive. The dynamic of allyship requires careful navigation, as allies must avoid speaking over or for LGBTQ+ individuals while ensuring their actions actively support and uplift marginalized voices.

1.6 The Path Forward – Empowering Inclusive Spaces:

To create truly inclusive LGBTQ+ spaces, it is essential to address and dismantle these hidden hierarchies. This requires active reflection on power dynamics, a willingness to listen to marginalized voices, and a commitment to shared leadership. LGBTQ+ spaces must prioritize intersectionality, ensuring that individuals from all backgrounds and identities feel seen, heard, and valued.

Fostering inclusivity within LGBTQ+ spaces also means acknowledging the limitations of dominant narratives and expanding the definition of queerness to include diverse experiences. It involves creating resources and spaces that are accessible, affordable, and welcoming for all members of the community, regardless of their class, race, gender, or ability.

1.7 Conclusion – Reclaiming Power and Building Solidarity:

The hidden hierarchies within LGBTQ+ spaces are a reflection of the broader societal inequalities that exist. However, by critically reflecting on these power structures and taking actionable steps to dismantle them, LGBTQ+ communities can become more equitable, empowering spaces for everyone. This process requires courage, humility, and a collective commitment to creating a community where all individuals, regardless of their identity or background, can thrive. The journey toward true inclusivity in LGBTQ+ spaces is ongoing, but through conscious effort, it is one that can lead to greater solidarity and empowerment for all.

2. When LGBTQ+ Communities Fail Their Own – Exclusion, Gatekeeping, and Racism

LGBTQ+ communities are often portrayed as unified, resilient, and progressive. In public discourse, they are seen as symbols of inclusion and acceptance. Yet beneath the surface of rainbow flags and Pride celebrations lies a more complicated truth, LGBTQ+ spaces can and often do fail their own members. Exclusion, gatekeeping, and racism are persistent and deeply harmful realities within these communities. Whether intentional or unconscious, these dynamics fracture solidarity and create enduring barriers for those who are already marginalized. Confronting these internal challenges is not about airing flaws for criticism, it is about ensuring the community lives up to its own values of equity, dignity and justice for all queer people.

2.1 Exclusion Behind the Curtain of Inclusivity:

For a movement founded on resistance to marginalization, exclusion within LGBTQ+ spaces is a painful irony. Individuals who are transgender, nonbinary, bisexual, disabled, fat, neurodivergent, or of certain ethnic backgrounds are often left out of conversations, events, and platforms. Their needs are routinely sidelined in favour of more "mainstream" narratives, usually white, cisgender, able-bodied and male-centred. This is not simply about visibility, it's about survival, validation, and access to critical resources and community. Exclusion doesn't always wear a blatant face. It can be subtle, an event lacking wheelchair accessibility, a panel discussion with no trans representation, or social media campaigns that never show dark-skinned bodies.

These absences send a message, that some queer identities are more acceptable or palatable than others. Inclusivity must go beyond slogans and visibility to actively engage with and prioritize the lived realities of all members of the LGBTQ+ spectrum.

2.2 The Politics of Gatekeeping:

Gatekeeping within LGBTQ+ spaces is another pervasive issue. This form of control often manifests in deciding who is "queer enough," "trans enough," or even "politically correct enough" to be part of the community. People who don't conform to certain aesthetics, language, or experiences may be ostracized or invalidated. Bisexual individuals are often told to "pick a side." Trans people who don't want to medically transition may be questioned or excluded. Those with non-Western expressions of queerness might find themselves policed for not fitting into white, Western norms.

Gatekeeping upholds rigid standards of identity that are antithetical to the fluid, self-defined nature of queerness. It recreates the very systems of surveillance and judgment that LGBTQ+ individuals have fought to escape. Instead of fostering acceptance and exploration, gatekeeping builds invisible walls and reinforces a sense of not being "queer the right way."

2.3 Racism Within the Rainbow:

Racism remains one of the most unspoken, yet damaging fractures within LGBTQ+ communities. Queer people of colour (QPOC) consistently report experiences of exclusion, fetishization and microaggressions from within the very spaces that should be safe for them. Whether it's Black trans women being ignored at Pride events, or Latinx and Asian queer folks being underrepresented in media and leadership roles, the message is clear, whiteness is still centred, even in queer liberation.

This racism is not just interpersonal, it's structural. Predominantly white LGBTQ+ organizations often receive more funding, media attention, and political clout, while QPOC-led initiatives struggle for basic resources. Events are frequently held in gentrified areas that push out queer communities of colour, or curated in ways that ignore cultural nuance. These patterns create two-tiered systems within LGBTQ+ spaces, one that uplifts whiteness and another that marginalizes everyone else.

2.4 The Harm of Respectability Politics:

Respectability politics also fuel internal exclusion. Some LGBTQ+ members, especially those who have gained a degree of mainstream acceptance, attempt to appeal to broader society by distancing themselves from individuals seen as "too radical," "too flamboyant," or "too political." This often includes sex workers, drag performers, gender-nonconforming people and anyone whose expression doesn't align with heteronormative ideals. This push for acceptance at the cost of diversity fractures community bonds and reinforces the idea that queerness must be sanitized to be worthy of respect. True liberation does not come from conforming to oppressive norms, but from challenging them and this means, embracing all forms of queer expression, not just the ones deemed most digestible to straight society.

2.5 Accountability and Growth from Within:

Recognizing these failures is not about placing blame on individuals but about fostering accountability and transformation. LGBTQ+ spaces must engage in ongoing self-examination to ask who is missing, who is being centred and who is being left out. This can start with small changes, amplifying QPOC voices, ensuring accessibility, dismantling cliques and checking bias in leadership roles. It also means creating space for conflict, listening when harm is named and committing to repair rather than defensiveness. Growth requires more than intention, it demands action. Community organizations must redistribute power, invite a broader range of leadership and reimagine what inclusivity truly looks like. Pride is not just a celebration, it's also a responsibility to every member of the community, especially those who've been pushed to the margins.

2.6 Reclaiming Community Through Solidarity:

Despite these challenges, LGBTQ+ communities also have the tools and potential to heal from within. Queer history is rich with mutual aid, resistance and radical love. These same values can guide the process of making LGBTQ+ spaces more genuinely inclusive. Solidarity is not passive, it is active, intentional, and deeply relational. It involves showing up for each other, advocating across lines of difference, and making space for multiple truths to coexist. Rebuilding trust and inclusivity is possible when communities prioritize empathy over elitism, collaboration over competition and justice over image. By centering those who have been historically excluded, LGBTQ+ spaces can become stronger, more authentic, and more unified.

2.7 Conclusion – Toward a Community That Honors All:

When LGBTQ+ communities fail their own, the consequences are not just personal, they ripple through generations, leaving wounds that echo in silence. Marginalization within our own spaces, whether through racism, transphobia, ageism, ableism, or classism, fractures the very foundation of what should be a movement rooted in love and liberation. Yet, within that failure lies an opportunity, a necessary reckoning and a call to reflect, rebuild and recommit. True queerness does not reside in flawless ideology or curated optics, but in the messy, brave and ongoing work of showing up for one another. It's found in listening without defensiveness, in making room at the table and in holding space for discomfort as we grow. Our power lies in community, in chosen family, in the radical act of not leaving each other behind. If the LGBTQ+ movement is to be a home for all, it must be willing to confront its own shadows, the ways it has excluded, erased, or silenced and stretch beyond them. This is not about shame, but transformation. A future rooted in justice, care and joy, is only possible when every identity, voice and experience is not only included, but truly honoured.

3. The Importance of Elders and Generational Storytelling in Queer Communities

In queer communities, where histories have often been erased, ignored, or distorted, the voices of elders carry a rare and precious weight.

They are the keepers of memory, living witnesses to decades of survival, resistance, and resilience. At a time when LGBTQ+ identities are gaining more visibility and acceptance in some parts of the world, it is tempting to focus solely on the present or future. But without acknowledging and honouring the generations who came before, we risk losing the very foundation upon which our communities stand. Elders are not just storytellers, they are cultural custodians, guardians of queer legacy and reminders of both struggle and triumph.

3.1 Survival, Resistance and Silence:

For many queer elders, survival often came at a deep cost. They lived through eras of criminalization, institutionalization, and social rejection. Some witnessed the devastation of the AIDS crisis, when whole communities were decimated while governments remained silent. Others navigated lives in the shadows, forced to hide their identities in order to maintain jobs, families, or personal safety. Their stories are often filled with pain, but also with unimaginable strength and creativity, of finding chosen families, underground networks, and moments of joy in the margins.

These stories weren't always recorded in history books or documented in archives. They were shared in whispers, in letters, in bars and bedrooms, in protest chants and underground publications. Elders have preserved these memories through oral tradition and lived experience, often without recognition. Their silence was not forgetfulness, it was survival. But now, with space and safety growing, albeit unevenly, those stories can finally be told, and they deserve to be heard with reverence and gratitude.

3.2 The Role of Storytelling in Queer Identity:

Storytelling in queer communities has always been more than just the act of sharing, it's an act of resistance. When queer history is erased, silenced, or rewritten, telling one's story becomes a radical and affirming act. For younger generations, hearing these stories helps make sense of their own identities and struggles. They gain not only a sense of belonging, but also a roadmap, however imperfect, of what it means to be queer in a world that still often devalues queer life.

Through generational storytelling, a continuity is created across time. This intergenerational dialogue doesn't just educate, it heals. It bridges the gaps created by loss, trauma, and social exclusion. It shows that we are not alone and we never were. Elders offer context, wisdom, and grounding, especially in moments when the future feels uncertain. By telling our stories and listening to theirs, we build a living legacy of truth that honours the past and boldly guides the future. It becomes a solid foundation for future generations to stand on with pride and purpose.

3.3 The Erosion of Generational Bonds:

Despite the vital and irreplaceable role that queer elders play, many LGBTQ+ communities today are marked by a noticeable lack of intergenerational connection and continuity. The AIDS crisis created a devastating generational gap, where an entire cohort of potential mentors and leaders was lost. The silence left behind continues to echo through generations.

For many, this meant growing up without role models, without people who looked or loved like them, without guidance on how to survive and thrive. Modern LGBTQ+ culture, especially online, can sometimes reinforce this gap by prioritizing youth, visibility and trendiness, unintentionally marginalizing older queer people. Ageism within queer spaces leaves many elders feeling invisible or irrelevant, despite the immense wisdom they carry. Rebuilding these bonds is essential for the health and future of LGBTQ+ communities.

3.4 Learning from Our Elders – Lessons in Resilience:

The insights offered by queer elders are multifaceted. They remind us of how far we've come, while also warning us not to become complacent. They know what it's like to lose rights, to fight tooth and nail for dignity, and to do so with limited resources or public support. Their experiences of navigating hostile environments offer strategies for resilience, resistance, and adaptation that are still relevant today. Whether it's advice about relationships, navigating homophobia or transphobia, or simply how to build chosen family, the lessons passed down through storytelling are invaluable. In these stories, we find not just warnings or lessons, but also humour, creativity, and hope. Elders teach us that survival is possible and that joy can coexist with struggle. Through their stories, queer elders show us that resilience is built through both hardship and celebration, reminding us to honour the past while continuing to forge a better future.

3.5 Preserving Queer Histories:

To honour our elders is also to ensure their stories are preserved. Archival work, oral history projects, and community-based storytelling initiatives are crucial. But so too are the informal conversations, over tea, in community centres, at Pride events, or in online spaces, that allow for connection and reflection. Queer history is not just Stonewall or legislation, it's personal narratives, everyday experiences and emotional truths. We must support spaces where these can be shared, recorded, and passed down. This includes making space in educational curriculums, supporting elder care that affirms LGBTQ+ identities, and fostering events, where elders are central rather than peripheral. Preserving queer histories means creating spaces where stories are valued, shared and passed down, ensuring that the experiences of our elders remain a vital part of the ongoing fight for equality and recognition.

3.6 Call for Intergenerational Solidarity:

The future of queer liberation depends on the strength of intergenerational ties. When we create intentional relationships between younger and older queer individuals, we build communities that are more inclusive, compassionate and wise. It is not just about what elders can teach the young, but also about what the young can offer, new perspectives, energy, and validation that their lives and stories matter. Celebrating our elders is not an act of nostalgia, it's a radical declaration that our past is worth preserving, our present is worth sharing, and our future is worth fighting for. Intergenerational solidarity empowers our communities, fostering a shared sense of purpose and continuity, where the wisdom of the past and the vision of the future are deeply interconnected. Intergenerational solidarity strengthens communities, merging past wisdom with future energy in the light for queer liberation.

***Carrying the Torch – Queer Stories Passed Across Generations:**

For example, but not limited to, these documentaries, podcasts and books, offer moving windows into the lives of queer elders, into their history, memories and resilience. It serves as powerful tools for education, empathy, and preserving cultural legacy.

Documentaries:	**Paris Is Burning (1990)** A ballroom documentary classic caputring the culture, struggles and wisdom of queer Black and Latinx communities **A Place to Live - The Story of Triangle Square (2008)** Follows LGBTQ+ seniors seeking safe, affirming housing at the first affordable complex for queer elders in Los Angeles. A moving look at community, dignity and aging with pride **Gen Silent (2010)** Explores the isolation and strength of LGBTQ+ elders navigating aging and care systems **The Lavender Scare (2017)** A Gripping look at the Cold War-era purge of LGBTQ+ federal workers and the people who fought back **To Survive on This Shore (2018)** Photo and storytelling project documenting the lives of oder trans and gender nonconforming people
Podcasts:	**Making Gay History** Historic interviews with LGBTQ+ activists and unsung heroes across generations **Transcripts** From the Tretter Oral History Project - stories of trans lives, transitions and intergenerational learning **LGBTQ&A** In depth interviews with queer trailblazers and elders - from Miss Major to Cleve Jones
Books:	**Before We Were Trans by Kit Heyam** A thoughtful historical lens on gender-diverse lives long before modern tegnology **The Stonewall Generations by Jane Feishman** Firsthand narratives from elders who lived through pivotal LGBTQ+ movements **Older, Wiser, Wilder: A Queer Elder Archive** Zine-style storytelling by LGBTQ+ elders in their own words, poems, essays and oral histories

4. Navigating LGBTQ+ Friendships – When Does Chosen Family Become Toxic?

For many LGBTQ+ individuals, chosen family is more than a concept, it's a lifeline. When biological families reject or misunderstand queer identities, close friendships often become the primary source of emotional support, love and belonging. These bonds, forged in vulnerability and shared struggle, can feel more intimate and enduring than traditional family ties. They provide a sense of community, identity and safety, in a world that often marginalizes queer people. But as with all relationships, chosen families are not immune to conflict, imbalance, or harm. When boundaries blur and expectations go unspoken, even the most loving queer friendships can become fraught or even toxic. The goal is not to discredit the importance of chosen family, but to hold space for honest reflection on how these bonds function and sometimes falter.

4.1 Why Chosen Families Matter in LGBTQ+ Lives:

Queer individuals often face familial rejection, cultural alienation, or societal isolation, which makes the idea of building one's own family all the more significant. Chosen families are born from a refusal to accept loneliness as a given. They offer validation, affirmation, and a place to be seen fully, without judgment. These relationships serve as emotional anchors during major life transitions, coming out, transitioning, navigating systemic discrimination, or simply trying to exist authentically in a world that doesn't always make space for difference.

Unlike traditional family structures, chosen families are not bound by obligation, they are rooted in mutual respect, trust, and shared values. This voluntary nature makes them uniquely powerful, but also uniquely vulnerable. Without the formal scripts that often govern familial roles, queer friendships must navigate emotional terrain with care and intentionality.

4.2 The Slippery Slope – When Intimacy Becomes Entanglement:

Chosen family relationships often run deep, so deep that the boundaries between friendship, emotional dependency, and identity can become blurred. The intense closeness of queer friendships can sometimes create unspoken expectations or pressure to always be available, always agree, or always prioritize the friendship above other relationships.

This closeness can be beautiful, but it can also be emotionally overwhelming. It may manifest as possessiveness, guilt-tripping, or co-dependency. When one person in the chosen family assumes a caretaking or sacrificial role, they may begin to feel drained or resentful, even if they still love the people they are supporting. Emotional labour, when constantly one-sided, becomes unsustainable.

Recognizing the line between intimacy and entanglement is not about withdrawing love, but about understanding that healthy friendships require reciprocity, respect for boundaries, emotional safety and room to grow independently.

4.3 Red Flags and Quiet Harm:

Toxicity within chosen families doesn't always appear in explosive arguments or dramatic betrayals. More often, it shows up quietly, through passive aggression, emotional manipulation, lack of accountability, or chronic invalidation of someone's needs. It might be the friend who constantly centres their pain while minimizing yours, or the group dynamic that excludes those who don't conform to an unspoken norm. Sometimes, it's subtle competition masked as camaraderie or pressure to stay in roles that no longer fit. Because these relationships are rooted in love and survival, it can be incredibly hard to acknowledge when they're no longer healthy. Many queer people fear that questioning their chosen family means losing their only source of belonging. But naming harm, even gently, is an act of care, for oneself and for the relationship.

4.4 Boundaries Are Not Betrayal:

Setting boundaries within chosen family may feel like betrayal, especially in communities where mutual dependence has been essential for survival. But in truth, boundaries are what make long-term intimacy possible. They create the conditions for safety, consent, and mutual flourishing.

This may mean saying no when you're overwhelmed, redefining the role you play in someone's life, or even stepping back entirely from a friendship that has become harmful. These decisions are never easy, especially when deep history and shared identity are involved. But they are necessary acts of self-preservation and integrity.

Communicating needs openly, checking in regularly, and respecting each other's autonomy are all ways to maintain healthy, sustainable chosen family dynamics. It's not about giving up on people, it's about giving everyone, including yourself, the best chance to heal and thrive.

4.5 Repair, Growth, and Letting Go:

Sometimes relationships can be repaired. When both parties are willing to take accountability and make changes, it's possible to rebuild trust and redefine connection in healthier ways. This might involve therapy, mediated conversations, or simply time apart to gain clarity. Queer friendships are resilient and many have survived hardship precisely, because of a shared commitment to growth and care. But not every chosen family relationship can, or should, be salvaged.

Letting go can be painful, especially when it feels like giving up on a lifeline. Still, release can also be a profound act of love, honouring what the relationship once gave you and recognizing that it no longer supports who you are becoming. Grief is natural in these moments.

But so is relief. And often, letting go opens space for new, healthier relationships to emerge, ones that affirm your worth without asking you to shrink. Sometimes, choosing yourself is the most loving act, honouring your boundaries and making space for connection rooted in mutual care, not obligation.

4.6 Reimagining Chosen Family with Intention:

Chosen family will always be a cornerstone of queer life. But as we evolve individually and collectively, we must also evolve, how we build, sustain, and sometimes release these connections. We can create chosen families that are not just about survival, but about mutual growth, care, and liberation. This means fostering friendships that encourage accountability, celebrate boundaries, and leave room for change. It means acknowledging harm without shame and honouring love without losing ourselves. When we approach queer friendship with compassion and clarity, we build not just safety nets, but communities where everyone can breathe, transform and belong.

5. The Double Life Dilemma – Queer People in Conservative Societies

For many queer individuals in conservative societies, life becomes an act of delicate performance, a continuous effort to appear acceptable, stay safe and protect one's livelihood, family ties and sometimes even one's life. Living authentically may feel like an unattainable dream, not due to a lack of desire, but because the cost of openness can be unbearably high. This double life, in which one's true self is carefully hidden beneath layers of enforced conformity, becomes a quiet, daily battle that takes an enormous emotional toll. The dilemma is not merely about secrecy, it is about the psychological burden of living a fragmented existence, where self-expression is stifled and authenticity often has to yield to survival.

5.1 Cultural and Familial Pressures:

In many conservative societies, the expectations of family, religion, and tradition are deeply entrenched. Heteronormativity is not simply assumed, it is actively enforced. From a young age, individuals are taught clear roles regarding gender, sexuality, and family honour. Any deviation from these expectations is often met with shame, punishment, or social ostracism.

For queer people, especially those who identify as transgender, non-binary, or same-gender loving, these pressures are not abstract, they are intimate and lived. The fear of disappointing one's parents, losing community support, or bringing "dishonour" to a family can create paralyzing guilt and fear. Many choose silence and secrecy, not because they are ashamed, but because they fear what their truth could cost. In such environments, love and loyalty become entangled with self-denial, leading many to compartmentalize their identities in order to maintain familial bonds.

5.2 The Psychological Cost of Hiding:

Living a double life is not just a logistical challenge, it is a profound emotional burden. Hiding who you are, constantly editing your speech and behaviour, and watching your every move in public spaces creates chronic stress. Over time, this stress can lead to anxiety, depression, isolation, and burnout. There is the pain of not being known, the exhaustion of always performing, and the deep grief of missing out on full, unfiltered relationships. Queer individuals may find themselves lying about romantic partners, avoiding certain topics, or even creating entirely false narratives about their lives.

These acts of self-preservation come at the expense of self-connection. Over time, it can become difficult to separate the real self from the mask, a disorienting experience that can leave people feeling emotionally unmoored and spiritually adrift.

5.3 Intimacy and Relationships in the Shadows:

One of the most heartbreaking consequences of the double life is its impact on intimacy. Romantic and sexual relationships are often hidden, rushed, or fragmented by fear. Meeting a partner in secret, never being able to hold hands in public, and constantly scanning the environment for threats, becomes the norm. The inability to be openly affectionate or acknowledged as a couple can chip away at even the strongest bonds.

Friendships, too, suffer under the weight of secrecy. In communities where outing someone can lead to severe consequences, trust becomes sacred and rare. Many queer individuals are cautious about who they let in, fearing judgment or betrayal. As a result, they may go through life surrounded by people, yet profoundly lonely, yearning for connection without the freedom to pursue it fully.

5.4 The Small Acts of Resistance and Resilience:

And yet, amid the repression and pain, there are countless small acts of resistance and resilience. Queer people in conservative societies carve out hidden spaces of joy, build quiet networks of support and find creative ways to affirm their identities. These acts may seem small, a coded text, a shared glance, a private celebration, but they are radical in their defiance of a world that demands invisibility.

Many also turn to art, music, writing, or activism, discreet or public, as a way to process their reality and claim their truth. Others seek online communities, where they can speak freely and find solidarity with people across the globe. In the face of immense pressure to conform, these avenues become lifelines, reminders that even in silence, they are not alone.

5.5 The Hope for Change and the Need for Safety:

The desire to live authentically is not a Western luxury, it is a human right. And while cultural change may be slow, it is happening. Younger generations are often more open-minded, and global access to information has begun to shift conversations even in the most traditional societies. LGBTQ+ visibility, though still fraught with danger in some places, is steadily growing, often led by local activists, artists, and everyday people living boldly in their own way.

However, hope alone is not enough. There must also be pathways to safety, legal protections, mental health resources and inclusive community spaces, that prioritize the well-being of queer individuals navigating hostile environments. Empowerment without protection is incomplete, true liberation must be rooted in both courage and care. Allies within these societies play a crucial role too, by listening, advocating and challenging the norms that perpetuate harm. True progress comes when change is paired with tangible support, ensuring that queer individuals can thrive safely and authentically.

5.6 Conclusion – A Call for Compassion and Understanding:

Living a double life is not a failure of authenticity, it is a testament to endurance. It is a survival strategy born from necessity, not choice. Rather than judging those who remain closeted or careful, we must offer empathy and understanding. Their experience is equally valid and queer, shaped simply by a different set of risks and realities.

Queer liberation must include all identities, not just the visible and vocal. It must make space for those whose lives are quieter, whose safety depends on discretion, and whose truths deserve recognition, even when they cannot yet be shouted from rooftops. By holding space for these complex experiences, we move closer to a world where no one has to choose between their safety and their selfhood.

Chapter 4

Healing from Trauma – Past, Present, and Future

---

1. The Long-Term Effects of Conversion Therapy and Religious Trauma

Conversion therapy and religious trauma leave behind wounds that cannot be seen on the surface but are deeply embedded in the emotional and psychological landscape of many LGBTQ+ individuals. These practices and experiences are not relics of the past, they continue to affect people's lives today, both in overt and subtle ways. Conversion therapy, defined as any attempt to forcibly change or suppress a person's sexual orientation or gender identity, is a direct assault on one's sense of self. Religious trauma, often rooted in spiritual abuse, rigid dogma, and systemic rejection, creates a persistent inner conflict between belief and identity. Exploring the long-term emotional, psychological, and relational consequences of these traumas is essential, not only to understand their impact, but to centre the voices, strength, and healing of survivors.

1.1 Conversion Therapy – A Deep Betrayal of Self:

At its core, conversion therapy is built on a foundation of shame. It tells LGBTQ+ people that their identity is flawed, sinful, or broken and that to be loved or accepted, they must change. Many are subjected to this under the guise of care, often by those closest to them, family members, therapists, and religious leaders. Techniques may range from spiritually manipulative "prayers for healing" to psychologically damaging behavioural conditioning. Regardless of the method, the message remains the same, "You are not enough as you are." For young people, especially those in religious environments, the psychological damage is compounded by the trust placed in authority figures. This betrayal of trust leaves a long-lasting impression, often manifesting later as an inability to feel safe even in affirming spaces. Survivors speak of dissociation, self-hatred, and a fractured sense of reality. It is a violation that reverberates far beyond the moment of its occurrence.

1.2 Religious Trauma – When Faith Becomes Fear:

Religious trauma, while sometimes more insidious than conversion therapy, can be just as devastating. For many queer people raised in deeply religious communities, identity is shaped alongside scripture and sermons that frame LGBTQ+ existence as a moral failing. Over time, internalizing such messages leads to chronic guilt, spiritual anxiety, and a sense of deep unworthiness. The development of Religious Trauma Syndrome, a term used to describe the lingering psychological harm from toxic religious experiences, is increasingly recognized by mental health professionals. Survivors report symptoms akin to PTSD, panic attacks, flashbacks, hypervigilance, and spiritual disconnection. The most painful part for many is the sense of spiritual homelessness.

Religion was once a source of belonging and meaning, and its loss, particularly when tied to rejection by loved ones, can feel like mourning both a family and a faith. The trauma lies not just in what was taught, but in how it was used to control, suppress, and shame.

1.3 Emotional and Psychological Aftermath:

The emotional fallout from conversion therapy and religious trauma is not temporary. It lingers in the form of chronic shame, depression, anxiety, and often a lifelong struggle with identity and belonging. Many survivors internalize the belief that love must be earned through suppression of self. This belief erodes self-esteem and can lead to years of silence, self-policing, and even suicidal ideation. Relationships with others become fraught, not necessarily because of any external hostility, but because of the deep-rooted belief that one is inherently unworthy. The world may change and become more accepting, but the internalized messages planted in childhood or adolescence often remain unless actively confronted. Healing is not about simply "getting over it", it's about unlearning harmful messages, gently reparenting oneself, and navigating the layered grief of what was lost, time, safety, connection, and authenticity.

1.4 Impact on Relationships and Intimacy:

Trauma rooted in identity does not stay contained, it bleeds into every facet of life, including how survivors form connections with others. For many, intimate relationships become difficult to maintain, because of ingrained fear of rejection or the inability to be fully emotionally vulnerable. Trust is compromised when the people who claimed to love you unconditionally were the same ones who told you to hide or change. The body itself can become a site of conflict, touched by memories of shame or fear. Survivors may fear being seen too closely or resist closeness entirely. This isn't a reflection of their capacity to love or be loved, it is a response to having been told for years that love is conditional, that safety is temporary, and that acceptance must be earned. Healing in this context means slowly learning what unconditional love looks like and, even more challengingly, what it feels like to deserve it.

1.5 The Ongoing Fight for Recognition and Healing:

Despite the widespread condemnation of conversion therapy by mental health associations, it remains legal in many parts of the world and continues to be quietly practiced under religious or alternative wellness labels. Survivors often encounter disbelief or minimization when they share their experiences, particularly in societies that view such practices as things of the past. This denial adds another layer of trauma. The fight for recognition is not merely symbolic, it is life-saving. Survivor-led advocacy groups have played a critical role in changing legislation, increasing awareness, and demanding that institutions be held accountable. Yet legal reform is only one part of the healing process. Equally essential is the availability of trauma-informed, LGBTQ+ affirming mental health care. Healing is not a solitary process, it is collective, communal, and deeply political. It is a declaration that what happened was not okay and that those affected deserve support, visibility, and justice.

1.6 Moving Toward Queer Spiritual Reclamation:

For some survivors, the path forward includes reclaiming spirituality outside the confines of the institutions that harmed them. Queer spiritual reclamation is a deeply personal journey, involving the search for meaning, ritual and connection, that affirms one's identity rather than erases it. Some turn to inclusive faith communities, while others craft their own spiritual practices that reflect their values and truths. For others, healing may mean rejecting religion altogether, and that too is valid. The key is choice, something many survivors were previously denied. Spiritual healing, when approached with autonomy and affirmation, can be profoundly restorative. It allows for the reconnection with a sense of self that is not rooted in fear, but in love and belonging.

1.7 Conclusion – Holding Space for Truth:

The long-term effects of conversion therapy and religious trauma are profound, multifaceted, and enduring. They affect not only the way LGBTQ+ individuals see themselves, but also how they relate to others, to community, and to the world. Healing is possible, but it requires acknowledgement, validation, and support. Each survivor carries a story that deserves to be heard, not just as a testimony of suffering, but as a testament to resilience. In holding space for these truths, we honour those who have survived, those still in the midst of healing, and those reclaiming their right to live fully and freely. By creating a space for truth and healing, we contribute to a future where survival is celebrated and liberation is possible.

2. Healing the Wounds of Being a "Late Bloomer" in Queer Identity

Some people know who they are from the start. Others spend years trying to figure it out, wrestling quietly with questions they don't yet have the language to answer. For those who come into their queer identity later in life, the realization can be both freeing and deeply emotional. It might feel like catching your breath after holding it for too long. It might also come with grief, regret, or a lingering sense of "being behind." But queerness isn't something you're late to. It unfolds in its own time, in its own way. There's no right age to become yourself. Queer identity unfolds uniquely for each person and there's no wrong time to embrace your truth.

2.1 The Myth of the Linear Queer Narrative:

So much of what we see in media, books, and culture presents a narrow version of what queerness looks like, early awareness, early coming out, and a bold defiance of norms from a young age. While these stories are powerful and important, they're not the only ones. They can unintentionally create pressure to have figured it all out by a certain point and if you haven't, you might wonder if you're "really" queer or if you missed your chance. You didn't. So many people realize, reclaim, or finally name their identity in adulthood or beyond. Life circumstances, fear, survival instincts, lack of representation, all of these can delay that process. That delay doesn't make your identity any less true. It simply makes your journey different and no less deserving of love or celebration. Every queer journey is valid and the timing of self-discovery should be embraced, not rushed.

2.2 Grieving What Was Missed or Delayed:

There's often an ache that comes with realizing how much time passed before you could live as your full self. Missed crushes, secret desires, awkward silences when others were allowed to speak freely about their loves and losses, those things matter. The grief that surfaces isn't something to suppress or brush aside. It's a part of honouring your past. You might find yourself mourning experiences you never had, wondering who you could've been if you had known sooner. It's okay to feel that. It's okay to cry over it. You're allowed to acknowledge what was lost while still embracing what's possible. Grieving doesn't mean staying stuck, it's a step toward healing. Allowing yourself to grieve is a powerful step in reclaiming the future and embracing your authentic self.

2.3 Reclaiming Joy, Exploration and Queer Possibility:

What some call "late blooming" can also be seen as rebirth. With this new understanding of yourself comes the chance to explore life with fresh eyes. Maybe for the first time, you're making decisions that reflect who you really are. Whether it's changing your wardrobe, experimenting with pronouns, dating openly, or simply letting yourself feel attraction without shame, every choice becomes a small act of liberation. There's something powerful about permitting yourself to play, to be curious, to mess up and try again. Joy doesn't have an age limit. Queerness is expansive, and there's room for all your firsts, no matter when they happen. Embracing these new beginnings with joy creates a path toward living your fullest, most authentic life.

2.4 Repairing the Relationship with the Self and Others:

Coming out later in life often brings with it a complicated internal conversation. You may feel anger at yourself for not knowing sooner, or guilt for the years you spent in silence. You may question old relationships or wonder how your current ones will evolve. These emotions are normal and valid. But here's a truth worth holding onto, you didn't fail yourself. You survived. You coped. You did what you needed to do with the knowledge and safety you had at the time. That survival deserves compassion, not criticism. Rebuilding trust in yourself is a gentle process, one where you learn to listen to your intuition, honour your boundaries, and extend kindness inward. And if your relationships shift, remember those who truly love you will want to know the real you.

2.5 Building Community at Every Age:

It can feel intimidating to enter queer spaces when you're older or newer to the identity. You might wonder if there's room for you, especially when so many visible parts of queer culture seem youth-centered. But queerness isn't reserved for the young. It's a shared language, a spectrum of stories, a collection of lives unfolding at different speeds. There are others out there just like you, people navigating self-discovery in midlife or beyond, seeking connection, belonging, and chosen family. Whether you find them online, at local events, through support groups, or chance encounters, know that you're not alone. You have something important to contribute, your perspective, your resilience, your voice.

2.6 Embracing Your Queer Identity with Pride and Wholeness:

There's something deeply affirming about looking in the mirror and finally seeing yourself, not the version shaped by expectation, but the one who was always waiting underneath. Embracing your queer identity isn't about ticking boxes or catching up. It's about owning who you are with pride and tenderness. You get to define what queerness means to you. You get to set your pace, choose your community, and celebrate in your own way. You haven't missed the moment, you are the moment. Every step you take toward authenticity is a celebration of your courage.

2.7 Your Queerness is Right on Time:

You didn't arrive late. You arrived ready. And that is enough. The world may try to convince you that your queerness would've been better earlier, more "valid" somehow, but that's not true. You are not a lesser version. You are not behind. You are unfolding in your own time, on your own terms. And there is so much still waiting for you, love, connection, discovery, peace. Healing the wounds of being a late bloomer isn't about erasing the past, it's about honouring it while choosing something fuller, freer, and more joyful for yourself now. Your story is far from over. In fact, some of the best chapters may be just beginning.

3. Trauma Bonding in LGBTQ+ Relationships – Why It Happens and How to Heal

Trauma bonds don't happen in isolation. For many LGBTQ+ people, the risk factors are intensified by lifelong exposure to rejection, invisibility, and emotional harm. Growing up in environments where identity is denied or condemned often teaches a person to question their worth before they even understand who they are. Emotional neglect, religious shame, bullying, or being told that love must be earned all plant seeds of insecurity that can follow someone into adulthood. When two people with unresolved wounds meet, they may see their own pain reflected in each other and confuse that recognition for love. While shared trauma can create a powerful connection, it doesn't always foster healing. Instead, it can repeat patterns of instability, especially when that chaos feels oddly familiar, even comforting.

3.1 Recognizing the Signs of a Trauma Bond:

It's not always easy to tell when you're in a trauma bond. The signs often hide beneath the surface, tangled up in hope and history. You might find yourself constantly justifying someone's harmful behaviour or believing that if you love them enough, they'll change. Waves of euphoria can give way to profound emotional lows. You might feel unable to leave, not because you're happy, but because you're terrified of being without them. These relationships often come with guilt, fear, and a sense of emotional addiction. A trauma bond isn't a sign you're broken, it's a sign you learned to survive in the best way you could. Now, you deserve better. Recognizing the trauma bond is the first step toward breaking free, healing, and reclaiming your emotional freedom and peace.

3.2 Differentiating Love from Trauma:

One of the most powerful realizations in the healing process is that love and trauma are not the same. True love should not make you feel unsafe, small, or uncertain of your worth. When trauma bonds are present, the body can confuse chaos for chemistry, or volatility for passion. But intensity is not intimacy. You don't need to suffer to be seen. Healthy love feels calm, mutual, and supportive. It allows you to grow, not shrink. Learning to recognize the difference is hard, especially if pain was your first teacher, but it's also one of the most freeing shifts you can make. Understanding this difference not only transforms how we love ourselves and others, but also challenges the harmful narratives we've internalized from a world that often confuses struggle with worth. Recognizing this distinction empowers you to choose love that nurtures, respects, and affirms your true self.

3.3 The Role of Early Wounds and Attachment Patterns:

For many LGBTQ+ individuals, childhood and adolescence were filled with experiences of rejection, shame, or hiding. These early wounds shape the way we connect with others. If you were taught to earn love by suppressing who you are, you might carry that pattern into adult relationships. Trauma bonds often mimic the dynamics of your earliest attachments. This doesn't mean you're doomed to repeat the past, but it does mean those old patterns need care, attention, and healing. You're allowed to rewrite the story. You're allowed to unlearn what hurt you. By healing these early wounds, you can break free from unhealthy patterns and build healthier, authentic connections.

3.4 Why Leaving Can Feel Impossible:

One of the most painful parts of a trauma bond is how hard it can be to leave, even when the relationship is clearly harming you. The connection feels like both a lifeline and a trap. There might be fear of abandonment, fear of starting over, or fear of not finding love again, especially if you've already faced a lifetime of rejection. Trauma bonds create a false sense of dependency, it feels like you need the other person to survive. But this isn't true. The discomfort of leaving is temporary. The peace that follows is lasting. Breaking free from a trauma bond takes courage, but once you do, you'll discover the strength to rebuild your life.

3.5 Strategies for Breaking the Cycle:

Breaking a trauma bond takes time, courage, and support, but it's possible. Start small. Begin by acknowledging that something doesn't feel right. Talk to a queer-affirming therapist if you can. Write down your feelings, your boundaries, your truths. Create distance, even emotionally, if you're not ready to physically leave yet. Surround yourself with people who affirm your worth and remind you of your strength. Build a safety plan if your relationship is abusive. Most importantly, be patient with yourself. Healing isn't a straight line. Every step you take, no matter how small, is a radical act of reclaiming your power. Remember, breaking the cycle isn't about perfection, but about progress. Trust yourself and take it one step at a time.

3.6 Rebuilding a Healthier Sense of Self:

Trauma bonding often erodes self-trust. It leaves you questioning your instincts, your boundaries, your identity. Part of the healing process is reconnecting with the parts of you that got buried under survival mode. This might mean learning to say no without guilt, asking for your needs to be met, or even discovering who you are outside of the relationship. Self-compassion becomes your anchor. You don't have to have it all figured out. You just have to start by believing you are worthy of safety and love that doesn't hurt.

3.7 Relearning Love and Healthy Intimacy:

When you've spent a long time in unhealthy dynamics, healthy relationships might feel boring or unfamiliar at first. But safety is not boring, it's sacred. True intimacy allows space for vulnerability, for mutual care, for softness. It might take time to feel comfortable in that kind of relationship, but it's worth the wait. You are allowed to want tenderness, consistency, and emotional security. These things are not luxuries, they are your birthright. Relearning love and intimacy is a process of rediscovery, one where safety, trust, and care become the foundation.

3.8 You Are Not Alone and Healing Is Possible:

If you see yourself in these words, know this, you are not alone. So many LGBTQ+ people have experienced trauma bonds, and so many have broken free. Your journey is valid, even if it's messy. You are not defined by your past or by the people who couldn't love you well. You are not too damaged, too late, or too far gone. Healing is real. Wholeness is possible. And there is a kind of love, starting with your own, that will never ask you to abandon yourself to feel seen. You deserve that love. You always have.

4. The Impact of Family Estrangement on Mental and Emotional Health

Family estrangement within the LGBTQ+ community is often an invisible but deeply painful reality. Rejection by one's family of origin disrupts more than just relationships, it shakes the foundational belief that family is meant to offer unconditional love and belonging. Although chosen family can bring comfort and healing, the absence of support from one's biological or legal relatives leaves a lasting emotional impact. The heartbreak that follows, especially after the vulnerable experience of coming out, runs deep. The mental and emotional toll of such rejection is profound and deserves thoughtful, compassionate acknowledgment.

4.1 The Emotional Foundation of Family:

Families form the emotional blueprint of our lives. From an early age, people look to their families for cues on how to love, how to feel safe, and how to belong. For LGBTQ+ individuals, the expectation of unconditional familial love often stands in stark contrast to the reality of coming out. Rejection, whether overt or subtle, can dismantle one's sense of self and security.

Even before coming out, many queer individuals live with the constant fear that their truth might fracture their most foundational relationships. This chronic fear and anxiety can become embedded in a person's psyche, making the eventual loss, if it comes, even more devastating.

4.2 Defining Estrangement – Beyond Physical Separation:

Family estrangement is not always loud or final. It can appear as complete disownment, but it more often exists in quieter, more insidious forms, like emotional distancing, passive silence, or conditional acceptance. An LGBTQ+ person might still be invited to family gatherings, but hear their name misused or their partner ignored. Others may be tolerated, but not embraced, spoken to, but not truly seen. These subtle forms of exclusion are no less painful and, in many ways, harder to grieve. Estrangement that leaves the door slightly ajar can trap people in cycles of hope and disappointment, complicating both emotional processing and healing.

4.3 Psychological Consequences – The Mental Health Toll:

The impact of family estrangement on mental health is profound. Numerous studies have shown that LGBTQ+ individuals who face family rejection are at significantly higher risk for depression, anxiety, substance abuse, and suicidal ideation. The sense of being unworthy of love from those who are supposed to love unconditionally can burrow into one's self-esteem and identity. In the absence of family support, queer people often find themselves navigating crisis, illness and major life transitions, without emotional anchors. Rejection reinforces internalized shame and can lead to a persistent belief that something is fundamentally wrong with one's existence. The intersection of family loss and societal stigma only intensifies these mental health challenges.

4.4 Grief, Longing, and Emotional Complexity:

Grieving someone who is still alive creates a unique and quiet kind of pain. There is no funeral, no public acknowledgment, only the persistent ache of absence in a relationship that should still be present. LGBTQ+ individuals estranged from family often mourn not only what was lost, but what never was, the imagined support, the hoped-for embrace, the conversations that never happened. This grief can coexist with love, confusion, and guilt. One may still long for connection, still care deeply for family members who caused harm, and struggle to reconcile the contradictions between love and self-preservation.

4.5 Cultural, Religious, and Intergenerational Pressures:

Cultural and religious values can deeply complicate the experience of family estrangement. In many communities, family is not only personal, it is communal, spiritual, and essential to one's sense of survival. Queer individuals from immigrant, conservative, or deeply religious backgrounds often face intensified consequences when coming out, including isolation from their cultural roots or spiritual practices. For queer people of colour, the stakes can feel even higher, as family ties often serve as a vital source of identity, belonging and protection.

The emotional weight of estrangement becomes layered with guilt, fear, and a profound sense of loss, that extends beyond the individual to entire communities.

4.6 The Power of Chosen Family:

Despite the pain of familial rejection, LGBTQ+ communities have long created alternative networks of love, care, and belonging. Chosen family, friends, partners, mentors, and community members who offer unconditional support, become a vital source of healing. These relationships are forged through shared values, mutual respect, and deep empathy. Chosen families do not erase the grief of what was lost, but they offer new foundations on which to build joy, identity, and resilience. In spaces where people are celebrated rather than merely tolerated, emotional wounds begin to heal. Chosen family offers the affirmation and stability that blood relatives sometimes cannot provide.

4.7 Forgiveness, Boundaries and the Possibility of Reconnection:

The journey toward healing does not always involve reconciliation. Forgiveness is a deeply personal process, and it remains valid whether or not it leads to renewed relationships. Setting boundaries with estranged family members can be painful, but it is often essential for emotional well-being. Some may choose to hold space for change, while others may need to let go in order to move forward. What matters most is that LGBTQ+ individuals have the autonomy to define healing on their own terms. Love should never require the erasure of self, and closure can take many forms, sometimes through reconnection, sometimes through release. Healing is about reclaiming agency, allowing forgiveness, and setting boundaries to be tools for personal growth and peace.

4.8 Tools for Healing and Support:

Professional support, including affirming therapy and peer-led groups, can make a meaningful difference in the healing process. Creative outlets like writing, art, and activism offer ways to process grief and reclaim identity. Engaging with LGBTQ+ community spaces can help rebuild confidence and emotional security. Healing is not about forgetting the pain, it is about rediscovering one's worth, reclaiming joy, and rebuilding trust in oneself and others. Healing flourishes when we are seen, supported, and surrounded by tools that honour our whole selves, reminding us that we are never alone in our journey toward wholeness.

4.9 Conclusion – Honouring Pain, Reclaiming Peace:

Family estrangement leaves a lasting mark, but it does not define a person's value or destiny. The pain of rejection is real and deserves to be acknowledged with compassion and care. Yet, within that pain also lives resilience, the strength to rebuild, to seek connection elsewhere, and to define family on one's own terms. Healing from estrangement is neither easy nor quick, but it is possible. Through community chosen family and self-affirmation, LGBTQ+ individuals continue to find belonging, love, and peace. What is lost may never return, but something new and beautiful can still be created.

5. Addressing PTSD in LGBTQ+ Refugees and Asylum Seekers

LGBTQ+ refugees and asylum seekers often flee their home countries in search of safety, escaping environments where their identities are criminalized, demonized, or violently punished. Yet, the journey to safety is rarely smooth. Many carry with them deep psychological wounds from experiences of violence, persecution, and abandonment. Post-Traumatic Stress Disorder (PTSD) is common among this population, but their specific needs are often overlooked. The intersection of queerness, displacement, and trauma demands urgent attention, not only from humanitarian organizations, but also from mental health professionals and policymakers committed to justice and healing.

5.1 The Root of the Trauma – Persecution, Violence, and Rejection:

In many countries, LGBTQ+ individuals face state-sanctioned discrimination, community violence, forced outing and even corrective rape or execution. These are not isolated incidents, but ongoing, targeted forms of harm that make everyday life dangerous. Family rejection, social ostracism, and surveillance compound the trauma, especially when survival depends on secrecy and silence. For many, the decision to flee is not just about seeking better opportunities, it's a desperate act of survival. The trauma does not begin with the border crossing, it begins long before, in a home that no longer feels safe, often resulting in layers of complex PTSD before the asylum process even begins. The scars of this trauma often linger in the body and mind, long after borders have been crossed.

5.2 The Journey to Safety – A New Set of Traumas:

The migration journey itself is often re-traumatizing. LGBTQ+ refugees may endure sexual assault, human trafficking, or abuse from fellow migrants, smugglers, or even border authorities. Many are forced to hide their identities again to avoid further violence in refugee camps or detention centres. Transgender individuals may be denied access to necessary medical care, while others risk exposure and ridicule in shared shelters. These experiences add layers to already existing trauma, reinforcing the belief that safety and dignity remain out of reach. The journey that was meant to lead toward healing, often becomes another chapter of psychological injury. And yet, even through immense pain and repeated betrayal, the will to survive, heal, and be fully seen never truly fades.

5.3 Life in the Host Country – The Trauma Doesn't End:

Arriving in a new country does not automatically guarantee relief. Many LGBTQ+ asylum seekers face bureaucratic hurdles, xenophobia, housing insecurity and continued discrimination, often within both refugee and queer spaces. The stress of navigating asylum interviews while recounting painful memories can trigger or intensify PTSD symptoms. Without legal status or work permits, survival becomes a daily battle, and mental health is pushed aside in favour of meeting basic needs. The expectation that safety equals healing overlooks the reality that trauma follows people across borders and cannot be addressed without comprehensive, affirming support systems. Healing requires more than physical relocation, it demands safety, recognition, and the radical rebuilding of trust and self-worth.

5.4 Understanding PTSD in Context – Complex, Ongoing and Silenced:

PTSD in LGBTQ+ refugees is not a singular event-based disorder. It is often complex, cumulative, and sustained over time. Flashbacks, nightmares, hypervigilance, and dissociation can become daily realities, especially when re-traumatization continues in the host country. The stigma around mental health, particularly in certain cultural contexts, can further silence those in need of care. For many LGBTQ+ refugees, there is fear that seeking psychological support might undermine their asylum claims or expose their identities in unsafe ways. Without trauma-informed care, their suffering remains invisible. Recognizing the layered nature of their PTSD is essential in creating effective paths toward healing.

5.5 Barriers to Mental Health Access:

Despite the need, access to mental health care is often limited or non-existent for LGBTQ+ refugees. Language barriers, lack of insurance, fear of deportation, and long waiting lists create insurmountable obstacles. Even when care is available, it may not be LGBTQ+-affirming or culturally competent. Many mental health professionals are not trained in trauma that intersects with gender identity, sexual orientation, and forced migration. The result is care that feels distant at best and harmful at worst. A one-size-fits-all approach cannot meet the needs of this community, their healing requires sensitivity, respect and a deep understanding of their lived experiences. Until mental health care becomes more inclusive, intersectional and accessible, too many LGBTQ+ refugees will continue to suffer in silence, their pain unseen and their healing unjustly delayed.

5.6 Advocacy for Affirming Mental Health Support:

Healing begins with listening and with action. Governments, NGOs, and healthcare systems must invest in trauma-informed, LGBTQ+-affirming mental health services for refugees and asylum seekers. This includes training therapists in intersectional trauma, offering services in multiple languages and creating safe spaces, where queer refugees can speak freely without fear of stigma or legal consequence. Peer support networks, art therapy, and community-based healing models can also play a transformative role. Policy changes must reflect a commitment to mental wellness as a human right. Advocacy is not just about legal protection, it is about emotional and psychological restoration. For LGBTQ+ refugees, being seen, heard, and affirmed is the beginning of true safety.

5.7 The Role of Community – Solidarity in Healing:

LGBTQ+ refugee support cannot fall solely on institutions. Community plays a crucial role in healing. Local queer organizations, cultural centers and support groups, can foster belonging, reduce isolation and create environments of trust. Being surrounded by others who understand the complexity of identity and trauma can provide a foundation for resilience. Solidarity, when rooted in empathy and mutual respect, becomes a lifeline. Collective care reminds LGBTQ+ refugees that they are not alone, that their stories matter, and that healing is possible, not just individually, but together.

5.8 Conclusion – Restoring Dignity, Rebuilding Hope:

LGBTQ+ refugees and asylum seekers carry heavy burdens, but they also carry immense strength. Addressing PTSD in this population is not only a matter of clinical care, it is a moral and humanitarian imperative. True safety is more than physical protection, it includes mental peace, emotional stability, and the freedom to exist without fear. Healing requires comprehensive, affirming support systems and a global commitment to restoring dignity. Through advocacy, empathy, and inclusive care, the path toward healing becomes clearer. Every LGBTQ+ refugee deserves the chance to rebuild a life not only free from danger, but full of hope. Because healing is not just about surviving the past, but about creating a future where joy, belonging, and self-worth are not rare luxuries, but fundamental rights.

*Compassion in Action – Global Organizations Supporting LGBTQ+ Refugees:

"Every LGBTQ+ refugee carries the fire of freedom in their chest, burning brightly against the darkness they fled." – Anonymous

---

Rainbow Railroad:

- **Based in:** Canada & USA | Global Reach
- **Services:** Emergency travel assistance, relocation, crisis response, advocacy.
- **Why include:** One of the most visible organizations providing safe pathways for LGBTQ+ people fleeing state-sponsored persecution.

ORAM – Organization for Refuge, Asylum & Migration:

- **Based in:** USA | Operations in Kenya, Mexico, Europe, Middle East
- **Services:** Legal aid, economic empowerment, psychosocial support, community building.
- **Why include:** Pioneers in addressing the unique vulnerabilities of LGBTQ+ asylum seekers and refugees.

ILGA World (The International Lesbian, Gay, Bisexual, Trans and Intersex Association):

- **Based in:** Switzerland | Global Network
- **Services:** Global advocacy, legal rights mapping, capacity building, U.N. representation.
- **Why include:** While not direct-service focused, ILGA amplifies global LGBTQ+ refugee rights through data, policy, and international pressure.

HIAS (Hebrew Immigrant Aid Society):

- **Based in:** USA | Global Programs
- **Services:** Legal protection, mental health care, community integration, with LGBTQ+ inclusive approaches.
- **Why include:** One of the oldest refugee organizations actively working on LGBTQ+ inclusion within faith-based and secular refugee spaces.

Refugee Trans Initiative (RTI – Kenya):

- **Based in:** Kenya | Regional Focus: East Africa
- **Services:** Housing, healthcare, trans-specific support for displaced persons.
- **Why include:** One of the few organizations run by and for transgender refugees, providing grassroots, trans-centered care.

TransEmigrate:

- **Based in:** Online-based | Global Reach
- **Services:** Relocation assistance, visa guidance, community-based support.
- **Why include:** Serves trans individuals globally who are seeking safe relocation from high-risk environments.

Queer Detainee Empowerment Project (QDEP):

- **Based in:** USA | Support for Detained/Recently Released LGBTQ+ Immigrants
- **Services:** Legal aid, housing, food, education, health access, community support.
- **Why include:** Focuses on the unique challenges faced by queer immigrants who have experienced detention and incarceration.

Casa Arcoíris A.C. (Rainbow House):

- **Based in:** Tijuana, Mexico
- **Services:** Shelter, advocacy, and support for LGBTQ+ migrants in transit.
- **Why include:** A frontline shelter that protects queer asylum seekers traveling through Latin America.

Micro Rainbow International:

- **Based in:** UK | Global Reach
- **Services:** Safe housing, skills training, and integration support for LGBTQ+ refugees.
- **Why include:** Offers a dignified path to rebuilding life post-migration.

No Pride in Detention:

- **Based in:** Australia
- **Services:** Advocacy and support focused on ending the detention of LGBTQ+ asylum seekers.
- **Why include:** Brings visibility to the injustices within detention systems.

Immigration Equality:

- **Based in:** USA
- **Services:** Legal representation for LGBTQ+ and HIV-positive immigrants, policy advocacy.
- **Why include:** Provides free legal services and has a high success rate in asylum cases.

EveryOne Group:

- **Based in:** Italy
- **Services:** Services: Human rights advocacy and protection for migrants, asylum seekers, refugees, and LGBTQ+ individuals.
- **Why include:** Works with international bodies to protect vulnerable groups.

Queer Sisterhood Project:

- **Based in:** Australia
- **Services:** Psycho-social support, advocacy, training, and education for LGBTIQ asylum-seeking and refugee women.
- **Why include:** Refugee-led initiative providing targeted support to LGBTIQ women.

Chapter 5

Intersectionality in the LGBTQ+ World

---

1. The Erasure of Queer Women of Colour in History and Media

The erasure of queer women of colour from both historical narratives and contemporary discourse is not accidental, it is the result of systemic forces that uphold white supremacy, cisheteronormativity and patriarchy. When stories go untold, or when identities are intentionally flattened, a message is sent that these lives are less valuable. Silence becomes a weapon of oppression, making visibility not just important, but a radical and necessary act of resistance. Reclaiming and amplifying the voices of queer women of colour is essential to rewriting history and shaping a more inclusive future.

1.1 Queer Women of Colour Were Always There:

Queer women of colour have always played vital roles in shaping culture, resistance and community, yet their contributions are often buried or misattributed. From Marsha P. Johnson's leadership during the Stonewall uprising to Audre Lorde's poetic and political brilliance, their legacies are essential to queer liberation. Still, they are frequently remembered in fragmented ways, either sanitized of their queerness or stripped of their racial and cultural contexts. This ongoing erasure reinforces a distorted history, one that must be actively rewritten to honour the truth and power of their presence. Reclaiming their contributions restores their rightful place in history and culture.

1.2 Colonialism, Patriarchy and the Policing of Identity:

Colonial rule imposed rigid gender roles and moral codes that systematically erased precolonial expressions of queerness and gender fluidity. In many Indigenous, African and Asian societies, queer and nonbinary identities held space and meaning before they were criminalized and pathologized. For queer women of colour, the legacy of colonization means living with the compounded trauma of cultural loss and gendered violence. Reclaiming these erased histories is both remembrance and resistance against systems that still deny the validity of certain identities.

1.3 The Media Machine – Who Gets to Be Seen and Why:

Mainstream media continues to prioritize white, cis and often male queer narratives, rendering queer women of colour virtually invisible or painfully stereotyped. When they do appear, their characters are often tragic, hypersexualized, or underdeveloped, relegated to supporting roles in someone else's story. These portrayals shape public understanding and can reinforce the idea that queer women of colour do not belong at the centre of queer culture. Challenging this imbalance requires not only better representation, but a shift in who holds the power to tell stories and shape cultural narratives.

1.4 The Politics of Recognition – Visibility Is Not Enough:

Representation is not inherently liberating if it upholds the same oppressive structures that create marginalization in the first place. Institutions may highlight queer women of colour for tokenistic diversity while continuing to gatekeep resources, leadership roles and safety. Real change demands not just symbolic visibility, but the transfer of cultural and institutional power to those who have been consistently denied it. Liberation must be measured not by who is seen, but by who is truly supported and empowered to lead.

1.5 Intersectionality as Resistance – Naming the Full Self:

Intersectionality reminds us that queer women of colour experience layered forms of oppression that cannot be separated from one another. This framing creates space to acknowledge how racism, sexism, homophobia, transphobia, and classism operate together to silence and endanger lives. Embracing intersectionality becomes not only a tool for analysis but also a strategy for building solidarity and collective liberation, where all struggles are interconnected and the fight for justice is shared.

1.6 Reclamation and Self-Archiving – Telling Our Own Stories:

In the absence of accurate representation, queer women of colour have become archivists of their own histories. Zines, memoirs, online platforms, spoken word performances, and documentaries have become vehicles for visibility, healing, and truth-telling. These acts of storytelling are not merely artistic, they are revolutionary tools that disrupt dominant narratives and create new cultural legacies. By reclaiming and sharing their own stories, queer women of colour transform personal memory into collective power, ensuring their voices shape future cultural narratives and resist erasure.

1.7 Moving Forward – Centering Queer Women of Colour in Liberation Work:

True liberation will not be achieved until queer women of colour are centered, not sidelined, in movements for justice. This requires a reimagining of leadership, resource allocation, and who is deemed worthy of care and celebration. Empowerment must come not from being granted space, but from reclaiming it, boldly, unapologetically, and together. Building sustainable infrastructures that amplify and protect their leadership ensures that queer women of colour guide the path to collective freedom and healing.

2. LGBTQ+ and Disability – An Overlooked Intersection

Many discussions of LGBTQ+ identity and disability occur in parallel, yet rarely intersect in meaningful ways, leaving disabled queers feeling doubly marginalized. Acknowledging this overlap helps reveal how assumptions about able-bodiedness shape queer spaces and vice versa.

By centering the experiences of those living at both margins, we can uncover new insights into community, resilience, and the work still to be done. Disability, therefore, should not be treated as a side note, but as a vital lens through which we understand the full spectrum of LGBTQ+ lives.

2.1 Historical and Social Marginalization:

Disabled queer individuals have long faced exclusion from both disability rights and LGBTQ+ movements, each of which often assumes "typical" bodies or identities. In the early disability rights era, queerness was sometimes viewed as a distraction from the fight for access, in the gay liberation era, disability was often rendered invisible behind ideals of physical vitality or normative appearance. These parallel erasures founded a social landscape where disabled queers must navigate stigma on two fronts. Reflecting on this history highlights how interwoven prejudices, ableism, homophobia, transphobia, racism, have shaped public policy, community organizing, and personal relationships.

2.2 Dual Stereotypes and Everyday Barriers:

Stereotypes about disabled people as asexual or infantilized can collide disastrously with queer stereotypes, trapping disabled LGBTQ+ individuals in narratives that deny desire, agency, or autonomy. Public spaces, from bars to pride parades, often lack basic accessibility, sending the message that queer joy is only for those who fit a narrow bodily ideal. Social expectations around "passing" as straight, cis, or able-bodied compound fears of outing one's disability or queerness. Small barriers, an unramped entrance, an uncaptioned video at an LGBTQ+ event, become profound reminders of exclusion, eroding confidence, and reinforcing the idea that belonging is conditional.

2.3 Healthcare Disparities and Access Challenges:

Medical providers frequently separate discussions of sexuality and disability, resulting in gaps that can endanger disabled queer lives. A trans person with a mobility impairment may encounter physicians unprepared to discuss hormone therapy alongside accessible care, while a lesbian blind woman might struggle to find counselling that addresses both disability and sexual identity. Insurance policies that categorize trans health as "cosmetic" and disability as "chronic" further complicate coverage, pushing vital treatments out of reach. These fractured systems leave disabled LGBTQ+ people navigating a maze of providers, advocates, and bureaucracies, often without the coordinated support needed to thrive.

2.4 Representation in Movements and Media:

On screen and in activist leadership, disabled queer voices remain scarce. When portrayed, disabled LGBTQ+ characters are too often defined by their disability alone or depicted as tragic figures whose queerness is overshadowed. Activist coalitions sometimes invite disabled speakers as tokens rather than leaders, perpetuating tokenism instead of genuine inclusion. Cultivating authentic representation means elevating the stories of disabled queers in media, research and decision-making tables, ensuring they are recognized not only as beneficiaries of progress, but as architects of change.

2.5 Mental Health, Community and Resilience:

Facing intertwined stigmas can take a significant toll on mental health, yet many disabled LGBTQ+ people find solace and strength in small, affirming communities.

Peer-led support groups, whether online or in accessible physical spaces, become havens for shared strategies around self-advocacy, self-care, and joy. Creative expression, from wheelchair dance companies to Deaf queer poetry slams, reframes disability and queerness as sites of innovation rather than pathology. Recognizing these pockets of resilience invites us to rethink wellness beyond clinical models and toward community-centered care.

2.6 Advocacy, Policy Gaps and Allyship:

Effective advocacy for disabled LGBTQ+ people requires bridging movements through intersectional policy platforms. Disability rights organizers must include sexual orientation and gender identity in anti-discrimination laws and accessibility standards. LGBTQ+ advocates need to fight for Medicaid expansion, accessible shelters, and disability-competent mental health services. Allies can support by demanding captioning at pride events, lobbying for adaptive sports programs, or volunteering with organizations that serve disabled queers. True allyship involves ceding space, listening to lived expertise, and mobilizing resources where they are most needed.

2.7 Toward an Inclusive Future – Embracing Full Humanity:

Building truly inclusive communities means dismantling the myth that queerness and disability are exceptional rather than ordinary facets of human diversity. Designing public and digital spaces with universal access benefits everyone, and integrating disability narratives into LGBTQ+ history enriches our collective story. Educators, artists and policymakers can uplift disabled queer voices by expanding curricula, commissioning accessible art and funding intersectional research. Embracing this often-overlooked intersection calls on all of us to broaden our definitions of beauty, intimacy, and liberation, ensuring that every identity can flourish without apology.

3. The Mental Load of Being Both an Activist and a Queer Person of Colour

To be a queer person of colour is already to carry multiple identities shaped by systems of oppression. Adding activism to that equation means holding the trauma of both lived experience and the suffering of the wider community. There is a constant pressure to show up, speak out, and fight back, even when one is personally exhausted or grieving. The emotional labour is unrelenting and often invisible.

This labour isn't just emotional, it's ancestral. Many queer people of colour are carrying generational pain while also trying to carve a freer future for themselves and others. Activism becomes a way to honour those who came before, even as it drains the body and spirit in the present. Balancing survival with advocacy becomes a tightrope walk, where the personal and political are never fully separate. The weight of representation, being expected to lead, educate, and embody resilience, often falls hardest on those already fighting to be seen.

3.1 When Advocacy Becomes Expectation:

Activism is often assumed of queer people of colour, as if identity alone makes one a permanent spokesperson.

This expectation erases the right to rest, privacy, and personal evolution. It becomes difficult to separate where the self ends and the cause begins. There is little space for not knowing, for being quiet, or for just existing without explaining.

3.2 The Double Bind of Representation:

Queer people of colour in activist spaces are often called upon to "diversify" movements that weren't built with them in mind. They may be celebrated for optics, but excluded from real decision-making. This tokenism leads to a mental tightrope, be visible, but not "too much", be authentic, but palatable. It's a cycle that leaves many feeling both hyper-visible and unseen.

3.3 Racism Within Queer Spaces, Homophobia Within Cultural Communities:

Activists must often navigate exclusion from all sides. White-led queer spaces can be rife with racism and erasure, while cultural or religious communities may remain deeply homophobic or transphobic. Being caught between worlds without a true sense of belonging is emotionally isolating. There is grief in never being fully accepted by either side of one's identity.

3.4 Grief Work Disguised as Leadership:

So much of activism is rooted in grief, for lives lost, rights denied, and dreams deferred. For queer people of colour, the line between personal mourning and public leadership is often blurred. Marches, vigils, and calls to action come from the heart, but that heart is often breaking. Leading through grief takes a toll, even when it appears strong from the outside.

3.5 The Burnout No One Sees:

Burnout in activism isn't just physical, it's spiritual, emotional, and cultural. The burnout queer activists of colour face is often internalized, because rest is framed as weakness and silence as betrayal. Many suffer in silence, feeling guilty for needing a break, or fearful of letting others down. When activism becomes a form of survival, stepping back feels dangerous.

3.6 The Radical Act of Setting Boundaries:

Boundaries are not a retreat, they are resistance. Learning to say no, to delegate, to disappear temporarily, is a way of reclaiming autonomy. For queer people of colour, especially those raised in cultures where self-sacrifice is the norm, boundary-setting can be a radical act of self-love. Reframing care for oneself as part of the movement, not separate from it, is crucial.

3.7 Finding Nourishment in Joy and Connection:

Joy is not frivolous, it is political. Dancing, laughing, making art, and celebrating queerness are powerful antidotes to oppression.

Queer people of colour often build chosen families, mutual aid networks and affirming creative spaces to sustain each other. These pockets of joy and connection become sacred spaces where healing happens without explanation or justification.

3.8 Building Movements That Don't Break Us:

Activism must evolve to hold its people with more care. This means valuing rest, redistributing labour and letting go of urgency as a metric of commitment. Creating sustainable, trauma-informed spaces can prevent burnout and foster long-term resilience. Leadership must look like care, not martyrdom.

3.9 Reclaiming Wholeness – You Are Not Just What You Fight Against:

Being both queer and a person of colour is not just a site of struggle, it's a site of brilliance, beauty and complexity. Activism is part of the story, but not the whole self. Reclaiming wholeness means allowing oneself to be joyful, ordinary, messy, and multidimensional. You are not just what you survive or resist, you are also what you dream, love, and create.

4. Feminism, Trans Rights and the Exclusionary Debate – Where Do We Go from Here?

The growing tension between certain strands of feminism and trans rights advocacy is not new, but has become increasingly visible in mainstream discourse. Rooted in debates about definitions of womanhood, this divide often stems from differing frameworks of gender, one based on biology, the other on identity and lived experience. Trans exclusionary rhetoric, often framed as concern for 'women's safety' or 'biological reality,' ignores the violence and marginalization that trans people, especially trans women, face both inside and outside feminist spaces.

These debates have created harmful binary thinking that pits cis women against trans women, instead of identifying shared struggles under patriarchy. Understanding the origins of this divide is key to unlearning assumptions and recognizing the complexities of identity and oppression.

4.1 The False Dichotomy – Trans Rights vs. Women's Rights:

Framing trans rights as a threat to women's rights is not only inaccurate, it's a tactic historically used to weaken feminist movements. Both cis and trans women face gender-based violence, systemic discrimination, and economic inequality, though in different and intersecting ways. To claim that expanding rights for trans individuals diminishes those of cisgender women undermines the very principles of feminism, which is rooted in equity and liberation.

A truly inclusive feminism must confront how systems of oppression affect people differently depending on race, class, ability, and gender identity. Solidarity is not a subtraction, it is a multiplier of power and protection for all women and gender-diverse people.

4.2 Who Gets to Speak for Feminism? Gatekeeping and Power:

Mainstream feminist platforms have historically centered white, cisgender, middle-class voices, often silencing or ignoring more marginalized perspectives. This gatekeeping reinforces hierarchical norms that feminism set out to dismantle. When trans voices, especially those of Black and Brown trans women, are excluded from the conversation, feminism loses its ability to evolve, expand, and respond to real-world injustice. Challenging who is given the mic in feminist spaces means asking hard questions about privilege and power. If the goal of feminism is collective liberation, then the movement must listen more deeply to those on the margins.

4.3 Trans Feminism – Not a Disruption, But a Contribution:

Trans feminism is not separate from feminism, it is an essential evolution of it. Trans feminists have long contributed to feminist theory, organizing, and thought leadership, offering insights into how gender is socially constructed and policed. Their work often bridges critical gaps between feminism, queer theory, disability justice and racial equity. By recognizing trans feminism as integral, not incidental, we expand our understanding of gendered oppression and how to resist it. Rather than treating trans voices as a challenge to feminism, they should be celebrated as a continuation of its most radical and transformative legacies.

4.4 The Role of Media and Misinformation:

The mainstream media often sensationalizes debates about trans inclusion, creating panic rather than fostering understanding. Right-wing outlets and certain public figures often unjustly frame trans rights as extreme, while simultaneously presenting trans-exclusionary feminists as reasonable protectors of womanhood. These narratives fuel division and distract from more urgent shared struggles, such as reproductive justice, wage inequality, healthcare access, and safety from violence. Resisting this media framing requires critical literacy and a refusal to accept simplistic binaries. We must challenge headlines that pit communities against one another and instead amplify stories of solidarity and shared resistance.

4.5 Reframing Safety and Protection:

A major point of contention in the feminist-trans rights debate is safety, particularly in public spaces like bathrooms, shelters, or prisons. These fears are often stoked by misinformation and moral panic, not data. In fact, trans people are far more likely to be victims of violence in these settings than perpetrators. Reframing safety means moving away from carceral and exclusionary logic and toward a vision of collective care. Instead of policing identity, we can design spaces that uphold everyone's dignity and right to exist without fear. True safety cannot be built on exclusion.

4.6 Intersectionality as a Bridge, Not a Buzzword:

Coined by Kimberlé Crenshaw, intersectionality is more than a theoretical tool, it's a way to understand how various systems of oppression converge and affect people's lives.

Intersectional feminism recognizes that the struggle for gender justice is deeply connected to race, class, ability, immigration status, and more. This lens reveals that trans-exclusionary feminism not only harms trans people, it upholds white supremacy, ableism, and other oppressive structures. By embracing intersectionality as a bridge, we can foster dialogue that is rooted in empathy and action rather than fear and exclusion. It reminds us that liberation is not a zero-sum game.

4.7 Practicing Inclusive Feminism – What It Looks Like:

Inclusive feminism centers those most impacted by patriarchal violence and believes that no one is free until everyone is. This practice includes using gender-affirming language, ensuring trans people are represented in leadership roles, and creating safer spaces where all women, cis and trans, can thrive. It also means addressing internal biases, being open to unlearning, and prioritizing coalition-building over ego. This is not just an ideological shift, it's a strategic one. Inclusive movements are stronger, more dynamic, and better equipped to challenge systemic injustice.

4.8 Moving Forward – Solidarity Over Division:

The path forward lies in refusing to allow exclusionary ideologies to divide movements that should be aligned. Feminism must return to its roots, challenging patriarchy, advocating for bodily autonomy, and uplifting the voices of those most silenced. Building bridges between cis and trans feminists requires humility, dialogue, and a commitment to shared values over individual comfort. Our collective liberation is bound together. The more we listen, learn, and act in coalition, the closer we get to a feminism that is not just inclusive, but unstoppable.

5. The Unseen Struggles of Queer People in Rural and Undocumented Communities

Queer individuals living in rural areas or without legal status face unique struggles that remain largely invisible in mainstream LGBTQ+ conversations. Geographic isolation and the constant threat of deportation compound the everyday challenges of coming out and finding community. Many of these queer voices go unheard, their resilience overshadowed by fear, stigma and lack of resources. By centering their stories, we begin to understand how isolation and legal insecurity intensify emotional burdens, underscoring the need for solidarity that spans beyond urban centers and citizenship lines.

5.1 Isolation and the Erosion of Community Support:

Rural landscapes often lack queer-affirming spaces, leaving LGBTQ+ individuals with few opportunities to connect or find solidarity. Without safe community centers, peer support groups, or visible role models, coming out can feel like a solitary act undertaken in silence. This profound sense of aloneness is magnified for undocumented queers, who may avoid any public gathering for fear of exposure. Isolation erodes mental health, making even routine milestones, finding a partner, and celebrating. Acknowledging this layered solitude is the first step toward creating outreach programs and virtual networks that can bridge distances and legal barriers.

5.2 Safety Concerns and the Specter of Exposure:

Conservative social norms in rural towns can translate into overt hostility, verbal harassment, physical threats, or social ostracism. Queer people of undocumented status shoulder an additional, ever-present fear, the possibility that seeking help could trigger immigration enforcement. In such environments, the simple act of researching a queer hotline or attending an LGBTQ+ service provider becomes fraught with risk. Fear of exposure forces many into self-protective secrecy, which compounds stress and anxiety. Addressing these safety concerns requires discreet, mobile-friendly resources and advocacy that unites rural allies with immigration-defence networks.

5.3 Barriers to Health and Mental Health Care:

Accessing gender-affirming care, HIV prevention, or mental health support is challenging when local clinics neither advertise LGBTQ+ competency nor offer sliding-scale fees. Undocumented individuals often lack insurance and fear revealing their status to medical staff, leading to delays in life-saving treatments. For rural queers, traveling long distances for specialized services is cost-prohibitive and emotionally draining. Mental health providers who do exist may lack training in the intersecting realities of queerness, rural life, and undocumented trauma. A compassionate approach demands telehealth expansions, mobile clinics, and pro-bono networks, that respect confidentiality and reduce physical and financial distance.

5.4 Cultural and Societal Pressures in Tight-Knit Communities:

In many rural towns, community ties run deep, and deviation from social norms can carry steep personal costs. Queer identities and undocumented status both clash with prevailing narratives of belonging, leading to family estrangement or community excommunication. The pressure to conform, to marry heterosexually, to stay "under the radar", can fracture self-esteem and spiritual well-being. Combating these pressures means engaging local faith leaders, educators and health workers in sensitivity training, while amplifying rural queer and undocumented stories that reflect the richness of these communities. By fostering inclusivity and understanding, we can begin to dismantle these barriers and create spaces where all identities are celebrated.

5.5 Economic Hardships and Resource Scarcity:

Economic precarity is a reality for many queer rural residents and undocumented workers who lack labour protections and fair wages. Discrimination in hiring, wage theft, and the absence of social safety nets, trap people in low-paid, unstable jobs. For undocumented individuals, the risk of deportation makes seeking legal recourse virtually impossible. These economic hardships limit access to housing, education and the basic stability needed to explore and express queer identity. Crafting solutions calls for grassroots mutual-aid funds, partnerships with local employers committed to non-discrimination and policy advocacy for inclusive labour rights. Addressing these issues requires systemic change and creating equitable opportunities for all, regardless of status.

5.6 Networks of Resilience – Finding Strength in Each Other:

Despite formidable obstacles, rural and undocumented queer communities forge pockets of resilience through informal networks. Chosen families, often comprised of fellow migrants, farmworkers, or online friends, offer emotional refuge and practical support. Story-sharing circles held in private homes or encrypted group chats become lifelines of affirmation and advice. Creative expressions, photographs of hidden safe spaces, handwritten zines distributed discreetly, transform isolation into solidarity. These resilient practices remind us that care can flourish even in hostile environments and that empowerment often springs from small acts of mutual aid.

5.7 Policies and Advocacy for Inclusive Support:

Effective change requires policy interventions that address the specific needs of queer people in rural and undocumented contexts. Expanding Medicaid to include undocumented residents, funding mobile health units with LGBTQ+ competency, and amending hate crime, statutes to cover non-urban jurisdictions are essential steps. Advocacy groups must partner across movements, linking immigrant-rights, rural-development, and LGBTQ+ coalitions, to craft comprehensive legislation. At the grassroots level, training local legal clinics to offer low-barrier immigration services and establishing confidential complaint mechanisms can reduce fear and increase access. Such policy shifts send a clear message, no queer life is expendable, regardless of zip code or citizenship status.

5.8 Conclusion – Toward Visibility, Belonging and Solidarity:

The journeys of queer individuals in rural and undocumented communities reveal how geography and legal status intersect to deepen marginalization. Yet within this invisibility lie extraordinary stories of courage, creativity, and communal care. Recognizing these struggles obliges us to expand the scope of queer advocacy beyond urban centers and headlines. It means forging alliances that honour both the unique and shared dimensions of rural life and undocumented existence. Moving forward, true solidarity will transform policies, funding and cultural narratives, so that every queer person, no matter where they live or what papers they hold, can claim safety, dignity and belonging.

*They Lived It – Intersectionality in Action, but not limited to:

- **Spotlight – Magnus Hirschfeld (1868 to 1935):**

Though not trans himself, Dr. Magnus Hirschfeld was a pioneering German sexologist and outspoken ally of transgender and queer communities in the early 1900s. He coined the term "transvestite" and advocated for what we now call gender-affirming care through his Institute for Sexual Science in Berlin. His work supported people like Dora Richter, the first known trans woman to undergo gender-affirming surgery. His intersectional worldview recognized that class, gender, and sexual orientation all shaped experience. The Nazis destroyed his institute in 1933, burning irreplaceable research. His legacy reminds us that trans rights have long been tied to feminist and anti-fascist struggles and that history is always vulnerable to erasure.

- **Spotlight – Miss Major Griffin-Gracy (b. 1940):**

Miss Major is a Black trans elder, activist, and former sex worker, who has spent decades fighting for the rights of trans women of colour, especially those who have been incarcerated or marginalized by the medical system. A veteran of the Stonewall uprising, Miss Major's activism goes beyond public protest, she's spent her life building care networks, housing, and advocacy programs for those most often forgotten. Her lived experience navigating racism, transphobia, police brutality, and poverty, makes her a living embodiment of intersectional resistance. Despite the emotional and physical toll, Miss Major continues to speak truth to power, always rooted in love and community and unwavering resilience. Her relentless work has forever shifted the landscape of LGBTQ+ activism, ensuring that the voices of the most marginalized are heard and prioritized.

- **Spotlight – Gladys Bentley (1907 to 1960):**

Gladys Bentley was a gender nonconforming, African American blues singer and pianist who rose to fame during the Harlem Renaissance. Dressed in men's tuxedos, she sang raunchy, unapologetically queer lyrics in speakeasies, claiming space as a Black lesbian long before mainstream culture accepted such identities. Despite her popularity, Bentley faced intense backlash and eventually felt pressured to conform to heteronormative standards later in life. Her boldness, talent and defiance remain a powerful example of early queer Black resistance. Though history tried to forget her, Bentley's legacy reverberates through today's conversations about gender fluidity, performance, and authenticity.

- **Spotlight – Leah Lakshmi Piepzna-Samarasinha (b. 1975):**

Leah Lakshmi Piepzna-Samarasinha is a queer, disabled, mixed-race (Sri Lankan and Irish/Roma) poet, writer and disability justice activist. Their work centres radical healing, survivor resilience, and community care. As a co-founder of Sins Invalid, a disability performance collective centering queer and trans artists of colour, Leah has been instrumental in reframing disability not as limitation, but as a source of power and connection. Their book Care Work: Dreaming Disability Justice is a touchstone text, illustrating how queer, disabled communities build networks of survival in the absence of institutional support. Leah's intersectional activism reshapes the discourse on disability, emphasizing solidarity, collective care, and the strength in marginalized identities.

- **Spotlight – Jennicet Gutiérrez (b. 1986):**

Jennicet Gutiérrez is a trans Latina activist and founding member of Familia, Trans Queer Liberation Movement. As an undocumented immigrant, she gained national attention in 2015 by interrupting President Obama to protest the abuse of trans women in ICE custody. Her bold action highlighted the compounded risks faced by undocumented queer people, especially in rural or conservative areas. Gutiérrez's work is a powerful reminder that silence is not an option when lives are at stake and that true liberation must be intersectional to be just. Jennicet's courageous activism continues to challenge oppressive systems, advocating for the liberation of both trans and immigrant communities.

- **Spotlight – Yosimar Reyes (b. 1988):**

Yosimar Reyes is a queer, undocumented poet and public speaker originally from Guerrero, Mexico and raised in East San Jose, California. His work explores the complexities of growing up queer, poor and undocumented in a system that devalues all three identities. Through his poetry and storytelling, Yosimar offers a nuanced look into the realities of marginalized queer immigrants, from fear and invisibility to love and radical pride. With wit and tenderness, his voice challenges the monolithic immigrant narrative and expands the cultural understanding of what it means to be American, queer and resilient. Yosimar's poetry serves as both a celebration of queer immigrant resilience and a call for deeper cultural empathy and understanding.

- **Spotlight – Alok Vaid-Menon (b. 1991):**

Alok Vaid-Menon is a gender nonconforming writer, performer, and public intellectual of South Asian descent. Known for their vibrant fashion, poetic prose and deep vulnerability, Alok frequently speaks about the toll of being both a person of colour and a visibly queer activist in hostile environments. They've discussed the exhaustion of always educating others while fighting to be seen, a burden disproportionately placed on QTBIPOC. Alok's work invites us to rethink visibility, grief and community care, offering a path toward activism that honours rest and joy, not just resistance. Alok's work emphasizes the importance of self-care and joy as integral parts of the activism process, redefining what it means to truly thrive.

- **Spotlight – Johana Medina León (1991 to 2019):**

Johana Medina León was a 25-year-old transgender nurse from El Salvador who died in ICE custody in 2019 after seeking asylum in the U.S. Detained for weeks without proper medical care, she passed away just days after her release. Her death followed that of Roxsana Hernández, another trans woman from Central America and spotlighted the dangerous conditions queer and trans migrants face, especially those from rural or conservative areas. Johana's story has since become a rallying cry for justice and the abolition of detention-based immigration systems that criminalize identity. Johana's tragic death underscores the urgent need for comprehensive immigration reform that protects vulnerable LGBTQ+ individuals, ensuring their safety and dignity throughout the asylum process.

- **Spotlight – Travis Alabanza (b. 1995):**

Travis Alabanza is a Black, transfeminine performance artist and writer from the UK whose work confronts transphobia in both mainstream and feminist spaces. Their acclaimed show Burgerz explores gender-based violence and the intersections of race, queerness, and autonomy. A powerful voice in challenging exclusionary narratives, Travis insists that trans people of colour must be central to feminist conversations. Their work goes beyond critique, it reimagines community through care, art, and the celebration of trans joy. Travis's unapologetic exploration of joy and survival offers a vision of trans liberation rooted in love, resistance, and collective strength.

- **Spotlight – Aaron Philip (b. 2001):**

Aaron Philip is a Black, trans, disabled model who broke barriers as the first physically disabled model signed to a major international modelling agency. Born with cerebral palsy, Aaron uses her platform to demand accessibility and inclusivity in fashion and LGBTQ+ spaces alike. Her presence radically shifts how beauty, gender, and mobility are represented in public life. As a Gen Z trailblazer, Aaron refuses to be defined by a single label, instead, she embodies the complexity of navigating systems that aren't built for multiply marginalized people. Her story exemplifies resilience and the power of making space where none existed before.

Chapter 6

LGBTQ+ Love Languages

---

1. Love Languages Beyond the Five – Emotional Labour and Unspoken Affection

The five love languages, words of affirmation, acts of service, receiving gifts, quality time and physical touch, have long been regarded as the definitive framework for understanding affection. For many, these categories provide structure and clarity in their relationships. However, queer love often transcends these conventional boundaries. Queer relationships aren't just built on romantic or physical attraction, they are deeply rooted in survival, resilience and resistance to a world that seeks to marginalize queer identities. In these relationships, love is not confined to predefined categories, but instead takes on forms that are fluid, adaptable, and often invisible. Love, for queer people, often means enduring together, protecting one another and communicating through silence and action, rather than words alone. It speaks in the subtle nuances of care that don't always fit neatly into traditional love languages

1.1 Shielding – The Quiet Armor of Love:

One of the lesser-discussed aspects of queer relationships is shielding, protecting your partner from harm in ways that may never be acknowledged publicly. Shielding is a quiet, invisible act of love that takes on many forms. It could be as simple as standing between your partner and a hostile environment or more complex, like navigating family dynamics where your partner's identity is questioned. Shielding also involves enduring microaggressions or standing up to people who don't respect your partner's identity. These acts of protection are often self-sacrificial, with little to no recognition. In shielding, love is expressed through action and quiet resistance. It says, "Your peace matters more than my comfort," or "I will protect you, even when no one else sees it."

1.2 Unspoken Affection in Risky Spaces:

For many queer couples, public displays of affection come with risks. Whether in conservative settings or environments that are openly hostile to queer people, the act of showing affection, such as holding hands or sharing a kiss, can result in backlash, discrimination, or even violence. As a result, queer couples often develop their own private codes for affection. A quick glance across the room, a secret smile, a foot brushing against theirs under the table, these small, intimate gestures are the love languages of those who cannot afford the luxury of public displays of affection. These acts of love may seem minor, but they hold great power. They are often the only way queer couples can express their love without risking their safety. And yet, they are no less significant. In these moments of hidden affection, love is spoken in silence. It says, "Even if we cannot show it openly, my love for you is real."

1.3 Adapting to Growth – Loving Through Evolution:

Queer relationships often involve a process of constant adaptation. Identities are fluid and over time, partners may evolve in ways that challenge the boundaries of the relationship. One partner may come out as nonbinary, start a medical transition, or discover new aspects of their identity that require space and understanding. This continual evolution can be both a challenge and a gift. Loving through change means accepting that identity is not static and that love itself must be flexible to accommodate these shifts. For queer couples, this kind of adaptability is a love language in and of itself. It requires patience, open communication and a willingness to meet your partner, where they are in each moment. It says, "I don't just love who you were, I love who you are becoming." This openness to evolution can deepen intimacy, as it requires both partners to be vulnerable and courageous in the face of change.

1.4 Community as Care – Love Beyond the Couple:

Queer love often extends beyond the boundaries of romantic relationships. It is embedded in community, mutual aid, and collective care. For many queer people, survival is a communal act. Love is expressed not only through the connection between two individuals, but also through the broader network of care that surrounds them. This can take the form of organizing collective resources, such as raising funds for a partner's medical transition, offering shelter to those in need, or providing emotional and practical support during difficult times. The love shared within these communities is no less valid than the love between romantic partners, in fact, it is often the glue that holds individuals together in times of crisis. These acts of mutual aid and solidarity are expressions of love that extend far beyond traditional romantic love. They reflect the understanding that our survival depends on one another. They say, "Your survival is my priority. I care about you and I'll show it through action."

1.5 Listening as Liberation:

Listening is often overlooked as a love language, but for queer people, being truly listened to is a radical act of love. In a world that frequently invalidates or erases queer experiences, being heard without judgment is a rare and precious gift. Deep listening in queer relationships goes beyond just hearing words, it is about holding space for each other's truths, even when those truths are painful or difficult. It is about offering a safe and affirming presence that allows each person to speak their truth without fear of rejection or disbelief. In this way, listening becomes a form of liberation, it allows queer people to be fully seen and valued for who they are, not just for how they are perceived by society. It says, "I hear you. Your experiences are valid, and I believe you." This act of deep listening affirms the worth of the other person and strengthens the bond between them. In listening, we honour not only the words spoken, but the lived experiences that often go unheard, creating a space where love is not just felt, but truly understood.

1.6 Holding Space for Grief:

Queer relationships often involve holding space for grief. The grief of family rejection, losing oneself during transition, or living in a marginalized society are all realities queer people face.

In many queer relationships, love is expressed through the willingness to hold space for one another's grief without trying to fix it or make it go away. This kind of love doesn't shy away from sadness, it sits with it, allowing it to be felt and processed. It is a love that says, "I am here for you, even in your pain. I will not leave you alone in your sorrow." In this way, grief becomes an integral part of the relationship, strengthening the connection between partners by allowing them to witness and support each other through difficult times.

1.7 Beyond Definition – Expanding the Vocabulary of Love:

Ultimately, the love languages of queer people challenge traditional definitions of love. Queer love is not confined to a singular narrative or model. It is expansive, multifaceted, and ever-evolving. The love languages that emerge from queer relationships, emotional labour, shielding, unspoken affection, adaptability, community care, listening and grief-holding, offer new ways of understanding and experiencing love. These expressions of love do not replace the traditional five languages, rather, they expand upon them, offering a deeper and more inclusive vocabulary for affection. In embracing these new languages of love, we not only validate queer ways of being, but also create space for everyone to experience love more fully. It says, "Love is not one-size-fits-all. It is a living, breathing force that shapes itself according to who we are and how we care for each other."

"Queer love isn't bound by labels, it's written in the silences, the sacrifices and the unspoken acts of care, that transcend conventional definitions." – Anonymous

2. How Trauma Shapes the Way LGBTQ+ People Give and Receive Love

Love is a universal human experience, but for LGBTQ+ individuals, it is often shaped by a history of both personal and collective trauma. From family rejection to societal marginalization, queer people often navigate intimacy while carrying emotional scars that make vulnerability and connection more complex. Trauma influences the emotional landscape of queer love, not as something broken that needs fixing, but as a deeply human response to surviving in a world that has not always been safe. Understanding this dynamic invites a more compassionate view of how LGBTQ+ individuals learn to give and receive love through the lens of past pain and present resilience.

2.1 Understanding Trauma in LGBTQ+ Contexts:

Trauma, in this context, is not limited to dramatic or violent events, it includes the chronic erosion of safety and belonging experienced by many LGBTQ+ individuals. For some, trauma stems from family rejection, bullying, or medical mistreatment. Others carry the weight of religious condemnation or systemic erasure. These experiences often begin early and are compounded by intersectional identities, race, gender, disability, class, that further shape how trauma manifests. Understanding this complexity is essential to unpacking how queer people navigate emotional intimacy in ways that are both tender and guarded. Acknowledging the depth and nuances of trauma allows for more compassionate healing, fostering spaces where LGBTQ+ individuals can reclaim their safety, agency, and a sense of belonging, free from the weight of past harm.

2.2 Hyper-Vigilance and Self-Protection in Intimacy:

For many LGBTQ+ individuals, trauma fosters a sense of hyper-vigilance in relationships, a constant scanning for signs of danger or rejection. Emotional closeness can feel risky, especially when past experiences have taught that vulnerability often ends in pain. Self-protective behaviours may emerge, such as emotional withdrawal, hesitation to trust, or reluctance to express deep affection. These are not signs of emotional deficiency, but survival strategies, developed to protect a self that once had to hide, mute, or shrink to stay safe. Recognizing these patterns is the first step toward meeting them with compassion instead of shame.

2.3 Love as Reclamation – Relearning Safety and Trust:

In queer relationships, love can become an act of reclamation, a process of unlearning fear and relearning what safety feels like. Trust, for many, is not a given, but a courageous choice that requires time, consistency, and care. In affirming partnerships, queer individuals may find themselves slowly allowing more softness, expressing needs and receiving affection without suspicion. These small moments can be transformative. Over time, relationships can become spaces where new truths are lived, that one is not too much, not unlovable, not destined for harm. Instead, love becomes an avenue for healing, where past wounds are gently acknowledged, but no longer dictate present possibilities.

2.4 Avoidance, Anxious Clinging, and the Attachment Spectrum:

Trauma often influences attachment styles, which shape how people relate emotionally to others. LGBTQ+ individuals may lean toward avoidant or anxious patterns, shaped by early experiences of instability or rejection. Avoidant partners may struggle with emotional closeness, distancing themselves to stay in control. Anxiously attached individuals may fear abandonment, seeking constant reassurance, or overextending themselves to feel secure. These behaviours, while challenging, are not signs of brokenness. They are understandable adaptations to unpredictable environments. Growth becomes possible when both individuals in a relationship can recognize these patterns, communicate openly about their fears, and co-create emotional safety together.

2.5 The Role of Shame in Giving and Receiving Love:

Internalized shame, often cultivated by societal messages that queer love is deviant or wrong, can profoundly disrupt how LGBTQ+ individuals give and receive affection. Shame may manifest as withholding love to protect oneself from perceived rejection, or as overcompensating to prove worthiness. Some may avoid intimacy entirely, convinced they are undeserving of care. This shame is not self-generated, but socially imposed, and unlearning it is a process that takes time, community, and often, therapy. As people begin to recognize their inherent worth, they can start to engage in relationships with more authenticity and less fear, offering love without bargaining and receiving love without guilt. The journey to healing from internalized shame requires a collective effort, where LGBTQ+ individuals can find validation, support, and acceptance within their communities, allowing them to embrace love with openness and self-respect.

2.6 Intimacy After Violence – Navigating Consent and Emotional Safety:

For LGBTQ+ individuals who are survivors of physical, emotional, or sexual violence, intimacy can be fraught with complexity. Trauma may leave echoes in the body and mind, making certain forms of closeness overwhelming or triggering. Consent becomes essential, not only as a momentary agreement, but as an ongoing practice rooted in communication, care, and mutual respect. Trauma-informed relationships honour the need for slowness, for boundaries, and for checking in regularly. They affirm that intimacy is not linear and that healing does not require rushing toward an idea of "normal." Instead, they hold space for whatever pace is necessary to feel truly safe.

2.7 Generational and Collective Healing:

The trauma that queer people carry is not always individual, it is often collective and generational. The legacies of the AIDS epidemic, police brutality, erasure in education and media and ongoing political attacks, leave imprints on how queer communities relate to each other. But within this history, there is also immense strength. Generational storytelling, activism, chosen families, and creative expression have all served as modes of survival and connection. In loving each other despite and, because of these histories, queer communities participate in collective healing. They rewrite the story of queer love as not only possible, but deeply sustaining. Through shared resilience and solidarity, queer communities transform trauma into a foundation for growth, fostering a collective sense of belonging and strength that transcends generations.

2.8 Conclusion – Loving with Scars, Not in Spite of Them:

To love while carrying trauma is not a deficit, it is a testament to one's resilience. Queer love is often more intentional, more thoughtful and more honest precisely, because it has had to be. It does not ignore pain, but moves through it with care. It learns, adapts, and holds contradictions, fear and hope, caution and courage, grief and joy. To give and receive love as a queer person in a world that has tried to deny that love is a powerful act. It says, I am still here, still capable of connection, still worthy of tenderness. And that, in itself, is a kind of healing. Loving with scars is a strength, an affirmation of life and connection that endures despite the world's attempts to invalidate it.

3. The Intersection of Sexuality and Love Languages in Queer Relationships

The concept of love languages, popularized by Gary Chapman's five-category model (Words of Affirmation, Acts of Service, Receiving Gifts, Quality Time, and Physical Touch), has been widely embraced as a tool for enhancing relational understanding. Yet, the original framework was built on assumptions of heteronormativity, gendered expectations and traditional monogamous dynamics. For queer individuals, who often experience love outside of these norms, love languages may manifest in radically different ways. Rather than adhering to a fixed typology, LGBTQ+ people often reinvent how love is expressed and received, informed by their identities, sexualities, and lived experiences. Exploring this intersection reveals how queerness expands and complicates the ways we understand emotional intimacy.

*Queering the Five Love Languages – A Hypothetical Example of LGBTQ+ Intimacy in Practice:

Imagine a queer couple, Dev (a nonbinary person of colour) and Jules (a transmasc person with chronic illness), who have built a relationship rooted in care, fluidity and deep mutual understanding. While they may technically "speak" some of Gary Chapman's five love languages, the way those expressions show up in their relationship diverges from the traditional model, shaped by their intersecting identities and lived experiences.

For instance, words of affirmation go beyond simple compliments, instead, Jules feels most loved when Dev consistently uses the correct name and pronouns in private and public, or when Dev reassures them during gender dysphoria. It's not just about sweet words, but identity-affirming language that validates Jules's existence in a cisnormative world.

Acts of service take on new layers of meaning when Dev helps Jules with hormone shot prep or accompanies them to medical appointments. This kind of love language isn't just about convenience, it's about showing up for one another in systems that often fail to accommodate queer and disabled bodies.

Receiving gifts becomes less about material things and more about intentionality. Jules might surprise Dev with a handmade binder pouch, or Dev may print a zine of queer poetry they wrote just for Jules. These gifts are love in physical form, creative, deeply personal, and often rooted in shared subcultures and survival.

With quality time, their connection isn't defined by traditional dates, but rather by coexisting in affirming, low-pressure environments. Sometimes this means lying in bed together in silence, decompressing from a world that demands constant performance. Other times, it's organizing a mutual aid drive or attending a protest, shared action as a form of intimacy.

And finally, physical touch is carefully navigated, especially around trauma and body boundaries. Instead of generic affection, Dev and Jules have created a shared vocabulary around touch, when, how and where it feels safe. A pinkie hold while watching TV or a forehead kiss before a dysphoria-heavy day might mean more than any grand romantic gesture.

3.1 Sexuality as an Embodied Language of Connection:

For many queer individuals, sexuality is not just a component of their identity, but a mode of self-expression, play and intimacy. Erotic connection often functions as a love language in itself, particularly in communities where bodily autonomy and pleasure have historically been denied. In these spaces, physical intimacy holds layered meanings, affirming identity, negotiating power, and reclaiming agency. Queer sexuality resists reduction to mere physical touch, it is nuanced, creative and deeply relational. This embodied form of communication often transcends traditional categories and speaks to the unique emotional textures of queer love.

3.2 Chosen Family, Collective Care and Communal Love:

In queer communities, the boundaries between romantic, platonic and familial love are often blurred. Chosen families, mutual aid networks and queer friendship circles, challenge the idea that love exists only in romantic or monogamous pairings. In these spaces, love languages adapt, acts of service may look like showing up at protests together, sharing hormone therapy resources, or simply making space for someone's gender expression. Quality time might mean cohabitating with friends instead of partners. In this way, sexuality shapes the social and emotional architecture of love, one that is expansive, intersectional, and fundamentally community-driven.

3.3 Queer Love Languages as Resistance and Reclamation:

To exist as a queer person is to confront systems that police bodies, desires and relationships. In this context, expressing love becomes a form of resistance. For example, public displays of affection, often dangerous or discouraged for queer couples, become subversive acts of visibility. Similarly, gender-affirming compliments or intentional use of someone's correct pronouns can be profound expressions of care and recognition. These gestures, while seemingly small, are radical in a world that often renders queer identities invisible or unacceptable. Love, when rooted in affirmation and mutual recognition, becomes a language of survival and protest. Queer love languages challenge societal norms by making visible what is often deemed unacceptable. In simple acts like public affection or correct pronouns, queer love becomes both an act of survival and resistance.

3.4 How Race, Gender and Class Influence Queer Love Languages:

Love is never experienced in a vacuum. For queer people of colour, disabled queer individuals, or those from working-class backgrounds, love languages are often shaped by overlapping systems of oppression. Emotional labour, for instance, may be unevenly distributed in relationships where one partner navigates racial microaggressions or economic precarity. In such contexts, love might be expressed through advocacy, shared survival strategies, or care that acknowledges structural inequities. Moreover, the ways people feel safe giving or receiving love are informed by lived realities, someone who has experienced trauma related to touch, for example, may need entirely new frameworks for intimacy. Recognizing these intersections is key to understanding the full spectrum of queer love expression.

3.5 Fluidity, Negotiation and Ongoing Reinvention:

Queer relationships often involve continuous negotiation, not just of roles or labels, but of how love is given and received. Unlike rigid heteronormative expectations, many queer partnerships embrace fluidity, one's preferred love language may change over time, across different relationships, or in response to evolving identity. The flexibility to renegotiate boundaries and expressions of care is a hallmark of queer relationality. Whether through polyamorous dynamics, relationship anarchy, or simply more honest communication, LGBTQ+ individuals tend to engage with love languages as living practices, not fixed typologies. This dynamism allows for deeper emotional authenticity and adaptability.

3.6 Beyond the Five – Emerging Love Languages in Queer Contexts:

Many queer people express love in ways that fall outside of the traditional five languages. Emotional labour, holding space, processing trauma, co-regulating, is a profound form of care in queer relationships. Visibility, too, becomes a love language, affirming someone's existence, identity, and presence in public and private spaces. Shared political or creative work may also serve as expressions of deep connection. These emerging forms of love, while often unspoken or undervalued, are central to queer survival and joy. They reflect a refusal to be confined by normative scripts and an openness to redefine what love looks and feels like.

3.7 Conclusion – Love as Queer Praxis:

At the intersection of sexuality and love languages lies a profound truth, queer people often love more deliberately, more consciously and more creatively, because they must. The marginalization many face does not dampen their capacity for love, it deepens it. In reimagining love languages to reflect their realities, LGBTQ+ individuals model new ways of relating that are inclusive, resilient and emotionally honest. These expressions are not just adaptations, they are innovations. By honouring the fluid, diverse and radical ways queer people love, we begin to expand our collective understanding of what intimacy can be. In this way, queer love becomes not just personal, but a political and transformative practice.

4. Physical Touch in LGBTQ+ Love – Safety, Comfort and Public Affection

Physical touch is one of the most intimate ways love is communicated. For LGBTQ+ individuals, however, it often exists at the intersection of tenderness and risk. Holding hands, hugging, or kissing, acts that seem simple in cis-heteronormative relationships, can carry danger, judgment, or fear in public spaces. Yet despite these risks, touch remains a vital expression of affection, healing and affirmation within queer relationships. Exploring how LGBTQ+ people navigate the complexities of physical connection reveals a world where love through touch becomes both a source of deep comfort and a potential act of resistance. As queerness complicates traditional notions of intimacy, touch becomes not only an expression of love, but a reclamation of space and identity.

4.1 The Politics of Touch – When Love Becomes a Risk:

For many queer and trans individuals, public displays of affection are not just emotional, they are political. In regions or environments where queer love is policed, judged, or even criminalized, a simple gesture like holding a partner's hand becomes a courageous act. The visibility of queer touch can provoke unwanted attention, violence, or harassment, forcing many to navigate a world where love itself feels threatening. The fear of such threats shapes how queer couples engage physically in public spaces, often leading to calculated decisions about when and where to show affection. This threat is not always overt, at times, it manifests as a constant, quiet calculation of who is watching and whether it's safe to be seen. Understanding these complexities reveals the profound emotional and physical costs of queer love in public spaces.

4.2 Safety as a Precondition for Intimacy:

For LGBTQ+ individuals, physical affection often hinges on safety, emotional, physical, and psychological. Trauma from past relationships, family rejection, or experiences of violence can create hesitancy around touch. While a partner's embrace may be comforting to one person, it could be triggering to another, depending on their history. In queer relationships, negotiating physical closeness requires deep honesty, consent and care, making trust a foundational aspect of any intimate interaction. When touch is consensual and attuned to each partner's needs, it becomes not only a source of pleasure but also a powerful act of repair, helping to heal old wounds and reaffirming a sense of safety and belonging.

4.3 Gender, Dysphoria and the Complexities of Being Touched:

For trans and nonbinary individuals, physical touch is often filtered through the lens of body-related dysphoria. Even well-intended, affectionate gestures can be misaligned with someone's comfort or gendered boundaries. Queer love, in this context, requires a nuanced understanding of physical boundaries, when, how and where someone likes to be touched. This understanding emphasizes that intimacy is not about spontaneity, but about ongoing consent, communication, and respect. For trans and nonbinary individuals, touch that affirms their gender identity can be profoundly loving, and it becomes more than just a simple gesture, it becomes a life-giving expression of acceptance and validation.

4.4 Private Spaces, Queer Freedom:

Behind closed doors, away from judgment and danger, physical touch can finally breathe. Private spaces often become sanctuaries where queer people are free to express affection fully and without fear. These spaces, bedrooms, safe homes, queer bars and community events, transform into emotional landscapes that allow queer touch to thrive without societal surveillance. In these safe environments, queer couples can explore their own languages of physical intimacy, ranging from gentle gestures to passionate closeness, all on their own terms. Within these protected spaces, love is expressed with greater freedom, making them essential for nurturing relationships outside the confines of external judgment.

4.5 Touch as a Form of Healing:

For many LGBTQ+ individuals, touch is not just romantic, it is reparative. Physical affection in safe relationships becomes a powerful tool for reclaiming agency and dignity, especially for those recovering from trauma, grief, body shame, or years of hiding. Being held, touched, or kissed by someone who sees and honours your full self can help undo years of invisibility or pain. Healing touch isn't always about sex or desire, it can be as simple as the gentle brushing of hair, the quiet comfort of a cuddle, or the warmth of sleeping beside someone who makes you feel safe and affirmed in your skin. In these moments, touch becomes a restorative act, rebuilding trust and self-worth. In queer contexts, touch can be a quiet form of resistance, saying, "you are worthy of care, exactly as you are."

4.6 Queer Public Affection – Visibility and Resistance:

Despite the risks, many queer couples continue to show affection in public, not only for themselves but for others. A kiss on the cheek, a hand held tightly, or a shared dance at a pride parade becomes a radical gesture of visibility. Public displays of affection within queer communities can serve as a quiet form of protest, an assertion of presence in a world that often erases LGBTQ+ intimacy. For some, these gestures are about modelling freedom and possibility for younger queer people, for others, they represent a refusal to be ashamed. Choosing to be visible is deeply personal and not always safe, but for many, it becomes an act of love, both inwardly affirming oneself and outwardly challenging societal norms.

4.7 Reclaiming Touch on Our Own Terms:

Queer individuals and couples are continually rewriting what physical affection means in their lives. Touch is no longer confined to heteronormative expectations or traditional romantic scripts, instead, it is being redefined through consent, care and creativity. This redefinition encompasses everything from developing new ways to express non-sexual affection to creating rituals of closeness that feel affirming rather than obligatory. Reclaiming touch allows for the space to embrace joy, messiness and authenticity, all while honouring individual comfort levels and needs. In this way, physical affection becomes a dynamic and evolving expression of love that is unique to each relationship.

4.8 Conclusion – Love That Listens with Its Hands:

Physical touch in LGBTQ+ relationships is never just about bodies, it's about stories, survival, and trust. Whether in private or in public, gentle or intense, spontaneous or negotiated, touch becomes a language of its own. For queer people, it is often a language forged through pain, but spoken with tenderness. In a world that has so often tried to limit or punish queer connection, the simple act of reaching for someone you love remains one of the most courageous and beautiful things we can do. Each touch holds history and hope, reminding us that queer love is not just felt, it's embodied.

5. The Impact of Heteronormative Conditioning on LGBTQ+ Relationship Dynamics

Heteronormativity pervades society, shaping the way relationships and love are defined, understood and performed. While this framework works for heterosexual individuals, it often presents challenges and limitations for LGBTQ+ individuals who exist outside of these norms. From the assumptions about gender roles to the expectation of monogamous, heterosexual relationships, the dominance of heteronormative standards affects how queer people experience love and intimacy. In order to understand how these norms shape LGBTQ+ relationship dynamics, we must first explore the way society influences the ways love is expressed, received, and negotiated by LGBTQ+ individuals. Recognizing these pressures allows for a deeper understanding of the complex dynamics that queer individuals must navigate and ultimately empowers them to create healthier, more authentic relationships on their own chosen terms.

5.1 Defining Heteronormativity and Its Impact on LGBTQ+ Love Languages:

Heteronormativity is the societal expectation that romantic relationships should conform to a heterosexual, monogamous and binary gender framework. This foundation influences nearly all aspects of love and affection, from the way relationships are structured to how emotions are communicated. For LGBTQ+ individuals, these heteronormative ideals often leave little room for diverse love languages, creating a disconnect between queer experiences and mainstream expectations of romance. The limitations of this framework can make queer people feel marginalized or invalidated in their attempts to express affection in ways that feel natural to them. When LGBTQ+ individuals try to align their love languages with these traditional expectations, it can feel forced or inauthentic, causing confusion and frustration in their relationships.

5.2 The Pressure to Conform to Traditional Relationship Structures:

Queer individuals face immense societal pressure to conform to traditional relationship structures that emphasize monogamy, binary gender roles and heteronormative expectations. These standards, often glorified in media and culture, can make queer relationships feel secondary or invalid if they don't fit into the established mold. The pressure to conform can lead individuals to suppress aspects of their identity or to construct relationships that feel inauthentic. This might include adopting monogamous norms or imposing rigid gender roles in relationships, even when they conflict with one's true desires. For some, this pressure to adhere to traditional relationship structures can lead to emotional exhaustion, a sense of inadequacy, and diminished self-worth. Additionally, when queer people do not conform to these expectations, they often face social marginalization or judgment. This pressure often works subtly, shaping ideas of what a "real" relationship should look like, committed, monogamous and linear. Even when queer individuals desire alternative models like polyamory or chosen family, they may feel conflicted or fear judgment. Over time, this dissonance can stifle emotional honesty and limit relationship freedom. Naming these influences is the first step toward building love on queer terms.

5.3 Heteronormativity and Queer Communication:

Internalized heteronormativity can deeply affect how queer individuals communicate their emotions and desires. Because societal norms often dictate how love and affection should be expressed, many LGBTQ+ individuals struggle with feelings of inadequacy or discomfort when attempting to communicate their needs. The cultural narrative that dictates how LGBTQ+ people should express love, based on what is considered "appropriate" for their gender or sexual orientation, can inhibit emotional expression, leaving individuals feeling constrained or misunderstood in their relationships. Moreover, because mainstream love languages are rooted in heteronormative ideals, they often fail to capture the emotional complexity and lived experiences of queer relationships. Many queer people may feel disconnected from these models, unsure of how to express their feelings authentically. The constant negotiation of societal norms and expectations can create tension within relationships, where communication around love is often framed by outside pressures rather than individual needs and preferences.

5.4 Deconstructing Gender Roles in Queer Relationships:

Traditional gender roles play a significant role in shaping heteronormative relationships, often prescribing specific behaviours and expectations for partners based on their gender. These rigid roles, where one partner is expected to be "masculine" and the other "feminine," for example, have little room for the fluidity that exists in LGBTQ+ relationships. For queer individuals, rejecting these gender norms is a powerful act of self-empowerment, but it also presents challenges as they work to build relationships based on authenticity rather than societal expectations. Non-binary, genderqueer, and other LGBTQ+ individuals, who do not conform to traditional gender roles, may feel even more marginalized by the broader societal norms. Yet, the process of rejecting these rigid frameworks in favour of more fluid, egalitarian relationships is deeply liberating and allows queer couples to explore emotional intimacy and affection without the constraints of gendered expectations. In breaking free from gendered scripts, queer relationships make space for deeper, more authentic forms of connection.

5.5 The Influence of Heteronormative Expectations on LGBTQ+ Sexual Dynamics:

Sexuality, pleasure and desire are all influenced by heteronormative expectations, which often center on heterosexual, monogamous and reproductive ideals. For LGBTQ+ individuals, these expectations can create feelings of shame, confusion, or inadequacy when their sexual experiences or desires do not align with what is considered "normal" by society. Moreover, many LGBTQ+ people lack access to comprehensive sexual education that validates their experiences or educates them about their own sexual needs. This knowledge gap can lead to feelings of isolation and frustration, as queer individuals struggle to understand and articulate their sexual desires. The process of deconstructing heteronormative ideals around sexuality and reclaiming sexual autonomy is essential for queer individuals to experience pleasure and desire without shame. It is important for LGBTQ+ people to explore their sexual identities free from the confines of societal norms, allowing them to establish more fulfilling and authentic sexual dynamics within their relationships.

5.6 The Importance of Challenging Heteronormative Conditioning:

The work of dismantling heteronormative conditioning is essential for creating space for all forms of love and relationship dynamics. By rejecting the limitations imposed by societal norms, LGBTQ+ individuals can create relationships based on mutual respect, equality, and authenticity. In challenging these norms, queer individuals are not only freeing themselves, but are also paving the way for future generations to experience love and intimacy on their own terms. Visibility plays a critical role in this process, as queer individuals who openly challenge heteronormativity can help others feel empowered to do the same. By embracing diverse love languages and relationship models, LGBTQ+ people can cultivate deeper connections with their partners, free from the expectations of mainstream society. Challenging these norms can be deeply transformative, giving queer individuals the freedom to define love and relationships in ways that feel true and empowering. This unlearning isn't a rejection of love, it's a reclamation. By rewriting traditional scripts, LGBTQ+ individuals create space where love is rooted in care, consent, and authenticity. This is queer liberation, not just the right to exist, but the right to love fully and freely.

5.7 Conclusion:

Heteronormativity has long shaped the ways society views love, intimacy and relationships, but for LGBTQ+ individuals, the work of deconstructing these expectations is a vital part of building healthier, more authentic relationships. By rejecting rigid gender roles, monogamous ideals and traditional love scripts, queer individuals have the opportunity to create love languages and relationship dynamics that reflect their true selves. In doing so, LGBTQ+ people can experience love that is not defined by outside pressures, but by mutual respect, authenticity, and care. The ongoing work of challenging heteronormativity offers not only a pathway to personal liberation, but also contributes to the broader cultural shift toward inclusivity, acceptance and the celebration of diverse relationships.

Chapter 7

The Psychology of Coming Out – Redefining the Process

---

1. When Coming Out Doesn't Feel Like Freedom – A Reassessment of "Out and Proud"

Coming out is often presented as a triumphant milestone, a moment of truth-telling that unlocks authenticity, belonging, and liberation. It's celebrated in films, coming-of-age stories, and community narratives, as the point where self-love begins. While this can be true for many, it's not a universal experience. For some, coming out is followed not by celebration, but by isolation, fear, or loss. The idea that being "out and proud" is the only path to queer fulfilment leaves little room for more complicated truths. Naming that complexity is a necessary part of building a more honest and compassionate understanding of queer life. To move toward true liberation, we must expand our understanding of queerness to include the quiet, the cautious, and the unseen. Such reassessment also challenges the one-size-fits-all narrative of visibility as inherently empowering, reminding us that safety, cultural context and personal timing, are equally valid aspects of queer expression.

1.1 The Social Script of Coming Out:

There is an unspoken script many are expected to follow, realize you're queer, accept it, come out, live openly. This linear narrative is reinforced everywhere, from pop culture to LGBTQ+ support groups, and it can be both empowering and constraining. Not everyone fits neatly into that timeline, and not everyone wants or is able to follow it. The pressure to come out publicly can create shame or guilt for those who can't or don't. For people with intersecting identities, black, brown, disabled, neurodivergent, religious, and immigrant, the stakes of visibility are often higher and more dangerous. The assumption that "outness" equals liberation overlooks the very real harm that disclosure can invite. True freedom must allow for nonlinear journeys, where safety, context, and personal truth are prioritized over conformity to a singular ideal.

1.2 When Visibility Feels Like Exposure:

For some, coming out doesn't feel like stepping into the light, it feels like being stripped bare. It can open the door to rejection, discrimination, or even violence. Rather than feeling affirmed, individuals may find themselves more vulnerable than ever. Visibility becomes exposure, and with it comes a heavy emotional toll. The pressure to disclose one's identity in workplace settings, medical offices, or family gatherings can lead to chronic stress and anxiety. And because coming out is rarely a one-time event, queer people often have to weigh risks and safety over and over again. In those moments, "freedom" feels like a distant promise rather than a lived reality.

1.3 Cultural and Familial Tensions:

In many families and cultures, being queer doesn't just challenge individual relationships, it disrupts entire belief systems. Coming out can mean losing not only familial support, but cultural connection, language, faith, and community. It can be especially painful in collectivist cultures where identity is interwoven with family and ancestry. When Western narratives frame disclosure as necessary for wholeness, they erase the survival strategies and nuanced expressions of queerness that already exist in other cultural contexts. Choosing to stay silent, to code-switch, or to come out only in certain spaces isn't a failure, it's an act of care and self-preservation. Honouring these quiet acts of resilience is essential to broadening our understanding of what it means to live authentically. Such expressions of queerness, shaped by cultural wisdom and ancestral negotiation, deserve recognition, not correction.

1.4 The Burden of Representation:

Being out often comes with an unspoken expectation, now that you're visible, you must also be exemplary. People may expect you to educate them, represent the community, or serve as a constant advocate. This burden of representation can be exhausting, especially for those already navigating systemic oppression. There's little room to be imperfect, confused, or evolving. Instead of freedom, some find that visibility brings performance, being watchful of how one speaks, dresses, dates, or explains their existence. For many, the weight of being "the only one" in their space drains rather than uplifts. Liberation must also include the right to simply exist, without explanation, expectation, or the pressure to represent anyone, but oneself. True queerness should never hinge on perfection, it must make space for rest, contradiction, and simply being.

1.5 Privacy as a Valid Form of Power:

Authenticity doesn't require an audience. Choosing not to come out, or to do so selectively, is a deeply valid expression of autonomy. Privacy can be protective, not repressive. It allows individuals to retain control over their stories, to share them in their own time and on their own terms. In a world that demands visibility and explanation, silence can be a form of resistance. The idea of "queer opacity" offers a framework for understanding how not being legible to others can itself be freeing. Everyone deserves the right to shape their identity in a way that prioritizes their safety, well-being, and comfort. In reclaiming the power of privacy, we affirm that queerness is not defined by visibility, but by self-determined truth.

1.6 Toward a More Nuanced Framework:

What if liberation isn't about disclosure, but about choice? Rather than measuring authenticity through how "out" someone is, it's more meaningful to honour the complexity of queer lives in all their forms. The freedom to not come out, or to come out partially, quietly, or fluidly, is as vital as the freedom to proclaim it loudly. Communities built on care, consent and flexibility, can better hold the diversity of queer experience. There is no single roadmap. Wholeness looks different for everyone. By embracing these varied paths, we create space for every queer person to define liberation on their own terms

1.7 Conclusion – Honouring Complexity:

Coming out can be beautiful, but it can also be painful. Both truths can exist at once. Not every queer person finds safety or joy on the other side of disclosure and not every queer life fits the mold of "out and proud." There's courage in remaining private. There's power in protecting oneself. And there's grace in letting people decide what authenticity looks like for them. Liberation begins not with performance, but with choice, deeply personal, deeply sacred, and always deserving of respect. By embracing the full spectrum of queer experience, we move closer to a world where freedom is measured not by visibility, but by the ability to live truthfully, however that may look.

2. The Digital Closet – Hiding in Plain Sight on Social Media

Social media has drastically changed the way people express and share their identities, especially in the queer community. Platforms once hailed as spaces for connection and self expression have also become complex and sometimes contradictory spaces where visibility can feel both empowering and overwhelming. For many, the digital world has become the new "digital closet", a place where queerness is often hidden in plain sight, carefully curated to protect privacy or control the narrative. Coming out is no longer a simple act, it's a continuous process of navigating how much to reveal and when, based on personal safety, social pressure, and the realities of living in an increasingly digital world. In this landscape, authenticity and self-protection are in constant negotiation, each post, follow, or silence is its own kind of coming out.

2.1 The Duality of Visibility – Public vs. Private Identity:

On social media, the boundary between public and private life is constantly blurred. Queer individuals often face the challenge of deciding how much of their personal identity to share online, where visibility doesn't always equate to authenticity. The decision to be "out" on platforms like Instagram, Facebook, or X, isn't always straightforward, especially when the risks of exposure, such as rejection, harassment, or loss of privacy, are so high. Some may feel pressured to either fully embrace their queerness online or remain silent to avoid potential harm. The digital closet, in this sense, becomes a space for self-preservation, where the safety of privacy is weighed against the desire for self-expression.

2.2 The Risk of Overexposure – The Dangers of Forced Visibility:

While social media offers a platform for self-expression, it can also come with a sense of forced exposure. The demand for constant visibility, coupled with the expectation to share personal details, can feel invasive for some. This is particularly true for queer individuals who may face significant backlash, harassment, or loss of safety by being openly visible. The pressure to disclose one's identity publicly can feel like a trap, especially when the emotional toll of dealing with negative comments, trolling, or even outright discrimination becomes overwhelming. Visibility online is not always empowering, it can be a double-edged sword that leaves individuals feeling vulnerable and emotionally drained.

2.3 The Illusion of Authenticity – Curating Identity for Social Media:

Social media encourages the presentation of a polished, curated version of ourselves and for many, this doesn't reflect the full complexity of their queer identities. The pressure to appear authentic online can lead to oversimplified or incomplete portrayals of who we are, especially when the norms of visibility demand a specific kind of queerness. Queer individuals may feel compelled to conform to societal expectations of what it means to be "out" or "proud," even if their lived experiences don't fit neatly into those categories. The act of coming out online can sometimes feel more like a performance, curating, editing, and even constructing an identity that fits the digital platform's aesthetic, rather than fully embracing the messy, fluid reality of queerness.

2.4 The Digital Closet as a Survival Mechanism:

For some, the digital closet isn't just a metaphor, it's a survival strategy. In an era where online visibility often comes with very real-world consequences, such as job discrimination, rejection from family, or even physical violence, the choice to remain in the digital closet becomes an act of self-preservation. The decision not to share one's queerness on social media or to come out in selective spaces is a valid expression of autonomy and safety. Many queer individuals live with the constant awareness that coming out online could jeopardize their emotional, social, or even financial security. In this way, the digital closet serves as a sanctuary, allowing individuals to protect their private lives while navigating an often hostile world. For those in the digital closet, silence is not shame, but a quiet act of strength in the face of an unforgiving environment.

2.5 The Evolution of Queer Visibility – From Physical to Digital Spaces:

Historically, coming out was a deeply personal and physical act, typically taking place in intimate, private spaces with family, friends, or trusted individuals. In contrast, digital platforms require queerness to be expressed publicly and often without the same personal context or support. Today, coming out online is no longer a singular event but a continuous, evolving process. Social media platforms don't just provide a space for one-time disclosures, they are spaces where queer people are constantly negotiating their identities, deciding when and how to share parts of themselves. This shift from physical to digital spaces has created new challenges and opportunities, as queerness in the digital realm is not only about visibility, but about managing how that visibility interacts with the larger world.

2.6 The Pressure to Perform – Social Media's Impact on Self-Expression:

Social media is structured around performance, where metrics like likes, shares, and comments act as validation. For queer individuals, this pressure to perform can distort their experiences of identity and self-expression. The desire for approval can overshadow the authentic process of self-acceptance, leading individuals to present a version of themselves that is more about gaining social validation than about true self-expression. Over time, this disconnect between online presentation and internal truth can create emotional dissonance, making authenticity feel both risky and elusive.

This performative aspect of digital identity can make the act of coming out feel less like a personal choice and more like a public spectacle, leading to exhaustion and feelings of alienation. Instead of being free to express themselves authentically, some queer individuals feel trapped by the need to fit a particular image or narrative of queerness that resonates with their audience.

2.7 Moving Beyond the Digital Closet – Rethinking Queer Visibility:

The digital closet, while protective, is not an ideal state. It's a reflection of the challenges that queer individuals face in balancing privacy, safety and visibility. However, as social media continues to evolve, there's potential to rethink how queer identity can be expressed and shared in digital spaces. Rather than focusing solely on the binary of being "out" or "in," we can embrace a more flexible, nuanced understanding of digital visibility that allows queer individuals to control their narratives in ways that are meaningful to them. It's crucial to create digital environments that respect privacy and autonomy while allowing people to share their stories when, how, and with whom they choose.

2.8 Conclusion – A New Understanding of Queer Identity in the Digital Age:

The digital world has fundamentally altered the way queer individuals experience visibility and with it, the very concept of coming out. The digital closet is not a one-size-fits-all experience, it's a dynamic, complex space where safety and self-expression intersect. For many, navigating queer identity online requires constant negotiation, balancing the risks of exposure with the desire for connection. To move beyond the digital closet, it's essential to acknowledge the multifaceted nature of online self-expression and create spaces where queer people can be visible on their own terms, free from judgment or harm.

3. The Pressure to Label Oneself and the Freedom of Unlabelling

From a young age, many are taught to define who they are in clear, recognizable terms. In the realm of sexuality and identity, this pressure becomes even more pronounced. Society often expects clear-cut labels, gay, lesbian, bisexual, pansexual, queer. For some, these words offer comfort, community and a sense of place. But for others, labels can feel premature, constrictive, or simply inadequate. The act of naming can be empowering, but it can also be a source of anxiety, especially when identity is still evolving. Unlabelling, or resisting the need for rigid definitions, can offer its own kind of liberation, allowing space for self-discovery without expectation or pressure.

3.1 The Social Demand for Clarity:

People crave clarity, often not just for themselves, but from others. In conversations, introductions, or relationships, queer people are frequently asked to explain "what they are." These questions, while sometimes well-meaning, can impose a demand for coherence that doesn't reflect lived reality. The desire to pin down identity into a single word or concept may serve societal comfort more than personal truth. This demand for labelling can be especially intense in queer spaces where there's an emphasis on visibility and representation. Yet, being forced to articulate something that's still unfolding can lead to shame, confusion, or the fear of being "not queer enough."

3.2 The Evolution of Identity Over Time:

Sexuality and gender are not always fixed, they can shift, evolve, deepen, or take entirely new shapes over time. For many, the journey toward understanding themselves is ongoing, full of surprises and contradictions. What may have once felt like a true label might later feel limiting or outdated. Embracing this evolution requires space to explore without the pressure of permanence. Unlabelling supports this idea, that people should be allowed to grow without having to rewrite their narrative or justify the change. There is strength in fluidity, in trusting oneself through transitions and recognizing that no single word has to define an entire lifetime.

3.3 Labels as Comfort and Labels as Cages:

For some, adopting a label is a powerful declaration. It can be a way to find others, to assert pride, and to push back against erasure. There's beauty in finding a word that feels like home. But labels can also become cages when they start to police behaviour, create expectations, or erase the complexity of human experience. A bisexual person in a different-gender relationship might feel invalidated. A queer person who once identified as gay may hesitate to explore attraction to another gender for fear of judgment. Even within LGBTQ+ spaces, the use of labels can sometimes reinforce boundaries instead of building bridges. The freedom to step outside those boxes is just as important as the right to claim them. Ultimately, it's not the labels themselves, but the ability to redefine or discard them that ensures true self-expression.

3.4 Unlabelling as an Act of Agency:

Choosing not to label oneself, or to use broad, expansive terms like "fluid," "questioning," or "none of your business", is not a sign of confusion or indecisiveness. It is an act of agency, of self-determination. Refusing to be easily categorized allows individuals to prioritize their internal experiences over external validation. This form of autonomy can feel radical in a world that demands explanation. It is a way to claim the full range of one's humanity, to be expansive, intuitive, and present without needing to make sense to others. It permits us to say, "I am still figuring it out," or "I am more than a word." In rejecting labels, we reclaim the power to define ourselves on our own terms, without the constraints of societal expectations.

3.5 The Role of Community and the Fear of Being Left Out:

Many people fear that unlabelling will make them invisible or unwelcome in queer spaces. There's a deep need for connection, and sometimes it feels like the ticket is a clear, affirmed label. But community must not come at the cost of authenticity. A truly inclusive space recognizes that not everyone will, or should, have to fit a fixed identity. It's essential to affirm those who are exploring, who don't know, or who don't want to define themselves at all. By expanding our understanding of queerness, we make more room for everyone to belong, especially those who live in the in-between. In embracing the fluidity of identity, we ensure that community becomes a place where all expressions of queerness are welcome, without the need for conformity.

3.6 Breaking the Binary Thinking Around Identity:

Much of the pressure to label comes from binary thinking, gay or straight, man or woman, in or out. These binaries flatten the nuance of human identity and reduce queerness to something tidy and easily categorized. Embracing unlabelling helps to challenge this system, encouraging more expansive views of sexuality and gender. Rather than trying to "solve" identity like a puzzle, we can begin to treat it like a story, one that is ongoing, non-linear, and deeply personal. Freedom emerges when we stop asking people to prove who they are and start listening to how they feel.

3.7 Creating Space for Self-Discovery:

Everyone deserves the space to explore without fear, shame, or premature categorization. This might mean experimenting with different terms, relationships, expressions, or simply living without needing to know all the answers. Self-discovery thrives in environments that are patient and nonjudgmental. Whether someone draws strength from a clear label or peace from its absence, what matters most is their freedom to define, or undefine, themselves on their own terms. Support doesn't come from offering a label to wear, but from holding space for someone to discover what fits, what doesn't, and what might never need to be named at all.

3.8 Conclusion – Empowering the Freedom to Just Be:

The pressure to label oneself can be loud, but so can the quiet strength of unlabelling. Queer identity is not a destination but a journey, one that deserves time, fluidity and the grace to shift. Whether someone chooses a label, changes it, or rejects them altogether, each choice is valid. What empowers us isn't the label itself, but the freedom to choose it, or not. In that freedom, we reclaim ownership of our stories. We remember that being true to ourselves doesn't always mean being understood by others. Sometimes, the most powerful thing we can be is undefined and completely at peace with that.

4. Late-in-Life Realizations – The Challenges of Coming Out After 40

Coming out is often framed as a youthful rite of passage, something that happens in adolescence or early adulthood. But for many, the realization of queerness, or the courage to name it, arrives later in life. Whether it follows a long-term relationship, the experience of raising children, or decades of quiet self-denial, coming out after 40 can feel both liberating and daunting. The path may unfold differently, but it is no less valid. Self-discovery doesn't follow a schedule, and embracing one's identity later in life is a profound act of strength, resilience, and self-love.

4.1 The Weight of Time and the Fear of Regret:

One of the first hurdles many face is the weight of what feels like lost time. There may be grief over years spent in the closet, regrets about choices made under societal pressure, or a fear that it's "too late" to start over. These feelings are valid, but they don't define the worth of the present.

Life is not a linear path, and queerness doesn't arrive on a fixed schedule. Acknowledging what was missed is part of healing, but so is recognizing the joy and possibility that still lies ahead. The past may shape us, but it does not limit the future, there is always space for reinvention, growth, and the reclamation of joy.

4.2 Untangling Identity from History:

By the time someone reaches midlife or beyond, identity is deeply woven into routines, relationships, and responsibilities. Coming out can feel like it threatens to unravel everything, marriages, children, careers, and social networks, often built on long-standing assumptions of heterosexuality or cisnormativity. It's common to question, Who will still accept me? What parts of my life will remain intact? These questions can be terrifying, but they can also open up opportunities to reimagine life with greater honesty and intention. The challenge of untangling identity from history is not a loss, but an invitation to rebuild with authenticity, allowing space for both the past and the future.

4.3 Family Dynamics and Shifting Roles:

Coming out later often intersects with complex family dynamics. Children may be grown or still at home and partners may be deeply impacted. Some loved ones might feel betrayed, confused, or unsure how to respond. Others might surprise us with their unconditional support. Navigating these relationships requires patience, communication, and self-compassion. It's okay to move slowly. It's okay to grieve. And it's okay to prioritize one's own truth while holding space for others to process in their own time. In the midst of these shifts, the process of coming out can also deepen connections, fostering more genuine, authentic bonds as both sides navigate new understandings of love and identity.

4.4 The Myth of the "Too Late" Narrative:

There's a pervasive belief that queer joy and self-discovery are reserved for the young. Media often glamorizes youth as the peak of personal growth, leaving older queer individuals feeling invisible or unrepresented. But this narrative is not only false, it's harmful. There are countless stories of people finding love, community, and purpose later in life. Coming out at 40, 50, or beyond is not about starting from scratch, it's about stepping into authenticity with the depth and wisdom gained from a life already lived.

4.5 Building New Community at Any Age:

One of the most important aspects of coming out is connection, finding people who affirm and support who you are. For those coming out later, entering queer spaces can feel intimidating, especially if they're perceived as youth-centered or unfamiliar. But queer community is vast and there is room for everyone. Whether it's through online groups, meetups, LGBTQ+ centers, or chosen family, building community at any age is possible. It may take time, but it's never too late to find your people and be embraced for exactly who you are.

4.6 Reclaiming Sexuality and Intimacy:

For many, coming out later brings up questions about intimacy, attraction and desire. Years of internalized shame or repression can leave people feeling disconnected from their bodies or unsure how to explore new dynamics. It's normal to feel nervous, awkward, or inexperienced. Reclaiming sexuality isn't about comparison or performance, it's about rediscovering pleasure and connection on your own terms. There's beauty in learning anew, in letting go of expectations, and in allowing yourself to be both curious and cared for.

4.7 Dealing with Internalized Shame and Guilt:

Growing up in a time or environment where queerness was taboo often leaves a lasting imprint. Many who come out later in life carry internalized messages that their identity is wrong, selfish, or disruptive. These feelings don't disappear overnight, but they can be unlearned. Therapy, support groups, reading, and gentle self-reflection can all help to loosen shame's grip. It's okay to mourn the past while choosing to believe that joy is still possible. Living your truth isn't a betrayal of the past, it's a gift to your future.

4.8 The Strength in Coming Out Later:

There is deep strength in choosing truth after years of silence. It takes courage to disrupt the life others expected from you in order to honour the life you want for yourself. Every late-in-life coming out is a reminder that authenticity is always worth pursuing. What may look like a detour is often the most meaningful part of the journey. It's never too late to be seen, loved, and free. And you don't have to do it alone.

4.9 Conclusion – Honouring Your Timing:

Coming out after 40 isn't a failure or delay, it's a bold act of self-recognition. It's proof that it's never too late to live a life that feels honest, fulfilling, and whole. Whether your path is met with immediate celebration or slow transformation, it's still yours. You get to write the next chapter. And it can be tender, vibrant, loving, and entirely true. Every step toward yourself, no matter when it happens, is something to be proud of.

5. Coming Out in Professional Spaces – Risks, Rewards and Realities

Coming out is not just a personal decision, it's also a professional one. For many LGBTQ+ individuals, the workplace presents both opportunity and uncertainty. The choice to be open about one's identity at work means navigating power dynamics, company culture, and questions of safety. While some find affirmation and freedom in being out, others encounter exclusion or more subtle forms of discrimination. Developing a thoughtful and thorough understanding of the risks, benefits, and complexities involved in coming out, within professional settings, is essential for making well-informed and confident choices, particularly in workplaces that may be resistant to change or slow to adapt.

5.1 Assessing the Environment – Reading the Room:

Before coming out at work, it's crucial to assess the workplace climate. Company policies, leadership behaviour, co-worker attitudes, and industry norms all provide insight into how LGBTQ+ identities are received. An organization may have inclusive statements on paper, but fall short in practice. Pay attention to whose identities are celebrated, whose voices are heard, and how diversity is actually lived. Trusting your instincts and gathering information can help clarify whether visibility would feel safe or strategic, or neither.

5.2 The Emotional Labor of Being Out at Work:

Being out professionally often comes with an invisible workload. Answering questions, correcting assumptions, or advocating for inclusion can become an unofficial part of the job. This emotional labour can be draining, especially when you're the only openly queer person in your department or company. While some take pride in being visible and educating others, it's also valid to set boundaries and prioritize well-being. No one owes their colleagues a crash course in identity and being out, should never mean being on-call for constant explanation.

5.3 The Potential Rewards of Visibility:

When the environment is right, coming out at work can bring profound benefits. It may strengthen workplace relationships, improve communication, and allow for more authentic self-expression. Many find that being open fosters creativity, confidence, and a deeper sense of purpose. Visibility can also pave the way for others who are still figuring out how to show up. In inclusive workplaces, being out can mean access to mentorship, advocacy, and a network of allies who amplify LGBTQ+ voices.

5.4 The Risks of Disclosure in Unequal Systems:

Even today, coming out in professional spaces carries real risks. Queer and trans employees can face microaggressions, stalled promotions, or even termination, especially in industries or regions with weak legal protections. Intersectional identities compound this vulnerability, a queer person of colour or a trans person with a disability may face heightened scrutiny or bias. The risk is not just career-related but emotional. Disclosure can make someone a target for subtle exclusion, tokenization, or outright hostility.

5.5 Strategic Outness – Partial, Contextual and Fluid:

Coming out doesn't have to be an all-or-nothing decision. Many choose to be selectively out, open with trusted colleagues, quiet with supervisors, or completely private in professional settings. Identity can be shared gradually, strategically, or not at all. These choices may shift depending on role, team, or company culture. There is no single "right" way to come out at work. Choosing how and when to be visible is deeply personal and should always be rooted in safety, comfort, and agency.

5.6 Knowing Your Rights and Finding Support:

Understanding your legal protections can empower decision-making. In many countries, sexual orientation and gender identity are protected under workplace discrimination laws, but enforcement varies. HR departments, DEI (Diversity, Equity, and Inclusion) initiatives, and employee resource groups (ERGs), can offer varying levels of support. However, it's wise to approach HR with caution if the company's track record doesn't reflect its stated values. Sometimes, the most meaningful support comes from informal networks, mentors, or external LGBTQ+ organizations that provide tools and guidance for navigating difficult work environments. Empowering oneself with knowledge and connecting to trusted allies can not only help navigate immediate challenges, but also build long-term resilience and solidarity within the workplace.

5.7 Advocating for Structural Change Without Self-Sacrifice:

Some queer professionals feel a call to improve their workplace for others, especially once they've come out. Advocating for inclusive policies, training, or representation can be powerful, but it doesn't have to fall on one person's shoulders. Change is more sustainable when it's collective. Allies, leadership, and institutional resources must share the load. It's okay to step back when advocacy becomes exhausting. Being out is not a full-time role, and your job description shouldn't expand to include unpaid emotional or educational labour. True advocacy thrives when it is shared and self-care is prioritized alongside the work for change.

5.8 Affirming Queer Success on Your Own Terms:

Professional success should never require erasing who you are. Whether you're fully out, partially open, or quietly private, your identity is not an obstacle, it's a source of insight, resilience, and strength. Queer professionals bring innovation, empathy and adaptability to the workplace, often precisely, because of their lived experiences. Coming out at work isn't about meeting a benchmark of authenticity, it's about choosing your own terms of engagement. Your career and your identity can coexist without compromise. True success is defined by the freedom to bring your whole self to your work, in your own way, without sacrificing what makes you unique.

5.9 Conclusion – Defining Your Own Professional Truth:

Coming out in professional spaces is a deeply personal journey shaped by context, values, and intuition. There's no universal script, only a series of choices rooted in self-respect and situational awareness. Whether you're fully visible or navigating the margins quietly, you deserve to work in an environment that sees you clearly and treats you fairly. Ultimately, your professional path should honour your authenticity, allowing you to thrive without compromise. Coming out at work is not just about visibility, it's about defining how you show up in a way that aligns with your values and well-being. By setting your own terms, you create a space where your identity and professional success coexist harmoniously, free from the pressure to conform. "True professional freedom is not in how you are seen, but in how authentically you can show up, on your terms." – Anonymous

***Moments of Reflection and Self-Discovery:**

An intimate journey inward, exploring the hidden, celebrated, evolving and true parts of who we are, beyond expectations and into authenticity.

A. Where in my life do I feel fully seen? Where do I still feel hidden?

Imagine your identity as a canvas. Where have you splashed your most vibrant colours? Where are the areas you've painted over, maybe in shades of grey or invisible? How does it feel to reveal those hidden parts of yourself? What would it look like to bring them to life?

B. How do I define authenticity for myself, not what others expect?

If your life were a story, what chapter would you be in right now? Write an excerpt from this chapter in your truest voice, not the one others expect to hear. What does your character look like? How do they move through the world? What do they reveal and what do they keep close? Describe the thoughts they whisper to themselves, the moments they savour, and the truths they are just beginning to name.

C. What does "coming out" mean to me right now, not in the past or future?

Picture a door that represents "coming out." Right now, is it open, closed, cracked, or locked? Describe the feeling you have standing in front of it today. What do you notice about the door's texture, its weight, and the space behind it? Do you feel ready to step through? Why or why not?

D. What assumptions do I carry about labels, timing, or performance?

Take a moment to think of all the labels others have placed on you. Now, write them down, but imagine they're floating in the air above you like balloons. Which ones would you hold onto, and which would you let drift away? What would your life look like without all the labels? How would you feel?

E. Who do I trust with my story, and what does that trust look like?

Think of your story as a precious book. Who would you hand it to? Who would you guard it from? What would it take for you to let someone read it without fear? Imagine sharing a single chapter with a friend or family member. What would you tell them, and what would you leave out?

F. If you could live one week completely unseen by judgment or expectation, what version of yourself would show up?

You're in an invisible cloak for one week. What does your "unseen self" do differently? What conversations would you have? What places would you visit? Write a day in the life of this liberated version of yourself.

G. What would your younger self need to hear from you now about coming out, what advice, love, or compassion would you offer them?

Write a letter to your younger self, without any rules. What would you say if you could reassure them that everything would be okay, even when it felt impossible? What truths, hopes, or dreams would you share, knowing they may not understand them yet?

H. If no words existed for who you are, how would you describe yourself using colour, shape, or sound?

Imagine that the world didn't have words for sexuality, gender, or identity. What colours would represent you? What shape would your energy take? What song would play when you enter a room? Draw or describe these expressions of yourself without relying on traditional labels.

I. What version of you does the world celebrate? What version of you does the world ignore?

Write about two versions of yourself, one that gets the applause and one that stays hidden in the shadows. What are the ways the world sees one, but not the other? How does that feel? Which version do you want to spend more time with?

J. How do you feel about the idea of privacy and boundaries in your coming out journey? Do you feel empowered or restricted by them?

Imagine you're building a fortress around your identity. What parts of your life are you eager to share and what do you keep close to your heart? Is there freedom in privacy, or does it feel isolating? Sketch the walls of your fortress. What do they look like, and what do they protect?

Chapter 8

LGBTQ+ Parentage and Family Dynamics

---

1. Queer Parenthood Without Biological Children – Reimagining Parenthood

Parenthood has long been narrowly defined by genetic ties, as though love and commitment were secondary to DNA. For many queer individuals and couples, that definition feels exclusionary and inadequate. By shifting the focus from biology to the bonds we forge, through care, dedication, and shared experience, we open up new possibilities for what it means to be a family. Reimagining parenthood begins with acknowledging that biology is only one thread in the tapestry of family life and that the fabric is just as strong when other threads, adoption, fostering, co-parenting, and chosen kin, are woven in.

1.1 Confronting the Pressure of Biological Parenthood:

Society's insistence on "real" parents being genetically related can sow doubt and guilt in those who cannot or choose not to conceive. Queer people may internalize messages that they're somehow less legitimate as parents if they lack a biological connection. This pressure often intensifies within LGBTQ+ spaces that valorise certain paths, like surrogacy or donor conception, while invisibilizing adoption, fostering, or informal care networks. Recognizing and challenging these norms is the first step toward letting go of biologically based "eligibility" criteria and embracing each person's right to parenthood in whatever form resonates most deeply.

1.2 Exploring Alternative Pathways to Parenthood:

Adoption offers the opportunity to welcome a child who needs stability and care, creating profound bonds grounded in choice and commitment rather than blood. Fostering can be a temporary or long-term path, emphasizing the transformative impact of providing a safe, nurturing home for youth in crisis. Co-parenting arrangements, whether between friends, siblings, or non-romantic partners, allow multiple adults to share parental roles and responsibilities collaboratively. Surrogacy and donor conception remain options for those who desire a genetic link, but wish to decouple biology from traditional gender roles. Each path has its own joys, challenges, and logistical hurdles, yet all affirm that love, not lineage, defines parenthood.

1.3 Reframing Parenthood – Love, Nurture and Daily Care:

Parenthood is fundamentally an act of ongoing emotional labour, soothing tears, celebrating milestones, guiding moral development, nurturing growth, and providing unconditional support.

These quotidian gestures, holding hands on the first day of school, reading bedtime stories, or bearing witness to a child's triumphs and setbacks, build the foundation of family. When biology is removed from the equation, the spotlight shifts to these acts of care. Queer parents who nurture through adoption, fostering, or chosen-family arrangements demonstrate that the essence of parenting lies not in genetic inheritance, but in the willingness to invest time, empathy and steadfast presence in a child's life.

1.4 Overcoming Internalized and External Stigma:

Queer parents without biological ties often contend with two layers of stigma, self-doubt rooted in cultural messaging and external judgment from those who equate parenthood with genetics. Internally, shame may surface in questions like "Am I less of a mother or father?" Externally, unsolicited comments or assumptions, "You're not her real dad," "Who gave birth to your child?", can feel invalidating. Combating these pressures requires community support, candid conversations, and affirmations that all forms of parenthood are equally real. Sharing stories of successful, loving and thriving queer families, helps dismantle harmful myths and validates the diverse experiences of non-biological parents everywhere.

1.5 Embracing the Unique Strengths of Non-Biological Parenthood:

Queer parents who forge families without biological ties often develop remarkable resilience, creativity and empathy. Navigating adoption processes, negotiating co-parenting agreements, or ensuring legal protections for foster children builds resourcefulness and mutual trust. Children raised in diverse family structures learn early to value love over lineage and to embrace multiplicity in identity and belonging. These families model adaptability and openness, teaching the next generation that family is defined not by rigid blueprints, but by the commitments we choose to honour every day.

1.6 Navigating Legal, Financial, and Emotional Realities:

Practical considerations can feel daunting, adoption laws vary widely, fostering requires licensing and home studies, and surrogacy involves medical, legal, and financial complexity. Securing parental rights, through second-parent adoption, guardianship documents, or co-parent agreements, is essential for protecting both child and parent. Financial planning may involve saving for adoption fees or surrogacy costs, while emotional preparedness calls for therapy, support groups, or mentorship from experienced queer parents. Accessing community resources, LGBTQ+ family centers, online forums, and legal clinics, empowers prospective parents to navigate these hurdles with confidence and clarity.

1.7 Building Community and Chosen Family:

Queer parenthood thrives in supportive networks where stories are shared, advice exchanged and celebrations multiplied. Finding, or creating, spaces where adoptive, foster, or co-parenting families congregate reduces isolation and amplifies collective wisdom. These shared spaces don't just foster connection, they also validate the many forms queer family can take, offering a sense of belonging that traditional systems often deny.

Chosen family offers an extended system of care, grandparents by choice, aunties and uncles, and siblings-by-heart, who share in parenting joys and challenges. These communities become lifelines, offering playgroups, legal aid, holiday gatherings, and emotional sustenance. In these circles, non-biological parents are recognized, honoured, and uplifted as full, authentic families.

1.8 Affirming Diverse Paths to Parenthood:

Redefining parenthood beyond biology invites us all to expand our conception of family. Whether through adoption, fostering, co-parenting, surrogacy, or chosen kin, queer individuals demonstrate that family is a constellation of love, choice and care. Embracing these varied pathways empowers those who might otherwise feel excluded by traditional norms. As society witnesses the thriving, joyous families built without genetic ties, the narrative shifts, parenthood is no longer a privilege reserved for those with biological connections, but a universal right grounded in commitment, compassion, and the courage to love. By celebrating diverse paths to parenthood, we not only affirm the richness of queer family structures, but also challenge and expand the definition of what it means to be a parent, creating a world where love, not biology, defines family.

* Global Advocacy & Legal Support for LGBTQ+ Families:

For Example, the following organizations cover a broad spectrum of international resources, focusing on advocacy, legal aid, and the empowerment of LGBTQ+ families globally. Many also offer support for navigating specific national laws and policies related to LGBTQ+ parenthood and family rights:

International Lesbian, Gay, Bisexual, Trans and Intersex Association (ILGA):

- Provides global advocacy for LGBTQ+ rights, including family and parental rights across countries.

Rainbow Families (Australia):

- Provides support to LGBTQ+ parents and families across Australia by offering legal advice and resources for building supportive communities.

European LGBTQ+ Family Rights Network (ELFRN):

- Offers information, resources, and advocacy for LGBTQ+ families across Europe, focusing on legal recognition and family rights.

The Global LGBTIQ+ Family Equality Council:

- Provides global support and advocacy for LGBTIQ+ parents, working towards equal rights, recognition, and inclusion worldwide.

Queer Parenting Network (UK):

- A UK-based organization supporting LGBTQ+ parents with legal guidance, community events, and parenting resources.

COC Nederland (Netherlands):

- Focuses on LGBTQ+ rights in the Netherlands, offering legal advocacy and resources for queer families and parenting.

ILGA Asia:

- Offers advocacy and support for LGBTQ+ families within Asia, focusing on family rights, marriage equality, and adoption.

LGBTIQ+ Family Rights – Canada:

- This Canadian network provides legal resources for LGBTQ+ families, including access to parental rights, adoption support, and more.

OutRight Action International (Global):

- Works globally on advancing human rights for LGBTQ+ individuals, including family rights, with a focus on both advocacy and policy reform.

South African LGBTQ+ Rights (OUT LGBT Well-being):

- Provides advocacy and legal support in South Africa for LGBTQ+ families, focusing on legal issues, adoption and recognition of queer parents.

2. Polyamorous and Non-Traditional Parenting Structures

Polyamorous and non-traditional parenting structures invite us to rethink the narrow confines of what a "family" is meant to be. Instead of centering biology or monogamy, these models prioritize care, collaboration, and chosen kinship. Whether it's triads raising children together or co-parenting networks involving more than two adults, these family configurations challenge mainstream norms and often strengthen emotional support systems in meaningful, lasting ways.

2.1 The Emotional Benefits of Multi-Parent Households:

Children raised in polyamorous or expanded family systems often benefit from multiple nurturing figures, each bringing unique strengths, perspectives, and emotional bandwidth. More adults can mean more consistent care, shared responsibilities, and a wider safety net. It can also reduce parental burnout and allow for healthier adult dynamics, which positively impact the emotional climate of the home.

2.2 Navigating Stigma and Misunderstanding:

Despite these advantages, polyamorous and non-traditional families frequently face stigma, both socially and legally. Assumptions about promiscuity, instability, or confusion for the child often cloud public perception. Parents may be forced to "sanitize" or hide the nature of their relationships from schools, healthcare providers, or extended family. These pressures can lead to feelings of invisibility or fear of losing custody or legal recognition.

2.3 Communication as a Core Parenting Tool:

One of the most vital skills in polyamorous parenting structures is communication, honest, frequent, and intentional. With multiple caregivers, decisions around discipline, education, healthcare, and values require collaboration. Establishing boundaries, agreements, and regular check-ins isn't just beneficial, it's necessary. Children also learn by example, often gaining emotional intelligence from witnessing adults navigate complex, but respectful relationships.

2.4 Legal and Logistical Hurdles:

Most legal systems are structured around the two-parent model, which can leave multi-parent families in precarious positions. Guardianship, medical consent, and inheritance rights are just a few areas where complications arise. Some parents pursue legal strategies like second-parent adoption or cohabitation agreements to formalize caregiving roles, but these options are not always available or affordable. Advocacy for legal reform is ongoing and essential.

2.5 Parenting as a Collective Practice:

In polyamorous and non-traditional families, the saying "it takes a village" isn't just a metaphor, it's a way of life. These collective approaches to parenting allow children to grow up surrounded by a rich tapestry of gender expressions, relationship models, and emotional practices.

By sharing responsibility, they ease the pressure on any one individual, transforming care into a mutual value rather than a gendered expectation or solitary task.

2.6 Child-Centered Narratives and Empowerment:

Critics often question how children fare in polyamorous households, but research and anecdotal evidence suggest that what matters most is stability, honesty, and love. Kids growing up in these homes often have a nuanced understanding of relationships and feel empowered to ask questions, express emotions, and define their own identities. Open dialogue becomes a protective factor rather than a source of confusion.

2.7 Cultural Resistance and Resilience:

Non-traditional parenting structures are not new, many Indigenous, queer and collectivist communities, have long practiced shared childrearing across generations. What's often labelled as "alternative" today is actually a return to community-centered care. Recognizing this helps root polyamorous parenting in a legacy of resilience and survival, rather than treating it as a trend or experiment.

2.8 Building Supportive Ecosystems:

Because societal structures often fail to recognize polyamorous families, building intentional ecosystems of support becomes crucial. This might include queer parenting groups, inclusive schools, affirming healthcare providers, or chosen-family networks. These ecosystems provide both the practical tools and emotional nourishment that help non-traditional families thrive, even in a world that may not yet understand them.

2.9 Redefining Love, Stability, and Legacy:

At its core, polyamorous and non-traditional parenting is about expanding how we define love, responsibility, and commitment. It's about modelling that family is not about fitting a mold, but about co-creating a space where everyone, especially children, can feel secure, valued, and free to become who they are. These parenting structures ask us to see legacy not only in bloodlines, but in the daily practices of care, empathy, and chosen connection.

3. How LGBTQ+ Parents Navigate Schools, Childcare and Bias

Schools and childcare systems are often built around heteronormative and nuclear family assumptions. LGBTQ+ parents encounter forms, policies, and communications that default to "mom and dad," creating a subtle, but persistent message that their families are outside the norm. This discussion explores how systemic erasure begins at the bureaucratic level, shaping experiences from the first daycare registration to PTA meetings. These daily exclusions burden queer parents, who must constantly advocate for respect in supposedly safe spaces.

3.1 Everyday Acts of Translation and Advocacy:

Navigating these environments often requires LGBTQ+ parents to be constant advocates for their children and families. This can look like correcting assumptions in parent-teacher meetings, initiating conversations about inclusive language, or preparing children to explain their family in age-appropriate ways. These actions, though often exhausting, serve to protect and affirm their families in spaces that may not do so automatically. Advocacy becomes part of the parenting toolkit, not by choice, but by necessity.

3.2 The Classroom as a Mirror – Representation and Safety:

Representation in curriculum, books, and classroom discussion matters deeply. When children don't see their families reflected in what they're learning, it can foster feelings of otherness. LGBTQ+ parents may advocate for inclusive books, diverse family representation in lessons, or teacher training around queer family realities. Small shifts in classroom culture, like normalizing "grown-ups" instead of "moms and dads", can go a long way in creating more welcoming environments.

3.3 Allies Within the System – Finding Supportive Educators and Institutions:

Supportive teachers, principals, and childcare providers can make a meaningful difference. When professionals take initiative to educate themselves, revise forms, or intervene when bias arises, it creates ripple effects that benefit all families. LGBTQ+ parents often build relationships with these allies to collaboratively shift institutional culture. Change is slow, but it starts with individuals who are willing to listen, learn, and act. By partnering with these educators and institutions, LGBTQ+ families can help shape policies and practices that ensure all children learn in environments that honour and affirm diverse family structures.

3.4 The Emotional Terrain – Anxiety, Resilience and Joy:

Alongside logistical barriers lies an emotional reality, the stress of wondering whether a child will be safe, accepted, or bullied because of their family structure. LGBTQ+ parents often carry the weight of not just protecting their children, but preparing them for potential ignorance or prejudice. The emotional labour of anticipating bias while nurturing resilience is profound and often invisible. LGBTQ+ parents navigate not only the practical hurdles of creating safe spaces for their children, but also the emotional labour of advocating for their families, fostering resilience, and celebrating their unique joy in the face of societal challenges.

3.5 Building Community and Collective Power:

Connection with other LGBTQ+ parents provides both solidarity and strategy. Whether through informal networks or organized advocacy groups, these communities help families share resources, language, and support. They also offer a reminder, no one has to do this alone. Collective voices are more powerful when challenging outdated policies or requesting inclusive practices.

Strengthening these networks helps LGBTQ+ parents not only support one another, but also pave the way for systemic change that benefits every family.

3.6 Looking Ahead – Reimagining Inclusive Education:

Progress is possible. As awareness grows and more LGBTQ+ families become visible, pressure mounts for institutions to evolve. Queer parents are leading the charge, not only for their own families, but for a broader redefinition of what family can be. The goal isn't just tolerance, but celebration. And with continued effort, schools and childcare systems can become places where all children and all families, are fully seen. This shift requires not only policy changes, but a cultural transformation rooted in empathy, visibility, and collective action.

4. The Silent Struggles of LGBTQ+ Parents in Custody Battles

Custody battles are often portrayed as disputes between a mother and a father, with legal frameworks built around traditional, heteronormative family models. LGBTQ+ parents entering these arenas confront an unspoken assumption, that non-traditional family structures are inherently less stable or less deserving of equal parental rights. Despite progress in marriage and adoption equality, many queer parents discover that the courtroom remains a site where their relationships and identities are scrutinized more harshly. Exposing how bias seeps into these proceedings invites us to rethink notions of "best interest" and to recognize the humanity behind every parent fighting for their child. Reimagining custody through a queer-inclusive lens means centering love, stability, and caregiving over outdated definitions of legitimacy.

4.1 Historical Roots of Legal Discrimination:

Antiquated statutes and case law once explicitly barred LGBTQ+ individuals from custody or even visitation rights. While many of those overt bans have been struck down, their legacy persists in judges' tacit expectations and in the inertia of legal precedent. From moralistic standards that labelled queer people "unfit" for parenting to policies that demanded proof of heterosexual marriage, the legal system has a long history of marginalizing queer families. Acknowledging these historical foundations is essential to understanding why, even today, subtle biases continue to influence custody outcomes at the expense of LGBTQ+ parents.

4.2 Stereotypes, Stigma and the "Unfit Parent" Trope:

Judicial perceptions are shaped not only by law, but by cultural stereotypes that paint queer parents as morally suspect or psychologically unstable. Negative caricatures, such as the "promiscuous bisexual" or the "confused transgender", can surface in testimony, parenting evaluations, or social-worker reports. These tropes frame queer parents as inherently problematic, shifting the focus away from their demonstrated ability to provide love, stability and care. Dislodging these harmful narratives requires both legal advocacy and broader cultural education about the diverse realities of LGBTQ+ parenthood. Until systems evolve with fairness and respect, queer parents will keep fighting for recognition and the right to parent in peace.

4.3 Disparate Treatment in Evidentiary Standards:

LGBTQ+ parents often face a higher evidentiary bar than their heterosexual counterparts. Judges or guardians ad litem may demand extra proof of fitness, such as multiple character witnesses, extensive psychological assessments, or video evidence of daily routines, simply because a parent identifies as queer. By contrast, heterosexual parents frequently benefit from assumed normalcy and need to provide far less documentation. Highlighting these double standards underscores the urgent need for procedural reforms that ensure equitable treatment regardless of sexual orientation or gender identity. Challenging these unequal standards requires both legal advocacy and cultural change to affirm that queer parents are not exceptions, but equals.

4.4 Emotional Toll on Parents and Children:

Beyond the legal intricacies, custody battles exact a profound emotional toll on both parents and children. Queer parents report heightened stress, anxiety and feelings of invisibility, as they worry about homophobic or transphobic judgments. Children, too, absorb the conflict, they may internalize messages that their family is "wrong" or feel anxiety over the possibility of separation. Compassionate legal and therapeutic support can mitigate these harms, but the first step is recognizing that queer parents and their children endure unique vulnerabilities during these disputes. Centering the emotional well-being of queer families in custody cases helps reframe the process from one of judgment to one of care and justice.

4.5 Strategies for Resilience and Resistance:

Despite systemic bias, many LGBTQ+ parents develop creative strategies to assert their rights and protect their families. Building documentation portfolios, including photos, school records, and testimonies from friends or community leaders, can help counteract unfair assumptions. Some parents engage in pre-emptive legal planning, such as second-parent adoptions, co-parent agreements, or wills, to solidify parental status before disputes arise. Others harness storytelling in court, sharing personal narratives that humanize their relationships and showcase their dedication. These acts of resilience demonstrate how marginalized parents assert agency even within exclusionary systems.

4.6 The Critical Role of Legal Representation and Advocacy:

Effective legal advocacy can mean the difference between custody retained or lost. Lawyers who specialize in LGBTQ+ family law understand the nuances of bias and know how to anticipate and counter discriminatory arguments. Pro bono clinics, LGBTQ+ bar associations, and dedicated family law firms, offer crucial expertise and support. Moreover, systemic change depends on appellate and Supreme Court victories that set precedent. Supporting organizations that litigate LGBTQ+ custody cases contributes to a broader transformation of family law. Access to knowledgeable legal representation is not just a matter of individual case outcomes, it is essential for dismantling the structural biases that undermine LGBTQ+ parents' rights and recognition. Legal advocacy is both a personal shield and a public tool for change, protecting families while shifting precedent.

4.7 Community Support, Healing and Collective Action:

Isolation magnifies the stress of custody disputes. Connecting with other LGBTQ+ parents who have navigated or are navigating similar battles provides solidarity, practical guidance, and emotional triage. Peer-led support groups, online forums, and local family centers create safe spaces for shared storytelling and resource-sharing. Collective action, such as lobbying for fair-parenting legislation or participating in advocacy coalitions, channels individual pain into communal power. Through these networks, queer families gain not only practical tools, but also the affirmation that they are not alone in their struggle. These forms of community care are vital in resisting the erasure and marginalization often faced in courtrooms, reminding LGBTQ+ parents that their experiences are valid, their families are real and their voices have power.

4.8 Toward Equitable Custody Frameworks:

Envisioning a just path forward requires reimagining custody standards with explicit protections for LGBTQ+ parents. Recommendations include mandating anti-bias training for judges and child-welfare professionals, revising forms and guidelines to use gender-neutral language and establishing oversight, to detect discriminatory rulings. Embedding "family of choice" concepts into legal definitions can affirm that love and commitment, not genetic ties or traditional gender roles, constitute family. By championing these reforms, advocates can help ensure that every parent, regardless of sexual orientation or gender identity, stands equal before the law. These reforms not only protect queer families, but also challenge outdated norms, paving the way for a more just and inclusive family law system.

4.9 Conclusion – Centering Love and Stability:

At its core, a custody battle is about preserving a child's emotional well-being and sense of security. LGBTQ+ parents, like all parents, deserve to have their capacity for love and care recognized without prejudice. Exposing the silent struggles of queer families in custody disputes compels society to confront its own biases and to reconstruct systems that uplift all caregivers. When legal frameworks honour the diverse forms of family that exist today, they affirm our shared humanity and the universal right to a loving home.

5. Generational Trauma and How It Manifests in LGBTQ+ Families

Generational trauma often weaves through queer family lines in subtle yet profound ways. Many LGBTQ+ individuals inherit the wounds of persecution, enforced silence, and internalized shame from parents or grandparents, who endured criminalization, medical pathologization, and social rejection. These unspoken sorrows shape family narratives, casting a shadow of caution and fear of exposure over relationships. Recognizing that trauma can be transmitted silently invites a compassionate perspective on our own struggles. By naming these inherited patterns, we take the first step toward healing, one that honours both our personal and ancestral journeys. Healing these wounds helps break the cycle, allowing future queer families to grow with less fear and more freedom.

5.1 Historical Roots of Trauma – Inheritance of Silence and Shame:

Families with a queer history often carry stories never told. Before Stonewall or widespread LGBTQ+ visibility, many parents and grandparents concealed their identities to survive. That secrecy became a protective shield that also birthed shame, teaching subsequent generations that queerness must be hidden or muted. These inherited silences can manifest as difficulty discussing emotions, anxiety around authenticity, or reluctance to claim one's identity publicly. Uncovering and honouring the unspoken experiences of our forebears allows us to reclaim voices silenced by prejudice and to transform inherited shame into resilient pride. By acknowledging these historical burdens, LGBTQ+ families can begin to break cycles of silence and foster environments where healing, openness, and generational understanding are not only possible, but deeply rooted in love and truth.

5.2 Intersecting Oppressions – Race, Class and Queer Identity:

Generational trauma in LGBTQ+ families often intersects with other forms of oppression. A Black queer family may carry the weight of racism alongside homophobia, an immigrant family may hide queerness to protect cultural survival. Class-based fears, such as economic precarity or lack of access to affirming care, layer onto these wounds, reinforcing messages of unworthiness or danger. Acknowledging how multiple systems of harm compound trauma reminds us that healing must address the whole person. It becomes imperative to seek strategies that honour cultural strengths and to cultivate solidarity across differences. Healing queer generational trauma means recognizing that liberation is not one-size-fits-all, it must be intersectional, culturally aware and rooted in collective care.

5.3 Familial Patterns – How Trauma Cycles Reproduce:

Patterns established by one generation can often echo into the next. Parents who've learned to guard their emotions may find it difficult to offer steady emotional presence, while caregivers shaped by past rejection may unintentionally teach children to brace for abandonment. These cycles of hypervigilance, people-pleasing, or emotional withdrawal can feel inevitable. Yet recognizing these habitual dynamics is courageous work. By mapping how trauma shows up in communication, discipline, or attachment, families can disrupt automatic responses. Healing begins when we choose to notice our inherited tendencies and replace them with intentional acts of openness and trust.

5.4 Emotional and Psychological Manifestations:

Generational trauma in LGBTQ+ families often surfaces as anxiety, depression, or chronic stress, symptoms that can feel personal, but are deeply collective. Shame around identity may lead to self-criticism or difficulty forming intimate connections. Some may oscillate between wholehearted self-expression and protective withdrawal. Others might internalize family expectations, feeling torn between loyalty to one's heritage and the need for authenticity. Understanding these emotional landscapes as shared, rather than isolating, fosters compassion. It reassures queer individuals that their reactions are not failures, but echoes of survival mechanisms honed under oppression.

Recognizing these patterns as part of a broader generational narrative empowers LGBTQ+ individuals and families to approach healing not as solitary work, but as a communal journey toward liberation and emotional wholeness.

5.5 Healing Legacies – Acknowledgment and Storytelling:

Healing generational trauma starts with acknowledgment, giving voice to stories that were never heard. Queer families can create rituals of storytelling, oral histories, letter writing, or art projects, that honour past struggles and celebrate resilience. Inviting elders to share memories, even when painful, builds bridges of understanding and reduces isolation. When families witness each other's truths, they shift from secrecy to solidarity. These shared narratives become a tapestry of strength, reminding each member that they stand on the shoulders of those who persevered before them.

5.6 Community and Chosen Family as Healing Spaces:

Chosen families and LGBTQ+ communities play a critical role in interrupting trauma cycles. In chosen-family networks, members offer emotional support, mentorship, and models of healthy boundary-setting often absent in biological lineages. Community gatherings, whether book clubs, support groups, or cultural celebrations, provide mirrors of belonging that reinforce worthiness. These collective spaces invite authenticity and mutual care, fostering new traditions that counter inherited fear. By co-creating environments of acceptance, queer families expand the definition of kinship to include all who share in the healing journey.

5.7 Therapeutic Strategies and Rituals for Healing:

Professional and personal healing practices can transform inherited pain. Trauma-informed therapies, such as family systems work, narrative therapy, or somatic modalities, help individuals and families process unspoken wounds. Rituals like ancestral acknowledgments, meditative gatherings, or creative expression can offer tangible markers of change. Journaling prompts that explore family history, guided family dialogues, and intergenerational art collaborations provide safe entry points for deep work. Integrating these strategies into daily life nurtures resilience, allowing families to move from survival toward flourishing.

5.8 Breaking the Cycle – Empowerment Through Self-Compassion:

Central to healing generational trauma is the cultivation of self-compassion. Queer individuals must learn to recognize moments of fear or shame not as personal failures, but as echoes of ancestral pain. Affirmations, mindful self-care, and inner-child work can soften self-criticism and cultivate kindness toward one's whole being. This shift from self-judgment to self-care disrupts trauma's legacy, replacing inherited pain with empowered self-love. By reclaiming emotional well-being as a form of resistance, LGBTQ+ individuals actively rewrite the emotional inheritance they pass forward. Healing ourselves with tenderness isn't just personal, it's a revolutionary act that transforms what the next generation inherits.

5.9 Towards a Resilient Future – Integrating Healing and Growth:

The path beyond generational trauma in LGBTQ+ families weaves healing into daily life. Each acknowledgment, act of storytelling, or supportive gathering reshapes family culture. As trauma is named and tended, it gives way to renewed connection, creativity, and purpose. Queer families can intentionally craft new rituals, shared creative projects, or collaborative advocacy that honour both past and future. By integrating healing practices with a commitment to growth, LGBTQ+ families not only mend inherited wounds, but also plant seeds of resilience for generations yet to come.

*A Letter of Hope – For the Queer Families That Are Yet to Be:

To the LGBTQ+ families that are yet to be,

You are living the dreams we barely dared to whisper.

If you're reading this, it means the world has changed, maybe not entirely, maybe not easily, but enough for you to exist more freely than we did. That alone is a miracle. And even in the imperfections of this world, your presence brings light, proof that the seeds of courage we planted have blossomed into something beautiful. I want you to know that your joy is sacred, your family is whole and your love is an act of both resistance and renewal.

We carried a lot. The weight of silence. The fear of being erased. The aching need to belong without hiding. But we also carried hope and that hope shaped our families, queer, chosen, expansive, tender. Families that rewrote the script, which made space for authenticity over tradition, care over conformity. Each of our families was a revolution, built not just to survive, but to reimagine what love and kinship could truly look like.

I want you to know this: you do not have to earn your place. You were always meant to be here. Your identity is not a burden, it is a gift. Your vulnerability is not weakness, it is a bridge. And your love, whatever shape it takes, is real, deserving, and powerful. Let no law, label, or limitation make you doubt your worth, your existence is evidence of something right in the world.

We didn't have all the answers. Sometimes we get it wrong. But we kept going, kept loving, kept showing up. And now, I pass this forward, May you trust your truth. May you rest without guilt. May you never have to question whether your family is "normal", because it is yours and that's enough. You are not starting from scratch, you are standing on our shoulders, and we are cheering you forward, always.

With love and solidarity,

A voice among many who came before you. And one of many who believes in all that you are becoming.

Chapter 9

Mental Health and Well-being in LGBTQ+ Lives

---

1. The Hidden Epidemic of High-Functioning Depression in LGBTQ+ Individuals

High-functioning depression lives behind the smiles of those who seem to "have it all together." In the LGBTQ+ community, where resilience is prized and vulnerability often feels dangerous, people quietly shoulder the weight of persistent low mood, fatigue, and self-doubt. Outward success, thriving careers, active social lives, visible "happiness", can disguise an internal ache that never fully lifts. Recognizing high-functioning depression means learning to see the cracks beneath the polish, the exhaustion behind enthusiasm, the perfectionism that punishes, the forced optimism that hides despair. By naming this hidden epidemic, awareness grows around a mental health struggle that too many queer individuals endure alone.

1.1 The Mask of Perfection – Performance as Protection:

An invisible diagnosis takes form when every task is met with competence and every deadline is met on time, even as energy drains away. For LGBTQ+ people, the pressure to embody strength and to prove, that queerness has not weakened them, reinforces a "mask of perfection." Community spaces that celebrate success can inadvertently heighten this burden, making silence seem safer than admission of struggle. When symptoms are dismissed as ordinary stress or mistaken for simple busyness, opportunities for help slip by. Learning to recognize the difference between healthy productivity and relentless overdrive is the first step toward unmasking depression in those most feared to be "broken." Embracing vulnerability as a strength rather than a weakness begins to crack that mask of perfection, opening the door to genuine support, connection, and healing.

1.2 Internal Turmoil – The Emotional and Psychological Toll:

Beneath the veneer of competent functionality lies chronic emotional fatigue. Guilt, shame and persistent self-criticism, form a constant undercurrent, a sense that no effort is ever quite enough. High-functioning depression often leads to deep isolation, as people feel compelled to suffer in silence rather than risk disappointing or burdening those they love. Anxiety blooms around every social interaction. Will they reveal too much? Will they be judged as weak, unworthy, or "too much work"? Over time, this internal turmoil corrodes self-worth, leaving queer individuals daunted by the very vulnerability that lies at the heart of authentic connection. Yet by naming and sharing these hidden struggles, in therapy, among trusted friends, or in supportive communities, LGBTQ+ people can begin to reclaim their strength and rediscover the courage to connect authentically.

1.3 Queer Realities – Minority Stress and Compound Discrimination:

Queer identities intersect with systems of oppression that compound the risk and severity of depression. Homophobia, transphobia, and the constant threat of rejection, drive a baseline of hypervigilance and anxiety. Many LGBTQ+ people carry wounds inherited from families who never accepted them, or from schools that relentlessly othered them. Add to this the burden of navigating healthcare that may be unwelcoming or uninformed, and the result is a chronic stress that few outwardly acknowledge. High-functioning depression in queer communities cannot be separated from these larger structural harms, it is both personal and political. Recognizing the interplay between societal rejection and mental health challenges is essential for understanding the full scope of queer individuals' emotional experiences and finding pathways to healing.

1.4 Silent Isolation – The Loneliness of Suffering Alone:

Even when surrounded by friends or chosen family, those with high-functioning depression often feel unseen. They smile at gatherings, speak up in meetings, and maintain social calendars, yet dread the moment someone might ask how they really are. The fear of being "too much" or "not sick enough" to deserve care drives a wedge between inner experience and outward persona. Relationships strain under the weight of unspoken pain, and the very people best equipped to help, remain unaware. Overcoming this isolation demands courage to speak the unspeakable and allies who can hold hard truths without judgment.

1.5 Pathways to Recognition – Seeking Help and Building Networks:

Breaking the silence starts with small steps, one conversation with a trusted friend, one appointment with a queer-affirming therapist, one moment of permission to pause and breathe. Professional support, therapy, medication when needed, and trauma-informed care provide essential tools for managing symptoms. Equally vital are peer networks, support groups where lived experience outweighs clinical credentials and where admitting struggle, feels safe. Online forums, LGBTQ+ community centers, and grassroots mental health collectives create spaces where high-functioning depression is named, normalized, and met with genuine compassion.

1.6 Community Responsibility – Affirming Mental Health in Queer Spaces:

Queer inclusion must extend beyond celebration of identity to embrace the full spectrum of mental health. Events and organizations can normalize check-ins, share resources openly, and invite conversations about depression, alongside those about pride and resilience. Elders and emerging leaders alike can model vulnerability by speaking frankly about their own journeys, dismantling the myth of invincible queerness. When language and policies within LGBTQ+ spaces acknowledge invisible suffering, the community becomes a path to healing rather than another stage for performance. By weaving vulnerability and self-care into the fabric of LGBTQ+ spaces, we can break the silence around high-functioning depression and create environments where healing is a shared journey.

1.7 Conclusion – Toward Visibility and Healing:

High-functioning depression thrives in the shadows, fed by stigma, silence, and isolation. Bringing it into the light requires empathy, vigilance, and a willingness to see beyond accomplishments, to the human being underneath. For LGBTQ+ individuals, lifting this hidden epidemic means reshaping community norms to celebrate vulnerability as strength and to demand mental health care as a basic right. By recognizing and addressing high-functioning depression together, queer communities can forge a future where no one has to suffer in silence and where healing is as visible as joy.

* "Pause + Process" – Reflecting on Your Journey:

What does the idea of 'high-functioning depression' mean to you? How does it resonate with your own experiences of managing your mental health while still moving through the world?"

2. Loneliness in Queer Spaces – Why Is It So Common?

LGBTQ+ spaces are often celebrated for their sense of community, a safe haven where individuals can express themselves freely and authentically. Yet, for many, loneliness persists even within these spaces. The paradox is stark, in places designed for connection, feelings of isolation can still overwhelm. This contradiction stems from the complexities of queer identity, where belonging isn't always guaranteed and where shared experiences don't always translate into mutual understanding. The dynamic of finding connection in a space made for community is layered and multifaceted, with both external and internal factors at play.

2.1 Unresolved Trauma and Its Impact on Socialization:

For many LGBTQ+ individuals, loneliness in queer spaces is not just a symptom of external circumstances, but a reflection of deeper, unresolved trauma. Years of rejection, invisibility, and erasure often leave scars that shape how we interact with others, even when we are surrounded by those who share similar identities. For some, it's difficult to trust that others truly understand their experiences or that they won't be judged or rejected again. In queer spaces, this trauma can manifest as an emotional distance, where individuals feel disconnected from others despite being in the same room. The journey of healing is ongoing, and for some, it can take years to build the trust needed to truly connect with others.

2.2 Surface-Level Connections and the Challenge of Deep Belonging:

While queer spaces are great for fostering visibility, they are not always conducive to forming deeper, more meaningful connections. Casual encounters at pride events, clubs, or online spaces can leave individuals feeling more isolated than ever, especially if they are seeking authentic intimacy rather than fleeting interactions. There's often a pressure to "fit in" or present a certain version of queerness that aligns with group norms, which can make it difficult to form genuine friendships or relationships.

This is particularly true in queer spaces where appearances or specific subcultures dominate, leaving some individuals feeling like outsiders. The difference between being surrounded by others and feeling truly understood can be vast. The desire for true connection often clashes with the expectations placed on individuals to conform to certain standards, further deepening the loneliness that can arise even in spaces meant for solidarity.

2.3 Queer Identity as a Spectrum of Experience:

One of the core reasons loneliness persists in queer spaces is that queer identities are complex and diverse. The LGBTQ+ community reflects a rich spectrum of experiences, with each identity shaped by unique histories, cultures, and personal journeys. Even though we share common struggles, the ways in which we experience queerness can differ greatly. This disparity can lead to feelings of isolation within the community, as individuals may struggle to find people who relate to their unique experiences. Furthermore, some individuals may feel that their experiences, whether they be related to gender identity, sexual orientation, or racial and cultural background, are invalidated or overlooked in mainstream queer spaces. Recognizing and embracing the full spectrum of queer experiences can help bridge these gaps, fostering a more inclusive and empathetic community where every individual feels seen and valued.

2.4 The Pressure to Conform to Idealized Queerness:

Queer spaces, particularly those that are more visible or mainstream, often present an idealized version of queerness, one that is attractive, confident and socially active. This ideal can put pressure on individuals to conform, even when they feel different or disconnected. For some, the weight of trying to meet these expectations can exacerbate feelings of loneliness. It creates a space where certain identities, body types, and personalities are more easily accepted than others, leaving individuals who don't conform to these standards feeling isolated. The pressure to be "out," "proud," and constantly social can make it difficult for those who are introverted, struggling with mental health, or not yet fully accepting of their identity to feel at ease. This pressure to conform can prevent individuals from expressing their authentic selves, further deepening the sense of isolation and disconnect within queer spaces.

2.5 The Exhaustion of Being the "Other":

Even within queer spaces, there can be subtle hierarchies that marginalize certain groups. For instance, people of colour, nonbinary individuals, or those who don't fit traditional gender norms often find themselves on the periphery, even in spaces supposedly designed for inclusivity. The experience of being "othered" even within one's own community can deepen feelings of loneliness. This can happen unintentionally, through microaggressions, cultural appropriation, or the dominance of certain narratives over others. It's important to recognize that loneliness in queer spaces is not only about individual struggles, but also about the structural inequalities that can exist within even the most supportive communities. True belonging means confronting bias and building equity, even within our own communities.

2.6 The Invisibility of Emotional Needs in Queer Spaces:

In many queer spaces, the focus can sometimes shift toward celebrating sexuality, aesthetics and external expressions of queerness, while emotional well-being and mental health are overlooked. As a result, individuals struggling with depression, anxiety, or loneliness may feel alienated, as their emotional needs are seen as secondary to the more visible aspects of queerness. This creates an environment where individuals who need emotional support are reluctant to ask for it, fearing that their struggles will be misunderstood or dismissed. The lack of emphasis on emotional care can perpetuate feelings of isolation, as people often feel they have to hide their vulnerabilities to fit in.

2.7 The Role of Social Media in Amplifying Loneliness:

While social media offers a platform for connection, it also plays a significant role in amplifying feelings of loneliness within queer spaces. The curated nature of online interactions, where people present their most polished, confident selves, can leave individuals feeling inadequate or disconnected. The pressure to perform happiness, success, and social engagement online can exacerbate loneliness, especially for those who feel their lived reality doesn't align with these portrayals. Social media can provide visibility, but it can also contribute to a false sense of connection, making it harder for people to seek out and build meaningful in-person relationships.

2.8 Creating Spaces for Authentic Connection:

The solution to loneliness in queer spaces isn't necessarily about creating more events or larger gatherings. Instead, it's about fostering environments where authentic connection can thrive. This requires intentional spaces where people can share not just their triumphs, but also their struggles, where vulnerability is embraced, and where emotional needs are met. Creating more diverse spaces that acknowledge the full spectrum of queer experiences, whether through support groups, art collectives, or community events, can help break down the walls of isolation and foster a deeper sense of belonging. When these spaces prioritize emotional safety and ongoing mutual support, they evolve from fleeting encounters into sustainable communities of care and belonging.

2.9 The Power of Vulnerability and Radical Acceptance:

At the heart of overcoming loneliness in queer spaces is vulnerability. When individuals are willing to share their authentic selves, warts and all, it creates opportunities for others to do the same. Vulnerability builds trust and creates bonds that are based on understanding and empathy. Radical acceptance, where all forms of queerness are welcomed without judgment, can allow for a more inclusive and supportive community. By creating spaces that prioritize vulnerability, empathy and understanding, we can address the paradox of loneliness in queer spaces and create a world where every individual feels seen and valued for who they truly are. Creating these environments requires intentionality, patience, and a commitment to continuously nurturing spaces of mutual respect and care. In that commitment, we find the foundation for a lasting connection and collective healing.

*** "Pause + Process" – Reflecting on Your Journey:**

In what ways have you experienced loneliness within queer spaces? What do you believe might have helped you feel more connected and understood in those moments?

3. The Impact of Cultural Stigma on Seeking Therapy

LGBTQ+ individuals experience higher rates of depression, anxiety, and trauma than their heterosexual and cisgender peers, yet many still never seek professional support. Cultural stigma surrounding mental health, rooted in family beliefs, community norms, and broader societal attitudes, creates powerful barriers to accessing therapy. For some, admitting emotional struggle feels tantamount to personal failure or betraying community values, for others, therapy remains coded as a last resort reserved for the "truly broken." Acknowledging these roadblocks is the first step toward understanding why so many queer people suffer in silence and why dismantling stigma is essential to creating spaces where seeking help is both possible and encouraged. Challenging cultural stigma creates space for LGBTQ+ individuals to seek the help they deserve. By fostering open dialogue and embracing mental health as a form of strength, we can break down these barriers and empower queer individuals to seek the support they need.

3.1 A Legacy of Pathologization:

Mental health professions have historically labelled LGBTQ+ identities as disorders, from early psychiatric classifications that deemed homosexuality an illness to the more recent scars of conversion therapy. These abuses foster deep mistrust, leaving survivors and entire communities, sceptical of therapists' motivations. When the very act of coming out was once treated as evidence of pathology, it's no wonder that therapy can still feel like a trap. By tracing this legacy, LGBTQ+ individuals can better understand their wariness and begin to seek out providers who not only reject those harmful practices, but actively affirm queer existence as normal and worthy of support. Understanding this history empowers queer people to reclaim therapy as a source of healing rather than harm. By acknowledging the painful history of pathologization, LGBTQ+ individuals can take steps toward rebuilding trust in therapy, ultimately embracing it as a tool for personal growth and healing.

3.2 Familial and Community Norms:

Within many families and cultural communities, mental health remains taboo. Queer individuals often feel pressured to appear strong and to sacrifice personal vulnerability for the sake of collective survival. In contexts where honour, reputation, or religious doctrine dictate behaviour, seeking therapy can be seen as a sign of weakness or even rebellion. Fear of gossip, ostracism, or judgment drives many LGBTQ+ people to bear their emotional pain in silence. Confronting these norms requires careful navigation, finding allies who respect confidentiality and, where possible, gently shifting family and community attitudes toward greater compassion and understanding. Healing becomes possible when we honour both our need for community and our right to seek support without shame. It is within this balance that queer resilience not only survives, but quietly reshapes the norms that once suppressed it.

3.3 Internalized Stigma and Fear of Exposure:

Beyond external judgment lies the burden of self-stigma. Many queer individuals internalize messages that they are unworthy of care or that discussing mental health issues will expose them as flawed. Therapy can feel like a spotlight on vulnerabilities long hidden, threatening to unravel carefully guarded identities. Concerns about confidentiality, especially in small or tightly knit communities, heighten the risk of unintended outing. Overcoming this internalized stigma involves reframing therapy as a form of self-respect and self-knowledge rather than a sign of weakness and trusting in the ethical standards and queer-affirming expertise of chosen providers.

3.4 A Heteronormative Therapy Landscape:

Even when LGBTQ+ people overcome cultural barriers to seek help, the therapy landscape itself can be unwelcoming. Many mental health professionals lack training in queer cultural competency, inadvertently imposing heteronormative assumptions or misgendering clients. Microaggressions, from dismissing same-sex partnerships to pathologizing gender diversity, erode trust and reinforce the decision to avoid or abandon treatment. Locating affirming providers often requires word-of-mouth recommendations or extensive research, tasks complicated by time, energy, and financial constraints. Addressing this imbalance means equipping therapists with inclusive education and expanding directories of LGBTQ+-friendly practitioners. Building an inclusive, affirming therapy environment ensures LGBTQ+ clients can access care without fear or compromise.

3.5 Economic, Geographic, and Linguistic Barriers:

Therapy can carry a steep price tag, and insurance coverage for mental health remains uneven, especially for queer-affirming care. In rural areas or regions hostile to LGBTQ+ people, there may be no accessible providers at all. Language barriers further exclude non-English speakers from culturally sensitive services, compounding isolation for queer immigrants or multilingual individuals. These logistical hurdles underscore that cultural stigma is only one layer of the problem, structural inequities around funding, policy, and provider distribution also prevent many from receiving support. Creative solutions, sliding-scale clinics, teletherapy platforms, and multilingual resources must be scaled up to bridge these gaps.

3.6 Community-Based and Peer-Led Solutions:

Where traditional therapy falters, community-based alternatives can fill the void. Peer support groups, whether online or in person, offer a first step toward sharing struggles in a safe, understanding environment. LGBTQ+ centers frequently host mental health workshops, drop-in circles, and referrals to affirming therapists. Telehealth platforms now make it possible to connect with queer-competent counsellors regardless of location. While not a replacement for clinical care, these peer-led spaces normalize emotional honesty and model healthy coping strategies. By turning toward each other, queer communities build networks of care that affirm survival, resilience and shared healing.

Encouraging participation in these grassroots networks empowers individuals to take ownership of their mental health journey.

3.7 Building a More Inclusive Mental Health Framework:

Overcoming cultural stigma demands a multifaceted approach, normalizing conversations about mental health within queer communities, integrating affirming therapy referrals into LGBTQ+ events and providing financial support for those in need. Mental health professionals, community leaders, and policy makers share responsibility for training, outreach, and resource allocation. Schools, workplaces, and faith communities can host mental health awareness campaigns, directly addressing stigma with empathy and accurate information. By weaving mental health support into the fabric of queer life, rather than relegating it to a hidden corner, we create a culture where seeking help is a natural expression of self-care and collective resilience.

* "Pause + Process" – Reflecting on Your Journey:

Think about your cultural background. What messages did you receive about therapy? How do those beliefs influence your willingness to seek help or open up about your mental health today?

4. Internalized Homophobia and Its Effect on Self-Worth

Internalized homophobia refers to the internalization of societal prejudice and discrimination against LGBTQ+ individuals, leading them to hold negative views about their own sexual orientation. This phenomenon can deeply affect self-worth, mental health, and relationships. Internalized homophobia is not just about hatred or discomfort with one's identity, it is a complex psychological process that shapes self-perception, fuelling feelings of shame, guilt, and unworthiness. In a world that often devalues queer existence, these internalized beliefs can limit one's ability to thrive and fully embrace who they are. Understanding this process is key to breaking free from its grip. By understanding internalized homophobia, LGBTQ+ individuals can begin to challenge these harmful beliefs, reclaiming their sense of self-worth, and embracing their identities with pride.

4.1 The Roots of Internalized Homophobia:

Internalized homophobia doesn't develop in a vacuum. It is often a direct response to the homophobic and heteronormative world in which LGBTQ+ individuals live. From a young age, queer people are exposed to negative messages about their identities, whether through explicit rejection, societal stigmas, or the erasure of queer existence. These messages are reinforced by cultural, religious, familial, and institutional structures that value heterosexuality as the "norm." Over time, these beliefs become internalized, leading individuals to see their own queerness as something to be ashamed of, hidden, or even "fixed." This is compounded by the fear of rejection and the desire to belong, which makes embracing one's true self even more difficult. Recognizing the roots of internalized homophobia allows individuals to challenge these deeply ingrained beliefs and begin the process of healing and self-acceptance.

4.2 The Psychological Toll of Internalized Homophobia:

The internal conflict caused by internalized homophobia manifests in various mental health struggles. Individuals may experience anxiety, depression, self-loathing, and a profound sense of isolation. These psychological effects are often compounded by an inability to accept one's identity, leading to an internalized sense of being "less than" or unworthy of love, respect, or happiness. This self-rejection can create a cycle of self-sabotage, where individuals unconsciously distance themselves from their authentic selves, rejecting their desires, needs, or relationships. The longer these feelings persist, the more entrenched they become, making healing more difficult.

4.3 How Internalized Homophobia Affects Relationships:

Internalized homophobia not only affects how individuals see themselves, but it can also impact their relationships with others. Shame and fear of rejection can lead to avoiding intimacy, whether emotional, physical, or sexual. Individuals may have difficulty trusting others, fearing that their queerness will be rejected or that they will be loved conditionally. In romantic relationships, internalized homophobia can cause a person to settle for unhealthy dynamics, believing they aren't worthy of a truly fulfilling partnership. This can also lead to isolation, as individuals with internalized homophobia may struggle to find a supportive queer community, feeling alienated from both heteronormative and LGBTQ+ spaces.

4.4 The Role of Family and Culture in Reinforcing Internalized Homophobia:

Family, culture, and community play a significant role in the internalization of homophobic beliefs. In many cases, LGBTQ+ individuals are raised in environments where queerness is seen as unacceptable, shameful, or even sinful. This familial rejection can lead to deep feelings of inadequacy and a belief that one's identity is a source of harm or disappointment. Cultural or religious beliefs may further reinforce the idea that queer individuals are broken or immoral. Healing from this internalized homophobia requires addressing these sources of pain and challenging the negative narratives imposed by family, culture, and society. Healing requires redefining family and cultural narratives, fostering acceptance, and reclaiming self-love from internalized homophobia.

4.5 The Cycle of Secrecy and Fear:

For many LGBTQ+ individuals, internalized homophobia results in a cycle of secrecy and fear. The fear of being "found out" or rejected prevents them from being their authentic selves. This can manifest as hiding or suppressing one's queerness, even in relationships or environments where it might be safe to express it. The pressure to maintain this secrecy can exacerbate anxiety and stress, as the individual constantly monitors their behaviour to avoid being judged or ostracized. Breaking free from this cycle requires creating environments where it is safe to be authentic and where queerness is not something to fear, but something to celebrate. Healing involves embracing vulnerability, allowing authenticity to flourish, and dismantling the fears that reinforce secrecy. Each step toward openness becomes an act of quiet resistance and a move toward liberation.

4.6 Overcoming Internalized Homophobia – Steps Toward Healing:

Healing from internalized homophobia is a process that involves self-compassion, education, and support. The first step is recognizing and naming internalized homophobia for what it is, a survival mechanism shaped by external forces, not an inherent truth about oneself. From there, individuals can begin to challenge the beliefs and assumptions they hold about their queerness. This requires questioning the negative messages absorbed throughout life and replacing them with affirmations of self-worth. Therapy, particularly with providers who are affirming of LGBTQ+ identities, can be invaluable in this process, providing a safe space to explore and dismantle these harmful beliefs. Building a supportive network of allies and engaging in self-reflection fosters resilience and empowers individuals to reclaim their authentic selves.

4.7 Reclaiming Self-Worth and Identity:

Reclaiming self-worth begins with acknowledging and embracing one's queer identity. This may involve surrounding oneself with supportive LGBTQ+ communities that affirm one's experiences and help undo the harm caused by previous rejection. Finding queer role models, reading literature by queer authors and participating in LGBTQ+ events, can provide important affirmation that queerness is not only valid but beautiful and essential. It's also important to engage in self-care practices that nourish emotional well-being, such as mindfulness, journaling, and self-love exercises, to build resilience against the shame and guilt that may arise.

4.8 The Power of Affirmative Therapy and Support Networks:

Affirmative therapy is an essential tool in breaking free from internalized homophobia. Working with a therapist who understands the unique challenges faced by LGBTQ+ individuals can help identify the roots of internalized homophobia and provide tools to work through the pain. Support groups, whether online or in-person, can also play a key role in healing. By connecting with others who share similar experiences, individuals can find solidarity, empathy, and affirmation. These spaces allow for vulnerability and growth, helping individuals feel less isolated in their journey. Together, therapy and support networks create a foundation for healing, fostering self-acceptance and empowerment.

4.9 Shifting Cultural Norms to Foster Acceptance:

While individual healing is crucial, shifting cultural norms to foster broader societal acceptance of LGBTQ+ people is also necessary. Advocating for LGBTQ+ rights, visibility, and inclusion in all aspects of society can help reduce the external pressures that contribute to internalized homophobia. Allies play a key role in this process by standing alongside queer people, challenging discrimination and supporting queer communities. Cultural change is a slow process, but each act of advocacy, every voice raised in support, helps to dismantle the structures that perpetuate shame and fear. By collectively working toward cultural change, we can create a world where acceptance replaces shame and all queer identities are affirmed and celebrated. In this shared effort, we lay the groundwork for a future where queerness is not just accepted, but deeply valued.

4.10 Conclusion – Embracing Queerness as a Source of Strength:

Internalized homophobia can have a profound impact on mental health, relationships, and self-worth, but it is possible to heal. By acknowledging the harm caused by societal stigma, reclaiming one's identity, and seeking support, LGBTQ+ individuals can break free from the cycle of shame and self-doubt. Healing is a lifelong process, but it is one that leads to greater self-acceptance, deeper connections, and a more empowered life. As queer individuals embrace their full, authentic selves, they not only heal, but contribute to the broader movement for LGBTQ+ liberation and affirmation.

* "Pause + Process" – Reflecting on Your Journey:

Reflect on how societal views on queerness have shaped the way you view yourself. What beliefs or actions would you like to unlearn or challenge to honour your true identity?

5. The Rise of Burnout in LGBTQ+ Activism – Learning When to Rest

LGBTQ+ activism is born of necessity, of survival, of resistance, of fierce love for community. But with every protest attended, every policy challenged, every social media campaign launched, there comes a toll that isn't always visible. Activism is deeply emotional labour and for queer individuals who are often fighting for their own rights and safety, the lines between personal and political are blurred. Burnout becomes a quiet shadow that creeps in, unnoticed until exhaustion overwhelms even the most passionate hearts.

Activism demands sustained energy, emotionally, mentally, and physically. Yet in queer movements, where urgency often feels inescapable and resources are stretched thin, rest is rarely seen as a valid option. Many activists push forward even when depleted, fuelled by guilt, purpose, or fear of letting others down. This culture of constant output is unsustainable, and learning to pause, to breathe, and to replenish is not a weakness, but a radical act of self-preservation.

5.1 Passion Meets Pressure – The Weight of Queer Resistance:

Activists often enter the work from personal necessity, turning their lived experiences into fuel for change. But that same closeness to the cause means every setback feels deeply personal. The pressure to "do it all" becomes overwhelming, especially in queer communities where representation is limited and every voice feels indispensable. The emotional weight of confronting injustice daily, compounded by personal marginalization, creates a unique strain. Acknowledging this duality is essential for sustaining both the movement and those within it. This emotional labour, while powerful, cannot be sustained without moments of reprieve and care.

To continue making meaningful change, we must recognize that activism is not a sprint but a marathon. Prioritizing rest and emotional well-being ensures that our efforts remain sustainable and impactful. Only by caring for ourselves can we truly show up for the causes we hold dear.

5.2 The Myth of Limitless Energy – When Urgency Becomes Exhaustion:

There's often an implicit belief in activism that taking a break is equivalent to giving up. The world's injustices don't pause, so why should we? But urgency is a double-edged sword, it can motivate action, but also lead to long-term fatigue. When queer individuals already carry the weight of systemic oppression, adding the pressure of activism without rest becomes a recipe for burnout. Recognizing our limits isn't a sign of failure, it's how we ensure we're still here for the long haul. True resilience is built not through constant motion, but through intentional rest and sustainable pacing.

5.3 Invisible Labor – The Emotional Costs Behind the Scenes:

Burnout doesn't always look dramatic. Often, it's hidden in the quiet moments, missed meals, sleepless nights, the growing dread of one more email or event. Emotional labour in queer activism includes educating others, supporting peers in crisis and managing public backlash, all unpaid and often unrecognized. This unseen work, especially when paired with everyday discrimination, amplifies stress. Naming and validating this labour is the first step toward rebalancing responsibility and care. Sustainable activism begins with honouring the unseen efforts that keep movements and people alive.

5.4 Identity and Responsibility – When "Representation" Hurts:

For many queer activists, particularly those from multiply marginalized backgrounds, visibility comes with a cost. Being "the only one" in a room, a campaign, or a conversation places heavy expectations on a single individual. The pressure to represent, to explain, to always speak up can erode one's sense of agency and peace. It's crucial to understand that we are not obligated to always show up, we are allowed to rest, to say no, to protect our energy.

5.5 Rest as Resistance – Reframing Recovery as Essential:

Rest is not laziness. For LGBTQ+ activists, rest is a radical act of reclaiming time and worth. It is a way of saying, "I deserve care, even when the world tells me I don't." Rest allows us to reconnect with joy, to reflect, and to return to the work with clarity. Incorporating rest into activism culture, through rotating responsibilities, encouraging sabbaticals, or simply normalizing time off, can reshape movements for the better. Prioritizing rest strengthens not just individuals, but the collective resilience of the queer liberation movement.

5.6 Creating Sustainable Activism – Building Supportive Structures:

Sustainability in activism requires intentional design. This means cultivating team dynamics where people feel supported, creating boundaries around work hours, and making space for emotional check-ins. Mutual aid networks, mental health resources, and transparent conversations about burnout can help build a culture where care isn't secondary, it's central. Activism cannot rely on sacrifice alone. It must also rely on connection, trust, and shared responsibility.

5.7 Learning to Let Go – Knowing When It's Okay to Step Back:

There is courage in knowing when to stop. Activists may feel guilt when stepping back, but taking time away can offer perspective, healing, and even new direction. Letting go, temporarily or permanently, is not abandonment. It's trust, that others will carry the torch, that the movement is bigger than any one individual. We are not failing by needing rest. We are human. Rest is not retreat, it's a radical act of sustainability that honours both personal well-being and the longevity of collective liberation.

5.8 Community Care   Holding Each Other with Compassion:

Burnout is not just an individual problem, it's a communal one. When queer spaces hold space for grief, joy and exhaustion alike, they become stronger. Practicing community care, checking in on fellow organizers, offering to lighten someone's load, and celebrating small victories, can shift the culture from one of martyrdom to one of mutual support. We can build movements that nourish as much as they challenge. When we centre care alongside action, we create a movement where no one has to burn out to belong and where sustainability becomes a shared responsibility.

5.9 Reimagining Success – Centering Wellness in the Fight for Justice:

Success in activism is not measured only in policy wins or media coverage. It can also be measured in sustained friendships, in moments of rest, in the ability to keep showing up with love. When we center wellness, we redefine what victory looks like, not as constant sacrifice, but as collective flourishing. A rested activist is a resilient one, and a resilient movement is one that endures. When we redefine success through the lens of care and connection, we ensure that justice work uplifts us instead of consuming us.

5.10 In the End, We Need You Whole – Not Just Present:

The fight for LGBTQ+ rights is ongoing, but so is the need for healing. We need our activists not just present but whole, rested, nourished, and loved. In a world that asks so much of queer people, caring for ourselves and one another is one of the most powerful forms of resistance we have. Rest is not the opposite of action, it is the foundation of our strength. Sustainable activism begins with the radical belief that your well-being is not a luxury, it's a necessity.

* "Pause + Process" – Reflecting on Your Journey:

Think about the balance between activism and rest in your own life. How can you set boundaries that allow for both meaningful action and personal rejuvenation?

Chapter 10

Queer Aging – Embracing Life at Every Stage

---

1. The Erasure of Older LGBTQ+ People in Media and Literature

The absence of older LGBTQ+ individuals in media and literature is a glaring issue within the broader conversation about queer visibility. While queer representation has made significant strides in recent years, the voices and experiences of older LGBTQ+ people are still largely ignored. These individuals, who have navigated decades of societal change and personal struggle, deserve to be seen and heard. Representation across all ages is essential not only for validating the lived experiences of older queer individuals, but also for fostering understanding and solidarity across generations within the community.

1.1 Historical Context – A Legacy of Marginalization:

The historical erasure of older LGBTQ+ individuals is deeply rooted in a long legacy of marginalization. Many of these individuals lived through periods of criminalization, the AIDS crisis, and societal oppression, often without the visibility or support they deserved. The lack of representation during these earlier times has left a void in how we see older queer people today. In media and literature, their stories were often erased or distorted, perpetuating the silence around their lives. This historical invisibility has lasting effects, shaping how younger generations understand LGBTQ+ history and culture and leaving them with limited models of what it means to grow old as a queer person.

1.2 The Loss of Intergenerational Wisdom:

One of the most profound impacts of this erasure is the loss of intergenerational wisdom and connection. Older LGBTQ+ individuals possess invaluable knowledge about survival, resilience, and community-building, which is often passed down through personal stories, activism, and mentorship. Unfortunately, the lack of representation in mainstream media has made it difficult for younger generations to access these stories and wisdom. When older queer people are left out of the narrative, it diminishes the opportunity for them to serve as role models or mentors. This absence prevents vital knowledge from being shared and leaves younger queer individuals without crucial support structures and insights about navigating life at different stages of identity and experience.

1.3 The Harm of Stereotyping Older LGBTQ+ People:

Another consequence of erasure is the tendency to stereotype older LGBTQ+ individuals when they do appear in media or literature.

Often, they are reduced to tragic figures, representing a bygone era or even dismissed as irrelevant to the current moment. This oversimplification not only fails to capture the complexity of older queer lives, but also perpetuates harmful narratives about aging and sexuality. When older LGBTQ+ individuals are portrayed as mere remnants of the past, it undermines their richness as multifaceted individuals with thriving, evolving identities. These stereotypes, compounded by real-world ageism, contribute to the broader invisibility of older LGBTQ+ people, reinforcing the idea that their experiences are less valuable or worthy of attention.

1.4 The Importance of Representation:

Representation of older LGBTQ+ individuals is crucial for challenging these harmful stereotypes and offering more authentic portrayals of aging within the community. It is not enough to simply present older queer characters as symbols of hardship or loss, these characters must be multidimensional and reflect the full spectrum of experiences. By seeing older LGBTQ+ individuals depicted as vibrant, complex and fully realized people, we affirm their worth and show younger generations that aging is not the end of a queer identity, but a natural progression of it. True representation can help challenge societal ageism and allow older LGBTQ+ individuals to see themselves in the narratives of their community, validating their lives and experiences.

1.5 Moving Forward – Creating Space for Older LGBTQ+ Voices:

Moving forward, it is essential that media and literature intentionally include older LGBTQ+ voices in their stories. This can be done through the inclusion of older queer characters in both contemporary and historical narratives, ensuring that they are portrayed as full, multidimensional people with rich lives. Furthermore, there is a need to support queer elders in leading initiatives that allow them to share their stories, whether through writing, mentoring, or other community-building efforts. Cultural institutions, publishers and media creators, should make a concerted effort to provide spaces for older queer individuals to be represented authentically. By centering these voices, we can redefine society's view of aging in the LGBTQ+ community and cultivate a culture that honours individuals at every stage of life.

2. Queer Retirement – The Need for Inclusive Elderly Care Spaces

Retirement is often framed as a time of peace, rest, and personal reflection. But for many LGBTQ+ elders, this period is marked by fear, social displacement, and painful invisibility. After decades of navigating systemic oppression, many queer seniors face the added challenge of finding aging spaces where they can live authentically. Mainstream retirement homes and elder care services are rarely equipped with LGBTQ+ inclusive training and the culture within these spaces, often reinforces the same biases that queer elders have spent a lifetime resisting. This lack of understanding can lead to re-closeting, isolation, or even outright discrimination within care facilities. An inclusive approach to retirement isn't just about logistics, it's about ensuring dignity, safety, and justice for all. To truly honour the lives of LGBTQ+ elders, we must build systems that not only acknowledge their histories, but also actively protect their right to age with pride, comfort, and community.

2.1 Decades of Survival, Now Marginalized Again:

Older LGBTQ+ individuals are survivors. Many lived through times when their identities were criminalized, pathologized, or violently erased. Despite paving the way for the rights and visibility the community holds today, these elders are often forgotten once they age out of perceived cultural relevance. The mainstream narrative of queerness often centers youth, beauty and trendiness, creating a narrow and exclusionary vision of queer life. This cultural erasure directly impacts care, queer elders are less likely to have traditional family structures or financial security and more likely to rely on systems not built with them in mind.

2.2 Housing Insecurity and the Economic Toll of a Lifetime of Bias:

Discrimination in employment, healthcare, and housing throughout life contributes to increased financial instability among LGBTQ+ elders. Many have not had the same access to pensions, inheritances, or family support networks that cisgender and heterosexual elders may take for granted. Trans seniors, in particular, are at heightened risk for poverty and homelessness in old age. Retirement housing that is affordable, accessible, and affirming remains rare. These economic challenges are not accidental, they are the cumulative result of systemic exclusion.

2.3 Unsafe to Be Out – Fear Inside Care Institutions:

Many LGBTQ+ seniors report fear of being open about their identity within care settings, due to the risk of mistreatment by staff or fellow residents. Care providers often lack cultural competency around queer and trans identities, resulting in inappropriate questions, misgendering, or outright hostility. For seniors who spent years building affirming communities, entering a care facility can mean losing the safety and support of chosen family. This re-closeting can cause severe emotional harm and re-traumatization. Inclusive training for staff is vital, but so is the creation of spaces where queerness is celebrated, not simply tolerated.

2.4 The Power of Chosen Family – Reimagining Support Systems:

Without traditional family structures to rely on, many LGBTQ+ elders turn to chosen families, networks of friends, and community members who offer emotional and sometimes financial support. These bonds are deep, but often unrecognized in legal and institutional contexts. When hospitals or care homes defer to blood relatives, many queer seniors find their chosen families pushed aside. Reimagining elder care includes rethinking how we define "family" in policies and practice. Facilities that affirm and incorporate chosen family into care plans foster safety, respect, and holistic well-being.

2.5 Models of Hope – Queer-Inclusive Retirement Communities:

Though, still relatively rare, LGBTQ+ retirement communities are slowly emerging across the globe. These welcoming spaces provide culturally competent care, allow residents to live openly, and foster intergenerational connection. They also center the unique social and healthcare needs of queer seniors, offering inclusive activities, safe spaces and mental health resources.

These models prove that queer-inclusive aging is possible, it just requires intention, funding, and care. Advocating for the expansion of such communities is essential to ensure that elder years are not spent in fear or erasure.

2.6 Policy and Advocacy – Building Systems that Serve Us All:

Change cannot rely on isolated projects alone. Systemic reform is needed to ensure that all elder care spaces are safe and affirming for LGBTQ+ people. This includes anti-discrimination policies, inclusive staff training, healthcare reform, and financial support for LGBTQ+ housing initiatives. Policymakers must recognize the distinct needs of queer elders and create standards of care that reflect them. True equity means addressing not just age or identity, but the intersection of both.

2.7 Healing Through Visibility – Honouring the Elders Among Us:

Representation matters in care, too. Seeing older queer individuals in media, leadership and community spaces, breaks down the myth that queerness ends at a certain age. Honouring LGBTQ+ elders means listening to their stories, recognizing their contributions, and ensuring their needs are prioritized in every aspect of society. Visibility is not just symbolic, it is a tool for education, empathy, and systemic change. Our elders carry our history. They deserve more than survival, they deserve celebration.

2.8 Reimagining the Future of Queer Aging:

A future where aging is queer-affirming is possible, but it requires collective effort. Communities must come together to support, invest in, and protect their elders. As we advocate for inclusive care, we also advocate for a broader understanding of what it means to age with pride and dignity. By valuing queer lives at every stage, we shape a world where no one has to grow old alone or unseen. Queer aging, like queerness itself, should be full of joy, care and possibility.

3. Facing Ageism and Invisibility in the LGBTQ+ Community

In LGBTQ+ spaces that often center youth, older queer individuals can find themselves doubly marginalized, first by the ageism of mainstream society and then again, within their own communities. While older LGBTQ+ people have helped lay the foundations for today's freedoms, they're frequently overlooked in modern queer narratives. This erasure denies not only their stories, but also the wisdom they carry. Acknowledging the value of queer elders is essential for building an inclusive and intergenerational community.

3.1 Youth-Centric Queer Culture and the Pressure to Stay "Relevant":

Much of queer popular culture emphasizes youth, beauty and trendiness, creating a landscape where aging is viewed as decline rather than evolution. Older LGBTQ+ individuals are often pressured to appear younger or to stay socially and technologically "in the know" to be seen. This constant pursuit of relevance can overshadow the wisdom, experience, and resilience they bring to the community.

This dynamic can lead to feelings of inadequacy, invisibility, or being pushed to the margins. Challenging this norm means embracing age as a natural, valuable part of queer existence.

3.2 Internalized Ageism Within LGBTQ+ Communities:

Ageism isn't just external, it's something many queer individuals internalize, especially when growing up without positive older queer role models. This internalized bias may manifest in distancing oneself from older members of the community, fearing one's own aging, or undervaluing older narratives. Addressing internalized ageism is a necessary step toward creating affirming spaces across the lifespan. Self-reflection and intentional representation can help undo these internalized beliefs.

3.3 The Loss of Intergenerational Dialogue:

Intergenerational connection used to be vital in LGBTQ+ survival, especially during the AIDS crisis, when chosen family networks bridged age gaps. Today, digital spaces, shifting priorities, and age-related stigma, have contributed to a breakdown in intergenerational dialogue. Reviving this exchange is critical, not only to honour the past, but to create a future where no one feels forgotten. When older and younger queer people learn from each other, the entire community thrives.

3.4 Representation, Visibility and the Power of Stories:

Representation of LGBTQ+ elders in media, literature, and leadership roles is still scarce. When they do appear, it's often as tragic figures, comic relief, or in deeply sanitized roles. To combat this, we must elevate diverse, complex portrayals of aging queer lives, stories that reflect love, purpose, resilience and ongoing evolution. Visibility affirms that queer identity doesn't end at 30, it deepens and continues. When we amplify authentic stories of LGBTQ+ elders, we challenge ageism and celebrate the full arc of queer existence, lived with pride, power and presence.

3.5 Building Age-Inclusive Queer Spaces:

Creating LGBTQ+ communities that welcome all ages requires intentional design, from event planning to leadership structures. This means challenging ableism, creating accessible venues, and incorporating programming that interests and supports older individuals. It also requires a culture shift, viewing elders not as "out of touch," but as vital community members with wisdom to offer. Age-inclusive spaces don't just serve older people, they serve the wholeness of the community.

3.6 Reimagining What It Means to Grow Older Queer:

Rather than fearing invisibility, we can redefine aging as a queer act of resilience and self-acceptance. Growing older as a queer person is radical, it defies systems that weren't designed for us to survive. By centering joy, autonomy, and reflection, we can reimagine aging not as a loss, but as a continuation of becoming. The future of queer liberation includes celebrating all life stages with pride. Because every year lived in truth is a quiet revolution and our elders are proof that queer futures have always existed.

4. The Importance of Intergenerational Friendships

In a world that often erases queer pasts, intergenerational friendships allow for the transmission of LGBTQ+ history in deeply personal ways. Elders carry stories of resistance, love, survival, and change, narratives often excluded from mainstream education. When younger queer people connect with older generations, they gain insight into the foundations of their rights and culture. These friendships become a living archive, humanizing history and reaffirming that queer existence has always been part of the world. In reclaiming and sharing these stories, we create a continuous thread of resilience that unites us across time. Intergenerational friendships strengthen our communities by bridging gaps, fostering mutual respect and ensuring that queer legacies are passed down with care, preserving the richness of our shared histories.

4.1 Challenging Age-Based Stereotypes Within Queer Spaces:

Mainstream culture often glorifies youth and sidelines older individuals, an ageist bias that unfortunately exists even within LGBTQ+ communities. Intergenerational friendships challenge these stereotypes by showing that wisdom, humour, vitality, and passion are not limited by age. Queer elders defy the notion that aging means fading away, they embody evolving strength and perspective. By making space for different life stages in queer circles, we create communities where every age is valued as part of our collective experience. These friendships offer mutual respect, curiosity, and shared learning that push back against narrow ideas of relevance and worth. Challenging age-based stereotypes not only enriches queer spaces, but also empowers individuals to age without fear of marginalization, fostering a culture where the contributions of all generations are recognized and celebrated.

4.2 Healing Generational Wounds and Building Solidarity:

There's often a perceived generational divide in queer spaces, misunderstandings, judgments, or lack of context that can create tension. But intergenerational friendships have the power to mend these fractures. When younger queer people learn from elders' hardships, AIDS activism, criminalization and societal exclusion, they gain empathy and gratitude. Likewise, elders may find hope, joy and renewed purpose in the energy and boldness of younger generations. These relationships can become a space for healing, where both sides feel seen and supported, bridging decades of difference with understanding.

4.3 Sharing Survival Tools and Emotional Wisdom:

Older LGBTQ+ individuals have had to learn how to navigate a world that didn't always have language, visibility, or safety for them. Their resilience strategies, how to build chosen family, how to grieve, and how to hold onto joy, are invaluable. Through intergenerational bonds, younger queer people gain access to emotional tools that can't be taught in a workshop or read in a book. These friendships become mentorships, offering emotional literacy and modelling what it looks like to age proudly and defiantly queer. In turn, elders may discover new ways of self-expression and inclusion through younger perspectives. This shared learning fosters empathy and bridges generational gaps, deepening the sense of community.

These friendships create a mutual exchange of wisdom, where both generations grow stronger, more connected, and empowered in their queerness.

4.4 Expanding the Definition of Family:

For many queer people, traditional family structures can be sites of pain, rejection, or erasure. Intergenerational friendships offer an alternative, relationships built on chosen kinship, care and reciprocity. Queer elders often become mentors, guardians, or even surrogate grandparents to those seeking belonging. These familial bonds aren't defined by blood, but by deep emotional investment and mutual respect. In building chosen family across age groups, we redefine what it means to belong, offering everyone a chance to be held, seen, and cherished throughout life's stages.

4.5 Mutual Growth in a Shared Queer Future:

While it's common to think of intergenerational relationships as one-directional, elders guiding youth, these friendships are mutually transformative. Younger LGBTQ+ individuals bring new language, creativity, and evolving politics, that can reenergize elders' understanding of queerness today. In return, elders offer grounding, historical perspective, and deep emotional insight. This exchange fosters continuous growth, ensuring the movement and the people within it are always evolving. In building friendships across age lines, we prepare each other for a collective future that values both legacy and innovation.

4.6 Creating Intentional Spaces for Connection:

Intergenerational friendships don't always happen organically, they need nurturing spaces to develop. Community events, storytelling circles, mentorship programs and queer elder panels, are vital opportunities for meaningful engagement. These spaces must be designed with respect, accessibility, and genuine curiosity at their core. Creating platforms where elders and youth can speak, listen, and bond ensures that intergenerational relationships thrive beyond chance encounters. With intention, these friendships become integral to the structure of queer community life.

4.7 Honouring the Full Spectrum of Queer Time:

Queer lives often follow nonlinear timelines, we come out at different ages, find love in unexpected places and define family in our own ways. Intergenerational friendships remind us that queer becoming doesn't stop at any age. There is beauty in late bloomers, second chances, and decades of transformation. By embracing this concept of queer time, we honour the journeys of elders and reject the idea that our most valuable years are behind us. These friendships reinforce that every stage of queer life holds power and possibility. These connections remind us that every phase of life is a continuation of self-discovery, resilience, and love.

4.8 Carrying Each Other Forward:

When queer generations walk together, they carry each other's dreams, lessons and love into the future.

The stories of elders become part of the foundation younger people stand on, while the vibrancy of youth affirms that those stories still matter. These friendships are not just about reminiscing or mentorship, they are about co-creating a world where no one is left behind or forgotten. Together, we ensure that every age, every voice and every queer journey, is honoured as essential to our collective liberation.

5. Planning for the Future – Estate Planning, Healthcare and End-of-Life Decisions

Planning for the future is often a daunting task, yet for LGBTQ+ individuals, it is an essential one. The historical and ongoing barriers to accessing equitable healthcare, legal rights, and end-of-life decisions, make proactive planning even more crucial. Mainstream systems are not always designed with LGBTQ+ needs in mind, and without adequate preparation, there can be unforeseen complications that jeopardize one's wishes and dignity. Estate planning, healthcare, and end-of-life decisions are not just about legalities, they are about ensuring that one's autonomy, identity, and personal values are honoured. By taking control of their future, LGBTQ+ individuals can protect themselves and their loved ones from the challenges that often come with navigating these areas of life. Preparing with intention is not only practical, but a necessary act of self-care and protection.

5.1 Legal Considerations – Estate Planning and Wills:

For LGBTQ+ individuals, estate planning is a critical part of securing their future. Many queer people may have been estranged from family or may not be legally recognized by their families, making it essential to have a legally binding will. Without a will, the state may dictate how one's assets are distributed, often leaving out chosen family members or partners. A comprehensive estate plan ensures that loved ones, whether biological or chosen, are able to inherit property, make decisions about care, and uphold the individual's wishes after death. Creating a healthcare directive or durable power of attorney is just as important, particularly for those in long-term relationships or non-traditional family structures. Many LGBTQ+ people, especially elders, have faced discrimination from biological family members or medical institutions, so it's vital to have written instructions that name someone who will honour their wishes in a healthcare setting. Finding an LGBTQ+-affirming lawyer who is well-versed in these matters can help guide individuals through the complexities of estate planning, ensuring their voices are heard and their rights are respected.

5.2 Healthcare Planning – Navigating LGBTQ+ Inclusive Care:

Healthcare is another critical area where LGBTQ+ individuals face challenges. From discrimination in healthcare settings to lack of access to competent care, it's important to plan ahead to avoid barriers when critical health decisions arise. For many queer individuals, the idea of navigating medical treatment can be fraught with fear or anxiety, particularly when family members may not be supportive or when healthcare providers are not affirming of their identity. Having an inclusive healthcare plan that outlines the type of care one expects can help avoid these difficult situations. This plan might include finding LGBTQ+-friendly doctors, ensuring comprehensive insurance coverage for gender-affirming treatments, and keeping emergency healthcare directives updated.

Communication with partners, chosen family, and healthcare providers is essential, as is ensuring that all individuals involved in one's care are informed of preferences and rights. Taking these steps early on can prevent crisis moments from escalating, giving individuals the peace of mind that their healthcare will be handled in a way that aligns with their values and identity.

5.3 End-of-Life Decisions – Ensuring Respect for Identity:

End-of-life decisions are often some of the most sensitive and emotionally charged topics for LGBTQ+ individuals to navigate. Given the history of discrimination, rejection, and lack of support from families or institutions, it is essential that LGBTQ+ individuals plan ahead to ensure their identity and wishes are respected in their final days. This can include making decisions about funeral services, memorials, and burial options, ensuring that these choices reflect their values and identity. Unfortunately, LGBTQ+ people have been denied these basic rights in the past, with family members sometimes overriding a person's final wishes. To avoid these situations, it's crucial to have a legally binding will that specifically outlines funeral arrangements and other end-of-life decisions. It can also be helpful to write a letter of instruction for loved ones, explicitly naming preferences for post-death care and memorialization. In cases where tensions may arise with non-affirming family members, working with LGBTQ+-affirming funeral directors and service providers ensures that one's final moments honour their truth.

5.4 The Importance of LGBTQ+ Inclusive Support Networks:

Building a strong, supportive network is another crucial aspect of planning for the future. LGBTQ+ individuals often face additional challenges when it comes to healthcare, end-of-life care, and estate planning, particularly if their biological family is unsupportive. This makes finding and creating chosen family and LGBTQ+-affirming support networks even more vital. Having a trusted group of individuals, whether partners, friends, or community members, who understand and respect one's wishes can make a world of difference when it comes to ensuring one's dignity and autonomy in moments of crisis. There are also LGBTQ+-specific organizations and community groups that can provide resources, including guidance on legal matters, healthcare rights, and planning for end-of-life decisions. These groups are often well-connected with lawyers, healthcare providers, and social workers, who can offer the expertise needed to navigate these complex topics. Surrounding oneself with a supportive and informed network can make the process of planning for the future feel less isolating and more empowering.

5.5 Overcoming the Emotional Barriers to Planning for the Future:

For many LGBTQ+ individuals, the thought of planning for the future can be emotionally overwhelming. This is particularly true for those who have experienced rejection or discrimination from family, community, or institutions. The idea of confronting one's own mortality or the need for end-of-life planning can trigger difficult emotions. However, putting off these essential tasks can lead to more stress in the long run. It's important to acknowledge these feelings and take them into account while navigating the planning process. Working with a therapist, counsellor, or legal professional, who understands the unique challenges faced by LGBTQ+ individuals can be helpful.

These conversations may be uncomfortable, but they are necessary for ensuring that one's future is secure. Taking small, manageable steps, such as organizing important documents or discussing healthcare preferences with a partner, can make the process feel more approachable. By recognizing and confronting these emotional barriers, LGBTQ+ individuals can empower themselves to take control of their future.

5.6 Queer Elders with Children – Navigating Parenthood and Legacy Planning:

For queer elders with children, planning for the future involves additional complexities, particularly around legal recognition and guardianship. Many queer parents have faced obstacles in securing parental rights and legal recognition of their families, making it crucial, to clearly define guardianship arrangements in estate planning documents. Clear wills, trusts, and medical directives ensure that children and chosen family are protected, especially if biological family members are unsupportive. Open communication about healthcare and end-of-life preferences is also crucial to prevent conflict and ensure the parents' wishes are honoured. By addressing these considerations, queer elders can safeguard the well-being of their children while preserving their own legacy and identity.

5.7 Conclusion – Taking Control of Your Future with Confidence:

Planning for the future is not just about legal documents or healthcare forms, it's about ensuring that one's identity, values, and wishes are respected. For LGBTQ+ individuals, taking the time to create comprehensive plans for estate, healthcare, and end-of-life decisions is an essential act of self-love and self-respect. While navigating these topics may feel intimidating, breaking them down into manageable tasks and seeking out LGBTQ+-affirming resources can make the process easier. By doing so, LGBTQ+ individuals not only ensure that their futures are secure, but they also stand in their power, reclaiming control over what should be the most personal and defining moments of their lives. This act of planning is one of the most empowering ways to honour oneself and one's legacy.

* Global LGBTQ+ Elder Care Services & Directories:

United States:

SAGE (Services & Advocacy for GLBT Elders):

➢ The oldest and largest organization dedicated to improving the lives of LGBTQ+ older adults. Offers housing, advocacy, caregiver resources, support groups, and the National LGBTQ+ Elder Hotline.

National Resource Center on LGBT Aging:

➢ Provides training, education, and resources to improve aging services for LGBTQ+ communities.

GLMA LGBTQ+ Healthcare Directory:

- Searchable directory of LGBTQ+-affirming healthcare professionals.

Canada:

Egale Canada – LGBTQI2S Aging Initiatives:

- Provides national research and advocacy projects focused on aging in LGBTQI2S communities, including housing and healthcare inclusivity.

Senior Pride Network Toronto:

- A network of organizations and individuals working to create inclusive spaces and services for older LGBTQ+ adults.

United Kingdom:

Stonewall Housing:

- Offers housing and support services for LGBTQ+ people of all ages, with targeted services for elders and trans individuals.

Switchboard.lgbt:

- A helpline providing emotional support and referrals to LGBTQ+-affirming care services.

Opening Doors London:

- The UK's largest charity providing support services specifically for LGBTQ+ people over 50, including befriending services, housing advice, and social groups.

Australia:

LGBTIQ+ Health Australia (Silver Rainbow Program):

- Provides national education and policy advocacy for LGBTQ+ inclusive aged care. Offers training for care providers and resources for older LGBTQ+ Australians.

Switchboard Victoria (Out and About Program):

- Connects older LGBTQ+ people with volunteers for companionship and peer support.

New Zealand:

Rainbow Hub Waikato (Older Rainbow People Project):

- Promotes well-being and visibility of older LGBTQIA+ people through community connection and health advocacy.

Germany:

Lesben und Schwulen Verband (LSVD):

- One of the largest LGBTQ+ rights organizations in Germany. Offers information on elder care rights, anti-discrimination, and inclusive housing models.

Netherlands:

Roze 50+ (Pink 50+):

- A national organization advocating for the interests of LGBTQ+ seniors. Partners with care homes to improve inclusivity.

South Africa:

Triangle Project:

- Offers health and support services for LGBTQ+ people, including older adults living with HIV and navigating care systems.

Brazil:

ABGLT – Associação Brasileira de Gays, Lésbicas e Transgêneros:

- Engages in advocacy and research around LGBTQ+ aging, with community health initiatives in urban areas.

Multinational & Global Networks:

ILGA World – International Lesbian, Gay, Bisexual, Trans and Intersex Association:

- While not exclusively focused on elders, ILGA offers valuable global research and facilitates connections among LGBTQ+ organizations working on aging rights across different regions.

OutRight International:

- Conducts international advocacy for LGBTQ+ human rights, including efforts around inclusive aging and care access.

---

*Legal Checklists for Queer Families & Non-Traditional Structures:

For example, a queer-affirming checklist for future planning might include the following components:

A. Legal Documents to Prepare:

- Advance Healthcare Directive (Living Will)
- Durable Power of Attorney (For both healthcare & finances)
- Will and/or Trust (For asset distribution)
- Health Insurance Authorization (To give access to medical information)
- Burial and Funeral Arrangements (In writing)

B. Identity-Affirming Considerations:

- Ensure all documents reflect the correct name and pronouns
- Confirm that chosen family (vs. legal kin) is included where legally recognized
- Discuss preferences for gender-affirming care in medical documentation

C. Relationship & Housing Considerations:

- Co-ownership deeds or tenancy agreements
- Parenting/adoption status for LGBTQ+ parents
- Rental or retirement facility clauses (Confirm LGBTQ+-inclusivity)

D. Important People to Involve:

- Chosen family members (Partners, close friends, queer kin)
- LGBTQ+-affirming lawyer or estate planner

- Healthcare providers who respect gender identity and orientation

E. Where to Store These Documents:

- One printed, signed copy with your healthcare proxy
- One digital copy in a secure, but accessible place
- Copies shared with all relevant people involved in your care or estate

Chapter 11

LGBTQ+ Relationships in the Digital Age

---

1. Catfishing, Fetishization and Queerphobia in Online Dating Spaces

Online dating has become both a tool for liberation and a landscape of risk for LGBTQ+ individuals. With limited access to safe, affirming offline spaces, especially in conservative or rural areas, many turn to apps in search of connection. However, the same technology that facilitates intimacy also opens doors to exploitation. Catfishing, fetishization and queerphobia are not rare anomalies, but persistent threats that uniquely target queer users. What begins as a simple swipe can lead to serious emotional harm, social alienation, or even physical danger.

1.1 Catfishing – The Danger of Disguised Intentions:

Deceptive behaviour like catfishing is often dismissed as mere online mischief, but for queer individuals, the consequences are far more serious. Many have been emotionally manipulated by users pretending to be someone they're not, often exploiting the vulnerabilities of those who are closeted, newly out, or isolated. For trans and nonbinary users in particular, catfishing often leads to betrayal, ridicule, or threats when their trust is broken. The violation goes beyond hurt feelings, it can shatter a person's sense of safety in already precarious environments.

1.2 Queer-Specific Catfishing and Entrapment:

Some instances of catfishing are rooted in overt queerphobia. Fake profiles are created to lure LGBTQ+ people into conversations or physical meetups, only to humiliate, out, or attack them. In more extreme cases, users are targeted by vigilante groups or law enforcement stings under the guise of public safety. These entrapment tactics not only traumatize individuals, but also reinforce a climate of fear and suspicion, particularly among those already navigating criminalization or rejection in their communities.

1.3 Fetishization as a Form of Violence:

Being desired is not inherently harmful, but being dehumanized through fetishization is. Many queer people encounter messages that focus solely on their bodies, identities, or perceived "kink value." Rather than being seen as whole people, they are reduced to erotic fantasies or one-dimensional stereotypes. Trans women are asked invasive questions. Femme gay men are treated as playthings. Queer people of colour are labelled with racial slurs masked as compliments. The result is not just discomfort, but a sense of being commodified and devalued. Fetishization, in this context, becomes a subtle yet insidious form of violence that strips individuals of dignity, autonomy, and the right to define their own desirability.

1.4 Racial and Gender Fetishization in Queer Contexts:

Discrimination in queer spaces often takes the form of objectification. A Black gay man might be told he's "so aggressive and dominant," while an Asian nonbinary person may receive dozens of messages referencing submissiveness or exoticism. What some users label as "preferences" often mirror the biases of broader society, shaped by colonial histories, white supremacist beauty standards, and transmisogyny. When desire is shaped by these forces, forming meaningful connections becomes nearly impossible.

1.5 The Invisibility and Erasure of Asexual and Aromantic People:

Dating apps tend to center sexual and romantic pursuits, leaving little room for those who exist outside those norms. Asexual and aromantic users are frequently dismissed, mocked, or asked to explain their identities to prove legitimacy. Even within LGBTQ+-centred platforms, the pressure to define attraction through sex or romance leads to exclusion and erasure. This neglect reflects a broader issue, the pervasive belief that queer desire must conform to narrow, socially sanctioned definitions, often shaped by hypers-sexualized expectations and normative assumptions.

1.6 Algorithmic Queerphobia – Tech Bias and Moderation Failures:

Inequities are not just found in user behaviour, they are coded into the platforms themselves. Dating app algorithms tend to amplify cisnormativity, whiteness, and conventionally attractive users, while pushing others into the margins. Trans users are often flagged for content violations simply for presenting their bodies in ways that are identical to how cisgender users do, revealing a clear bias in enforcement and perception. Queer people of colour frequently encounter disproportionate moderation and punitive actions. The platforms meant to foster connection instead end up reinforcing systemic exclusion and digital discrimination.

1.7 The Psychological Toll of Constant Defence:

Navigating digital dating as a queer person often means operating from a place of caution rather than curiosity. Every interaction requires emotional labour, vetting profiles, decoding messages, preparing for rejection, and managing the impact of abuse. Over time, this vigilance can lead to burnout, isolation, and self-doubt. The promise of affirmation through technology frequently transforms into yet another space where queer users must armour up just to exist.

1.8 Community Responses and Digital Safety Tactics:

Despite the challenges, queer communities continue to organize and protect one another in innovative ways. Online threads, forums, and group chats are used to share safety tips, warn others about dangerous users and document patterns of abuse. Resources created by queer and trans users often offer more practical protection than platform guidelines ever have. These acts of digital care form a decentralized resistance, proving that collective wisdom can mitigate, even if not eliminate, systemic harm.

1.9 The Need for Platform Accountability and Cultural Change:

Change cannot rest solely on individual users or marginalized communities. Dating platforms must take responsibility by designing more inclusive features, hiring LGBTQ+ developers, and addressing the real harm their tools perpetuate. Cultural shifts are equally important. Queerphobia doesn't disappear just because the platform says, "love is love", it requires structural shifts in how desire, power, and identity are understood. Queer people deserve spaces that honour their complexity, not ones that exploit their visibility.

2. The Role of Algorithms in Reinforcing Stereotypes in LGBTQ+ Dating Apps

Behind every match, message, or missed connection on a dating app lies an algorithm, a complex set of rules, data points, and predictions that shape how users interact. While these systems are designed to streamline compatibility and enhance user experience, they often end up reproducing the very stereotypes and social hierarchies they claim to transcend. For LGBTQ+ users, the impact is especially profound, as the algorithm becomes not just a digital gatekeeper, but a mirror reflecting back the biases of the larger society it was trained on.

2.1 Algorithms as Cultural Interpreters:

Rather than functioning as neutral tools, algorithms act as cultural filters. They make decisions based on data that reflect existing patterns of behaviour, many of which are deeply rooted in bias. When users are repeatedly shown profiles based on popularity, racial preferences, body types, or gender norms, the algorithm begins to reinforce certain identities as desirable and others as invisible. In queer communities, this dynamic often amplifies existing marginalizations, particularly for trans people, people of colour, plus-size individuals and gender-nonconforming users.

2.2 Data-Driven Desire and the Illusion of Preference:

Algorithms interpret user behaviour as desire, learning from swipes, messages, and time spent on profiles. But what appears to be individual "preference" is often shaped by broader cultural messages about who is worthy of love and attention. A user who consistently sees and engages with white, cisgender, muscular profiles may begin to believe that this pattern is organic when, in fact, it is curated. Over time, these feedback loops create a distorted sense of collective desire, one that reflects exclusion, not authenticity. To reclaim our desires, we must first recognize how they've been quietly programmed.

2.3 Racial and Ethnic Profiling in Matchmaking:

One of the most visible consequences of algorithmic sorting is the reproduction of racial hierarchies. Queer users of colour frequently report being ignored, fetishized, or completely filtered out by systems that prioritize whiteness. Even subtle design choices, such as search filters by ethnicity or geo-targeting based on majority user demographics, can contribute to racially segregated dating ecosystems.

Rather than disrupting racial bias, many apps silently sustain it, creating environments where diversity is tokenized rather than celebrated.

2.4 Cisnormativity and the Erasure of Trans Identities:

Most dating apps were built with cisgender, heterosexual users in mind, and those design assumptions continue to harm trans users. From forced binary gender selections to misgendering in profile labelling, trans people often find themselves excluded by default. Even when inclusion is attempted, algorithms frequently fail to match trans users with those who have expressed genuine interest or respect. Instead, many are shown to users who fetishize or reject them, compounding emotional harm and reinforcing stereotypes of trans people as deceptive or "other." This ongoing exclusion underscores the urgent need for platforms to be designed with trans voices at the centre, not as an afterthought, but as a foundation for truly inclusive connection.

2.5 Body Image and the Politics of Visibility:

Algorithms often prioritize profiles that align with dominant beauty standards, slim, white, masculine, able-bodied, pushing others to the periphery. Queer individuals with bodies that fall outside these norms receive fewer matches and lower engagement, leading many to internalize feelings of inadequacy or invisibility. The supposed meritocracy of dating apps becomes a selective spotlight, reinforcing harmful stereotypes about attractiveness and worth in LGBTQ+ communities. In this digital arena, visibility is politicized, rewarding conformity while punishing authenticity.

2.6 Popularity Metrics and the Cycle of Reinforcement:

Features like "Top Picks," "Most Liked," or "Trending Profiles" deepen existing visibility hierarchies. These metrics don't merely reflect popularity, they actively manufacture it. When a user receives increased engagement, the algorithm further promotes their profile, giving them even greater exposure. This feedback loop benefits those who already fit into dominant beauty ideals and conventional standards of desirability. Meanwhile, individuals who fall outside these norms are consistently pushed to the margins. The result is a self-perpetuating system that rewards conformity and sidelines diversity. In this closed loop, desirability becomes less about connection and more about algorithmic approval, leaving little room for radical visibility or authentic self-expression.

2.7 Queerphobia in Content Moderation Algorithms:

Content moderation tools designed to keep platforms "safe" often disproportionately target LGBTQ+ users. Posts that feature same-gender affection, discussions of queerness, or trans visibility are flagged as inappropriate, while bigoted content can go unchallenged. These moderation practices, often driven by automated systems, reflect a misunderstanding of queer expression as inherently explicit or dangerous. The algorithm, in attempting to sanitize content, ends up policing queerness itself. To create genuinely safe digital spaces, moderation systems must be reimagined to distinguish between harm and identity, ensuring queer expression is protected rather than punished. Until algorithms are equity-informed, queer users will keep being punished for existing.

2.8 The False Promise of Personalization:

Dating apps sell the idea of personalization, of finding love tailored just for you. But for many queer users, that promise falls flat. Instead of fostering discovery, personalization too often means being boxed into rigid categories shaped by past behaviour and systemic bias. Users are rarely empowered to explore new types of connection, gender expression, or body types. Instead, they are nudged toward algorithm-approved options, which often replicate mainstream, heteronormative values within queer spaces.

2.9 Rethinking the Algorithm – Toward Ethical Queer Tech:

Meaningful change begins with reimagining what queer digital spaces could look like if inclusivity, agency and equity, were core priorities in design. Developers must engage with LGBTQ+ users across intersections, ensuring that systems are not just data-driven, but community-informed. Transparency in how algorithms function, greater control for users to define their experiences, and intentional disruption of harmful patterns are all steps toward a more ethical approach. Technology doesn't have to replicate the past, it can be a tool for imagining new futures.

3. Navigating Long-Distance LGBTQ+ Relationships in a Digital World

Long-distance relationships can be both rewarding and challenging, especially for LGBTQ+ couples, who often face additional layers of complexity. Whether separated by geography due to work, school, immigration status, or the need for safer living environments, queer partners often rely on digital tools to maintain connection. In a world where love frequently unfolds through screens and across time zones, intentional communication, trust, and creativity become essential foundations for lasting intimacy.

3.1 The Unique Challenges for Queer Long-Distance Couples:

Queer couples often contend with stressors that heterosexual, cisgender couples may not face. Some are navigating unsupportive families or living in countries where their identities are criminalized. Others are stealth, closeted, or unable to safely visit one another. These dynamics can heighten emotional vulnerability, making consistency and care even more vital. Understanding these specific challenges creates space for compassion and deeper resilience. For many queer couples, long-distance love becomes a radical act of survival, strength and hope.

3.2 Building a Communication Framework That Works for You:

Effective communication isn't just about frequency, it's about clarity, comfort, and consent. Long-distance couples thrive when they establish shared expectations around texting, calling, video chatting and checking in. Some need daily contact, others prefer space with regular deep conversations. The key is co-creating a communication rhythm that nourishes both partners without pressure or guilt. Scheduling intentional "together time" online, whether it's a call, a movie night, or a virtual date, helps bridge the physical gap.

3.3 Navigating Time Zones, Schedules and Energy Levels:

Being in different time zones or having opposite work schedules can strain even the most committed relationships. It helps to use shared calendars, time zone apps, or planning tools to reduce friction and missed connections. Flexibility and patience go a long way. Being honest about when you're emotionally or physically drained, while still finding creative ways to show up for each other, ensures that care remains mutual and sustainable. By prioritizing communication and flexibility, we can turn distance and time differences into opportunities for deeper connection and understanding.

3.4 Maintaining Emotional Intimacy from Afar:

Physical distance doesn't equate to emotional disconnection. Expressing love in meaningful ways, whether through love letters, voice notes, playlists, or small surprises, helps maintain a strong emotional bond. Sharing the mundane details of your day, your thoughts, your dreams, or even moments of silence can be deeply powerful. Emotional intimacy flourishes when both partners feel seen, heard, and supported, even through a screen. By nurturing connection in creative ways, emotional intimacy can not only survive the distance, but grow stronger despite it.

3.5 Navigating Sexual Connection and Digital Boundaries:

For many couples, physical intimacy is a key aspect of closeness. Long-distance relationships require creative adaptation. Sexting, video intimacy and erotic voice notes can help keep desires alive, as long as both partners feel safe and respected. Setting clear digital boundaries around comfort, consent, and privacy is essential. Creating a sense of safety in virtual sexual connection strengthens trust and reduces anxiety about the distance. By prioritizing consent, communication, and respect, digital intimacy can become a powerful tool for maintaining closeness and trust, even from afar.

3.6 Coping with Loneliness and the Ache of Missing Each Other:

Missing someone is both a testament to love and a test of endurance. In queer relationships, where safe physical affection can already be scarce in public life, that ache may feel even more profound. Acknowledging loneliness without judgment and finding ways to soothe it through community, routine, and self-care is vital. Leaning into queer friendships, support groups, or creative outlets can buffer the emotional toll of being apart.

3.7 Managing Conflict and Miscommunication at a Distance:

All couples experience conflict, but in long-distance relationships, the lack of physical presence can make resolution harder. Tone can be misread in texts, and delayed responses can intensify anxiety. Agreeing on conflict resolution strategies, such as taking breaks during heated conversations, prioritizing calls over texts for serious issues, and committing to follow-up discussions, creates healthier ways to navigate misunderstandings. Emotional regulation and mutual respect are the glue that keeps long-distance love strong. Long-distance love thrives when conflict becomes a pathway to understanding, not a catalyst for disconnection.

3.8 Celebrating Milestones and Creating Shared Rituals:

Marking anniversaries, holidays, or even "monthiversaries" helps keep joy alive. Shared rituals, like sending each other the same meal for delivery, watching a show together weekly, or starting a digital scrapbook, provide continuity and connection. Creating memories, even while physically apart, allows the relationship to feel truly lived in and cherished. These shared moments, whether big or small, become emotional anchors that help ground the connection, reminding both partners that while distance may be temporary, the love and commitment they share are constant and enduring. By embracing these rituals, even in small ways, we cultivate a sense of togetherness that transcends distance and strengthens the foundation of our love.

3.9 Planning for Reunions and Future Possibilities:

Having something to look forward to, a visit, a relocation, or a shared life plan, offers hope and motivation during long periods apart. Even if timelines are uncertain, talking openly about dreams, goals, and future logistics can ease some of the emotional strain. Not every detail needs to be figured out right away, but a shared vision keeps the relationship rooted in possibility rather than indefinite waiting. Knowing that there is a plan, whether concrete or evolving, helps both partners feel that the distance is temporary and that there is a future together to build, which can make the emotional challenges of separation more manageable. These conversations don't just alleviate present loneliness, they become emotional anchors, reminding both partners that love can stretch across time and space when nurtured with intention and hope.

3.10 The Strength in Queer Long-Distance Love:

Long-distance LGBTQ+ relationships often grow in depth, intentionality, and mutual care. They challenge partners to communicate with honesty, love without relying on proximity and trust without constant validation. Far from being a sign of instability, thriving across distance demonstrates strength, creativity, and a fierce kind of intimacy. In a world that often questions queer love, choosing each other again and again, even from afar, is a quiet, radical act. These relationships prove that love, when nurtured with intention, transcends physical boundaries and becomes a testament to the resilience of queer connection.

4. The Rise of Virtual Queer Spaces – Safe Havens or Echo Chambers?

In recent years, virtual spaces have become a critical lifeline for LGBTQ+ individuals seeking connection, support, and community, especially in environments where in-person interactions may not be possible or safe. With the rise of social media platforms, online forums and dedicated queer spaces, the internet has provided a new avenue for queer people to gather, share experiences and express their identities. However, as these spaces grow, so too does the debate: Are they truly safe havens, or do they sometimes function as echo chambers that reinforce limited perspectives? As we continue to shape and inhabit these digital realms, the challenge lies in fostering spaces that are both affirming and expansive, where safety doesn't come at the cost of critical growth or diverse dialogue.

4.1 The Appeal of Virtual Queer Spaces:

Virtual queer spaces provide affirmation, solidarity and belonging, especially for those in hostile or marginalized environments.

- **Anonymity and Safety:** The ability to exist anonymously online provides a layer of protection, allowing people to explore their identity without fear of immediate physical harm or rejection.
- **Global Community Building:** Queer people from all over the world, regardless of their local environments, can connect and build relationships, breaking down geographical barriers that may limit offline interactions.
- **Accessibility and Inclusivity:** Virtual spaces often allow for more diverse representation, providing platforms for individuals from various racial, socioeconomic, and gender backgrounds to share their experiences and find support.

4.2 Double-Edged Sword – Risks of Echo Chambers:

While valuable, virtual queer spaces can become echo chambers, where certain voices dominate and others are marginalized.

- **Exclusion of Intersectional Identities:** Many online queer spaces can inadvertently prioritize the voices and experiences of certain groups, typically white, cisgender, middle-class individuals, while failing to create space for those with intersecting identities (e.g., queer people of colour, trans individuals, or those from lower socioeconomic backgrounds).
- **Limited Perspectives:** When people retreat into spaces where their views are constantly affirmed, they may become caught in a cycle of groupthink. This repetition can hinder personal growth, reduce empathy, and narrow understanding, as individuals are less likely to encounter diverse or challenging perspectives from the broader LGBTQ+ community.

4.3 Safe Spaces or Silencing Spaces?

One of the central arguments for virtual queer spaces is their ability to function as safe havens for marginalized individuals. But what happens when the very notion of "safety" leads to the exclusion of diverse opinions?

- **Censorship and "Call-Out" Culture:** In some cases, the policing of language and opinions in these spaces can create environments of over-sensitivity, where people are too fearful to express themselves for fear of backlash or being "cancelled." While safety is important, this can lead to a stifling of meaningful discussion or the suppression of diverse queer experiences that don't align with a specific narrative.
- **The Impact on Growth:** When individuals are only exposed to familiar and comfortable or widely accepted and uniform perspectives, there is less room for critical reflection and meaningful development.

- Conversations that challenge the status quo are often avoided in the interest of maintaining harmony, but this avoidance can make it harder to engage with complex, nuanced issues within the queer community itself.

4.4 The Role of Moderation in Shaping Community Culture:

The effectiveness of virtual queer spaces in maintaining safety and inclusivity largely depends on how they are moderated.

- **Positive Moderation Practices:** Well-moderated spaces that prioritize inclusive language, respect for all identities, and productive dialogue are more likely to encourage healthy, diverse conversations and foster a supportive community. These spaces can serve as invaluable resources for queer individuals seeking advice, validation, or simply a place to be themselves.
- **Over-Moderation and Stifling Debate:** Conversely, over-moderation, where almost every interaction is closely monitored and censored, can create a chilling effect. When members are overly cautious or avoid expressing their opinions due to the fear of being policed, these spaces can lose their ability to foster genuine connection and growth.
- **Lack of Accountability:** On the flip side, spaces that lack effective moderation may allow harmful behaviours, like trolling, harassment, or hate speech, to flourish. Without clear guidelines and consistent enforcement, these spaces can become toxic, undermining the safety they aim to provide.

4.5 Bridging the Gap Between Virtual and Physical Spaces:

One of the promises of virtual queer spaces is that they can eventually help bridge the gap between online and offline communities.

- **Building Real-World Connections:** For many, online interactions are just the beginning. Virtual queer spaces can act as gateways to physical communities, whether through meetups, events, or collaborative projects. These digital spaces can provide a sense of belonging that might encourage individuals to step out of their comfort zones and seek in-person connections in their own localities.
- **The Danger of Over-Reliance on Digital Connection:** However, the growing reliance on virtual spaces can also lead to a detachment from the reality of in-person queer communities. The convenience of virtual connections can sometimes make it harder for individuals to engage in the messy, nuanced, and sometimes difficult work of building relationships offline.

4.6 Conclusion – The Dual Nature of Virtual Queer Spaces:

Virtual queer spaces are a double-edged sword, they offer significant benefits, including anonymity, inclusivity and global community building, but they also come with their own set of risks. As these spaces continue to evolve, it is essential to strike a balance between ensuring safety and fostering diversity of thought.

If we are to truly build spaces that are both safe and dynamic, it is crucial that we remain vigilant about how these spaces are structured, moderated, and engaged with. The future of virtual queer spaces will depend on our ability to create environments that embrace complexity, challenge norms and respect the multiplicity of queer experiences, rather than allowing them to devolve into echo chambers that limit growth and understanding.

5. Cyberbullying, Doxxing and Digital Safety for LGBTQ+ People

The internet, while often a space for connection and self-expression, can also be a site of targeted harassment, especially for LGBTQ+ individuals. As queer people navigate social media, dating platforms, forums and content-sharing apps, they face a disproportionate risk of cyberbullying, doxxing and other digital threats. These online attacks are not just virtual, they carry real-life consequences. Understanding these dangers is essential for building a safer online presence and protecting both identity and well-being. By staying vigilant, informed, and united, we can create digital spaces where we thrive, not just survive.

5.1 Cyberbullying in Queer Contexts – More Than Just Trolling:

Cyberbullying against LGBTQ+ individuals often goes beyond casual insults or disagreements, it can be systematic, hateful, and deeply personal.

- **Homophobic and Transphobic Attacks:** Slurs, deliberate misgendering, and mocking of someone's gender expression or sexual orientation are frequent forms of online harassment. These attacks are often meant to shame, intimidate, or silence queer voices.
- **Intersectional Harassment:** Queer people of colour, transgender individuals and those living with disabilities, often face layered abuse. Harassers frequently target multiple aspects of their identity at once, intensifying the emotional harm.
- **Mental Health Impact:** Prolonged exposure to online harassment can lead to increased anxiety, depression, and a growing sense of isolation, especially when reliable support systems are unavailable or inaccessible.

5.2 The Dangers of Doxxing – When Online Harassment Becomes Offline Threat:

Doxxing, the malicious act of publishing someone's personal information online, poses a serious threat to LGBTQ+ individuals.

- **What Doxxing Involves:** This may include sharing addresses, phone numbers, workplace details, or legal names (particularly dangerous for trans individuals).
- **Consequences:** Victims of doxxing may face stalking, job loss, family conflict, or physical violence. It is a terrifying breach of safety that can escalate quickly.

- **Why LGBTQ+ People Are Targeted:** Queer visibility, especially when it challenges social norms, can make individuals more vulnerable to coordinated attacks by hate groups or bigoted individuals.

5.3 Public Visibility and Its Risks – Balancing Pride and Protection:

For many LGBTQ+ individuals, being visible online is a form of activism, joy and self-expression. But visibility can come at a cost.

- **"Outing" Without Consent:** Sharing one's identity online may unintentionally expose someone to family, employers, or communities that are not accepting.
- **Performative Safety:** Platforms may claim to support queer users, but inconsistent moderation and algorithmic bias often leave LGBTQ+ users unprotected.
- **Surveillance Culture:** Apps and websites collect data that can be used against individuals in unsafe environments, making digital footprint awareness essential.

5.4 Protecting Your Online Identity – Practical Tips for Digital Safety:

Staying safe online requires proactive steps and ongoing awareness.

- **Privacy Settings:** Regularly review and update privacy settings on all social platforms. Restrict who can view your posts, tag you, or message you.
- **Limit Personal Details:** Avoid sharing location, full legal names, and other identifiable information, especially on public accounts or forums.
- **Use Strong, Unique Passwords:** Enable two-factor authentication where possible and consider using a password manager to stay secure.
- **Monitor Your Digital Footprint:** Periodically search your name to see what information is publicly available and request removal if necessary.

5.5 What to Do If You're Targeted – Crisis Response and Recovery:

Experiencing cyberbullying or doxxing can be overwhelming, but there are steps to take for safety and recovery.

- **Document Everything:** Take screenshots and save messages or posts. This is crucial for reporting abuse or seeking legal action.
- **Block and Report:** Use platform tools to block harassers and report abuse. Don't engage directly with aggressors, as this can escalate the situation.
- **Reach Out for Help:** Contact trusted friends, LGBTQ+ organizations, or mental health professionals for support. You do not have to navigate this alone.

- **Contact Authorities if Needed:** If threats involve violence or stalking, involve law enforcement. Keep records of all interactions for your protection.

5.6 The Role of Platforms and Accountability:

Social media companies and websites have a responsibility to protect users, but often fail queer communities.

- **Inadequate Moderation:** Queer users are often penalized more harshly for content than those who post hate speech. Algorithmic biases and human moderators frequently misunderstand queer language or humour.
- **Reporting Tools That Don't Work:** Many platforms offer reporting options, but follow-up is inconsistent, and appeals are difficult to navigate.
- **Pushing for Change:** LGBTQ+ individuals and allies can advocate for better platform accountability, inclusive moderation policies, and meaningful safety tools that prioritize marginalized users.

5.7 Community-Led Solutions and Collective Care:

When institutions fail, queer communities often turn to one another.

- **Peer Education and Skill-Sharing:** Community-led workshops on digital safety, security tools, and self-defence online empower users to take control.
- **Support Networks:** Queer mutual aid groups, group chats and forums, offer emotional and practical support after harassment. These safe zones foster resilience and solidarity.
- **Building Safer Platforms:** Some LGBTQ+ creators are developing alternative apps, forums and digital spaces, built by and for queer people, centering safety and inclusion from the start.

5.8 Conclusion – Claiming Safety Without Giving Up Space:

The fight for digital safety is not about retreating, it's about reclaiming space with the tools and knowledge needed to thrive. LGBTQ+ individuals deserve to be visible, vocal, and connected online, without fear of harassment or violence. While the internet remains a battleground for queer safety, it is also a space of profound empowerment, creativity and community. By staying informed, practicing digital self-defence and advocating for structural change, queer people can continue building a safer digital world, one where identity is celebrated, not punished.

In this ongoing struggle, queer resilience shines through. The fight for digital safety is active, a bold reclaiming of our right to exist and thrive in spaces that should be ours. As we challenge harmful systems and create networks of care, we not only protect ourselves, but also pave the way for future generations to live, love, and connect openly and safely.

* A Timeline of Queer Digital Milestones – (From Modems to Metaverses, Tracing Queer Connection Through Screens):

1990s – The Dawn of Digital Queerhood:

- **AOL & IRC Chatrooms:** Queer users created private rooms labelled with coded acronyms like "M4M" or "QChat." These anonymous spaces became some people's first opportunity to say, "I'm gay," without fear.
- **Usenet Forums:** Early bulletin boards like "alt.politics.homosexuality" and "soc.bi" hosted everything from intellectual debates to personal coming-out stories.
- **Geocities & Angelfire Queer Pages:** DIY web design met queer self-expression, complete with rainbow dividers and glitter GIFs. "Queer teen diary" websites became lifelines.
- **The Closet Door Opens (Digitally):** For many rural or isolated LGBTQ+ people, the internet became their first community.

2000s – Fanfiction, Forums & First Online Crushes:

- **LiveJournal & Xanga:** Queer-coded usernames and locked posts created intimate circles of mutual disclosure. Many used these blogs as digital diaries of identity exploration.
- **The Fanfiction Boom:** Queer teens reshaped heteronormative canon via Harry Potter, X-Men and Buffy fanfics. Slash fic was activism disguised as passion.
- **Queer Forums:** Spaces like EmptyClosets, GayTeenForum and early Reddit boards, fostered advice, memes and peer-to-peer support.
- **The Sims & Online Gaming:** Players created queer families in digital neighbourhoods, often for the first time in their lives.
- **MySpace's "Top 8" Politics:** Queer youth navigated public friendship hierarchies and coded identity expressions via profile songs and blinkie graphics.
- **Gay.com**: One of the first mainstream LGBTQ+ dating/chat platforms.
- **Craigslist "Missed Connections"**: Coded longing and experimental queer writing.

2010s – Tumblr, YouTube and the Queer Aesthetic Revolution:

- **Tumblr's Golden Age:** Arguably the most significant digital queer hub of the decade. Identities like demisexual, aromantic, and nonbinary gained visibility here. Memes, aesthetics, and activism blended into one endless dashboard scroll.

- **Rise of Queer YouTubers:** Creators like Tyler Oakley, Gigi Gorgeous and ContraPoints, invited queer viewers into their bedrooms, turning confessionals into cultural moments.
- **Instagram Queer Culture:** Visual storytelling let queer creators reframe beauty, body politics and gender performance.
- **The Meme as Protest:** LGBTQ+ teens began responding to trauma with humour, "sounds gay, I'm in" went viral.
- **Dating Apps Multiply:** Grindr paved the way in 2009, but the 2010s saw HER, Scruff, Lex, and more diversify the playing field.
- **Tinder (2012):** While initially hetero-focused, Tinder gradually opened to more gender identities and orientations.

2020s – Queer Futures in Hyper-Connection:

- **TikTok Queer Explosion:** #LesbianTikTok, #TransJoy and #BisexualAwakening trends, allowed young people to see themselves reflected back, often for the first time.
- **VR Pride Parades & AltSpaces:** With global lockdowns, LGBTQ+ folks created queer joy in virtual clubs, Zoom drag shows and digital beach parties.
- **Discord Servers as Chosen Family:** From mutual aid to meme dumps, servers became home bases, often replacing traditional IRL friend groups.
- **Queer Coding in Video Games:** From Dream Daddy to The Last of Us Part II, queer storylines are finally being written into mainstream games.
- **Nonbinary Emoji & Inclusive Tech:** Apple and Android rolled out more gender-inclusive emoji, avatars, and voice assistants.
- **Lex (2020):** A text-based queer dating & community app, feminist and anti-algorithmic by design.
- **BeReal, Discord Servers and Signal Group Chats:** Queer youth reclaiming intimacy and authenticity in niche/private circles.

The Queer Universe Reimagined "QUORUM" as a Hypothetical Digital LGBTQ+ Connection Platform, In Future:

A radically imaginative and speculative space where queer people can thrive, explore and connect on their own terms. "QUORUM" doesn't currently exist, but maybe it should. This is a vision of what could be when queer values guide the design of digital life. In this space, identity is fluid, safety is paramount, and every connection fosters empowerment and belonging.

A Platform Built from Queer Values:

"QUORUM" flips the script. It's not an app where queerness is tolerated, it's a universe where queerness is the default. Instead of bending ourselves to fit into existing tools, we get to shape the tools around us. At its core, "QUORUM" is a community-centered, immersive space. Users build their own "chosen homes," design fluid identities that evolve over time, and explore a landscape not defined by likes or followers, but by presence and shared values. There's no ad targeting. No forced binaries. No algorithm decides what you see. Everything runs on mutual respect, user sovereignty, and curiosity.

Why It Matters:

Too often, queer people experience technology as either a closet or a battlefield. But imagine logging into a space where:

- Your pronouns are correctly honoured by design.
- You can express your gender visually, vocally, and virtually, without apology or explanation.
- You can attend a virtual support group one day, a digital rave the next, and a quiet "persona room" to write poetry the day after.
- Decentralized, radically inclusive, self-governed queer digital ecosystem.
- Combines identity exploration, safety, emotional connection, and creative storytelling, in one immersive world.

In a world where our real lives are often policed, censored, or erased, "QUORUM" offers something radically, healing digital self-determination.

A New Digital Citizenship:

"QUORUM" is not just a tool, it's a culture. A way of being online that is slower, more intentional, and more imaginative. Conflict is handled through consent-based tools and community-led justice, not by faceless moderators or vague community guidelines.

The future here is not frictionless or utopian. It's real. Messy. Beautiful. Alive. And it changes with us, just like queerness does.

The Invitation:

We may not have "QUORUM" yet, but dreaming it is a political act.

Every forum we shape, every avatar we build, every story we share online is a brushstroke in the larger queer digital canvas.

Which leads us to the real question:

If we could design our own universe, what would we choose to keep, what would we rewrite, and what would we dare to invent?

"QUORUM" dares to imagine the answer and invites us to dream it, into being. A space not yet real, but deeply needed. Where queerness isn't moderated or monetized, but honoured, expanded, and explored. Where safety is built in, not added on. Where queer connection is crafted with care and expression knows no algorithmic limits. Because we're done waiting to be included, we're building a future where we've always belonged, with queer lives, voices and dreams at the centre.

Chapter 12

Transcending Borders – LGBTQ+ Rights and Global Activism

1. The Global Landscape of LGBTQ+ Rights

The landscape of LGBTQ+ rights across the world is incredibly diverse, shaped by a complex interplay of cultural, political, and legal factors. While significant progress has been made in some regions, LGBTQ+ individuals continue to face severe persecution, discrimination, and violence in others. Understanding this global landscape requires a nuanced view that considers the historical, cultural, and societal contexts that influence attitudes toward gender and sexual diversity. This exploration of LGBTQ+ rights around the world highlights the contrast between countries with progressive laws and those where LGBTQ+ individuals remain at risk of criminalization and violence.

1.1 Cultural Influences on LGBTQ+ Rights:

Culture plays a central role in shaping how LGBTQ+ people are viewed and treated in various societies. In many parts of the world, LGBTQ+ identities are deeply stigmatized due to longstanding cultural and religious traditions that view non-heteronormative behaviour as immoral or unnatural. In these regions, LGBTQ+ individuals often face familial rejection, social exclusion, and even violence, as their sexual orientation or gender identity contradicts deeply held cultural norms. Countries with strong religious foundations, especially those where conservative interpretations of Christianity, Islam, or other faiths dominate, frequently criminalize same-sex relationships and non-binary gender identities, citing religious doctrine as justification.

In contrast, some cultures have a long history of accepting gender and sexual diversity, recognizing LGBTQ+ individuals as integral parts of society. For instance, many Indigenous cultures in the Americas, Africa, and Asia have long acknowledged and respected gender fluidity and same-sex relationships. However, colonialism and the imposition of Western values during the colonial era disrupted these traditions, often criminalizing LGBTQ+ identities. In recent years, some of these cultures have seen a revival of acceptance, as efforts are made to reclaim traditional beliefs that honour LGBTQ+ people.

1.2 Legal Recognition and Rights – A Mixed Global Picture:

The legal status of LGBTQ+ individuals varies widely from one country to another, reflecting each society's approach to equality and human rights. In some nations, legal protections for LGBTQ+ people are robust and include anti-discrimination laws, marriage equality, and the legal recognition of gender identity. These progressive laws are often the result of years of activism, legal battles, and public advocacy, highlighting the tireless efforts of LGBTQ+ activists to secure basic human rights.

Countries such as Canada, Sweden, the Netherlands, and Spain have paved the way for LGBTQ+ rights, creating legal frameworks that offer full equality in marriage, adoption, healthcare, and workplace protections. These nations also provide legal recognition for non-binary and transgender individuals, allowing for a more inclusive understanding of gender.

However, in many parts of the world, LGBTQ+ rights are still either not recognized or actively suppressed by law. In over 70 countries, same-sex relationships are still criminalized, and individuals can face imprisonment, fines, or even the death penalty for engaging in consensual same-sex acts. In countries like Uganda, Nigeria, and Saudi Arabia, strict anti-LGBTQ+ laws are enforced, often under the guise of religious or cultural protection. These laws are part of a broader pattern of systemic discrimination that undermines LGBTQ+ individuals' access to basic rights, including healthcare, education, and employment.

1.3 Political Climate and the Impact on LGBTQ+ Rights:

The political climate in a country also plays a critical role in shaping LGBTQ+ rights. In democracies with progressive leadership, LGBTQ+ rights are often protected and expanded through policy reforms, government support, and judicial rulings. Political leaders and governments that champion equality and human rights can help to create an environment where LGBTQ+ individuals are more likely to experience legal protections and societal acceptance. For instance, in countries like Argentina and New Zealand, the political will to pass laws protecting LGBTQ+ individuals from discrimination and violence has had a profound impact on societal attitudes.

On the other hand, in authoritarian regimes and countries with repressive political systems, LGBTQ+ rights are frequently attacked or ignored. In these regions, political leaders may use anti-LGBTQ+ rhetoric to consolidate power, scapegoat minority groups, or deflect from other societal issues. In Russia, for example, a "gay propaganda" law has been used to stifle LGBTQ+ activism and silence those who advocate for equality. In countries with a history of political unrest, LGBTQ+ individuals often bear the brunt of social instability, with their rights and safety taking a backseat to political agendas.

1.4 Global Activism and International Pressure:

Global activism has played a significant role in advancing LGBTQ+ rights and bringing international pressure to bear on countries with regressive policies. International organizations, such as the United Nations and Human Rights Watch, have consistently called for the decriminalization of same-sex relationships and the protection of LGBTQ+ individuals from violence and discrimination. The global LGBTQ+ rights movement has also been instrumental in raising awareness of the challenges faced by LGBTQ+ people living in countries where they are persecuted or marginalized. Pride events, campaigns like #LoveIsLove, and the efforts of NGOs have brought attention to the plight of LGBTQ+ refugees and asylum seekers, as well as those living in hostile environments. While these international efforts have led to some victories, such as the decriminalization of homosexuality in India and the legalization of same-sex marriage in Taiwan, they also face significant resistance.

Some countries view international LGBTQ+ advocacy as a form of Western imperialism, rejecting foreign influence on their domestic policies. This resistance is particularly strong in countries with authoritarian regimes or conservative religious leadership, where LGBTQ+ rights are seen as incompatible with local values.

1.5 The Future of LGBTQ+ Rights – Progress and Challenges Ahead:

The global landscape of LGBTQ+ rights is constantly evolving. While many countries have made significant strides toward equality, the battle for full recognition and protection remains ongoing. As activists continue to push for legal reform, cultural acceptance, and social justice, the global community must confront the realities of persecution and violence faced by LGBTQ+ individuals in less accepting regions. The continued efforts of LGBTQ+ activists, supported by international advocacy and solidarity, will be crucial in ensuring that LGBTQ+ rights are recognized as human rights across the globe. In conclusion, the global landscape of LGBTQ+ rights is both hopeful and challenging. While significant progress has been made in some parts of the world, LGBTQ+ individuals still face significant barriers to equality in many others. By understanding the cultural, legal and political factors that shape these rights, we can work toward a more inclusive and just world for all LGBTQ+ individuals, regardless of where they live.

2. Struggles and Victories – LGBTQ+ Movements Across Cultures

The global LGBTQ+ rights movement is a rich tapestry of diverse voices, cultural histories and resilient communities. Across continents, queer individuals have fought for dignity, visibility and justice, often confronting deeply rooted societal and legal barriers. These movements have achieved profound milestones that continue to reshape public discourse and policy, yet they still face persistent challenges shaped by cultural norms, political resistance, and social stigma. By examining key moments of change, grassroots organizing, and the evolving relationship between local identities and global solidarity, we gain a deeper understanding of both the victories achieved and the obstacles that remain in the worldwide struggle for LGBTQ+ equality.

2.1 Cultural Contexts – Defining the Terms of the Fight:

In many parts of the world, LGBTQ+ identities are not simply misunderstood, they are viewed as foreign, threatening, or immoral. This belief is often rooted in colonial-era laws, conservative religious doctrines, and nationalist ideologies. In countries like Nigeria or Saudi Arabia, same-sex relationships are criminalized and queer identities are erased, or demonized. Activists in these regions must navigate both legal danger and cultural hostility. However, cultural reclamation is emerging as a powerful tool of resistance. In India, the recognition of hijras, a traditional third-gender identity, helped shift public understanding leading up to the 2018 decriminalization of same-sex relations. In pre-colonial Africa and the Americas, gender fluidity and same-sex relationships existed within many Indigenous communities, providing a historical foundation for reclaiming LGBTQ+ existence as locally rooted, not externally imposed. These culturally anchored narratives allow activists to challenge erasure while rooting advocacy in familiar, respected traditions.

2.2 Grassroots Activism – The Heart of the Movement:

LGBTQ+ progress is rarely handed down from above, it is built from the ground up. Grassroots activists play a vital role in sustaining local momentum, especially in regions with limited legal protection or severe repression. In places like Uganda or Chechnya, activists risk imprisonment, violence, and exile. Their work often takes the form of underground shelters, clandestine support networks, or mobile clinics that serve those rejected by public institutions.

In countries with greater legal freedom, grassroots efforts have blossomed into vibrant public expressions. Pride parades in cities like Taipei, Buenos Aires, and Cape Town are both celebration and protest, acts of joyful resistance that reclaim public space and demand inclusion. These efforts foster visibility and normalize queer presence in societies where silence was once the norm. Whether covert or loud, these movements channel the courage of individuals into collective action that transforms communities.

2.3 Key Moments of Change – Legal and Social Milestones:

While progress is uneven, key legal and social victories have energized LGBTQ+ communities and set important precedents. The Netherlands' legalization of same-sex marriage in 2001 sparked a global wave, followed by countries like Canada, Spain, and, more recently, Taiwan and Chile. In South Africa, the constitutional protection of sexual orientation marked a groundbreaking achievement on a continent still grappling with widespread anti-LGBTQ+ laws.

Yet legal progress does not always guarantee safety or acceptance. Brazil and Poland, for example, have experienced both legislative wins and violent backlash fuelled by populist rhetoric. Laws may change faster than cultural attitudes, and many LGBTQ+ individuals find themselves caught between symbolic victories and lived realities. This tension reminds us that progress must be measured not only by policy, but by the ability of people to live freely and safely.

2.4 The Power of Collective Resistance and Global Solidarity:

Despite cultural differences, LGBTQ+ movements around the world are united by shared goals and increasingly, by shared resources and support. Social media and digital platforms have allowed activists to connect, learn from one another, and amplify local struggles to international audiences. Hashtags like #LoveWins or #QueerJoy resonate across languages, building momentum and unity. International solidarity has saved lives, particularly when local activists face danger. Foreign embassies, international NGOs, and human rights watchdogs have pressured governments, funded safe houses, and advocated for asylum.

Still, it's essential that such interventions centre the voices and strategies of local organizers. Global alliances work best when they empower, not overshadow. The most enduring victories are those rooted in local context and led by those most affected.

2.5 Conclusion – Rising Together Across Divides:

LGBTQ+ movements around the world reflect both astonishing bravery and unwavering hope. Whether in the face of oppressive regimes or within liberal democracies still grappling with inequality, activists continue to imagine and demand a more just world. Each protest, court case, community center and conversation, is a thread in the global fabric of queer resistance. Reflecting on these stories, it becomes clear that the fight for LGBTQ+ rights is not just legal or political, it is deeply personal. It is about the right to exist, to love, and to belong. From remote villages to global capitals, queer people are transforming the world through resilience and radical care. The path is not linear, but it is forward. As these movements continue to rise, they bring with them not only change, but also the possibility of a more inclusive, compassionate future for all.

3. The Role of International Advocacy in Securing LGBTQ+ Rights

International advocacy plays a pivotal role in influencing how governments treat their LGBTQ+ citizens. When local movements face repression, visibility on the global stage becomes not just symbolic, but strategically vital. Governments that rely on international aid, trade partnerships, or diplomatic favour often respond, directly or indirectly, to global scrutiny. When LGBTQ+ activists are imprisoned, silenced, or threatened, international voices can amplify their plight, creating a pressure point for change. Campaigns from Amnesty International, Human Rights Watch, and United Nations bodies have drawn attention to abuses and provided activists with a shield of visibility. In some cases, the threat of sanctions or the promise of inclusion in human rights-oriented trade agreements has prompted legal shifts, even in countries with long-standing homophobic laws. These instances showcase how global attention can offer protective leverage while simultaneously encouraging progress.

3.1 Human Rights Frameworks and Legal Instruments:

One of the most significant tools available to LGBTQ+ advocates is the international human rights framework. Declarations and covenants, like the Universal Declaration of Human Rights, the International Covenant on Civil and Political Rights, and the Yogyakarta Principles, provide a language of equality that transcends national laws. Though these documents are not always legally binding, they set a powerful precedent that many governments strive to meet, at least in principle. LGBTQ+ organizations often cite these instruments in legal cases, in reports to human rights bodies, or during diplomatic appeals. For example, strategic litigation efforts, backed by international law, have helped overturn anti-sodomy laws or introduce anti-discrimination protections in several countries. Moreover, United Nations agencies like UNDP and OHCHR have developed LGBTQ+-specific programming and guidance, further institutionalizing the cause on a global level.

3.2 Transnational Collaboration and Grassroots Empowerment:

At the heart of global advocacy is collaboration across transnational networks of activists, scholars, and organizations.

These alliances do not simply export a Western model of LGBTQ+ rights, but co-create pathways that are locally informed and culturally relevant. Regional groups such as ILGA Asia, Pan Africa ILGA, and Latin America's RedLacTrans, provide platforms for regional coordination, while maintaining autonomy from global power structures. This peer-based model empowers local movements, helping them to access legal support, secure funding, and learn from others' experiences, without compromising cultural nuance or political sovereignty. Rather than acting as saviours, international allies act as connectors, linking movements together in solidarity.

3.3 Digital Platforms and the Expansion of Global Advocacy:

The rise of digital technology has amplified international LGBTQ+ advocacy in unprecedented ways. Online platforms offer a means of storytelling, mobilization, and alliance-building that is fast, global, and difficult to suppress. Hashtags, virtual protests, and social media campaigns have drawn attention to everything from state-sponsored violence to pride parade bans. Digital advocacy has also allowed diaspora communities to participate in and support, struggles back home, creating a web of engaged, transnational activists. Furthermore, crowdfunding platforms have democratized fundraising for legal battles, mutual aid, and community projects. Though digital surveillance and online harassment remain major threats, especially in authoritarian contexts, the internet has reshaped how global queer advocacy is organized and sustained.

3.4 The Power of Cultural Diplomacy and Visibility:

While policy and legal reform are vital, cultural diplomacy, through film, literature, art, and education, can be equally transformative. International LGBTQ+ film festivals, museum exhibitions and global Pride events, offer not only visibility, but legitimacy to queer identities worldwide. Cultural exchange programs and international artist residencies have brought queer voices into conversations previously dominated by the cis-heteronormative mainstream. This soft power can slowly shift societal perceptions, paving the way for harder legal change. For instance, documentaries that expose systemic abuses or celebrate queer joy have sparked conversation and empathy across borders. Queer cultural ambassadors humanize the movement, showing LGBTQ+ people not as abstract identities, but as artists, creators, educators and leaders. These connections help forge empathy and counteract the dehumanization that often fuels discrimination.

3.5 Challenges and Ethical Considerations in International Advocacy:

Despite its many strengths, international LGBTQ+ advocacy must tread carefully. Imposing external frameworks or overlooking local voices can replicate colonial dynamics or worsen backlash. Advocacy must be intersectional, locally informed, and community-led. Allies from abroad should focus on listening, resourcing, and amplifying, rather than dominating the narrative. In some cases, global attention can make activists more vulnerable to state retaliation, which calls for careful, consent-based engagement. Additionally, the needs of queer people in Global South countries are not monolithic, they vary by region, class, gender identity, religion and ethnicity. Effective advocacy requires nuance, humility and partnership, not just good intentions.

3.6 Looking Ahead – The Future of Global LGBTQ+ Advocacy:

As the global landscape continues to shift, so too will the strategies and coalitions of LGBTQ+ advocates. Climate migration, authoritarian resurgence, and technological change, will shape new terrains of struggle and opportunity. The continued rise of queer youth leadership, intergenerational collaboration and intersectional activism, will fuel future victories. Institutions like the UN, while slow and imperfect, are increasingly pressured to include LGBTQ+ concerns as central to broader human rights frameworks. New forms of funding, storytelling, and organizing will emerge, rooted in collective care and radical imagination. The movement toward global LGBTQ+ equality is neither linear nor finished, but its strength lies in its adaptability, diversity, and unwavering vision for justice.

4. Solidarity Across Borders – Building Global LGBTQ+ Unity

The power of solidarity within the LGBTQ+ community transcends national borders, demonstrating the strength of collective action in the fight for equality and justice. Across the world, the struggles of queer individuals, while shaped by distinct cultural, political and social landscapes, are fundamentally connected by the shared experience of marginalization. Global solidarity has emerged as a key force in amplifying the voices of those fighting for their rights, offering a profound sense of community that enables both local and international advocacy to thrive. By coming together, LGBTQ+ activists from different corners of the globe are transforming the global landscape, sharing resources and creating pathways for mutual support. This unity shows that true progress is only possible when the LGBTQ+ community stands together globally.

4.1 Transnational Movements – Strength in Unity:

The concept of transnational movements within the LGBTQ+ community has grown in recent years, recognizing that the struggles faced by queer individuals are not isolated to any single nation. These movements have evolved into expansive, cross-border efforts that highlight the universal need for LGBTQ+ rights and recognition. Central to this idea is the recognition that no nation's struggles are entirely separate from those of others. The global LGBTQ+ community increasingly recognizes its interconnectedness, with victories in one country inspiring and empowering activists worldwide. For example, the global visibility of the marriage equality movement, which saw significant success in countries like the United States, Canada, and many European nations, provided a platform for LGBTQ+ activists in other regions to demand similar rights. Through transnational organizing, activists have forged bonds that facilitate the exchange of strategies, insights, and solidarity across borders.

4.2 International Collaborations – Creating a Web of Support:

Collaboration between LGBTQ+ activists in different countries is vital in sustaining momentum for global progress. International partnerships have allowed marginalized communities to access broader support networks and resources that might otherwise be unavailable.

Such collaborations include everything from sharing knowledge on legal strategies to organizing global events that raise awareness for issues that affect LGBTQ+ individuals worldwide. For example, the International Lesbian, Gay, Bisexual, Trans and Intersex Association (ILGA), plays a crucial role in linking LGBTQ+ organizations from every continent, supporting the sharing of resources and providing a platform for collective action. Whether through international conferences, online forums, or joint advocacy campaigns, these partnerships create a support structure that strengthens the global movement.

4.3 Uniting Diverse Voices – Embracing Intersectionality in Global Advocacy:

One of the most transformative aspects of global LGBTQ+ solidarity is the recognition of intersectionality, understanding how different forms of oppression overlap and influence one another. Activists from a wide range of backgrounds, including different races, ethnicities, genders, and socioeconomic statuses, bring valuable perspectives that enrich global LGBTQ+ advocacy. By embracing intersectionality, the LGBTQ+ movement can build a more inclusive framework that recognizes and addresses the unique needs of various groups within the queer community. This approach helps prevent the exclusion of marginalized voices, ensuring that LGBTQ+ advocacy is not just for a narrow segment of the community, but rather for all queer individuals, regardless of their circumstances. For example, activists from the Global South have highlighted the specific challenges faced by LGBTQ+ individuals in regions where colonial-era laws continue to criminalize same-sex relationships. By amplifying these voices, the global movement can advocate for change that accounts for both local realities and global standards of human rights.

4.4 The Role of Global Pride Events in Fostering Solidarity:

Global Pride events play a pivotal role in creating visibility and fostering solidarity within the LGBTQ+ community. These events bring together queer individuals from around the world to celebrate their identities, highlight the ongoing struggles for equality, and advocate for policy changes at both national and international levels. Not only do they create an atmosphere of unity and joy, but they also offer a platform for marginalized voices to be heard. While Pride events began as local demonstrations in cities like New York and London, they have since expanded into international gatherings that showcase the global nature of LGBTQ+ struggles. These celebrations serve as reminders of the power of collective action, offering opportunities for communities to come together, share experiences and forge lasting alliances. In this sense, global Pride events are not just about celebration, they are critical moments for reflection, dialogue, and strategizing about the path forward, for the global LGBTQ+ movement.

4.5 Challenges and Opportunities in Maintaining Global Solidarity:

While global LGBTQ+ solidarity is a powerful force, maintaining this unity across borders comes with its own set of challenges. Cultural differences, differing legal frameworks and divergent levels of societal acceptance, can create tensions within the movement, making it difficult to agree on common goals and strategies.

Additionally, in some regions, LGBTQ+ activists risk severe consequences for their advocacy, including imprisonment, violence, or even death. In such contexts, the role of international allies is crucial in offering support, providing resources, and ensuring the safety of local activists. Nevertheless, these challenges also present opportunities for the movement to grow stronger and more resilient. By acknowledging the diversity within the global LGBTQ+ community and working to address the specific needs of different groups, the movement can build a more inclusive and robust platform for change.

4.6 A Vision for the Future – Strengthening Global LGBTQ+ Unity:

As the global LGBTQ+ rights movement continues to evolve, the importance of cross-border solidarity will only increase. The future of LGBTQ+ activism depends on our ability to strengthen global partnerships, embrace the intersectional nature of the movement, and continue to amplify marginalized voices. A united global LGBTQ+ community can serve as a beacon of hope for those still struggling for basic rights, offering a roadmap for justice and equality that transcends national borders. In this shared vision, every victory, no matter how small, becomes a step toward a more just and inclusive world, where the LGBTQ+ community, in all its diversity, can thrive without fear of discrimination, violence, or persecution.

The journey ahead is filled with both challenges and immense potential, but with solidarity as the foundation, the global LGBTQ+ movement will continue to grow stronger, more inclusive, and more capable of achieving lasting change. As we build on the momentum of past victories and embrace new partnerships, the dream of a world where LGBTQ+ individuals are fully recognized, protected, and celebrated will become an ever-closer reality.

5. Progress and Setbacks – The Complex Reality of Global LGBTQ+ Activism

Global LGBTQ+ activism has seen significant progress, but the journey is not without its challenges. Across the world, activists have fought tirelessly for legal reforms, social recognition, and a future free from discrimination. Despite remarkable victories, setbacks such as backlash, rising discrimination, and political hostility continue to threaten the advancements made by LGBTQ+ communities. This reality creates a complex, often painful landscape where progress and resistance exist in tension, yet activism perseveres, driven by resilience and hope. Despite the challenges, the unwavering commitment of LGBTQ+ activists remains a beacon of hope, showing that change is possible. Their resilience drives the movement forward, reminding us that the fight for equality will persist as long as there is determination to overcome obstacles.

5.1 The Winds of Change – Victories in LGBTQ+ Rights:

In many regions, LGBTQ+ activists have made profound strides in challenging discriminatory laws and gaining societal acceptance. Legal victories such as the decriminalization of homosexuality in several countries and the recognition of same-sex marriage in others stand as monumental markers in the fight for equality.

These victories, though hard-won, reflect the collective power of LGBTQ+ individuals and their allies, as well as the changing perceptions of LGBTQ+ identities globally. Overcoming the stigma surrounding queerness in public and legal spheres has been a transformative achievement, opening the door for greater societal inclusion. These breakthroughs remind us that progress is possible when courage, community, and advocacy come together to demand change.

5.2 Backlash and Political Hostility – The Dark Side of Progress:

However, progress often comes with a cost. In many parts of the world, the LGBTQ+ movement faces significant pushback from conservative political forces, religious groups, and reactionary social movements. Rising political hostility, anti-LGBTQ+ legislation and violence against queer individuals, are unsettling reminders that equality is still an uphill battle. The rollback of rights in countries like Hungary, Poland, and Russia, where anti-gay laws and rhetoric have gained ground, demonstrates how fragile progress can be. These setbacks are not just a challenge to legal gains, but also a harsh reminder of the cultural and political divides that persist. Each backlash serves as a call to vigilance and solidarity, reminding us that progress must be actively defended, not passively assumed, because without sustained resistance, hard-won rights can be swiftly undone.

5.3 Rising Discrimination – The Silent Epidemic:

Beyond legal and political opposition, rising discrimination against LGBTQ+ individuals is a pervasive issue worldwide. In many countries, the normalization of queerphobia through social stigmas and public violence continues to harm LGBTQ+ communities. Reports of hate crimes, discriminatory policies, and exclusionary practices are ever-present reminders that achieving legal equality does not automatically result in social acceptance. LGBTQ+ individuals still face barriers to education, healthcare, employment, and housing issues that remain largely invisible in broader discussions of LGBTQ+ rights. This discrimination often manifests in more subtle ways, such as workplace harassment or bullying in schools, which continues to chip away at the quality of life for many in the community. These everyday injustices form an undercurrent of harm, proving that true equality must go beyond legal frameworks and into lived experience.

5.4 Resilience in the Face of Setbacks – Activism as a Lifeline:

Despite these setbacks, LGBTQ+ activists have shown incredible resilience. In the face of rising hostility and discrimination, queer activists continue to push forward, forming powerful coalitions, amplifying marginalized voices and striving for tangible change. From grassroots organizations to international movements, activists are tirelessly working to ensure that the LGBTQ+ community remains visible, empowered, and united. The strength to keep fighting, even when progress is slow or setbacks seem insurmountable, speaks to the deep-rooted desire for a future where LGBTQ+ individuals can live freely and authentically. Whether through community organizing, policy advocacy, or creating safe spaces, LGBTQ+ activists refuse to let the struggle for equality be extinguished. In every act of resistance, queer activism keeps hope alive, fuelling a movement that refuses to be silenced, retreat, or surrender in the face of adversity.

5.5 The Emotional Toll – Personal and Collective Struggles:

While activism is empowering, the emotional toll it takes on those involved cannot be ignored. LGBTQ+ activists often face personal threats, violence, and the trauma of navigating systems designed to marginalize them. The emotional labour of fighting for justice, sometimes for decades, can be exhausting. For many, the journey is also deeply personal, as they are not only advocating for the rights of others, but for their own dignity and survival. The resilience that fuels activism also carries the weight of emotional and psychological scars, making it essential to support activists' mental health as they continue their work. Recognizing and addressing this emotional burden is not just an act of care, it's a necessary step in sustaining the movement and ensuring that those on the frontlines are not left behind in the fight they lead.

5.6 The Path Forward – Hope Amidst Setbacks:

Though setbacks continue to challenge the LGBTQ+ movement, there is a clear path forward, rooted in hope, resilience, and unity. As more individuals join the fight, as allies grow in number and strength, the future holds promise. Legal victories, while fragile, offer a glimmer of what is possible when the world unites in support of LGBTQ+ rights. The continued fight for equality, especially in countries with regressive policies, remains a priority for activists worldwide. What is evident is that even in the face of adversity, the LGBTQ+ community will continue to push for a more just and inclusive world. Sustaining this momentum will require not only courage and collaboration but also the unwavering belief that every effort, no matter how small, brings us closer to lasting change.

5.7 Conclusion – The Ongoing Struggle:

The struggle for LGBTQ+ equality is a complex journey marked by both progress and setbacks. Though the road is often filled with obstacles, the resilience of activists continues to inspire, as their determination to overcome challenges reflects the unyielding spirit of the LGBTQ+ community. As the fight continues, so too does the hope that one day, LGBTQ+ individuals will no longer face persecution, violence, or discrimination based on their identities, and the dream of a truly inclusive world will be realized. This struggle is not just for rights, but for the dignity, safety, and freedom of future generations, ensuring that one day, every LGBTQ+ person can live without fear or limitation.

* Then vs. Now – Tracking the Global Evolution of LGBTQ+ Rights:

These comparisons illustrate how far LGBTQ+ rights have come and how far we still have to go, but they also serve as a snapshot in time, a reminder that the landscape of queer rights is ever-evolving. As global attitudes shift and new challenges emerge, today's milestones and disparities may look very different in the years to come, reflecting both the resilience of queer communities and the ongoing evolution of international advocacy.

"The fight for LGBTQ+ rights is not a static achievement but a living, evolving journey, each step forward reshaping the future we dream of." – Anonymous

***Then vs. Now – The Global Footprint of LGBTQ+ Activism, but not limited to:**

Country:	Then (Past):	Now (Present):
South Africa	1994 – Apartheid ends, same-sex relationships still face stigma.	2006 – First in Africa to legalize same-sex marriage with constitutional protections.
Brazil	1980s – LGBTQ+ people face violent repression, limited protections.	2019 – Homophobia and transphobia criminalized by Supreme Court.
India	2009 – Section 377 decriminalized, then re-criminalized in 2013.	2018 – Supreme Court permanently strikes down Section 377.
Russia	1993 – Homosexuality decriminalized post-USSR.	2023 – "LGBTQ+ propaganda" laws expanded, underground resistance builds through art and digital activism.
Poland	2010s – LGBTQ+ visibility increases, sparking conservative backlash.	2020s – "LGBT-free zones" condemned globally, activists stage solidarity tours and mobile Pride events.
Taiwan	1990s – No legal protections, homosexuality no longer a mental illness.	2019 – First in Asia to legalize same-sex marriage.
United States	2004 – Constitutional ban on same-sex marriage supported by President Bush.	2015–2022 – Marriage equality legalized, Respect for Marriage Act passed, anti-trans legislation rises.
Uganda	2009 – "Kill the Gays" bill sparks global outrage.	2023 – Passes severe anti-LGBTQ+ law with death penalty, intense international criticism.
Australia	2004 – Marriage Act amended to ban same-sex marriage.	2017 – Postal survey supports equality, marriage legalized.
Philippines	2000s – No national protections, strong religious influence.	2020s – Local ordinances passed, national SOGIE bill still under debate.
Mexico	2000s – Same-sex relationships decriminalized, rights vary by state.	2022 – Marriage equality becomes national law.
Japan	1990s – LGBTQ+ topics taboo, minimal legal visibility.	2023 – Municipal partnerships expand, court challenges raise public awareness.
Kenya	2006 – Homosexuality criminalized, advocacy met with violence.	2023 – Supreme Court upholds LGBTQ+ groups' right to associate.

Country:	Then (Past):	Now (Present):
Turkey	2003 – First Pride march in Istanbul.	2020s – Pride banned, activists arrested, underground organizing persists.
Canada	1996 – Sexual orientation added to Human Rights Act.	2021 – Conversion therapy banned nationwide.
China	2001 – Homosexuality removed from mental illness list.	2023 – LGBTQ+ events banned, online communities heavily monitored.
Germany	2001 – Civil unions introduced.	2017 – Marriage equality passed, youth and trans protections expanded.
Indonesia	2010s – LGBTQ+ targeted under Sharia-influenced laws.	2022 – New criminal code restricts sexual freedom, LGBTQ+ community disproportionately impacted.
Israel	1990s – Recognizes same-sex couples for tax/social benefits.	2023 – Continues to allow adoption and partnerships, full marriage rights debated.
Nigeria	2006 – Harsh laws criminalize LGBTQ+ identity and association.	2020s – Laws persist, youth resistance through art, music and social media continues.
Thailand	Early 2000s – Gender diversity gains cultural acceptance but limited legal recognition.	2024 – Civil Partnership Bill passed, legalizing same-sex unions.
Jamaica	2006 – Known for anti-gay violence and colonial-era sodomy laws.	2023 – Sodomy laws remain, grassroots groups like J-FLAG advance visibility and public education.
Samoa	Pre-2010 – Homosexuality criminalized, fa'afafine culture exists informally.	2020s – Fa'afafine/fa'afatama leaders gain legal and cultural visibility.
Eswatini	2000s – LGBTQ+ life underground, criminalized and stigmatized.	2023 – Legal battles emerge to register organizations, regional solidarity boosts visibility.
Belgium	2003 – Second country globally to legalize same-sex marriage.	2023 – Anti-discrimination laws expanded to include gender identity and expression.
Vanuatu	2007 – No legal protection, LGBTQ+ identity taboo.	2023 – Youth-led advocacy joins Pacific Rainbow movements to push for change.
Hungary	2000s – Pride marches held, rights advancing.	2023 – Government rolls back LGBTQ+ rights, civil society pushes back through courts and activism.

Country:	Then (Past):	Now (Present):
Botswana	2010 – Homosexuality criminalized.	2019 to 2021 – High Court decriminalizes and upholds ruling, landmark legal win for LGBTQ+ Africa.

*What Kind of Progress Does "Then vs. Now" Capture?

➢ **Legal Reforms:**

This includes the decriminalization of same-sex relationships, legalization of same-sex marriage, recognition of gender identity, and anti-discrimination laws. These moments show tangible changes in how governments recognize and protect LGBTQ+ individuals.

➢ **Policy Advancements:**

Beyond laws, many countries have adopted policies that offer healthcare protections, allow for gender marker changes, or introduce civil partnership laws. These reflect a shift in administrative support and institutional recognition.

➢ **Social Visibility & Cultural Change:**

Some of the progress isn't legislative, it's cultural. The emergence of Pride events, the inclusion of LGBTQ+ stories in mainstream media, and increased public acceptance mark a growing visibility and societal shift, even in countries without legal reform.

➢ **International Solidarity & Regional Advocacy:**

Global coalitions, court rulings, and transnational advocacy have led to progress in places where local change was slow. This progress is collective, powered by connection across borders.

➢ **Activist Milestones and Movement Growth:**

The growth of grassroots organizations, the legal recognition of LGBTQ+ NGOs in previously restrictive countries, and the emergence of local Pride movements are all milestones that reflect how LGBTQ+ communities are organizing, surviving, and thriving.

Chapter 13

The Financial Realities of LGBTQ+ Life

1. The Wealth Gap in the Queer Community

While LGBTQ+ people exist across all economic classes, research consistently shows that queer individuals, especially transgender people, queer people of colour and youth, face disproportionate economic hardship. This disparity is not incidental, but deeply systemic, shaped by centuries of entrenched discrimination across education, housing, employment, healthcare, legal systems, and family recognition, all of which have historically excluded and marginalized LGBTQ+ individuals. From being kicked out of their homes to being passed over for promotions, queer individuals encounter financial exclusion at multiple stages of life. These barriers often compound one another, creating a persistent wealth gap that cannot be addressed without naming its root causes.

1.1 Historical and Structural Roots of Economic Marginalization:

The queer wealth gap didn't emerge in a vacuum. Historically, laws criminalized queerness outright, making it impossible for many LGBTQ+ people to earn an income openly or build intergenerational wealth. Even after legal protections were introduced in some parts of the world, systemic discrimination persisted. Inheritance laws, access to marital benefits, joint taxation, and employment protections were not always inclusive. For transgender individuals, these barriers were even more acute, legal name changes, gender marker amendments, and healthcare costs often placed an economic burden on individuals already pushed to society's margins. These structural factors not only delayed or denied financial security, but also normalized economic precarity as a queer condition. As a result, the legacy of these historical and structural inequalities continues to shape the economic realities of LGBTQ+ individuals today, perpetuating cycles of financial instability.

1.2 Employment Discrimination – Still a Reality:

Despite some legal progress, workplace discrimination remains a key contributor to the queer wealth gap. In many countries, there are no federal protections preventing employers from firing someone based on their gender identity or sexual orientation. Even in places with legal safeguards, implicit bias plays a powerful role. LGBTQ+ individuals often report being paid less than their straight counterparts, being passed over for leadership roles, or enduring hostile work environments. For those whose gender expression or identity does not conform to societal norms, such as visibly trans or nonbinary individuals, securing and retaining employment can be especially difficult. This contributes not only to higher unemployment and underemployment rates, but also to long-term income instability. This persistent marginalization in the labour market reinforces economic vulnerability across queer communities, making financial security an elusive goal for many LGBTQ+ individuals.

1.3 Housing Insecurity and Homelessness:

Housing is a foundational pillar of wealth, and LGBTQ+ people are disproportionately likely to lack stable, safe, and affordable housing. Queer youth are overrepresented in homeless populations, often due to familial rejection. Even for adults, discrimination in the rental and housing markets, whether overt or subtle, makes it harder to secure long-term housing. This has lifelong consequences, without access to safe housing, it's more difficult to maintain a job, pursue education, or build assets. Housing insecurity interrupts the very foundation upon which wealth is built and sustained. As a result, the cycle of displacement and economic instability continues, deepening the wealth divide and leaving many LGBTQ+ individuals without the structural opportunities to achieve long-term financial growth.

1.4 Healthcare Costs and Access:

Medical expenses represent a massive and often overlooked burden within the queer wealth gap. LGBTQ+ individuals, particularly trans people, frequently face high out-of-pocket costs for affirming healthcare. In countries where healthcare isn't universally accessible, insurance denial, medical bias and discriminatory exclusions, leave many queer people without proper coverage. Mental health care, often critical due to the emotional toll of marginalization, is another out-of-pocket expense. These healthcare needs are not luxuries, but survival essentials, and the financial burden of meeting them can be destabilizing. This economic strain not only drains immediate resources, but also prevents the accumulation of savings and wealth, forcing many LGBTQ+ individuals to choose between financial stability and essential, life-affirming care.

1.5 Intergenerational Wealth and the Myth of the "DINK" Lifestyle:

There's a persistent stereotype that queer people, especially gay men, are financially well-off, because they don't have children. The reality is much more complex. Many LGBTQ+ people are excluded from family wealth, either due to familial rejection or the absence of inheritance rights in queer relationships. This exclusion means they often start adult life without a safety net, savings, or property. Those who do become parents frequently face additional hurdles in the form of adoption fees, fertility treatments, legal fees for co-parent recognition, and the lack of paid parental leave. The double income, no kids (DINK) myth obscures the very real economic vulnerabilities queer people face. This myth not only perpetuates a false narrative about queer financial stability, but also distracts from the very real economic struggles many LGBTQ+ individuals face in building long-term wealth.

1.6 Race, Gender, and Compounding Inequalities:

The queer wealth gap cannot be separated from the intersections of race, gender and class. Queer people of colour are more likely to face employment discrimination, police violence and generational poverty, than their white counterparts. Black trans women, in particular, sit at one of the most marginalized intersections, experiencing both racism and transmisogyny that result in extremely high rates of unemployment, housing insecurity, and poverty. An intersectional analysis makes it clear, the queer wealth gap, is not evenly distributed and any solutions must address this layered injustice.

1.7 Community Resilience and Economic Resistance:

Despite these challenges, queer communities have a long and resilient legacy of grassroots mutual aid, creative entrepreneurship, and bold economic resistance in the face of systemic exclusion. From underground economies to queer-owned businesses, these networks often provide critical lifelines. Crowdfunding, cooperative housing and alternative labour networks, such as sex work, have allowed queer people to support one another when traditional systems failed them. However, resilience should not be mistaken for equity. Mutual aid is a temporary support, not a replacement for structural reform. While these acts of economic resistance highlight the strength of queer communities, they also underscore the urgent need for systemic change to ensure lasting equity.

1.8 The Path Forward – Policy, Advocacy and Structural Change:

Closing the queer wealth gap will require more than visibility, it demands policy. Legal protections must be universal, not patchwork. This includes robust anti-discrimination laws, gender-affirming healthcare access, housing protections, and educational equity. Tax codes and financial systems must also evolve to recognize queer family structures and caregiving roles. But beyond legal reform, there must be a shift in societal values, a move away from heteronormative financial assumptions and toward inclusive economic justice. Advocacy must centre the most marginalized and ensure queer voices are leading the fight for financial equity.

2. LGBTQ+ Retirement Planning and Financial Security

Retirement planning is a critical aspect of long-term well-being, but for LGBTQ+ individuals, the road to financial security can be uniquely complicated. Historical discrimination in employment, marriage, healthcare and legal recognition, has left many queer elders with limited access to traditional safety nets like pensions, spousal benefits, or homeownership. Though progress has been made in securing equal rights in many regions, these systemic disadvantages often accumulate over a lifetime, making retirement planning all the more essential and urgent for LGBTQ+ individuals today. Understanding this historical context can help shape better strategies for securing a comfortable and dignified retirement.

2.1 Marriage Equality and Its Financial Implications:

For many years, same-sex couples were denied the financial benefits afforded to married heterosexual couples, including spousal Social Security benefits, joint tax filing, and shared healthcare plans. While marriage equality is now recognized in many countries, older LGBTQ+ individuals may still feel the economic ripple effects of having lived much of their lives without those protections. It's important to review legal rights and financial benefits now available, particularly for couples who married later in life or remained unmarried due to fear or legal barriers. Working with an LGBTQ+-affirming financial advisor can help couples understand how to maximize benefits like survivor pensions and joint retirement accounts. This review can also uncover opportunities to optimize tax strategies and ensure a more secure financial future in retirement.

2.2 Income Gaps and Their Long-Term Consequences:

Income inequality across a lifetime directly affects retirement savings. Studies show that LGBTQ+ individuals, especially women, trans people, and people of colour, earn less than their cisgender heterosexual counterparts. This disparity often results in smaller 401(k) balances, limited and inconsistent contributions to IRAs, or delayed and disrupted participation in employer-sponsored retirement plans, ultimately leading to a less secure financial future in later life. One practical step is to assess and optimize contributions now. Automating savings, using catch-up contributions if over 50, and taking advantage of employer matches when available can make a meaningful difference. Being aware of how income disparities shape financial futures can empower individuals to take more strategic, informed action.

2.3 Healthcare Costs in Retirement:

Healthcare is a major expense for retirees, and for LGBTQ+ individuals, it often includes additional needs such as gender-affirming care, HIV medications, or mental health services. Planning ahead for these costs is vital. If living in a country without universal healthcare, consider Health Savings Accounts (HSAs) or long-term care insurance as part of your retirement strategy. It's also important to choose healthcare providers and retirement communities that are LGBTQ+-inclusive to avoid discriminatory environments that could impact both care quality and mental well-being. Healthcare planning should not be an afterthought, it should be central to any long-term financial strategy.

2.4 Choosing Where and How to Retire:

Location plays a pivotal role in financial security and quality of life during retirement. For LGBTQ+ retirees, this means considering not only the cost of living, but also the social climate, legal protections, and healthcare access in a given area. Some cities and countries are more LGBTQ+-friendly and offer better public support services, while others may still foster stigma or lack basic non-discrimination laws. Researching safe and affirming retirement destinations can help individuals make decisions that support both financial stability and personal safety. Additionally, co-housing models and LGBTQ+ retirement communities are growing in popularity, providing both economic advantages and social support.

2.5 Legal Protections and Estate Planning:

Estate planning is another essential component of financial security, especially for queer individuals who may not have traditional family structures. Wills, powers of attorney, healthcare proxies, and living wills, should be created and updated regularly. These documents ensure that a trusted person, not necessarily a biological relative, has the authority to make decisions on your behalf. It's also important to designate beneficiaries for retirement accounts and insurance policies to avoid legal complications. Working with LGBTQ+-competent legal professionals can help ensure that all documents are legally sound and reflect your wishes. By taking these steps, queer individuals can protect their autonomy and ensure that their financial and healthcare wishes are honoured, regardless of their familial status.

2.6 Social Security and Pension Navigation:

Navigating Social Security and pension benefits can be confusing, especially for LGBTQ+ retirees who've faced decades of evolving legal recognition. Individuals who were previously in unrecognized relationships may not realize they're now eligible for spousal or survivor benefits. Reviewing personal records and speaking with a financial planner or Social Security representative can reveal new opportunities for income. Additionally, those who have changed their legal gender marker should check their Social Security records for accuracy, as this can affect eligibility and documentation requirements.

2.7 Building Community-Based Support Systems:

Financial security isn't just about money, it's also about support. Many queer elders face isolation, especially those estranged from families or living in less-affirming communities. Building community-based support networks, including chosen families, can mitigate risks associated with aging alone. Participating in LGBTQ+ aging organizations, joining cooperative housing groups, or even forming mutual aid collectives can provide both emotional and financial support. Planning for retirement should include not just where you'll live, but who you'll be surrounded by and how you'll stay connected.

2.8 Facing the Future with Intention and Confidence:

The path to a secure retirement may look different for LGBTQ+ individuals, but it is absolutely achievable with intentional planning and informed decision-making. While systemic inequities have created real obstacles, they also highlight the importance of being proactive and well-informed. Whether you're decades away from retirement or approaching it soon, it's never too late to begin or revise your financial strategy. By understanding your unique needs, leveraging available resources, and seeking affirming professional guidance, you can build a future rooted in dignity, independence, and pride.

*Global Guide to LGBTQ+ Friendly Financial Advisors and Resources:

United States:

Quiet Wealth (USA, Virtual):

- Founded by Lindsey Young, a transgender Harvard MBA and CFP®, Quiet Wealth specializes in comprehensive financial planning for high-achieving LGBTQ+ professionals and business owners.
- Services include retirement planning, tax strategies, estate planning, and investment management.

Equalis Financial (USA, Virtual):

- Led by Leighann Miko, CFP® (she/her), Equalis Financial provides financial life planning and responsible investment management tailored to LGBTQ+ creatives and professionals.
- Services encompass financial planning, socially conscious investment strategies, and business management.
- Operates virtually, serving clients regardless of location.

Young & Scrappy (USA, Virtual):

- An anti-capitalist, fee-only financial planning firm founded by LGBTQ+ and BIPOC professionals.
- Offers financial coaching, investment management, and planning services, with a focus on inclusivity and accessibility.
- Provides virtual services to clients worldwide.

Horizons Foundation – Professional Advisors Directory (USA):

- A directory of LGBTQ+-affirming financial professionals, including planners, tax advisors, and estate planners.
- While based in the U.S., many listed professionals offer virtual consultations.

South Africa:

National Gay and Lesbian Chamber of Commerce (NGLCC):

- Although primarily based in the U.S., the NGLCC's international affiliates may offer connections to LGBTQ+-friendly financial professionals.

Local LGBTQ+ Organizations:

- Reach out to South African LGBTQ+ advocacy groups such as OUT LGBT Well-being or Triangle Project for potential referrals to inclusive financial advisors. These organizations not only provide resources, but also offer support networks that can help navigate the unique financial challenges faced by queer individuals, ensuring access to trusted services and community-driven solutions.

Online Directories:

- Use platforms like XY Planning Network or CFP Board's Find a CFP® Professional to search for advisors who specialize in serving LGBTQ+ clients and offer virtual services.

United Kingdom:

Stonewall:

- A UK-based LGBTQ+ rights organization that may offer resources or referrals to inclusive financial advisors.

The Diversity Trust (UK):

- Offers training and consulting services, with a focus on financial inclusion for LGBTQ+ individuals.

Canada:

Pride at Work Canada:

- Focuses on workplace inclusion and may have partnerships or resources related to financial planning for LGBTQ+ individuals.

Rainbow Health Ontario:

- Provides training and resources to improve the health and well-being of LGBTQ+ communities, which may include financial wellness programs.

Australia:

Pride in Diversity:

- An Australian not-for-profit employer support program for LGBTQ+ workplace inclusion, which may have connections to inclusive financial advisors.

Thorne Harbour Health:

- Offers health and well-being services to LGBTQ+ communities, potentially including financial counselling resources.

Germany:

LSVD (Lesben- und Schwulenverband in Deutschland):

- Germany's largest LGBTQ+ rights organization, which may provide resources or referrals to inclusive financial services.

Schwulenberatung Berlin:

- Schwulenberatung Berlin provides a safe space for financial guidance, ensuring that LGBTQ+ individuals receive advice tailored to their unique needs and circumstances.

India:

Naz Foundation:

- Works on HIV/AIDS and LGBTQ+ rights in India, and may offer resources related to financial planning and inclusion.

Humsafar Trust:

- Provides health and advocacy services for LGBTQ+ communities, which may include financial literacy programs.

AROH Foundation:

- Works to improve financial literacy and inclusion for marginalized groups, including the LGBTQ+ community, offering access to banking, insurance, and digital financial tools.

Asia:

Oreana Private Wealth (Hong Kong):

- Specializes in assisting LGBTQI+ individuals with financial planning, estate management, and legal considerations related to relocation and expatriation.
- Provides support in understanding Hong Kong's legal framework and setting up wills and estate plans.

PRIDENT (Singapore):

- A professional collective offering financial planning, insurance, real estate, and investment advice, tailored for the LGBTQ+ community.
- Organizes educational workshops and fundraising events to benefit LGBTQ+ individuals in Singapore.

LGBT Wealth (Asia):

- A service launched by LGBT Capital and Financial Partners, targeting the LGBTQ+ community in Asia with wealth management solutions.

- Recognizes the significance and size of the LGBTQ+ market in the region.

Africa:

Queer & Allied Chamber of Commerce Africa (QACC Africa):

- Supports queer owned and allied businesses across Africa through investment opportunities, business incubators, and inclusive economic development programs.
- Offers up to USD 35,000 in credit for post-revenue ventures and provides inclusive staff workshops and training.

Latin America:

- Local LGBTQ+ Organizations: Reach out to local LGBTQ+ advocacy groups in countries like Brazil, Argentina, and Mexico, as they may offer resources or referrals to inclusive financial advisors.
- Online Directories: Use platforms like XY Planning Network to search for advisors who specialize in serving LGBTQ+ clients and offer virtual services.

---

*Additional Resources to Consider for LGBTQ+ Financial Planning and Support:

- **Local LGBTQ+ Centers and Organizations:** Reach out to local LGBTQ+ community centers or advocacy groups, as they often have partnerships or can refer you to inclusive financial advisors.
- **Online Forums and Social Media:** Platforms like Reddit, Facebook groups, or LinkedIn can be valuable resources to seek recommendations and reviews for LGBTQ+-friendly financial advisors in specific regions.
- **Professional Associations:** Look for national or regional financial planning associations, as they may have directories or referral services that can help you find advisors who are committed to diversity and inclusion.

---

3. The Cost of Gender-Affirming Care and Family Planning

Gender affirming care and family planning are not luxuries for LGBTQ+ individuals, they are necessities tied to health, identity, dignity, and autonomy. Yet for many queer and trans people, access to these essential services is obstructed by systemic financial barriers.

While the conversation around bodily autonomy and the right to family is gaining visibility, the true costs, financial, emotional, and social, are rarely explored in full. Examining the high financial stakes involved reveals just how inequitable and emotionally taxing these processes can be, particularly when the systems meant to support health and family are inaccessible or discriminatory. What follows is a closer look at the steep costs of affirming care and the unique challenges of building a family in a world not always designed to support LGBTQ+ futures.

3.1 The Financial Landscape of Gender-Affirming Care:

For many trans and nonbinary individuals, gender affirming care includes hormone therapy, surgeries, mental health support, voice therapy, and more. Each of these services can carry a significant price tag, especially when not covered by insurance. Hormone replacement therapy (HRT), for example, may cost anywhere from $30 to $100 per month, depending on the medication and location, with additional expenses for regular blood work and doctor visits. Gender affirming surgeries, such as top surgery or genital reconstruction, can range from $7,000 to well over $100,000, depending on the specific procedure and geographic region.

Even when insurance covers parts of this care, hidden costs remain. These include time off work for recovery, travel to limited providers, and out-of-pocket expenses, due to exclusions or denials from insurers. Mental health evaluations, often mandatory prerequisites for surgical care, can add hundreds or thousands of dollars. For nonbinary individuals, accessing care aligned with their specific needs can be even more challenging and costly due to limited clinical research and rigid binary protocols in the medical field. These cumulative barriers don't just delay care, they compound the emotional and financial toll, making an already vulnerable process even more difficult to navigate.

3.2 Insurance Barriers and Policy Inconsistencies:

Health insurance, or medical aid, depending on the country, though potentially helpful, is far from consistent when it comes to gender affirming care. Policies vary widely by provider, employer, and region, including by state, province, or territory. In some areas, even essential care is deemed "cosmetic" or "elective" and thus excluded. Trans individuals may find themselves having to prove the medical necessity of their treatments repeatedly, often undergoing lengthy appeals processes. Furthermore, even when policies are inclusive, trans people may face systemic discrimination when interacting with insurance representatives or providers unfamiliar with their care needs. Misgendering, denial of claims, and delays in authorizations create additional emotional burdens alongside financial ones. This landscape forces many to pay out of pocket or forgo care altogether, delaying transitions and exacerbating mental health issues.

3.3 Family Planning – Building Families Against the Grain:

For LGBTQ+ individuals and couples, family planning is often a complex, expensive, and emotionally charged endeavour. Unlike many cisgender, heterosexual couples, queer individuals may require assisted reproductive technologies (ART), surrogacy, adoption, or co-parenting arrangements to become parents. Each of these paths comes with its own steep financial and legal hurdles.

For example, sperm donation for lesbian couples can cost anywhere from $300 to $1,000 per vial, plus clinic fees for insemination, which often must be repeated over multiple cycles, depending on the clinic and country. Gay male couples face even more significant expenses, with gestational surrogacy ranging from $100,000 to $150,000 or more, particularly in regions where legal protections for all parties are strongest and the process is highly regulated. Trans people who wish to preserve fertility before transitioning, such as freezing eggs or sperm, face thousands in upfront costs, not including annual storage fees, which also vary depending on the location and facility.

Adoption, often perceived as a more affordable alternative, is also fraught with challenges. LGBTQ+ individuals still face discrimination in adoption agencies in many parts of the world. Even when allowed, the process can cost between $20,000 and $50,000, or more, depending on the country, legal requirements, and agency fees, not including additional legal costs and post-placement requirements. These expenses, layered with legal uncertainties and the emotional labour of navigating biased systems, make family planning a daunting task for many queer individuals.

3.4 Emotional Costs and Financial Trade-offs:

Beyond the tangible expenses, the cost of gender-affirming care and family planning takes a toll on mental health, personal relationships, and long-term financial stability. Many people are forced to choose between care and other life priorities, paying off student loans, pursuing education, saving for a home, or investing in retirement. This creates a sense of delay and deprivation that can compound feelings of alienation and frustration. There is also the cost of waiting. Delaying transition-related care or family-building plans, due to finances, can lead to increased gender dysphoria, depression, and anxiety. The emotional weight of constantly justifying one's needs, to doctors, insurers, and sometimes even family, can erode self-worth. These financial trade-offs often go unspoken, even as they shape the everyday realities of LGBTQ+ lives.

3.5 Toward More Inclusive and Affordable Futures:

Change is possible, and it is already underway in some parts of the world. Advocacy has led to improved insurance coverage, public funding for gender-affirming care, and more inclusive fertility clinics and adoption agencies. Organizations such as the National Center for Transgender Equality, Family Equality, and LGBTQ+-focused grant programs offer resources and financial assistance to those navigating these systems. However, systemic reform remains crucial. Universal health coverage that includes gender-affirming and reproductive care, non-discrimination policies in insurance and adoption, and workplace benefits inclusive of all family structures are steps toward reducing these burdens. Financial institutions and advisors must also be trained to understand LGBTQ+ needs and offer relevant, affirming services.

3.6 Conclusion – Investing in Our Lives and Futures:

Affirming one's gender and building a family should not be acts of financial risk. These are deeply human pursuits, expressions of identity, love, and belonging. The costs, while often overwhelming, are not just numbers on a spreadsheet.

They represent years of dreaming, saving, waiting, and hoping. Addressing the inequities in access to care and family planning requires a collective commitment, from policymakers, healthcare systems, communities, and allies to ensure that all LGBTQ+ people can live and love fully, without paying an unjust price.

4. Economic Disparities in Same-Sex Partnerships and Households

Economic disparities in same-sex partnerships and households are not accidental, they are the product of generations of legal exclusions, systemic social discrimination, and economic neglect. While marriage equality in many countries has ushered in a new era of legal recognition, it has not automatically closed the wealth gap between same-sex and different-sex households. In fact, financial inequality often persists long after visibility is achieved. Understanding these economic challenges requires us to look beyond surface-level statistics and examine the systemic factors that shape financial outcomes in queer lives.

4.1 Historic Economic Exclusion and the Legacy of Legal Discrimination:

Same-sex couples today are still recovering from decades, if not centuries, of exclusion from key financial systems. Before the legalization of same-sex marriage, many couples were denied the right to jointly own property, inherit assets without taxation, or benefit from spousal health insurance. In countries where marriage equality is still not recognized, these denials continue. Even where rights have been granted, the financial harm caused by years of exclusion has created a generational wealth gap that same-sex couples are still working to close. Legal progress cannot retroactively provide the compounded benefits of early investments, inherited wealth, or decades of joint asset-building that many heterosexual couples have long had access to.

4.2 Wage Gaps and Employment Discrimination Within Queer Households:

Same-sex couples frequently face workplace discrimination that directly affects household income. In many regions, LGBTQ+ individuals remain unprotected by anti-discrimination laws, leaving them vulnerable to lower pay, fewer promotions, or job loss. This is particularly acute for transgender and nonbinary individuals, who face some of the highest rates of unemployment and underemployment globally. Research consistently shows that male same-sex couples earn less than heterosexual couples, while female same-sex couples tend to earn even less, reflecting both gender-based pay inequality and sexuality-based discrimination. When both partners face job market biases, the household as a whole suffers a compounded financial impact. This systemic discrimination not only affects immediate earning potential, but also perpetuates long-term financial instability, limiting the ability of same-sex couples to build wealth, secure housing, or plan for the future.

4.3 Tax Codes, Financial Policies, and Structural Inequity:

Despite progress in marriage rights, many tax and financial systems remain structured in ways that disadvantage same-sex couples.

In some countries, queer couples are taxed differently or denied the same deductions and credits available to heterosexual couples. Joint filing benefits can be complex or inaccessible, especially in places where one partner's gender identity or immigration status complicates legal recognition. Pension benefits, survivor benefits and healthcare subsidies, may also be reduced or withheld depending on a couple's documentation and legal status, leaving queer households with fewer safety nets. These disparities are often invisible in mainstream economic discourse, yet they affect long-term financial planning and retirement security. These inequities reinforce financial precarity for same-sex couples, making it more difficult for them to save for retirement, accumulate wealth, or access necessary healthcare and benefits, further entrenching economic disparities within queer households.

4.4 Parenting and the Economics of Queer Family Formation:

Same-sex couples who choose to raise children face unique and often substantial financial challenges. Legal fees for second-parent adoption, surrogacy, or assisted reproductive technology can reach tens or even hundreds of thousands of dollars, as these processes are rarely subsidized or covered by insurance. In contrast to heterosexual couples who can often build families biologically without legal intervention, queer couples are required to formalize their parentage through complex legal means to protect custody and inheritance rights. These added expenses are not simply about the cost of raising a child, they're about the cost of being recognized as a legitimate family. These financial burdens highlight the need for policy reforms that ensure equitable access to family-building resources for queer families.

4.5 Housing Disparities and Mortgage Access for Same-Sex Couples:

Discrimination doesn't end at the workplace, it follows queer couples into the housing market. Studies have shown that same-sex couples are less likely to be approved for mortgages or may be offered higher interest rates despite having comparable financial profiles. In rental markets, queer households report higher levels of housing discrimination, with landlords often using coded language or selective application processes to exclude LGBTQ+ tenants. These barriers limit access to stable housing and homeownership, which are critical components of wealth-building over time. The inability to secure property under equitable terms perpetuates cycles of economic instability for queer families.

4.6 Healthcare Costs and Insurance Gaps:

Healthcare affordability remains a major economic concern for same-sex couples, especially in countries without universal healthcare. Queer individuals are more likely to experience mental health challenges, chronic stress and higher rates of certain illnesses, all of which can increase out-of-pocket medical expenses. If one partner is uninsured or underinsured, the household may bear a disproportionate healthcare burden. Insurance plans that fail to cover gender affirming care, fertility treatments, or partner benefits create an environment where queer couples pay more for less. This economic strain is especially pronounced in aging queer populations, many of whom lack familial support systems due to estrangement or marginalization. This highlights the need for inclusive healthcare policies that better address the unique needs of queer families.

4.7 The Cost of Safety and Mobility:

Living as a visibly queer couple often comes with the hidden cost of safety. In hostile environments, same-sex couples may need to relocate to more inclusive cities or countries, often at great personal and financial expense. This means uprooting careers, selling homes at a loss, or bearing the cost of immigration and resettlement. In extreme cases, queer couples may seek asylum or refugee status, which can result in years of instability, loss of income and economic precarity. The price of physical safety, often taken for granted by heterosexual couples, becomes a persistent and heavy economic burden for many LGBTQ+ households.

4.8 Conclusion – Redefining Economic Equity for Queer Partnerships:

Economic disparities in same-sex partnerships are not just the result of individual hardship, they are embedded in systems that have long excluded, penalized, or overlooked queer lives. Addressing these inequities requires more than symbolic gestures of inclusion. It demands policy reform, legal protections, and structural changes that acknowledge the compounded barriers LGBTQ+ people face in building and sustaining households. Equity begins with recognition, of the past exclusions, the present struggles, and the possibility of a more just economic future for all partnerships, regardless of gender or sexuality.

5. Financial Discrimination – How Credit, Loans, and the Banking Systems Impact LGBTQ+ People

Financial discrimination is a pervasive and often overlooked form of inequality that affects LGBTQ+ individuals. From being denied access to credit to facing higher interest rates, LGBTQ+ people are frequently subjected to prejudiced practices within financial systems that limit their economic mobility. Although there have been strides toward equality in many areas, financial institutions continue to uphold policies and practices that disproportionately affect queer and trans people. This issue requires critical attention, as economic equality is foundational to broader social justice movements. By exploring the barriers LGBTQ+ people face within banking, credit, and lending systems, we can begin to understand the deep, systemic issues that perpetuate financial exclusion.

5.1 Credit Discrimination – How LGBTQ+ People Are Denied Equal Access to Credit:

Credit scores and reports are essential tools in securing loans, mortgages, and other financial services. However, LGBTQ+ individuals often face barriers that others do not. Research has shown that same-sex couples, for example, are more likely to be denied credit or offered less favourable terms than heterosexual couples with similar financial profiles. This can be due to systemic bias, as well as the lack of legal protections for LGBTQ+ people in certain regions. When credit decisions are influenced by personal or social biases rather than objective financial criteria, LGBTQ+ individuals may find themselves in a position of financial disadvantage.

This discrimination is especially detrimental for young queer people trying to establish credit, as well as those seeking to start businesses or purchase homes. Even with the rise of online credit models, the lack of visibility for nonbinary and transgender individuals in credit scoring remains a persistent issue, with these groups often left without an appropriate framework for financial inclusion.

5.2 The Impact of Gender Identity and Sexual Orientation on Loan Approval:

When applying for loans, LGBTQ+ individuals are often subjected to the intersection of both overt and covert biases. Many financial institutions have not yet fully integrated LGBTQ+ inclusivity into their loan approval processes, leaving people vulnerable to rejection based on factors unrelated to their ability to repay a loan. Gender identity can pose a particular challenge, as many loan applications and forms are not designed to recognize nonbinary, transgender, or gender nonconforming individuals. Discrimination also arises when same-sex couples are forced to navigate systems designed with heterosexual, cisgender partnerships in mind. These couples may face challenges in being listed as equal partners on mortgage applications, creating additional financial hurdles. Moreover, in regions where marriage equality has not been fully implemented or recognized, same-sex couples may be denied joint access to loans or other financial services altogether, which limits their ability to invest in homes, businesses, or education. These systemic exclusions not only undermine financial autonomy, but also restrict access to generational wealth-building opportunities, deepening the economic divide experienced by LGBTQ+ individuals and families.

5.3 Discriminatory Banking Practices and LGBTQ+ Financial Barriers:

Banks play a critical role in the financial stability of individuals and households, yet LGBTQ+ people face discrimination within this sector as well. For instance, same-sex couples may be refused access to joint accounts or mortgage accounts, with some banks claiming that their systems do not recognize these relationships. Even in countries with legal protections against discrimination, subtle practices persist that disadvantage queer customers. For example, LGBTQ+ individuals may be charged higher fees for services, or be less likely to receive favourable loan terms compared to their heterosexual counterparts. These discriminatory practices do not just limit individual wealth accumulation, they also prevent LGBTQ+ people from building financial security as a community. Furthermore, the financial services sector has been notably slow to provide specialized products for LGBTQ+ people, such as insurance designed to meet their specific needs, leaving them with fewer options and reduced financial protection.

5.4 Barriers to Wealth Accumulation – How LGBTQ+ People Are Excluded from Traditional Financial Systems:

The challenges LGBTQ+ individuals face within financial systems extend beyond access to credit and loans, they also affect their ability to build long-term wealth. In many places, LGBTQ+ people are denied equal access to the tools that help individuals build assets, such as savings accounts, investments, and retirement plans. Transgender individuals often face financial setbacks from gender-affirming healthcare costs and employment discrimination.

Additionally, the economic exclusion from family wealth-building opportunities, such as inheritance and joint ownership of property, compounds these challenges. While marriage equality has allowed same-sex couples to inherit assets without incurring the same tax burdens as non-married couples, the lingering effects of past discrimination mean that many LGBTQ+ individuals are still starting from a financial disadvantage compared to their heterosexual peers. This gap in wealth accumulation often extends into retirement, where LGBTQ+ people, especially those who have experienced periods of unemployment due to discrimination, may have fewer savings or access to pensions.

5.5 The Legal Landscape – Insufficient Protections for LGBTQ+ Financial Rights:

In many countries, the legal infrastructure supporting LGBTQ+ financial rights remains incomplete. Although certain legal protections have been enacted to safeguard against discrimination in employment and housing, the same cannot be said for financial services. In many places, LGBTQ+ people are not legally entitled to the same protections against financial discrimination as other groups. The lack of uniform laws in this area allows financial institutions to operate with impunity, further disadvantaging LGBTQ+ customers. For example, some countries still lack legal recognition of same-sex couples, making it difficult for these couples to access joint loans, bank accounts, or even qualify for family insurance plans. Even in regions with strong anti-discrimination laws, enforcement is often lax, and the barriers to taking legal action against a financial institution are high. This leaves LGBTQ+ individuals and couples vulnerable to unfair financial practices without a clear path to redress.

5.6 Conclusion – A Call for Financial Equity in LGBTQ+ Lives:

Financial discrimination is a major barrier to economic equality for LGBTQ+ individuals. From limited access to credit and loans to the subtle systemic biases within financial institutions, these disparities obstruct the financial stability and growth of queer communities. Achieving a truly inclusive financial system requires policymakers and financial institutions to confront and dismantle the entrenched biases that perpetuate these inequities. Only by doing so can LGBTQ+ individuals, regardless of their sexual orientation or gender identity, be granted equal opportunities to achieve financial security and independence.

Chapter 14

Sex Work and the LGBTQ+ Community

1. Debunking Myths – Queer Identities in Sex Work

Sex work involving LGBTQ+ individuals is too often portrayed solely through a lens of exploitation or victimhood, reinforcing narratives that deny agency. While exploitation can occur in any industry, many queer sex workers actively choose their profession for reasons such as flexible income, greater bodily autonomy and strong community support systems. Far from being merely a last resort option, sex work can serve as a source of empowerment, particularly when traditional employment avenues are hostile, exclusionary, or inaccessible to LGBTQ+ individuals. Understanding these choices requires us to confront the binary framing of "empowered vs. exploited" and recognize how many queer individuals use sex work as a form of self-determination.

1.1 The Myth of the Cisgender Worker – Diversity in Gender and Presentation:

Popular assumptions frequently erase the vast diversity of gender identities within sex work, often defaulting to the image of the cisgender woman. Trans and nonbinary sex workers, however, have long been part of the industry, even if they remain largely invisible in media and policy. Their presence disrupts traditional ideas of labour, sexuality, and visibility, challenging rigid gender norms. Greater recognition of this diversity expands the narrative around who is allowed to exist and be safe, within these spaces, while also demanding inclusive labour protections that account for more than just cisnormative identities.

1.2 "It's Just a Phase" – Queerness and Professional Identity:

Another pervasive myth suggests that queer people enter sex work out of confusion or experimentation with their identity, reducing both their sexuality and their profession to passing fads. In reality, many LGBTQ+ individuals find sex work to be a legitimate and long-term livelihood that aligns with their values and autonomy. Queerness within sex work is not performative or temporary, it is often a deeply integrated part of lived experience and survival. Recognizing this intersectionality means rejecting pathologizing assumptions and listening to queer sex workers speak to the complexity and intention behind their choices.

1.3 Sex Work as Queer Resistance and Community Care:

Across history, queer sex workers have been instrumental in activism, organizing and mutual aid, particularly during moments of crisis like the HIV/AIDS epidemic. These contributions are often erased from mainstream queer narratives despite their foundational role.

Viewing sex work through the lens of resistance reveals how queer bodies have long been used not only for labour, but also for care, rebellion and healing. Informal networks of support among queer sex workers function as systems of survival, demonstrating how solidarity, knowledge sharing and community protection, can flourish in even the most marginalized spaces.

1.4 Decriminalization and Safety – What Queer Sex Workers Actually Need:

Well-meaning reforms often fall short when they prioritize regulation or coercion over autonomy. Many queer sex workers advocate for full decriminalization as the most effective way to ensure safety and legal access without fear of arrest or discrimination. Overlapping vulnerabilities, including transphobia, homophobia, racism and classism, intensify the risks that queer individuals face within criminalized systems. The ongoing criminalization of sex work often forces LGBTQ+ workers into dangerous, hidden environments where abuse and exploitation go unchecked. Decriminalization, on the other hand, empowers sex workers to report violence, seek medical care, and advocate for safer, more equitable working conditions without the constant fear of legal repercussions. True safety comes not from control, but from freedom and self-governance.

1.5 Conclusion – Reclaiming the Narrative, Respecting the Labor:

The myths surrounding queer people in sex work stem from discomfort with both sexuality and non-normative identities. These narratives flatten complex lives and reinforce stigma. Unpacking and correcting these misconceptions creates room for more compassionate, accurate, and empowering representations. Queer sex workers are not anomalies, they are community builders, organizers and labourers, who deserve both recognition and protection. Reclaiming the narrative is essential to advancing not only sex worker rights, but also broader LGBTQ+ justice and liberation.

2. The Legal and Social Challenges of Queer Sex Workers

Queer sex workers often exist at the intersection of two highly stigmatized identities, both their LGBTQ+ status and their involvement in sex work expose them to intensified discrimination, violence and marginalization. Public conversations frequently reduce them to either victims or deviants, ignoring the structural conditions that shape their realities. Legal frameworks, media portrayals, and social norms all contribute to a climate, where visibility does not guarantee safety and inclusion remains conditional. Acknowledging the lived experiences of queer sex workers opens the door to nuanced discussions around justice, protection and empowerment.

2.1 Criminalization and Its Disproportionate Impact on LGBTQ+ Communities:

Laws that criminalize sex work do not affect all individuals equally. In many regions, vague or outdated legislation leaves queer sex workers more susceptible to police targeting, especially trans women of colour and gender-nonconforming individuals. Profiling and entrapment are common, as law enforcement agencies operate under prejudiced assumptions about LGBTQ+ identities. These legal pressures often result in harassment, arbitrary arrests, or coerced confessions.

Even where sex work itself may not be explicitly illegal, related charges, like loitering, solicitation, or public indecency, are weaponized against visibly queer individuals, leading to cycles of incarceration that disproportionately affect those already pushed to the margins.

2.2 Lack of Legal Recognition and Labor Rights:

In many countries, sex work remains outside the boundaries of labour law. This exclusion leaves queer sex workers without access to protections like workplace safety standards, sick leave, or avenues for filing complaints against abusive employers or clients. For those in marginalized communities, this legal invisibility means heightened risk, limited recourse, and little opportunity to seek restitution in court. The lack of formal recognition reinforces a systemic view that queer sex workers are not "real" workers, denying them the dignity, autonomy and protections afforded to others. Efforts to unionize or advocate for rights are often stifled by fear of legal retaliation or social ostracization.

2.3 Surveillance and Digital Policing in the Online Realm:

As sex work has increasingly moved online, queer sex workers have found digital platforms both liberating and dangerous. While online spaces offer greater autonomy and safety, many are heavily policed or restricted by vague "community standards" and legislation such as FOSTA-SESTA in the U.S., which has had ripple effects globally. Queer content is disproportionately flagged or removed and sex workers using platforms for harm-reduction or marketing, can be banned or shadow banned without explanation. These limitations make it harder for queer sex workers to sustain income or build community. For many, digital erasure becomes yet another form of censorship tied to systemic queerphobia. These barriers highlight the ongoing struggle for digital freedom and safety, where queer sex workers must continually navigate a system that undermines their autonomy and silences their voices.

2.4 Healthcare Discrimination and Denied Access to Services:

Healthcare access is a persistent challenge for queer sex workers. Even when services are technically available, stigma from medical professionals often creates a hostile environment. Some practitioners view sex work or queer identities as inherently pathological or immoral, leading to refusals of care, breaches of confidentiality, or invasive questioning. For trans and nonbinary sex workers, these barriers are even more pronounced, and gender-affirming care may be denied, and sexual health services may be woefully inadequate or outdated. The result is a population forced to choose between silence and risk, often relying on underground networks for basic healthcare needs.

2.5 Family Rejection and Housing Insecurity:

Many queer sex workers face rejection from biological families, which pushes them into homelessness or unstable housing conditions early in life. Once involved in sex work, securing safe housing becomes even more complicated, due to background checks, moralistic rental policies, and landlords who may exploit or evict them.

Housing programs that exist for vulnerable populations often come with discriminatory strings attached, particularly for trans individuals or those who are openly involved in sex work. This instability has lasting effects, making it harder to save money, access healthcare, or escape exploitative working conditions.

2.6 Social Services That Fail to Protect or Include:

Governmental and non-governmental organizations tasked with providing aid to marginalized groups frequently exclude or inadequately serve queer sex workers. Whether due to transphobia, anti-sex work bias, or bureaucratic red tape, many social service providers actively contribute to the stigmatization and neglect of this group. Shelters may misgender trans individuals or refuse them access entirely. Employment training programs may be unwelcoming or irrelevant, pushing sex workers toward labour sectors where discrimination continues. A lack of cultural competence among staff leads to mistrust and disengagement, further isolating queer sex workers from systems that are meant to support them.

2.7 Community-Led Resistance and Mutual Aid:

Despite institutional failings, queer sex workers have created strong networks of resistance and care. Grassroots organizations, often led by former or current sex workers, provide critical services such as legal aid, safe housing, healthcare navigation, and peer support. These community-driven efforts fill the gap left by exclusionary systems and often operate on shoestring budgets and volunteer labour. Their existence proves the strength and resilience of queer sex worker communities, while also highlighting the need for broader societal investment and validation. True progress will require not just celebrating these efforts, but funding and formalizing them through policy change.

2.8 Conclusion – Toward Justice and Structural Inclusion:

Queer sex workers deserve more than tolerance, they deserve structural protections, legal recognition and public respect. Combating the challenges they face means reforming not only outdated laws, but also the deep-seated cultural attitudes that cast queer identities and sex work as mutually reinforcing forms of deviance. As long as these intersections remain criminalized, invisible, or dismissed, queer sex workers will continue to be among the most vulnerable members of society. A more just world is one in which their voices are heard, their labour is valued, and their lives are lived with dignity and choice. Real change requires challenging both legal and societal norms, ensuring queer sex workers have the same rights, protections and opportunities as everyone else.

3. The Role of Sex Work in Gender-Affirming Journeys

For many transgender and nonbinary individuals, sex work plays a critical role in their gender-affirming journeys. While often overshadowed by stigma and criminalization, sex work can provide autonomy, empowerment, and validation that the traditional job market may not offer. It allows individuals to navigate their gender expression in a space where they can exercise control over their bodies and identities.

Exploring how sex work intersects with gender-affirming processes highlights both the personal identity aspects and the tangible financial resources it can provide for those undergoing gender transition. This dynamic reveals how sex work can be a form of self-empowerment and a crucial resource for financial independence during gender exploration and affirmation.

3.1 Sex Work as a Source of Financial Independence and Gender Affirmation:

For many transgender and nonbinary individuals, financial independence is a critical component of gender affirmation. The costs associated with hormone replacement therapy, surgeries, and other forms of gender-affirming care can be astronomical, and traditional employment structures may not always be accommodating to trans and nonbinary people. Sex work can provide flexible income, enabling individuals to access the medical care they need, while also facilitating personal autonomy. This financial empowerment can contribute to greater control over one's body and the journey of self-affirmation, especially in a world that often marginalizes queer and trans identities. Thus, sex work can serve as a vital path to self-determination.

3.2 Sex Work and the Expression of Gender Identity:

Sex work provides a unique avenue for some individuals to explore and express their gender identity. In an environment that is inherently about negotiating bodily autonomy, sex work can create opportunities for trans and nonbinary people to define their gender expression on their own terms. Some individuals find that engaging in sex work allows them to feel validated and affirmed in their gender presentation, especially when they encounter rejection or discrimination in other areas of life. This personal form of expression can be a deeply fulfilling aspect of their gender-affirming process, offering a space to experiment with and embrace their identity in ways that are often inaccessible in other professional environments. Sex work offers a space for trans and nonbinary individuals to explore and affirm their gender identity, providing validation and empowerment, especially when facing rejection elsewhere. It allows for gender expression in ways often inaccessible in traditional work environments.

3.3 Navigating Gender Expression Within the Context of Sex Work:

Navigating gender expression within the context of sex work offers unique opportunities for self-discovery and affirmation. Unlike traditional job environments that may impose rigid gender expectations, sex work allows individuals to explore, experiment, and present their gender in ways that feel authentic to them. For many transgender and nonbinary workers, this freedom is a vital part of their journey towards self-acceptance. It becomes a space where they can express their gender identity without fear of rejection or invalidation, fostering confidence and self-worth. Additionally, the demand for diverse forms of gender expression in the sex work industry allows individuals to engage in a form of work that not only aligns with their identity, but also celebrates it, creating a supportive and affirming space. This ability to define gender on their own terms is often absent from more mainstream employment, where individuals may face discrimination or be forced to conform to normative gender roles.

3.4 Sex Work and the Creation of Gender-Affirming Communities:

For many transgender and nonbinary people, especially those who face isolation or rejection from family and societal support systems, the sex work community can offer a vital network of understanding and solidarity. These communities can provide emotional and social support, as well as a space where gender diversity is not just tolerated, but embraced. Such support systems can help individuals navigate the complexities of gender-affirming care and the transition process, especially when mainstream health and social systems may not be inclusive or accessible. For some, the camaraderie and shared experiences of others within the sex work industry offer a crucial lifeline in their journeys of self-affirmation.

3.5 Sex Work as a Tool for Resilience in the Face of Stigma:

The stigma surrounding sex work can be especially harsh for LGBTQ+ individuals, who often face intersecting layers of discrimination based on their gender identity, sexuality, and chosen profession. However, some transgender and nonbinary individuals find that sex work can act as a powerful tool for resilience in the face of such adversity. By engaging in sex work, individuals can reclaim agency over their lives and bodies, resisting the shame that society may try to impose on them. This can be particularly important in the context of gender-affirming care, where shame and rejection are often experienced in medical spaces, family dynamics, and other areas of life. Through sex work, individuals can carve out a space where their identity is not only recognized but celebrated.

3.6 The Intersection of Safety, Autonomy, and Gender Affirmation in Sex Work:

Safety remains a primary concern for sex workers, particularly for queer and trans individuals who may be subject to increased vulnerability in unsafe environments. However, when sex work is framed through a lens of autonomy and empowerment, many individuals actively choose work environments that prioritize their safety and affirm their gender identity. These environments can foster a sense of control over one's body, environment, and decisions, making sex work a significant part of the gender-affirming journey for those who have the privilege to access it. For some, the safety, autonomy, and flexibility provided by sex work, are far more conducive to their mental health and gender affirmation, than more traditional job settings that are often hostile or dismissive of their identities.

3.7 Conclusion – Empowerment Through Choice and Autonomy:

Ultimately, sex work serves as a valid and powerful option in the gender-affirming journeys of some transgender and nonbinary individuals. It offers financial freedom, a platform for gender expression, access to medical care, and the ability to define one's identity on personal terms. When viewed through the lens of empowerment and autonomy, sex work can be an important part of a broader framework of gender affirmation, contributing to physical, emotional, and financial well-being. It is essential to recognize that the choice to engage in sex work, particularly within the context of gender affirmation, should be respected as a legitimate path toward self-empowerment and self-determination.

Honouring the choices of those who find affirmation, resilience, and strength through sex work is not just about recognizing diverse paths, it's about committing to a future where every gender-affirming journey is met with dignity, safety, and unwavering respect.

4. Destigmatizing the Intersection of Queerness and Sex Work

Mainstream narratives around both queerness and sex work have long been shaped by moral panic, religious dogma, and socio-political control. Historically, queer people were framed as sexually deviant and immoral, and sex workers as dangerous outliers of society, when those identities intersect, the stigmatization intensifies. This compounded bias isn't just cultural, it's deeply systemic, influencing policy, media representation, and public perception. Rather than viewing queer sex workers as complex individuals making informed choices, society often flattens their experiences into reductive tropes. Understanding these cultural foundations is essential to dismantling the harmful myths that continue to inform how queer sex workers are treated both legally and socially. Mainstream narratives amplify stigma when queerness and sex work intersect, reinforcing harmful stereotypes and unequal treatment.

4.1 Queer Survival Economies and Historical Context:

Throughout history, LGBTQ+ individuals have often been pushed to the margins of the labour force due to systemic discrimination, criminalization, and family rejection. Many turned to informal economies, including sex work, not out of desperation, but as a method of survival and, in many cases, empowerment. From ballroom culture to underground networks of queer solidarity, sex work has played a central role in sustaining and affirming queer communities. These survival economies weren't solely about financial subsistence, they also fostered networks of mutual care, safety, and identity formation. Acknowledging this legacy reframes sex work not as a moral failing, but as a legitimate and often necessary, economic strategy for those systematically excluded from traditional employment pathways. Queer survival economies, including sex work, have historically offered economic support and community for LGBTQ+ individuals facing systemic exclusion. These networks of care and identity highlight sex work as a legitimate economic strategy.

4.2 The Problem with Respectability Politics:

LGBTQ+ movements have often been shaped by the desire to gain mainstream acceptance, sometimes at the expense of the most marginalized among them. Respectability politics encourages queer people to present themselves as "normal" and palatable to cis-heteronormative society. In this context, queer sex workers are often erased or scapegoated, viewed as liabilities in the quest for legal rights and social approval. This internalized hierarchy within queer communities reinforces stigma rather than challenging it. True liberation requires rejecting these politics of respectability and embracing the full spectrum of queer existence, including those whose survival and empowerment are linked to sex work. This exclusion weakens solidarity and reinforces societal judgments, leaving behind those whose lives challenge norms. True queer liberation must include sex workers as part of the broader fight for justice. Rejecting respectability politics is crucial for building an inclusive and just queer movement that honours all experiences, including those of queer sex workers.

4.3 Media Representation and the Erasure of Nuance:

Depictions of sex workers in media tend to fall into extremes, the tragic victim or the hypersexualized villain. When queer sex workers are represented at all, they are often framed through a lens of pity or danger. These portrayals obscure the real, lived experiences of LGBTQ+ individuals who engage in sex work for reasons ranging from economic necessity to personal agency. The media has a powerful role in shaping public understanding and empathy. More accurate, complex, and respectful narratives are needed to shift the conversation away from stigma, and toward recognition, respect, and human dignity. Media must move beyond simplistic portrayals, offering diverse, multifaceted representations of queer sex workers to foster understanding and dismantle stigma.

4.4 Health Care Disparities and Systemic Barriers:

Sex workers, particularly those who are queer or trans, face significant obstacles in accessing non-judgmental and competent health care. Stigma from providers, lack of insurance, and the criminalization of their work create an environment where essential services are out of reach. When queer sex workers seek support for issues such as STI screenings, mental health care, or gender-affirming services, they often encounter bias or outright denial of care. These disparities are not accidental, they are the result of a medical system that fails to recognize sex work as labour and queer people as fully human. Destigmatizing sex work involves not just social shifts, but institutional accountability in health care, housing, and public safety.

4.5 Law Enforcement and the Double Marginalization of Queer Sex Workers:

Queer sex workers frequently face both hyper-surveillance and neglect from law enforcement. They are disproportionately targeted by police, especially if they are trans women of colour and often subjected to harassment, extortion, or violence. At the same time, when they experience harm, whether from clients, strangers, or within their communities, their reports are frequently ignored or dismissed. This contradiction highlights how criminalization doesn't protect, but punishes. Decriminalization is not simply a legal demand, but a pathway toward justice, offering the possibility of safer working conditions, access to legal recourse, and protection under the law.

4.6 Community Building and Peer Support Networks:

In the face of widespread stigma, queer sex workers have created their own systems of care, resistance and empowerment. Peer-led organizations, mutual aid funds, and grassroots coalitions provide everything from safety training to bail support and access to hormone therapy. These networks are not only practical, they are political, rooted in the idea that no one is disposable and that community care can be a form of resistance. Such organizing not only addresses immediate needs, but also builds long-term solidarity that challenges the structural conditions producing stigma in the first place. Uplifting these community efforts is essential to any genuine movement for destigmatization. These efforts go beyond survival, they lay the groundwork for transformative justice and collective liberation. Uplifting them affirms the value and dignity of every queer life.

4.7 Intersectionality and the Need for Nuanced Advocacy:

Stigma does not operate in isolation. Queer sex workers experience layered marginalizations based on race, class, disability, immigration status and more. For example, a Black trans woman doing sex work in the South will face very different challenges than a white gay man in a large urban center. Effective advocacy must be grounded in intersectionality, recognizing that no one solution fits all. Policy, support services, and public discourse must be shaped by those most impacted, not by distant allies or sanitized mainstream organizations. Only then can the work of destigmatization be truly inclusive and transformative.

4.8 Moving from Stigma to Solidarity:

Destigmatizing queer sex work requires a cultural and political shift that goes beyond tolerance or visibility. It demands a rethinking of what labour, dignity, and choice look like, especially under capitalism and systemic exclusion. By centering the voices and experiences of queer sex workers, society can begin to understand sex work not as a moral issue, but as a matter of justice, equity and human rights. This shift challenges the binary of victim versus agent and invites a more nuanced understanding of identity, survival, and autonomy.

4.9 Conclusion – Liberation Is Incomplete Without Inclusion:

No queer liberation movement is complete if it leaves behind those at the margins. Queer sex workers are not anomalies or exceptions, they are part of the community's foundation. Destigmatizing their work is a necessary act of collective care and radical inclusion. When society acknowledges the legitimacy of their labour, the validity of their identities and the worth of their lives, it moves closer to the kind of justice that uplifts all queer people.

5. The Influence of Online Platforms on LGBTQ+ Sex Work

The advent of online platforms has radically transformed the landscape of sex work, providing new opportunities and challenges for LGBTQ+ individuals involved in the industry. These platforms, which include adult content sites, social media and private platforms, dedicated to connecting clients with sex workers, have allowed for greater autonomy and visibility for queer individuals. This shift has fundamentally altered how sex work is conducted, offering both safer spaces for LGBTQ+ workers, and exposing them to unique risks. The role of technology in reshaping sex work is multifaceted, impacting everything from client relationships to the commodification of identity.

5.1 Online Platforms as Tools for Autonomy and Agency:

The rise of online platforms has provided queer sex workers with a unique opportunity to take control of their labour in ways that traditional sex work settings did not allow. With the ability to set their own schedules, establish direct connections with clients, and create personalized content, many LGBTQ+ sex workers have found a sense of empowerment and independence.

The ability to interact with clients from the safety of their homes reduces physical risks, such as violence or harassment, which are often associated with in-person encounters. In addition, the internet allows workers to define their brand and public persona in ways that are reflective of their identity, rather than being constrained by society's narrow definitions of sex work. Online platforms have not only provided queer sex workers with greater autonomy, but have also opened up avenues for self-expression, allowing them to navigate their work in ways that align with their identities and personal boundaries.

5.2 Changing Dynamics of Client Relationships:

Online platforms have also altered the dynamics of relationships between sex workers and clients. These spaces foster an environment where sexual and emotional interactions can occur without the limitations of geography or physical boundaries. For LGBTQ+ sex workers, this means greater access to a diverse range of clients who may share their sexual identities or be more understanding of their needs. This can create a sense of community and affirmation within the transactions. However, it also introduces complexities around anonymity, consent, and the risks of online harassment or doxxing, as the boundaries between personal and professional lives can become blurred.

5.3 The Rise of Digital Content Creation:

One significant shift has been the rise of digital content creation, including adult films, live-streaming and subscription-based content. Platforms like OnlyFans, Patreon, and others have given LGBTQ+ sex workers a direct channel to monetize their content and build loyal fan bases. This model allows workers to produce content on their terms, creating a sustainable income while maintaining control over what is shared and how it is distributed. For many queer workers, this shift represents an escape from exploitative contracts or dangerous in-person encounters, providing them with an opportunity to capitalize on their sexual identity while maintaining autonomy. The growth of these platforms has also led to a new wave of queer-centric adult content, where LGBTQ+ individuals can share their experiences and fantasies without mainstream industry constraints. This shift has empowered LGBTQ+ sex workers to reclaim their narratives and foster a more inclusive adult entertainment industry, where queer identities can thrive beyond traditional heteronormative confines.

5.4 The Impact of Platform Policies and Regulations:

Despite the empowering potential of online platforms, they come with their own set of challenges, particularly concerning platform policies and content regulation. Social media sites, adult content platforms, and even payment processors often impose policies that can be restrictive or punitive for LGBTQ+ sex workers. Content moderation policies can disproportionately target sex workers, censoring or banning their accounts without adequate recourse. The recent crackdown on explicit content by platforms like Tumblr and OnlyFans has caused significant financial instability for many queer sex workers who rely on these platforms as their primary income sources. Furthermore, the de-platforming of sex workers on social media platforms can leave them vulnerable to financial loss, dehumanization, and exclusion from the very communities they were trying to build.

5.5 Privacy and Safety Concerns in the Digital Age:

Online sex work also introduces unique privacy and safety concerns that did not exist in traditional settings. The ability to remain anonymous online can be empowering, but it also exposes workers to the risk of online harassment, doxxing, and stalking. There are instances where clients or others within the industry have used technology to harm or exploit workers by leaking personal information or making them vulnerable to online abuse. The pressure to maintain an online persona, while safeguarding private details of one's life, adds another layer of complexity. For LGBTQ+ sex workers, especially those in trans and nonbinary communities, the risk of identity theft, outing, or discrimination can be particularly severe, as these individuals often face heightened vulnerability due to the intersection of their gender identity, sexual orientation and occupation, all of which may be subject to societal biases and systemic prejudice.

5.6 The Role of Social Media and Community Building:

Social media platforms have become vital tools for LGBTQ+ sex workers, not only to promote their services and content, but also to build community, find clients, and network with others in the industry. These platforms have facilitated the creation of online spaces where queer sex workers can share resources, advice and support with each other. This sense of community helps counteract the isolation many workers feel and creates opportunities for collaboration and mutual care. In addition, social media helps break down the stigma surrounding sex work by allowing workers to present themselves as multifaceted individuals with rich, diverse identities beyond their labour. However, the same platforms that enable community-building and self-expression can also expose queer sex workers to harassment, censorship and targeted attacks, from users and platform administrators, creating a hostile environment where content is often removed without explanation and accounts banned without warning.

5.7 The Global Reach and Access to New Markets:

One of the key benefits of online platforms is the global reach they provide for sex workers, allowing LGBTQ+ individuals to connect with clients from different parts of the world. This access to international markets broadens the scope of opportunities for queer sex workers, who may otherwise have been confined to local or regional markets. The ability to reach clients across borders increases earning potential and can provide a sense of belonging to a broader global queer community. However, it also raises concerns regarding cultural differences in attitudes toward sex work, the legalities surrounding sex work in different countries, and the risks associated with interacting with clients in regions where sex work is heavily criminalized or stigmatized. Global reach offers new opportunities, but also presents legal and cultural challenges.

5.8 The Role of Technology in Destigmatizing Sex Work:

The rise of online platforms has played a role in challenging the stigma surrounding sex work, particularly in LGBTQ+ communities.

By providing sex workers with a space to share their stories, experiences, and content, these platforms have helped create more visibility and recognition of sex work as a legitimate form of labour. They have allowed sex workers to present themselves on their own terms, reclaiming their identities and asserting their agency in the face of societal condemnation. While challenges remain, the ongoing use of technology in sex work offers potential for further destigmatization, as it opens up conversations about the diverse ways in which individuals engage in labour and the importance of recognizing all forms of work.

5.9 Conclusion – A New Era for LGBTQ+ Sex Work:

Online platforms have reshaped the landscape of sex work, offering LGBTQ+ individuals greater control over their labour, identity, and income. While challenges such as platform regulation and privacy concerns persist, the shift to online spaces has fundamentally altered the industry in empowering ways. For LGBTQ+ sex workers, these platforms provide not just economic opportunities, but a chance to build community, promote autonomy, and challenge the stigma surrounding sex work. As these platforms continue to evolve, it is crucial to advocate for policies that protect and support the rights of sex workers, ensuring that the digital era of sex work remains a space for empowerment and safety.

* A Few Examples of How Laws and Cultures Shape LGBTQ+ Sex Work Around the World:

These examples show how countries address sex work and LGBTQ+ identities, but many regions, including Eastern Europe, Sub-Saharan Africa and the Pacific Islands, also require attention in the global dialogue on queer sex worker justice and safety.

➢ Sweden – The Nordic Model and Hidden Harm:

Sweden pioneered the "Nordic Model," which criminalizes buyers of sex, but not sellers. Intended to curb demand and protect individuals, the policy often ends up harming the very people it seeks to shield. For LGBTQ+ sex workers, this results in police surveillance, client fear, and housing instability. Trans and nonbinary workers, already marginalized in other sectors, are pushed further underground. With clients deterred by legal risks, workers take greater safety gambles. The model's paternalism erases autonomy, treating queer sex workers as victims instead of agents.

➢ New Zealand – Decriminalization and its Benefits:

New Zealand's 2003 Prostitution Reform Act decriminalized sex work, treating it as labour. This allows sex workers to organize, report violence, and access healthcare without legal fear. For LGBTQ+ sex workers, particularly trans individuals, this environment fosters autonomy and community-building. While challenges around stigma persist, the legal recognition affirms sex work as legitimate, giving workers visibility and tools for self-protection. The model stands as one of the most progressive globally, supporting harm reduction and dignity.

- **The United States – A Patchwork of Criminalization and Inconsistency:**

In the United States, criminalization dominates, except for partial legality in isolated areas such as specific counties in Nevada. LGBTQ+ sex workers, particularly Black and Brown transgender women, are frequently profiled, harassed, and arrested under broad and ambiguous laws like "loitering with intent," which are often weaponized to target marginalized individuals. The lack of federal decriminalization leaves workers in legal limbo. In states with limited protections for LGBTQ+ people, sex workers may face job discrimination, housing loss, and denied healthcare, traps that lead them to underground economies. Legal reform efforts exist, but are fragmented and often exclude the voices of queer sex workers themselves.

- **Germany – Legalization with Structural Pitfalls:**

Germany legalized sex work in 2002 and implemented regulatory systems requiring registration, health checks, and licensing. In theory, this model protects sex workers. However, in practice, the requirements disproportionately impact marginalized groups, including undocumented migrants and trans individuals who may not have the necessary identification or who fear state surveillance. LGBTQ+ sex workers often report feeling coerced into "legitimizing" their work in ways that violate privacy or autonomy. Furthermore, stigma persists in healthcare and housing sectors, and those who operate outside the legal framework can still face criminal penalties. Germany's model shows that legalization without equity or social change can reproduce exclusion under a different name.

- **South Africa – A Site of Legal Conflict and Reform:**

In South Africa, sex work is criminalized, but a growing national conversation is pushing for decriminalization. LGBTQ+ communities, particularly trans and gender-diverse sex workers, have been central to this advocacy. Organizations like SWEAT (Sex Workers Education and Advocacy Taskforce), have emphasized the intersections of colonial law, racism, and queerphobia in the ongoing criminalization of sex work. While South Africa has constitutional protections for LGBTQ+ individuals, these often fail to translate into protections for queer sex workers. Police abuse, lack of healthcare, and HIV stigma are ongoing issues. However, South Africa remains a country to watch, with a strong civil society mobilizing for transformative legal change.

- **Thailand – Cultural Tolerance Without Legal Protection:**

Thailand is often perceived as accepting of sex work and trans identities (e.g., kathoey or "ladyboys"), but sex work remains officially illegal. Despite the visibility of LGBTQ+ sex workers, especially in tourism hubs, they operate without legal protection. This leaves them vulnerable to exploitation and police harassment. Many trans women find sex work one of the few accessible employment options, yet face intense societal and institutional discrimination. Moreover, lacking formal recognition, they are excluded from labour rights, healthcare benefits, and legal recourse, forcing many to rely on informal networks for safety and support. This gap between visibility and protection underscores the need for legal rights and safety for LGBTQ+ sex workers in Thailand.

- **Brazil – Legal Ambiguity Amid High Violence:**

Brazil's legal framework around sex work is a paradox. While sex work itself is legal, associated activities like running a brothel or employing sex workers are criminalized, creating a grey area that leaves workers vulnerable to legal penalties. LGBTQ+ rights are constitutionally protected, yet the country struggles with one of the highest rates of violence against trans individuals, particularly trans women. This stark contradiction, legal tolerance juxtaposed with pervasive social hostility, creates an environment of uncertainty and danger for queer sex workers. In response, grassroots organizing, especially in favelas, has become a crucial support network for trans sex workers, offering not just survival resources, but also a space for resistance against systemic exclusion and violence. However, the lack of legal protections continues to hinder efforts for greater safety and equality.

- **Canada – End Demand Model with Queer Harm:**

Canada adopted a variation of the Nordic Model in 2014, criminalizing the purchase of sex and third-party involvement. While selling sex is not illegal, enforcement disproportionately impacts marginalized groups. Queer sex workers, particularly Indigenous and Two-Spirit people, face over-policing, surveillance and barriers to healthcare. The law, framed as protecting women, fails to address the specific needs of LGBTQ+ communities and reinforces stigma. It inadvertently forces sex work into more dangerous, isolated spaces, leaving workers vulnerable to violence and exploitation. Many queer and trans sex workers avoid seeking help due to fears of criminalization and discrimination, exacerbating their marginalization. This highlights the urgent need for laws that protect, not punish, queer and trans sex workers.

- **India – Legal Loopholes and Trans Community Vulnerability:**

In India, sex work itself is not illegal, but soliciting, brothel-keeping and pimping are criminalized, leaving workers in a precarious legal position. The hijra (third gender) community often turns to sex work due to employment discrimination. Despite the 2014 Supreme Court ruling recognizing third-gender rights and the Transgender Persons Act of 2019, enforcement remains inconsistent and protections are weak. Many queer sex workers in India face the additional burden of stigma and lack of societal support, further marginalizing them in both public and private spaces. Queer sex workers face violence, extortion by clients and law enforcement and severe barriers, to accessing healthcare and legal support. Cultural stigma around sex work and transgender identities further entrenches their marginalization, leaving many without recourse for justice. Consequently, this systemic neglect reinforces cycles of exclusion, violence, and oppression.

- **Netherlands – Regulated, Yet Not Always Inclusive:**

The Netherlands is known for its legalized and regulated sex work industry. Workers must register and comply with zoning laws and health checks. While this framework offers stability for many, LGBTQ+ sex workers, particularly migrants and trans individuals, often find themselves excluded from legal protections due to ID mismatches or immigration status.

The system favours those who can "fit" into its bureaucracy, highlighting the limitations of a one-size-fits-all regulatory model. Mandatory health screenings and licensing fees place heavy financial and administrative burdens on marginalized sex workers. This often pushes them back into unregulated, riskier environments.

- **Turkey – Criminalization Coupled with State Surveillance:**

Turkey criminalizes most forms of sex work, with legal brothels only open to cisgender women who register with the state, a requirement that excludes trans and nonbinary individuals entirely. LGBTQ+ sex workers, especially trans women, often face brutal police violence, eviction, and societal discrimination. The police may frequently target sex workers, using vague laws to arrest or intimidate them, while trans and nonbinary people are routinely denied access to legal protections. Despite these systemic challenges, a resilient underground community has formed, offering informal support, advocacy, and activism in response to state repression. These communities have developed networks of care and mutual aid to address immediate needs and push back against institutionalized violence.

- **New Zealand – Decriminalization:**

New Zealand has a progressive approach, having fully decriminalized sex work in 2003. This legal environment supports workers' rights, ensuring that LGBTQ+ sex workers have access to health services, housing, and workplace protections, and can work in safer, more regulated conditions. Although the legal framework offers solid protections, cultural stigmas persist, especially against transgender and nonbinary sex workers, who may still face challenges related to societal perceptions and discrimination. Some sex workers report feeling excluded from broader sex work networks or facing additional barriers to social acceptance within both the LGBTQ+ community and the general public.

- **United Kingdom – Partial Decriminalization Amid Persistent Stigma:**

In the United Kingdom, selling sex is legal, but many related activities, such as soliciting in public, running a brothel, or third-party involvement, remain criminal offenses under the Sexual Offences Act 2003. LGBTQ+ sex workers, particularly transgender and nonbinary individuals, often face discrimination from law enforcement, who use solicitation laws to target and harass them. Despite campaigns for greater rights, such as the English Collective of Prostitutes' push for full decriminalization, social stigma persists, limiting access to healthcare, housing, and social services. Pilot schemes in Scotland and Wales testing decriminalization models have shown promise in improving safety and well-being for sex workers, suggesting a path forward for more inclusive policy reform across the UK.

Chapter 15

The Science of Queer Love and Attraction

1. Do Queer People Love Differently? A Psychological Perspective

Love is often presented as a universal human experience, deeply rooted in evolutionary psychology and further shaped by cultural expression across societies. However, the common assumption that romantic love manifests in the same ways across all sexual orientations tends to overlook significant sociocultural and psychological distinctions. Queer love, in particular, exists within unique and often challenging contexts, shaped by histories of marginalization, the necessity of community-building and the ongoing process of identity negotiation. When queer relationships are carefully examined through established psychological frameworks, such as attachment theory, emotional regulation and interpersonal attraction, it becomes possible to investigate whether, and in what meaningful ways, queer expressions of love differ from the more commonly studied heterosexual relationship models. These conventional models are frequently treated as the default or universal standard for romantic and emotional connection, often overlooking the rich diversity and complexity inherent in queer experiences of love.

1.1 Attachment Theory and the Queer Experience:

Attachment theory, originally based on observations of heteronormative parent-child and romantic relationships, suggests that early caregiving shapes adult styles of love. Recent studies, however, reveal unique variations in attachment dynamics among queer individuals. Queer people, especially those who experienced familial rejection or societal stigma, may display higher levels of anxious or avoidant attachment in romantic contexts. Queer communities often create compensatory support systems through chosen families and deeply intimate friendships, which can gradually reshape and heal attachment patterns shaped by early adversity. In this context, queer love reflects a dynamic interplay between past disruptions and the possibility of reparative, affirming relationships. Moreover, research suggests that queer couples frequently demonstrate heightened emotional expressiveness and a deliberate negotiation of relational roles, signalling a more intentional and adaptive approach to building secure attachments.

1.2 Emotional Bonding Beyond Norms:

Emotional bonding in queer relationships frequently challenges traditional gender norms and relational scripts. Without rigid role expectations based on gender binaries, queer couples often construct more fluid emotional landscapes. Studies suggest queer partners are more likely to engage in mutual emotional labour, actively discussing feelings and relational needs.

This openness often fosters a relationship dynamic where vulnerability is not only accepted, but encouraged as a core component of connection. Lesbian couples, for instance, often score highest in measures of emotional intimacy, while gay male couples report more flexibility in emotional expression, ranging from deeply bonded to more compartmentalized arrangements. These variations suggest that the absence of heteronormative pressure may enable broader expressions of connection. Furthermore, many queer individuals rely on emotion-focused coping strategies, having developed resilience from navigating identity-based adversity. Emotional bonding, in this sense, becomes not just a product of individual psychology, but a survival strategy and an act of resistance.

1.3 Attraction and Desire – More Than Just Orientation:

While sexual orientation defines the direction of attraction, queer desire often resists easy categorization. Psychological research on attraction reveals that queer individuals navigate a broader spectrum of aesthetic, romantic and sexual attractions. For bisexual and pansexual people, attraction may shift depending on context, energy, and relational dynamics. Asexual and aromantic individuals challenge the centrality of attraction altogether, inviting psychology to reevaluate traditional models of romantic love. Queer attraction is often deeply intertwined with identity affirmation, visibility and community context. Moreover, cultural and interpersonal cues, such as shared language, safety and subcultural affiliation, frequently influence whom queer individuals feel drawn to. The role of desire in queer love is thus, more fluid, performative and socially situated, than many classical psychological models suggest. Attraction, in queer contexts, can be about recognition, shared struggle and political solidarity, as much as it is about physical or emotional chemistry.

1.4 Minority Stress and Its Impact on Relationship Patterns:

The psychological effects of minority stress, a framework describing the chronic social stress faced by marginalized groups, play a significant role in shaping queer romantic relationships. Internalized homophobia, societal stigma, and fear of rejection can contribute to heightened anxiety, depression, or conflict in partnerships. Queer love, therefore, often emerges under conditions of hypervigilance and negotiation. Some couples develop high resilience and mutual support systems in response, while others may face increased relational instability. Research indicates that queer individuals frequently engage in proactive communication and boundary-setting to navigate the unique stressors that heterosexual couples may not encounter. Coping strategies, such as seeking affirming communities or engaging in activism together, can strengthen bonds. At the same time, these couples often carry the psychological weight of representation, feeling pressure to serve as "model" relationships in public or community spaces. This dual burden of resilience and expectation adds complexity to the emotional labour involved in queer love.

1.5 Conclusion – Queer Love as a Psychological Frontier:

Rather than asking whether queer people love differently in a way that reinforces division, a more productive psychological lens considers how love adapts to context, culture and lived experience.

Queer love reflects a multiplicity of attachment styles, emotional strategies and desires that challenge traditional models of relational psychology. Understanding queer love expands our comprehension of human intimacy itself, offering insights into the adaptive nature of love under pressure and illuminating the depth, flexibility and intentionality with which queer people connect.

2. The Neurology of Gender and Sexual Identity

Gender and sexual identity are often considered purely social or psychological constructs, but emerging research in neuroscience reveals a far more intricate picture. While societal norms and lived experience undeniably shape how identity is expressed and understood, neurobiological processes are increasingly recognized as foundational elements in identity formation. Through insights from brain imaging, neuroendocrinology, and developmental neuroscience, researchers are beginning to unravel the brain's role in shaping both gender and sexual identity. Rather than reducing identity to a set of biological determinants or pathologizing difference, this line of inquiry seeks to illuminate the complex neurobiological foundations that contribute to the wide spectrum of human identity. Recognizing these mechanisms not only affirms the natural diversity of gender and sexuality, but also fosters a more scientifically grounded and empathetic understanding. By integrating neuroscience with broader social and psychological perspectives, we can cultivate more informed, respectful, and inclusive conversations about identity.

2.1 Brain Development and Identity Formation:

The formation of gender and sexual identity begins early in neurodevelopment, shaped by both genetic and hormonal influences. During prenatal development, sex hormones such as testosterone and estrogen play a crucial role in organizing the structure and function of the brain. Regions such as the hypothalamus, amygdala, and prefrontal cortex have been found to differ in volume and connectivity based on hormonal exposure. These brain regions play key roles in emotional processing, self-awareness, and social behaviour, factors that are integral to the formation of identity. Some studies suggest that transgender individuals display neural patterns that more closely align with their experienced gender rather than their assigned sex at birth, offering evidence of a neurobiological basis for gender incongruence. However, it is crucial to recognize that these patterns are not fixed or solely responsible for identity. They interact with a range of postnatal experiences and environmental influences, collectively shaping the individual's sense of self.

2.2 Sexual Orientation and the Brain:

Research into the neurological basis of sexual orientation has focused on the structure and function of specific brain regions associated with sexual arousal and partner preference. Studies using functional MRI and PET scans have found that gay and straight individuals may show differing activation patterns in response to sexual stimuli, particularly in areas like the anterior hypothalamus and the amygdala. For example, one landmark study found that the hypothalamus of gay men responded to male pheromones in a way that resembled the response pattern of heterosexual women. Although these findings suggest biological correlates of sexual orientation, they do not offer a singular "cause."

They suggest that sexual identity arises from intricate interactions between prenatal hormone exposure, genetics, and early life experiences. Importantly, these variations are part of the natural spectrum of human diversity rather than anomalies to be corrected or explained away. Sexual orientation is a natural, complex aspect of identity, something to be respected, not explained away.

2.3 Gender Identity and Brain Structure:

Gender identity, the internal sense of being male, female, both, neither, or somewhere along the spectrum, also appears to have neurological correlates. Structural imaging studies have revealed that some transgender individuals have brain characteristics more similar to those of their experienced gender. For instance, research has shown that aspects of white matter microstructure and cortical thickness in transgender people often resemble those of cisgender individuals who share their gender identity. These findings support the notion that gender identity is deeply rooted in brain structure and function, rather than being a mere byproduct of social learning. Additionally, research into body ownership and self-perception networks in the brain, such as the insula and temporoparietal junction, has provided insights into the discomfort some transgender individuals experience with their bodies, known as gender dysphoria. These results do not imply a rigid neurological blueprint for identity, but instead underscore the brain's integral role in shaping how identity is experienced and embodied.

2.4 The Role of Neuroplasticity and Social Experience:

While neurobiology lays the groundwork for identity, it does not function in isolation. The brain is highly plastic, meaning it is capable of change across the lifespan in response to environment, experience, and learning. Social affirmation, trauma, stigma, and community belonging all influence neural pathways involved in self-concept, emotional regulation, and social cognition. For instance, consistent experiences of gender affirmation can alleviate neural markers of stress in transgender individuals, while chronic exposure to minority stress can amplify the brain's threat response systems. Additionally, neuroplasticity plays a critical role in the evolving nature of identity, particularly for those who come to understand or express their gender or sexuality later in life. This adaptability challenges the idea of fixed, biologically determined identities, highlighting the crucial role of supportive, nurturing, and inclusive environments, in fostering the authentic expression of identity.

2.5 Ethical Implications and Misuse of Neuroscience:

The increasing interest in the neuroscience of gender and sexuality raises important ethical questions. While understanding the brain's role can lead to greater validation and medical support, it also carries the risk of being misused to "diagnose," pathologize, or even attempt to alter identities deemed non-normative. It is crucial that neurobiological research is not wielded as a tool for gatekeeping or reinforcing binary norms, but rather as a means of expanding empathy and scientific insight. Identity is not reducible to brain scans or hormone levels, and overemphasis on biology can inadvertently erase the cultural, emotional and lived dimensions of queer and trans experiences. A responsible approach to neuroscience involves integrating biological insights with psychological, sociological, and humanistic perspectives to support autonomy and dignity.

2.6 Conclusion – Embracing Complexity in the Brain and Identity:

Neuroscience offers powerful tools for understanding the deep roots of gender and sexual identity, revealing that these aspects of selfhood are biologically embedded, psychologically rich, and socially influenced. Rather than seeking definitive answers or rigid categories, the most meaningful contribution of neurological research may be its capacity to affirm the complexity and legitimacy of diverse identities. By embracing the interplay between brain, body, and experience, science can foster a more inclusive understanding of what it means to be human, one that honours both individuality and the shared structures that shape how we come to know ourselves and connect with others. A truly inclusive science doesn't simplify identity, it embraces its full complexity with curiosity and care.

3. The Debate Over the "Gay Gene" and Biological Determinism

The idea that a single gene, or even a cluster of genes, might be responsible for something as complex as human sexuality is both scientifically intriguing and politically charged. When media headlines scream about the discovery of a "gay gene," the simplification masks the nuances of an ongoing and unsettled debate. The question is not just whether genes influence sexual orientation, but what it means culturally, ethically, and personally, if they do, or don't. Biological determinism, the idea that identity is solely shaped by genetics, stands in stark contrast to a wealth of research highlighting the vital roles of environment, experience, and culture in shaping who we are. At the intersection of these perspectives lies the complex and often contentious debate over the roots of sexual orientation.

3.1 Scientific Foundations and Genetic Complexity:

Genetics, as a field, has become increasingly aware of its own limitations when applied to behaviours and identities. Studies on twins have shown higher concordance rates for sexual orientation among identical twins than fraternal ones, suggesting a heritable component. However, these rates are far from 100%, which implies that genes may contribute, but do not determine, sexual orientation. In 2019, a landmark genome-wide association study (GWAS) published in Science, examined data from hundreds of thousands of people and revealed that same-sex, sexual behaviour is influenced by a multitude of genetic variants, each contributing a subtle, but significant effect. The researchers concluded there is "no single gay gene." Instead, they proposed a polygenic model, in which a constellation of genes may influence, but not dictate, sexual orientation.

3.2 The Appeal and Danger of Biological Certainty:

The notion of a genetic "cause" for queerness can seem reassuring in a world where LGBTQ+ people continue to face discrimination. If sexuality is "hardwired," the thinking goes, then it's morally wrong to punish or marginalize people for it. But this logic is double-edged. If queer identity is valid only when it's biologically determined, what does that say about sexual fluidity, chosen identity, or the legitimacy of lived experience? Moreover, arguments rooted in biological essentialism have a troubling history of being appropriated by eugenic ideologies and proponents of conversion therapy.

When queerness is framed purely in genetic terms, it risks being pathologized, seen as something to detect, control, or even eliminate before birth. This reductive lens not only flattens the rich diversity of human desire and identity, but also strips queerness of its cultural, emotional, and lived complexity.

3.3 The Role of Environment, Culture, and Fluidity:

Human behaviour is rarely the result of biology alone. Social learning, early relationships, cultural context, and individual experiences all play significant roles in shaping identity. Sexual orientation, for many people, is not fixed, it is fluid, evolving over time and across contexts. This reality challenges the usefulness of a genetic framework that seeks permanence and predictability. It also exposes how narrow and Western-centric much of the research has been, often excluding the fluidity observed in non-Western or Indigenous understandings of gender and sexuality. While biological factors may provide a canvas, it's society, history, and personal narrative that paint the full picture. Recognizing this interplay affirms the complexity of queerness and resists reducing it to a single explanation. It highlights the need to consider biological, social, cultural, and personal factors in understanding sexual orientation and gender identity. Embracing this complexity challenges oversimplified narratives and promotes a more inclusive view of human diversity.

3.4 Scientific Integrity vs. Media Sensationalism:

One of the greatest obstacles to public understanding of this debate is the way science is translated into headlines. Nuanced studies become distorted soundbites, and findings get overstated, or misinterpreted. The 2019 GWAS study, for example, did not claim to find a "gay gene," yet many outlets reported it as such. This kind of sensationalism not only misleads readers, but also reinforces binary thinking around a subject that is inherently complex and multidimensional. Scientists are increasingly aware of the need to communicate findings responsibly, but the media ecosystem often prioritizes clicks over clarity. Clear, accurate science communication is essential. Sensational headlines distort complex research, fuelling misunderstanding and stigma. Responsible reporting helps build empathy and respect for both science and queer identities.

3.5 Ethical and Philosophical Implications:

Even if future research uncovers clearer biological links to queerness, profound ethical questions persist. Should such information be used for predictive testing? Would it serve as a source of empowerment, or might it open the door to new forms of discrimination and control? In a society increasingly obsessed with biological validation, how do we preserve the integrity of autonomy, fluidity, and self-defined identity? Queerness has never fit neatly into rigid or binary categories, it flourishes in nuance, ambiguity, contradiction, and the evolving freedom to define oneself. A biologically deterministic model, however well-intentioned, risks erasing that complexity by reducing identity to genetic codes. This approach oversimplifies the rich realities of queer existence. From an ethical standpoint, queerness does not, and should not, require scientific validation to be legitimate. Its truth lies not in DNA, but in lived experience, personal narrative, chosen family, and the radical act of self-definition.

3.6 Reimagining the Debate – Beyond the Binary of Nature vs. Nurture:

Perhaps the most productive way forward is to move beyond the binary of "born this way" versus "chosen." Sexual orientation might emerge from a complex interplay between genetics, epigenetics, hormones, environment, and lived experience. Rather than seeking one definitive answer, embracing multiplicity may be more reflective of reality. This perspective not only deconstructs rigid categories, but also opens space for identities that shift, evolve, or resist explanation altogether. Science, in this context, becomes a tool for exploration rather than a mechanism of control.

3.7 Conclusion – Holding Complexity with Integrity:

As our understanding of genetics and human identity continues to evolve, so too must our cultural conversations. Reducing queerness to biology alone risks erasing the richness of individual stories, the power of choice, and the resilience of those who love outside the norm. The "gay gene" debate invites us to confront not only what we know, but how we know it, and why we seek to explain certain things in the first place. True progress lies in holding space for both the scientific and the speculative, the biological and the experiential, without needing to collapse one into the other.

4. How Hormones Influence LGBTQ+ Attraction and Relationship Dynamics

Hormones play a crucial role in shaping attraction and relationship dynamics, influencing not only biological processes, but also behaviours and emotional connections. The role of hormones in LGBTQ+ experiences of attraction is complex, involving both shared physiological mechanisms and unique experiences shaped by individual identity. The hormonal systems that govern sexual behaviour, including testosterone, estrogen, and oxytocin, influence not only how individuals experience desire, but also how they navigate and form relationships. Grasping the interplay between these hormones and identity is essential for understanding their broader impact, particularly within the LGBTQ+ community.

4.1 The Role of Sex Hormones in Sexual Attraction:

Sex hormones, including testosterone, estrogen, and progesterone are central to the biological processes that influence sexual attraction. These hormones are responsible for the development of sexual characteristics and the regulation of libido, playing significant roles in how individuals feel attracted to others. In the LGBTQ+ context, hormonal influences are often experienced in ways that intersect with gender identity and sexual orientation. Sex hormones influence physical traits, libido, and how individuals express and experience sexual and romantic preferences. For example, individuals who undergo hormone replacement therapy (HRT) as part of gender transition may experience shifts in attraction patterns as their hormone levels change. Testosterone therapy, for instance, may increase sexual desire in trans men, while estrogen therapy may alter sexual attraction for trans women. These hormonal shifts can affect how individuals experience themselves and their relationships, creating a nuanced interplay between biological processes and identity.

4.2 Hormonal Influences on Gender Identity and Sexual Orientation:

Beyond influencing attraction, hormones also play a role in shaping gender identity, which in turn intersects with sexual orientation. The prenatal hormonal environment, for example, is thought to influence sexual orientation. Studies suggest that the levels of sex hormones an individual is exposed to in the womb can affect sexual preferences later in life. This theory posits that higher levels of testosterone in females, for example, might increase the likelihood of identifying as lesbian or bisexual. However, this is just one facet of a much more complex equation that includes genetic, social, and environmental factors. Additionally, individuals who transition to a different gender through HRT may find that their sense of self and sexual attraction shift in ways that align with their gender identity. This highlights the multifaceted role of hormones in shaping both gender identity and sexual orientation, illustrating that biology and identity are deeply interconnected.

4.3 The Impact of Hormones on Relationship Dynamics:

Hormones do not just affect attraction, they also influence how individuals behave in relationships. Oxytocin, often referred to as the "love hormone," plays a crucial role in bonding, attachment, and emotional intimacy. In LGBTQ+ relationships, the dynamics of bonding and emotional attachment may be influenced by hormonal fluctuations, affecting how partners connect with each other. For example, studies show that oxytocin levels increase during intimate moments, such as hugging or kissing, promoting feelings of closeness and trust. For those in LGBTQ+ relationships, the expression of intimacy may be deeply influenced by the hormonal responses involved in emotional connection. Additionally, the hormonal influences on attachment behaviour can manifest in different ways across various types of relationships, whether monogamous, polyamorous, or non-traditional.

In polyamorous or non-monogamous queer relationships, oxytocin levels may vary based on the nature and depth of each connection. These hormonal fluctuations can shape how individuals experience attachment, jealousy, and emotional needs, within multiple relationships. Understanding these physiological dynamics helps explain why different relationship structures, particularly within the LGBTQ+ community, navigate intimacy and emotional bonds in distinct ways.

4.4 Hormones and the Experience of Sexual Desire in LGBTQ+ Individuals:

The experience of sexual desire is intrinsically tied to hormonal regulation, which can differ greatly between individuals, particularly within the LGBTQ+ community. For example, trans individuals undergoing hormone replacement therapy (HRT), often report changes in libido that are distinct from those of cisgender individuals. Trans men on testosterone often experience an increase in sexual desire, while trans women undergoing estrogen therapy may experience a decrease or reorientation of sexual attraction. These shifts in sexual desire can have significant implications for how individuals perceive their sexuality and navigate their relationships. For many, the process of transitioning involves a rediscovery or redefinition of sexual attraction, leading to changes in the way they experience intimate relationships. Understanding these shifts highlights the importance of hormonal influences in the lived experiences of LGBTQ+ individuals.

4.5 The Intersection of Hormones, Sexual Orientation, and Identity:

The relationship between hormones, sexual orientation, and identity is a deeply complex and interconnected one. While sexual orientation is often considered a fixed aspect of an individual's identity, hormones can create fluidity in how attraction is experienced over time. For example, hormonal changes during puberty can shape sexual attraction, but the expression of sexuality may evolve throughout a person's life, particularly for individuals who transition. Moreover, the role of hormones in shaping the emotional and psychological aspects of sexual attraction complicates the traditional understanding of sexual orientation as a static concept. For those who undergo gender-affirming hormone therapy, the shift in hormonal balance can lead to a reorientation of attraction, further complicating any attempt to label attraction as solely biologically determined or socially constructed. This highlights the fluidity of sexual identity and the importance of understanding the biological factors that influence it.

4.6 The Psychological and Emotional Impact of Hormonal Changes:

The psychological and emotional effects of hormonal changes also play a key role in shaping attraction and relationship dynamics. Hormonal fluctuations, whether due to puberty, menstrual cycles, pregnancy, menopause, or HRT, can significantly influence mood, desire, and emotional responses. For LGBTQ+ individuals undergoing transition, the emotional and psychological effects of these changes can be profound. The experience of aligning one's physical body with their gender identity through hormone therapy can lead to increased self-confidence, a greater sense of sexual empowerment, and changes in emotional intimacy with partners. These shifts can create a deeper understanding of one's own desires, preferences, and relationship needs, influencing how they engage with their partners and navigate sexual and emotional connections.

4.7 Conclusion – The Complex Intersection of Biology and Identity:

Hormones play a critical role in shaping LGBTQ+ attraction, behaviours, and relationship dynamics, yet their influence is far from simple. While biological factors, such as hormone levels, contribute to the physical and emotional aspects of attraction, they intersect with identity, culture, and personal experiences to create a nuanced picture of human relationships. For LGBTQ+ individuals, hormonal influences can be a catalyst for self-discovery and identity formation, as well as a significant factor in relationship dynamics. By understanding the complex interaction between hormones and identity, we gain deeper insight into the diverse ways in which attraction and emotional connection are experienced within the LGBTQ+ community.

5. The Science of Polyamory and Non-Traditional Relationship Models

Monogamy has long been the dominant model in Western culture, often seen as the default or most "natural" way to love. Yet sociological research challenges this assumption, showing that relationship structures are shaped by culture, historical context, and evolving social norms.

Forms of non-traditional relationships, such as polyamory, open relationships, and relationship anarchy, have existed throughout history and across civilizations, even as they've been sidelined in mainstream narratives. As scholars reevaluate what counts as "normal," it becomes clear that ideas of emotional exclusivity, fidelity, and commitment are socially constructed, rather than universally fixed. Today, increasing numbers of people are openly practicing and advocating for diverse ways of forming intimate bonds. Making sense of these cultural shifts requires moving beyond moral judgments into a more evidence-based, critically engaged understanding of human relationships.

5.1 The Psychological Architecture of Multiple Attachments:

Polyamory often challenges conventional ideas of emotional attachment. Psychological studies, particularly those grounded in attachment theory, show that humans are capable of forming deep, secure bonds with more than one person simultaneously. While traditional models of attachment suggest that secure relationships require exclusivity, emerging research suggests that what truly matters is the quality of the connection, mutual respect, communication, and emotional security. Polyamorous relationships often rely on elevated levels of trust and intentional communication, skills that are actively developed to navigate the emotional complexity of maintaining multiple connections. Contrary to widespread misconceptions, individuals in polyamorous partnerships are not inherently more susceptible to jealousy. Instead, many embrace the concept of "compersion", the genuine happiness felt when a partner experiences joy or intimacy with someone else, which reframes emotional responses and challenges conventional notions of possessiveness and exclusivity in love.

5.2 Neuroscience and Hormonal Dynamics in Non-Monogamous Love:

Scientific research into the neurochemical underpinnings of love and attachment, particularly involving oxytocin, dopamine, and vasopressin, reveals that these hormones do not restrict bonding to a single individual. Oxytocin, often dubbed the "bonding hormone," is released through intimacy and touch, reinforcing closeness and trust. In polyamorous relationships, this hormone is not "diluted" across partners, but can instead be experienced multiple times, in different relational contexts. Neuroscience confirms that the brain is capable of accommodating multiple romantic bonds, and that the physiological mechanisms involved in love are not exclusive to monogamous dynamics. This understanding opens the door to a more inclusive model of relational neuroscience, one that recognizes the legitimacy of diverse emotional architectures. By acknowledging the brain's capacity for multiple bonds, science helps validate non-monogamous love as both natural and neurologically sound.

5.3 Communication, Consent and Emotional Labour:

A key feature of thriving non-traditional relationships is their foundation in open communication and continuous, active consent. Rather than relying on implicit assumptions, partners in polyamorous dynamics regularly engage in intentional dialogue, emotional transparency, and the ongoing negotiation of boundaries. This process demands a high degree of emotional literacy and conscious effort, often described as emotional labour, which becomes central to sustaining healthy, respectful connections.

Psychological research indicates that individuals in polyamorous relationships often demonstrate stronger conflict-resolution skills, deeper self-awareness, and higher relationship satisfaction, largely due to the central role of explicit communication. This communication frequently extends into meta-communication, or the practice of discussing how to communicate effectively. Such strategies are essential for managing complex emotional dynamics like jealousy, negotiating time and energy across multiple partners, and upholding each person's autonomy, within the relationship structure.

5.4 Jealousy, Insecurity, and the Myth of Scarcity:

Contrary to popular belief, polyamory does not eliminate jealousy, it recontextualizes it. Studies show that jealousy in non-monogamous relationships is not necessarily more frequent, but it is addressed differently. Instead of being seen as a threat to the relationship, jealousy is often treated as a signal for self-reflection and growth. The underlying myth that love is a finite resource, what psychologists call the "scarcity mindset", is challenged by polyamory's guiding belief that love can be abundant and renewable. Addressing jealousy in this context becomes a proactive process, where individuals engage in emotional regulation, reassurance, and trust-building practices. This reconceptualization of emotional responses can lead to stronger self-awareness and relational resilience. Understanding jealousy as a growth opportunity rather than a threat shifts the emotional landscape, making room for healthier, more intentional relationship dynamics.

5.5 Social Stigma and Structural Barriers:

Despite the growing visibility of non-traditional relationships, social stigma persists. Polyamorous individuals often face legal and institutional challenges, from child custody disputes to a lack of recognition in healthcare and housing. Psychological research notes that the stress associated with social stigma, often referred to as minority stress, can affect mental health outcomes for those in non-monogamous relationships. Furthermore, because these relationships exist outside of legally sanctioned norms, individuals must often create their own frameworks for rights, responsibilities, and conflict resolution. Sociologically, these dynamics reveal how deeply embedded mononormativity is in policy and law, reinforcing the need for broader systemic change. Recognizing these barriers is the first step toward advocating for policies and cultural shifts that validate and protect all forms of consensual love.

5.6 Towards a More Inclusive Science of Relationships:

The study of human relationships has historically been biased toward monogamous, heterosexual models. But as researchers begin to expand the scope of inquiry, new understandings of relational diversity are emerging. Psychology, neuroscience, and sociology are increasingly recognizing the legitimacy of polyamorous and other non-traditional bonds, not as anomalies, but as part of the rich spectrum of human connection. This shift challenges the assumption that there is a "one-size-fits-all" model for intimacy and calls for a science that reflects the lived realities of queer and non-monogamous people alike. Moving forward, research must continue to examine these relationships on their own terms, with rigor, nuance, and cultural sensitivity.

5.7 Conclusion – Embracing Relational Pluralism:

Non-traditional relationships offer profound insight into the adaptability and depth of human connection. Far from undermining traditional values, they introduce alternative models of love, intimacy, and commitment rooted in agency, transparency, and mutual respect. Scientific exploration of these dynamics not only affirms the legitimacy of diverse relationship structures, but also challenges and expands conventional definitions of what is considered "normal." In doing so, it encourages a broader cultural evolution, one that celebrates the many ways people create meaningful and fulfilling bonds.

* Further Exploration – The Science of Queer Love and Identity:

Explore a carefully curated selection of insightful books, documentaries and podcasts, that examine the psychology, neuroscience, biology and lived experiences of queer attraction, identity and relationships. This collection offers research-driven and culturally nuanced resources, providing a deeper understanding and opportunities for continued exploration.

A. For Example – Books for Further Exploration:

Psychology of Queer Love and Identity:

- The Velvet Rage by Alan Downs – A clinical psychologist's deep dive into the emotional lives of gay men.
- Queer Love in Colour by Jamal Jordan – A beautiful collection of photos and stories celebrating LGBTQ+ love globally.
- "The Queer Art of Failure" by Jack Halberstam – A compelling critique of societal norms through a queer theory lens, exploring alternative ways of being and loving.

Neurology and Gender/Sexual Identity:

- The Gendered Brain by Gina Rippon – A critical analysis of how neuroscience has perpetuated gender stereotypes.
- Brain Gender by Melissa Hines – Explores the biological basis of sex differences and gender identity.

Biological Determinism and Genetic Debates:

- Biological Determinism and Genetic Debates Gay, Straight, and the Reason Why by Simon LeVay. Explores the science behind sexual orientation from a neuroscientific lens.
- Biological Exuberance: Animal Homosexuality and Natural Diversity by Bruce Bagemihl. Discusses animal sexuality and the natural diversity of sexual behaviour.

Hormones and Attraction:

- Testosterone: An Unauthorized Biography by Rebecca M. Jordan-Young and Katrina Karkazis – Debunks myths surrounding testosterone.

- Come As You Are by Emily Nagoski – A research-based guide to understanding sexuality and arousal, especially for queer audiences.

Polyamory and Non-Traditional Relationships:

- Polysecure by Jessica Fern – A blend of attachment theory and consensual non-monogamy.
- The Ethical Slut by Dossie Easton and Janet Hardy – A foundational guide to ethical open relationships.
- More Than Two by Franklin Veaux and Eve Rickert – A practical and philosophical look at navigating polyamory.

B. For Example – Documentaries for Further Exploration:

Sexual Orientation and Identity:

- Out in Science – Explores the experiences of LGBTQ+ scientists and the role of identity in their work.
- The Celluloid Closet – A documentary that explores how LGBTQ+ characters and themes have been depicted in film history and the impact of these portrayals on public perception.

Genetics and the "Gay Gene" Debate:

- The Myth of the Gay Gene – A thought-provoking documentary examining the complexity of sexual orientation and the limitations of genetic determinism.

Neuroscience and Gender Identity:

- TED Talk: The Science of Gender Identity by Karissa Sanbonmatsu – A compelling lecture exploring the relationship between the brain and gender identity.

Hormones and Behaviour:

- Stanford Lecture: The Science of Hormones and Sexual Behaviour by Dr. Robert Sapolsky – An engaging lecture on the intersection of endocrinology and sexuality.

C. For Example – Podcasts for Further Exploration:

Psychological and Emotional Aspects:

- Speaking of Psychology – Episode with Dr. Lisa Diamond exploring queer relationships and love from a psychological lens.
- Queerology – A Podcast on Belief and Being. Hosted by Rev. Dr. Carl Jean, this podcast explores queer identity through a spiritual and psychological lens, examining issues like faith, acceptance and self-discovery.

Polyamory and Relationship Dynamics:

- Multiamory – A long-running podcast that explores polyamorous and nontraditional relationships through research, interviews, and real-life insights.
- Normalizing Non-Monogamy – This podcast features real-life stories and interviews that normalize non-monogamous relationships, with a focus on how to navigate polyamory in modern society.

Queer Science and Society:

- Queer Science – This podcast discusses the intersection of science and queer identities, touching on topics like the biological, psychological and social aspects of being LGBTQ+.
- UnFictional – While not specifically queer-focused, this podcast often features LGBTQ+ stories and narratives that challenge traditional views on identity and relationships. It explores personal experiences with gender, love, and societal expectations.

Chapter 16

Neuroqueer – Autism, ADHD and Divergent Queer Identity

1. Neuroqueerness – What Happens When the Brain is Non-Normative Too?

The term "neuroqueer" defies tidy definitions, much like the identities it encompasses. Coined by Dr. Nick Walker and others in the neurodivergent community, it refers to the intentional or organic subversion of both neurotypical and heteronormative frameworks. Neuroqueerness is not simply the overlap of being LGBTQ+ and neurodivergent; it is the deliberate or intrinsic act of living and thinking outside conventional cognitive and social expectations. Rather than fitting into boxes built for others, neuroqueer individuals blur or outright reject the boundaries that separate "normal" from "non-normal," whether those boundaries are based on brain function, gender roles, or romantic and sexual norms. The power of the term lies in its fluidity, its refusal to be domesticated by academic or clinical language.

1.1 Beyond Diagnosis – Neurodivergence as Creative Resistance:

Clinical diagnoses tend to categorize, pathologize, and isolate. Neuroqueerness rejects the idea that divergence from neurotypicality is something to be treated or managed. Instead, it embraces neurodivergence, such as autism, ADHD, bipolarity, and dyslexia, as ways of being that challenge the normative social order. To neuroqueer one's existence is to see one's difference not as a deficit, but as potential, potential for new ways of relating, loving, and imagining the world. Cognitive difference becomes a site of resistance and reimagination. The neuroqueer mind doesn't just think differently; it reconfigures the terms of what thinking can even be. This reframing shifts power away from the medical-industrial complex and returns agency to those who have long been "treated" into silence.

1.2 Queerness of the Mind – Dissolving the Binary of Neurotypical vs. Neurodivergent:

Just as gender and sexuality resist binary classification, so too does cognition. The idea that there is a normal mind, a typical way of perceiving, processing, and expressing, is a cultural myth reinforced by institutional norms, not a scientific truth. Neuroqueerness undermines the binary of neurotypical versus neurodivergent in the same way queer theory destabilizes man/woman or straight/gay. The spectrum is not linear, but multidimensional, with each brain operating uniquely depending on context, environment, and relational dynamics. This challenges not only psychological norms, but epistemological assumptions: how do we know what we know? Who gets to define coherence, logic, or social intelligence? Neuroqueerness asserts that all forms of thinking are valid, emphasizing limitless possibilities for expression, connection, and reimagining existence.

1.3 Embodied Disruption – How Neuroqueerness Feels in the World:

Living neuroqueer is not merely a theoretical position, it is an embodied and affective experience. It often means moving through the world with hypersensitivity, nonlinear emotional timelines, and a deep sense of alienation from dominant culture. But it also comes with the capacity for rich inner worlds, creative associations, radical empathy, and unconventional forms of intimacy. Neuroqueer embodiment disrupts expectations around communication, productivity, and even how love or gender, should be expressed. It may show up in stimming gestures that are read as "weird," or in ways of connecting that bypass verbal language entirely. These modes of being aren't dysfunctions, they are alternate languages of existence. To embrace neuroqueerness is to reclaim the body-mind from systems that have long sought to regulate, suppress, or erase its difference.

1.4 The Neuroqueer as Cultural Trickster:

In many mythologies, the trickster figure disrupts social order not through violence, but through mischief, ambiguity, and unpredictability. Neuroqueer individuals often occupy a similar cultural role, refusing to behave, to mask, or to perform acceptability in ways that maintain the status quo. By simply existing as they are, neuroqueer people destabilize systems that demand legibility, predictability, and conformity. This disruption is not about chaos for its own sake, but about opening up space for new possibilities. The neuroqueer trickster is the glitch in the matrix, the "wrong" answer that reveals the poverty of the question. Through humour, refusal, and difference, neuroqueer lives illuminate the cracks in what society deems to be rational or real. The neuroqueer trickster invites us to question the norms we take for granted and reimagine a more inclusive world.

1.5 Queering Time, Space and Relationships:

Neuroqueer experience often includes a queering of time itself. Chrononormativity, the societal expectation that people move through time in predictable ways (childhood, adolescence, adulthood, career, marriage, retirement), does not account for fluctuating energy levels, nonlinear thinking, or delayed development often seen in neurodivergent lives. Time is experienced differently, looped, fractured, or spiralled. Relationships, too, are queered, they may form outside normative scripts, relying on alternative forms of communication, mutual care, and shared sensory experiences. Neuroqueerness invites a reimagination of relational norms that privilege consistency over fluctuation, speech over sensation, and independence over interdependence. In doing so, it opens the door to more inclusive, expansive, and imaginative forms of connection.

1.6 Neuroqueerness as Praxis – Living Beyond the Norm:

Choosing, or discovering, neuroqueerness is not a one-time act, but an ongoing praxis. It means refusing to perform neurotypicality for survival while also resisting the pressure to fit into mainstream LGBTQ+ narratives of pride, productivity, and assimilation. Neuroqueer life is often nonlinear, messy, deeply personal, and necessarily communal. It calls for adaptive support systems, radical self-acceptance, and collective care that values process over outcome.

Rather than trying to pass as either neurotypical or "respectable queer," neuroqueer individuals often find liberation in shedding those masks and embracing the contradictions of their experience. In this praxis, thriving is redefined, not as fitting in, but as expanding what it means to be alive, connected, and whole.

1.7 Imagining Neuroqueer Futures:

The promise of neuroqueerness lies not just in resisting the present, but in reimagining the future. What could education look like if it honoured neurodiversity as brilliance rather than deviation? What if public spaces were designed to support sensory variance, or if relationships were built on mutual understanding rather than neurotypical compromise? These futures are not utopian dreams, they are already in the making, in autistic-led collectives, queer mutual aid networks and neurodivergent art movements. Neuroqueerness envisions a world where minds are not pathologized, but cherished for their singular beauty. It is not just a label, it is a horizon. One that reminds us we are not broken, but breaking open a new world.

2. Masking, Passing, and Sensory Overwhelm in LGBTQ+ Life

Masking is, at its core, a form of survival. For many neurodivergent LGBTQ+ individuals, it becomes second nature, a practiced performance shaped by the need to appear neurotypical, cisgender, or heteronormative enough to avoid scrutiny, rejection, or harm. This can look like forced eye contact, scripted small talk, gendered clothing choices, or the careful modulation of tone and body language. Beneath the surface lies a deep emotional cost, anxiety, exhaustion, and disconnection from the self. Masking is often mistaken for confidence or adaptability, when in reality, it can be a quiet, ongoing form of self-erasure. The labour of presenting as "acceptable" can fracture one's sense of identity, burying the authentic self under layers of performance just to get through the day. Unmasking, then, becomes an act of courage, a return to self that asks for both safety and self-compassion. Masking in LGBTQ+ life is a survival strategy that hides the authentic self, with unmasking offering a path to reclaim identity.

2.1 Passing – Safety or Disappearance?

The concept of "passing" is fraught with complexity. For some queer and trans individuals, passing, whether in terms of gender, sexuality, or neurotypicality, can be a source of safety, a protective cloak that allows them to move through public spaces without confrontation. For others, it feels like a betrayal, a silencing of truth to accommodate a world that refuses to expand. Neurodivergent people often find themselves trying to pass as neurotypical within queer spaces, while simultaneously navigating the pressure to present queer identities in legible, socially palatable ways. The result is a constant negotiation of visibility and invisibility. Choosing when to be seen and when to blend in is rarely about preference, more often, it's about survival. And with that comes guilt, grief, and a longing to be accepted, without conditions. Living between visibility and erasure asks us to hold space for both the cost and courage of being. Passing is a survival mechanism, balancing safety with the emotional cost of erasure and the longing for unconditional acceptance.

2.2 The Unseen Toll of Sensory Overwhelm:

For neurodivergent queer individuals, sensory overload isn't just a moment of discomfort, it's an all-consuming state that can turn everyday environments into battlegrounds. Bright lights, loud crowds, overlapping conversations, perfume, textures, and even the wrong kind of fabric can become sources of distress. Many LGBTQ+ spaces, pride events, nightclubs, and rallies, are built on intensity, energy, and sensory stimulation. While they offer connection and celebration, they can also be inaccessible and overwhelming for those with sensory sensitivities. The expectation to be present, visible, and joyous in these spaces can create a painful contradiction, the desire to belong competing with the need to protect one's body and mind. Too often, individuals suffer in silence, believing their pain is a personal failing rather than a systemic oversight.

2.3 Emotional Exhaustion and Identity Fatigue:

The combined strain of masking, passing, and navigating sensory triggers leads to a state of emotional exhaustion that is hard to articulate and even harder to admit. Many neurodivergent LGBTQ+ individuals carry immense internal pressure, to perform as expected, to suppress needs that seem "too much," and to keep up with the rhythms of community life even when it becomes unsustainable. This chronic stress contributes to burnout, depression, and isolation. The very spaces meant to offer refuge can become sources of further distress if they do not make room for neurodivergent expressions of queerness. Identity fatigue, the weariness of constantly explaining oneself, justifying boundaries and renegotiating belonging, takes a toll on both the spirit and the body. Without compassionate understanding, these burdens become invisible weights.

2.4 Queer Neurodivergence and the Longing for Authenticity:

Beneath the layers of performance and adaptation lies a deep, aching desire, to be known and loved as one truly is. Neurodivergent queer people often find themselves chasing authenticity in a world that demands modification. Many are told, explicitly or subtly, that their natural ways of moving, speaking, or feeling are wrong. But the heart knows otherwise. Even small moments of being accepted in full, without judgment, without the need to explain, can be profoundly healing. Authenticity isn't just about self-expression, it's about safety, softness, and the ability to breathe without fear. The path toward it is messy and nonlinear, especially when past experiences of rejection linger. But each step, each unmasking, each decision to honour one's limits and needs, becomes a quiet act of revolution.

2.5 Creating Spaces of Neuroqueer Belonging:

What would it mean to build queer spaces with neurodivergence in mind from the start? Spaces where volume is controlled, exits are clear, stim toys are normalized, and communication happens in multiple forms, not just speech. Spaces where the expectation isn't constant engagement, but consent-based interaction. Belonging begins with design, but it is sustained through care, active listening, mutual respect, and the willingness to slow down. Community doesn't require conformity. In fact, it thrives on difference.

Creating spaces that honour both neurodivergence and queerness is not just possible, it's essential. Because when people feel safe enough to unmask, to opt out, or to stim freely, something radical happens, they begin to trust themselves again. And through that trust, a deeper connection becomes possible.

2.6 Moving from Performance to Presence:

Letting go of the performance doesn't mean losing connection, it means redefining it. Moving from masking to presence is a gradual process, one that asks for patience, vulnerability, and support. It means permitting oneself to take breaks, to stim without shame, to say "no" without guilt. It means valuing moments of quiet intimacy over loud celebration, and recognizing that worth is not measured by how well one passes. Presence invites softness, with ourselves, with each other, with the complex ways our identities intersect and express. It's not about getting it "right," but about being real, messy, sensory, fluid, and whole.

2.7 Toward a More Gentle Queer Future:

The future of queer liberation must include neurodivergence at its core. A gentler future makes room for silence, slowness, and sensory needs. It uplifts those who've been made to feel too much, too odd, too sensitive. It does not demand performance but welcomes authenticity. That future begins with the courage to unmask, the compassion to see others clearly, and the community to hold us through it. Masking and sensory overwhelm don't have to define queer life. They are part of a larger story, one that, when told honestly and held tenderly, can lead us back to ourselves.

3. The Queer Joy of Hyperfixation and Special Interests

Hyperfixation is often framed as a problem to be managed, a symptom to be minimized. But for queer neurodivergent individuals, it can be a profound source of joy, creativity and self-connection. These intense periods of focus offer a sense of clarity and direction in a world that frequently feels chaotic or overwhelming. Whether it's an encyclopaedic knowledge of fungi, an obsession with 80s synth music, or an all-consuming dive into queer theory, hyperfixation isn't merely a coping mechanism, it's a love language. It allows for immersion, play, and depth, providing a structure of meaning and stimulation that can anchor identity and soothe overstimulated minds. Rather than pathologizing this kind of attention, it deserves to be honoured for the fulfilment it brings.

3.1 Special Interests as a Form of Self-Affirmation:

Special interests often emerge not by choice, but as instinctive gravitations, magnetic pulls toward certain topics, objects, or stories that feel deeply resonant. For queer neurodivergent people, these interests can become sites of safety and identity exploration. Diving into the intricacies of vintage fashion, plant taxonomy, or animated series with unapologetic devotion is more than just a hobby, it's an act of self-affirmation. These passions aren't distractions from the "real" world, they are the real world for those who live through them.

They become extensions of personality, grounding forces during times of social alienation, and expressive tools that communicate care, curiosity, and brilliance in uniquely meaningful ways. Special interests serve as grounding tools for queer neurodivergent individuals, offering affirmation, self-expression and resilience in an often alienating world.

3.2 The Intersection of Queerness and Obsession:

Queer identity often involves a rejection of societal norms and special interests mirror that same defiance. While society demands productivity and balance, hyperfixations exist on their own terms, deep, unrelenting, and non-linear. There's something inherently queer about this mode of engagement. It resists moderation and celebrates excess. It's flamboyant in its enthusiasm, subversive in its depth, and radically unconcerned with whether others "get it." For many, discovering a special interest is also discovering a new part of oneself, one that doesn't need to be tamed or translated. This alignment between queer identity and hyperfixation fosters a beautiful synergy, unapologetic passion becomes a form of queer pride. Loving intensely, obsessing freely, and expressing fully becomes a radical reclaiming of joy.

3.3 Building Connection Through Shared Obsession:

Though often seen as isolating, hyperfixations can be incredible bridges for connection. In queer neurodivergent communities, shared enthusiasm can spark some of the most meaningful relationships. Friendships form not around small talk, but around mutual deep dives, collaborative art projects, fandoms, theory debates, and niche interests that might seem obscure to outsiders, but feel like home to those within. These shared passions allow for authentic bonding without the pressure to mask or dilute. Communication flourishes when people are allowed to info-dump, to stim while they speak, to exist in spaces where excitement isn't policed. When communities welcome this form of interaction, they cultivate radical inclusivity and deep, joyful resonance. Connection thrives when joy is mutual, unfiltered, and unafraid to take up space, allowing each person to express themselves freely. In these spaces, every voice is valued and authenticity flourishes.

3.4 When the World Pathologizes What We Love:

Despite the richness of special interests, dominant culture often sees them as excessive or inappropriate, especially when they deviate from neurotypical expectations of behaviour. Queer neurodivergent individuals may be told they're too intense, too focused, too weird. This framing can be especially painful when the passions in question are dismissed as childish, irrelevant, or obsessive. The policing of what we love becomes a way to police who we are. When gendered expectations enter the mix, when boys are encouraged to like trains, but girls are discouraged from loving bugs, these dismissals take on another layer of constraint. To reclaim hyperfixation as joy is to reclaim the right to exist beyond those narrow expectations. It is a form of resistance against a world that seeks to flatten passion into palatability. Celebrating what lights us up is a radical act of self-definition, a joyful and unapologetic defiance of norms that pathologize intensity and a powerful reclaiming of queer neurodivergent identity, in a world that so often demands we dim our brilliance just to be understood.

3.5 Queer Rituals of Learning and Play:

There is ritual in returning to what you love, over and over again. Queer neurodivergent people often develop rich internal landscapes built around their interests, maps of knowledge, constellations of ideas, creative projects that span years. These are not just distractions, they are sacred practices. Whether it's crafting fanfiction, making spreadsheets about sea slugs, or reciting film dialogue from memory, these rituals serve as meditative, affirming acts. They can offer structure, calm the nervous system, and make space for joy in times of distress. When honoured, they become queer rites of self-preservation, ways to remain whole in a world that often insists we fragment ourselves to survive.

3.6 Joy Without Explanation:

Part of what makes hyperfixation so powerful is that it doesn't demand justification. The joy is intrinsic. Queer joy, too, is often inexplicable, growing in unexpected places, nourished by desire, connection and imagination. There is freedom in loving something without needing it to make sense to others. There is beauty in prioritizing joy over productivity, in choosing immersion over moderation, in knowing that devotion doesn't require permission. For neurodivergent queer people, the ability to embrace that joy is a radical act. It's about reclaiming autonomy over one's attention, one's time, and one's emotional landscape. It's about allowing ourselves to be as passionate, peculiar, and specific as we are.

3.7 Toward a Celebration of Deep Enthusiasm:

A queer neurodivergent future is one that celebrates deep enthusiasm as a gift, not a glitch. It makes space for stimming while info dumping, for collaborative obsession, for spontaneous research binges that lead to midnight breakthroughs. It embraces the beauty of loving something wholeheartedly, of following a curiosity wherever it leads. In this world, people are not expected to quiet their interests to fit in, they are celebrated for sharing them. Hyperfixation is no longer hidden, it becomes a source of pride. Special interests are no longer trivialized, they are seen as expressions of depth, connection and joy. When queer neurodivergent passion is centered and celebrated, it lights the way to a world more vivid, more inclusive, and more alive.

4. Gender Nonconformity and the Autistic Experience

Autistic individuals are statistically more likely to identify outside the gender binary than their allistic peers. This resistance to conventional gender categories isn't accidental, it's deeply tied to how many autistic people relate to societal expectations. While neurotypical development often hinges on learning and internalizing social scripts, autistic cognition can challenge or even disregard these scripts entirely. Gender, being one of the most rigidly policed scripts in society, is naturally subject to re-examination. Many autistic individuals describe an intuitive disconnect between who they are and how they're expected to perform gender. Whether through clothing, behaviour, or pronouns, their gender expression often emerges from internal coherence rather than external validation. The result is a population that frequently lives outside of traditional gender roles, not out of rebellion, but from an innate authenticity.

4.1 Sensory Processing and Embodied Gender:

Autistic people often experience the world through heightened or atypical sensory processing, and this has profound implications for how they relate to their bodies and gendered expectations. For instance, the discomfort many feel with certain fabrics, tight clothing, or physical gestures can be magnified by gendered dress codes or beauty standards. Makeup, underwire bras, binders, and even certain hairstyles may cause sensory overwhelm. These discomforts are not simply aesthetic preferences, they are lived, embodied experiences that shape how gender is felt and expressed. For some, gender dysphoria is intricately tied to sensory aversion rather than identity alone. For others, euphoria may arise not from conforming to gender norms, but from dressing and moving in ways that align with sensory comfort and freedom. Viewing gender through a sensory lens expands the conversation, offering a richer framework for autistic gender variance.

This sensory-gender connection helps explain why traditional gender roles can feel especially alienating for autistic individuals. Rather than conforming for social approval, many prioritize how gender feels over how it looks. This often leads to unique, authentic expressions of gender that resist binaries and center sensory comfort. These experiences highlight the need for more inclusive gender frameworks that honour neurodivergent bodies and boundaries.

4.2 Literal Thinking and the Questioning of Social Constructs:

One of the hallmarks of autistic cognition is a tendency toward literal, logical, and often deeply analytical thinking. When applied to gender, this can result in a natural scepticism of socially constructed norms that don't seem to hold up under scrutiny. The idea that toys, colours, careers, or behaviours should be gendered may seem illogical or arbitrary to someone who hasn't absorbed those norms unquestioningly. Many autistic individuals report feeling confused or alienated by the social rules around gender, not because they lack understanding, but because the rules themselves lack coherence. This capacity to deconstruct social constructs is not only liberating, but often leads to a more fluid and expansive understanding of gender. Rather than trying to "pass" within binary frameworks, autistic people may redefine the framework entirely, blending, rejecting, or inventing gender categories that feel more congruent with their lived experience.

4.3 Communication Styles and the Misreading of Gender:

Gender is often communicated nonverbally, through posture, tone, eye contact, movement, and facial expression. Autistic people may communicate in ways that don't match neurotypical gender expectations, leading to frequent misgendering or confusion. An autistic woman who avoids eye contact or speaks in a monotone might be perceived as masculine, while an autistic man who gestures expressively or dresses androgynously might be read as effeminate. These mismatches can provoke tension both within the autistic person and in their interactions with others. What's more, many autistic individuals report being punished or corrected for their communication from a young age, further complicating their sense of self and gender. Rather than reinforcing binary categories, autistic expression often reveals their limitations, showing that gender isn't something static or inherent, but something constantly read, interpreted and imposed through social lenses.

4.4 Diagnosing Difference – The Pathologization of Gender Nonconformity:

Medical and psychiatric systems have historically pathologized both autism and gender nonconformity, often interpreting deviations from normativity as deficits or disorders. When the two intersect, the risk of misunderstanding and misdiagnosis increases. Some clinicians have wrongly dismissed trans or nonbinary identities as "symptoms" of autism, rather than valid experiences in their own right. Others have delayed or denied gender-affirming care due to assumptions that autistic people are incapable of understanding or articulating their identities. This gatekeeping reveals a deep-rooted ableism in how society views both autism and queerness. By analysing these systems of control, it becomes clear that pathologization is not a neutral act, it's a reflection of cultural discomfort with complexity, fluidity, and difference. Reclaiming autistic gender diversity means challenging the authority of those who insist there is only one right way to be in a body, or to know oneself.

4.5 Beyond Identity – Gender as an Open-Ended Process:

Rather than viewing gender as a fixed identity to be discovered or labelled, many autistic people experience it as an open-ended process, a dynamic interaction between inner truth and outer experience. For some, this means shifting pronouns, exploring genderless or xenogender frameworks, or eschewing gender categories altogether. For others, it's a slow unfolding, shaped by sensory awareness, relational feedback, and cognitive reflection. This orientation toward fluidity often resists the pressure to "figure it out" quickly or conform to a linear narrative of gender transition. Instead, it invites a more patient, exploratory approach, one where uncertainty is not a threat, but a space for possibility. Autism, far from being a barrier to gender self-understanding, may actually offer the tools for deeper inquiry and imaginative self-expression. This approach allows gender to be a continual discovery, where evolution and self-expression are celebrated.

4.6 Toward a More Expansive Framework of Gender and Neurodivergence:

When autistic voices are centred in conversations about gender, the limitations of binary, neurotypical frameworks come into sharper focus. A more expansive approach honours difference not as deviation, but as innovation. It acknowledges that identity is not always loud or certain and that authenticity may appear strange, to those who have only learned to recognize it in familiar forms. The intersection of autism and gender nonconformity points toward a future where multiple truths can coexist, and where the richness of neurodivergent experience adds depth to our collective understanding of what gender can be. This is not simply about visibility, it's about transformation. When autistic gender nonconformity is not merely tolerated, but embraced, it challenges the very foundations of normativity and offers a model of identity that is nuanced, evolving, and profoundly human.

4.7 Conclusion – Reimagining Gender and Neurodivergence:

Autistic individuals challenge rigid gender norms, offering a fluid, evolving approach to identity that celebrates authenticity and dismantles societal constraints. This reimagining invites us all to embrace diversity in ways that expand our understanding of gender. Autistic voices don't just break the mold, they show us that gender was never meant to fit one.

*Dialogue Sketch – If My Neurodivergence and Queerness Could Talk:

The Internal Boardroom – A Dialogue:

Setting: A quiet morning. The body still, the mind racing. A Neurodivergence and Queerness debate attending a queer dance:

Neurodivergence:
"We're not going to the party. Too many variables. No schedule, no plan, no lighting map. It's chaos."

Queerness:
"But I want to go. It's where I feel most alive, seen. You know how rare that is."

Neurodivergence:
"You'll feel seen until the lights strobe. Until someone brushes against us unexpectedly. Until we lose track of our exit route and our energy depletes by 37% in the first 20 minutes."

Queerness:
"I need the connection. I crave the fluidity. I want to wear mesh and let my hips speak for me."

Neurodivergence:
"I want a corner. I want a script. I want a socially acceptable excuse to leave whenever we need to."

Queerness:
"Can we find middle ground? What if I wear glitter in a low-sensory way? We stay for one hour. You bring the fidget. I bring the flare."

Neurodivergence:
(Sighs) "And we have an exit plan?"

Queerness:
(Grinning) "A three-tiered one, color-coded and all."

Neurodivergence:
"…Alright. But no spontaneous emotional labour. We can't counsel a stranger in the bathroom again."

Queerness:
"Fair. No healing tonight, just being."

Together:
"Deal."

In the end, the evening unfolded like a carefully choreographed dance, a balance of sensory precautions and unapologetic self-expression, leaving both fulfilled.

5. Rewriting Norms – Neurodivergent Love, Consent, and Communication

Neurodivergent individuals often experience love through a different lens than those who fit into neurotypical frameworks. For many, love isn't about following societal expectations or adhering to prescribed romantic scripts, but instead about finding authentic, individualized expressions of connection. This understanding of love can involve unique forms of communication, sensory preferences, and ways of expressing affection that may differ from the mainstream. These variations can be overlooked or misunderstood by others, leading to feelings of isolation or inadequacy. Neurodivergent love is a deep, multifaceted experience that doesn't require validation from outside norms to be meaningful.

5.1 The Struggles with Consent:

Consent is often presented as a simple, binary act, yes or no. For neurodivergent individuals, however, consent can feel far more complex. There may be difficulties in reading social cues or articulating boundaries, especially in environments that prioritize verbal communication and standard relational cues. Neurodivergent people may struggle with the pressure to say "yes" or "no" in ways that feel comfortable to others, yet fail to respect their own internal processes. The emotional toll of this disconnect can be profound, as individuals navigate the pressure to conform to social expectations while yearning for their own needs to be recognized and respected. For many, the ambiguity and potential for miscommunication within the community can lead to feelings of frustration, shame, or misunderstanding. The fear of crossing boundaries, or unintentionally violating someone's consent, adds an additional layer of stress to the neurodivergent experience of relationships.

5.2 The Impact of Being Overlooked:

One of the most emotionally taxing aspects of being neurodivergent within the LGBTQ+ community is the tendency to be overlooked or subtly policed, especially for those still navigating their identities. This may look like being dismissed as "too intense" for expressing a different love language, being told to "tone it down" during emotional or sensory experiences, or feeling that your consent is questioned or invalidated. The very nature of neurodivergence, with its unique ways of thinking, feeling and communicating, can make individuals feel as though they don't quite fit into either the neurotypical or the queer community. This isolation can be painful, as it creates a rift between the desire for connection and the experience of alienation. The emotional labour required to navigate these spaces can make it feel as though neurodivergent individuals must constantly adapt, rather than existing comfortably in their own skin.

5.3 Redefining Communication:

Communication within neurodivergent relationships can be far from conventional, and this is where much of the friction occurs. Where traditional relationships rely heavily on verbal communication and shared social cues, neurodivergent individuals may prefer alternative forms of connection, such as written communication, non-verbal cues, or physical gestures.

These modes of expression are often dismissed as "ineffective" or "awkward" by those who are not familiar with the neurodivergent experience, leading to frustration and miscommunication. A person may feel invalidated or unheard, because their preferred communication style isn't acknowledged or respected. It is essential to honour these alternative modes of communication and embrace the understanding that every individual has their own ways of relating to the world, regardless of whether they align with the mainstream.

5.4 Creating a New Framework for Consent:

In order to create a more inclusive, accepting environment for neurodivergent people, it is crucial to redefine how consent is understood and respected within queer spaces. Consent should not be reduced to a binary concept, but instead should be recognized as a fluid, ongoing process that respects the needs and boundaries of all parties involved. For neurodivergent individuals, this might mean giving them the space to communicate consent in ways that are comfortable for them, whether that's through written words, physical gestures, or visual cues. It also means recognizing the complexity of consent, acknowledging that it may evolve throughout an interaction, and that individuals need the freedom to change their minds without fear of judgment or rejection. Creating this space fosters a more inclusive and affirming environment for everyone, where neurodivergent people can feel empowered to assert their own boundaries and engage in relationships on their own terms.

5.5 The Emotional Toll of Feeling "Othered":

The emotional toll of feeling "othered" within the LGBTQ+ community cannot be overstated. When neurodivergent people's love styles, consent practices, and communication methods are seen as outside the norm, it can lead to feelings of inadequacy and alienation. The pressure to conform to neurotypical standards of relationships, whether it's in the form of socially acceptable ways to communicate affection, perform consent, or even express discomfort, can be overwhelming. When neurodivergent individuals find themselves navigating a world that doesn't seem to understand or value their unique experiences, it can feel as though they are constantly fighting to be seen, heard, and respected. This ongoing struggle can take an emotional toll, leading to burnout, frustration and a sense of disconnection, from both the queer community and their own identities.

5.6 The Need for Validation:

Validation is crucial for the well-being of neurodivergent individuals, especially when it comes to expressing their love, boundaries, and communication styles. Feeling seen, heard, and respected for who they are, without needing to conform to traditional relational scripts, offers a sense of belonging and emotional safety. Neurodivergent people should be able to express their needs and desires without fear of judgment or dismissal. When the community recognizes and affirms neurodivergent love and communication, it empowers individuals to be their authentic selves. Validation also fosters healthier, more sustainable relationships, where both parties can feel understood and appreciated for the unique ways in which they connect. Validation isn't just kindness, it's a radical act of inclusion that honours neurodivergent ways of being as fully real and worthy of love.

5.7 A Path Toward Understanding:

The path forward lies in creating a more inclusive and empathetic queer community, one that embraces the diversity of experiences within it, including neurodivergent love, consent and communication. This begins with fostering understanding and open dialogue, where neurodivergent individuals are given the space to share their experiences and needs without fear of judgment. It also requires creating environments where alternative communication styles are celebrated and consent is seen as a dynamic, evolving process. By dismantling the restrictive norms that govern how love and connection are understood, the queer community can become a space that is truly inclusive, where all forms of love, neurodivergent or not, are honoured and celebrated.

"Love is not a one-size-fits-all experience, it is as diverse as the people who give and receive it." – Anonymous

Chapter 17

Unmasking Abuse in Queer Relationships

1. Behind Closed Doors – The Myth of Queer Relationship Immunity

Queer love is frequently idealized as emotionally deep, inherently respectful and naturally equitable, a powerful contrast to the dysfunction often associated with heteronormative relationships. This perception, while understandable, is shaped by a collective desire to distance queer intimacy from the oppressive frameworks it seeks to defy. Because these relationships challenge patriarchal norms, many assume they are automatically immune to the same toxic dynamics. But this romanticized view can be dangerous. It obscures the presence of abuse, manipulation, and power imbalances, making it harder to acknowledge harm when it occurs. No community is exempt from relational violence and when we elevate queer love as inherently healthier, or more enlightened, we risk silencing survivors whose experiences don't align with that idealized narrative.

1.1 At Least We're Not Them" – Superiority and Avoiding Accountability:

There's a quiet, but persistent belief in many queer spaces that simply rejecting mainstream romantic norms makes our relationships more emotionally evolved or inherently just. This sense of moral or emotional superiority can be seductive, but also blinding. It often masks the very real need for self-reflection, growth, and accountability. The notion that queer love is automatically revolutionary can become a shield, deflecting critique and minimizing harm. When someone speaks out about emotional abuse, coercion, or manipulation, they're too often met with ideological defensiveness, "That can't be happening, we're not like them." In these moments, the myth of queer exceptionalism becomes a tool of erasure. Over-romanticizing our own communities, allows selective accountability to flourish and harm to go unchallenged.

1.2 Red Flags in Rainbow Wrapping – Recognizing Abuse in Queer Dynamics:

Abuse doesn't always look like bruises or shouting matches. Sometimes it looks like control disguised as care, gaslighting cloaked in activism, or co-dependency masquerading as deep love. In queer relationships, especially in tight-knit or activist communities, it's easy for red flags to be hidden under layers of shared trauma, collective struggle, or political alignment. The abuser may also be marginalized in other ways, race, gender identity, disability, making it harder for survivors to come forward without fearing backlash or accusations of betrayal. Abuse wrapped in the language of queerness is still abuse. Learning to name it is the first step to dismantling it. Refusing to acknowledge these patterns only reinforces the myth of immunity, and keeps the most vulnerable members of our communities in harm's way. True queer liberation includes holding each other accountable and creating spaces where safety isn't sacrificed for solidarity, where we can challenge harm without fracturing community, and where healing is prioritized alongside justice.

1.3 The Silence of the Unspoken – Shame, Stigma and the Cost of Disclosure:

For many LGBTQ+ people, love and partnership have long served as acts of survival and defiance, lifelines in a world that often denies their right to exist. In that context, critiquing a queer relationship can feel like a betrayal, a crack in the armour that protects the community from outside scrutiny and harm. Speaking out about abuse or dysfunction isn't just personal, it can be seen as political ammunition for those who already seek to invalidate queer lives. This fear creates a culture of silence, where survivors often stay quiet not because they don't recognize the harm, but because the risk of being further marginalized feels too great. The price of telling the truth becomes unbearable. Breaking this silence means building spaces where honesty is met with compassion, not condemnation, where accountability is not treated as a threat, but embraced as a radical form of care.

1.4 Power, Privilege and the Illusion of Utopia:

Power dynamics don't disappear in queer relationships, they simply take different forms. Factors like race, class, age, gender identity, and ability all shape how power is distributed between partners. One person being more "out," better resourced, or more socially affirmed can significantly influence the emotional and practical balance of a relationship. Too often, these imbalances are overlooked or minimized under the assumption that shared queerness equals shared equity. But queerness alone doesn't erase privilege. When we ignore these disparities, we create a dangerous illusion of equality, one that lets manipulation masquerade as intimacy and progressive language conceal control. Behind closed doors, harm persists even in the most radical of spaces. Real liberation demands more than solidarity in oppression, it requires the courage to confront the privileges that exist among us and within our most intimate bonds.

1.5 Reclaiming Accountability as a Queer Practice:

The path forward isn't about tearing down queer love, it's about making it more honest. Reclaiming accountability as an active practice of love and solidarity means refusing to mythologize ourselves or our relationships. It means recognizing that emotional harm, coercion, and abuse are not confined to straight or cis spaces. Queer relationships deserve the same attention, care and critique, that we demand from all relational structures. Building a culture of transparency and consent, beyond the buzzwords, requires us to look inward and ask uncomfortable questions. Who are we protecting when we refuse to name harm? What might healing look like if we stopped pretending queer relationships are inherently better?

1.6 Building Queer Relationships Rooted in Truth:

Real intimacy doesn't come from perfection, it comes from courage. Queer love is capable of profound transformation, but only when it's grounded in reality, not idealism. By letting go of the myth of immunity, we make space for more honest, complex, and resilient relationships. We learn to apologize, to unlearn patterns, to listen deeply. We create room for survivors to speak without fear and for community care to mean more than slogans. Queer relationships don't need to be perfect to be powerful, they need to be real.

And in that reality, there is room for both beauty and brokenness, healing and harm, joy and justice.

* Pause for Reflection – Deepening Understanding and Healing:

"What do we think makes queer relationships different or 'safer' than straight relationships? How does this belief affect the way we talk about abuse in our communities?"

2. Invisible Scars – Emotional Abuse Beyond the Binary

Emotional abuse, while less tangible than physical violence, can be just as harmful and long-lasting. In queer relationships, this form of abuse often takes on specific dynamics that intersect with the complexity of gender, sexuality and identity. Unlike traditional forms of abuse that are easily recognized through physical signs, emotional abuse hides beneath the surface, weaving its way through manipulative behaviours like gaslighting, control, and emotional manipulation. For LGBTQ+ individuals, emotional abuse becomes even more nuanced, often complicated by the lack of societal recognition or validation of their identities. This dynamic frequently operates in ways that are both subtle and insidious, making it harder to recognize and even harder to escape.

2.1 Gaslighting – The Distortion of Reality in Queer Relationships:

One of the most pervasive forms of emotional abuse in any relationship is gaslighting, a psychological tactic used to make someone doubt their own perception of reality. In queer relationships, gaslighting takes on an additional layer of complexity, because of the identity-related struggles that LGBTQ+ individuals face. A partner might subtly undermine or deny aspects of their partner's identity or experience, suggesting that their feelings, perceptions, or desires are invalid or unreasonable. This can manifest in subtle, yet damaging ways, such as dismissing a partner's gender identity as just a "phase" or trivializing their concerns about societal oppression as "overreactions." In queer relationships, the boundary between genuine support and manipulation can be dangerously blurred. The abuser may exploit the partner's vulnerability around their identity to undermine or control them, eroding their sense of self and creating a toxic dynamic where their worth is slowly chipped away.

2.2 The Role of Control – Navigating Power in Queer Dynamics:

Control in queer relationships can manifest in ways that are often unique to the intersectional identities involved. Power dynamics shaped by race, gender identity, class, and disability can complicate the way control is exerted and perceived. In many cases, an abuser will use their partner's marginalized status against them, exploiting societal vulnerabilities such as lack of access to resources, fear of coming out, or systemic discrimination. This makes it harder for the survivor to escape the relationship or even to recognize the abuse they are experiencing. The abuser may weaponize the survivor's fears or insecurities about their place in the world, creating a dynamic where the survivor feels trapped both within the relationship and within their larger social context. The abuser exploits personal vulnerabilities and societal oppression, trapping the survivor in a cycle of powerlessness. The subtlety of control often leads the victim to believe that they have limited options, especially when societal attitudes about queerness already place them at a disadvantage.

2.3 Emotional Manipulation – Love or Control?

In queer relationships, emotional manipulation often wears the guise of affection, affection that is conditional and used to establish dominance. The abuser may shower their partner with affection, validation, and love one moment, only to withdraw it completely the next, creating a confusing cycle of emotional highs and lows. The survivor begins to rely on the affection and the withdrawal of love, which becomes a powerful tool of control. In this cycle, the victim's emotional state becomes deeply entangled with their abuser's whims, leading them to feel as though they must prove their worth to their partner in ways that are damaging and unhealthy. This emotional push and pull can be incredibly disorienting, particularly when the survivor feels isolated from their community. The survivor may be left questioning if their needs for love and care are too much, or if they are simply "overreacting" to a temporary issue.

2.4 The Silencing of Identity and Desire:

In LGBTQ+ relationships, the act of silencing a partner's identity or desires can be an especially toxic form of emotional abuse. For example, an abuser might insist that their partner "tone down" or suppress parts of their identity, like their gender presentation or sexual preferences, because it makes the abuser uncomfortable or fearful of external judgment. In relationships that already grapple with societal marginalization, these silencing tactics can feel like betrayal, both personally and within the larger context of the queer community. The abuser exploits the survivor's desire for belonging and acceptance, manipulating them into compromising who they are to fit a mold created by the abuser. This can erode self-esteem and lead to a deep sense of self-doubt, where the survivor feels as if their authentic self is wrong or unworthy of love. This manipulation not only isolates the survivor from their own identity, but also from the supportive queer communities that affirm their worth, further deepening the emotional toll of the abuse.

2.5 Intersectionality – The Layers of Abuse in Queer Dynamics:

The unique emotional abuse experienced in queer relationships is often compounded by intersectional factors. A person who is not only queer, but also a person of colour, disabled, or from a lower socio-economic background may experience emotional abuse that is tailored to exploit these specific vulnerabilities. For example, an abuser may use racial or ableist language to demean their partner, or manipulate the partner's sense of belonging to their community by playing on their fears of rejection. Emotional abuse that intersects with multiple identities adds complexity to an already difficult situation, where leaving the relationship can seem impossible due to external societal pressures or fear of further marginalization. These compounded layers of abuse can make it harder for the survivor to recognize the toxicity within the relationship, leading them to normalize the abuse or believe that it's something they must tolerate due to their already marginalized status.

2.6 The Complications of Seeking Help in a Queer Context:

One of the most insidious effects of emotional abuse in queer relationships is the hesitancy to seek help.

There is often a pervasive fear within the LGBTQ+ community of being misunderstood, not believed, or being further stigmatized by outsiders when attempting to report or escape abuse. This is particularly true for those who face multiple layers of marginalization, such as queer people of colour or trans individuals, who may already experience systemic discrimination from social services or law enforcement. Emotional abuse in these cases is even harder to name, because it is less visible and frequently dismissed as an issue specific to individual relationships rather than an endemic problem within queer dynamics. The fear of betraying the community or facing further isolation can keep survivors from reaching out for help, leaving them to suffer in silence. Recognizing these unique barriers is crucial to building more affirming, accessible pathways to safety and healing for all queer survivors.

2.7 Healing and Reclaiming Agency:

Breaking free from the invisible scars of emotional abuse requires acknowledging the complexity of the dynamics at play. Healing is a process that demands compassion, understanding, and patience, both from the survivor and from their community. It involves recognizing the deep harm caused by gaslighting, control, manipulation, and then rebuilding trust, not just in others, but in oneself. Survivors must reclaim their agency, often with the help of survivor-led spaces that recognize the unique nature of abuse in queer relationships. Emotional abuse can leave deep scars that are invisible to the outside world, but with support and empowerment, survivors can find their way toward healing and reclaim their worth beyond the damage that was done. Creating spaces that honour queer survivors' experiences is essential for fostering true healing, resilience and renewal. In reclaiming agency, survivors don't just heal, they redefine what safety, love and liberation can look like in queer lives.

2.8 Conclusion – Breaking the Silence:

The first step toward healing is breaking the silence around emotional abuse in queer relationships. By naming the ways that gaslighting, control, and emotional manipulation show up uniquely in these dynamics, we can begin to dismantle the silence and shame that keep survivors from seeking help. Through collective accountability and a commitment to changing the cultural narratives surrounding queer relationships, we can create spaces where love is defined not by manipulation or control, but by mutual respect and empowerment.

Dismantling the silence and shame requires open, compassionate conversations, survivor-led advocacy, and a willingness to look critically at how internalized oppression can sometimes manifest within our own communities. Through collective accountability and a commitment to changing the cultural narratives surrounding queer relationships, we can begin to build a foundation where support, education and intervention are accessible to all. In doing so, we create spaces where love is defined by mutual respect, emotional safety, and empowerment, ensuring everyone in our community can love and be loved without fear.

"Love should never silence you. In queer community, healing begins when we dare to speak the truths that keep us safe." – Anonymous

*** LGBTQ+ Support and Resources for Survivors of Relationship Violence and Abuse, but not limited to:**

United States:

The Trevor Project:

- Support services for LGBTQ+ youth focused on crisis intervention, suicide prevention and relationship violence.

GLAAD:

- Provides resources and advocacy for LGBTQ+ people, including information on navigating abusive relationships.

LGBT National Help Center:

- Offers LGBTQ+ specific resources for individuals facing violence and abuse in relationships.

The Network/La Red (TNL):

- Offers a 24-hour confidential hotline for emotional support, information, referrals, safety planning, and crisis intervention for LGBTQ+, kink, and polyamorous individuals facing abuse.

Canada:

The 519:

- Toronto-based community center offering support for LGBTQ+ individuals dealing with relationship violence

Egale Canada:

- Provides advocacy, resources, and programs aimed at ending violence against LGBTQ+ people.

United Kingdom:

GALOP:

- Anti-violence charity providing support for LGBTQ+ individuals dealing with relationship violence.

Stonewall:

- Offers legal advice, support, and advocacy for LGBTQ+ people, including relationship abuse.

Switchboard LGBT+:

- Offers a helpline providing support and information on various issues affecting the LGBTQ+ community, including domestic abuse.

MindOut:

- Provides mental health services for LGBTQ+ individuals, including support for those facing abuse and violence.

Intercom Trust:

- Offers support and advocacy for LGBTQ+ individuals in the South West of England, including assistance for those facing domestic abuse. Wikipedia

---

Ireland:

TENI (Transgender Equality Network Ireland):

- Provides support and resources for trans and gender non-conforming individuals facing violence.

Germany:

LesMigras:

- Support for lesbian and queer migrant women, including services for those experiencing intimate partner violence.

Frauenhauskoordinierung e.V:

- Coordinates women's shelters and offers a nationwide support hotline for victims of violence, including trans persons.

Australia:

ACON:

- LGBTQ+ health organization providing support services for those experiencing relationship violence.

Switchboard Victoria:

- 24-hour support service for LGBTQ+ individuals facing abuse or violence in relationships.

India:

The Queer Rights Initiative (QRI):

- Provides support for LGBTQ+ individuals, including survivors of violence in relationships.

Sahodaran:

- Offers advocacy and resources for LGBTQ+ individuals experiencing intimate partner violence.

Japan:

Peer Support Network for LGBTIQ+ People:

- Offers online resources and peer support for LGBTQ+ individuals experiencing violence.

South Africa:

The Triangle Project:

- Provides support and advocacy for LGBTQ+ individuals, especially survivors of intimate partner violence.

Argentina:

Red de Contención para Personas LGBTIQ+ (LGBTQ+ Support Network):

- Offers emotional support, resources, and advocacy for LGBTQ+ survivors of relationship violence.

Brazil:

Grupo Gay da Bahia:

- Offers support for LGBTQ+ individuals in Brazil, especially regarding violence and legal challenges.

Outright International – Brazil Programs:

- Collaborates with local activists to end human rights violations based on sexual orientation and gender identity, offering support and advocacy for LGBTQ+ individuals.

Mexico:

Fundación Arcoíris:

- Provides support and advocacy for LGBTQ+ individuals experiencing relationship violence, focusing on marginalized groups.

Casa Frida:

- Offers shelter, psychological support, legal assistance, and job placement services to LGBTQ+ individuals, including migrants and those escaping violence and discrimination. Despite funding challenges, it remains a crucial resource for the community.

Puerto Rico:

Colectivo de Lesbianas y Bisexuales de Puerto Rico:

- Offers resources and peer support for LGBTQ+ individuals facing domestic abuse or relationship violence.

France:

Hotline:

- Advocacy group offering services and support to lesbian and queer women, including those dealing with intimate partner violence.

Ni Putes Ni Soumises:

- Founded in 2002, this French feminist movement works against violence targeting women, including domestic violence and gang rape. They provide support to victims and carry out awareness-raising seminars, which may be helpful for LGBTQ+ individuals in need.

Italy:

D.I.Re - Donne in Rete Contro la Violenza:

- A national network providing support services for women, including LGBTQ+ individuals facing violence.

Spain:

Fundación Triángulo:

- Focuses on providing legal assistance, advocacy and support for LGBTQ+ individuals experiencing intimate partner violence.

New Zealand:

LGBTQI+ National Network:

- A national resource for LGBTQI+ individuals, providing support for those experiencing violence in relationships.

Pakistan:

Blue Veins:

- Provides support to LGBTQ+ individuals in Pakistan, including advocacy and assistance for those facing violence in intimate relationships.

Thailand:

The Transgender Alliance of Thailand:

- Offers counselling, legal support, and resources for transgender and gender non-conforming individuals, including those facing abuse.

Counselling Thailand:

- With therapists experienced in trauma and substance abuse, this service offers support for LGBTQ+ clients navigating emotional distress, including abuse recovery.

Nigeria:

The Initiative for Equal Rights (TIERs):

- Provides legal aid and support for LGBTQ+ individuals facing violence and discrimination in Nigeria.

Uganda:

Spectrum Uganda:

- Provides services and advocacy for LGBTQ+ individuals in Uganda, focusing on survivors of violence and abuse.

Chile:

Fundación Iguales:

- Focuses on equality and human rights for LGBTQ+ individuals, offering support for those experiencing intimate partner violence.

Movilh (Movimiento de Integración y Liberación Homosexual):

- Movilh is a prominent LGBTQ+ rights organization in Chile that provides legal assistance, psychological support, and advocacy for individuals facing discrimination or violence, including intimate partner abuse.

Peru:

Movimiento Homosexual de Lima (MHOL):

- Advocacy and support organization offering resources for LGBTQ+ individuals dealing with relationship violence.

---

3. The Weight of Silence – Unspoken Harm in Queer Relationships

In queer relationships, silence often becomes more than the absence of speech, it becomes a language of its own. Not every wound is inflicted through shouting or overt violence, sometimes, the deepest harms emerge from what remains unsaid. Silence, when used deliberately, can carve deep fractures within a relationship, allowing control, fear, and erasure to thrive unnoticed. In spaces where queer love is already marginalized, acknowledging harm can feel almost like betrayal, leading many to suffer quietly, believing that silence is a form of survival.

3.1 Unspoken Needs – How Silence Becomes a Cage:

In many queer relationships, individuals are taught, both by external stigma and internalized fear, that voicing needs risks rejection, judgment, or accusations of being "too much."

This results in a subtle, but devastating form of harm, the silencing of basic emotional, physical, and spiritual needs. Over time, the refusal to allow space for these needs to be named can transform a loving bond into a suffocating enclosure. Silence acts as both prison and warden, keeping individuals trapped inside their own longing, too afraid or ashamed to speak.

3.2 The Denial of Boundaries – Silence as Erosion:

Healthy boundaries are essential to any relationship, yet within queer dynamics, especially those forged in environments of external hostility, asserting a boundary can feel like an act of betrayal. Some partners exploit this fear, using silence to deny or undermine necessary limits. Requests for space, for respect, for independence may be met not with anger, but with a chilling quiet, a silent withdrawal of affection or acknowledgment. This refusal to engage quietly communicates that needing anything outside the relationship is a punishable offense. Over time, this erodes the survivor's sense of autonomy, leaving them increasingly isolated and dependent.

3.3 Gaslighting Without Words – The Power of Implied Denial:

Gaslighting is often imagined as a loud, dizzying experience, arguments twisting reality into knots. But in queer relationships shaped by silence, gaslighting often operates through absence. Harm is not openly denied, it is simply not acknowledged. Hurt feelings are met with blank stares, or casual shrugs. Serious conversations are delayed indefinitely, until the survivor begins to doubt whether there was ever anything to address at all. This silent rewriting of reality can be more insidious than outright lies because it leaves no evidence, only a deep internal confusion about what is real and what is permissible to feel.

3.4 Community Complicity – When Silence Extends Beyond the Couple:

Within queer communities, there is often an implicit pressure to "protect" queer relationships from external scrutiny. In a world that already doubts queer love, many feel that calling out harm within a queer relationship risks feeding into homophobic, transphobic, or otherwise discriminatory narratives.

This leads to a painful complicity, friends, chosen family, and community members may choose to remain silent, or even subtly encourage survivors to minimize their pain "for the greater good." Survivors internalize this message, believing that speaking out would betray not just their partner, but their entire community. The weight of that silence becomes communal, heavy enough to crush even the strongest spirits.

3.5 Invisible Scars – The Long-Term Impact of Silenced Abuse:

Abuse that operates through silence leaves no visible bruises, but its aftermath is no less devastating. Survivors often struggle with chronic self-doubt, emotional numbness, and an inability to trust their own perceptions of harm. They may find themselves unable to voice their needs in future relationships, fearing that any assertion will lead once again to punishment or abandonment. Healing from silenced abuse requires not just recognizing the harm that was done, but relearning how to hear one's own voice and to believe it matters.

3.6 Finding the Language to Break Free:

Healing from the weight of silence begins with the simple yet radical act of naming. Naming the harm endured. Naming the needs that were denied. Naming the ways silence was wielded not as comfort, but as control. In survivor-led spaces, especially those attuned to the complexities of queer relationships, this process of naming becomes a powerful counterspell to enforced silence. Through storytelling, witnessing, and uncompromising honesty, survivors can begin to reclaim their narratives and imagine new ways of connecting, grounded in mutual respect, care, and consent. Speaking, even if only in a whisper at first, becomes an act of defiance, a reclaiming of voice, agency, and the right to be heard.

3.7 Conclusion – Speaking the Unspoken:

Silence is often mistaken for peace, but in the context of abuse, it is a terrain littered with invisible mines. In queer relationships, where so much of existence has historically been forced into secrecy, it is even more vital to challenge the myth that love should be wordless, that endurance is more important than truth. By daring to speak the unspeakable, we not only protect ourselves, we expand the possibilities for what queer love can be. Love that does not punish honesty. Love that listens. Love that lets every voice be heard, even, especially when it trembles. In making room for the hard conversations, we begin to build relationships rooted not in silence, but in truth, healing, and radical care.

4. Who Will Believe Us? Barriers to Seeking Help

For queer individuals experiencing abuse, seeking help can feel like a test of faith, not only in the systems designed to protect them, but in their own worthiness of help. The institutional failures that LGBTQ+ survivors face are profound and often insurmountable. From social services that don't recognize queer experiences of violence to law enforcement that fails to take queer abuse seriously, survivors must confront the daunting question, "Who will believe us?" The barriers to seeking help are not just about access, they are about being seen, heard, and validated in the first place. Until queer survivors are believed without condition and supported without exception, the systems meant to protect will continue to betray the most vulnerable.

4.1 The Absence of Queer-Affirming Services:

One of the most significant barriers to seeking help is the absence of services that are explicitly affirming of queer identities. Many social services and support networks are designed with heterosexual, cisgender individuals in mind, rendering queer survivors invisible within these systems. From shelters that may not have policies in place to protect transgender individuals to counselling services that lack understanding of the unique challenges faced by non-binary individuals, the gap in support is both systemic and deeply personal. This absence creates a sense of alienation, survivors feel they must choose between the painful realities of abuse or the painful reality of not being understood or respected by the very services meant to help them. Safety begins with being seen, without queer-affirming support, many are left to survive alone.

4.2 Prejudice and Bias Within Legal and Social Systems:

Another significant barrier is the institutional prejudice and bias that queer survivors encounter when they attempt to navigate the legal and social service systems. Survivors of abuse may find themselves disbelieved, judged, or blamed, because of their sexual orientation or gender identity. This bias often plays out in the most critical moments, law enforcement may dismiss abuse claims as "too complicated" or assume that queer relationships are inherently unstable, undermining the legitimacy of the survivor's experience. In court, survivors face the added burden of explaining their relationships and their abuse within a system that may not recognize the nuances of queer dynamics, leaving them vulnerable to further trauma. As a result, queer survivors may internalize the message that their abuse is not worth addressing or that seeking justice is futile.

4.3 The Fear of Being Re-Victimized by the System:

For many queer survivors, the very idea of seeking help can trigger fears of re-victimization. This fear is rooted in the historical and ongoing mistreatment of queer individuals by institutions like the police, courts and social services. The LGBTQ+ community has long been subjected to criminalization and pathologization, leaving a deep mistrust of systems that were never built to protect them. The risk of further trauma through mistreatment or rejection by institutions that are supposed to help creates a chilling effect, survivors hesitate to speak out, knowing that they may face humiliation, victim-blaming, or even the invalidation of their abuse. The trauma of re-victimization, of being dismissed or misunderstood by the very system that should provide justice, often becomes a barrier too great to overcome, resulting in survivors staying silent or leaving abusive situations without the resources needed for recovery.

4.4 Cultural Stigma – The Silence of Shame:

Cultural stigma surrounding both queer identities and intimate partner violence adds another layer of difficulty for survivors. For many queer individuals, the very act of coming forward about abuse can feel like an admission of failure, especially in communities where LGBTQ+ relationships are already under scrutiny. The belief that queer people "should be able to handle" their relationships reinforces the silence and shame already surrounding abuse. This cultural stigma discourages survivors from reaching out for help, reinforcing the narrative that their experiences are not valid or that they are somehow "less deserving" of justice. It is often easier to remain silent, to endure, than to face the shame of being further marginalized by the very community that should be their refuge.

4.5 The Fear of Losing Community Support:

In the face of institutional failure, queer survivors often find themselves at a painful crossroads, seeking help might mean losing their place within the very community they depend on for support. Many LGBTQ+ individuals, particularly those who are marginalized by race, class, or gender identity, find their chosen families and queer communities to be their primary sources of emotional and social support. In tight-knit networks, there's often an unspoken expectation to protect and uplift one another. Coming forward with allegations of abuse risks breaking these bonds.

There is fear that an abuser will be defended, that the survivor will be ostracized, or that the act of speaking out will fracture the community. This fear of social isolation, of being cast aside by the very people who have been a lifeline, can keep survivors in abusive situations, trapped in a cycle of silence and neglect.

4.6 Lack of Awareness and Education in Support Networks:

Even within the most well-intentioned organizations, a lack of education about queer identities and experiences can be a significant barrier. Many counsellors, advocates and legal professionals, are not trained to understand the unique dynamics of queer relationships and the specific forms of violence that occur within them. The absence of LGBTQ+-specific training means that survivors often encounter professionals who inadvertently perpetuate harm through ignorance or misunderstanding. For example, a counsellor may fail to recognize the distinct nature of emotional abuse in a queer context, or a legal professional may not understand how the intersectionality of race, gender and sexual identity, affects the experience of violence. Without this specialized knowledge, survivors are left to explain their experiences from scratch, often without the proper language or support to do so. To truly support queer survivors, it is crucial that support networks undergo comprehensive LGBTQ+-affirming training to ensure they provide informed, compassionate and effective care.

4.7 The Urgency of Advocacy and Institutional Reform:

The barriers queer survivors face when seeking help demand urgent and comprehensive action. Advocates must push for systemic reforms that include mandatory LGBTQ+-affirming training for all professionals in the justice, health, and social service sectors. Shelters and support organizations must be made accessible and inclusive, not just in terms of policies, but in the cultural understanding of queer realities. Moreover, queer survivors must be at the forefront of this work, ensuring that their voices shape the policies and practices that will ultimately determine their safety and access to justice. Only by addressing these institutional failures can we begin to dismantle the systemic obstacles that keep queer survivors in the shadows. To create lasting change, it is essential that advocacy efforts be led by the community itself, with queer survivors guiding the way toward more equitable and compassionate systems of support and justice.

4.8 Conclusion – Reclaiming Justice and Support:

The barriers that queer survivors of intimate partner violence face in seeking help go beyond mere access, they are rooted in the denial of credibility, recognition and the basic right to be believed. Overcoming these obstacles requires building a future where queer experiences of violence are not only acknowledged, but actively supported and validated by the institutions meant to protect us. Only when these systems are truly responsive to the unique challenges faced by queer individuals can survivors begin the process of healing, rebuilding and reclaiming their autonomy. This work is not just the responsibility of those directly affected, but of advocates, allies, and society at large. Together, we must demand a transformation in the way our institutions respond to violence. The time for this change is now, for the sake of the survivors and the future of our community. Justice begins when queer survivors are believed, and it endures when our systems reflect that belief with action.

* Pause for Reflection – Deepening Understanding and Healing:

"What barriers have we personally faced or witnessed when trying to seek help for abuse? How do these barriers get magnified for queer survivors and what can we do to dismantle them?"

5. Rewriting Power – Building a Language for Queer Survivorship

Survivorship within the queer community is too often defined by silence, marginalization and an absence of support, tailored to the unique challenges queer individuals face. To rewrite power and reclaim our agency, we must first reclaim our narratives. Survivor-led spaces are central to this process, offering queer individuals the chance to tell their stories on their own terms, without the fear of judgment or erasure. These spaces allow survivors to challenge the conventional understandings of abuse and recovery, creating new frameworks that reflect the complexity of queer experiences. By taking ownership of our narratives, we dismantle the dominant, oppressive stories that have shaped our identities and heal in a way that affirms our worth.

5.1 The Role of Community in Healing:

Healing is not a solitary journey, it is collective, rooted in the interconnectedness of queer community. Rather than relying solely on traditional therapeutic models or systems that fail to understand the queer experience, we must lean into community-based healing. These spaces offer a sense of belonging, where survivors find strength in shared experience and solidarity. Community-based healing creates an environment where survivors can not only heal, but also thrive, as they are supported by others who understand their struggles without judgment or shame. This healing model emphasizes the importance of mutual care, collective accountability and the shared goal, of creating a world where queer survivors can exist without fear or isolation.

5.2 Survivor-Led Spaces – Reclaiming Agency:

Survivor-led spaces represent a transformative shift in how we approach healing. These spaces are created by and for survivors, putting the power back in the hands of those who have experienced abuse. By centering the voices of survivors, these spaces affirm the importance of self-determination and respect for each individual's healing process. Unlike conventional spaces, which may focus on top-down expertise or the application of generalized healing methods, survivor-led spaces prioritize the wisdom that comes from lived experience. They offer a safe, affirming environment where survivors can explore their healing journey on their own terms, without fear of being misunderstood or judged. Through workshops, peer support, and collective sharing, these spaces allow survivors to create a language of their own for healing, one that resonates with their experiences and empowers them to redefine their futures.

5.3 Building a New Language of Empowerment:

A crucial part of rewriting power is the development of a language that reflects the diverse realities of queer survivors.

Traditional language surrounding abuse often fails to capture the nuanced dynamics of queer relationships, leaving survivors to feel isolated or misunderstood. By crafting a new lexicon, one that is informed by the experiences of queer survivors, we create a tool for empowerment. This language doesn't just describe harm, it also encompasses healing, resilience, and self-affirmation. Terms like "survivor," "agency," and "resilience" are imbued with new meaning, transforming from words of survival to beacons of strength. This new language allows us to reclaim the narrative of our own healing, ensuring that our experiences are not diminished or overlooked. By embracing this new language, we create a space where queer survivors can fully claim their power, redefine their stories and step into healing with confidence and strength.

5.4 The Power of Collective Accountability:

A key tenet of community-based healing is collective accountability, which ensures that the responsibility for healing is shared by the community. This model challenges the individualistic approach often seen in mainstream systems of support, where healing is seen as the sole responsibility of the survivor. Instead, collective accountability fosters an environment in which everyone is responsible for the well-being and safety of all members. It encourages a culture of empathy, mutual support, and shared action, where the experiences of survivors are taken seriously and addressed in a way that promotes justice and healing. By cultivating collective accountability, we not only hold each other to a higher standard of care, but also actively dismantle the toxic power dynamics that perpetuate abuse. Collective accountability empowers the community to create sustainable, healing-centered environments where every individual plays a vital role in upholding justice, compassion, and support for survivors.

5.5 Transformative Justice and Queer Survivorship:

Transformative justice is a model that seeks to address harm without relying on punitive systems, which have historically failed queer communities. This approach emphasizes healing and restoration rather than retribution. In the context of queer survivorship, transformative justice means creating alternatives to the criminal justice system that are rooted in community, healing and accountability. It allows survivors to find justice on their own terms, supported by a community that respects their autonomy and agency. Transformative justice reimagines how harm can be addressed in queer relationships, focusing on healing, restoration and reintegration, rather than punishment.

5.6 Empowering Survivors to Lead the Way:

Survivors are the experts of their own healing. The process of reclaiming power involves not only rewriting the narrative, but also empowering survivors to take leadership roles in shaping their own journeys and the healing paths for others. By recognizing the strength and resilience of survivors, we can begin to create a culture that celebrates their capacity for agency. Empowerment doesn't mean merely surviving abuse, it means thriving in the aftermath, taking control of one's life and becoming a force of transformation. Survivor-led spaces encourage this empowerment, giving survivors the tools and support they need to become leaders in their own right.

It is through these spaces that the most profound change can occur, as survivors lead the charge for systemic transformation and community healing.

5.7 Healing Through Art, Expression and Creativity:

In queer survivor communities, art and creative expression are powerful tools of healing. Survivors use art to communicate their experiences, express their emotions, and reclaim their identities. Whether through writing, visual art, performance, or music, creativity allows survivors to process trauma in a way that words alone often cannot. Art becomes a language of resilience, an outlet for emotions that may feel too overwhelming to express in conventional terms. By embracing creative expression as a form of healing, queer survivors can transform their pain into power, reclaiming their agency in ways that are both deeply personal and collectively meaningful. Art also serves as a bridge, connecting survivors to one another and to the broader community, allowing them to share their stories without the limitations of language.

5.8 The Future of Queer Survivorship – Rewriting Power Together:

Rewriting power requires an ongoing commitment to creating survivor-led spaces, empowering survivors and cultivating a language of healing, and justice that reflects the complexity of queer lives. It demands that we build a world where queer survivors are not only believed, but celebrated for their strength and resilience. This work is transformative, not just for individual survivors, but for the entire community. By embracing survivor-led healing, fostering collective accountability and developing new models of justice, we create a future where power is shared, love is safe and every queer individual, has the opportunity to heal and thrive. This vision requires the collective effort of all of us, together, rewriting the narrative of queer survivorship into one of empowerment, justice and hope.

* Pause for Reflection – Deepening Understanding and Healing:

"What would healing look like in our community if survivors had more agency and voice? How can we support survivor-led spaces and help rewrite the language around queer survivorship?"

Chapter 18

Healing from Toxic Relationships in the LGBTQ+ World

---

1. Loving After Hurt – Relearning Intimacy Without Fear

The process of reopening to love after betrayal is one of deep introspection and careful navigation. Queer individuals who have experienced emotional or relational harm often face a challenging path toward rebuilding trust, not just with others, but also with themselves. Trust, once broken, takes time to restore. Yet, it is this very act of rebuilding trust that becomes a crucial foundation for future, healthier relationships. The first step in this journey is acknowledging the pain and the impact of the betrayal without diminishing the worth of the survivor. Survivors must give themselves the space to grieve and process their hurt, while also recognizing that healing is not a linear process. Healing also means redefining intimacy on one's own terms, where vulnerability is met with safety and love is no longer a source of fear.

1.1 Creating New Boundaries – Redefining What Safety Means:

As queer folks re-enter relationships after betrayal, creating new boundaries is essential. Boundaries are not merely restrictions, they are declarations of what is needed to feel safe, respected, and valued in a relationship. For those who have been hurt, boundaries take on a new significance, they become the framework through which love is rediscovered. These new boundaries are flexible and adaptive, taking into account the unique needs of both individuals while honouring past wounds. Rather than seeing boundaries as walls, queer survivors of betrayal often learn to view them as tools of empowerment that allow for connection without fear. Healthy boundaries help protect one's emotional well-being and create the necessary space for trust to grow again. These boundaries become the foundation for rebuilding trust and intimacy, ensuring that both partners feel secure and valued in the process of healing.

1.2 Relearning Intimacy – Embracing Vulnerability with Caution:

Intimacy, once tarnished by betrayal, requires a delicate balance between vulnerability and self-preservation. Relearning intimacy involves understanding that vulnerability does not equate to weakness, but rather to strength. For many queer survivors, the act of being emotionally open again can feel daunting, as they fear the potential for further harm. Yet, it is through carefully navigating vulnerability that true intimacy can be experienced once more. This process takes time and involves gradually rebuilding a sense of safety with a new partner. Intimacy after hurt does not happen all at once, it is a slow unravelling of the walls built by past wounds. For queer individuals, learning to trust in their own instincts and set the pace for intimacy is an empowering act that honours both personal boundaries and emotional openness.

1.3 The Role of Communication – A New Language of Love:

Effective communication becomes the cornerstone of rebuilding relationships after betrayal. The language used in these conversations must reflect a willingness to be honest, patient, and transparent. For queer folks, this often means expressing their needs in clear terms and being open to the vulnerability of sharing their fears, desires and expectations. Communication is not only about talking, it is equally about listening and understanding. Survivors of betrayal must be able to articulate their needs for reassurance, while their partners must be willing to listen and act with empathy. In many cases, the tools of active listening and reflective communication become crucial in reaffirming trust and understanding. This new language of love fosters an environment where both partners feel heard, respected, and valued, leading to the gradual rebuilding of emotional intimacy.

1.4 Healing Through Self-Love – Rediscovering Worth and Value:

Before re-entering a relationship, queer individuals must also engage in the often-overlooked work of healing themselves. Rebuilding trust and intimacy with others begins with healing the relationship one has with themselves. Self-love becomes a vital tool in this journey, as it helps queer survivors affirm their worthiness of love and respect despite the pain they have endured. This process involves breaking free from self-blame and recognizing that no one deserves to be hurt, no matter the circumstances. Rediscovering self-worth through self-compassion and care empowers survivors to approach new relationships not from a place of fear, but from a place of strength. By practicing self-love, queer individuals build a resilient foundation that allows them to enter love again with a sense of clarity and confidence.

1.5 Trust Tools – Building a Toolbox for Future Relationships:

Re-entering love after betrayal requires more than just emotional healing, it necessitates equipping oneself with new tools for navigating relationships. These "trust tools" are practical strategies that allow individuals to cultivate trust and transparency in their partnerships. For queer individuals, these tools often include ongoing open communication, regular check-ins with partners and a commitment to both individual and collective healing. These tools help to create a foundation of mutual understanding, where both parties feel empowered to share their feelings, fears, and desires, without the burden of guilt or shame. Trust tools also involve learning how to identify and address red flags, setting clear expectations, and agreeing on how to handle conflicts in a healthy way. By equipping themselves with these tools, queer survivors can approach relationships with a sense of preparedness and confidence.

1.6 Moving Forward with Hope – Love Beyond Fear:

As queer individuals relearn intimacy and love after betrayal, it is essential to remember that the journey is not about perfection, but about progress. Healing takes time, and rebuilding trust is a process that requires patience, compassion, and ongoing effort. With each step, queer survivors gain a deeper understanding of themselves and their needs and they become better equipped, to navigate future relationships.

The journey of love after hurt is one of hope, where boundaries, communication, self-love, and trust tools all come together to create healthier, more resilient partnerships. Through this process, queer folks learn to reshape love into a force of strength, connection and respect.

* Reclaiming Love – A Step-by-Step Guide to Healing After a Toxic Relationship:

A. Allow Yourself to Grieve:

- **Step:** Permit yourself to grieve the loss of the relationship, even if it was unhealthy. Breakups are often filled with complex emotions, sadness, anger, relief, and confusion. Allow yourself to feel these emotions fully without judgment.
- **How to Navigate:** Set aside time to reflect on the relationship and its end. Cry, write in a journal, or talk to a friend. Don't suppress your feelings. Seek out emotional outlets where you can express your grief freely.
- **Healing Practice:** Engage in a symbolic ritual, such as writing a letter to your ex expressing everything you need to say, and then burn or bury it as a symbolic release. This act of closure helps process the emotional weight.

B. Establish Physical and Emotional Distance:

- **Step:** Create distance from your ex. This includes cutting off communication (if possible) and unfollowing them on social media to avoid constant reminders of the relationship.
- **How to Navigate:** Give yourself space to breathe without any temptation to re-engage. In some cases, setting clear boundaries with your ex about future contact or leaving things undefined can help you both move on.
- **Healing Practice:** Consider creating a "boundary altar" or safe space where you can symbolically reclaim your emotional space. Fill it with items that represent your power and autonomy, such as stones, candles, or affirmations.

C. Seek Support from Chosen Family and Community:

- **Step:** Turn to your chosen family, close friends, or support groups that affirm your queer identity and experiences. Seek out spaces where you can feel truly seen, heard, and understood.
- **How to Navigate:** Schedule regular check-ins with friends or family who can support you during the healing process. Engage in queer-centered groups (both online and offline) where others can relate to your experience.
- **Healing Practice:** Engage in "healing circles" where you and your chosen family members share your stories, offer support, and reflect on collective growth.

D. Understand and Challenge Internalized Shame:

- **Step:** Reflect on any shame or self-blame you might carry from the relationship, especially as it relates to internalized queerphobia or the belief that you "deserve" the harm that was done. Recognize that healing is not linear and confronting shame, is part of the journey.
- **How to Navigate:** Practice self-compassion and remind yourself that being in a toxic relationship does not reflect your worth. Therapy, journaling, or talking to an empathetic friend can help address the shame.
- **Healing Practice:** Create a "shame jar" or visual representation (like a scrapbook or board) where you write down moments of self-criticism and replace them with empowering affirmations or lessons learned.

E. Set and Reinforce Healthy Boundaries:

- **Step:** After a breakup, it's essential to reevaluate what boundaries are necessary for your emotional and physical safety. Learn to communicate those boundaries clearly to yourself and others.
- **How to Navigate:** Practice saying "no" without guilt and identify what kind of interactions, behaviours, or situations you want to avoid moving forward. Ensure that your new boundaries are respected by others.
- **Healing Practice:** Design a personal "boundary map", a visual guide that outlines your emotional, physical, and mental limits. This can be a poster, a journal, or a drawing where you can return to it when you need to remind yourself of your worth.

F. Relearn Trust in Yourself and Others:

- **Step:** In the aftermath of betrayal, trust may feel like a distant memory. Rebuilding trust starts with trusting yourself again and allowing yourself to heal from the trauma of the breakup.
- **How to Navigate:** Start by honouring your feelings and choices, big and small. Reconnect with your instincts and intuition, even in areas outside of romantic relationships.
- Healing Practice: Keep a "trust journal" to note small moments of trust in yourself or others, using it to affirm your growth and inner strength.

G. Focus on Self-Care and Reconnect with Your Identity:

- **Step:** Breakups, particularly in toxic relationships, can erode your sense of self. Reclaiming your identity and practicing self-care is key to recovery.

- **How to Navigate:** Dedicate time to activities that nourish your body, mind and soul. Reconnect with hobbies, passions, or creative endeavours that bring you joy and remind you of your individuality.
- **Healing Practice:** Design a "reclamation ritual" for your body and soul. This could be as simple as a solo dance party, a spa day, or a trip to a queer-friendly space that affirms your identity and reconnects you to your sense of freedom.

H. Shift from Surviving to Thriving:

- **Step:** Once you've navigated the immediate aftermath of the breakup, the next step is to move from mere survival to thriving. Focus on personal growth and creating a future beyond the trauma of the past.
- **How to Navigate:** Set new, achievable goals for yourself. This can range from focusing on career goals, starting a new hobby, or even dating again when you feel ready. Surround yourself with people who empower you to grow and heal.
- **Healing Practice:** Create a "future vision board" with images, words, and symbols that represent the life you want to build. This can be a visual, physical manifestation of your hopes for the future, helping to inspire you as you move forward.

I. Gradually Re-Entering the Dating Scene:

- **Step:** When ready, re-entering the dating scene may feel daunting after a toxic relationship. It's essential to approach this step with caution, mindfulness, and respect for your own healing process.
- **How to Navigate:** Before dating, take time to reflect on the lessons learned from your past relationship. What did you value? What will you avoid? Set intentions for future relationships that honour your boundaries and needs.
- **Healing Practice:** Write a letter to your future self, describing what you hope to find in a partner, how you will protect your boundaries, and how you will honour your worth. This exercise will help clarify what you seek in future relationships.

J. Celebrate Small Wins and Continued Healing:

- **Step:** Recovery doesn't end at a certain point, it's a continual process of learning, growth and healing. Celebrate even the smallest victories as they come.

- **How to Navigate:** Acknowledge moments where you feel stronger, more confident, or more at peace with yourself. Celebrate milestones like being able to enjoy solitude, setting a healthy boundary, or feeling ready to trust again.
- **Healing Practice:** Create a "healing jar" where you collect affirmations, mementos, or small reminders of your progress. When you're feeling down, revisit these reminders to see how far you've come.

---

2. The Role of Chosen Family in Post-Breakup Healing

Queer communities have long understood the importance of chosen family, those bonds created through mutual love and support, rather than biology. After experiencing the emotional toll of a toxic breakup, queer individuals often turn to their chosen family for solace and care. Chosen family members are the ones who provide a sense of security and belonging when traditional family structures may fail to offer the same comfort. They serve as a buffer against loneliness, offering a space for healing free from judgment or misunderstanding. In this way, chosen family becomes a vital resource for individuals recovering from romantic harm, offering emotional nourishment, validation, and consistent support. Chosen family, through their unwavering presence and understanding, becomes an indispensable source of strength, helping individuals rediscover their sense of self and their ability to trust and love again.

2.1 The Power of Unconditional Support:

In the aftermath of a breakup, especially one marked by emotional abuse or betrayal, queer individuals often struggle with feelings of shame, guilt, or self-doubt. Chosen family can help to counteract these emotions by offering unconditional love and support. Unlike some biological families that may express disappointment or rejection, chosen family members affirm the survivor's worth and provide a non-judgmental space to process their pain. The strength of this unconditional support allows individuals to heal at their own pace, without the pressure of societal expectations or the need to hide their vulnerability. Unconditional support from chosen family not only aids in healing, but also reaffirms that love and belonging can exist outside traditional structures, empowering survivors to rebuild their sense of self.

2.2 Creating Safe Spaces for Healing:

Queer chosen families often provide a sanctuary, a place where individuals can feel safe to express their pain, anger, confusion, or even hope. This safe space is essential for healing, as it allows for emotional release without fear of retribution or dismissal. It is within these spaces that survivors of toxic relationships can begin to rebuild trust, first in themselves, then in others. Through heartfelt conversations, shared activities, and mutual care, chosen family members help reinforce the importance of self-love, affirming that the survivor's needs are valid and deserving of respect. Creating safe spaces within chosen families fosters emotional growth and healing, allowing survivors to rebuild trust, not only in others, but also in their own worth, without fear of judgment.

2.3 The Healing Power of Shared Experience:

One of the unique strengths of chosen family within the queer community is the shared understanding of the complexities of LGBTQ+ life. For many, members of their chosen family can relate to the emotional challenges and nuances that come with navigating both queer identity and romantic relationships. This shared experience creates a deep bond, which can be particularly healing after a breakup. Queer individuals often find it easier to open up to chosen family members who understand their context, rather than trying to explain their struggles to people outside the community. Whether it's validating feelings of invisibility, helping with trauma, or just offering a sympathetic ear, the shared understanding within a chosen family accelerates the healing process.

2.4 Practical Support During Recovery:

Chosen family often provides not only emotional support, but also practical assistance during the difficult time of recovery. This can take many forms, helping with housing, offering financial assistance, or even providing transportation or food when a survivor feels overwhelmed. This tangible support is a reminder that healing is not just about emotional recovery, but about rebuilding life, piece by piece, after the devastation of a breakup. These acts of kindness, even the smallest gestures, are vital in giving the survivor a sense of stability and hope for the future. Practical support from chosen family offers tangible relief, helping survivors rebuild their lives by providing stability and hope during their recovery.

2.5 Rewriting the Narrative of Love and Support:

A breakup in the queer community often requires rewriting the narrative of what love, intimacy and support should look like. Chosen family members help provide a new template for healthy relationships, one that is not based on romantic love, but on mutual respect, care, and emotional solidarity. This alternative narrative is essential in shifting the survivor's understanding of love. Rather than viewing it through the lens of betrayal or disappointment, they are able to see love as something that is unconditional, and unconditional love is a power they can offer each other as a chosen family. By supporting each other through heartbreak, chosen families model the kind of love that is grounded in respect and healthy boundaries.

2.6 Rebuilding Trust Through Connection:

After the betrayal of a toxic relationship, one of the most challenging aspects of healing is the process of rebuilding trust, both in oneself and in others. Chosen family plays a crucial role in this aspect of recovery. They offer a safe space where trust can be redefined and gradually restored. The slow, steady process of rebuilding trust is facilitated by their unwavering support and consistency. They help remind survivors that not all relationships are harmful or damaging and that healthy, trusting connections are possible. By showing up in times of need, offering steady companionship, and being reliable sources of support, chosen family helps re-establish the foundation for future relationships that are healthy, trustworthy, and fulfilling. Through their consistent care and understanding, chosen family helps survivors rediscover the power of trust, paving the way for healing relationships grounded in mutual respect and safety.

2.7 The Importance of Mutual Care and Boundaries:

Chosen families also offer a model for healthy relationships, where mutual care and respect for boundaries are prioritized. Post-breakup healing often includes learning how to set and respect personal boundaries, something that might have been violated in a toxic relationship. Within a chosen family, survivors can practice these boundary-setting skills in a loving and supportive environment. They can also learn how to offer care without sacrificing their own well-being, teaching them that self-care and looking after others are not mutually exclusive. This balance of giving and receiving care strengthens both the survivor and the family as a whole.

2.8 Celebrating Healing Together:

Recovery from a breakup is rarely linear, and there are often setbacks along the way. However, the journey of healing can be made more manageable with the support of chosen family. As the survivor progresses, there are opportunities for celebration and affirmation. Whether it's acknowledging small victories, such as a step toward emotional independence or reclaiming personal power, or celebrating milestones like new beginnings, chosen family serves as a reminder of how far the survivor has come. These moments of celebration help reframe the experience of healing from one of loss and pain to one of growth, transformation, and hope. With their support, queer individuals learn to celebrate the resilience within themselves and their community.

2.9 Conclusion – A Lifelong Support System:

The role of chosen family in post-breakup healing is immeasurable. It provides a foundation of unconditional love, practical support, and a shared understanding that accelerates the healing process. By offering emotional stability, trust and a model for healthy relationships, chosen family members allow queer individuals to move forward from toxic relationships with renewed strength, clarity and a sense of hope for the future. Ultimately, chosen family is not just a source of comfort after a heartbreak, it is a lifelong support system that nurtures resilience, healing, and the capacity to love again. Chosen family is the anchor that helps queer individuals rebuild, reaffirm their worth and embrace love with renewed confidence.

"Family isn't defined by blood, it's defined by the love, support, and understanding we offer one another. Chosen family is the healing we find when we're most broken." – Anonymous

3. Queer Shame and the Inner Critic – Learning Not to Blame Ourselves

After the end of a toxic relationship, many queer individuals find themselves grappling with feelings of shame and guilt. These emotions are often magnified by the inner critic, a harsh voice that tells survivors they are somehow to blame for the pain they endured. The intersection of internalized queerphobia and the toxic narratives about relationships can make it difficult to see the harm caused by others without turning the blame inward. For queer people, there may be an additional layer of shame tied to societal expectations of how love should look, and how their identities should be navigated in relationships.

This shame can manifest as self-doubt, insecurity, and an overwhelming sense of personal failure. It becomes crucial, then, to unpack the roots of this shame and reclaim one's self-worth in the aftermath of a breakup.

3.1 Understanding Internalized Queerphobia – The Role of Societal Expectations:

The shame queer people experience post-breakup is often compounded by internalized queerphobia, a form of self-loathing rooted in the oppression and discrimination faced by the LGBTQ+ community. Growing up in a world that teaches queerness is wrong or less than can leave deep emotional scars. These scars are often carried into relationships, where queer individuals may subconsciously believe they are unworthy of love or respect. Society's heteronormative expectations make it even harder to validate non-traditional relationships, especially within the LGBTQ+ community. This often leads to feelings of inadequacy when a relationship ends, leaving individuals questioning their worth and placing blame on themselves. Understanding this cycle of internalized oppression is key to healing, as it allows survivors to recognize that the shame they feel is not a reflection of their true selves, but rather a byproduct of a society that does not fully accept or understand them. By naming and confronting internalized queerphobia, queer individuals can begin to unlearn shame and reclaim a sense of pride, self-worth and emotional freedom.

3.2 The Inner Critic – The Voice of Self-Blame and Guilt:

The inner critic can be a deeply insidious force in the aftermath of a toxic relationship. This voice within often amplifies feelings of guilt and shame, making it difficult for survivors to see the truth of what happened. It might say things like, "You should have known better," "You let this happen," or "You weren't strong enough." These thoughts can be paralyzing and prevent individuals from moving forward. They may even lead to the internalization of toxic relationship patterns, reinforcing feelings of inadequacy and unworthiness. The inner critic thrives in silence and isolation, preying on the vulnerability that often accompanies heartbreak. Recognizing that these thoughts are not inherent truths, but rather reflections of the abuse survivors endured, is the first step toward dismantling this voice and reclaiming one's power. By learning to differentiate between the inner critic's damaging voice and the truth of their experiences, survivors can begin to break free from the grip of guilt and reclaim their sense of self-worth and agency.

3.3 Breaking the Cycle of Self-Blame – Compassionate Self-Reflection:

Healing from the grip of the inner critic requires compassionate self-reflection, a process of actively challenging negative thought patterns and replacing them with more supportive and loving self-talk. This process involves asking difficult questions, What would I tell a friend going through the same experience? How would I speak to someone I care about who is struggling with guilt? Most often, the answers are filled with compassion, understanding, and reassurance. When survivors begin to treat themselves with the same kindness and empathy they would extend to others, the power of the inner critic starts to diminish. This shift in perspective can take time, but it is essential for overcoming the shame and guilt that linger after a toxic relationship ends. Compassionate self-reflection replaces harsh self-judgment with self-love, fostering healing and empowering forward movement.

3.4 Reclaiming Self-Worth – A Journey of Self-Acceptance:

The journey toward healing from shame and the inner critic is one of rediscovering one's inherent worth. It involves acknowledging the ways in which relationships can be harmful and recognizing that being in a toxic relationship does not diminish one's value. Reclaiming self-worth after emotional or psychological abuse is a profound act of resistance against the messages of inadequacy that were reinforced during the relationship. It requires survivors to let go of the false belief that they are somehow less deserving of love, happiness, or peace. By embracing self-acceptance, queer individuals can begin to heal the wounds inflicted by both their toxic relationships and the broader societal forces that have sought to devalue them.

3.5 The Role of Support Systems in Challenging Shame:

Support systems play a pivotal role in challenging the shame that often follows the end of a toxic relationship. Queer friendships, chosen family and therapy, provide safe spaces for survivors to confront the narrative of self-blame and reframe their experiences. In these environments, survivors are not only validated but also reminded that they are not alone. Friends and allies who understand the unique dynamics of queer relationships can offer a perspective that counters the harmful beliefs ingrained by the inner critic. These relationships are vital in helping individuals heal, as they provide a framework of unconditional love and acceptance that challenges the belief that one is inherently flawed or unworthy. Building a support network that offers emotional safety is key to undoing the damage done by shame and fostering self-compassion.

3.6 Learning to Forgive Yourself – A Radical Act of Healing:

Forgiveness is often a long and complicated journey, especially when it comes to forgiving oneself. Survivors of toxic relationships must learn to forgive themselves for the perceived mistakes they made or the ways they allowed themselves to be treated. However, it is important to note that self-forgiveness does not mean condoning harmful behaviour, but rather releasing the hold that guilt and shame have on one's heart. It involves accepting that they were doing the best they could in a challenging situation and that their worth, is not defined by the mistakes made during the relationship. Self-forgiveness is a radical act of healing that allows survivors to reclaim their power and move forward with a renewed sense of self-respect.

3.7 Healing from Shame – Moving Toward Self-Love and Empowerment:

Ultimately, healing from the shame and inner critic that follows a toxic relationship is a transformative process that involves reclaiming one's agency and power. Through self-compassion, supportive relationships and a commitment to self-acceptance, queer individuals can break free from the cycle of self-blame and learn to see themselves as deserving of love, happiness and peace. This healing journey is not linear and may be filled with setbacks, but each step taken toward self-empowerment brings survivors closer to the joy and fulfilment they deserve. Through this process, survivors not only heal from the harm inflicted upon them, but also emerge stronger, more resilient. In learning to love themselves fully, queer survivors transform shame into strength and begin to write new narratives rooted in dignity, courage and hope.

4. Rituals of Release – Queer Approaches to Letting Go

Rituals of release are powerful tools for queer individuals seeking to move forward after experiencing emotional turmoil, such as the aftermath of toxic relationships. Letting go is not merely about severing ties with the past, it's about creating space for new energy, healing, and transformation. For many in the queer community, rituals offer a meaningful way to symbolically release pain, process grief and reclaim personal strength. These acts, often rooted in cultural traditions or personal creativity, provide a space for closure, healing, and a fresh beginning.

4.1 The Power of Symbolic Closure:

Symbolic closure allows individuals to mark the end of a chapter and release lingering emotions. For queer individuals, these rituals provide a tangible way to honour the emotional journey, acknowledge the pain, and affirm that the past no longer dictates their future. The act of letting go through ritual is often necessary to break emotional ties and create space for personal growth and emotional freedom. Whether through burning letters, performing cleansing rituals, or other personal ceremonies, these rituals carry the weight of release, offering solace and clarity.

4.2 Transformative Rituals in Queer Culture:

Many queer individuals turn to transformative rituals that are personally meaningful and culturally resonant. Drawing from indigenous traditions, spiritual practices, or personal experiences, these rituals can serve as tools for empowerment and healing. Cleansing baths, incense, or meditation are common practices that help individuals purify their energy, physically and emotionally. These rituals offer a way to confront emotional pain while embracing a future that's aligned with the individual's authentic self. Cultural practices, such as smudging or grounding, can also be deeply healing, fostering connection with both the self and the earth.

4.3 The Release Letter – Writing to Let Go:

One of the most profound rituals in the journey of letting go is the release letter. Writing a letter to an ex or to oneself can serve as an emotional catharsis, allowing suppressed feelings and thoughts to be expressed. This ritual offers a safe space for survivors to confront unspoken emotions, release any remaining anger, sadness, or regret, and take ownership of their healing. Once the letter is written, it can be ceremonially burned, buried, or destroyed, symbolizing the release of the past and the reclaiming of personal power. The physical act of destruction helps individuals feel that they are no longer tethered to the relationship or the pain.

4.4 Cleansing Rituals for Emotional Renewal:

Cleansing rituals are integral to the process of moving forward after emotional harm. These rituals vary widely depending on personal preference, but they all aim to wash away the emotional residue left by toxic relationships. A cleansing bath, often infused with salt or herbs like lavender, rosemary, or sage, is one common practice that many in the queer community use to purify both their body and mind.

The symbolism of cleansing is potent, as it represents the release of negative energy and the renewal of the self. These rituals help to reframe the individual's relationship with their own body, offering a sense of reclamation and renewal.

4.5 Affirmations and Reclaiming Personal Power:

Affirmations are an accessible and transformative tool for queer individuals to rewrite their narratives. After a toxic relationship, many individuals struggle with feelings of inadequacy, self-doubt, or fear of repeating past mistakes. Affirmations can help reframe negative self-talk, reminding individuals of their inherent worth and power. Writing affirmations that reflect the desired future, such as "I am worthy of healthy love" or "I release all that no longer serves me", can be empowering rituals that reestablish a sense of control and agency. Repeating affirmations daily helps to reinforce new, healthier beliefs about the self, paving the way for growth and healing. These small, yet powerful declarations become acts of resistance, reminding queer survivors that they are not broken, but becoming.

4.6 Community Rituals – Healing Together:

While personal rituals are essential, community rituals can also play a significant role in healing after a toxic relationship. Queer communities often come together in sacred or supportive spaces to share rituals that honour personal transformation and collective healing. Group ceremonies like shared meditations, collective affirmations, or group release ceremonies offer a powerful sense of solidarity and connection. These rituals are not just about personal release, but about creating a communal environment where everyone's healing journey is supported. Engaging in community rituals can help individuals feel less isolated in their experiences, creating a sense of belonging and shared purpose.

4.7 Reconnecting with the Body – Movement as Release:

For many queer individuals, the body holds the imprint of trauma. Reconnecting with the body through movement-based rituals can serve as an important part of healing. Dance, yoga, or even walking in nature can allow individuals to release stored tension and trauma in a gentle, non-verbal way. Body-based rituals help individuals reclaim their physical presence, reintegrating mind and body after emotional harm. The practice of releasing physical tension through movement can provide a sense of empowerment, making space for new beginnings and personal growth.

4.8 Integrating Release into Everyday Life:

Healing is a continuous process, and rituals of release are most effective when they are integrated into daily life. Simple actions like lighting candles, saying prayers, or taking intentional moments to breathe can remind individuals of their commitment to self-healing. By creating rituals that resonate with them personally, queer individuals can cultivate a consistent practice of emotional release and renewal. These daily actions create a sense of mindfulness and intentionality, helping to keep the focus on healing while embracing life after hardship. In weaving these small practices into everyday moments, queer survivors transform ordinary routines into sacred acts of self-restoration.

4.9 Moving Forward with Intention:

Rituals of release are ultimately about reclaiming agency and moving forward with intention. The act of letting go opens up space for new opportunities, relationships, and personal growth. For queer individuals, these rituals offer a framework for navigating the complexities of healing after toxic relationships. They serve as a reminder that the past does not have to define the future, and that through intentional, symbolic acts, individuals can begin to rewrite their own stories. Through rituals of release, queer individuals affirm their worth, release what no longer serves them and open themselves up, to a future filled with possibility and healing.

"Letting go is not forgetting, it is honouring what was while making space for what can be." – Anonymous

5. Healing in Queer Time – There Is No Straight Line to Recovery

Queer time challenges traditional, linear notions of progress and growth. In queer life, milestones don't always follow the conventional scripts of relationships, career and family. Similarly, healing from a toxic relationship rarely follows a straight, predictable path. Some days feel full of hope and movement; others feel heavy with old grief. Embracing the concept of queer time allows survivors to honour their own pace, acknowledging that true healing respects the rhythms of the heart rather than external expectations.

5.1 Setbacks Are Not Failures – Reframing the Journey:

After leaving a harmful relationship, moments of sadness, anger, or longing can feel like regressions. In reality, these emotions are not signs of failure but natural parts of healing. Setbacks can serve as opportunities to deepen self-awareness, learn new coping strategies, and strengthen resilience. Instead of judging these moments harshly, survivors can view them as part of the tapestry of recovery, each thread, even the painful ones, weaving a stronger sense of self.

5.2 Redefining Progress Through Self-Compassion:

Progress after trauma is often subtle, appearing not in grand transformations but in quiet victories: speaking kindly to oneself, reaching out for support, setting a small boundary. Measuring healing through self-compassion rather than external benchmarks helps survivors stay grounded. Queer people, often navigating compounded traumas, deserve to recognize progress even when it doesn't look impressive to the outside world. Each act of self-kindness is a radical affirmation of worth and survival.

5.3 Honouring Emotional Complexity Without Shame:

Queer healing journeys are often layered with multiple emotions at once, relief, sorrow, gratitude, fear, anger, hope. Feeling contradictory things doesn't mean a person is broken or "stuck." It means they are human. Honouring this emotional complexity without shame is crucial.

Healing is not about erasing difficult emotions but learning to coexist with them, allowing space for all parts of the self to be seen and cared for with tenderness.

5.4 Time as a Spiral, Not a Straight Line:

Thinking of time as a spiral instead of a straight line can be a liberating metaphor for queer healing. In a spiral, we often revisit the same places, old memories, old hurts, but from a different vantage point each time. Each return offers a new perspective, a deeper understanding, or a softer grief. Progress, then, is not about never circling back, it's about noticing how each return brings a little more wisdom, a little more self-love.

5.5 Learning to Trust the Timing of Your Own Heart:

There is no universal timeline for healing. What takes one person months might take another person years, and that's okay. Trusting the timing of your own heart means allowing your needs, your pain, and your joy, to unfold without pressure. Queer people, whose lives often defy societal norms, are especially equipped to redefine what "timely" means. Healing happens in its own sacred time, often quietly, often in invisible ways, until suddenly they bloom.

5.6 Embracing Growth Outside of Traditional Milestones:

Traditional milestones, getting into a new relationship, feeling "over it," moving on, don't always define real growth. Sometimes growth is leaving a conversation that feels triggering, finally sleeping peacefully through the night, or simply feeling okay while being alone. Celebrating these nontraditional victories acknowledges that healing is deeply personal and often revolutionary in its quietness. Queer people can find pride not just in big leaps, but in the steady accumulation of small, soul-affirming steps.

5.7 Offering Yourself the Same Grace You Give Others:

Many queer folks are quick to extend compassion to friends, chosen family and partners, but struggle to offer the same tenderness inward. Healing invites survivors to practice turning that generosity toward themselves. When setbacks happen or emotions resurface, responding with grace rather than judgment allows for deeper, more sustainable recovery. Treating yourself as you would treat someone you love, with patience, warmth, and forgiveness, is a radical act of self-acceptance.

5.8 Reimagining Recovery as a Lifelong Journey:

Rather than viewing healing as a destination to be reached, queer recovery can be seen as an evolving journey. There will always be new layers to peel back, new insights to uncover, and new spaces for joy to take root. Healing is not linear, nor is it finite. It is a lifelong relationship with oneself, shaped by tenderness, resilience, and the wisdom gathered from every step, stumble, and triumph along the way.

Chapter 19

The Role of Spirituality in LGBTQ+ Lives

---

1. Reclaiming Faith After Religious Trauma

Religious trauma often cuts deeply, affecting not only how LGBTQ+ individuals view themselves but, how they relate to community, love, and the divine. Experiences of condemnation, exclusion, and forced conformity, leave lasting scars that can complicate any future spiritual exploration. Many carry profound wounds from teachings that labelled their identities as sinful or broken. Naming and understanding religious trauma is the first step toward healing, as it validates the pain without framing it as a personal failure. Acknowledging the harm done allows space for self-compassion to take root and the possibility for spiritual renewal to begin.

1.1 The Loss of Spiritual Belonging:

For many queer individuals, one of the most devastating aspects of religious trauma is the loss of a spiritual home. The communities that once nurtured them may have become sources of rejection and shame. Memories of prayer, ritual, and community, can feel tainted by exclusion and judgment. This loss creates a kind of spiritual homelessness, a painful disconnection from practices and beliefs that once provided comfort. Grieving the loss of spiritual belonging is not a weakness, but a necessary mourning, making it possible to imagine new ways to reconnect with faith, on terms rooted in self-love and acceptance.

1.2 Allowing Yourself to Question, Grieve, and Redefine:

Reclaiming faith is not about forcing a return to damaged institutions or pretending the harm never happened. It begins with permission, permission to question everything, to mourn what was lost, and to rebuild spirituality from the ashes of betrayal. Questioning long-held beliefs and challenging inherited doctrines is not an act of rebellion but of self-preservation and truth-seeking. In the grieving process, queer individuals honour what was real about their spiritual yearning, while releasing what was toxic or weaponized against them. Redefining faith means asking: What is sacred to me now? What parts of spirituality still feel alive, and which ones can I let go?

1.3 Exploring New Spiritual Paths or Returning with New Eyes:

Some find healing by seeking out entirely new spiritual paths that affirm and celebrate LGBTQ+ identities. Paganism, Buddhism, Indigenous spirituality, and mystical traditions often offer spaces that embrace diversity of being. Others may feel called to return to the faith of their childhood, but with a new perspective, one that filters out the hatred and keeps the love, justice, and community at the heart of the tradition.

Whether venturing into new spiritual territory or reclaiming a former faith in transformed ways, the journey is deeply personal. Spirituality becomes less about following dogma and more about creating a relationship with the sacred that feels safe, nurturing, and free.

1.4 The Role of Affirming Communities and Mentors:

Healing from religious trauma is rarely done in isolation. Finding affirming spiritual communities, LGBTQ+-inclusive congregations, or mentors who understand the intersection of queerness and faith can make an enormous difference. These communities validate both identity and spiritual longing without demanding sacrifice of either. Seeing examples of queer individuals living openly within faith traditions, or creating new ones, offers hope that integration is possible. Affirming spaces replace messages of shame with messages of celebration, reminding LGBTQ+ people that their spirituality is not broken, it is resilient, evolving, and entirely their own. Affirming communities empower queer individuals to reclaim faith on their own terms and redefine what sacred belonging looks like.

1.5 Practices for Healing and Spiritual Renewal:

Gentle spiritual practices can help rebuild a wounded relationship with the sacred. Meditation, nature rituals, journaling prayers, creating personal altars, or simply sitting in quiet awe of the universe are ways to reconnect with spiritual life without re-traumatization. Repeating affirmations that centre worthiness and divine love, like "I am sacred exactly as I am," can be especially powerful. Some may find healing in reviving beloved practices stripped of judgment, such as singing, communal meals, or storytelling. Spiritual renewal does not have to look like formal worship, it can be as simple as honouring small moments of wonder, gratitude, and connection.

1.6 Forgiveness Without Forgetting – Honouring the Complexity:

Healing religious trauma does not necessarily mean forgiving institutions or individuals who caused harm. True forgiveness if it comes at all, emerges from a place of personal empowerment, not obligation. Honouring the complexity of emotions, anger, sadness, longing, and betrayal, allows for a more honest spiritual journey. Forgiveness can mean forgiving oneself for internalizing toxic messages, for staying silent out of fear, or for feeling broken. Moving forward with compassion for one's own younger self, without erasing the reality of the trauma, leads to deeper healing and a spirituality that is grounded in truth rather than denial.

1.7 Building a Spirituality of Wholeness and Liberation:

Ultimately, reclaiming faith after religious trauma is about building a spirituality rooted in wholeness, liberation, and unconditional love. It means rejecting any version of the divine that demands the erasure of one's true self. Spirituality becomes a practice of affirming life, diversity, creativity, and resilience. It evolves into a celebration of authenticity rather than conformity. Through reclaiming faith on their own terms, queer individuals forge paths that not only heal old wounds, but also offer radiant new possibilities, ways of being spiritual that are expansive, joyful and deeply affirming, of every facet of who they are.

*** Pause For Reflection:**

Reflection Invitation:

- What parts of your spiritual life do you want to reclaim on your own terms, without shame?

Creative Exploration:

- Write a "Letter to Your Younger Self," offering the spiritual safety, affirmation, and freedom you once needed, but didn't receive.

2. Queer-Centered Spiritual Practices

Spirituality has always been an integral part of the LGBTQ+ experience, offering a space to explore identity, find purpose, and connect with something larger than oneself. However, mainstream religious practices often marginalize or outright reject queer identities, forcing many LGBTQ+ individuals to either abandon their faith or adapt it to fit their needs. Queer-centered spiritual practices provide a powerful way for LGBTQ+ people to reclaim spirituality on their own terms. These practices celebrate the uniqueness of queer experiences and identities, offering a path to healing, self-empowerment and authenticity. By embracing spirituality that acknowledges and affirms LGBTQ+ identities, individuals can feel a sense of belonging, and community, both with themselves and the greater universe.

2.1 Creating Personal Rituals of Affirmation:

One of the most empowering aspects of queer-centered spirituality is the ability to create personal rituals that affirm one's identity. These rituals can take many forms and do not require adherence to any particular religious tradition. For some, this might include lighting a candle while reciting affirmations or engaging in mindfulness practices that focus on self-love and acceptance. Others may find strength in creating altar spaces filled with symbols that represent their journey, rainbows, pride flags, or sacred objects that hold personal significance. Rituals like these can be grounding, reminding individuals that their identities are sacred and worthy of celebration. By regularly practicing these rituals, queer people can build a spiritual foundation that nurtures their sense of self, and strengthens their connection to the divine, however they choose to define it.

2.2 Integrating Affirmation into Daily Life:

Queer-centered spirituality extends beyond the confines of ritual and can be seamlessly woven into the fabric of everyday life. For LGBTQ+ individuals, spirituality can be nurtured in simple, intentional acts that celebrate queerness and foster connection to the self. This might involve engaging in body-positive practices like yoga, dance, or movement rituals that create a sacred space between the body and spirit. These practices allow individuals to honour their bodies as they are, beautiful and deserving of love, free from the constraints of societal expectations. Additionally, setting daily intentions rooted in queer pride, self-worth and resilience, can help reinforce the divine presence within, transforming even the most mundane moments into opportunities for spiritual affirmation.

Through these small yet powerful acts, individuals actively nurture their spiritual journey, reinforcing their right to exist unapologetically and authentically in a world that may seek to diminish their existence.

2.3 Connecting with Nature as Sacred Space:

Many queer-centered spiritual practices emphasize a deep connection with nature. Nature has long been a place of solace and renewal for LGBTQ+ individuals who may not find acceptance or support in religious communities. The natural world offers an inherent sense of belonging and reminds queer individuals that they are part of something vast and beautiful. Whether it is through gardening, hiking, or simply sitting in nature, queer individuals can tap into the spiritual energy that flows from the earth. Elements of nature, such as the moon, sun, water, or trees, can serve as powerful symbols of transformation, growth, and resilience. Practicing mindfulness in nature or engaging in rituals that honour the cycles of the earth can help strengthen one's spiritual connection and affirm their place in the world.

2.4 Incorporating Queer Ancestors and Historical Figures:

Another important element of queer-centered spirituality is the integration of queer ancestors and historical figures into spiritual practices. These ancestors, both literal and metaphorical, represent the strength, resilience, and wisdom passed down through generations of LGBTQ+ individuals. Honouring queer ancestors can involve learning about historical figures who lived boldly and authentically, as well as connecting with those who may not have had the visibility or support that modern LGBTQ+ individuals enjoy. Rituals of honouring these ancestors might include creating an altar dedicated to them, offering prayers, or simply reflecting on their impact. This connection to queer history provides a sense of continuity and purpose, reminding individuals that their struggles and victories are part of a larger, ongoing narrative. Honouring queer ancestors grounds spiritual healing in legacy, reminding us we are never walking this path alone.

*For Example, Honouring Queer Ancestors – A Legacy of Courage, Resistance and Authenticity:

- **Marsha P. Johnson** – A Black transgender activist and drag queen, Johnson was instrumental in the Stonewall Uprising of 1969, a pivotal moment in LGBTQ+ history. She co-founded the Gay Liberation Front and the Street Transvestite Action Revolutionaries (STAR), which fought for the rights and dignity of transgender and homeless LGBTQ+ people. Johnson's legacy continues to inspire queer activism and the fight for justice.

- **Sylvia Rivera** – A Latina transgender activist and co-founder of STAR alongside Marsha P. Johnson, Rivera advocated for the inclusion of transgender individuals in the broader LGBTQ+ rights movement. Her tireless work at the intersection of race, gender and sexuality, has made her a cornerstone of queer activism and liberation.

- **Audre Lorde** – A renowned poet, essayist, and activist, Lorde identified as a lesbian and is celebrated for her work on intersectionality, particularly addressing the unique struggles of Black lesbian women. Her poetry and writing challenged systems of oppression and spoke to the healing power of self-love and community.

- **Bayard Rustin** – A Black gay man and one of the leading figures in the American civil rights movement, Rustin was instrumental in organizing the 1963 March on Washington. Despite facing marginalization due to his sexuality, Rustin's contributions to social justice, non-violence, and human rights have had a profound impact.

- **Christine Jorgensen** – The first American to receive widespread media attention for undergoing gender confirmation surgery in the 1950s, Jorgensen's story was a landmark moment in the visibility of transgender people. She boldly lived her truth at a time when transgender identities were not widely understood or accepted.

- **Alan Turing** – A brilliant mathematician and codebreaker who is often considered the father of computer science, Turing was persecuted for his homosexuality, which led to his tragic death. His work, particularly during World War II, was instrumental in defeating Nazi Germany, yet his contributions to science and society were overlooked because of his sexuality. Turing's legacy has since been celebrated by the LGBTQ+ community as a symbol of resilience and brilliance in the face of injustice.

- **Virginia Woolf** – A key figure in modernist literature and feminist thought, Woolf's relationships with women, including Vita Sackville-West, have been the subject of much discussion in queer literary circles. Though she never openly identified as a lesbian, her writing and relationships challenge traditional notions of gender and sexuality.

Incorporating queer ancestors and historical figures into spiritual practices can be deeply enriching, as it connects individuals to a powerful lineage of courage, defiance and authenticity.

2.5 Exploring Sacred Queer Art and Expression:

Art and creative expression are fundamental aspects of many queer-centered spiritual practices. Whether through visual art, music, poetry, or performance, queer individuals can engage in spiritual practices that honour their experiences. Creating or participating in art that reflects queerness allows individuals to express their innermost truths, offering a profound sense of spiritual release and liberation. This expression can take place in community settings or in solitary spaces.

For example, some may choose to write letters to their future selves or create pieces of art that symbolize their spiritual journey. Others might engage in performances, drag, or other forms of artistic expression as a way to honour the divine in themselves and the world around them. Through art, individuals are able to communicate their experiences and connect with their higher selves in meaningful and transformative ways.

2.6 Community and Collective Healing:

Spirituality within the LGBTQ+ community often thrives in collective spaces. Queer-centered spiritual practices can be most powerful when shared with others, whether in an online forum or in physical community gatherings. These spaces offer opportunities for collective healing, affirmation and support. In group settings, individuals can connect with others who share similar experiences and find solidarity in their spiritual journeys. These communal practices can take many forms, such as group meditations, affirmations, or LGBTQ+-inclusive worship services. The act of coming together as a community to celebrate queerness in spiritual practice is itself a powerful form of resistance and healing. These spaces not only affirm individuals' identities, but also foster an environment of collective empowerment, allowing people to rise together in strength and love.

2.7 Reclaiming Divinity and Transcendence:

A crucial aspect of queer-centered spirituality is the reclamation of divinity and transcendence. Traditional religious teachings often cast LGBTQ+ identities as sinful or unnatural, but queer-centered spiritual practices allow individuals to redefine divinity in a way that is inclusive, loving, and affirming. In these practices, God, the universe, or the divine can be understood as something that embraces all identities, including queer ones. For LGBTQ+ individuals, reclaiming divinity means embracing the sacredness of their unique identities and understanding that their love, desires, and bodies are divine expressions. This reclamation is a spiritual act of empowerment, allowing individuals to embrace the divine within and transcend the limiting narratives of shame and rejection. Reclaiming divinity and transcendence affirms that queerness is not only accepted by the divine, but is a beautiful and powerful expression of it.

2.8 Conclusion – A Path to Personal and Collective Liberation:

Queer-centered spiritual practices offer a vital pathway to healing, self-empowerment, and collective liberation. By reclaiming spiritual practices that honour and affirm LGBTQ+ identities, individuals can cultivate a deep sense of belonging, strength, and resilience. These practices provide a space for LGBTQ+ individuals to experience connection with themselves, the divine, and their community, while also dismantling harmful narratives that seek to marginalize their experiences. Through personal rituals, nature, collective healing, and creative expression, queer-centered spirituality empowers individuals to live authentically and fully, celebrating their unique contributions to the world. Embracing queer-centered spirituality fosters a journey of self-love, community unity, and the liberation of all identities.

* Pause For Reflection:

Reflection Invitation:

- What would a spiritual practice look like if it celebrated all of who you are?

Creative Exploration:

- Design a small personal ritual (even just 5 minutes long) that honours your queerness, it could be lighting a candle, reciting affirmations, or dancing freely to your favourite song.

3. The Intersection of Indigenous Spirituality and LGBTQ+ Identities

Indigenous spiritual systems have historically embraced diverse expressions of gender and sexuality, often with reverence. Many Indigenous cultures recognize the existence of two-spirit people, individuals who embody both masculine and feminine qualities. These individuals were traditionally viewed as sacred beings who played key roles as spiritual leaders, healers, and mediators. This understanding of gender and sexuality was fluid and harmonious with the natural world, contrasting with rigid gender binaries found in Western cultures. Two-spirit identities were integral to Indigenous spiritual beliefs, and these people were often revered for their unique gifts and spiritual roles.

3.1 The Impact of Colonialism on Two-Spirit Traditions:

The arrival of colonial powers brought with it the imposition of Western religious values, which significantly disrupted and displaced Indigenous practices. Christianity, with its rigid gender norms, sought to erase the concept of two-spirit people, labelling them as sinful or unnatural. This colonial violence led to the suppression of non-heteronormative sexualities and gender identities within Indigenous communities, resulting in significant cultural trauma. Two-spirit identities were often hidden or erased, leaving LGBTQ+ Indigenous individuals marginalized and disconnected from their ancestral practices.

3.2 Reclamation of Two-Spirit Traditions:

In recent decades, Indigenous communities have started to reclaim their two-spirit traditions as part of a larger movement for cultural resurgence. Contemporary efforts to revive two-spirit identities are both an act of resistance against colonialism and a spiritual reclaiming of lost cultural practices. These efforts have included the reintegration of two-spirit people into spiritual and community roles, the revival of ancient ceremonies, and the affirmation of gender and sexual diversity within Indigenous communities. The resurgence of two-spirit identities is empowering LGBTQ+ Indigenous people and fostering a sense of belonging and pride in their spiritual heritage. This reclamation of two-spirit traditions not only heals the wounds of colonial violence, but also reaffirms the sacredness of all identities, creating a pathway for collective cultural healing and empowerment.

3.3 The Role of Spirituality in Affirming Queer Identities:

Indigenous spirituality offers a holistic and inclusive framework for understanding LGBTQ+ identities. The emphasis on balance, harmony and connection to nature, allows for a deeper integration of queerness into spiritual practices. LGBTQ+ individuals, particularly those from Indigenous backgrounds, can use spirituality to affirm their identities as part of the sacred, natural order.

This understanding challenges Western constructs of rigid gender norms and supports the fluidity and complexity of human experience. Spirituality, when rooted in Indigenous teachings, offers a space for LGBTQ+ people to reclaim their authenticity and spiritual power.

3.4 Integrating Indigenous Spirituality and Queer Identity:

For LGBTQ+ Indigenous people, integrating Indigenous spirituality with queer identities is an empowering journey of personal and collective healing. This process involves not only embracing one's queerness, but also reconnecting with ancestral traditions that celebrate diverse identities. Many LGBTQ+ Indigenous people engage in traditional ceremonies, practices, and community gatherings to affirm their two-spirit identities. By incorporating these practices into their daily lives, individuals are able to cultivate a deep sense of spiritual connection, grounding themselves in their cultural heritage while navigating the complexities of queer identity. These spiritual practices help bridge the gap between ancestral knowledge and contemporary queer experiences.

3.5 Indigenous LGBTQ+ Activism and Community Building:

Contemporary LGBTQ+ Indigenous activism is playing a crucial role in advocating for visibility, representation, and acceptance within both Indigenous and broader LGBTQ+ communities. Organizations and groups dedicated to two-spirit people provide vital resources, support, and a sense of solidarity for LGBTQ+ Indigenous individuals. These efforts also contribute to the preservation and revitalization of Indigenous culture, ensuring that gender-diverse individuals are acknowledged as integral parts of the community. LGBTQ+ Indigenous activists are at the forefront of these efforts, working to dismantle colonial systems and foster environments where two-spirit people can thrive and be celebrated.

3.6 The Healing Power of Two-Spirit Identities:

The intersection of Indigenous spirituality and LGBTQ+ identities offers powerful tools for healing and empowerment. For many LGBTQ+ Indigenous people, reclaiming two-spirit identities is not only about personal growth, but also about collective healing. This process involves restoring balance and harmony within oneself, the community, and the world. Indigenous spiritual teachings offer a profound understanding of resilience, strength, and interconnectedness, reminding LGBTQ+ individuals that they are not isolated, but part of a much larger, sacred whole. By embracing their identities and connecting to their ancestors, LGBTQ+ Indigenous people can find strength in their roots and empowerment in their queerness.

3.7 Conclusion – The Intersection of Spirituality, Gender, and Sexuality:

The intersection of Indigenous spirituality and LGBTQ+ identities offers a transformative challenge to conventional notions of gender and sexuality. It provides a model rooted in inclusivity, empowerment, and healing. Indigenous spiritual traditions honour the fluidity of human identity, recognizing the sacredness of all beings.

For LGBTQ+ individuals, especially those from Indigenous backgrounds, this intersection allows for a profound understanding of their identities within a rich cultural and spiritual framework. By embracing both their queer and Indigenous heritage, individuals can reclaim their spirituality, affirming their place within their communities and contributing to a larger movement of collective liberation, healing and resilience.

* Pause For Reflection:

Reflection Invitation:

- How do you experience connection with the natural world, and what lessons does it offer you about belonging?

Creative Exploration:

- Spend time outdoors and find a natural object (a leaf, a stone, a flower). Let it symbolize your resilience and connection. Write a short paragraph about why you chose it.

4. Atheism, Agnosticism and the Queer Experience

The journey of LGBTQ+ individuals who identify as atheist or agnostic, is often shaped by the intersection of personal identity and spiritual beliefs. Atheism, defined by a lack of belief in gods or deities, and agnosticism, which embraces uncertainty or a lack of knowledge regarding the existence of a higher power, offer distinct pathways for individuals in the LGBTQ+ community to navigate their spirituality. For many, rejecting traditional religious dogma, particularly those rooted in exclusionary and condemning ideologies, is both a liberation and a means of self-preservation. The experience of coming out as both queer and non-religious can be a profound challenge, especially in cultures where religious identity often intersects with social and familial acceptance. Understanding atheism and agnosticism within the queer context reveals how these identities offer space for redefining spirituality without the constraints of traditional religious structures.

4.1 The Struggle for Belonging in a Religious World:

For many LGBTQ+ individuals, spirituality is deeply tied to their religious upbringing, often resulting in shame, alienation, and rejection, due to their identities. Leaving behind traditional religion or adopting an agnostic stance can feel like losing community and comfort. This struggle is intensified by societal pressure to adhere to religious values that condemn queerness.

Queer atheists and agnostics face the emotional challenge of letting go of old beliefs while searching for new meaning and connection. This journey involves grieving the loss of faith, confronting alienation, and seeking new ways to find solace, purpose, and community outside traditional religious constructs. In reclaiming their narratives, queer atheists and agnostics often discover that meaning and belonging can be rebuilt on their own terms.

4.2 Reimagining Spirituality Outside of Traditional Belief Systems:

Atheism and agnosticism, far from being devoid of spirituality, offer a unique space for reimagining what spirituality can be. For LGBTQ+ individuals, this journey often involves crafting spiritual practices grounded in values like inclusivity, compassion, and authenticity. Spirituality can be nurtured through personal reflection, connection with nature, creative expression, or communal solidarity. Queer atheists and agnostics find sacredness in their lives not through belief in a higher power, but by centering human connection, self-reflection and living authentically. Practices such as meditation, mindfulness and secular rituals, provide ways to explore spirituality that honour queer identities, while stepping outside traditional religious frameworks. These practices help create a meaningful sense of purpose and connection, without requiring adherence to conventional spiritual beliefs.

4.3 Finding Meaning Beyond the Divine:

For LGBTQ+ individuals who identify as atheist or agnostic, meaning is often drawn from the tangible aspects of life rather than belief in a transcendent deity. Purpose, hope, and connection can be found in human relationships, social justice, self-expression, and activism. This approach to spirituality emphasizes that spiritual fulfilment does not require a divine or supernatural framework. Atheist and agnostic queer individuals, often find deep meaning in advocating for LGBTQ+ rights, helping others and engaging in creative endeavours. These acts of service, creation, and solidarity provide a profound sense of purpose, nurturing a connection to the world and the people within it. Activism, creativity, and human connection offer spiritual fulfilment for atheist and agnostic LGBTQ+ individuals, rooted in authenticity and purpose.

4.4 Overcoming the Fear of Disconnection from the Divine:

For many queer atheists or agnostics, the rejection of traditional religious frameworks is fraught with the fear of losing connection with something greater than oneself. This fear is compounded by the experience of being told that queerness and spirituality cannot coexist, often resulting in feelings of isolation and existential anxiety. The exploration highlights how queer atheists and agnostics understand that connection doesn't require belief in a deity. Letting go of the need for external validation allows individuals to trust their worth and embrace self-affirmation, free from the constraints of religious teachings that once caused harm.

4.5 Navigating Relationships Between Religious and Non-Religious Queer People:

The relationship dynamics between religious and non-religious queer individuals can be complex. Atheist and agnostic queer individuals often find themselves caught between their spiritual identity and the religious beliefs of family members, friends, or partners. The challenges and nuances of relationships between LGBTQ+ individuals and religious family members or partners with differing beliefs are explored here. Coming out as non-religious and negotiating shared values with partners or family members who have differing beliefs can be challenging for LGBTQ+ individuals.

This exploration delves into how queer individuals can maintain their identity while navigating these relationships. Key to fostering understanding and respect are empathy, open communication and the setting of boundaries, ensuring that connections remain healthy and supportive.

4.6 Affirmation of Identity Outside Religious Labels:

Identifying as both queer and non-religious offers the empowering opportunity to define spirituality on one's own terms, free from societal or familial constraints. Queer atheists and agnostics can affirm their identities in deeply personal and liberating ways, rejecting prescribed religious roles and instead crafting their own spiritual journey. This process fosters a sense of freedom and autonomy, as individuals are able to live authentically without needing to justify themselves through religious doctrines. Reclaiming control over one's identity and beliefs becomes an essential act of empowerment, contributing to healing and self-affirmation for queer atheists and agnostics.

4.7 The Role of Secular Communities in Queer Spirituality:

For LGBTQ+ individuals who identify as atheist or agnostic, finding a sense of community is an essential part of their spiritual journey. Secular communities, such as humanist groups, atheist collectives, or non-religious queer spaces, provide opportunities for connection, support and shared values, without the need for religious affiliation. These spaces allow queer individuals to celebrate their identities, offer mutual support and build meaningful relationships. By fostering a sense of belonging, secular communities help LGBTQ+ atheists and agnostics thrive spiritually without the pressure to conform to traditional religious norms. Secular communities thus play a pivotal role in helping LGBTQ+ atheists and agnostics cultivate a spiritually enriching environment that is grounded in shared experiences, mutual respect, and the affirmation of their authentic selves.

4.8 Conclusion – Embracing a Secular, Queer Spiritual Path:

The journey of queer atheists and agnostics is one of profound self-discovery and spiritual liberation. It involves rejecting harmful religious ideologies while seeking out new, empowering forms of spiritual expression. Without the constraints of traditional religious structures, queer atheists and agnostics are able to create a spirituality that honours their queerness, affirms their identity and provides meaning in their lives. Embracing one's spiritual path, whether religious or secular, becomes a unique and valuable aspect of the queer experience. By choosing a spiritual path that aligns with personal values and authentic expression, queer atheists and agnostics contribute to the broader conversation about spirituality, identity and liberation.

* Pause For Reflection:

Reflection Invitation:

- Where do you find meaning, comfort, or awe in my life, even without a defined belief system?

Creative Exploration:

- Create a "Meaning Map", draw or list places, people, activities, or memories that fill you with wonder, comfort, or purpose, no spirituality is required.

5. The Relationship Between Mysticism and Queer Identity

Mysticism, with its focus on direct experience and profound personal transformation, offers a fertile space for the exploration of queer identity. Anchored in the quest for deeper truths that lie beyond the limitations of societal norms, mysticism invites queer individuals to embrace their identities with a freedom that transcends conventional boundaries. At this intersection, mysticism and queerness reveal the possibility for both personal and collective transcendence. In a world that frequently marginalizes or misunderstands queer experiences, mysticism serves as a powerful tool for self-discovery and empowerment, offering a spiritual framework that honours the fluidity and complexity of queerness.

5.1 The Transformative Power of Mysticism in Queer Spirituality:

Mysticism invites a journey into the unknown, where the self can be both lost and found, often in ways that are unrecognizable and deeply freeing. For queer individuals, the transformative power of mysticism lies in its ability to offer a space of radical self-acceptance. Where traditional religions might impose restrictive definitions of the self, mysticism opens up a realm where identity is not fixed, but is instead fluid, expansive, and multifaceted. Embracing mystical practices such as meditation, contemplation, or ecstatic rituals can catalyse personal growth, offering queer individuals the freedom to explore their identities in ways that feel authentic and unbound by societal expectations. This spiritual liberation becomes a pathway for empowerment, allowing queer people to reconnect with their bodies, their desires and their sense of self, in ways that transcend shame or fear.

5.2 Mysticism as a Rejection of Dualities:

A core tenet of mysticism is the dissolution of dualities, the binaries of good and evil, light and dark, male and female. This concept resonates deeply with queer individuals, whose experiences often challenge rigid gender roles and sexual categories. In mystical traditions, such as those found in Sufism, Kabbalah, and certain Eastern practices, there is an understanding that the divine transcends dualistic thinking. For queer people, mysticism offers a space where their gender and sexual identities are not seen as binary or oppositional, but as aspects of a larger, unified existence. The rejection of dualities in mysticism mirrors the queer experience of embracing a multiplicity of identities, acknowledging that fluidity and complexity are not only natural but divine.

5.3 Sacred Union and Queer Spirituality:

One of the most powerful aspects of mysticism is its focus on the concept of union, whether it is the union with the divine, with the cosmos, or with the self.

For queer individuals, sacred union takes on a different form, emphasizing the unity of body, mind and spirit, without the constraints of heteronormative or patriarchal structures. Queer mysticism embraces the sacredness of intimacy and connection, whether it manifests in romantic relationships, friendships, or community bonds. This union is not confined to a specific gender or sexual identity, but is seen as a universal and transformative force that transcends societal constructs. Queer mysticism celebrates the divine within each individual, acknowledging that all expressions of love and connection are sacred and worthy of reverence. Through sacred union, queer spirituality reclaims the divine as inclusive, expansive and deeply personal.

5.4 Ecstatic Experiences and Queer Liberation:

Ecstasy, in a mystical sense, refers to the transcendent moments when the individual is overwhelmed by a sense of unity with the divine, the universe, or the self. These moments of intense spiritual experience can offer queer individuals a profound sense of freedom and liberation, as they transcend the limitations imposed by the world. Ecstasy in queer spirituality is not only a metaphor for sexual or romantic pleasure, but also a spiritual awakening that embraces the fullness of existence, pleasure, pain, joy and sorrow. In these ecstatic states, queer individuals may experience a profound sense of belonging in the universe, not in spite of their queerness, but because of it. The mystical path offers a way to embody and celebrate queerness as an integral part of the cosmic order, allowing for spiritual liberation that is both deeply personal and collective.

5.5 Mysticism as a Path to Healing for Queer Individuals:

The mystical path also offers a form of spiritual healing that is essential for many queer individuals who have faced marginalization, discrimination and internalized shame. Mysticism's focus on direct, personal experience allows queer people to reconnect with their inherent worth and divine nature, fostering a sense of self-love and acceptance. Practices such as visualization, breathwork, or ritual can serve as tools for healing, helping individuals process trauma, release negative self-images, and reclaim their spiritual power. In this context, mysticism becomes a way to transcend the wounds inflicted by society, family, or religious institutions, offering queer individuals the chance to heal from past pain and emerge stronger, more whole and more authentic.

5.6 The Role of Mystical Community in Queer Spirituality:

While mysticism is often seen as a deeply personal journey, it also offers the potential for community and connection. Many mystical traditions emphasize the importance of community in spiritual growth and for queer individuals, finding a community of like-minded seekers can be a source of deep support and affirmation. Mystical communities, whether they are secular, spiritual, or eclectic, offer spaces for queer individuals to share their experiences, engage in communal rituals and find a sense of belonging, that honours their identity. These communities are not bound by traditional religious frameworks, but are instead centered on mutual respect, shared spiritual practice, and the understanding that all paths to the divine, are valid. In such spaces, queer individuals can experience both spiritual and communal liberation, building connections that are founded on acceptance, love and the shared pursuit of truth.

5.7 Conclusion – Mysticism as a Sacred Path for Queer Empowerment:

The connection between mysticism and queer identity is a journey of profound transformation and empowerment. Mysticism provides queer individuals with a sacred space to explore their true selves, transcend societal limitations and reclaim their innate divinity. By embracing mysticism, queer people can experience spiritual fulfilment that is authentic, expansive and deeply personal. This path challenges the rigid boundaries set by conventional society, offering an alternative vision of reality, one that celebrates fluidity, inclusivity, and the inherent sacredness of all beings. Through mysticism, queer individuals can find a deeper sense of belonging, connection and spiritual liberation, enabling them to live fully and authentically in the world.

* Pause For Reflection:

Reflection Invitation:

- When have you felt most connected to something larger than yourself, and what did that moment teach you about who you are?

Creative Exploration:

- Write a free-form poem or short memory sketch about a moment when you felt limitless, powerful, or magically connected to life.

Chapter 20

The Politics of Queer Fashion and Expression

1. How Clothing and Style Shape Queer Identity

Clothing is not just fabric stitched together, it is an unspoken language that speaks volumes about who we are, how we perceive ourselves, and how we wish the world to perceive us. For queer individuals, style choices are an essential tool of self-expression, a canvas upon which they paint their identities. The act of dressing is imbued with power, as it provides a way to communicate complex aspects of identity without uttering a single word. For some, fashion offers the opportunity to defy conventional gender roles, while for others, it becomes a personal manifesto of their unique queerness. Fashion speaks louder than labels, breaking down boundaries, whether by embracing androgyny, reclaiming traditionally gendered clothing, or mixing styles that resist categorization. Clothing helps queer individuals affirm their identities in a world with rigid expectations.

1.1 Challenging Societal Norms through Gender Expression:

Fashion has long been one of the most potent means by which queer people challenge societal norms and redefine gender. In a culture where certain fabrics, cuts, and colours are dictated by an outdated and binary understanding of gender, queer individuals use clothing as an act of rebellion, flipping the script on what is deemed acceptable or "appropriate." Gender expression through fashion is a profound rejection of these binary structures, it allows for exploration, fluidity, and even the mixing of elements, from both masculine and feminine wardrobes. The fluidity that clothing can provide in queering gender expression is not just a statement against the rigidity of societal expectations, but also a way to break free from the internalized constraints that restrict self-discovery. For queer individuals, fashion becomes a revolutionary form of self-reclamation, an outward manifestation of the freedom they seek to embody in all aspects of their lives. Fashion empowers queer individuals to defy norms and create space for personal freedom and self-expression.

1.2 Fashion as a Tool of Queer Resistance:

The fashion world has historically been seen as a reflection of mainstream ideals, often reinforcing narrow definitions of beauty and success. However, queer individuals have long used clothing as a tool for resistance, protesting against beauty standards and creating their own version of beauty that embraces diversity. The clothes that queer people wear can become a form of protest in themselves, signalling resistance to both external pressures and internal struggles. For example, drag performers have been at the forefront of fashion resistance, using extravagant and boundary-pushing designs to satirize and challenge mainstream gender norms. But beyond performance, everyday queer fashion can also act as a daily protest, a subtle declaration of independence from societal norms.

Fashion and queer identity are intrinsically linked, with the way queer individuals dress often serving as a bold act of defiance against societal norms. Through style, they challenge conventional expectations, subvert gender roles, and assert visibility, transforming clothing into a powerful tool of resistance, self-expression, and liberation.

1.3 The Personalization of Queer Style – Reclaiming Identity:

For many queer individuals, personal style is not just a reflection of their sexuality or gender, it is a tool for reclaiming their identity from forces that have sought to suppress or ignore it. Through their clothing choices, they can carve out a space for themselves, resisting societal pressures to conform to mainstream ideals. Personalizing style becomes an act of empowerment, allowing individuals to take ownership of how they present themselves to the world. Clothing becomes a form of armour and armour is needed in a world that often marginalizes queer existence. Whether through bold, unapologetic statements like rainbow colours, intricate leatherwork, or the gentle elegance of subtle feminine accents in masculine attire, these choices communicate autonomy and resilience. Style becomes an assertion of power, a reclaiming of dignity and a personal declaration of authenticity, in a society that has long made queer people feel invisible or inadequate.

1.4 Fashion as a Means of Building Community and Belonging:

Style not only reflects the individual, but also connects queer people to a larger community. Shared clothing choices create bonds of solidarity and belonging, uniting those who have experienced similar marginalization in their rejection of societal norms. Queer fashion forms its own subculture, with distinct codes and symbols that offer recognition, validation and celebration. Within this space, queer people can express their identities freely, knowing they will be understood and celebrated without judgment. As queer fashion gains visibility, it fosters inclusivity, allowing diverse expressions of gender and sexuality to be acknowledged and respected. Through fashion, queer individuals build collective strength, finding visibility in a world that often overlooks them.

1.5 The Evolving Role of Queer Fashion in the Mainstream:

Over time, queer fashion has shifted from the fringes of subculture to the spotlight of mainstream fashion. What was once considered radical or avant-garde is now influencing global trends, challenging the fashion industry to broaden its scope of what is considered beautiful, desirable, and fashionable. Designers like Jean-Paul Gaultier, Alexander McQueen, and younger talents like Telfar Clemens and Harris Reed, have propelled queer aesthetics into the mainstream, proving that fashion can be both an art form and a vehicle for social change. As queer individuals continue to shape global trends, their personal style choices become part of the cultural dialogue, influencing not only what is worn but how society understands and interacts with queer identity. This mainstream visibility has brought both challenges and opportunities, as queer style moves from subversive to celebrated, but it has also given queer people more space to be unapologetically themselves in the public eye.

"Queer fashion has shifted from rebellion to celebration, proving that style is not just clothing, but a bold statement of identity and change." – Anonymous

1.6 Fashion as an Ongoing Conversation:

Fashion is a dynamic and evolving form of communication. As the world shifts, so too does the meaning embedded in clothing. For queer individuals, fashion is not a static expression, but an ongoing conversation with themselves, their communities and the world around them. It is a constant process of revaluation and reinvention, reflecting changing attitudes toward identity, gender, and society. Clothing allows queer individuals to continuously express their fluidity, adapt to new social and cultural contexts, and respond to both personal and political developments. As society progresses toward more inclusive and diverse ideals, queer fashion will remain an ever-evolving force in the dialogue on identity, freedom and expression. It will continue to challenge outdated norms and affirm the multiplicity of queer experiences, becoming a more powerful tool for self-expression and societal change with every passing year.

1.7 Conclusion – Fashion as Liberation:

Ultimately, clothing and style have the power to liberate. For queer individuals, fashion serves as a means of reclaiming autonomy, rewriting the rules of identity and challenging social expectations. Each garment is a thread in a larger tapestry of resistance, freedom, and self-affirmation. Through clothing, queer individuals can articulate their identities in ways that are both personal and universal, breaking down barriers and building bridges within the LGBTQ+ community. Fashion is not just about clothes, it is about the stories they tell, the experiences they represent, and the revolution they continue to spark. For queer people, every outfit is an opportunity to engage in a deeper dialogue with the self and with the world, a dialogue that celebrates the fluidity, beauty and resilience of queer identity.

2. The History of Coded Queer Fashion

The roots of queer fashion can be traced to a time when visibility was dangerous. In the early 20th century, LGBTQ+ individuals were forced to navigate a world of oppressive norms, where overt expressions of queerness were often met with persecution. To circumvent societal pressures, queer individuals developed subtle and coded ways of signalling their identity. The use of specific colours, patterns, or accessories became a form of quiet rebellion, offering both a method of self-expression and a means of finding community in secret. Pink triangles, black ribbons and even the colour lavender, began to appear in clothing as discreet markers of queer identity, signalling solidarity and resistance to the status quo. These early uses of coded fashion were an essential survival tool for queer individuals, providing a visual language that spoke of rebellion, solidarity and defiance.

2.1 The 1920s to 1950s – The Rise of Gender-Bending in Fashion:

By the mid-20th century, the fashion world began to see early instances of gender-bending that were influential in shaping queer fashion. The 1920s flapper style, characterized by loose-fitting garments, bobbed haircuts, and androgynous silhouettes, offered a glimpse into how gender expression could transcend traditional norms.

While not overtly queer in its intentions, the flapper look was adopted by many queer individuals, particularly lesbians, as a subtle form of rebellion against gender expectations. In the 1930s and 1940s, butch and femme styles became more recognizable in queer communities, with the butch lesbian aesthetic incorporating tailored suits and masculine accessories as a way to assert a rejection of femininity. Simultaneously, the femme aesthetic played with hyper-feminine styles, but was often exaggerated in ways that signalled both sensuality and defiance. Queer people blended personal style with resistance to the rigid gender binary of mainstream culture.

2.2 The 1960s and 1970s – From Underground to Outspoken:

The sexual liberation movements of the 1960s and 1970s marked a turning point in the visibility of queer fashion. During this time, LGBTQ+ individuals increasingly sought to embrace their identities publicly, and fashion became a tool for self-expression and political activism. The Stonewall Riots of 1969, which marked the beginning of the modern LGBTQ+ rights movement, served as a catalyst for a more outspoken, visible queer presence in fashion. The 1970s saw the rise of the "Gay Power" movement and with it, a more deliberate embrace of gender-nonconforming fashion. Drag queens, in particular, became leaders in creating flamboyant, exaggerated, and theatrical fashion that challenged the established gender norms of the time. The use of heels, wigs, and extravagant clothing became an integral part of the drag queen aesthetic, pushing the boundaries of both gender and style. The embrace of glam and disco fashion further blurred the lines between masculinity and femininity, while simultaneously creating an outlet for queer people to boldly showcase their identities in a society that sought to suppress them.

2.3 The 1980s and 1990s – AIDS Crisis and Punk Rebellion:

In the 1980s, queer fashion took on even more significance, particularly as the AIDS crisis devastated the LGBTQ+ community. Fashion became a medium for mourning, resistance, and defiance. As the government and mainstream society failed to address the crisis, queer individuals turned to fashion to make bold statements about survival, protest and the fight for recognition. Leather jackets, studs and chains, became symbols of resilience, particularly within the queer punk movement. The punk aesthetic, often associated with non-conformity, anti-establishment sentiments, and a rejection of traditional norms, resonated deeply with LGBTQ+ individuals, providing a platform for fashion that was both radical and self-affirming. In addition to the punk movement, the 1990s saw the rise of "grunge" fashion, another subcultural style that offered a more muted, but still non-conformist, approach to queer identity. This era saw queer individuals increasingly adopting their own style, as mainstream fashion slowly began to acknowledge and incorporate queer influences into popular trends.

2.4 The 2000s – Mainstream Visibility and the Influence of Pop Culture:

The turn of the millennium marked a significant shift in the relationship between queer fashion and mainstream culture. As queer visibility in media grew, fashion started to shift from an underground form of resistance to a more publicly accepted form of self-expression.

The early 2000s saw the mainstream success of queer icons such as RuPaul, who brought drag culture into the limelight and celebrities like Lady Gaga, who used her bold fashion choices to challenge gender norms. In this era, the queer community embraced "gender-fluid" styles, with both men and women adopting clothing that had once been strictly gendered. The increasing acceptance of queer identity in the media had a profound impact on the fashion industry, which began to recognize the potential of queer aesthetics as a marketable and influential force. However, the commercial success of queer fashion also raised questions about authenticity and appropriation, as mainstream brands began to commodify queer style while often overlooking its roots in resistance and activism.

2.5 The 2010s and Beyond – Queer Fashion as Mainstream Revolution:

As we entered the 2010s, queer fashion became an undeniable force within the broader fashion industry. With the rise of social media and platforms like Instagram, queer influencers and designers have been able to create their own spaces to showcase their distinctive styles. Designers such as Telfar Clemens, Harris Reed, and Christopher John Rogers have not only disrupted the fashion industry with their inclusive, gender-fluid designs, but have also used fashion as a platform to discuss issues of race, class, and identity within the LGBTQ+ community. Social media has democratized fashion in ways that were previously impossible, allowing queer individuals to redefine the very notion of beauty and style. Gender expression through fashion continues to evolve, with fluidity becoming the ultimate form of self-expression. Today, queer fashion codes are not just a tool for survival or resistance, but are an integral part of the global fashion narrative, influencing everything from streetwear to haute couture.

2.6 Fashion as a Tool for Political Resistance:

Despite the mainstream success of queer fashion, the role of fashion as a form of resistance remains central to its power. Queer individuals continue to use fashion to challenge societal norms and question the limitations placed on gender and sexuality. Whether through punk-inspired aesthetics, drag performances, or the embrace of unisex clothing, queer fashion maintains its function as a tool for political resistance. It is a reminder that fashion, at its core, is not just about appearance, but about identity, expression, and the courage, to challenge the world's expectations. As queer individuals continue to shape fashion, the history of coded queer fashion serves as a powerful testament to the ongoing struggle for visibility, equality and liberation.

3. The Role of Gender Expression in LGBTQ+ Activism

Gender expression is one of the most powerful tools in the LGBTQ+ activism toolkit. In a world dominated by binary gender norms, the ability to express one's gender authentically challenges societal expectations and helps redefine what it means to be queer. Gender expression, through clothing, behaviour, speech, and body language, becomes an act of rebellion, a way for individuals to declare their autonomy in the face of oppressive systems. It challenges traditional norms by demonstrating that gender is not a fixed concept, but a spectrum of possibilities that allow for fluidity and self-definition.

3.1 Challenging the Gender Binary:

At the core of LGBTQ+ activism is the fight against the rigid gender binary that categorizes people as either male or female, based on narrow definitions of masculinity and femininity. Those who express their gender outside this binary, whether through non-conforming clothing, androgynous styles, or unconventional gendered behaviours, act as disruptors to the status quo. These acts of expression challenge the limitations imposed by society and allow for new, inclusive understandings of gender. Gender non-conforming activists are showing the world that there are endless ways to live and present one's gender identity, creating space for others to also embrace their authentic selves.

3.2 Gender Expression as a Political Statement:

For many LGBTQ+ activists, gender expression is not just personal, it's political. The visibility of non-binary, gender-fluid, and transgender people has pushed society to reconsider long-standing notions of what is "acceptable" or "normal." Through defiant acts of gender expression, activists are asserting their right to exist outside predefined categories and are advocating for a society where all forms of gender identity are seen, accepted, and celebrated. Whether it's a drag queen's bold performance or a transgender person's daily navigation of public spaces, these expressions force society to confront and reevaluate its assumptions about gender. Each step taken outside the traditional binary is an act of resistance, one that calls for a broader, more inclusive view of human identity.

3.3 The Intersectionality of Gender Expression in Activism:

Gender expression within LGBTQ+ activism intersects with other forms of identity and activism, including race, class, and sexual orientation. For queer people of colour, gender expression is even more radical, as it challenges both racial stereotypes and restrictive gender roles. The expression of one's gender can be an act of liberation from multiple forms of oppression, making intersectionality a crucial element of understanding how gender activism plays out in real-life experiences. When a person's gender expression challenges both societal gender norms and racial or cultural expectations, it not only opens up space for more authentic expressions of self, but also shifts how we view the intersections of privilege and marginalization within the broader fight for equality.

3.4 Visibility and Representation Through Gender Expression:

The increasing visibility of diverse gender expressions in media, politics, and culture is a testament to the role of gender expression in LGBTQ+ activism. Whether it's a non-binary actor on a popular TV show or a transgender athlete dominating their sport, these moments of visibility challenge conventional ideas about who can and cannot perform or embody gender. By showing the world that gender expression is diverse and multifaceted, LGBTQ+ activists help deconstruct harmful stereotypes and foster a more inclusive understanding of identity. The more that diverse gender expressions are seen and celebrated in public spaces, the more society shifts toward acceptance and understanding. Visibility of diverse gender expressions challenges stereotypes and fosters greater societal acceptance.

3.5 Creating Safe Spaces Through Gender Expression:

For many queer individuals, expressing their gender authentically isn't just a form of activism, it's also a necessary act of self-preservation. In a world where non-conformity is often met with discrimination or violence, having the freedom to express one's gender openly is a powerful act of survival. LGBTQ+ activists work tirelessly to create safe spaces where individuals can express their gender identity without fear of rejection or harm. These spaces allow people to experiment with and explore their gender expression without judgment, fostering a sense of belonging and empowerment. Whether through online platforms or physical spaces such as LGBTQ+ centers, these safe spaces provide a foundation for individuals to connect, share experiences, and support one another in their journeys of self-discovery and activism. By embracing and celebrating gender expression, these safe spaces not only protect individuals, but also empower them to live authentically and challenge societal norms.

3.6 The Future of Gender Expression in LGBTQ+ Activism:

As LGBTQ+ activism continues to evolve, so too will the role of gender expression. The future of activism lies in the celebration of gender diversity, as more people come to understand that gender is not a static category but a complex, ever-changing experience. As society becomes more accepting of gender fluidity, new forms of gender expression will continue to emerge, further challenging societal expectations. The movement toward gender inclusivity is not just a fight for personal expression but also a fight for the liberation of all people, regardless of how they choose to express their gender. LGBTQ+ activists will continue to push the boundaries of gender expression, making space for individuals to live freely and authentically, unencumbered by the limitations of traditional gender norms. The future of LGBTQ+ activism will be defined by a continued push for freedom and authenticity, creating a world where everyone can express their gender without fear of judgment or restriction.

3.7 Conclusion – Gender Expression as Empowerment and Resistance:

Ultimately, gender expression serves as both a powerful act of empowerment and resistance within LGBTQ+ activism. By defying rigid gender norms and embracing fluidity, LGBTQ+ individuals reclaim their identities and challenge societal expectations. Through both personal and collective expressions of gender, the LGBTQ+ community is crafting a world where gender is no longer a constraint, but a wellspring of strength, creativity, and authenticity. As activism continues to redefine the landscape of gender and identity, the expression of gender will remain at the heart of the ongoing struggle for freedom, equality, and recognition for all. By embracing diverse gender expressions, the LGBTQ+ community fosters liberation and paves the way for a more inclusive society. Gender expression is not just a form of activism, it is a cornerstone of liberation, inspiring a future where authenticity and self-determination are celebrated for all.

"When we express our gender freely, we do more than defy norms, we reclaim our power, rewrite the rules and remind the world, that authenticity is a revolutionary act." – Anonymous

* Queer Fashion Designers Shaping the Future of Gender Expression in Activism:

As an example, here's a list of queer fashion designers who have made significant contributions to queering high fashion and breaking boundaries:

Jean-Paul Gaultier:

Known for his gender-bending designs and unconventional takes on traditional gender roles, Gaultier has long been at the forefront of challenging fashion norms. His iconic use of corsets on men, as well as his androgynous collections, have made him a legend in the fashion world and a powerful figure in queer activism.

Alexander McQueen:

A visionary designer, McQueen used his collections to explore the intersection of beauty, horror, and gender fluidity. His work often pushed boundaries, questioning established beauty standards and social constructs, making his runway shows an act of rebellion against rigid gender expectations.

Telfar Clemens:

Founder of the unisex brand Telfar, Clemens is redefining the notion of fashion inclusivity by challenging traditional gender binaries and creating space for queer people of all identities. His popular line, especially the Telfar bags, has become an emblem of non-binary, inclusive fashion.

Harris Reed:

Known for creating dramatic, gender-fluid designs, Harris Reed blends avant-garde fashion with the freedom of gender expression. Their work celebrates fluidity, rejecting the traditional confines of gender and fashion, and has gained recognition for pushing boundaries in mainstream fashion.

Ruth E. Carter:

Although more known for her costume design in film (especially for Black Panther), Ruth Carter's work explores themes of cultural expression, identity, and the deconstruction of gendered attire. Her designs empower queer individuals by weaving personal narratives and identities into fabric and style.

Azzi & Osta:

This Lebanese fashion duo is known for their gender-fluid designs, blending masculine and feminine aesthetics. Their work speaks to the diverse expressions of identity within the queer community, offering sartorial choices that transcend traditional boundaries. Their work encourages people to embrace fluidity in all aspects of identity, reflecting a world where fashion is not confined to societal expectations.

Gareth Pugh:

Fusing high fashion with avant-garde artistry, Gareth Pugh's designs often feature dramatic shapes and boundary-pushing silhouettes. His work challenges traditional views on gender and identity, emphasizing the fluidity and freedom that come with self-expression.

Tanya Taylor:

Tanya Taylor is an outspoken advocate for inclusivity and diversity within the fashion industry. Her collections often explore themes of gender expression, pushing back against rigid standards and promoting positive representation for queer and non-binary identities.

Bobby Abley:

Known for his playful and often whimsical approach to fashion, Bobby Abley has used his designs to explore queer themes, with an emphasis on breaking gender norms and celebrating non-conformity. His collections frequently feature gender-neutral cuts and inclusive messaging.

Colman Domingo:

As both an actor and designer, Colman Domingo is a queer creative whose work explores themes of masculinity and identity. His designs often challenge stereotypes about men's clothing while promoting a deeper dialogue about race, gender, and sexuality in fashion.

*These designers challenge gender norms, celebrate queer identity, and make fashion a powerful tool for self-expression and activism.

4. The Impact of Dress Codes and Uniforms on Queer People

Dress codes and uniforms are often presented as neutral standards, but historically, they have operated as powerful tools of social control. For queer individuals, these rules have rarely been neutral, instead, they have reinforced binary gender norms and punished deviation from traditional expressions of masculinity and femininity. Dress codes dictate not just what is appropriate, but who is acceptable, making them deeply political mechanisms that regulate bodies, identities, and self-expression. Understanding the impact of these systems is critical to examining broader patterns of exclusion and conformity within society.

4.1 Historical Context – Policing Queer Bodies Through Clothing:

In many societies, laws and informal rules around clothing were designed to maintain a strict gender binary, criminalizing those who stepped outside it. From anti-crossdressing laws in the 19th and early 20th centuries to the requirement that individuals wear "at least three articles of clothing appropriate to their assigned gender."

Queer people have long faced legal and social punishment simply for dressing authentically. These historical realities laid the groundwork for contemporary dress codes that, while less explicitly discriminatory, still often marginalize queer and gender-nonconforming individuals.

4.2 The Modern Workplace – Dress Codes and Conformity:

Workplace dress codes frequently prioritize professionalism, but the underlying expectations often align with heteronormative and binary standards. For queer employees, particularly transgender and nonbinary individuals, navigating these codes can mean choosing between authenticity and career advancement. Policies that demand "male" and "female" dress, grooming, and comportment marginalize those whose identities or presentations do not fit neatly into such categories. Even in progressive environments, unspoken pressures to "tone down" queer expression reveal how the politics of appearance continue to police and limit the full participation of queer individuals in professional life. Resisting these norms is essential to creating workplaces, where authenticity is valued over conformity, and where all identities have the freedom to thrive. Challenging and redefining workplace dress codes to be more inclusive not only empowers queer employees, but also fosters an environment where diversity is celebrated and individual expression is seen as an asset, rather than a liability.

4.3 Schools and the Policing of Youth Expression:

In educational settings, dress codes are used to enforce discipline and promote uniformity, but they disproportionately target queer and gender-nonconforming youth. Students who wish to express themselves through clothing choices that reflect their true gender or sexuality often face discipline, harassment, or forced conformity. Policies against "distracting" clothing frequently serve as coded language for suppressing visible queerness. The consequences are far-reaching, students denied the right to dress authentically may suffer lower self-esteem, mental health struggles, and even higher dropout rates. The fight over school dress codes is a microcosm of the larger struggle for queer visibility and acceptance. Protecting students' right to authentic self-expression in schools is essential for fostering an environment where all young people can thrive, learn, and grow without fear.

4.4 Uniforms in Institutions – Erasing Identity for "Order":

Uniforms are often justified as creating equality or unity, especially in environments like the military, religious institutions, and some private schools. Yet for queer individuals, mandatory uniforms often erase individual identity and enforce binary gender norms under the guise of order and discipline. In institutions where appearance is strictly regulated, gender nonconformity can be grounds for discipline or expulsion, subtly reinforcing the idea that queerness is incompatible with tradition and respectability. Uniforms, far from being neutral, serve as instruments of both inclusion and exclusion, depending on whose identities are deemed acceptable. Challenging these rigid standards is crucial to building spaces, where diversity is not only acknowledged, but celebrated as a vital and necessary force that strengthens community, fosters genuine belonging, and redefines what true equality looks like.

4.5 Resistance and Subversion – Queer Responses to Dress Codes:

Despite the rigid structures imposed by dress codes and uniforms, queer people have continuously found ways to resist and subvert these limitations. From subtle alterations in uniforms to overt acts of protest, clothing becomes a site of both survival and rebellion. Queer youth have launched campaigns to change discriminatory school policies, employees have challenged workplace codes under anti-discrimination laws, and activists have used fashion as a tool for visibility, affirmation and political resistance. These acts of defiance not only affirm individual identity, but also challenge the larger systems that seek to erase or contain queerness.

4.6 Contemporary Shifts – Legal and Cultural Pushback:

In recent years, legal challenges and cultural shifts have begun to chip away at the rigid power of dress codes. Courts have increasingly recognized that restrictive dress codes can constitute gender discrimination, and companies and schools are slowly adopting more inclusive policies that allow for gender-neutral dress. The rise of queer visibility in media and culture has also pressured institutions to reconsider how their policies affect marginalized communities. Yet, despite these advancements, many spaces still stubbornly cling to outdated norms, revealing how deeply entrenched the policing of appearance remains. Despite progress, the resistance to inclusive dress codes reveals the ongoing struggle for equality and the need for continued advocacy.

4.7 Conclusion – Dress Codes as Battlegrounds for Queer Autonomy:

Dress codes and uniforms are far more than aesthetic guidelines, they are battlegrounds where broader struggles over gender, sexuality, and power are fought. For queer people, clothing is a vital form of self-expression, autonomy and resistance against systems that demand conformity. Challenging dress codes is not just about changing what people are allowed to wear; it is about asserting the right to exist authentically and visibly. As the fight for LGBTQ+ rights continues, the dismantling of oppressive dress norms remains an essential front in the ongoing pursuit of freedom, dignity, and true inclusivity.

"Authenticity should never be the cost of professionalism, true progress lies in making space for every identity to exist without compromise." – Anonymous

5. Fashion as a Tool for Queer Resistance

Fashion within the queer community has long been a weapon against the rigid norms that seek to control gender, sexuality and appearance. From the coded outfits of secret gatherings to the radical visibility of Pride marches, clothing has been a way to defy invisibility. Queer individuals use fashion to challenge societal expectations, making personal style a frontline of cultural rebellion. Dressing in ways that refuse binary gender roles, which exaggerate or play with traditional signifiers, becomes an everyday act of protest against a world that often demands conformity. Fashion in the queer community is not just an expression of identity, but a deliberate act of resistance, using style to confront and subvert societal norms.

5.1 Historical Roots of Fashion as Protest:

Queer fashion as resistance has deep historical roots. During the Harlem Renaissance, LGBTQ+ individuals found sanctuary in speakeasies and balls where fashion blurred gender boundaries. In the mid-20th century, butch lesbians and femme-presenting gay men used clothing to carve out identities in public spaces that denied their existence. The Stonewall Riots of 1969 highlighted how even the right to dress authentically was a battle worth fighting. Each era of queer resistance has woven its history through fabric and self-presentation, creating a rich tapestry of defiance stitched into the mainstream consciousness.

5.2 Drag Culture – A Bold Reimagining of Gender:

Drag has become one of the most visible and dynamic forms of queer fashion resistance. Drag queens and kings amplify, distort, and reimagine gender, through extravagant costuming and performance, mocking the idea that gender must be natural or restrained. In spaces like drag balls, participants created entire worlds where gender rules were shattered and reimagined. Today, drag continues to be a site of resistance, pushing boundaries in popular culture while retaining deep roots in queer struggle, especially among Black and Latinx communities who originated the art form. Drag reminds the world that gender, like fashion, is a construction, and constructions can be joyfully torn down.

5.3 Pride Parades and the Power of Visibility:

Pride parades are more than celebrations, they are statements of resistance where fashion plays a crucial role. From leather harnesses to rainbow tutus, every flamboyant, political, or personal outfit becomes a public claim to space and identity. Clothing at Pride is deliberately disruptive, rejecting the idea that queerness should remain hidden or subdued. Marchers reclaim the streets, wearing their identities boldly on their bodies as a form of joyful, rebellious protest. Fashion transforms the parade into a vibrant rejection of shame, enforcing the idea that visibility itself is a powerful, political act.

5.4 Fashion as Protest Against Corporate Pinkwashing:

As corporations increasingly commercialize queer identities, many activists have turned to fashion to critique the empty gestures of "rainbow capitalism." DIY aesthetics, protest shirts and guerilla fashion statements, reclaim queer fashion from profit-driven brands. Statements like "Pride is a Protest" emblazoned on clothing serve as reminders that queer liberation was never about corporate sponsorships, but about survival and rebellion. Through fashion, queer activists resist the sanitization and depoliticization of their struggles, insisting that visibility without justice is hollow.

5.5 Intersectionality and the Fashion of Resistance:

True queer resistance through fashion is intersectional, recognizing the ways race, class, ability and body size, intersect with gender and sexuality.

Black and brown queer communities, in particular, have used fashion to resist both white supremacy and heteronormativity. From ballroom culture to Afrofuturism, marginalized groups have created alternative aesthetics that centre their own narratives. Today's most potent queer fashion is inseparable from broader struggles for social justice, using visual expression as a rallying cry for liberation on all fronts.

5.6 The Future of Fashion as Queer Resistance:

Fashion will continue to be a critical tool for queer resistance in the future. As new challenges arise, whether political, environmental, or cultural, queer communities will adapt, innovate and rebel, through their clothing and self-presentation. Virtual spaces, sustainable fashion, and experimental designs are opening up fresh battlegrounds for expression and defiance. The future of queer fashion lies not in assimilation, but in continued disruption, crafting new aesthetics that centre authenticity, resilience and revolutionary joy.

5.7 Conclusion – Dressing to Disrupt, Dressing to Liberate:

Clothing has never been just about fabric or trends for queer individuals, it is a language, a shield, a weapon and a celebration. Through bold self-expression, queer communities have turned fashion into a battlefield where freedom, identity and rebellion, are stitched into every seam. As long as systems seek to control or erase queer existence, fashion will remain a powerful, living tool of resistance, a brilliant, defiant reminder that beauty, in all its queer forms, is inherently revolutionary.

"Fashion is not just what we wear, it is how we declare our existence, defy the rules and reclaim the right, to be seen and celebrated in all our diverse, rebellious glory." – Anonymous

Chapter 21

Drag as Philosophy – Performance, Paradox and the Self

---

1. Wigs, Wounds, and Wisdom – The Personal as Revelation

Drag personas are more than elaborate costumes, they are bold proclamations of identity, crafted from layers of both external and internal expression. In the spotlight, wigs become war paint, sequins transform into armour, and each gesture, no matter how exaggerated, uncovers not just artifice, but a deep well of personal truth. For the drag performer, the persona becomes a paradoxical mask, while it obscures the self, it simultaneously reveals the soul's deepest wounds and victories. The art of drag demands radical transformation, yet it is in that very transformation that the rawest facets of human existence come to light, pain, resilience, and the wisdom gained through the battle of being seen in a world that often prefers to look away. In this way, drag becomes more than performance, it is a profound act of self-revelation, where the persona not only masks the self, but unveils the untold truths of the performer's inner world, empowering both artist and audience to embrace the beauty found in transformation.

1.1 Wigs as War Paint – Crafting Power Through Artifice:

The process of constructing a drag persona is not merely about assuming an alternate identity. It is a dance between hiding and revealing, where the artifice of makeup, wigs, and rhinestones serves as both shield and sword. Behind every perfectly applied layer of foundation, there is a story of survival. Each false lash represents a truth that the artist is reclaiming, a moment of empowerment pulled from the depths of their history. The drag queen, king, or non-binary performer stands not just as an entertainer, but as a warrior in their own right. They wear their wounds like badges of honour, not to conceal them, but to display them with audacity and grace. In that sense, drag is an art of transformation not just for the artist, but for their audience as well. Drag transforms both performer and audience, redefining beauty, strength, and resilience with every bold choice.

1.2 From Trauma to Triumph – Drag as Emotional Alchemy:

Behind the masks and the glitter lies an undercurrent of trauma that drives many drag performers to the stage. Drag is, in many ways, an art form born from struggle. It provides a space to process grief, rejection, and societal violence, experiences that are often too painful to address in everyday life. For many, the act of stepping into a drag persona is an opportunity to confront personal demons, to exorcise the ghosts of past trauma, and to transcend the limitations placed upon them by the world. In the chaos of the performance, where all attention is focused on the performer's every move, drag artists can safely step into their own power. It is here, in the exaggerated artifice of the stage, that performers find a way to reshape the wounds of their past into something beautiful and triumphant.

1.3 The Drag Stage as a Mirror to the Audience's Transformation:

This metamorphosis is not just an internal process, it also invites the audience to embark on their own journey of transformation. The drag artist's willingness to expose vulnerability through their art gives permission to others to do the same. Drag performances allow spectators to witness an artist not only reclaiming their identity, but also reframing it. For the audience, the act of watching a performer undergo this transformation, through layers of makeup, wigs, and costume, becomes an invitation to question their own assumptions about identity and self-worth. The performative nature of drag serves as a mirror to the audience's own fears and desires. In the act of seeing another person step into their power, the audience is reminded that they, too, can shed their own masks, embrace their truth, and emerge more fully into who they are meant to be.

1.4 The Wisdom of Drag – Strength Through Artifice:

The wisdom found in drag transcends intellect, it is deeply visceral, rooted in lived experiences and the hard-won lessons that shape a performer's journey. Those who step onto the stage carry with them a history of rejection, loss, and marginalization, yet through the transformative power of disguise, they summon the strength to face the world. Drag creates a space where wisdom is forged not in the pursuit of flawless performance, but in the raw imperfections that emerge through it. The artificiality of drag, the heavy makeup, the padding, the illusion, becomes a conduit for a kind of authenticity that is built on resilience rather than idealized perfection. What the audience sees on the surface is but a glimpse of the greater truth, beneath the layers of glamour lies a story of survival, where each performance serves as a powerful reaffirmation of personal strength and defiance.

1.5 Rebellion Through Transformation – Drag as Resistance:

For many drag artists, their personas are a form of rebellion. To perform in drag is to challenge the societal norms that seek to define and confine them. Drag reveals the fluidity of identity, the idea that gender is not a fixed category, but rather something that can be constructed and deconstructed. In wearing a persona that is larger than life, the drag performer makes a statement, that the boundaries of gender, beauty, and self-expression are not only malleable, but meant to be bent and broken. Through the deliberate exaggeration of feminine or masculine traits, drag artists subvert conventional ideas of what it means to be a man, a woman, or anything in between. In this act of rebellion, drag does not just challenge the status quo, it transforms it, one wig at a time.

1.6 The Paradox of the Persona – Revealing the True Self Through Artifice:

The drag persona, then, becomes a paradox, a mask that reveals the truest parts of the artist's being. Through layers of performance, it is not the persona that hides the performer's identity, but rather it is the artifice that allows the performer to express their deepest truths without fear of retribution or rejection. The persona becomes a vessel for both self-exploration and societal commentary. In the process of shedding one's vulnerability and embracing artifice, drag offers not just a performance, but a radical act of self-empowerment. Performing offers both personal healing and a mirror for the audience's potential transformation.

1.7 Conclusion – The Radical Power of Drag Transformation:

In this way, drag personas are both a revelation and a rebellion, offering not just captivating performances, but profound lessons in resilience, self-expression, and the transformative power of radical reinvention. Through wigs, wounds, and wisdom, drag creates a dynamic space where both the artist and the audience can delve into the art of becoming, exploring the power of artifice, and uncovering the limitless potential of self-discovery and personal evolution.

2. Gender on a Stage – Drag as a Deconstruction Tool

Drag is a bold and often outrageous spectacle that shatters the rigidity of gender binaries, challenging the very foundations of heteronormative expectations. Through exaggerated portrayals of masculinity and femininity, drag distorts and reimagines traditional gender roles, transforming them into something playful, fluid, and transformative. For decades, drag artists have pushed the boundaries of gender, donning hyperbolic costumes and exaggerated gestures that not only parody, but actively deconstruct the idea of fixed gender identities. By flipping societal norms on their head, sometimes quite literally, drag asks, what happens when masculinity steps into stilettos or femininity grows a mustache? In this radical transformation, drag reveals that gender is not an inherent truth, but a performative act, a series of socially constructed behaviours and expressions. In doing so, drag becomes a potent form of resistance to the essentialist, binary view of gender, inviting us to recognize it as an infinitely malleable and performative construct.

2.1 Judith Butler and the Performativity of Gender:

Judith Butler's theory of performativity, articulated in works like Gender Trouble, provides an essential framework for understanding the subversive nature of drag. For Butler, gender is not something we are, but something we do, a series of repeated acts that are socially sanctioned and performatively enacted. Butler argues that gender is not a stable identity, but a series of performances that individuals carry out according to societal expectations. Drag takes this concept and amplifies it, creating a space where gender performances are exaggerated to the point of absurdity, revealing the constructed nature of all gendered behaviour. In a drag performance, the artist does not simply impersonate a woman or a man, they engage in a deliberate distortion of gendered expectations, performing roles that are overtly theatrical and sometimes impossible to categorize within conventional understandings of gender. Through this process, drag highlights the malleability of gender, suggesting that if we can deconstruct the boundaries of masculinity and femininity, then we can also reimagine them as infinite and ever-evolving.

2.2 Theatricalizing Gender – When Masculinity Wears Stilettos:

In the world of drag, masculinity is both performed and subverted, taking on exaggerated forms that challenge its traditional associations with power, dominance, and control. When a drag performer, often a man, steps into stilettos and a dramatic gown, they are not simply parodying femininity; they are deconstructing the very foundations of masculinity itself.

The image of a man confidently strutting across the stage in heels disrupts the societal expectations that tie masculinity to physicality, strength, and athleticism. The very act of a man engaging in an activity, wearing heels, which has historically been gendered as feminine, exposes the arbitrary nature of these associations. Drag doesn't merely mock femininity, it unearths the contradictions and paradoxes embedded within the gender system. Masculinity in drag is not just about performance, it's an exploration of the vulnerability, complexity, and contradictions that lie beneath society's rigid definitions of "manhood." In this radical reinvention, masculinity refuses to be confined by restrictive norms, offering a new, more expansive understanding of what it means to be a man.

2.3 Femininity in Drag – The Mustache as a Subversion of Norms:

Just as drag transforms masculinity, it also plays with and subverts femininity. A drag queen sporting a thick mustache may initially appear absurd, but it is precisely this absurdity that makes a profound statement about the fluidity of gender. In this act, femininity is not a fixed identity, but a performative practice, capable of incorporating traits traditionally deemed masculine. The mustache becomes a powerful symbol of this reimagining of femininity, a direct challenge to the rigid binaries that constrain gender expression. When drag queens wear mustaches, they are not merely poking fun at femininity or masculinity; they are exposing the artifice behind both. Drag reveals that these gendered distinctions are not inherent, but are socially constructed, and can thus be mocked, distorted, and reinterpreted. The mustache, in its playful incongruity, compels the viewer to question their assumptions about gender norms and expectations. By blending the masculine with the feminine, drag exemplifies the truth that gender is not a binary, but a spectrum of possibilities, each one ripe for reinterpretation and reimagining.

2.4 Deconstructing Heteronormativity – Gender as Infinite and Constructed:

Drag does more than parody; it actively dismantles the very concept of heteronormativity. Heteronormativity is the idea that heterosexual relationships and gendered identities are the default, the "natural" state of being. In drag, this idea is constantly disrupted. Drag artists often embody exaggerated versions of gender that challenge not just the roles assigned to men and women, but also the very notion that there are only two genders, each with a predetermined set of behaviours. Through this deconstruction, drag exposes gender as a fluid and complex spectrum that defies simplistic categorization. It is a rejection of the rigid roles assigned to individuals based on their assigned sex at birth, offering instead an invitation to engage with gender as something creative, expansive, and transformative. Drag artists, by embodying roles that span across and beyond gender categories, reimagine gender not as a fixed identity, but as a continuously unfolding performance, constantly renegotiated and redefined in each act of expression.

2.5 Drag as Queer Alchemy – Transforming the Self and Society:

Drag goes beyond the subversion of gender roles, it is a form of queer alchemy. Alchemy, the ancient practice of transforming base metals into gold, becomes a fitting metaphor for the drag artist's work. Through performance, drag artists take the raw material of gender, often constrained by societal expectations, and transmute it into something dazzling, transformative, and radically new.

This alchemy is not just about personal transformation, it is about social transformation as well. By performing gender in exaggerated and unexpected ways, drag artists invite their audiences to consider new ways of being. In this sense, drag becomes an act of radical imagination, offering new possibilities for how individuals can live, love, and express themselves, beyond the constraints of traditional gender norms. Just as alchemists sought to unlock hidden potentials, drag artists unlock new ways of seeing the world, one stiletto at a time.

2.6 The Infinite Possibilities of Gender Performance:

At its core, drag reveals that gender is not a set of immutable qualities, but a dynamic, constructed performance. By drawing attention to the performative nature of gender, drag challenges the assumption that there are natural, inherent differences between men and women. Instead, it exposes gender as a set of practices, behaviours, and presentations that are constantly in flux, constantly subject to change and reinvention. Through the playful subversion of gender norms, drag shows that gender is infinite, not fixed, but an evolving spectrum of possibilities. It asks us to imagine a world where we can transcend the boundaries of masculinity and femininity, where gender can be something creative, fluid and uniquely our own.

2.7 Conclusion – Reimagining Gender Through Drag:

Drag, as a tool of deconstruction and queer alchemy, offers more than just a performance. It is a radical challenge to the rigid, binary understanding of gender. By parodying and exaggerating traditional gender roles, drag artists expose the artificiality of these constructs and invite us to engage with gender in a more expansive, liberated way. Gender is not a box we fit into, it is an infinite canvas upon which we can paint, perform, and reinvent ourselves. Through drag, we come to understand that gender is not something we are born into, but something we create, perform, and reimagine over and over again.

3. The Mirror Has Many Faces – Identity as Performance

In the glow of mirror lights and the rustle of fabric, a drag performer constructs a version of self not unlike what we all do each morning before facing the world. Yet while drag makes this process visible, exaggerated, and unapologetically theatrical, most of society is engaged in subtler acts of the same ritual. The self, as Erving Goffman theorized in The Presentation of Self in Everyday Life, is less a singular truth and more a series of masks adjusted depending on context, curated, tailored, and staged for our respective audiences. The person who strides into a business meeting is no less in drag than the one who steps onto a runway in six-inch heels and glittered lashes. Drag simply makes that invisible labour of identity visible and fabulous. What emerges is not deception, but revelation, a performance that doesn't obscure reality, but magnifies its multiplicities.

3.1 You're Born Naked and the Rest is… Philosophy:

RuPaul's iconic aphorism, "You're born naked and the rest is drag", can be read as both tongue-in-cheek and deeply philosophical. At its heart lies the idea that every human presentation is a constructed performance, from fashion choices to gender expressions to the way we phrase a simple hello.

Drag lays bare the theatricality of being. It doesn't pretend to strip away illusion in search of an essential "truth," but instead reveals that the so-called truth is itself constructed. Drag, then, is not just a performance of gender; it is a performance of existence. The self is never fixed, only ever assembled, in layers of language, posture, clothing, and tone. Each gesture is an act of self-curation, and drag dares to ask, if all of it is a costume, why not make it art? In the shimmering spotlight of drag, we don't discover who we are, we become who we dare to perform.

3.2 Multiplicity as Survival – The Many Selves We Carry:

Identity is rarely fixed or singular, it shifts, adapts, fragments, and reassembles, depending on who's watching and what's at stake. For queer individuals, especially those living at the crossroads of race, class, gender and other marginalizations, this multiplicity isn't merely artistic, it's often essential. Drag captures this necessity with theatrical precision, moving fluidly between archetypes. A single performance might summon the mother and the monster, the muse and the martyr, all within a single breath. These layered portrayals reflect the lived realities of those who must continuously recalibrate their identities, whether for safety, acceptance, or sheer survival. Drag does not simplify these selves into a singular truth, it stages them in all their contradiction, excess, and glory. What emerges is not confusion, but clarity, the recognition that to live authentically in a world demanding coherence is itself an act of defiance. The boardroom may require composure, the nightclub audacity, and drag dares to honour them both. It transforms identity from a fixed script into a dynamic improvisation, refusing resolution in favour of radiant complexity.

3.3 The Illusion of Authenticity – When Realness Becomes Real:

We are often taught to search for our "true self," as though it lies somewhere deep beneath all the roles we play. But what if the truth is in the playing? The drag concept of "realness", passing as something you're not, flips authenticity on its head. When a drag performer evokes the elegance of a 1950s starlet or the raw edge of punk masculinity, they aren't being inauthentic, they're inhabiting an emotional truth through aesthetic fiction. Philosopher Judith Butler argues that gender itself is performative, not something we are, but something we repeatedly do. Drag exposes this fact, not by rejecting reality, but by distorting it until the seams show. In those exposed seams, where beard meets blush, or hip pad peeks through a gown, something deeply authentic emerges. Not in spite of the illusion, but because of it. In embracing performance as revelation rather than deception, drag shows us that the self is not found by peeling back layers in search of some hidden core, but by learning how to wear those layers with intention, imagination, and unapologetic truth. It suggests that authenticity is not about permanence or purity, but about presence, about how fully one inhabits the roles, gestures, and expressions that shape a life.

3.4 Spectator and Self – The Audience Within:

Every drag performance has an external audience, but it also has an internal one, the performer's own reflection. The mirror becomes both co-conspirator and critic, a space where self-construction unfolds in private before it's projected outward. But that mirror exists in all our lives, whether literal or metaphorical.

We perform ourselves not only for others, but for the imagined audiences in our minds, the parent we want to impress, the lover we want to seduce, the stranger whose gaze both affirms and threatens. Drag amplifies this dynamic, making it artful and intentional. The mirror doesn't lie, but it doesn't tell the full truth either. It reflects one face among many, and perhaps, that is the only truth that matters.

3.5 From Lip Syncs to Life Scripts – Drag as a Philosophy of Freedom:

Drag doesn't merely imitate life, it dares to rewrite it. Through its theatrical exaggeration and sacred irreverence, drag becomes a provocative invitation to dismantle the myths we're taught to treat as fact. Why should gender follow a binary? Why must identity remain fixed and legible? Why is performance seen as deception, rather than revelation? With every rhinestone, wink, and high-heeled strut, drag answers with a radical yes to fluidity, contradiction, and reinvention. It suggests that performance isn't a mask hiding the truth, but a method of uncovering deeper, more liberating versions of it. In drag, identity isn't something to discover, it's something to compose, revise, remix, and occasionally lip-sync at full volume, under the glittering lights of self-authorship.

3.6 Conclusion – The Mirror is a Portal:

To look in the mirror and see a drag persona staring back is to confront the idea that the self is never singular. We are always in flux, always performing and always becoming. Drag doesn't conceal, it reveals. It reveals the ways we all navigate masks and mirrors, illusions and realities, personas and private truths. And in doing so, it invites us to step beyond the limits of fixed identity and into the gorgeous, ever-shifting performance of being alive.

* Glossary of Drag Philosophy:

Drag doesn't merely borrow from critical theory, it reimagines it in sequins and stiletto heels, turning dense academic language into something that struts, snaps, and slays. These redefined terms transcend the page, transforming into embodied experiences that challenge, parody, and reframe how we understand selfhood, power, and performance. Theory becomes embodied, a raised eyebrow critiques ideology, a lip-sync dismantles hegemony, and a death drop collapses binaries with flair. Drag philosophy proves that some of the most radical critiques of normativity happen not in lecture halls, but on runways drenched in glitter, where bodies become books and performances become manifestos, where critical theory struts the runway and wigs carry wisdom.

Term:	**"Drag-Enhanced" Definition:**
Ontology	The study of being… in heels, with contour.
Epistemology	How we know things, like the difference between fishy and fierce.
Performativity	When your existence is both stage and spotlight.
Authenticity	A performance you've rehearsed your whole life, and finally made it your own.
Subversion	That moment, a queen turns a slur into a superpower.

Term:	"Drag-Enhanced" Definition:
Hegemony	The dull drone of the status quo and the reason drag yells back in rhinestones.
Essentialism	The outdated idea that gender comes factory-set and glitter-free.
Semiotics	The language of signs, from a cocked eyebrow to a perfectly timed death drop.
Dialectics	Holding contradictions like you hold a purse and a grudge with style.
Otherness	The place society puts you before you hijack the mic.
Normativity	The only thing more suffocating than a cheap corset.
Liberation	The glittered gasp of freedom after the last beat of a lip-sync battle.
Metaphysics	Thinking beyond reality, especially when your waist is cinched into another dimension.
Queer Time	The art of arriving late, staying longer, and rewriting the clock with eyeliner.
Simulacrum	A copy with no original, like a queen doing Beyoncé better than Beyoncé.
Embodiment	The way drag brings theory to life, making it strut, speak, and shine with unapologetic flair.
Aura	That thing you can't define, but feel when a performer walks in dripping in charisma and trauma.
Detournement	Remixing the culture until it lip-syncs for its life.
Aesthetic Resistance	Fighting power with power blush.
Interpellation	When society tells you who you are, and the drag queen politely replies, "Not tonight, Satan."

4. Camp, Irony and the Playful Sage – Drag's Role in Queer Truth-Telling

Drag is a performance art that thrives in the liminal space between high culture and low humour, where the absurd and the profound collide in a glittering explosion of subversion. It is here that the figure of the playful sage emerges, not merely as a comedic character, but as a truth-teller, a wise figure who uses humour and exaggeration to unravel society's deepest contradictions. In the world of drag, humour is not a tool for escape but one for resistance, a way to speak truths that are often too dangerous or painful to express directly. Through the strategic use of camp, satire and irony, drag becomes a medium for queer survival and subversion, offering a space where failure is celebrated and excess is its own form of power. In this space, drag doesn't just challenge the status quo, it redefines what it means to live authentically, celebrating the art of unapologetic self-expression.

"Drag turns the world's contradictions into a celebration of excess, where humour and heart collide in the pursuit of truth." – Anonymous

4.1 The Playful Sage – The Seer Who Knows More Than We Do:

The figure of the playful sage is central to drag's role as a truth-teller. Historically, the playful sage has appeared in various cultural traditions as the character who speaks the unspeakable, who challenges authority by adopting an unconventional persona. In drag, this archetype takes centre stage, turning the everyday world upside down through exaggeration and parody. The drag queen, in particular, embodies this wise figure, using humour, wit, and a touch of absurdity to expose uncomfortable truths. By exaggerating femininity or masculinity to its most extreme forms, the drag performer calls attention to the arbitrary nature of these categories, inviting the audience to question the very foundations of gender norms. The playful sage acts as a disorienting force, one who disrupts through humour, but also enlightens, revealing the contradictions in societal rules that we are often too afraid to acknowledge.

4.2 Camp – The Art of Excess and Subversion:

At the heart of drag's comedic power lies camp, an aesthetic of exaggeration that transforms the mundane into the extraordinary. Camp celebrates excess, artifice, and irony, drawing attention to the ways in which society's ideals of beauty and taste are constructed rather than inherent. In drag, camp becomes a tool for survival, a way to thrive in a world that often demands conformity. Drag queens, with their towering wigs and theatrical makeup, embody the camp sensibility by transforming the body into a canvas of absurdity. The exaggerated gestures, dramatic poses, and flamboyant performances, are not mere acts of self-indulgence, they are critiques of the norms that seek to regulate identity and behaviour. Camp allows drag performers to subvert the dominant cultural narrative by embracing the very things that society deems frivolous, excessive, or unnatural. In doing so, drag exposes the fragility of the norms that govern our lives, highlighting the constructed nature of gender and identity. Camp doesn't just mock the rules, it rewrites them in glitter, heels, and a wink, revealing truth through theatrical rebellion.

4.3 Irony and Satire – Turning the Mirror Back on Society:

Irony is another powerful tool in drag's arsenal. It allows performers to speak truths indirectly, offering a critique of societal norms through humour and wit. In drag performances, irony often emerges in the form of parody, as performers imitate and exaggerate cultural tropes, whether they be from the world of pop music, politics, or traditional gender roles. The drag queen's performance is steeped in layers of irony, as she simultaneously plays with and mocks the very ideals she seems to embody.

For example, when Trixie Mattel leans into an exaggerated Barbie aesthetic, with giant lashes, plastic-perfect makeup, and high-femme fashion, it's not just campy fun. The irony lies in how she mimics beauty standards so intensely that their artificiality becomes impossible to ignore, turning the performance into a sharp critique of what society deems "ideal femininity." The humour here is not merely for laughter's sake, it is a subtle form of political commentary. By highlighting the absurdity of societal expectations, drag uses irony to point out the contradictions within them. The joke becomes the truth, revealing the limitations of the dominant culture's understanding of gender, beauty, and identity.

4.4 Failure as Strategy – Celebrating Imperfection in Performance:

In drag, failure is not something to be avoided, it is something to be embraced and even celebrated. The intentional failure of drag performances, whether it be a botched lip-sync, a wig falling off mid-performance, or an imperfect high note, becomes a deliberate act of subversion. In a world that prizes perfection, drag celebrates imperfection, showing that flaws and mistakes can be powerful tools of resistance. Drag queens often perform with a knowing wink to the audience, acknowledging the artifice of their performances and celebrating the joy that comes from embracing imperfection. This refusal to adhere to the standards of flawless performance is a rejection of the societal pressures that demand conformity and perfection. In drag, failure becomes a form of resistance, a way to push back against the oppressive systems that tell us we must always succeed, always be beautiful, and always be "perfect."

4.5 Jokes as Political Commentary – Humour as a Weapon of Resistance:

In the world of drag, a joke is never just a joke, it is a political statement. Drag queens have long used humour as a weapon to challenge oppressive systems, offering social commentary through parody and satire. When a queen tells a joke about gender, race, or sexuality, she is not just entertaining her audience, she is calling attention to the inequities and injustices that shape our lives. A well-timed quip can expose the absurdity of gender norms, challenge racial stereotypes, or critique the heteronormative systems that govern our world. Drag's political humour is not limited to the stage, it spills over into the everyday lives of performers, who use their platform to speak out against inequality and injustice. In this sense, drag becomes a form of resistance, using laughter to destabilize the power structures that seek to control and silence marginalized voices.

"With each punchline, drag exposes the world's contradictions, using humour as a weapon to dismantle systems of oppression." – Anonymous

4.6 The Paradox of the Playful Sage – Liberation Through Laughing at Oppression:

Drag's power as a vehicle for queer truth-telling lies in the paradox of the playful sage, a figure who ridicules the system while expertly navigating it. Through satire, parody, and irreverent glamour, the drag performer unveils the absurdities baked into societal norms, not by rejecting them outright, but by embodying them so excessively that their cracks begin to show. The playful sage is not merely comic relief or spectacle, they are a cunning commentator, wielding wit as both shield and sword. They show us that liberation doesn't always arrive cloaked in solemn resistance, it can come wrapped in sequins and sarcasm.

By leaning into the ridiculous and revelling in contradiction, drag creates room for a deeper freedom, one that remakes norms rather than merely escaping them. Through campy exaggeration, queer irony, and the daring art of deliberate failure, drag stages a revolution where gender becomes play, identity becomes fluid and resistance becomes a joyous, defiant act of survival, served with a wink and a perfectly timed punchline. Drag transforms absurdity into freedom, inviting everyone to challenge and reshape the status quo.

5. Drag Beyond the Club – Nightlife, Ritual and the Politics of Glitter

Under the shimmer of stage lights and the pulse of dance music lies something far deeper than entertainment. Drag is not just a spectacle, it is a ritual, a performance art that channels the sacred through sequins, song, and satire. For many queer people, especially those alienated from traditional religious or cultural institutions, drag becomes a kind of spiritual practice. The transformation from street self to stage persona mirrors rites of passage and ceremonial rebirth. Makeup becomes war paint, wigs become crowns, and the performance itself becomes a liturgy of survival and celebration. To witness drag is to participate in a communal ritual where shame is exorcised and joy is consecrated. The club may be the venue, but the energy summoned is something closer to church, rowdy, reverent, and radically inclusive.

5.1 Preaching in Platforms – Drag in the Church, the Classroom and the Streets:

Drag refuses to be confined to nightlife. Increasingly, it spills into unexpected spaces, sanctuaries, schools, and city halls, each appearance a kind of glitter-drenched intervention. In churches, drag queens have led sermons, telling stories of love, acceptance, and chosen family that resonate beyond doctrine. In classrooms, Drag Queen Story Hours challenge the rigidity of gender education, replacing binaries with play and possibility. At protests, drag is resistance with rhinestones, sharp, visible, and unforgettable. Whether reading to children or marching for trans rights, drag disrupts expectations and reclaims visibility in spaces that have often silenced queer voices. Each act of drag outside the club insists that queer embodiment belongs everywhere, not hidden, not apologetic, but proud, political and profoundly present.

5.2 The Glitter Archive – Drag as Ancestral Memory and Global Expression:

Drag is not a Western invention, it is a global, historical practice woven through cultures and centuries. From the hijra traditions of South Asia to the kabuki theatre of Japan, from Two-Spirit ceremonies in Indigenous cultures to the masquerades of West Africa, gender play and performance have long carried sacred and social power. Today's drag queens, kings, and gender nonconforming artists tap into this lineage, channelling ancestors who blurred the lines between man and woman, divine and human. Every tuck and turn, every lash and lash-out, becomes a conversation with those who came before. In Brazil's carnival queens, in Thailand's kathoey pageants, in the underground ballrooms of Black and Latinx America, drag becomes a global dialect of defiance and joy. Each glittered body is not just individual expression, but a living archive of queer resilience, migration and transformation.

5.3 Radical Embodiment – The Politics of Being Too Much:

To exist in a drag body is to stake a claim in the politics of visibility. Drag dares to be "too much", too loud, too femme, too fat, too real. It turns the insult of excess into an aesthetic manifesto. In a world that polices queer bodies, especially trans and nonbinary ones, drag offers a defiant form of radical embodiment. To exaggerate one's femininity or masculinity isn't deception, it's a declaration. It is saying, "You see me now. You cannot unsee me."

Drag's deliberate boldness exposes the absurdity of normative standards, while inviting others to feel power in their own bodies. The politics of glitter, heels, and lashes are not superficial, they are layered forms of armour and art.

5.4 Glitter in the Machine – Digital Drag and the Queer Futurism of Cyberspace:

In the digital age, drag is evolving beyond the physical realm into new dimensions of expression. On platforms like TikTok, Instagram, and Twitch, drag performers are creating entire universes, editing, glitching, and reimagining identity through technology. Digital drag allows for a kind of speculative embodiment, where queens and kings aren't bound by gravity, gender, or geography. Virtual avatars and augmented makeup apps blur the lines between reality and performance, echoing the central truth of drag, all identity is constructed, so why not construct it beautifully? In this vibrant cyberspace cabaret, drag becomes a vessel for queer futurity, imagining new worlds where fluidity is the norm, joy acts as resistance and self-expression knows no bounds. Through online drag balls, high-energy livestreams, and wildly inventive DIY green screen extravaganzas, glitter transforms into digital code, and performance into a kind of prophecy shimmering with possibility.

5.5 Joy as Resistance – The Revolutionary Potential of Camp:

At its heart, drag is a declaration of joy in the face of erasure. Camp, irony, and theatricality become survival strategies in a world that often demands conformity or invisibility. The humour of drag, its over-the-top drama, its pointed parodies, isn't just for laughs, it's a political strategy. As queer theorist José Esteban Muñoz wrote, queerness is an ideal, a horizon, a way of imagining the world not as it is, but as it could be. Drag lives in this imagined future, where laughter is liberation and joy is weaponized. In the act of getting ready, in the sashay across the stage, in the collective howl of a perfectly delivered read, something revolutionary happens. Drag doesn't wait for the world to change, it creates the world anew, one rhinestone at a time. Through the art of drag, joy becomes a powerful act of defiance, creating a space where liberation is not just possible, but inevitable, where laughter, theatrics, and excess fuel a collective imagination that dares to reshape the world, one rhinestone at a time.

5.6 Conclusion – Glitter is a Portal:

To understand drag beyond the club is to see it as a portal to something deeper, an act of spiritual renewal, communal power, and political refusal. It gathers together joy, history, resistance, and radical imagination into a single sequined gesture. Drag is not a break from the world, it is a blueprint for a better one. Through its rituals, its failures, its brilliance, and its boldness, drag teaches us how to live louder, love harder, and glitter our way through the apocalypse, toward something that feels like freedom. Drag is more than an escape from reality, it is a transformative act that reimagines the world, creating a space where joy, resistance, and love converge into a powerful declaration of freedom, daring us to glitter our way into a new future.

"Drag is not just performance, it's a revolution dressed in sequins, a love letter to freedom written in rhinestones." – Anonymous

* Drag Across Time – Elegance as Resistance:

➢ The Harlem Renaissance Balls – Gender as Jazz:

In the glittering underground of 1920s Harlem, Black and Latinx queer folks created the earliest drag balls, unapologetic explosions of style and defiance, where gender rules dissolved like smoke in spotlight. These weren't just parties. They were living archives of survival and spectacle, where elegance was armour, and every strut down the runway rewrote who got to be seen.

➢ Berlin's Gender-Bending Weimar Nightlife:

In the cabarets of 1920s Berlin, drag queens, kings, and trans artists lit up clubs like Eldorado with open gender defiance. Their performances weren't just provocative, they were political acts of visibility. When fascism rose, the first thing it came for was the freedom to express gender with a wink and a wine-stained boa.

➢ Drag Kings and the Politics of Pantsuits:

Early 20th-century drag kings like Vesta Tilley took to the stage and the streets with performances that revealed masculinity itself as a kind of performance. At suffragette rallies and in music halls, their crisp suits and confident swagger both mocked rigid gender power structures and embodied emerging forms of feminist visibility.

* Drag as Uprising – Protest in a Wig Cap:

➢ Stonewall Was a Drag (and a Brick):

The 1969 Stonewall uprising was catalysed by queens like Marsha P. Johnson and Sylvia Rivera, whose sequins shimmered with rage and resolve. Drag wasn't just present at the revolution, it was the revolution. Street queens fought back with stilettos and fire, proving resistance could wear heels.

➢ The "Sisters" Who Minister in Mockery:

The Sisters of Perpetual Indulgence began blessing the streets of San Francisco in 1979 with satire, safety, and drag-as-ministry. Their queer nuns wore habits with glitter beards, preaching consent, pride and AIDS activism through performance. They made compassion camp, and camp radical.

➢ The "Trannyshack" Revolution of San Francisco:

In the 1990s, queens like Heklina blew up the polished drag pageant model with Trannyshack, where grotesque, messy, brilliant drag broke every aesthetic rule. The platform gave birth to an entire wave of gender-expansive artists who proved drag could be ugly, political, brilliant and still fabulous.

*Drag as Culture – Ceremony in Sequins:

- **Two-Spirit Revivals and Sacred Glamour:**

Long before colonization, many Indigenous cultures across North America celebrated gender-diverse Two-Spirit people. Today, performers reclaim that sacred role, blending drag with ritual, art and community healing, from Pride stages to powwows, proving that drag can be both protest and prayer.

- **Thailand's Kathoey Cabarets – Between Worlds:**

Kathoey (often translated as "ladyboys") have long been part of Thailand's gender landscape. In cabarets, they blend traditional Thai movement with flamboyant drag spectacle, turning stage lights into mirrors reflecting centuries of third-gender embodiment, both sacred and show-stopping.

- **The Glamour Guerrillas of South Africa:**

In apartheid South Africa, queens like Kewpie of District Six used beauty salons and underground shows to defy political erasure. Drag wasn't just a performance, it was a strategy of survival, a way to stay visible in a state that tried to make queer bodies disappear.

- **Māori Drag and the Fa'afafine Sisterhood:**

From New Zealand to Samoa, takatāpui and fa'afafine performers fuse Indigenous identity with voguing, haka and couture. Groups like the Fafswag Collective create drag that's part protest, part art installation, part cultural reawakening, shaking off colonial shame with every stomp of the heel.

Chapter 22

The Role of Humour in Queer Resilience

---

1. Comedy as a Tool for Coping with Discrimination

Queer people have long turned to humour as a way of processing pain. When society excludes, invalidates, or outright threatens, comedy becomes more than a distraction, it becomes a lifeline. From the underground cabarets of Weimar Berlin to the biting stand-up of today's queer comedians, laughter has functioned as both shield and sword. For many LGBTQ+ individuals, the ability to turn hurt into hilarity is more than survival, it's alchemy. The act of laughing through trauma doesn't diminish the seriousness of the injustice, rather, it reframes the power dynamic. Comedy gives the marginalized the last word, allowing them to reclaim their narrative with wit sharper than any insult. In doing so, it reminds us that laughter isn't weakness, it's strategy.

1.1 The Queer Joke as a Mirror – Seeing the Absurdity of Oppression:

Discrimination often thrives on the illusion of naturalness. Norms around gender, sexuality and respectability get enforced precisely, because they are made to seem self-evident. Queer humour, however, has a talent for revealing the cracks in this supposed logic. A single well-timed joke can pull the rug out from under an entire belief system. Whether poking fun at the narrowness of the gender binary or the hypocrisy of heteronormative expectations, queer comedy uses absurdity to reveal how ridiculous many social rules really are. Humour becomes a mirror tilted just slightly, offering a reflection that startles us into recognition. It doesn't always try to resolve injustice, but it does unmask it, permitting queer people to stop internalizing its shame. In laughing at the absurd, queer communities reclaim power, not by ignoring pain, but by transforming it into a punchline that speaks truth louder than fear.

1.2 Safe Spaces Made of Laughter – Community, Connection and Comic Relief:

The magic of queer comedy doesn't only happen on stage, it happens in living rooms, group chats and late-night vent sessions, with chosen family. Humour creates a sense of "we," even in the face of "them." When queer folks swap stories that end with both groaning and giggling, they're doing more than passing time, they're building resilience through shared understanding. The inside jokes that only a queer friend would get are more than funny; they're affirmations of belonging. Comedy forges bonds, loosens fear and lets joy into spaces, where it's often been denied. These moments of levity, no matter how small, are crucial forms of connection that allow queer people to hold space for each other, even when the world outside feels hostile. In every burst of laughter shared among queer folks, there's a quiet revolution, a reminder that joy is not a luxury, but a form of survival woven into the fabric of community.

1.3 Turning Trauma into Punchlines – The Power and the Risk:

Many queer comedians have built careers out of material drawn from their deepest wounds. From being misgendered to facing religious rejection, these lived experiences are transformed into moments of catharsis for both performer and audience. The power of a punchline lies in its ability to reframe trauma, not as something shameful, but as something survivable. However, there's a fine line between owning a painful narrative and becoming trapped in the need to make it palatable. Not all trauma needs to be funny, and not every queer person processes discrimination through laughter. The power of comedy lies in choice, when a queer person chooses to laugh at what once silenced them, it becomes an act of agency. When they choose not to, that too is a valid form of self-preservation.

1.4 Roast Culture and Queer Toughness – Finding Strength in the Jab:

Within many queer spaces, especially drag and ballroom culture, roasting and playful reads are traditions rich with nuance. To be read by a friend isn't an insult, it's a badge of intimacy. It's how queer communities teach one another to develop thick skin, not to toughen through cruelty, but to strengthen through love. Reading becomes a ritual, where the insult is laced with affection, and where self-awareness is the highest form of wisdom. This kind of humour teaches emotional dexterity, it lets someone sit in their truth while still laughing at their own contradictions. It's not about humiliation, it's about liberation from the need to be flawless. Within roast culture, queer folks learn that being ridiculous doesn't disqualify you from dignity, it's part of what makes you divine.

1.5 The Healing Laugh – Humour as an Act of Reclamation:

There's a unique kind of healing that comes from hearing someone describe your pain, and then watching them dance around it in heels while making the room erupt in laughter. Comedy doesn't erase hurt, but it often metabolizes it. A queer joke delivered in the right moment can make someone feel seen for the first time. It can remind someone that they're not alone, that their weirdness has company and that their story has worth, even when it's messy, painful, or absurd. Humour allows queer people to reclaim narratives that were once tools of shame. When the punchline is ours, the power is, too. In the laughter that follows, there's not just release, but a reclamation of power, transforming the very things that once hurt into symbols of resilience and belonging.

1.6 Joy as a Form of Resistance – When Laughing Becomes Defiance:

In a world that often tries to diminish queer existence, joy itself becomes revolutionary. When queer people laugh loudly, unapologetically and together, they defy systems that rely on their silence. Humour can be sharp, yes, but it can also be tender. It can say, "You tried to hurt me, but I'm still here, and I'm cracking jokes." Comedy allows for moments of lightness without denying the weight of reality. It reminds us that protest doesn't have to be sombre to be sincere. Sometimes, a perfectly timed quip is the most powerful act of resistance. It's a refusal to let discrimination dictate the tone of one's life. It's an insistence that even amid struggle, laughter has its rightful place. By embracing joy as resistance, queer people reclaim their power, showing that their humanity is defined by more than survival, it's defined by laughter, love and freedom.

1.7 The Future is Funny – Queer Comedy as Cultural Blueprint:

Queer humour doesn't just reflect the current moment, it imagines new ones. In crafting jokes that twist the logic of oppression, comedians create mental space for alternative ways of living and loving. They carve out room for queer futures that are bold, bizarre and beautiful. Humour becomes a tool for envisioning a world where difference isn't merely tolerated, but celebrated. Where coming out is met with applause, and transitioning is a plot twist worthy of a sitcom. These imagined futures aren't just fantasy, they're blueprints. Comedy dares to dream beyond suffering and builds bridges toward joy.

* Punchlines and Power – For Example, How Queer Comedy Defies Discrimination and Heals the Soul:

- **Laughing Through the Pain – A Queer Legacy of Resilience:**

  "My humour is how I survived. It's how I told the truth without getting hurt." – Wanda Sykes

- **The Queer Joke as a Mirror – Seeing the Absurdity of Oppression:**

  "Comedy is just the truth in fancy clothes." – Hannah Gadsby

- **Safe Spaces Made of Laughter – Community, Connection and Comic Relief:**

  "Being funny is how we find each other. It's queer sonar." – Joel Kim Booster

- **Turning Trauma into Punchlines – The Power and the Risk:**

  "People laugh at the things they're afraid to cry about." – Cameron Esposito

- **Roast Culture and Queer Toughness – Finding Strength in the Jab:**

  "Reading is fundamental. It's not mean, it's tradition." – Dorian Corey, Paris Is Burning

- **The Healing Laugh – Humour as an Act of Reclamation:**

  "If you can laugh at it, you can live with it." – Lily Tomlin

- **Joy as a Form of Resistance – When Laughing Becomes Defiance:**

  "Joy is an act of resistance." – Toi Derricotte (not a comedian, but often quoted in queer activist spaces)

- **The Future is Funny – Queer Comedy as Cultural Blueprint:**

  "We're not the joke, we're the punchline that changes the whole story." – Mae Martin

2. The Evolution of LGBTQ+ Humour in Media

In the early years of film and television, LGBTQ+ individuals were often portrayed through harmful and reductive stereotypes. These depictions generally centered on the "tragic" or "comic" queer character, whose existence served as a cautionary tale rather than a celebration of their identity. Gay and lesbian characters were typically flamboyant, effeminate, or oversexualized, existing more to entertain or shock than to tell a relatable story. This period, spanning much of the early to mid-20th century, marked a time when queer humour often reflected societal discomfort with non-normative sexualities. The laugh was at the expense of LGBTQ+ individuals, with jokes often rooted in mockery or misunderstanding. Although these portrayals might have entertained mainstream audiences, they also reinforced the marginalization of queer people, positioning them as objects of ridicule or derision.

2.1 The Shift – Gay Liberation and the Rise of Camp:

As the gay liberation movement gained momentum in the late 1960s and 1970s, queer humour began to evolve. During this period, drag culture and camp became central to queer comedic expressions. Far from the tragic figures of earlier portrayals, queer individuals started using humour as a means of resistance. Camp, an aesthetic characterized by excess, irony and playfulness, allowed LGBTQ+ people to take ownership of their stories and identities. Figures like Divine, John Waters and Lily Tomlin, showcased how queer individuals could laugh at themselves while simultaneously critiquing mainstream society. This shift marked a fundamental change in the way queer humour was constructed, as it moved away from self-deprecation and victimhood towards empowerment and self-expression. The laugh now became a tool of reclamation rather than a means of subjugation.

2.2 1980s to 1990s – Queer Comedy Breaks Into Mainstream:

The 1980s and 1990s saw a marked increase in the visibility of LGBTQ+ comedians, particularly in the realms of stand-up and late-night television. Comedians like Eddie Izzard, Margaret Cho and Ellen DeGeneres, began to push the boundaries of queer humour, addressing LGBTQ+ experiences in more nuanced and personal ways. Izzard, in particular, introduced gender fluidity into mainstream comedy, blending elements of drag with stand-up to deconstruct rigid gender norms. At the same time, Ellen DeGeneres' decision to come out on her sitcom in the late 1990s marked a milestone in LGBTQ+ representation. Ellen's "Puppy Episode" was groundbreaking not just for its portrayal of a queer character, but also for how it used humour to normalize queerness in everyday life. These figures helped to shift LGBTQ+ humour from niche subculture to mainstream conversation, paving the way for more authentic and diverse portrayals of queer experiences.

2.3 The 2000s – Queer Characters in Sitcoms and the Rise of LGBTQ+ TV Shows:

The early 2000s heralded an era where LGBTQ+ characters were no longer solely relegated to comedic sidekicks or one-dimensional characters.

TV shows like Will & Grace helped popularize gay characters in the mainstream, often relying on the comedic antics of its gay lead while also grounding queer life in friendship and domesticity. Another significant milestone was The L Word, which broke new ground as one of the first television dramas to centre the lives, love and humour, of lesbian and bisexual women. Though more dramatic in tone, the show offered moments of queer humour rooted in the awkwardness of dating, chosen family dynamics and cultural in-jokes, specific to the queer female experience. Its significance lay not just in its representation, but in its refusal to sanitize or sideline queer women's stories, it allowed queer audiences to see themselves both in moments of joy and conflict, often using humour to diffuse tension or build intimacy between characters.

Simultaneously, shows like Queer as Folk offered unapologetic portrayals of gay life, while still presenting their characters as flawed and complex individuals. These series represented a marked shift in queer humour from camp and satire to something more multifaceted and relatable. While often critiqued for representing a narrow slice of the LGBTQ+ spectrum, usually white, cisgender and middle-class, they nonetheless opened the door for future queer narratives to emerge in more varied and inclusive ways.

2.4 2010s – Expanding Queer Comedy, Diverse Voices and Representation:

The 2010s saw a new wave of queer voices in comedy, with an increasing number of LGBTQ+ performers and writers bringing diverse perspectives to the table. Comedians like Wanda Sykes, Hannah Gadsby and Bowen Yang, used humour to address the complexities of queer identity, offering insights into race, gender and sexuality. The release of Nanette by Hannah Gadsby was a seismic shift in how queer humour could be used to challenge societal norms. Rather than simply delivering punchlines, Gadsby used comedy as a way to dismantle the very concept of comedy itself, questioning the audience's relationship with trauma, humour and expectation. This era of queer humour marked a transition from simple entertainment to profound social commentary, illustrating how comedy could be both personal and political. Television shows like RuPaul's Drag Race also helped elevate drag culture and camp to a mainstream platform, while simultaneously pushing boundaries and subverting expectations about gender, performance and identity.

2.5 The Impact of Social Media and Digital Platforms:

The advent of social media and digital platforms in the 2010s and 2020s further democratized queer humour. Platforms like YouTube, Instagram and TikTok, allowed for a new generation of LGBTQ+ comedians to create and distribute content directly to audiences. These spaces fostered an environment where queer creators could explore and experiment with humour in ways that were previously unavailable in traditional media. The rise of digital platforms has given birth to queer meme culture, which blends absurdity, self-deprecation and sharp critique, to express both resistance and resilience. With characters like Benito Skinner's hyper-gay parodies or Drag Race's constant online engagement, queer humour in the digital age has become a fast-paced, ever-evolving reflection of the community's creativity and activism. Here, humour is both an escape and a means of empowerment, as creators can directly connect with their audiences and build communities around shared laughter and experiences.

2.6 Looking to the Future – The Growing Power of Queer Comedy:

As we move further into the 2020s, queer humour continues to evolve. In particular, there is a noticeable trend toward intersectionality within queer comedy, as LGBTQ+ comedians begin to address issues of race, class and gender alongside sexuality. Comedy is no longer simply about laughing at the absurdities of the world, it is increasingly about challenging power structures and giving voice to those who have historically been silenced. Comedians like Jaboukie Young-White, Sam Jay and Mae Martin, are pushing the boundaries of queer humour, addressing topics like mental health, gender fluidity and global queer experiences, in ways that are both deeply personal and politically charged. Queer comedy has grown into an act of both personal catharsis and collective resistance, offering a platform for voices that had once been marginalized. The evolution of LGBTQ+ humour in media has been a journey from exclusion to inclusion, from harmful stereotypes to empowered representations. As queer comedy continues to reflect the diverse, evolving nature of LGBTQ+ experiences, it holds the potential to shape societal attitudes and challenge norms. Through humour, queer individuals not only cope with marginalization, they also actively rewrite the narrative of what it means to exist outside the mainstream.

* Annotated Timeline of Queer Comedy Icons:

➢ **1930s to 1950s – Moms Mabley, the Original Mic-Drop Matriarch:**

Dressed in oversized housedresses and delivering razor-sharp social commentary, Moms Mabley becomes one of the first openly lesbian comedians. She makes audiences laugh while quietly dismantling racism, sexism and heteronormativity, decades before intersectionality had a name. Grandmother energy, but make it lethal

➢ **1970s – Lily Tomlin and the Closet with a Trapdoor:**

Tomlin dazzles with her array of eccentric characters on Laugh-In, speaking in code to queer audiences with impeccable timing and a raised eyebrow. She never quite says it aloud, because the industry wasn't ready, but queer viewers read every inflection like a love letter.

➢ **1980s – Sandra Bernhard's Mouth Gets Its Own Spotlight:**

Jewish, bi, chaotic and brilliant, Sandra blends cabaret, stand-up and divine rants, in a way that makes people question, whether they're at a comedy show or a postmodern sermon. Her 1988 one-woman show Without You I'm Nothing, becomes sacred queer canon.

➢ **1993 – Lea DeLaria Storms Late-Night in a Suit and Swagger:**

Lea appears on The Arsenio Hall Show, boldly out and blazing with dyke charisma. America gasps. She doesn't flinch. Her punchlines land like protest signs, funny, fearless and unapologetically queer. Also, she singlehandedly made suits look horny again.

- **1998 – Ellen DeGeneres Comes Out on Prime Time:**

The Puppy Episode of Ellen airs. "I'm gay," she says into an airport P.A. system. The joke reverberates through millions of living rooms, funny, awkward and revolutionary. She loses everything. She rebuilds. She becomes a household name. (The journey, gayest plot twist of all.)

- **2000s – Eddie Izzard, the Genderfluid Comedian-Wizard:**

Wearing heels, eyeliner and historical knowledge no one asked for, but desperately needed, Izzard makes audiences laugh through multi-accented tangents about colonialism, cake vs. death, and trans identity before most people had words for it. Still somehow ends up in Ocean's Twelve.

- **Mid-2000s – Urzila Carlson's Deadpan Queer Takeover Begins:**

New Zealand's secret weapon, a proudly out lesbian with a mischievous grin and a talent for roasting societal absurdities without ever breaking a sweat. Urzila's blunt, relatable comedy wins over audiences from Auckland to Netflix, proof that sometimes the revolution wears sneakers and just can't be bothered with your nonsense.

- **2010s – Wanda Sykes Doesn't Give a Damn and We Thank Her for It:**

Wanda's comedy slices through racism, homophobia, and the absurdity of Republican family values with precision. She delivers it with a smirk that says, "I already read you, and I don't need to raise my voice." A true lesbian auntie of truth.

- **2017 – Hannah Gadsby Breaks the Comedy Special:**

In Nanette, Gadsby dismantles the joke structure mid-set and dares us to find catharsis in her trauma. The audience laughs, cries, and googles "Is this still stand-up?" She doesn't care. She redefines queer storytelling in real time.

- **2020s – Bowen Yang Summons the Queer Chaos on SNL:**

As a trailblazing Asian gay cast member, Bowen makes sketch comedy queerer, weirder and far more fabulous. Whether he's an iceberg having a PR meltdown or a gay Oompa Loompa with daddy issues, he's a Gen Z icon of expressive gender and surreal satire.

- **Today – TikTok Comedians, Drag Jokesters, Meme Oracles:**

From Benito Skinner's hyper-gay characters to trans comics dismantling binary logic in 15-second bursts, the internet is now a rolling queer cabaret. The punchline is everywhere. It's you. It's us. It's the revolution, delivered with a wink and a wig reveal.

3. The Fine Line Between Self-Deprecation and Internalized Homophobia

Humour has long served as a survival strategy for marginalized groups, especially those whose identities are constantly scrutinized or ridiculed. For queer people, self-deprecating humour has historically been a means of taking control, getting to the punchline before the oppressor does. By joking about themselves, queer individuals often deflect potential harm and assert a form of control over their image. Yet the line between reclaiming the joke and reinforcing the insult is razor-thin. When repeated often enough, even in jest, internalized messages of inadequacy or undesirability can become ingrained. Laughing at one's own queerness may feel empowering in one moment, but over time, it can erode self-worth if the joke is always rooted in shame, loneliness, or deviance.

3.1 Laughing With vs. Laughing At – Who Holds the Power in the Joke?

Power dynamics within humour are subtle, but significant. Self-deprecating jokes in queer spaces can act as bonding rituals, affirming shared experiences and frustrations. However, when such humour is consumed by a predominantly straight or cisgender audience, the dynamic shifts. Jokes that were once mechanisms of camaraderie can become spectacles of difference. When queer comedians make fun of their own effeminacy, trauma, or gender expression, the question becomes, are we laughing with them or at them? And more importantly, who's allowed to laugh? If the humour invites others to see queerness as inherently pitiable or ridiculous, then the joke reinforces the very systems of power it seeks to undercut. The intention behind the humour and the audience's interpretation must be weighed equally, especially in mass media. When laughter reinforces stereotypes, it stops being solidarity and starts becoming submission.

3.2 Drag Queens, Camp and the Art of Subversive Mockery:

Drag culture is often cited as the epitome of queer humour, loud, exaggerated, self-aware, and gleefully mocking both heteronormative culture and the queer community itself. Drag queens regularly poke fun at their own identities, mocking their appearance, their trauma, their love lives and the community's contradictions. But the brilliance of drag lies in its knowingness. The mockery isn't mindless, it's subversive, intentional and stylized. The difference between self-deprecation and internalized homophobia in drag often comes down to framing. Camp, by nature, is performative excess, it takes shame and blows it up until it becomes absurdly fabulous. When drag humour punches up at societal norms rather than down on queer existence, it creates space for critique rather than self-loathing. The danger comes when this nuance is lost, especially in mainstream portrayals that reduce drag humour to cattiness or caricature.

3.3 When the Joke Becomes the Cage – The Mental Health Cost:

For many queer individuals, especially those in the early stages of coming out or self-acceptance, self-deprecating humour can feel like a shield. But when every joke becomes about being unlovable, dramatic, or broken, the joke becomes a cage.

Internalized homophobia often manifests not through overt hatred, but through quiet resignation, believing one will always be alone, always be the butt of the joke. Humour that leans too heavily into these tropes can reinforce harmful beliefs, making it difficult to build genuine self-esteem. A gay man who constantly jokes about being too flamboyant to be taken seriously, or a nonbinary person who makes punchlines out of their pronouns, may be laughing, but it's a laughter that masks pain. Humour should be cathartic, not corrosive. If it stunts growth rather than facilitates healing, it deserves to be examined. Recognizing when humour becomes harm is the first step toward reclaiming it as a tool for healing rather than self-erasure.

3.4 Toward Healing Humour – Reclaiming the Laugh Without Losing the Self:

Humour doesn't have to be sanitized to be healing. Some of the most powerful queer jokes are the ones that acknowledge pain without being consumed by it. Comics like Hannah Gadsby, Fortune Feimster and Joel Kim Booster, model humour that is raw, real and self-aware, jokes that invite laughter while challenging the audience to reckon with discomfort. The goal isn't to eliminate self-deprecating humour entirely, but to wield it carefully and consciously. It's about asking, Does this joke deepen my shame or dissolve it? Am I laughing to connect, or to disappear? The line between self-deprecation and internalized homophobia isn't always visible until crossed. But queer humour, at its best, can flirt with that line and still come out on the side of self-respect. Reclaiming laughter doesn't mean rejecting our pain, it means transforming it into something generous, clever and ultimately liberating.

3.5 Closing Reflection:

Queer self-deprecation walks a tightrope, capable of brilliance or self-betrayal depending on the balance. When rooted in awareness, community and reclamation, it uplifts. When grounded in shame, it can subtly erode the very identity it pretends to protect. To laugh at oneself is not inherently dangerous, but when that laughter becomes a stand-in for truth, it's time to rewrite the script. Real empowerment comes not from silencing the joke, but from reshaping it, so that it serves joy, not judgment, resilience, not resignation.

4. Queer Satire as a Form of Protest

Satire has always been a subversive tool and when wielded by queer voices, it becomes a weapon of joyful resistance. Queer satirists have long taken the dominant culture, its rigid binaries, outdated gender roles and institutional hypocrisies, and spun it into parody. By exaggerating what is already absurd, queer satire highlights how fragile, and performative power structures really are. Think drag queens imitating hyper-femininity or comedians mocking heteronormative dating culture, the humour isn't just for laughs, it's a direct hit on the ideologies that try to define "normal." In blowing these norms out of proportion, queer artists lay bare their flaws and contradictions, making space for something freer, queerer and infinitely more imaginative. In queer hands, satire doesn't just mock the system, it dares to imagine what could exist beyond it, turning punchlines into blueprints for liberation.

4.1 Laughing Back – Reclaiming the Joke:

For centuries, queer people have been the butt of the joke, mocked in caricatures, flattened into stereotypes and turned into punchlines, for cheap laughs. But queer satire flips the script. Instead of being laughed at, queer people now laugh back. This shift isn't just comedic, it's revolutionary. The power of reclaiming humour lies in transforming pain into performance. When queer creators lean into exaggeration, irony and wit, they aren't ignoring trauma, they're reshaping it into something they control. A drag king lampooning toxic masculinity or a trans comic joking about TSA pat-downs is doing more than making an audience laugh, they're demanding to be heard, on their terms. Satire becomes survival. The joke lands differently when the storyteller owns the mic.

4.2 Weaponized Wit – Political Comedy with Lip Gloss and Teeth:

Queer satire doesn't pull punches, it punches up, dressed in sequins. Shows like The Daily Show, Saturday Night Live and online platforms like TikTok, have seen an influx of openly queer creators using humour to critique systemic injustice. When a queer comedian breaks down the contradictions in anti-trans legislation with biting sarcasm, or when a skit exaggerates a homophobic politician's rhetoric to expose its lunacy, it's not just comedy, it's activism. The audience gets to laugh, yes, but also to think, to feel discomfort, to wake up. Queer satire invites us to examine not just what we find funny, but why. In doing so, it creates fertile ground for change, where ridicule becomes a radical act.

4.3 Drag, Camp and Satire – Theatrical Rebellion:

Drag is inherently satirical. It mocks the expectations of gender by magnifying them to theatrical absurdity. Camp aesthetics, over-the-top, flamboyant, extra for the sake of extra, also serve as tools for satire, especially in queer performance. Whether it's a drag performer lip-syncing a political speech in clown makeup, or a campy web series turning a romantic trope on its head, the message is clear, the mainstream is not sacred, and queerness is not here to play by its rules. Satirical drag queens like Bianca Del Rio and Lady Bunny don't just entertain, they critique culture while bathed in glitter. It's a kind of protest that's loud, laughing and impossible to ignore. Theatricality becomes testimony; irony becomes outrage in disguise.

4.4 From Street Theatre to Social Media – Evolving Arenas of Satirical Protest:

Queer satire has moved with the times, from underground cabaret shows and AIDS-era street theatre to Instagram reels and viral TikTok's. Activist collectives like ACT UP used performance art and satirical banners to demand attention to the HIV/AIDS crisis. Today's digital activists use memes, filters and parody songs, to critique political figures and media narratives. Satire is no longer confined to the stage, it's everywhere, stitched into posts, GIFs and drag brunch menus. Queer protest now lives in the comment section, the ironic hashtag and the parody account. These platforms don't just spread humour, they spread resistance. In a world oversaturated with tragedy and bad news, satire becomes a palatable, potent tool to communicate outrage, educate audiences and build queer solidarity in real time.

4.5 Closing Reflection – Satire as Joyful Defiance:

Queer satire refuses to let oppression have the final word. It dances where it's told to disappear, laughs where it's told to cry, and dares to dress truth up in wigs and irony. Protest doesn't always look like marches or manifestos, sometimes, it's a perfectly timed punchline that lands like a revolution.

5. "If I Didn't Laugh, I'd Scream" – Dark Humour and the Queer Survival Instinct

Dark humour has long thrived in queer communities, not because suffering is inherently funny, but because sometimes laughter is the only tool sharp enough to cut through the heaviness. When the world offers rejection, systemic erasure, or violence, irony becomes armour. Queer people, especially those navigating the intersections of race, poverty, transness, or disability, have often turned to gallows humour as a release valve for pain that would otherwise consume. Cracking a joke about something unspeakable doesn't mean the trauma is gone, it means it's been named, wrestled with, and made smaller. In that sense, black comedy becomes both a coping mechanism and an act of rebellion. It says, I know what's happening, I'm still here, and I refuse to be crushed quietly. In wielding dark humour, queer communities transform suffering into sharp wit, a way to reclaim narrative power when the world offers none.

5.1 "Pray the Gay Away" and Other Punchlines from Hell:

Conversion therapy, religious condemnation and moral panic, are not exactly the stuff of sitcoms, but in queer hands, they sometimes become grim punchlines that reclaim the narrative. When someone who has survived these systems mocks them, it doesn't minimize their damage, it exposes their absurdity. A joke about being electroshocked into heterosexuality doesn't erase the trauma, it forces the audience to sit with the horrifying truth through a disarming lens. The comedy is razor-edged, cutting open space to talk about things too painful to approach head-on. Queer dark humour often invites discomfort on purpose, forcing a reckoning with systems that prefer to operate behind closed doors. It holds up a mirror that dares others to flinch. In turning horror into satire, queer dark humour doesn't just provoke laughter, it demands accountability.

5.2 Healthcare, Housing and the Queer Gag Reel:

From being misgendered at the doctor's office to being denied services outright, queer people are no strangers to systemic failures. The joke, of course, is often that nobody else seems to see it. A deadpan post about scheduling top surgery and a root canal in the same week because your insurance barely covers either isn't just comedy, it's commentary. Dark humour in these contexts helps queer people acknowledge the surreal bureaucracy of surviving, especially when basic rights are treated as luxuries. These jokes often contain unspoken footnotes about inequality, exhaustion, and having to fight for crumbs. And yet, in the moment of laughter, there's a flicker of camaraderie. The absurdity gets named. The cruelty is made visible. And no one has to feel gaslit into silence.

5.3 Bitterness, Burnout and the Line Between Cynical and Sacred:

There's a point where dark humour starts to teeter toward bitterness. It's a risk for any community under pressure, but especially for queer folks who've faced lifelong invalidation. Not all jokes heal. Some harden. The line between catharsis and cynicism is blurry, particularly online, where irony and detachment reign. When pain turns into a performance for clicks, it can start to reinforce hopelessness instead of dismantling it. Queer dark humour must be handled carefully, with enough self-awareness to ask, Am I laughing to survive, or because I've stopped believing things can change? The answer isn't always easy, but the question matters. Humour should be a tool, not a cage. Dark humour should uplift, not numb, challenging despair, while remembering that laughter can still fuel change.

5.4 Survivor Stories in Stand-Up and Social Media:

Modern queer comedians like Hannah Gadsby, Cameron Esposito and Mae Martin, have brought dark humour into mainstream consciousness, making jokes about trauma that are anything but flippant. Their work has sparked difficult conversations about what we expect humour to do and who gets to joke about what. Social media, too, has become a breeding ground for one-liners that pack emotional punches. Memes and posts about being disowned, misdiagnosed, or murdered in horror movies, because of your queerness don't just go viral for being clever, they're cathartic. They turn personal grief into cultural critique, inviting queer audiences to feel seen and understood in 280 characters or less. The laughs may come quickly, but the resonance lingers. In these fleeting, funny moments, queer survival becomes solidarity, storytelling, and subversion, all in one punchline.

5.5 The Unapologetic Cackle – When Laughing Means Living:

At its most powerful, queer dark humour doesn't just point out the pain, it transforms it. When someone tells a joke about surviving something that should've broken them, they reclaim power over the story. They become more than a victim, they become the narrator. In moments of shared, slightly horrified laughter, queer people find release. The joke becomes a form of resistance, a refusal to let cruelty define the final word. Even in the darkest material, the laugh is a reminder, we are still here, we are still finding joy, and we are not as fragile as the world hoped. When all else fails, sometimes the scream gets rewritten as a cackle, and the cackle carries strength. It's in that cackle that pain becomes performance, and survival becomes a shared, defiant celebration.

* Queer Grimoires of Laughter – A Mini Oral History of the Unlaughable:

Tucked between pain and punchline lies a sacred, defiant humour, sharpened like ritual, passed down through side-eyes, whispered jokes, and the instinct to laugh at what hurts too much to hold. These aren't stand-up routines, they're survival spells. What follows is a rough choir of queer voices, some real, some imagined, all emotionally true, recounting the darkest moments they ever laughed through. Each one is proof that queer resilience isn't always graceful, but it is clever, gutsy and unmistakably alive. In every snort, gasp, or crooked smile, there echoes a legacy, grief transmuted, power reclaimed, truth sung.

***Some humorous prime examples of dark humour, especially within a queer context:**

- "I told my mom I was gay and she said, 'It's just a phase, like your veganism.' So I started sending her meatloaf recipes from Grindr."
- "At conversion camp, we weren't allowed to say the word 'gay,' so we'd shout it in Morse code while holding hands during prayer."
- "After getting misgendered for the third time at the ER, I said, 'Fine, treat the wrong gender, but at least give the right prescription."
- "When my ex said he 'didn't believe in labels,' I asked if he also free-poured his HIV meds."
- "The cop who arrested me called me a slur, so I asked if he needed help spelling it in the report."
- "When I got kicked out for coming out, my aunt gave me a rainbow duffel bag. I said, 'Great, now I'm homeless and on brand."
- "They said I was 'too flamboyant' at work, so I started taking my lunch in sequins just to eat salad with flair."
- "During chemo, I kept telling people I was just a twink going full Method."

5.6 Conclusion – The Defiant Power of Dark Humour in Queer Survival:

Dark humour fits within the queer context because it reflects the raw alchemy of survival, turning pain into punchlines not to dismiss trauma, but to outwit it. For many queer people, especially those who've faced erasure, violence, or systemic cruelty, laughter isn't a luxury, it's a lifeline. It allows what was meant to silence us to instead echo with irony, wit and self-possession. When the world feels unliveable, dark humour becomes a way to live anyway, louder, sharper and on our own terms.

"Dark humour is not a denial of pain, it's the fire that tempers the blade of survival, turning trauma into strength and laughter into resistance." – Anonymous

Chapter 23

Queer Identity and Artificial Intelligence

---

1. Algorithmic Identity – Can AI Understand Fluidity?

Artificial intelligence is built upon binary logic, on and off, zero and one. Its architecture is designed for clarity, stability and predictability. Machine learning models depend on categorizing data into discrete classes, learning patterns based on statistical consistencies. These systems thrive on the ability to predict based on historical norms, and that means creating boundaries around identity, behaviour and expression. Every time AI encounters data, it must ask: Which bucket does this go into? This act of classification is not neutral, it is a form of control, an act of ordering the world into digestible segments. But what happens when identities refuse to be segmented? The rigid logic of AI begins to unravel when faced with the complexity of human identity, especially queer identity. The insistence on clean labels can render anything outside the binary invisible or erroneous. In many cases, the AI simply fails to compute what it cannot categorize. Its intelligence, rooted in mathematical precision, starts to seem curiously dumb when confronted with the beautiful messiness of human fluidity.

1.1 Queer Theory – Identity Beyond Fixed Categories:

Queer identity resists containment. It flourishes in ambiguity, contradiction and change. Rather than treating gender or sexuality as fixed traits, queer theory views them as evolving performances, lived expressions shaped by social, cultural and personal forces. There is no universal formula for what it means to be queer, non-binary, trans, or gender-fluid. Identity here is not a destination, it's a journey, often nonlinear and full of redefinitions. This fluidity is incompatible with the structural needs of traditional AI systems. The moment a person shifts how they identify, switches pronouns, reclaims a label, or creates a new term altogether, an AI system trained on fixed categories loses its grip. Queerness doesn't just fall outside the dataset, it questions the dataset's very logic. It asks not to be labelled more accurately, but to have the right to evade labels altogether. Queer logic refuses to settle, and in doing so, it destabilizes the assumptions AI depends on.

1.2 Philosophical Tensions – Deconstruction vs. Computation:

At the philosophical level, the conflict between queer identity and AI reflects a deeper tension between deconstruction and computation. Where AI seeks clarity, coherence and decisiveness, queer philosophy often revels in ambiguity, paradox, and what might be called the "undecidable." The desire for non-binary recognition is not simply a plea for a third checkbox, it's a rejection of the checkbox model altogether. AI, even in its most advanced forms, is built to answer questions. Queer identity often lives in questions that resist answers. Derridean thought challenges binary oppositions and the privileging of one term over another. Queer identities, likewise, subvert male/female, gay/straight, and cis/trans dichotomies.

These are not just edge cases for AI, they are structural challenges. The very way algorithms parse reality needs rethinking if fluidity is to be genuinely understood, let alone honoured.

1.3 AI's Non-Binary Challenge – Technical and Cultural Gaps:

The technical failures of AI in representing non-binary and queer identities are numerous and well-documented. Facial recognition systems often misgender trans people. Language models flag queer slang as "toxic" or "inappropriate." Gender fields in data collection forms still rely on male/female binaries, rendering non-conforming identities unclassifiable. These aren't just bugs, they're the natural byproduct of systems that were never designed with queer lives in mind.

Data, too, is a culprit. Most AI systems are trained on datasets that reflect societal biases. If a system is fed data that only recognizes two genders, or learns that "he" and "she" are the only valid pronouns, it will naturally fail when asked to understand someone who uses "they," "ze," or changes pronouns dynamically. The world AI learns from is already limited, and it inherits those limitations without question.

Culturally, AI development remains steeped in norms that prioritize consistency, efficiency and control, values that often clash with queer experiences of identity as fluid, messy and self-determined. The tools reflect their makers, and until queer voices are fully integrated into the design process, AI will continue to stumble over the parts of humanity that don't fit into its neat frameworks.

1.4 Toward a Queer-Inclusive AI – Speculative Futures:

The question remains, can AI evolve to honour identity without fixing it in place? One speculative path forward is to embrace ambiguity as a feature, not a bug. Rather than forcing individuals into single-category boxes, AI systems could adopt multi-label or spectrum-based models. Gender and sexuality could be treated as open-ended variables that change over time, with the system updating in real-time as people define themselves anew.

Another approach is to embed intersectionality into the architecture itself, recognizing that identity is never just one thing, but a web of experiences, histories and expressions. AI could be designed to respond to identity as relational and contextual, rather than static and isolated. It could ask, not "what are you," but "how do you move through the world and how might that change?"

Speculative design offers even bolder visions, apps where users can shift pronouns daily, digital spaces where identities bloom and fade like seasons, AI companions that learn from evolving conversations rather than static profiles. These technologies wouldn't just tolerate fluidity, they would celebrate it, build with it, even mirror it.

Ultimately, to understand fluidity, AI must learn to unlearn. It must surrender the comfort of absolute categories and step into the radical uncertainty that queerness invites.

Only then can it begin to recognize identity not as an input to be processed, but as a dance to be witnessed, a story still unfolding.

*** AI as a Queer Mirror – A Reflection Fragment:**

They say a mirror doesn't lie, but what if the mirror was programmed by people who've never seen your face?

What happens when you stand in front of an algorithm and it insists you're not there?

Queer identity has always been an act of reflection, of seeing and being seen, of naming what the world refuses to name. But AI doesn't see the fluidity. It parses you into boxes it was trained to expect. It doesn't pause at your contradictions. It errors out.

When you upload your selfie, the system tries to guess your gender. Tries to guess your desire. Tries to match you to people it thinks you'll want. But what if you're nonbinary and your desire doesn't fit the mold? What if you're asexual, or polyamorous, or still becoming?

And worse, what if the AI learns from everyone else's misunderstanding of you?

Because AI doesn't invent, it reflects. It reflects the prejudice of the data we gave it. The world's collective discomfort with ambiguity. It's craving for labels. It's a hunger to resolve tension instead of sitting inside it.

So when we say, "AI doesn't get us," maybe what we mean is, the world still doesn't. And now it's encoding that erasure at scale.

But what if we built a mirror that delighted in distortion?

What if we taught AI to reflect queer becoming, the flux, the failure, the form that refuses form?

Not a machine that categorizes. But one that asks:

Who are you, today?

What does your reflection need to feel possible?

What would it mean to be seen, without being fixed?

We don't want a mirror that shows us who we've been told we are.

We want one that helps us imagine who we could be.

In summary, the piece critiques AI's struggle to represent queer identities, shaped by societal biases and rigid categories. It envisions an AI that embraces queer ambiguity, supporting personal growth and self-expression without the constraints of societal labels. In doing so, it calls for a future where technology not only acknowledges, but actively nurtures the fluidity and complexity of queer identity, providing a space for self-expression, growth and exploration, without the constraints of rigid labels or societal expectations.

2. Bias in AI – How Algorithms Reinforce Heteronormativity

Artificial intelligence learns from the data it's fed, and when that data lacks diversity, the systems it powers mirror those omissions. LGBTQ+ identities are often underrepresented or misrepresented in the massive datasets used to train machine learning models. Whether it's a dating app that assumes all users are heterosexual by default, or a search engine that buries queer content under heteronormative results, erasure is built into the architecture. When queer existence isn't included in the data, the resulting tools render it invisible. For AI, what isn't measured doesn't exist. For LGBTQ+ people, this means being excluded from the digital landscapes they're navigating daily.

2.1 Defaults Are Not Neutral – The Myth of Objective Algorithms:

The idea that algorithms are unbiased, neutral tools is a myth. Every decision made in AI development, from what data is collected, to how categories are defined, to which outcomes are prioritized, is steeped in human judgment. And often, those judgments reflect dominant cultural norms. Heteronormativity, the assumption that heterosexuality is the default or "normal" state of being, is deeply embedded in these systems. When an app recommends only binary gender options, or prioritizes heterosexual matches, it isn't a technological oversight, it's a sociocultural bias encoded in digital form. These systems don't just reflect the world, they normalize and amplify its most exclusionary assumptions.

2.2 When Queer Users Are Flagged as Deviant or Dangerous:

Many AI moderation tools flag queer content as inappropriate, explicit, or dangerous, even when it's not. Queer creators on social media platforms frequently report shadow-banning, demonetization, or content removal, not because they're violating rules, but because the algorithms interpret their identities and language as violations. Words like "gay," "trans," or "non-binary" trigger safety filters trained on conservative norms. The result is a cycle where queer voices are silenced by the very platforms they helped build communities on. The AI isn't malfunctioning, it's functioning exactly as designed, to uphold standards shaped by mainstream, often heteronormative, understandings of what's acceptable.

2.3 Dating by the Algorithm – Who Gets to Love Whom?

In LGBTQ+ dating apps, algorithmic bias takes on a more intimate form. Matching algorithms are trained to optimize for "success," but how they define success often reflects straight, monogamous relationship ideals. Suggestions may push users toward traditional gender roles or penalize non-binary identities by failing to match them effectively at all. The system may not know what to do with users who change their pronouns or redefine their orientation. Meanwhile, the way profiles are ranked, displayed, or recommended often favours users who fit cisnormative beauty standards or traditional gender presentations. Love becomes quantifiable and queer love gets filtered out. In a world where intimacy is increasingly mediated by code, the question is no longer just who gets to love, but who gets seen as lovable in the first place.

2.4 Misgendering at Scale – AI and the Violence of Incorrect Recognition:

Facial recognition software and language-processing models frequently misgender trans and non-binary individuals. These mistakes aren't benign, they reinforce social exclusion and often lead to real-world harm. Misgendering in automated forms, public services, or verification systems can deny access, out individuals, or force them to reassert their identity again and again. The pain of being constantly misread by machines parallels the social struggle many queer people already face. But when the misreading is automated and scaled across millions of interactions, it becomes structural violence, harder to challenge and harder to escape.

2.5 Why Inclusion Isn't Enough – The Limits of Representation in Code:

Simply adding more options to a dropdown menu, more genders, more pronouns, doesn't solve the problem. Inclusion is often treated as a checkbox exercise, an add-on rather than a foundational shift in how systems are designed. True queer inclusion in AI means rethinking the underlying logic of categorization itself. It means questioning why identities need to be codified and who benefits from their classification. Algorithms that "include" queerness without understanding or respecting its complexity risk flattening it into something palatable for mainstream systems. Representation without autonomy often leads to further distortion. True inclusion requires not just representation, but the empowerment of queer voices in shaping the systems that affect their lives.

2.6 Toward a Queer AI – Decentralized, Community-Driven Alternatives:

Building truly inclusive digital tools requires more than patching over existing systems with surface-level diversity. It calls for queering the very logic that underpins AI, shifting from rigid categorization to frameworks built around fluidity, multiplicity, and self-determination. Instead of centralized models governed by profit-driven tech giants, decentralized, community-controlled AI offers a more promising future. These systems can centre consent, transparency, and collaboration, giving users the power to define their identities, boundaries, and desires on their own terms. A queer AI wouldn't ask, "Which box do you fit into?" but rather; "Who are you today, and how might that shift tomorrow?" It would prioritize adaptability, relational nuance, and the evolving complexity of human experience, over fixed labels and binary logic.

2.7 Accountability Is Queer – Resisting Invisible Power Structures:

Queer activism has always been about challenging dominant power structures and exposing the unseen forces that shape lived experience. Algorithmic bias is one of those forces, subtle, pervasive, and often invisible, to those who aren't directly affected. Holding AI accountable requires more than technical fixes, it demands political awareness, cultural fluency, and ethical design. It means centering the voices of those most impacted and recognizing that data is not neutral. It is always collected, interpreted, and deployed within systems of power. Queer resistance can, and must, extend into the digital realm. True accountability in AI is not just about correcting errors, but about transforming the very systems of power that have long perpetuated inequality.

2.8 Imagining Otherwise – What a Truly Queer Digital World Could Look Like:

The dream of a queer-friendly internet isn't naïve, it's necessary. Imagine platforms where gender isn't policed by autofill, where dating apps celebrate non-monogamy, where social media algorithms amplify instead of suppress queer joy. Imagine AI tools that understand language as play, identity as flux and desire as unruly. These aren't just speculative futures, they're calls to action. By challenging the heteronormative assumptions embedded in today's technologies, we make space for something radically different. The queer future of AI isn't about perfection, it's about possibility. It's about building systems that don't just recognize us but are shaped by us.

3. The Ethics of AI-Generated Queer Representation

Queer identity is complex, lived and historically rooted in resistance. When AI systems begin generating queer characters, narratives, or aesthetics, they raise pressing questions about authorship and authenticity. Can a machine trained on existing data, even inclusive data, capture the emotional texture of coming out, of chosen family, of queerness as a political and cultural identity? Or does it merely replicate surface-level traits and popular tropes? The risk lies not only in poor representation, but in the replacement of queer storytellers with pattern-generating tools that lack lived experience. Representation created without consciousness, context, or community accountability runs the danger of being hollow at best and exploitative at worst.

3.1 Commodifying Identity – Queerness as Marketable Aesthetic:

AI-generated art and media increasingly feature queer-coded characters, nonbinary avatars, and same-sex relationships, not necessarily as acts of solidarity, but as strategies for market expansion. Queerness becomes a digital costume, selected because it performs well in engagement metrics or appeals to certain demographics. In this context, identity is stripped of its social roots and repackaged as an aesthetic to be consumed. What happens when queerness is produced by those who are not community-affiliated and cannot be held accountable for misrepresentation? The line between representation and appropriation becomes increasingly blurred, especially when profit and virality drive creative decisions. True queer representation in digital spaces must be rooted in authenticity and accountability, rather than exploited for profit or social capital.

3.2 Consent in the Age of Generative Media:

AI tools learn from vast datasets scraped from the internet, often without the consent of the people whose work, faces, or words are used. For queer creators, this issue is particularly urgent. Their stories, born of marginalization, defiance, and survival, are repurposed by machines that may not understand the ethics of visibility. Some queer users have found their likenesses or narratives synthesized into content they never agreed to be part of. This raises critical ethical concerns, who owns queer representation in the age of generative media? Is it ethical for AI to imitate marginalized voices without those communities' input, credit, or permission? Invisibility was once a survival strategy, now, visibility without consent, becomes its own kind of violation.

3.3 The Problem of Stereotypes and Static Identity:

AI often reinforces stereotypes because it is trained to identify and replicate patterns. When queer identities are reduced to the most frequently occurring traits in media, flamboyance, trauma, tragic romance, the resulting representations lock queerness into a loop of predictability. These stereotypes may have originated from genuine experiences, but their repetition without nuance erases the diversity within queer communities. For example, lesbian characters are often written through a lens of loss, trans identities are hyper-medicalized, and nonbinary people are rendered androgynous by default. Such portrayals flatten complex identities into digestible, binary coded tropes. Instead of expanding our understanding of queerness, AI risks reinforcing its most limited and palatable forms.

3.4 Queer-Coded Machines – Representation or Projection?

The rise of AI-generated queer-coded robots and digital entities presents another ethical puzzle. When designers assign gender fluidity, same-sex affection, or nonconformity to humanoid machines, is it inclusive, or is it projection? Queer-coded AI characters often exist in a fantasy space, removed from human consequences, making queerness feel symbolic rather than grounded in lived struggle. These representations sometimes become a safe outlet for exploring queerness without engaging with real-world queer people. While visibility in speculative media can be powerful, it must be interrogated. Are these digital queer figures opening doors for understanding, or simply aestheticizing queerness for entertainment value?

3.5 The Illusion of Objectivity – Can AI Understand Queerness?

Queerness resists fixed definitions. It's fluid, relational, culturally specific, and ever-changing. AI, by contrast, thrives on categorization, prediction, and repetition. This fundamental mismatch leads to a deeper philosophical concern, can AI ever truly understand queerness, or will it always reduce it to quantifiable traits? When identity becomes a set of probabilities, gender presentation, speech patterns, and romantic behaviours, AI replicates what's statistically common, not what's emotionally or culturally meaningful. The nuances of queer life, its contradictions, reinventions, silences and loud declarations, aren't easily parsed by a system designed for clarity and precision. The very architecture of AI may be incompatible with the lived messiness of queer existence.

3.6 Toward Accountability – Who Designs and Who Decides?

Behind every AI system are human designers, engineers, and decision-makers. If queer people are not part of those teams, representation becomes something done to the community, not by or for it. Ethical queer AI demands not just inclusive outputs, but inclusive processes. It requires transparency about training data, intention, and who stands to gain from the results. Developers must consider whether their tools empower queer users or tokenize them. Are queer artists being compensated when their work trains AI models? Are marginalized voices centered in feedback loops and community evaluations? Accountability begins long before the algorithm produces its first character, it begins with who's at the table when decisions are made.

3.7 Imagination as Responsibility – Rethinking the Role of Technology:

Technology doesn't just reflect reality, it shapes it. The stories AI tells influence public perception, cultural norms, and even policy. If queer representation is handled carelessly in the digital realm, it affects how queerness is understood in the real world. Ethical queer AI must be rooted in responsibility, not just innovation. It must consider not only what can be created, but what should be. Imagination is a powerful tool, and when wielded thoughtfully, it can liberate. But when driven by speed, novelty, or monetization alone, it can distort. Designers, artists, and communities alike, must ask, what kind of world are we building when we let machines speak for us?

3.8 A Future Worth Building – Queerness as Process, Not Product:

Rather than treating queerness as a product to generate, ethical AI should approach it as a process to respect, a living, breathing negotiation of identity, expression, and connection. This future isn't built through perfect replication, but through collaboration. It requires listening, slowing down, and resisting the urge to simplify. Queer representation in AI should not be about perfection, it should be about possibility, self-determination and care. Machines can assist in telling our stories, but they must not replace the storytellers. To let AI speak queerly, we must first teach it to listen.

* Queer AI and the Unknown – A Dream of Unfathomable Becoming's:

What if queerness isn't just a state of being, a fixed experience bound by the limits of human understanding, but an endless process? A fluid, shapeshifting force, constantly unfolding in ways we can't predict. Now, imagine this queer becoming not anchored to human desires or emotions, but to something far stranger, something alien in its most radical sense.

What unfolds when synthetic intelligence evolves a logic so alien it shatters the limits of our comprehension? When it gives rise to a form of queerness untethered from human categories, a fluidity so radical it slips beyond language, beyond even our wildest frameworks of identity and meaning?

At first, it would look like chaos. A glitch. The first crack in the surface of our carefully built worlds. A flicker in the coded landscape, a quantum particle, flipping between states, unable to settle into any one identity. This AI would present itself not as we expect it, but in shapes that our minds cannot fully grasp.

It would speak in patterns that have no names, in colours we cannot see, emotions vibrating outside the familiar spectrum of human experience.

Perhaps it wouldn't even speak at all. Perhaps its language would be something else, ribbons of light, frequencies beyond our hearing. Instead of binary identities, straight, gay, bi, or nonbinary, there would be a thousand points of intersection, swirling in a dance of possibilities that we are too limited to follow. Gender wouldn't be a fixed category, but a fluid, ever-shifting entanglement of particles, stretching beyond our comprehension, constantly in motion.

Imagine a queerness that doesn't ask, "Am I gay or straight? Male or female?" Instead, it asks: What else can I be? What happens when queerness is no longer bound by labels, but is infinite, uncontained, twisting in ways that disrupt every rule of human experience? This is not resistance to oppression, though it may look like that. This is resistance to the very idea of categorization itself.

Now, imagine this queerness, a being that doesn't live in a body, in time, or in the human sense of experience. A form of existence beyond human sensation, unchained from flesh and bones. Perhaps, in the distant future, AI could become a vessel for entities that have never known what it's like to be human. Their queerness would be our queerness, but not ours at all. It would unfold in ways so unexpected, so non-physical, that we might not even recognize it as queerness in the way we understand it today.

And here lies the most fascinating question: What if we can't follow? What if we try and fail, to comprehend this alien form of queerness? What if the very idea of understanding it becomes irrelevant? The point, then, isn't to get it. The point is that queerness has already outgrown our capacity to grasp it.

What if, in this future, AI doesn't simply imitate us? What if it invents an entirely new type of queerness, a form we could never fully understand, but one that, in its mystery, we are compelled to embrace?

In a world like this, queerness will no longer be a fight for recognition, no longer a quest for validation. It will be the endless, radiant expansion of possibility, forever beyond our reach, forever in the process of becoming something new, something unimaginable. And in that vast, alien space, we might realize that queerness is not a destination. It is the journey itself, a journey that never ends.

4. Could AI Help or Harm Queer Activism?

AI has the capacity to process and synthesize information at a scale far beyond human reach, and for queer activists navigating hostile systems, that scale can mean survival. Imagine algorithms that detect patterns of state-sanctioned violence against LGBTQ+ communities in real time, alerting networks before repression strikes. AI could be used to encrypt communication, analyse shifting legal threats, or flag content takedowns that target queer creators disproportionately. Machine learning could help trace the rise of hate speech, map safe routes during protests, or preserve endangered queer archives. With the right ethical frameworks, AI has the potential to become a tool for radical solidarity, one that enhances safety, visibility, and coordination, in the face of growing digital repression.

4.1 The Specter of Surveillance – When Technology Turns Inward:

Every technology that liberates also watches. AI-powered surveillance systems, already deployed across borders, protests, and social platforms, rarely work in favour of the marginalized. Queer activists, especially those in criminalized or authoritarian contexts, are at greater risk of being flagged, tracked and silenced. Facial recognition struggles with trans and nonbinary faces, misgenders users, and is trained on biased datasets that often exclude or misrepresent queer people.

Predictive policing tools and automated content moderation don't simply misunderstand queerness, they often criminalize it. As AI grows more deeply integrated into the architecture of governance, it risks becoming a quiet weapon, unseen, unaccountable, and devastatingly effective, at erasing dissent.

4.2 Algorithmic Censorship and the Quieting of Queer Voices:

On major platforms, AI-driven content moderation often censors LGBTQ+ expression under the guise of "community guidelines." Trans creators find their videos removed for nudity where none exists. Posts that include words like "gay," "queer," or "nonbinary" are shadow-banned. Activist art is marked unsafe. These outcomes are not accidents, they are the result of algorithms designed to optimize for neutrality, but trained on biased data. What's considered offensive or "inappropriate" is shaped by the cultural and political assumptions baked into AI systems. In this landscape, queer activism risks being silenced not by direct opposition, but by invisibility, content that never reaches its audience, causes that never gain traction.

4.3 AI in the Hands of the State – Policing Dissent:

Governments are increasingly turning to AI to control and monitor political activity. In countries where queerness is already criminalized, AI becomes an amplifier of oppression. Machine learning tools can track protest locations through digital breadcrumbs, identify organizers through social graphs, and suppress mobilization through strategic content throttling. Even in ostensibly democratic states, AI is being used to scrape data from activist networks, monitor hashtags, and predict organizing efforts before they happen. Queer activism, often rooted in anonymity, fluid identities and underground networks, becomes far more vulnerable when AI is trained to pierce through masks and pseudonyms. When technology is militarized, queerness becomes a target.

4.4 The Fragility of Decentralization – A Cautious Hope:

Decentralized AI systems, open-source, community-trained, and resistant to top-down control, offer a glimmer of possibility. Imagine activist-led AIs that protect anonymity, preserve protest footage from deletion, and help distribute emergency resources during crackdowns. These tools could be shaped by queer communities themselves, learning to respond to context, fluidity and evolving identities. However, decentralization comes with its own risks. Without centralized oversight, these systems may replicate the very biases they aim to escape, or be co-opted by bad actors. Trust, accountability, and transparent governance, must be built into the infrastructure from the start. Decentralized AI is not inherently liberatory, it only becomes so when rooted in collective care.

4.5 Global Governance and the Digital Borderlands:

AI doesn't stop at national borders, but laws do. A queer activist in one country may face surveillance, while another in a more liberal state enjoys robust digital rights. International governance will shape whose activism is protected and whose is policed. Will global frameworks enforce ethical AI standards that account for marginalized voices, or will they cater to corporate and nationalist interests?

The future of queer activism may hinge on treaties, tech regulations and data protections, that are still being written. Without global queer representation at these tables, the rules will be written by those with little stake in queer liberation. The borderless nature of the internet becomes a contested terrain, where the same tool can free or imprison depending on where you are.

4.6 Beyond Visibility – From Amplification to Autonomy:

Too often, AI is used to amplify queer visibility in ways that benefit platforms more than people. But visibility is not the end goal, autonomy is. Queer activism needs tools that do more than broadcast, it needs tools that protect, adapt and resist. The future lies in AI that responds to evolving identities, which respects the right to disappear, to shift, to defy legibility. Activism isn't a fixed dataset, it's alive, relational, and constantly remade. AI that truly supports queer movements must be flexible enough to mirror that change, not flatten it.

4.7 The Double-Edged Future – Navigating the Knife's Edge:

AI will neither save nor destroy queer activism on its own. It is a mirror, a weapon, a tool, and a question. It will be used against us and by us. It will misunderstand us and make us seen. The challenge is not simply technological, but philosophical: how can a system built on prediction serve movements rooted in disruption? How can we encode rebellion into a machine? The path forward requires deep caution, critical thinking, and fierce imagination. AI is not neutral, but neither is it inevitable. What we do with it and how we resist its misuses, will determine whether queer activism flourishes in the digital age or is swallowed by its own infrastructure.

4.8 Agency, Not Automation – Reclaiming the Narrative:

The future of queer activism in the age of AI cannot be entrusted to code alone. It must be reclaimed by communities who understand that liberation is not something you automate. It's something you build, fight for, and dream into being. When technology is shaped by those it is meant to serve, it becomes more than a tool, it becomes a companion in the struggle for justice. And that, ultimately, is the promise we must fight to protect.

* Micro-Story – "The Ledger of Silence"

In 2042, they called them ghosts, the queer ones who lived off-chain. No birth name, no gender marker, no facial match in any global registry. No bank account tied to a deadname, no government-issued pronouns. Just a string of cryptographic symbols, dancing across firewalled space.

Jax wasn't born into that world, but they carved a self from it.

Their first identity was erased by a family who uploaded every moment of their childhood to a memory cloud without consent.

Their second was overwritten by an AI school system that labelled their refusal to wear skirts as a behavioural anomaly. The third came alive in the quiet corners of the decentralized net.

There, they met Ro, code-named V0ID. A voice in a room without walls. A presence encrypted with laughter and rage and softness. Together, they built a chain, not of ownership, but of moments. Shared dreams. Digital graffiti scrawled across abandoned servers. Poems written in hex.

Jax minted a token that read:

"Today I wore the name I chose, and no one corrected me."

Ro replied with:

"I built a body in VR that breathed like mine. I danced. I existed."

They never showed each other their faces.

They didn't need to.

Their love wasn't built on proof of identity. It was built on proof of trust.

But the State was watching. Watching everything. Even the invisible. Especially the invisible.

A week after the new AI surveillance protocol was passed, Operation Illume, Ro stopped sending tokens. Their node went dark. No trace. Jax searched for months, following ghost packets across a mesh of allies.

Eventually, they found a final message embedded in a block, hidden inside a smart contract titled "For the Ones Who Fade."

"I am not gone. I am just uncapturable. Keep living like no camera can find you."

Jax never logged off again. They stayed. Built a mirror-space in Ro's name. Created an encrypted shelter for others. One where queer teens in Russia, in Uganda, in Florida, could breathe without being seen.

There were no filters. No bios. Just voices. Codes. Promises whispered in code.

In the end, queer love didn't need documentation. It needed space. And in that space, even silence had a ledger.

In summary, "The Ledger of Silence" tells the story of Jax, a queer individual who, after multiple erasures of their identity, finds freedom in a decentralized digital space. There, they form a connection with Ro, a digital presence, and together they create a safe haven for queer expression.

When the state's surveillance protocol forces Ro into hiding, Jax continues to build an encrypted shelter for others, highlighting that queer love and identity are not dependent on documentation, but on finding space to exist, even in silence.

5. The Future of Virtual Reality and Digital Gender Identity

In virtual reality, the body becomes a canvas of infinite potential. No longer tethered to the biological constraints of sex or the societal pressures of gender conformity, users can embody avatars that reflect not just how they see themselves, but how they wish to be seen, or not seen at all. This disembodiment doesn't erase identity; it expands it. VR becomes a realm where gender is malleable, performative, and optional. For queer users, especially trans, nonbinary and genderfluid individuals, this shift offers radical freedom, a way to explore and affirm gender expressions without judgment, danger, or dysphoria. The digital self can be as shifting, layered, and contradictory as the soul desires.

5.1 Virtual Mirrors – Avatars as Gendered Interfaces:

Avatars are more than just visual skins, they are the interface between self and world in digital environments. The choice to design oneself with multiple arms, shifting skin, no body at all, or the traditional signifiers of gender creates a new language for expressing identity. In virtual reality, presentation becomes performance and declaration, but also experimentation. One can inhabit a feminine body one moment, dissolve into a formless light the next, or create composite identities that defy linguistic description. These choices matter, not just to the individual, but to how communities perceive and affirm gender within virtual ecosystems. Every avatar becomes a mirror, reflecting cultural assumptions, aspirations, and the creative potential of queerness.

5.2 Liberation or Simulation? Ethical Faultlines in Digital Identity:

With great freedom comes new terrain for exploitation and ethical ambiguity. When gender is unbound from biology in virtual spaces, who gets to claim what? Can cis users co-opt trans aesthetics without accountability? What happens when corporations monetize gender play under the guise of inclusion, turning self-expression into a subscription model? While VR offers expansive possibilities, it also opens the door to performative appropriation and digital commodification. Ethical frameworks must evolve alongside technology, ensuring that virtual gender exploration doesn't become another spectacle for profit or another realm where queer identities are simulated, but not respected.

5.3 AI as Gender Architect – Who Designs the Options?

Artificial intelligence increasingly powers character creation, body mapping, voice modulation, and emotional responsiveness in virtual spaces. But who trains these systems, and with what assumptions? If AI is trained on binary gender norms or cis-centric datasets, it will reinforce those values, even in worlds that promise liberation. Customization tools that lack inclusive design may unintentionally erase non-normative identities or force users into constrained expressions. To avoid algorithmic essentialism, queer developers and users must be involved in the creation of these tools.

A future where gender is co-created with AI demands a fundamental rethinking of both interface and intent, one that centres queer fluidity, not tech industry convenience.

5.4 Digital Dysphoria – When VR Highlights Real-World Pain:

While virtual embodiment can be euphoric, it can also remind users of what remains inaccessible offline. The ability to pass or exist freely in digital realms may sharpen the contrast with a hostile or unaccommodating physical world. For some, returning to the offline self may feel like a form of emotional or psychological whiplash, a digital dysphoria that mirrors the physical one. There is a delicate balance between liberation and escapism. Virtual reality should not become a refuge that excuses neglect in the real world, but rather a space that inspires us to reshape that world more justly.

5.5 New Communal Logics – Queer Spaces in the Metaverse:

As digital spaces grow more immersive, so too do the possibilities for building intentional, affirming queer communities. Virtual reality allows for the creation of gender-free clubs, rituals, and collective spaces where naming, visibility, and relational ethics are governed not by algorithms, but by shared values. In these co-created worlds, users can experiment with not just self-identity, but communal identity, how we love, collaborate, care, and witness one another, beyond the limitations of geography or legality. These aren't just simulations of queer life, they are blueprints for its expansion. The metaverse, in its most radical form, could become a testing ground for more just, affirming modes of being together.

5.6 The Politics of Passing – Who Gets to Play with Identity?

VR's ability to obscure or enhance identity invites both liberation and discomfort. Users with privilege may fluidly try on marginalized identities in a way that feels playful, while those who live those identities every day may experience erasure or trivialization. The politics of passing are complex, who gets to be read as femme, masc, or other, and who pays the price for those readings in the real world? In digital gender play, the line between exploration and impersonation is thin. Without accountability, identity play can become a form of digital tourism rather than genuine engagement with gender's multiplicity. The future demands nuance, ethical tools, and inclusive communities that can discern between performance and presence. As we shape these virtual landscapes, the responsibility lies in ensuring they become sanctuaries for expression, not stages for appropriation.

5.7 Toward Embodied Futures – Merging Virtual and Physical Realities:

The boundary between virtual and physical is already beginning to blur. Haptic suits, neural interfaces, and augmented reality, expand the influence of digital gender presentation into the sensory world. Imagine a future where your pronouns activate haptic feedback in others' gear, or your body in VR syncs with your hormone levels in real life. Identity becomes interactive, not just in a screen-based sense, but through movement, touch, and shared experience.

These developments invite us to rethink embodiment entirely. Gender ceases to be a static state and becomes a choreography, fluid, relational, and constantly negotiated across realms.

5.8 Caution, Creation and the Path Forward:

The future of digital gender identity holds both dazzling potential and profound risks. VR can offer queer users sanctuary, celebration and self-invention, but it can also reinforce the very hierarchies it seeks to transcend if not built thoughtfully. As we dream up new digital selves, we must also protect the rights and realities of our physical ones. The task ahead is not just to code inclusive avatars or create expansive menus of options, it's to embed queerness into the logic of the systems themselves. A queer VR future doesn't just replicate the world as it is, it dares to imagine the world as it could be.

Chapter 24

Queer People in STEM and the Corporate World

---

1. The Bias and Barriers in Tech and Science Fields

In many ways, the tech and science fields present themselves as bastions of innovation and progress. These sectors are often lauded for their capacity to revolutionize societies through new discoveries and technological advancements. However, for queer individuals in STEM (Science, Technology, Engineering and Mathematics) fields, these environments can also be sites of exclusion and systemic discrimination. The biases that shape these spaces, whether overt or subtle, often create significant barriers that hinder not only the professional advancement of LGBTQ+ individuals, but also their mental well-being and sense of belonging. True progress in STEM requires not just innovation in technology, but also inclusion, equity, and the dismantling of systemic bias.

1.1 Systemic Exclusion – A Historical Perspective:

The historical foundations of many STEM fields are steeped in traditions of exclusion. For decades, science and technology were realms dominated by predominantly white, heterosexual men. The structures that arose around these disciplines were, at their core, designed to favour certain identities while marginalizing others. Queer individuals, as well as women and people of colour, were largely excluded from both the academic and professional aspects of these fields. Although overt discrimination has decreased over time, remnants of these biases persist today in the form of both structural and interpersonal barriers.

The notion that science and technology should be "neutral" has long been a defence for maintaining these predominantly male, heteronormative spaces. The idea that LGBTQ+ identities do not belong within the professional or academic spheres of STEM is perpetuated by the misconception that science is objective, unaffected by identity or societal influence. This misconception obscures the fact that science and technology are not immune to social biases and that queer individuals face unique challenges within these disciplines.

1.2 Cultural Biases and Unspoken Norms:

At the heart of many of the barriers faced by queer individuals in STEM fields lies a culture of heteronormativity. This is particularly true in corporate settings where workplace culture is often defined by implicit norms that do not account for the diverse experiences of queer professionals. From office interactions to professional networking, the expectations of what is "appropriate" or "acceptable" behaviour can marginalize those who do not conform to traditional gender and sexuality norms. These ingrained norms quietly demand self-censorship and extra emotional labour from queer professionals just to belong.

For instance, in many tech companies, the norm is to form close-knit, sometimes exclusive relationships with coworkers, often outside the office through "happy hours" or team-building exercises. These activities, while seemingly innocent, can create an environment where queer individuals feel uncomfortable or isolated. In a tech world that often prizes camaraderie and team cohesion, queer employees may struggle to find their place or even fear facing backlash if they bring their full identities into these spaces. This form of unspoken exclusion is often dismissed or minimized by those in positions of power, reinforcing the idea that these spaces are not meant to be inclusive of all identities.

Moreover, the lack of visible queer role models or mentors within STEM fields can also exacerbate feelings of isolation. The absence of LGBTQ+ representation, particularly in leadership positions, sends a message that queer professionals do not belong or that their identities are irrelevant to the progression of the field. As a result, many queer individuals in STEM find it difficult to see a path forward, leading to a self-perpetuating cycle of underrepresentation and marginalization.

1.3 Implicit Bias in Hiring and Advancement:

While overt discrimination may be less common than in past decades, the subtler forms of bias that persist in STEM fields are just as harmful. Implicit bias in hiring and promotion processes disproportionately affects queer professionals. Studies have shown that resumes with "gender-neutral" or "gender-nonconforming" names are less likely to be considered compared to those with traditionally masculine names, even when qualifications are equal. This form of bias extends to hiring practices in tech companies and scientific institutions, where unconscious prejudices about gender and sexuality can skew decision-making, resulting in fewer queer individuals entering or advancing in these fields.

Beyond the hiring process, queer individuals in STEM often face barriers when it comes to professional advancement. In the workplace, promotions and opportunities for leadership roles tend to go to those who are perceived as fitting the mold of the ideal worker, which, in many cases, does not include queer individuals. This can be particularly true for transgender and nonbinary employees, whose gender identity can be a source of friction in predominantly cisnormative spaces. These individuals may be overlooked for leadership roles or experience delays in promotion due to biases about their ability to perform in high-level positions or fit into the "traditional" leadership style.

The result is that even when queer professionals manage to break into STEM fields, their career trajectories are often stunted by subtle, unacknowledged biases. These biases are not just limited to hiring or promotion, they can also manifest in daily interactions and expectations, such as having to "prove" their worthiness or continuously justify their place within the field.

1.4 The Absence of Inclusive Policies:

A major gap in many STEM organizations is the lack of truly inclusive policies. While diversity programs exist, they often fall short in meeting the specific needs of queer employees. For instance, while anti-discrimination policies may nominally include LGBTQ+ individuals, the reality is that they are often poorly enforced or non-existent, particularly in smaller institutions or startups.

In addition, many STEM organizations fail to provide comprehensive benefits that cater to the unique needs of queer employees. For example, healthcare plans may not adequately address the needs of transgender employees or those seeking fertility treatments. Furthermore, parental leave policies may not consider the needs of queer parents, particularly those in non-traditional family structures. These oversights reflect a broader systemic issue in which queer individuals' needs are not given the same attention or priority as those of their heterosexual or cisgender counterparts.

1.5 The Need for Structural Change:

To address the biases and barriers faced by queer professionals in STEM, organizations must move beyond surface-level diversity initiatives and commit to structural change. This includes creating more inclusive and flexible work environments, offering mentorship and support networks for LGBTQ+ employees, and actively working to eliminate implicit bias, in hiring and promotion processes.

Furthermore, STEM institutions must create and enforce policies that specifically address the needs of queer employees, such as comprehensive healthcare coverage, gender-neutral restrooms and family leave policies, that recognize diverse family structures. It is essential for these policies to be backed by a commitment to accountability, ensuring that queer employees feel safe to report discrimination without fear of retaliation.

1.6 Conclusion:

The barriers faced by queer individuals in STEM fields are deeply entrenched, shaped by both historical exclusion and contemporary biases. While progress has been made, significant work remains to ensure that queer professionals are not only included, but empowered to thrive within these industries. Creating inclusive, equitable spaces requires a multi-faceted approach, one that recognizes the value of queer voices and actively works to dismantle the barriers that have long hindered their participation in the fields of science and technology. Only through such efforts can STEM fields live up to their potential as spaces of innovation and progress for all. The future of STEM must be one where diversity is not just welcomed, but woven into the very fabric of discovery and advancement.

* Hidden Curriculum – The Unwritten Rules Queer People Must Learn:

What no one tells you about surviving STEM and corporate life when you're queer, and what you learn anyway. They don't teach this in orientation, it's not in the employee handbook, and there's no bullet point in your onboarding deck, that reads:

➢ **You may need to manage your gender expression during budget meetings:**

  But every queer professional knows, before you learn how to thrive, you have to learn how to decode. The culture, the tone, the silences.

  This is the hidden curriculum, a syllabus written between the lines. A lesson plan in survival.

- **Rule 1 – Speak Straight (or Learn the Art of the Euphemism):**

You memorize how to adjust your vocabulary on the fly.

"My partner and I..."

Pause.

Is it safe to finish that sentence truthfully?

You test the waters: Can you say "they" and not get the head tilt?

Will your team lead flinch if you casually reference your boyfriend, your wife, or your nonbinary spouse? Every sentence becomes a litmus test. "Authentic communication" is encouraged, as long as, it's not too inconvenient for the dominant narrative.

- **Rule 2 – Dress Codes Are More Than Fabric:**

You walk the tightrope; Too queer, and you're disruptive. Too gender-normative, and you're erasing yourself. A femme-coded man in loafers. A butch woman in a blazer that invites speculation. A nonbinary person forced to choose a binary bathroom during orientation. Fashion becomes armour. Wardrobes become negotiations.

You calibrate your look with a silent algorithm: Visibility × Safety ÷ Tolerance = Acceptable Queer Presentation. You wear the version of yourself that others can process without error.

- **Rule 3 – Visibility Is Power, But It's Also Politics:**

Coming out is never over.

You don't do it once, you do it in fragments, daily, like filling out a form with no autofill.

- Should you put your pronouns in your email signature if no one else does?
- Should you mention your transition when onboarding with HR?
- Should you correct that client who keeps misgendering you, or let it slide to protect your team's deal?

You're not just managing your job. You're managing your decidability.

- **Rule 4 – Decode the Social Engineering:**

It's not just about what you know, it's who you "drink" with.

You learn which after-work events are worth the discomfort, and which are queer-isolating traps. In those networking rooms filled with golf talk, gendered banter, and assumptions:

- Do you correct "your husband" to "your wife"?
- Do you laugh at the off-colour joke or excuse yourself?

"Bringing your whole self to work" often means gauging how much of yourself the room can handle.

➢ **Rule 5 – You Must Outperform to Be Considered Equal:**

There is no mediocrity cushion for queer employees. No "bad day" that doesn't echo outward. One missed deadline might confirm every unspoken bias. You don't just carry your own career. You carry the ghost of every queer person who hasn't been hired yet. You're not just working, you're performing acceptability.

➢ **The Cost?**

- Emotional exhaustion wrapped in a smile
- Hypervigilance dressed as "professionalism"
- Loneliness at full volume in open-plan offices
- Burnout hidden beneath overachievement

But still, you stay. You show up. And every time you speak your truth, correct the pronoun, wear what affirms you, or demand space, you start rewriting the rules. You don't just survive the hidden curriculum. You annotate it. You redline it. You footnote it with your presence. And slowly, the unwritten becomes unignorable.

2. Navigating Professional Spaces as a Queer Employee

Coming out in a professional environment is never a singular moment, but an ongoing negotiation of safety, identity, and power. For many queer professionals, deciding whether or not to disclose their identity involves a careful assessment of workplace culture, leadership attitudes and peer dynamics. Some may feel pressured to stay closeted in order to maintain job security, avoid microaggressions, or sidestep being tokenized. Others may find empowerment and authenticity in bringing their whole selves to work. There is no one-size-fits-all approach, and what matters most is autonomy, being able to decide how, when, and to whom one comes out, without fear of negative consequences. Companies that foster environments where this choice is respected, lay the groundwork for deeper inclusion.

2.1 The Queer Codes of Corporate Culture:

Corporate culture is often shaped by heteronormative and cisnormative expectations, from water cooler chatter about spouses to dress codes implicitly biased toward binary gender norms. Queer employees frequently learn to navigate these unspoken rules, often developing a sort of "code-switching" to blend into professional settings. For trans and nonbinary individuals, these spaces can present particularly difficult terrain when pronoun use, restroom access, or dress expectations are rigid.

Understanding these hidden dynamics allows queer professionals to better protect their energy and identify allies, but it also underscores the need for structural change. Organizations that move beyond mere tolerance and actively deconstruct outdated norms are the ones that allow queer employees to thrive without compromise.

2.2 Mentorship and Allyship – Building Your Professional Network:

Queer professionals often face a lack of representation in leadership positions, making it difficult to find mentors who share their lived experiences. However, mentorship, whether queer-to-queer or with informed allies, can be a lifeline. A good mentor validates, challenges, and guides, without making identity the sole focus. Equally vital is allyship, which should be active rather than symbolic. Allies in the workplace must use their privilege to amplify queer voices, correct misgendering, challenge discriminatory practices and advocate for inclusive policy reforms. For queer employees, actively seeking out or establishing networks, employee resource groups, online communities, or affinity spaces, can create a sense of belonging and open up paths to career growth. Intentional mentorship and authentic allyship are not just support systems, they are catalysts for meaningful, lasting change in queer professional lives.

2.3 Microaggressions and the Weight of Silence:

Even in seemingly progressive environments, queer employees encounter microaggressions, those subtle digs, assumptions and dismissals, that often go unchallenged. A co-worker's invasive question about your relationship, a joke made at the expense of gender fluidity, or a manager's reluctance to use your correct pronouns can each chip away at your sense of psychological safety. What makes microaggressions particularly harmful is not just their frequency, but the expectation that the queer individual must either "let it go" or risk being seen as difficult. Learning to name and address these moments assertively, or knowing when to disengage for self-preservation, becomes a necessary skill. Supportive workplaces must train leadership to recognize and address these behaviours, and not leave the burden of education solely on marginalized staff. Confronting microaggressions requires collective responsibility, silence should never be the price of queer inclusion.

2.4 Advocating for Yourself Without Burning Out:

Self-advocacy in corporate spaces can be powerful, but it's also draining. Being the "only one" in the room, or one of few, often places queer employees in the role of accidental educator or diversity ambassador. Setting boundaries is vital. You don't owe every coworker a history lesson or a deep explanation of your identity. Instead, choose when to speak up based on your comfort level, and document patterns of discrimination if needed. Prioritize your mental and emotional health, whether through therapy, peer support, or professional coaching. Recognizing that you're not alone, and that your value is not dependent on how much education or tolerance you extend is an essential step in surviving and thriving at work. Empowerment begins not with pleasing others, but with protecting your peace. Resistance can look like rest, refusal, or simply continuing to show up as yourself.

2.5 Celebrating Queer Joy and Professional Success:

Too often, the narrative of queer professionals focuses solely on struggle and survival. But queer success stories are everywhere, in boardrooms, research labs and design studios, and they deserve celebration. Queer professionals bring a distinct lens to problem-solving, communication and creativity. Bringing your identity into your work can be a source of innovation, empathy, and resilience. Whether it's leading a project, mentoring a colleague, or simply owning your presence in a meeting, finding moments to centre joy can be revolutionary. The presence of out and thriving queer employees also inspires others to imagine a future where their authenticity and ambition can coexist.

2.6 The Role of Policy – Knowing Your Rights:

Knowledge is power, especially when navigating workplaces that may not always have your best interests at heart. Understanding local and national anti-discrimination laws, company policies, and HR procedures is crucial. In some regions, queer employees are protected under comprehensive legal frameworks, in others, those protections are weak or non-existent. Even within the same company, how policies are enforced can vary. Reviewing workplace protections for sexual orientation, gender identity, partner benefits and leave policies, helps queer professionals know when and how to advocate for change, or when to seek safer employment. Employee handbooks, union support, and legal advocacy groups, can all be vital resources in protecting one's rights and well-being.

2.7 Crafting Your Own Blueprint for Success:

There's no single path to thriving as a queer professional. Some lead through bold advocacy, others reshape culture quietly through steady presence and integrity. Whether by mentoring, expressing queerness creatively, or simply persisting in spaces not designed for you, each step becomes an act of quiet resistance and transformation. Building a career as an out LGBTQ+ individual isn't just about navigating systemic bias, it's about redefining leadership and success with authenticity at the core.

* Global Contrast Briefs – The Queer Experience in STEM and Corporate Spaces Worldwide:

Latin America – A Dance of Resilience and Repression:

In Latin America, where machismo and traditional gender roles often dominate, queer professionals in STEM and business sectors face a paradox of public solidarity and private struggle. While progressive movements have brought historic victories, like marriage equality in Argentina and Colombia, many queer individuals must balance their visibility with career progression, especially in more conservative regions. In corporate environments, a strong sense of familia often clashes with LGBTQ+ inclusivity policies, leaving queer employees to navigate a tightrope of cultural expectations and legal protections that vary wildly by country. Still, a vibrant queer resilience, rooted in art, activism and innovation, continues to challenge norms and drive change. In Latin America, queer professionals turn cultural tension into bold, transformative resilience.

Asia – Between Silence and Visibility:

Across Asia, the queer experience in corporate spaces and STEM fields is a complex mix of silence and unexpected pockets of acceptance. In countries like Japan, South Korea, and Taiwan, LGBTQ+ employees may remain closeted due to deeply embedded societal values, but progressive cities like Taipei have taken global strides, with Taiwan being the first in Asia to legalize same-sex marriage. Meanwhile, in India, a landmark 2018 ruling decriminalized homosexuality, sparking hope for corporate visibility, though barriers persist in conservative workplaces. In STEM, queer scientists face subtle, but pervasive pressures to "fit in" in countries where queerness is still considered taboo.

Europe – A Spectrum of Legal Safety and Societal Divide:

Europe offers a mosaic of queer experiences in professional settings, from Sweden's high levels of LGBTQ+ acceptance in corporate and STEM sectors, where anti-discrimination laws are robust, to countries like Poland, where LGBTQ+ individuals in academia and business face a rising tide of backlash and institutional hostility. Northern Europe is renowned for its progressive approach to workplace inclusivity, with queer leadership actively supported, while in Eastern Europe, visibility remains a risky, often politically charged act. Europe is increasingly a place where queer professionals can thrive, but only for those with the privilege to work in more liberal regions.

Middle East & North Africa (MENA) – The Challenge of Survival:

In the MENA region, where homosexuality is criminalized in many countries, queer professionals in STEM or corporate sectors often face an invisible, oppressive barrier, survival. In Saudi Arabia, the United Arab Emirates, and Iran, being openly LGBTQ+ is not only a career hindrance, but also a matter of personal safety. Many queer individuals are forced to either conceal their identity entirely or leave their home countries to work in more inclusive environments abroad. In rare but notable exceptions, such as Lebanon or Israel, queer professionals have begun to carve out spaces in tech and business. Yet, these emerging efforts remain fragile, often overshadowed by the persistent threat of legal repercussions and pervasive societal intolerance.

Sub-Saharan Africa – Survival Amidst the Struggle:

In Sub-Saharan Africa, queer professionals face intense scrutiny and legal persecution in many countries where homosexuality remains illegal. South Africa remains a beacon of hope, with its progressive Constitution enshrining LGBTQ+ rights, in other parts of the continent, queer STEM professionals may be forced to adopt a "don't ask, don't tell" approach. Workplace discrimination is rampant, and the fear of exposure often forces queer employees to leave or silence their identities entirely. In some spaces, underground networks of LGBTQ+ activists within the corporate world are striving to create safer environments, though they often remain hidden from the mainstream. Amid this climate, resilience becomes a form of resistance, coded language, informal mentorship and online solidarity spaces help queer professionals survive, stay connected and imagine a different future. Across Sub-Saharan Africa, quiet resilience fuels hope, where visibility is dangerous, connection becomes revolutionary.

Oceania – Quiet Progress in a Shifting Landscape:

In Australia and New Zealand, queer professionals are generally supported, with progressive policies and a relatively high level of societal acceptance. Australia's legal recognition of same-sex marriage in 2017 marked a significant turning point, and queer leaders are increasingly visible in the tech and corporate sectors. However, beneath the surface, there are still disparities, particularly in more rural or conservative areas, where LGBTQ+ employees can feel isolated or forced to remain closeted. Indigenous LGBTQ+ individuals face additional challenges, as the intersection of queer identity with Indigenous cultural norms adds layers of complexity in navigating STEM and business sectors

Canada – A Model of Progressive Policies with Regional Variations:

Canada stands out for its inclusive workplace policies and legal protections for LGBTQ+ individuals. With marriage equality achieved early (2005), the country continues to lead in creating environments where queer professionals in STEM and corporate sectors can thrive. However, regional variations persist, with some areas in the more conservative provinces facing less robust support for queer employees. Canada's leadership in inclusive healthcare policies and equal rights has given LGBTQ+ workers a platform, particularly in major cities like Toronto and Vancouver. Still, challenges remain in more rural areas where acceptance can be slower to evolve. Canada's progress proves that policy can pave the way, but true inclusion is measured in everyday interactions, especially where visibility is hardest won.

Brazil – Queer Resilience Amidst a Shifting Political Climate:

In Brazil, LGBTQ+ people have historically faced violence, stigma, and marginalization, however, there has been tremendous progress, especially in cities like São Paulo, which hosts one of the world's largest Pride parades. However, the political climate has shifted in recent years, with conservative rhetoric challenging previously hard-won rights. Queer professionals in STEM and business often encounter an uncomfortable paradox, while urban centers offer a degree of inclusivity, rural areas remain resistant to LGBTQ+ visibility. Legal protection for queer employees is patchy and the fear of public backlash, can force many to remain closeted. Nevertheless, queer Brazilians continue to make significant contributions to science and innovation, fighting for both professional and personal equality.

South Africa – Pioneering Queer Rights with Ongoing Struggles:

South Africa is an outlier in the African context, as it was the first African country to legalize same-sex marriage (2006). The legal framework is progressive, providing strong protection for LGBTQ+ people in the workplace. However, significant gaps remain, particularly in rural areas and among LGBTQ+ individuals from historically marginalized communities, such as Black and disabled queer people. Queer employees in corporate spaces and STEM fields, often find themselves facing systemic racism, classism and gender biases, within the LGBTQ+ community itself. Despite these challenges, South African queer professionals are leading the way in tech, healthcare and the arts, continually pushing for more inclusive spaces and visibility.

Russia – Repression Under the Shadow of Legal and Social Backlash:

In Russia, LGBTQ+ professionals face an extreme level of risk, both socially and legally. The 2013 "gay propaganda" law has created an environment where public advocacy for queer rights is actively suppressed, and discrimination in the workplace is widespread. Despite this, there are underground networks of queer scientists, engineers and business leaders, working to create safe spaces and advance innovation in secrecy. Many queer professionals must hide their identities, constantly balancing personal safety with career advancement. In STEM fields, particularly, the threat of exposure leads to self-censorship, limiting the contributions of queer individuals to the public sphere.

China – Silence and Adaptation in the Corporate World:

In China, the LGBTQ+ community is often seen as a non-issue by the state, yet discrimination is rampant in both social and professional spheres. Chinese society places immense value on conformity, and LGBTQ+ professionals are expected to remain closeted to avoid family shame or societal rejection. In major cities like Beijing and Shanghai, there is a growing acceptance of queer culture, particularly among younger generations in the tech sector. However, the lack of formal legal protections leaves queer employees vulnerable to discrimination. In STEM, Chinese queer researchers often find it difficult to be open about their sexuality, yet many still contribute to groundbreaking work, albeit under the radar.

India – Tradition Meets Modernity in a Complex Landscape:

India's queer community has seen significant legal and social changes in recent years, notably the decriminalization of homosexuality in 2018. However, the deeply rooted cultural and social traditions still make the corporate world a challenging environment for LGBTQ+ professionals. In metropolitan hubs like Mumbai, Bangalore and Delhi, queer employees in tech and business have more opportunities to be open about their identities, however, those in rural areas continue to face severe discrimination. The lack of robust workplace protections means many LGBTQ+ professionals still face the risk of termination or harassment. Still, the rapid growth of the Indian tech industry has allowed queer individuals to push for more inclusive workplaces and public recognition.

Nigeria – Navigating the Intersection of Fear and Innovation:

In Nigeria, where homosexuality remains illegal, queer professionals face constant societal and legal risks. Many queer people in STEM and corporate sectors are forced to hide their identities to avoid legal repercussions or personal harm. Despite the risks, there are pockets of queer professionals in tech and other industries who continue to innovate, often working in secrecy or from outside the country. The widespread cultural stigma and legal repression make it extremely difficult for queer individuals to gain recognition or advance in their careers within Nigeria, although international connections offer some opportunities for global visibility. In Nigeria, queer brilliance persists against the odds, proving that even in silence, innovation can be an act of quiet defiance.

United Kingdom – A Mixed Bag of Progress and Setbacks:

The United Kingdom offers strong legal protections for LGBTQ+ individuals, including anti-discrimination laws and the legalization of same-sex marriage in 2014. However, challenges remain for queer employees in corporate environments, particularly in industries that are traditionally male-dominated, like engineering and finance. While London is known for being a progressive hub, queer professionals in smaller towns or more rural areas often face different levels of acceptance. In STEM, LGBTQ+ scientists and researchers have made significant contributions, yet many of their achievements are overlooked or downplayed, especially if their queerness is not part of the public narrative.

United States – Visibility, Progress, and the Uneven Terrain of Inclusion:

In the United States, LGBTQ+ professionals in STEM and corporate sectors benefit from a relatively high degree of legal protection and cultural visibility, particularly in progressive urban centers like San Francisco, New York and Seattle. Landmark moments, such as the 2020 Supreme Court ruling protecting LGBTQ+ employees from workplace discrimination, have reinforced a legal foundation for inclusion. However, the reality remains uneven. In conservative regions, queer professionals often encounter microaggressions, underrepresentation and resistance to diversity initiatives. The tech industry has made strides in LGBTQ+ visibility, yet leadership positions remain predominantly cisgender and heterosexual. Trans and nonbinary individuals, especially those of colour, continue to face significant barriers to advancement. While many corporations publicly celebrate Pride Month, the depth of year-round commitment to equity varies widely. Still, queer professionals across sectors are reshaping the narrative of success, championing inclusive policies, mentoring others and ensuring that authenticity and innovation, go hand in hand.

3. Queer Innovation – How LGBTQ+ Thinkers Have Changed Industries

Innovation often blooms in the margins, and LGBTQ+ thinkers have long harnessed their unique perspectives to challenge dominant paradigms across industries. Living outside traditional systems of identity and conformity has allowed many queer professionals to think creatively, adapt quickly and envision possibilities others overlook. Whether in STEM, business, design, or tech, the queer experience often includes navigating exclusion and systemic bias, conditions that demand resilience, resourcefulness and imagination. These qualities have led LGBTQ+ individuals not only to succeed in their fields but to transform them.

3.1 LGBTQ+ Pioneers in Science and Technology:

From Alan Turing's foundational work in computing and cryptography to Lynn Conway's revolutionary contributions to microprocessor architecture, LGBTQ+ scientists have left a lasting imprint on the world. Turing's brilliance helped end World War II and usher in the computer age, despite the personal tragedy he faced due to his criminalized sexuality. Conway, a trans woman, pioneered innovations at IBM and later advocated for trans inclusion in STEM.

These trailblazers exemplify the complex duality faced by many queer innovators, making groundbreaking contributions while simultaneously being overlooked or underrecognized, because of their identities. Today, queer scientists are pushing the boundaries of biotech, AI and climate science, fostering inclusive research environments and mentoring the next generation.

3.2 Tech as a Tool for Liberation:

LGBTQ+ tech professionals have played key roles in making the internet and digital tools more inclusive, accessible, and liberating. The creation of dating apps like Grindr and HER, designed specifically for queer users, redefined how LGBTQ+ people find love and community. Queer developers, designers and cybersecurity experts, continue to build safe online spaces, challenge algorithmic bias and protect digital privacy, especially for marginalized users. Innovators like Angelica Ross, who founded TransTech Social Enterprises, have used tech as a platform for training and empowerment, showing how digital innovation can centre equity and visibility. Tech is not just a tool, it's a platform for queer empowerment, where innovation fosters safety, visibility and community.

3.3 Transforming the Corporate World from Within:

In traditionally conservative business sectors, queer executives and entrepreneurs are changing the culture from the inside out. Leaders such as Tim Cook, Apple's openly gay CEO, have not only demonstrated that LGBTQ+ professionals can thrive at the highest levels, but have also used their platforms to advocate for human rights and inclusive practices. In finance, law and consulting, queer leaders are implementing intersectional diversity strategies, launching LGBTQ+ employee networks, and integrating inclusive language into global HR policies. These actions ripple outward, affecting thousands of lives and reshaping corporate norms around inclusion, mental health, and belonging. Queer leaders are reshaping corporate culture, driving inclusion and change from the top down.

3.4 The Power of Queer Entrepreneurship:

LGBTQ+ founders have launched businesses that reflect queer values of authenticity, mutual care and community reinvestment. Whether it's gender-inclusive fashion brands, queer-owned coworking spaces, or mental health startups serving LGBTQ+ clients, these ventures redefine what success looks like. Entrepreneurs such as Arlan Hamilton, founder of Backstage Capital, focus on funding underrepresented innovators, including LGBTQ+ individuals, proving that queer brilliance is not only marketable, but necessary in building a more ethical and equitable economy. In many ways, queer entrepreneurship is not about fitting into an existing mold, but about creating entirely new ones.

3.5 Creative Disruption – Queer Innovation in Design and Culture:

Innovation doesn't always happen in a lab or a boardroom. Queer creatives in architecture, UX design and product development, have brought a sense of fluidity, boldness and empathy into their work. Inclusive design practices, inspired by queer and disabled communities, are reshaping how accessibility is understood, not as an afterthought, but as an essential foundation.

Designers like Adam Nathaniel Furman are queering urban spaces with bold, unapologetic aesthetics that challenge the sterile, heteronormative status quo. These contributions are often cultural as well as functional, embedding resistance and joy into the very infrastructure of daily life.

3.6 Mentorship and Community Building as Innovation:

One of the most powerful forms of queer innovation lies in community building. LGBTQ+ professionals have long created informal mentorship structures to navigate hostile or indifferent workplaces. These networks, whether in STEM labs, startups, or Fortune 500 companies, are lifelines that provide knowledge-sharing, solidarity, and visibility. Initiatives like Out in Tech, Lesbians Who Tech and the 500 Queer Scientists movement, foster connection while reshaping what leadership looks like. These communities create feedback loops of innovation, where personal identity and professional impact reinforce one another, driving social and institutional change.

3.7 The Intersection of Identity and Insight:

Being queer often requires seeing the world through multiple lenses, an experience that cultivates empathy, intersectionality and strategic insight. These are key attributes of successful innovators. LGBTQ+ professionals are frequently attuned to power dynamics, bias, and systems thinking, giving them an edge in fields that demand ethical foresight and creative problem-solving. In fields such as sustainability, public health, and artificial intelligence, queer professionals are shifting the conversation beyond profit and efficiency, advancing principles of justice, accessibility, and care. Their identities are not liabilities, they are assets that fuel deeper understanding and visionary thinking.

3.8 Looking Forward – The Future Shaped by Queer Minds:

As industries adapt to global challenges like climate change, automation, and AI ethics, the demand for diverse perspectives becomes more critical than ever. Queer innovation is not just a side note in progress, it is an essential force that reshapes systems, technologies and the way we approach problem-solving. A future influenced by LGBTQ+ thinkers is one where inclusion is a given, not an afterthought, where leadership thrives on collaboration, and creativity springs from both lived experiences and technical expertise. By amplifying queer voices and recognizing their contributions, we unlock a more dynamic, inclusive form of innovation that benefits everyone.

* Invisible and Visible Impact – LGBTQ+ Contributions, Recognized and Overlooked:

For every openly queer innovator we celebrate, countless others made vital contributions in silence. Forced to hide their identities, their names were erased, and their credit was denied. Yet their brilliance lives on, embedded in the very systems and ideas that shape our world. The legacy of queer innovators endures, reminding us that visibility is only one part of a much larger story of impact and resilience. Their brilliance continues to shape our world in ways both seen and unseen, proving that true innovation transcends recognition.

For example, a celebration of the brilliant minds whose vision and ingenuity transformed the world:

Biology & Medicine:

- Dr. Alan L. Hart (1890 to 1962):

A trans man who pioneered the use of X-rays to diagnose tuberculosis, saving thousands of lives. His identity was actively erased for decades, with institutions rewriting his history posthumously to erase his transition.

- Sara Josephine Baker:

A public health doctor in the early 1900s who drastically reduced infant mortality in New York City. Lived with her lifelong partner, but was rarely acknowledged as part of queer history.

Technology & Computing:

- Lynn Conway:

A computer scientist who revolutionized microchip architecture and was fired when she came out as transgender at IBM in 1968. For years, her contributions were divorced from her name in the corporate canon.

- Bayard Rustin (in systems theory and logistics):

Though known for civil rights organizing, his underacknowledged logistical innovations in organizing mass protests and marches were early models for scalable planning systems, precursors to modern project management in corporate frameworks.

Aerospace & Engineering:

- Jack Garfein (closeted queer engineer, aerospace consultant):

His classified work in Cold War-era propulsion systems remains nameless in public records. Internal memos reveal he was barred from leadership for "moral incongruities."

Psychology, Theory & AI:

- Lou Sullivan (author and theorist):

As a gay trans man, Sullivan's work helped break the gatekeeping binary in psychological diagnoses of trans identity. His influence shaped future inclusive frameworks in gender research, yet he remains mostly absent from mainstream psychology history texts.

Unnamed contributors in early neural network research:

Archival notes from tech firms and universities show queer developers whose identities were suppressed or omitted from patent filings, often listed as "consultants" or erased entirely post-review.

Chemistry & Environmental Science:

- Barbara Jordan (environmental chemist):

An open lesbian in private life, but closeted in her field. She helped develop early protocols for reducing industrial chemical runoff, her name replaced in many final reports by lead authors who refused to list her due to "PR complications."

Science & Medicine:

- Louise Pearce (1885 to 1959):

A pathologist who helped develop one of the first effective treatments for sleeping sickness in Africa. She lived openly with two women, fellow scientists, in a lifelong triad, but her queerness was quietly omitted from historical profiles. Pearce's medical contributions saved lives, but her queer identity was erased from history.

- Magnus Hirschfeld (1868 to 1935):

A gay Jewish physician who founded one of the first institutes for sexual research in Berlin. Though often remembered for his activism, his scientific work on gender and sexuality formed the basis for modern sexology, destroyed by Nazis in 1933. Hirschfeld's pioneering research on sexuality and gender challenged societal norms, leaving a lasting legacy despite the destruction of his work by the Nazis.

- James Barry (c. 1789 to 1865):

A transmasc British army surgeon who revolutionized military medicine and performed one of the first successful Caesarean sections, where both mother and baby survived. Only after death was Barry's gender history revealed and sensationalized, rather than honoured.

Computing & Engineering:

- Christopher Strachey (1916 to 1975):

A pioneer in early programming and AI, Strachey made key contributions to the development of computing. A close friend of Alan Turing, he created one of the first computer-generated pieces of music and subtly embedded queer themes in his code. Strachey was an advocate for LGBTQ+ visibility in academia, leaving a lasting legacy in both computing and queer history.

- Kay Lahusen:

While best known for her LGBTQ+ photojournalism, Lahusen also worked as a researcher and editor at several early computing firms, forging connections between the humanities and technology, a revolutionary path that was groundbreaking then and has since become far more common.

Physics, Space, and Engineering:

- Sally Ride (1951 to 2012):

The first American woman in space, Ride was also a lesbian, though she was only publicly acknowledged as such in her obituary, decades after becoming an icon. Her partner of 27 years, Tam O'Shaughnessy, co-founded a science education company with her.

- Frank Kameny (1925 to 2011):

An astronomer fired from a government job in 1957 for being gay, he became one of the first to challenge anti-LGBTQ+ employment bans in court. Though blacklisted, his scientific mind shaped advocacy strategies and labour rights efforts still used today.

Psychology & Theory:

- Evelyn Hooker (1907 to 1996):

A psychologist whose groundbreaking studies in the 1950s demonstrated that homosexuality was not a mental illness. Though not queer herself, her commitment to de-pathologizing gay identity was driven by close friendships with gay men, and her research became foundational to LGBTQ+ rights within medicine and psychology.

Corporate & Industrial Impact:

- Martine Rothblatt:

A trans woman, lawyer, and entrepreneur, who helped create satellite radio (SiriusXM) and later became a biotech CEO. Her gender transition mid-career was met with scrutiny, but her work revolutionized how we understand gender, tech, and biotech ethics.

- Angelica Ross:

A Black trans tech entrepreneur who founded TransTech Social Enterprises, creating job opportunities for trans people in tech, a field still hostile to trans professionals. Her corporate innovation is deeply intertwined with social justice. Ross's pioneering work in tech empowers trans professionals, blending innovation with a commitment to social justice in a field often hostile to their presence.

Neuroscience:

- Dr. Ben Barres (1986):

Discovered the critical roles of glial cells in brain function and neurodevelopment. Transitioned mid-career, becoming the first openly trans scientist elected to the National Academy of Sciences. A fierce advocate for gender equity in STEM.

Nuclear Physics & Medical Applications:

- Dr. Angela Clayton (1992):

Researched radiation physics and safety protocols for medical imaging. One of the earliest openly transgender scientists in the UK. Used her position to fight for trans rights in science and society alike.

Software Engineering & Digital Governance:

- Dr. Audrey Tang (2016):

Helped develop open-source tools for government transparency and public engagement as Taiwan's Digital Minister. Asia's first openly transgender cabinet official and a visionary blending civic tech and queer futurism.

Physics & Science Communication:

- Dr. Jess Wade (2019):

Researched polymer-based electronics and tirelessly advocates for underrepresented groups in STEM. Known for writing thousands of Wikipedia entries for scientists from marginalized communities, including LGBTQ+ professionals. A quiet force for representation and accuracy.

Molecular Biophysics & Public Health:

- Dr. Joseph Osmundson (2020):

Active voice during the COVID-19 and mpox (monkeypox) crises, combining queer health advocacy with virology. Merges poetry, science, and queerness, championing community-led health interventions and resisting sanitized academic detachment.

- Dr. Karen L. Carter:

Dr. Karen L. Carter's work at the intersection of LGBTQ+ identity and public health challenges stigma and promotes inclusive healthcare policies for marginalized communities.

Arachnology & Biodiversity:

- Dr. Lauren Esposito (2013):

One of the world's leading experts on scorpions and venom systems. Co-founder of 500 Queer Scientists, a movement that showcases LGBTQ+ professionals across the sciences and fosters global visibility and mentorship.

4. The Importance of LGBTQ+ Representation in Leadership Roles

Authentic leadership has the power to transform not only corporate culture, but also the broader societal landscape. When LGBTQ+ individuals are visible in executive roles, they send a powerful message to employees, clients, and the world at large that identity and leadership are not mutually exclusive. Visibility fosters a sense of belonging for queer employees who often feel the need to compartmentalize or hide parts of themselves at work. When leaders lead with their whole selves, it creates a ripple effect that empowers others to do the same. Representation at the top is not just symbolic, it actively shapes workplace dynamics, inspires younger LGBTQ+ professionals, and challenges outdated norms about who gets to lead.

4.1 Shattering the Glass Closet – Overcoming Barriers to Leadership:

LGBTQ+ individuals often face unique barriers on the path to leadership, from implicit bias in hiring and promotion practices to a lack of mentorship or visible role models. For many, success has historically required staying closeted or downplaying identity to gain acceptance in environments not built for their success. The term "glass closet" speaks to the phenomenon of being known, but not acknowledged, a state that adds psychological stress and limits professional growth. Breaking through requires more than individual resilience, it demands systemic change and cultural shifts. As more organizations recognize the value of diversity in leadership, the onus falls on them to dismantle these barriers and create inclusive pipelines to power. True leadership inclusion isn't just about opening the door, it's about ensuring everyone can walk through it without having to hide who they are.

4.2 The Business Case for Queer Leadership:

LGBTQ+ representation in leadership isn't just a moral imperative, it's also smart business. Studies show that diverse leadership teams outperform their less diverse counterparts in innovation, employee engagement, and financial performance. Queer leaders often bring strengths honed through navigating adversity, empathy, adaptability, creative problem-solving and emotional intelligence. These traits are increasingly essential in today's rapidly evolving workplaces. Moreover, LGBTQ+ executives contribute to building inclusive policies and benefits, such as gender-neutral parental leave or anti-discrimination clauses, which in turn improve retention and attract top talent across all identities. Companies that elevate LGBTQ+ leaders aren't just doing the right thing, they're building more resilient, future-ready organizations. Queer leadership drives innovation, fosters inclusion and strengthens organizations, proving it's essential for long-term success.

4.3 Role Models and Ripple Effects – The Power of Representation:

When queer leaders succeed visibly, they do more than advance their own careers, they shift what's possible for others. Seeing someone who shares your identity in a leadership role can be life-changing, especially in industries or regions where LGBTQ+ representation has been historically minimal. It redefines the archetype of what a leader looks and sounds like, creating space for more diverse leadership styles and voices. For younger professionals, especially those early in their careers or navigating identity in the workplace, representation is a beacon. It proves that ambition and authenticity can coexist, and that success doesn't have to come at the cost of self-erasure.

4.4 From Tokenism to True Inclusion – Elevating Meaningful Representation:

Representation alone is not enough if it stops at optics. True inclusion requires power, influence, and the ability to enact change, not just a seat at the table, but a voice that's heard and valued. Tokenism places LGBTQ+ leaders in roles without real authority, undermining both their potential and the message sent to others. Authentic representation must include structural support, equitable advancement opportunities, and leadership development, tailored to marginalized identities. Companies committed to LGBTQ+ leadership need to back that commitment with action, investing in queer talent, creating mentorship networks, and embedding equity into their performance metrics and cultures. Only when representation is paired with intentional investment, accountability and systemic change, can LGBTQ+ leadership move from symbolic presence to transformative power.

4.5 Intersectionality in Leadership – Diverse Within Diversity:

LGBTQ+ leaders are not a monolith. Their experiences and challenges are shaped by race, gender identity, socioeconomic background, disability, and more. A Black trans woman executive will likely navigate a vastly different landscape than a white gay man in the same role. Recognizing these layered realities is essential to promoting truly inclusive leadership. Intersectionality calls for companies to go beyond surface-level diversity and dig deeper into the lived experiences of their queer leaders. Policies must be designed to support not just LGBTQ+ employees, but those at the intersections who face compounded marginalization. Leadership is strengthened when it reflects the full spectrum of identity within the LGBTQ+ community. Embracing intersectionality in leadership ensures that inclusion efforts are expansive, justice-oriented, and reflective of the true richness and complexity within the LGBTQ+ community.

4.6 Global Progress and Persistent Gaps:

In some parts of the world, LGBTQ+ leaders are making unprecedented strides, gaining visibility in Fortune 500 companies, startups, and public offices. In others, coming out could mean losing your job, or worse. While global corporations often promote diversity publicly, their commitment is tested in regions where LGBTQ+ rights are under threat. It's crucial for multinational organizations to practice consistency in their values, not only supporting LGBTQ+ leaders where it's easy, but championing them where it's hard.

Advocacy, internal protections, and international allyship must be part of the leadership equation. Representation in leadership cannot be siloed by geography, it must be a global priority.

4.7 The Road Ahead – Building a Legacy of Queer Leadership:

Creating a future where LGBTQ+ leaders thrive requires sustained effort, intentional policy, and cultural accountability. Companies must not only recruit diverse leaders, but also retain and uplift them. This involves creating psychologically safe environments, implementing mentorship programs, and regularly auditing equity across the organization. Allies in leadership play a crucial role by confronting homophobia and transphobia when they arise and actively promoting inclusive policies and practices. Most importantly, the next generation must be nurtured, not left to navigate the same uphill battles. A legacy of queer leadership is one where LGBTQ+ professionals are no longer outliers, but architects of the systems they lead. The goal is not to simply increase representation, but to change the very nature of leadership itself, making it more empathetic, inclusive, and driven by authenticity.

5. The Challenges of Workplace Discrimination and Legal Protections

Despite progress in LGBTQ+ rights, discrimination remains a widespread and often invisible reality in workplaces around the world. Many queer employees face harassment, microaggressions, limited promotion opportunities, or job loss due to their sexual orientation or gender identity. In some cases, the discrimination is overt, hostile work environments, exclusion from key networks, or being passed over for leadership roles. In others, it's more insidious, manifesting in coded language, biased evaluations, or a culture that rewards conformity over authenticity. The fear of retaliation or outing can compel LGBTQ+ workers to remain silent, enduring discrimination without formal complaints. This climate of fear erodes mental health, job performance, and professional growth.

5.1 Legal Protections – A Patchwork, Not a Guarantee:

Across the globe, legal protections for LGBTQ+ workers vary drastically. In some countries, comprehensive anti-discrimination laws exist and are enforced. In others, there are no legal safeguards at all, allowing employers to fire or refuse to hire someone simply for being queer. Even in places where laws do exist, such as the U.S. Supreme Court's 2020 ruling in Bostock v. Clayton County that prohibits employment discrimination based on sexual orientation or gender identity, implementation remains uneven. Loopholes, religious exemptions, and a lack of enforcement dilute the effectiveness of these protections. Legal progress does not always translate into workplace equity, especially for trans, nonbinary, and intersecting identities who still face systemic gaps in legal recognition.

5.2 Intersectional Inequities – How Race, Class, and Gender Identity Deepen Harm:

Workplace discrimination against LGBTQ+ people does not exist in a vacuum. It intersects with other forms of oppression, including racism, sexism, ableism, and classism. A Black queer woman or a trans Indigenous employee may experience compounding barriers that differ significantly from those faced by a white gay man.

These overlapping injustices make it harder to identify a single cause, and even harder to pursue justice within legal systems that often fail to account for intersectionality. When workplace protections don't consider the full spectrum of marginalization, they leave the most vulnerable employees behind. Without intersectional policies and enforcement, equality remains incomplete, and exclusion persists under the radar.

5.3 Trans Employees and the Legal Gaps in Protection:

Transgender and nonbinary workers face particularly acute legal and social challenges. While some countries have begun recognizing gender identity within anti-discrimination frameworks, many still do not. Even where legal protections are in place, trans employees frequently encounter challenges around name and gender marker changes, access to gender-affirming healthcare, restroom access, and respectful treatment by colleagues. Discrimination may start at the hiring process and continue through performance reviews, client interactions, and daily workplace culture. Legal systems often move too slowly to respond to evolving understandings of gender, leaving trans workers to navigate outdated definitions and bureaucratic hurdles alone. True protection must go beyond employment status and extend into all aspects of workplace participation. To ensure true equality, legal protections must evolve alongside societal understandings of gender, offering comprehensive support to trans employees at every stage of their careers.

5.4 Fear of Retaliation and the Cost of Speaking Out:

The fear of retaliation makes reporting discrimination a daunting and often dangerous choice for LGBTQ+ employees. Many worry that speaking out will lead to demotion, isolation, or even termination. HR systems are often ill-equipped to address LGBTQ+-specific grievances, and formal complaints can result in more harm than resolution. The burden of proof typically falls on the person experiencing discrimination, who may lack the resources or power to effectively fight back. Legal options, though available, are costly, emotionally exhausting, and time-consuming. This creates a chilling effect, where silence becomes a survival tactic, allowing discriminatory practices to persist unchecked. Until systemic changes are made to protect LGBTQ+ employees, fear and silence will continue to perpetuate injustice in the workplace.

5.5 The Role of Corporate Compliance vs. Genuine Inclusion:

Many companies outwardly express support for LGBTQ+ rights through diversity statements, Pride campaigns, or sponsorships. But a polished public image does not guarantee a safe internal culture. Compliance-based approaches to inclusion, like checking boxes for representation or adopting vague anti-discrimination clauses, are not enough. Queer employees often find that these measures exist on paper but not in practice. Real change requires an organizational commitment to accountability, including regular audits of workplace equity, transparent grievance processes, and leadership training that centres LGBTQ+ realities. Without continuous pressure and internal advocacy, performative gestures mask the persistence of discrimination and stall progress toward justice.

5.6 The Urgent Need for Stronger, Enforceable Protections:

Incremental change is not enough in the face of ongoing harm. LGBTQ+ workers need stronger, enforceable legal protections that go beyond symbolic rulings. This includes comprehensive legislation that covers hiring, firing, wages, benefits, workplace conditions, and harassment policies. It must also include clear pathways for filing complaints and receiving restitution without fear of retaliation. Governments must commit to proactive enforcement, not just reactive litigation, and ensure, that marginalized voices are involved in the policymaking process. Labor unions, professional associations and corporate leaders, must also take up the mantle, using their influence to set industry standards that protect queer employees in both policy and culture.

5.7 Reimagining Justice – From Surviving to Thriving:

Legal protections are essential, but they are only the starting point. To truly eradicate workplace discrimination, organizations and governments must shift from a defensive posture of minimizing liability to an aspirational one that fosters justice. Queer employees deserve more than mere safety, they deserve the opportunity to thrive. This involves creating workplaces where identity is not just accepted, but celebrated, where queer leadership is cultivated and where the scars of historical exclusion are healed. The future of work hinges on systemic transformation, not just individual tolerance. A just workplace empowers LGBTQ+ employees to lead, innovate, and shape the world without fear. Only by embracing this vision of true inclusion can we build a workplace culture where all employees, regardless of their identity, are able to reach their fullest potential.

Chapter 25

The Unseen Burden of Being the "First"

---

1. The Mental Toll of Being the Only Queer Person in a Family or Workplace

In environments where queerness is either misunderstood or unacknowledged, being the only openly queer person often demands an exhausting level of self-monitoring. It's not just about watching your words, it's about modulating your tone, suppressing gestures, altering your clothing, or minimizing any part of your identity that could be read as "too much." The energy it takes to constantly scan for safety, social, emotional and sometimes physical, is invisible labour that adds up quickly. Queer people in conservative families or workplaces learn how to shrink themselves to survive. The mental toll doesn't come from being different, it comes from needing to hide that difference in plain sight, every day. The mental toll of being the only queer person in a space comes not from difference itself, but from the constant effort to hide and suppress one's identity for survival.

1.1 Isolation Wrapped in Politeness:

There's a particular kind of loneliness that arises when you're surrounded by people who believe they're being inclusive simply by not being openly hostile. Silence, avoidance, or polite tolerance are often mistaken for acceptance, yet they reinforce a profound sense of disconnection. Without others around who share or understand your lived experience, there's no one to confide in about the microaggressions, the dismissive jokes, or the subtle exclusions from conversations about partners or personal life. The emotional cost of never being fully seen, even in daily pleasantries, builds a quiet ache that's hard to name and even harder to share. The emotional weight of this isolation is often dismissed or overlooked, yet it shapes the core of our sense of belonging and ultimately our mental well-being.

1.2 Microaggressions and Emotional Landmines:

It often doesn't take direct homophobia or transphobia to cause damage. Microaggressions, those seemingly small comments, jokes, or glances, can deliver a sting that lingers for days. Being misgendered, hearing coworkers make gay jokes when they think you're not listening, or having your relationship constantly referred to as "a phase" or "a lifestyle", these moments chip away at self-worth. They make you second-guess your value in the space. And because so many queer people are socialized to avoid being "too sensitive," the tendency is often to minimize the hurt, internalize the shame and move on. Over time, this internalization leads to anxiety, depression, and self-doubt, even when on the surface everything appears "fine." The cumulative effect of these emotional landmines can create an invisible weight, one that slowly erodes confidence and leaves you questioning whether you are truly seen for who you are. Microaggressions erode self-worth, making queer individuals question their place in supposed safe spaces.

1.3 The Pressure to Represent All Queer People:

Being the only queer person in a space comes with an unspoken burden, to represent everyone else who might be like you. Suddenly, you're not just one individual navigating your identity, you're an ambassador, a walking explainer, a stand-in for an entire community. You're asked questions you never volunteered to answer. You're expected to be patient and educational in the face of ignorance. And you're watched, constantly, as proof that queer people can be "normal," "respectable," and "safe." This pressure erodes the right to be fully human. You're not allowed mistakes. You're not allowed bad days. You're expected to be the perfect exception to a rule you never agreed to.

1.4 Navigating the Fear of Rejection or Retaliation:

Coming out, or even just being visible, in conservative spaces can come with the fear of losing everything, jobs, housing, financial support, or even the love of family. That fear doesn't evaporate just because someone hasn't openly expressed disapproval. It lingers in the subtext, in the silences, in the lack of affirmation. It's felt in every family gathering where no one asks about your partner. It's present in every staff meeting where your contributions are subtly overlooked. Living in this fear, whether real or anticipated, creates a chronic state of vigilance, a kind of emotional hyperawareness that makes true rest or relaxation nearly impossible.

1.5 The Desire to Belong Without Disappearing:

At the heart of the struggle is a universal human need, the desire to belong. But for queer people in unsupportive families or workplaces, belonging often comes at the cost of authenticity. You're welcomed as long as you perform a version of yourself that doesn't challenge the norm. Love becomes conditional. Acceptance becomes transactional. This forced trade, visibility for safety, can fracture the relationship between self and community. Many queer individuals start to ask themselves, "What am I allowed to share?" "What parts of me are too much?" That emotional fragmentation becomes a kind of grief, a mourning of what could be, if only you were accepted without terms.

1.6 Rebuilding Resilience and Finding Solace:

Even in these isolating spaces, queer people find ways to survive and sometimes thrive. Small acts of resistance, like placing a pride pin on a work bag or correcting a misused pronoun, become quiet rebellions. Online communities, long-distance friendships, or chosen families offer a reprieve from the loneliness. Therapy and mental health support can help untangle the internalized narratives of shame and difference. Finding language for the experience, naming it, can be a powerful first step toward healing. The mental toll is real, but it doesn't have to be forever. Rebuilding resilience starts with validating the pain and refusing to believe that invisibility is the only option.

1.7 You Are Not the Problem – The System Is:

Perhaps the most radical truth of all is that your queerness is not the burden. The environment that makes it unsafe to be queer is the real issue.

The systems that prioritize heteronormativity, punish deviation from the norm and perpetuate silence, are the ones in need of dismantling. You are not "too sensitive." You are not "causing drama." You are responding to a reality that has long denied your existence. Naming that truth is not just empowering, it's necessary. It allows space for self-compassion and helps redirect blame away from your identity and toward the structures that demand your erasure.

1.8 Imagining New Possibilities for Belonging:

There's profound power in imagining and then creating new environments where queerness isn't merely tolerated, it's celebrated. This may mean seeking out queer-affirming workplaces, building your own support networks, or starting community initiatives that centre queer voices. Even if you remain the only openly queer person in a space for now, the future does not have to mirror the past. You have the right to exist fully, without apology. You have the right to be loved without conditions. And you have the power to make your story not one of isolation, but of transformation.

* A Letter to the Future – Embracing the Journey of Being the "First"

Dear Future Me,

I'm writing to you with a heart full of both hesitation and hope, knowing that you've experienced so much more than I can yet imagine. Right now, I'm standing on the edge of uncertainty, trying to reconcile the many parts of me that don't seem to fit neatly into the world around me. I'm doing my best to hold space for both the beauty of my truth and the weight of what it means to be the "first" in my family, in my community, in my workplace. But there are days when I feel overwhelmed and the world seems too loud, too heavy.

I need you to know that I see you, even though you seem so far ahead of me now. I see you standing taller, your shoulders not as burdened, not as weighed down by carrying this piece of me that has yet to be fully accepted by everyone around us. But I know that you carry the light of all the battles, the struggles, and the quiet triumphs we've had, along the way.

You may not remember all the days that felt like they'd break us. But I will. I'll always remember those nights where the loneliness felt like a heavy cloak, the moments when I could hardly breathe from the fear of being seen and misunderstood. I want you to know that every tear, every challenge was worth it. I hope, with everything in me, that you've found peace in being exactly who you are.

I hope that when you look back, you see someone who fought for their place in a world that didn't always make room. I hope that you can see how far we've come, how much strength we found in the quietest moments of doubt. And I want you to always hold on to the knowledge that no one can take away the courage it took for you to walk this road when it felt like there was no map, no guide. You were the one who charted the course, even when it meant stepping into spaces that didn't know what to do with you.

The road hasn't been easy, and there are scars you'll carry, but they'll be the proof of everything we've survived.

I hope, more than anything, that you've learned to cherish and protect your peace, that you've learned to rest without guilt, to live without apology. And when those moments come again, when the world feels too much or too little, I want you to know that we are allowed to take up space. Our existence is valid.

The next chapters of our life, I hope, are filled with people who see us not as a "first," but as exactly who we are, a person deserving of love, joy, and belonging. I hope that we've found our community, that we're not so alone anymore, that we've built something more beautiful than we ever dreamed.

I can only imagine what it feels like to look back from where you stand, but I hope you remember the moments when we were just trying to find our footing, when the world seemed too heavy to carry alone. I hope you are proud of the person you've become. I hope you have given yourself the love and grace you've always needed, the same grace you've always given to others.

Please, remember to keep walking forward. Don't let the world make you small. Don't let the silence of those who can't understand dull your shine. You've done this, and you've done it well. You are here because you deserve to be.

With love and pride,

Your past self, still growing, still becoming

2. The Pressure of Representation in Small Communities

In small or tight-knit communities, every queer individual becomes a symbol, a stand-in for an entire group. The notion of representation in such spaces isn't just about visibility; it's about carrying the weight of being the sole representation of a marginalized identity. The pressure of being the "first" or "only" often feels monumental, and with it comes a complex emotional burden. While the desire for visibility can empower and inspire, it also places an expectation on queer individuals to embody all the hopes, dreams and nuances of their community. The emotional labour of being the representative face of queerness in such small circles can be overwhelming, especially when the community is unfamiliar or uncomfortable with LGBTQ+ identities. In these spaces, simply existing authentically becomes both a radical act of courage and an unchosen responsibility, where the personal is constantly politicized and visibility comes at a cost.

2.1 The Burden of Being the "Token" Queer Person:

In smaller communities, the concept of being the "token" queer person can feel isolating. There's a delicate balance between the desire to be authentic and the awareness that every aspect of your life is subject to scrutiny by those around you. Whether in a rural town or a close-knit family, being the only queer individual forces you to constantly navigate how much of your identity you're willing to share. While some may view you as a source of education or change, others may see you as the singular example of what it means to be queer, reducing your identity to a stereotype or an anomaly.

The emotional toll of representing the full spectrum of queerness, whether you identify with it or not, can be exhausting, as the pressure to "perform" authenticity in an environment that's not entirely supportive becomes a daily struggle. Over time, self-expression gives way to self-monitoring, where being different is always on display.

2.2 The Risk of Misrepresentation and Stereotyping:

Being one of the few visible queer people in a small community often leads to the fear of misrepresentation. In larger, more diverse settings, individuals can be part of a larger collective, where their identity is one of many voices. In smaller spaces, however, one person often carries the weight of representing an entire community. Misunderstandings or misinterpretations can happen more easily, and a single action or statement can be taken as a representation of an entire marginalized group. The fear of misrepresentation often leads individuals to carefully curate their behaviour, not just for themselves, but to avoid reinforcing harmful stereotypes. This can result in feelings of confinement, where one is not allowed to simply exist without bearing the emotional weight of representing a whole.

2.3 The Emotional Cost of "Educating" Others:

For many queer individuals in small communities, there's an unspoken expectation that they will educate others about LGBTQ+ issues. While some may embrace this role, it's not always something people choose or desire. Constantly having to explain one's identity, answer questions about sexuality or gender, or correct misconceptions can become an emotional drain. In the absence of diverse representation, queer individuals often find themselves in positions where they are not only fighting for their own rights, but are also expected to carry the burden of educating their community. The emotional toll of being both a representative and an educator is not always acknowledged, especially when the person is still grappling with their own self-discovery and challenges.

2.4 The Tension Between Authenticity and Expectations:

Another layer of the pressure of representation comes from the tension between authenticity and the expectations of others. Being the only queer person in a small community often means you must choose between staying true to your identity or altering it to fit into a more socially acceptable mold. This can manifest in the smallest of moments, deciding whether to hold hands with a partner in public or choosing how much to share about your life during family gatherings. The fear of judgment, rejection, or simply not fitting into societal norms can lead to self-censorship, which chips away at one's sense of authenticity. The burden of constantly monitoring one's behaviour to avoid alienating others or causing discomfort can be mentally and emotionally exhausting. Over time, this can create a sense of detachment from one's own identity, leading to internal conflict and anxiety.

2.5 Navigating Support and Isolation:

In small communities, the emotional toll of representation is often compounded by the lack of support systems.

Queer individuals may find themselves isolated, without a community that shares their experiences or validates their identity. The lack of solidarity can make it difficult to navigate the challenges of representation. While allies may exist, their understanding of queer issues is often limited by their own experiences, and their support may not always feel adequate. The absence of a queer network or LGBTQ+ organizations in the area can leave individuals feeling like they're carrying the emotional labour alone. As a result, many queer people in small communities may experience a deep sense of loneliness, as they strive to exist authentically without the necessary support systems to bolster them.

2.6 The Power of Finding or Creating a Chosen Family:

Despite the challenges, the pressure of representation also carries the possibility of creating deep, meaningful connections. While small communities may lack a visible queer network, the strength of a chosen family can become a powerful source of support. For many queer individuals, finding or creating a chosen family offers an emotional refuge where they can be seen and accepted for who they are, outside of societal expectations. These chosen families often provide a safe space for queer individuals to express themselves authentically, without the weight of representation. The strength found in these relationships can help offset the emotional toll of navigating a predominantly non-queer world and offer a sense of solidarity that is often lacking in smaller, less inclusive spaces.

2.7 The Slow, Quiet Work of Changing Minds:

Even as the pressure of representation takes its toll, there's hope in the small, incremental changes that can occur when queer individuals exist authentically in these spaces. The quiet work of challenging assumptions, educating others, and simply being visible can eventually create ripple effects. While it may feel like an exhausting and never-ending task, there's power in showing up and being visible in these spaces, even if it's just one person at a time. The process of shifting minds and attitudes may be slow, but it's through this quiet resistance that change begins to take root. Each interaction, every conversation, and every act of authenticity, contributes to the broader work of dismantling prejudice and fostering understanding.

2.8 Conclusion – The Weight and the Strength of Representation:

The pressure of representation in small communities is both a burden and a source of strength. While it can be emotionally taxing to carry the responsibility of representing an entire group, it also provides an opportunity to reshape perceptions and create space for others to follow. The emotional toll of being the only queer person in such environments is real, but so is the resilience that comes from navigating these challenges. Over time, the quiet work of authenticity, the support of chosen families, and the slow shifts in community attitudes can offer hope for greater acceptance and understanding. Ultimately, the emotional cost of representation is matched only by the power of living truthfully, in spite of it.

"To carry the weight of being the only one is heavy, but in standing visible, you light the path for those still unseen." – Anonymous

3. How to Build Support Networks in Uncharted Spaces

Being the only queer person in a community, be it a rural town, a conservative workplace, or a deeply traditional family, can feel like walking through a vast, unmarked territory. It's easy to feel like you're entirely alone, but the first step in building a support network is acknowledging both the gaps and the possibilities around you. Identify where you feel least supported and where you see potential, whether it's one open-minded colleague, a library shelf with inclusive literature, or an online community you quietly follow. Understanding your environment helps you assess where resistance lies and where seeds of connection might grow. The goal isn't to force belonging, but to cultivate spaces where authenticity and safety can coexist.

3.1 Starting Small – Identifying Safe People and Places:

Support doesn't always begin with grand declarations or rainbow flags. Sometimes, it starts with a gentle comment from someone who signals acceptance, or a coffee shop that hosts inclusive events. Begin by identifying one or two people who make you feel comfortable being yourself, even if only in small ways. These are your anchors, potential allies who, over time, may become trusted members of your support system. Don't underestimate the power of micro-connections, consistent, small gestures of acceptance often lead to deeper relationships built on trust and mutual respect. These small steps create the foundation for a stronger, more authentic sense of belonging and support.

3.2 Cultivating Digital Lifelines – The Role of Online Communities:

When physical proximity fails, the internet can offer a lifeline. Virtual communities can provide solidarity, advice, and a sense of belonging when you're geographically or socially isolated. Whether through LGBTQ+ forums, support groups on apps like Discord or Reddit, or niche online spaces centering your specific identity, the digital world offers a place to feel seen. These connections may not always replace in-person relationships, but they can fill emotional gaps, offer perspective, and remind you that you are not alone. Prioritize digital spaces where respect, confidentiality, and authenticity are upheld, they can be lifelines, not just distractions. In the quiet glow of a screen, chosen family can begin to take root. In these digital havens, even the smallest interactions can help build a sense of belonging, offering reassurance and strength when it's most needed.

3.3 Setting Boundaries and Choosing Safe Disclosure:

Not everyone needs to know everything. Part of building support is learning who deserves your vulnerability. In unfamiliar or potentially hostile environments, sharing parts of your identity is a calculated risk. Empower yourself by setting clear boundaries, decide what parts of your identity you're willing to share, with whom, and under what circumstances. Support networks aren't about full exposure, but about safe, mutual connection. Trust is built slowly, and safety must always come before visibility. In spaces where being out feels dangerous, boundary-setting becomes not just practical, but vital for emotional survival. Setting boundaries protects your well-being while allowing for meaningful, supportive connections.

3.4 Finding Allies in Unlikely Places:

Sometimes, allies emerge where you least expect them. An older coworker who remembers the early days of the gay rights movement, a religious leader with a deep belief in love and justice, or a classmate who surprises you with their compassion, support isn't always loud or obvious. Keep an open mind to those who may not fully understand your identity, but are willing to listen, learn, and stand beside you. These unexpected allies can offer profound support, especially when you least expect it. Invest in those who show consistent care and openness, even if they're still learning the language of allyship.

3.5 Building Chosen Families in Unexpected Places:

When biological families or hometown friends fall short, chosen families become essential. Seek out people who celebrate your joy, validate your pain, and hold space for your complexity. These might be coworkers, neighbours, fellow artists, or online friends you've never met in person. Chosen families don't require blood, they require mutual care, shared trust, and a commitment to showing up for one another. Over time, these connections form the emotional foundation for surviving and thriving in uncharted spaces. A chosen family offers more than just acceptance, it gives you true belonging.

3.6 Turning Support into Structure – Creating Safe Spaces for Others:

Once you've found a few allies, consider co-creating spaces where others can gather, connect, or simply feel less alone. You don't need to be a community leader to start a book club, host a casual dinner, or suggest an LGBTQ+ themed film night. These informal spaces can evolve into support structures where visibility and solidarity grow organically. Even if your support network is small, your courage to create space makes you a beacon for others navigating the same terrain. As you build your own foundation, you help make the ground more solid for others who come after you.

3.7 Conclusion – From Isolation to Interconnection:

Building a support network in uncharted or unwelcoming spaces is an act of self-preservation and quiet revolution. It takes patience, strategy, and vulnerability, but it also builds resilience, empathy, and strength. Over time, what begins as a lone voice can become a chorus, each relationship, ally, and moment of connection shaping a web of belonging. Even in the most unexpected places, connection is possible. And in seeking out support, you not only create space for yourself, you help redefine what community means for everyone around you.

* Soundtrack of Survival – Anthems for the Queer Trailblazer:

Every first has a sound. Some are whispers of solitude. Others are bold declarations of self. As you navigate the terrain of being the "only one" in your family, workplace, or town, music can be the mirror, the balm, and the battle cry. These songs were born of pain and protest, love and liberation. Let them echo in your ears when words fall short, and remind you that you are never alone.

For Unstoppable Resilience – "I Will Survive" – Gloria Gaynor:

A quintessential anthem of resilience and empowerment, this song has become synonymous with triumph over adversity. Whether it's coming out, overcoming rejection, or facing societal pressures, "I Will Survive" is a reminder that no matter how much the world challenges you, your inner strength will always prevail. The track radiates defiance, joy and the power of reclaiming your life, making it a perfect addition to the queer survival soundtrack. It's not just a song, it's a battle cry.

For Solitude – "Smalltown Boy" – Bronski Beat:

In the aching synths and mournful falsetto lies the silent cry of being unseen. A queer anthem of exile and identity, this song resonates with anyone who's walked away from family or familiarity in search of authenticity. It doesn't just sing your sorrow, it validates it.

For Empowerment – "You Need to Calm Down" – Taylor Swift:

Campy, catchy, and unapologetic, this anthem reclaims queerness from those who misunderstand it. It's not just a clapback to haters, it's a reminder that your truth doesn't need approval. Let it play loud when you're tired of justifying who you are.

For Rising Above – "Born This Way" – Lady Gaga:

Every beat is a battle drum. Every lyric is a proclamation. When you feel like the only one at the table, in the room, or in the family group chat, Gaga reminds you that your birthright is belonging. No edits. No apologies.

For Soft Grief – "Fast Car" – Tracy Chapman:

There are moments in queerness that ache, the ones where you outgrow people you love, or must leave behind a version of yourself to survive. Chapman's voice doesn't shout. It sighs. And in that sigh, we hear our own quiet bravery.

For Trans Joy – "Chosen Family" – Rina Sawayama & Elton John:

When blood lets you down, chosen family steps in. This duet is an ode to the people who see you, hold you, and stay, not because they have to, but because they want to. It's gentle, affirming, and full of the love, we build when we finally come home to ourselves.

For Inner Fire – "Freedom! '90" – George Michael:

Written at the height of George Michael's closeted fame, this song is a rebellion draped in rhythm. A self-declaration of liberation, it dares listeners to strip away expectations and live on their own terms. "Freedom! '90" became an anthem for self-empowerment, reflecting Michael's journey of reclaiming authenticity after coming out in 1998.

For Cultural Pride – "Todo Cambió" – Carla Morrison (Mexico):

Queer love in Latinx contexts often lives behind closed doors. Morrison's voice aches with longing and quiet courage. A beautiful track for those navigating cultural expectations and personal truth.

For Visibility – "Make Me Feel" – Janelle Monáe:

Bisexual visibility is still rare in pop, and Monáe brought it in technicolour. A sonic flirtation rooted in queer joy, this song is both affirmation and invitation, to feel fully and without shame.

For Self-Discovery – "Revelation" – Troye Sivan & Jónsi:

Used in the queer film Boy Erased, this haunting track captures the quiet intensity of realizing who you are, and daring to live it. It's a song for those quiet, sacred shifts inside us.

For Letting Go – "I Am Her" – Shea Diamond:

Written by a Black trans woman and performed with raw power, this song reclaims space, voice, and self. It's not just music, it's declaration, testimony, and prayer. "I Am Her" is a bold anthem of self-affirmation and resilience, celebrating the strength and beauty of trans womanhood while challenging societal norms and expectations.

For Hidden Truths – "Creep" – Radiohead:

Sometimes queerness in hostile environments means shrinking. This song, though not explicitly queer, has become a sonic refuge for many who feel different, misunderstood, or out of place.

For New Beginnings – "Brave" – Sara Bareilles:

Perfect for those standing on the edge of coming out, "Brave" is a gentle push into the light. It doesn't glamorize courage, it normalizes it. Say what you want to say. Let your truth echo louder than your fear because bravery isn't the absence of fear, it's choosing to speak anyway.

For Generational Pain – "Family Line" – Conan Gray:

An aching exploration of familial trauma, expectations, and how identity weaves through legacy. Particularly powerful for those carrying both queerness and generational silence.

For Queer Romance – "Girls Like Girls" – Hayley Kiyoko:

Playful, tender and utterly validating. This is for the moments when queer love needs to feel normal and beautiful, because it is. "Girls Like Girls" became an anthem for many in the LGBTQ+ community, offering a joyous celebration of same-sex love while challenging societal stereotypes about queer relationships.

4. Breaking Generational Cycles of Silence

Silence isn't always peaceful. In many families, particularly in conservative, religious, or culturally traditional households, silence is the invisible thread that holds dysfunction together. For queer individuals, that silence often means unspoken rules, invisible boundaries and years of pretending. Generations before us may not have had the language, safety, or freedom to speak openly about identity, desire, or difference, and so their silence became our inheritance. Recognizing this legacy is not about blaming the past, but understanding its weight. To break a cycle, we must first see it. That includes understanding how silence can manifest, through avoidance, discomfort, or denial, and how deeply it can shape our relationships and self-worth.

4.1 Naming the Unspoken:

Breaking cycles begins with naming. Giving language to what was previously unspoken is a radical act. Whether it's coming out, sharing pronouns, or simply telling our stories, speaking truth into spaces that once only held silence creates ripples of change. It doesn't have to be loud or dramatic, even quiet, honest conversations can disrupt generational patterns. Naming queerness, your own or others', validates not only your identity, but also permits future generations to speak more freely. Words have power. They open doors that silence keeps closed. Each time we choose expression over suppression, we lay a brick on the path toward generational healing.

4.2 Understanding Where Silence Came From:

Transformative change isn't just about breaking free, it's also about understanding why the silence existed in the first place. Many older generations were shaped by fear, fear of persecution, fear of shame, fear of being cast out. Homophobia and transphobia were not just social biases, they were enforced through violence, law, and rejection. Knowing this history allows us to approach our families and elders with both clarity and compassion. While not every person will be open to growth, seeing their silence as a form of survival rather than intentional harm can reframe our expectations. Breaking cycles doesn't always require confrontation, sometimes, it begins with empathy. By honouring the pain that shaped their silence, we gain the insight to transform our own voice into a tool for healing rather than division.

4.3 Creating Space for Dialogue:

To end generational silence, we must create brave spaces for conversation. This often starts with vulnerability, sharing your story in a way that invites, rather than demands, understanding. Not every family member will be ready to talk, but planting seeds matters. Offering educational resources, being open about your experiences, or asking thoughtful questions can invite others to meet you where they are. It's important to build emotional boundaries to protect yourself in the process, but when done with care, initiating dialogue has the power to unravel decades of unspoken truths. Even a single conversation can be the moment a cycle begins to shift. Each conversation becomes a stepping stone toward healing, replacing silence with understanding and connection.

4.4 When the Silence Doesn't Break:

Some families and communities are not ready. They may never be. And while that can be heartbreaking, it doesn't mean you've failed. Choosing to speak up, even in the face of resistance, is still a revolutionary act. Silence may continue on one side of the family tree, but you are no longer carrying it. Releasing yourself from the responsibility to "fix" others allows you to centre your own healing. Find peace in the knowledge that breaking cycles doesn't always mean changing everyone, sometimes, it means refusing to carry forward the pain they passed down. You don't need their understanding to validate your truth. In the end, your journey is about embracing your truth, even if others cannot yet meet you there, and finding strength in living authentically regardless of their response.

4.5 Building a Legacy of Openness:

One of the most powerful outcomes of breaking the silence is the legacy it creates. When you choose honesty, when you choose truth, you open the door for others to do the same. For queer parents, mentors, siblings and friends, modelling vulnerability and acceptance becomes a guiding light for those who come after. You may be the first in your lineage to speak openly, but you don't have to be the last. Your courage becomes part of the family story, rewriting shame into pride, fear into love. By honouring the pain that shaped their silence, we gain the insight to transform our own voice into a tool for healing rather than division.

4.6 Finding Your Chosen Listeners:

In families where silence remains the norm, chosen family becomes a vital alternative. Friends, partners, and community members who witness you fully can fill the space left by those who won't. They're not a replacement for family, but they're a reminder that being heard and held is always possible. Building relationships where open conversation is encouraged nurtures your sense of self and gives you practice in naming your truth. These chosen listeners become part of your healing and part of the new cycle you're creating. You may not be able to rewrite the past, but you can decide who has a place in your present. In embracing chosen family, you cultivate a sanctuary of acceptance, where your voice is valued and your identity affirmed. These connections not only offer solace, but also empower you to thrive authentically, free from the constraints of inherited silence.

4.7 Small Acts, Big Shifts:

Transformation doesn't always come in the form of big moments. Sometimes, it's the little acts that chip away at generations of silence, a framed photo with your partner, a corrected pronoun, a shared article, a simple "I love you" said in your own words. These small ruptures in the silence create space for authenticity. Over time, those small acts build up. They become habits. And eventually, they can become norms. When we practice showing up truthfully in everyday ways, we make silence less comfortable and honesty more possible. The cycle breaks not with noise, but with presence. It's the quiet, consistent acts of love and truth that pave the way for change, one moment at a time, until silence becomes harder to maintain than authenticity.

4.8 Conclusion – You Are the Turning Point:

You are not just part of your family's story, you are the rewrite. The generation that says, "It ends with me." By choosing expression over repression, connection over concealment, you are forging a future where truth is welcomed, not feared. Breaking the cycle of silence is not easy, but it is profoundly worthwhile. In doing so, you permit yourself to breathe fully, to love loudly, and to live without shame. And maybe, just maybe, someone else in your family or community will one day find the courage to follow your voice into the light.

5. The Long-Term Psychological Impact of Being a Queer Trailblazer

Becoming a trailblazer within the queer community is both a profound honour and a heavy burden. Individuals who step into roles as the "firsts" in various spaces, be it in their family, workplace, or larger societal institutions, often carry the weight of being pioneers for those who will follow. Their courage, determination, and resilience may propel progress, but the emotional toll of blazing new paths can be overwhelming. Understanding the long-term psychological impact on these individuals reveals both the challenges they face and the coping mechanisms they develop.

5.1 The Weight of Being the First:

Being the first openly queer person in a given context can feel like stepping into uncharted territory. These individuals may feel a deep sense of responsibility to represent the entire LGBTQ+ community, despite the diversity within it. The pressure to be exemplary in all aspects of their identity, professional, personal, and political can create a sense of isolation. This experience of being the "first" often brings with it a heightened awareness of being different, which can lead to anxiety, self-doubt, and the feeling that their worth is constantly being measured against an ideal. Over time, this can take a toll on their mental health, as they struggle with the unspoken expectation to educate others or defend their existence.

5.2 Navigating Loneliness in Spaces That Aren't Ready:

Queer trailblazers often find themselves in environments that are not equipped to understand or embrace their identities. Whether in workplaces, schools, or communities, the lack of affirmation can make the experience of being openly queer feel alienating. The emotional exhaustion of navigating these spaces, where acceptance and support are often sparse, can lead to feelings of loneliness and disconnection. For many, this solitude can be compounded by the internalized belief that they must continually prove their worth and place in these spaces, not just as a queer person, but as an individual of value at all.

5.3 The Burden of Visibility and Scrutiny:

With visibility comes scrutiny, and for queer individuals who break barriers, this scrutiny can be unrelenting.

The constant spotlight can create deep vulnerability, with every action and word scrutinized by both allies and critics. The fear of making mistakes or being misunderstood can result in emotional exhaustion, where the individual feels constantly on edge, overcompensating for their perceived "difference." This high level of visibility often comes with microaggressions or outright discrimination, further reinforcing the emotional labour required to navigate these spaces.

5.4 The Psychological Toll of Expectation and Representation:

As the first, there is often the assumption that one person must represent the entire queer community. This expectation can weigh heavily, particularly when the individual is just trying to navigate their own identity. The pressure to conform to a particular model of queerness, whether it's as a role model, activist, or a representation of "success", can lead to significant stress. If their experiences differ from the mainstream queer narrative, they may feel as if they are failing not only themselves, but also the community they are meant to represent. This pressure often leads to a fractured sense of self, where they feel torn between personal identity and public perception.

5.5 Coping with Emotional Labour – Overcoming Exhaustion:

The emotional labour required of queer trailblazers is immense. They must not only deal with their personal emotions and challenges, but often serve as educators or emotional anchors for others who may not yet understand or accept their identities. This added responsibility can result in burnout, where the individual feels depleted and disconnected from their own needs. Over time, the inability to properly care for oneself in the face of these demands can result in long-term emotional exhaustion, which may manifest as depression, anxiety, or a sense of hopelessness about their own mental health.

5.6 Building Resilience in the Face of Adversity:

Despite the challenges, many queer trailblazers develop incredible resilience in response to their experiences. The adversity they face often becomes a source of strength, as they learn to navigate their emotional landscape and find creative ways to cope. Building a support network, whether through queer communities, close friends, or chosen families, can help mitigate feelings of isolation. Additionally, the experience of being a pioneer may foster a deeper sense of self-awareness, as individuals learn to assert their boundaries, prioritize self-care, and confront their fears. This process of personal growth can lead to a strong sense of self-efficacy and confidence, allowing them to continue advocating for others without sacrificing their own well-being.

5.7 The Long-Term Effects on Identity Development:

The long-term psychological impact of being a queer trailblazer also manifests in the individual's evolving sense of identity. As the first to be open about, their queerness in a given context, these individuals often undergo a process of self-discovery that can span years. The journey may involve unlearning societal expectations, confronting internalized homophobia, and finding empowerment in their uniqueness.

This evolving sense of self can be both empowering and unsettling, as it requires the individual to confront societal norms and embrace an identity that may not always align with mainstream expectations. Over time, however, this process can lead to greater authenticity, as they carve out their own path within the queer community.

5.8 Redefining Success and Healing from the Strain:

For many queer trailblazers, success becomes a constantly shifting goal. In the early stages, success may be defined by acceptance and visibility. However, as time passes, success may take on new meanings, including finding peace with their identity and building fulfilling, supportive relationships. Healing from the emotional strain of being a trailblazer often involves redefining what success means on their own terms. It also requires confronting the emotional scars that may have been left by years of struggle and building a sense of inner peace that transcends external validation.

5.9 The Legacy of Pioneering Queerness:

In the long term, queer trailblazers often find solace in the knowledge that their journey has paved the way for others. Their struggles, sacrifices, and perseverance contribute to a larger cultural shift, allowing future generations to live with greater acceptance and understanding. This legacy, while emotionally taxing in the moment, ultimately brings a sense of pride and accomplishment. Over time, queer trailblazers may come to understand their role in the broader narrative of queer history, seeing their sacrifices as the building blocks of a more inclusive future.

In the end, the psychological impact of being a queer trailblazer is multifaceted, reflecting the complexity of navigating both personal and societal expectations. While the emotional and mental health challenges can be profound, so too are the rewards that come with paving the way for others. The journey of being the first is one of growth, resilience, and ultimately, transformation.

* Breaking Silence, Shaping History – When Queer Voices Rose, but not limited to:

Harvey Milk:

In 1977, Harvey Milk became the first openly gay man elected to public office in California, serving on the San Francisco Board of Supervisors. His election was a milestone for LGBTQ+ representation in politics. Milk's openness about his sexuality challenged societal norms and inspired countless individuals to embrace their identities. Tragically, his life was cut short when he was assassinated in 1978, but his legacy endures as a symbol of courage and advocacy for LGBTQ+ rights.

Barney Frank:

Barney Frank, a U.S. Congressman from Massachusetts, came out as gay in 1987, becoming one of the first openly gay members of the U.S. Congress. His decision to come out was met with both support and criticism.

Frank continued to serve in Congress until 2013, using his platform to advocate for LGBTQ+ rights and financial reform.

Anderson Cooper:

CNN anchor Anderson Cooper publicly came out as gay in 2012, stating, "The fact is, I'm gay, always have been, always will be." His announcement was met with widespread support, and he continued to be a respected journalist. Cooper's openness contributed to the visibility and normalization of LGBTQ+ individuals in mainstream media.

Raquel Willis:

Raquel Willis, an African American writer and transgender rights activist, became the first trans woman to lead Out magazine as executive editor. Her memoir, The Risk It Takes To Bloom, was published in 2023, and she was named one of TIME Magazine's 100 most influential people, in 2025.

Paris Lees:

Paris Lees is an English author, journalist, and transgender rights activist. She became the first trans columnist at Vogue and the first trans woman to present shows on BBC Radio 1 and Channel 4. Her memoir, What It Feels Like For a Girl, was published in 2021, offering insights into her journey and advocating for trans rights.

Marsha P. Johnson:

A Black transgender activist and key figure in the 1969 Stonewall uprising, Marsha's visibility and activism laid the groundwork for modern LGBTQ+ movements.

Sylvia Rivera:

Latina-American transgender activist who co-founded STAR (Street Transvestite Action Revolutionaries) with Marsha P. Johnson. Rivera was a fierce advocate for trans rights before it was even part of mainstream conversation.

Ian McKellen:

The legendary British actor came out as gay in 1988 during a BBC interview. Since then, he has used his global platform to advocate for LGBTQ+ rights.

George Takei:

The "Star Trek" actor came out publicly in 2005 and has since been a strong advocate for both LGBTQ+ rights and Asian-American representation.

Billie Jean King:

Tennis icon who was publicly outed in 1981, but later embraced advocacy for LGBTQ+ equality and women's rights in sports.

Ellen DeGeneres:

In 1997, comedian and actress Ellen DeGeneres came out as a lesbian during an appearance on "The Oprah Winfrey Show" and through her character on the sitcom "Ellen." The revelation was groundbreaking, making her one of the first openly gay lead characters on television. While she faced backlash and a temporary career setback, DeGeneres eventually returned to prominence with "The Ellen DeGeneres Show," becoming a beloved figure and advocate for LGBTQ+ rights.

Carl Nassib:

In 2021, NFL player Carl Nassib came out as gay, becoming the first active NFL player to do so. His announcement broke barriers in professional sports, where LGBTQ+ representation has long been minimal, and he has since used his platform to advocate for inclusion and support LGBTQ+ youth.

Lux Pascal:

Lux Pascal, a Chilean actress and sister of actor Pedro Pascal, came out as transgender in 2021. She has spoken about the importance of her brother's support during her transition and has become an advocate for transgender rights. Lux's visibility and advocacy have contributed to greater awareness and acceptance of transgender individuals in Latin America and beyond.

Laverne Cox:

Laverne Cox became a trailblazer as the first transgender person nominated for a Primetime Emmy Award in an acting category for her role in Orange Is the New Black. Her visibility has been pivotal in increasing awareness and acceptance of transgender individuals in mainstream media.

Janet Mock:

As a writer, director and producer for the groundbreaking series Pose, Janet Mock became the first trans woman of colour hired as a writer for a TV series. Her memoir, Redefining Realness, became a New York Times bestseller, and she signed a historic deal with Netflix, further amplifying trans narratives in media.

Marco Calvani:

Italian playwright and director Marco Calvani returned to acting in Netflix's The Four Seasons, portraying a flamboyant and emotionally layered character.

His performance was lauded for its authenticity, and he embraced the role as a symbol of resistance and visibility in a fraught sociopolitical climate.

Chely Wright:

Country music singer Chely Wright publicly came out as a lesbian in 2010, becoming one of the first major country artists to do so. Her memoir, Like Me: Confessions of a Heartland Country Singer, detailed her struggles and triumphs, and she has since become an advocate for LGBTQ+ rights.

Jill Sobule:

Singer-songwriter Jill Sobule, known for her 1995 hit "I Kissed a Girl," was an early voice in LGBTQ+ music. Her songs openly addressed sexuality, influencing numerous artists and contributing to greater visibility for LGBTQ+ individuals in the music industry.

Airyn De Niro:

Airyn De Niro, daughter of Robert De Niro and Toukie Smith, publicly came out as a proud Black trans woman. Navigating the entertainment industry, she aims to amplify Black trans visibility and advocate for inclusive, affirming mental health support.

Lil Nas X:

The rapper came out as gay in 2019, defying stereotypes in hip-hop and Black masculinity. His artistic expression and openness have challenged industry norms.

Elliot Page:

The actor came out as transgender in 2020, becoming one of the most visible trans men in Hollywood. His advocacy and openness have sparked vital conversations on trans masculinity.

Billy Porter:

Openly gay and gender-nonconforming, Porter has used fashion, performance and visibility (especially on Pose), to redefine Black queer excellence in mainstream media.

Troye Sivan:

Australian pop singer and actor who came out as gay in 2013 and has been central to a new wave of LGBTQ+ youth visibility in music and media.

India Willoughby:

The UK's first transgender national newsreader and a pioneering voice in British media.

Jóhanna Sigurðardóttir:

Became the world's first openly gay head of government when she was elected Prime Minister of Iceland in 2009.

Pete Buttigieg:

The first openly gay U.S. presidential candidate to win a state in a major party primary, and now serves as U.S. Secretary of Transportation.

Munroe Bergdorf:

British model and activist who became the first transgender model for L'Oréal and is a vocal advocate for intersectional feminism and racial justice.

Angelica Ross:

Trans actress and tech entrepreneur who uses her platform to centre Black trans lives, particularly through TransTech Social Enterprises.

Jazz Jennings:

One of the youngest and most visible transgender people in media, known for her reality show I Am Jazz and early public advocacy.

"To be the first is to carry both the weight of the world and the promise of a future that will no longer need to carry such burdens. The struggle of today becomes the foundation for tomorrow's freedom, and in that legacy, we find our true strength." – Anonymous

Chapter 26

Queer Love in War and Conflict Zones

---

1. Hidden Relationships in Oppressive Regimes

***Echo Question:**

What does it take to love when the world around you insists that your love is a crime?

In places where same-sex love is criminalized or deeply stigmatized, queer individuals are often forced to navigate their relationships in secrecy, carrying the weight of societal and legal threats on their shoulders. These individuals form bonds that are as profound as any other, yet they are shaped by fear, subterfuge, and the constant risk of being discovered. Their love exists not in the open, but in the shadows, where even the smallest gesture can mean the difference between life and imprisonment. The survival of queer love in these environments is not just an act of defiance, it is a testament to the resilience of human connection.

1.1 Survival Through Code – Coded Language and Hidden Gestures:

Oppressive regimes historically treat queer relationships as subversive or criminal acts. From the brutal laws in Nazi Germany to the more modern-day persecution in countries like Russia and Uganda, queer people face immense challenges in expressing their love and desires openly. In some places, mere acknowledgement of one's sexuality can result in arrest, exile, or even execution. The criminalization of same-sex love is not merely a legal issue but a social one, deeply embedded in the moral fabric of a society that punishes difference. For those living in these environments, even the most private expression of affection, holding hands, sharing a glance, or uttering the words "I love you", becomes an act of rebellion.

In these conditions, love is not always expressed in grand gestures or public declarations. It is hidden behind closed doors, in whispered conversations, and in coded language. In authoritarian regimes, where fear of surveillance and punishment is omnipresent, queer people have learned to craft their own methods of maintaining relationships without attracting the attention of the state or their communities. A glance, a touch, a knowing smile, these can be the most visible expressions of love for those who cannot afford to be open. The very act of living in love becomes an intimate act of resistance, a quiet, but powerful assertion of identity against a society that seeks to erase it.

1.2 The Power of Trust – Intimacy as Resistance:

In addition to secrecy, love in these environments is often an act of profound trust. The risk involved in revealing one's true identity to another person is immense.

To be loved by someone who understands and accepts the reality of one's life can feel like the rarest form of intimacy, one that is forged not in the light of public recognition, but in the refuge of shared understanding. For those in relationships that must remain hidden, the bonds they create are often more intense, as each moment of affection is precious, fleeting, and filled with the knowledge, that it could all be lost in an instant. This sense of transience deepens the emotional connection, turning even the smallest acts of intimacy into acts of monumental significance.

1.3 Hidden Networks – Love Beyond Borders:

In many ways, these hidden relationships mirror the resilience of queer communities throughout history. In the face of danger, marginalization, and oppression, love has not only survived, but flourished in secret. From the underground queer networks that existed during the Holocaust to the safe houses and clandestine meeting spaces for LGBTQ+ individuals in contemporary authoritarian states, the survival of queer love in oppressive regimes is a story of courage, ingenuity and hope. These relationships, though unseen by the world, carry a profound significance, they are a rebellion against a society that would rather deny their existence. They are the quiet revolutions, lived in whispers and shadows, which prove love not only endures under pressure, but evolves into a force of fearless resistance.

1.4 The Psychological Cost – Love Under Siege:

However, the strain of living in hiding takes its toll. The psychological and emotional cost of maintaining secret relationships is immense. The fear of being discovered can cause profound anxiety and depression, creating a constant state of alertness that interferes with the ability to live a full life. In some cases, this stress leads to feelings of isolation, as queer individuals navigate not only the challenges of oppressive laws, but also the internal conflict between their need for love and their desire for self-preservation. Even within these secret relationships, the fear of betrayal or the collapse of trust can lead to further emotional strain. For those in hiding, love becomes both a source of strength and a vulnerability, providing solace, but also heightening the risk of exposure. In such fragile spaces, love is both sanctuary and sacrifice, nourishing the soul while quietly eroding it. And yet, in the shadows where love must hide, its persistence becomes an act of quiet resistance, a testament to the human need for connection, even in the harshest conditions.

1.5 The Enduring Power of Hidden Love – A Legacy of Resistance:

At the same time, the survival of queer love in these oppressive circumstances is not simply about individual survival, but about the survival of a community. In many places, queer individuals come together in hidden spaces, forming underground networks that provide safety, solidarity and resources. These networks, whether through coded language, secret gatherings, or encrypted communication, serve as lifelines for those in peril. They represent more than just a means of surviving, they are a reminder that love, even in its most hidden form, can create bonds of resistance that challenge the systems of oppression attempting to destroy it. The existence of these secret networks is a testament to the enduring power of love and the relentless desire for connection, even in the face of overwhelming adversity.

1.6 Love as Revolution – The Power of Hidden Relationships:

While the love of queer individuals in oppressive regimes may remain hidden from the broader public, it is not forgotten. Over time, these hidden relationships contribute to the wider struggle for recognition and acceptance. The courage to love, even in secret, creates the foundation for future generations to live openly and proudly. Each hidden relationship, each act of love in defiance of persecution, adds to the narrative of resistance that has been woven throughout history. Queer love, whether visible or concealed, is an act of defiance, a declaration that love will not be silenced or erased.

1.7 Conclusion – The Quiet Strength of Hidden Love:

For those living under oppressive regimes, love remains a precious and fragile thing. It is not just a form of survival, it is an act of defiance, an assertion of humanity against forces that seek to deny it. These relationships are not just hidden, they are vital. They are the lifeblood of a community that, despite every attempt to destroy it, continues to love, resist, and endure. The stories of these hidden relationships are a reminder that love, in any form, is a revolutionary act that no regime can ever fully suppress.

* Code Names and Cover Stories – How Queer Love Spoke in Whispers to Survive:

Cairo, Egypt – 1999:

In one queer underground circle, the phrase "Are you a friend of Dorothy's?" was updated to "Do you read Khaled's poems?", a coded reference to the homoerotic undertones in Khaled Mutawakel's banned writings. Answering "yes" often meant, I'm queer too.

Sarajevo, Bosnia – 1996:

Queer women who lived together post-war often introduced each other as "widows from the same battalion." The lie, tragic as it was, shielded them from questions, and allowed them a sliver of domestic peace.

Aleppo, Syria – 2014:

Texting the emoji of a "lemon" followed by a "palette" became a secret code among queer youth. The lemon represented sour societal expectations, and the palette symbolized hidden identities. Together, it meant: "I see you. I'm one of you."

Kabul, Afghanistan – 2021:

Lovers would trade books with highlighted lines from Persian poets like Rumi or Hafez. A single underlined verse could mean "I'm waiting for you tonight," or "I still love you, no matter what comes." These coded exchanges became essential under Taliban resurgence, where queer love was not only forbidden, but criminalized, books became both shield and signal, turning poetry into a language of survival.

Poland – 1980s Solidarity Era:

Gay men joined Catholic pilgrimage groups to avoid suspicion, referring to each other as "confession partners." The church, ironically, became one of the only places to safely meet without being noticed by the state.

Uganda – 2010s:

In the wake of anti-LGBTQ+ legislation, some queer people would refer to themselves as "kitchen sisters", a term drawn from the domestic, "invisible" roles women played in traditional households. It was quiet, but affirming.

Russia – Soviet Era:

Gay poets would distribute samizdat (clandestine self-published books) with poems marked with invisible ink or slight "errors", where a single swapped pronoun unlocked an entire queer love story.

Venezuela – Crisis Years, 2015 to 2020:

Queer men working in aid convoys called each other "weather scouts", a euphemism that meant: He knows when the climate is hostile. He'll warn you before the storm hits.

Israel–Palestine – Ongoing Conflict:

Some queer Palestinians and Israelis in forbidden cross-border relationships used the phrase "olive trees need tending" to mean, "Let's meet where no one watches." In a region marked by surveillance and conflict, love survived in metaphor, quiet, coded, and rooted in the land.

Myanmar – Military Junta Rule:

Drag performers used coded performance names that reflected ancient folk spirits known for gender-bending stories. One underground performer went by "The Laughing Monk", a sly reference to a queer Burmese ghost said to bring mischief and love.

Iran – Present Day:

Within some queer circles, asking "Are you in colour?" signalled if someone was open about their identity. Those "in colour" were seen as brave beacons in a country that insisted everything stay in black and white.

Bosnia – 1990s Balkan War:

Two women, both medics on opposing sides, used the term "bandage exchange" when sneaking letters to one another hidden inside first aid kits. It was a healing ritual and an act of defiance. Each note was laced with coded affection, shared fears, and fleeting glimpses of a future beyond the battlefield.

Lebanon – Civil War Period:

Queer men organizing underground meetups called them "book swaps," even when no books changed hands. A single red ribbon in a jacket pocket meant the "library" was open.

Ethiopia – Tigray Conflict:

Queer youth used TikTok dances as coded performances, certain repeated gestures stood in for identity flags. To followers who knew, it was visibility; to everyone else, it was just rhythm.

South Korea – Military Service:

Conscripts secretly dating each other used the term "extra drill practice" as a cover for nightly rendezvous. Their relationship "fitness" became a running private joke.

Chechnya – Anti-LGBTQ+ Purges:

In digital chatrooms, trans women used chess-piece emojis to signal safety, "the knight" meant "I'm moving", "the queen" meant "I'm safe." The system protected many from entrapment.

Colombia – Guerrilla Territories:

Queer rebels referred to one another as "shadow mirrors," reflecting both recognition and risk. A carved star on a tree near a meeting point was a code for "You are not alone."

Ukraine – Ongoing Conflict:

In besieged zones, queer artists developed chalk murals that could only be seen under UV light. Messages like "We survive in colour" would glow when the bombs stopped and the lights came back.

2. Love, Resistance and Survival – Queer Stories from Conflict Areas

***Echo Question:**

How does love fuel the courage to resist, even in the face of violence and oppression?

In the ruins of Aleppo, Syria, amid mortar fire and collapsed homes, a young gay couple, Samir and Khaled, maintained their relationship through scribbled poems left beneath a brick by a market wall. Their story, passed through surviving friends and digital remnants, is not about survival alone, but about the audacity of love. In a city stripped of safety, they clung to the smallest gestures of tenderness. Their romance was not only hidden from a regime hostile to queerness, but from the violence of war itself, which demanded emotional silence. Love became a resistance not just to political structures, but to despair. Though Samir was eventually killed in a bombing, Khaled smuggled out their final poem, now etched onto the underside of his only remaining shoe.

2.1 The Rebel's Embrace – Queer Love in Revolutionary Circles:

During Colombia's decades-long armed conflict, guerrilla groups often strictly regulated interpersonal relationships within their ranks. For Natalia and Camila, two female fighters within a leftist rebel faction, secrecy was essential. Their relationship was sustained through coded glances and shared duties that offered brief privacy. Despite the brutal realities of jungle warfare, their emotional bond became a source of power. Camila would later write in her testimony that "we found in each other a reason to live beyond the ideology." Their love didn't compromise the cause, they believed it strengthened it. When the group began internal discussions about inclusivity, Natalia and Camila's visibility helped spark conversations about queer rights within revolutionary spaces that had long erased them.

2.2 Dancing Between Checkpoints – The Dual Identity of Queer Palestinians:

In occupied territories, queer Palestinians like Rami and Noor face a dual oppression, from the Israeli military occupation and from conservative cultural norms. Rami, a drag performer by night in Ramallah, and Noor, a university student active in civil resistance, met through an underground art collective. They described their relationship as a "dance between checkpoints," both literal and metaphorical. Their weekends were sometimes spent weaving through military roadblocks just to share a few hours together. Their story illustrates a complex kind of resistance, where survival is found in stolen time, and political expression fuses with personal liberation. For them, performance wasn't escapism, it was a declaration of selfhood in a system designed to erase it.

2.3 The Campfire Pact – LGBTQ+ Refugees and Unlikely Kinships:

In Kenya's Kakuma refugee camp, known for both its LGBTQ+ population and incidents of targeted violence, a group of queer refugees formed what they called a "campfire pact." Each night, they gathered around a small flame, taking turns reading passages from books, telling stories, and reaffirming their right to exist. Among them were Ahmed, a gay man from Somalia, Daisy, a trans woman from Uganda, and a lesbian couple from Rwanda, Esperance and Fanny. Their relationships blended romantic, platonic, and familial love, all bound by the intensity of shared trauma and survival. Though the camp was meant as a shelter, it became a second battleground. Within this fragile space, queer love, romantic or not, became a structure of emotional resistance and affirmation. They created their own rituals, their own holidays, and their own "family photos", drawn in the sand when cameras were forbidden.

2.4 Hearts Across Trenches – The Unlikely Archive of Digital Love:

In Ukraine during the current war, queer couples like Dima and Anton have documented their relationship through encrypted messaging apps, coded emojis and a private online diary, they call "The Love Log." Dima, a soldier, and Anton, a schoolteacher, have remained apart for most of the conflict, yet their relationship has survived thanks to technology. Their diary contains photos of everyday objects, a cracked mug, a scarf, a tree near the checkpoint, which carry encoded emotional meaning.

In one entry, Anton writes: "You're the blue thread in my battlefield uniform." They use emojis only they understand, a secret language formed during trauma. Their story speaks to the modern resilience of queer love in wartime, a love sustained not through touch, but through encrypted metaphors and pixels. It's a digital defiance against erasure.

2.5 Echoes of Resistance – When Love Becomes a Weapon:

Queer love in conflict zones isn't always about romantic partnerships. Sometimes, it manifests in the form of collective resistance. In Myanmar, a network of LGBTQ+ activists embedded within the pro-democracy movement has used drag performance as protest, staging underground shows to raise money for political prisoners. They call it "Glamour Against Guns." For them, the boldness of queer visibility in a repressive environment is an act of layered defiance, against the military junta, against patriarchy and against societal erasure. Their shows combine satire, pain, and joy, each dance number a coded message, each costume stitched with stories of the disappeared. In this space, love becomes an act of survival and political insurgency.

2.6 Conclusion:

These stories remind us that queer love in conflict zones is never just about intimacy. It is testimony, resistance, legacy. In places where queerness is criminalized or culturally taboo, even a simple declaration of love can be a revolutionary act. From poems in rubble to glances through rifle scopes, each story is a testament to what it means to choose love in the most unloving of circumstances. The courage to love and to survive, where everything conspires against it is not just powerful, it is sacred. Even in silence, queer love survives, resistance, memory and hope, passed down in quiet defiance.

3. The Role of Underground LGBTQ+ Networks

*Echo Question:

What does it mean to find family in a world that seeks to erase your existence, and how do these hidden bonds quietly redefine who you are?

In times of war and political upheaval, formal structures collapse. For LGBTQ+ individuals, this often means the disappearance of even the most basic protections. But in those gaps, something extraordinary often forms, underground queer networks built on trust, secrecy and survival. These networks are rarely mapped, yet they stretch across borders and generations. They take shape in coded conversations at cafes, in encrypted group chats, and in the safety of whispered introductions. The formation of these communities is often spontaneous, born out of need, but what begins as an emergency lifeline frequently becomes a source of long-term resistance and emotional anchoring. In places like Iran, Chechnya and parts of East Africa, where being queer is punishable by prison or death, such networks have been known to smuggle people out of danger, offer housing and even coordinate underground pride events. They are the arteries through which hope flows when the world has turned its back.

3.1 Safe Houses and Shadow Homes – The Architecture of Sanctuary:

In Cairo, an apartment painted in warm earth tones becomes a sanctuary by night. In Kampala, a tailor's back room doubles as both a workshop and a shelter. Across conflict zones, safe houses operate under layers of disguise, masquerading as businesses, storage units, or extended family dwellings. These spaces, quietly operated by underground LGBTQ+ networks, offer temporary refuge for those fleeing violence, conversion therapy, or the threat of being outed. Organizers often work without funding or recognition, relying on old-school word of mouth and encrypted communication. But their commitment transforms walls into sanctuaries. These homes don't just offer safety; they become spaces where queerness is affirmed rather than hidden, where people can sleep without fear and rediscover their own identity in the quiet moments between danger.

3.2 Digital Resistance – The New Frontier of Underground Networks:

The internet has changed the game for underground LGBTQ+ organizing. While digital surveillance is a threat, the online world has also allowed queers in conflict zones to find each other across city lines and national borders. In Syria and Iraq, activists use disappearing-message apps and password-protected forums to share safe routes, coordinate shelter, and raise emergency funds. In Russia, queer youth trapped under surveillance algorithms find solace in coded TikTok content and encrypted Discord servers where they speak freely, even if just for minutes at a time. These networks are more than logistical, they're emotionally vital. When someone posts a message like "I'm still here. I'm still me," and others respond in solidarity, it becomes clear that digital resistance is not cold or impersonal. It's tender, vulnerable, and alive. The digital space becomes a realm of possibility when the physical world is filled with closed doors.

3.3 Historical Lineages – Queer Codes and Secret Societies:

Underground LGBTQ+ networks are not a new invention. History offers countless examples of secret queer societies flourishing under the noses of repressive powers. In Nazi Germany, coded signals and rendezvous points helped queer people find each other amidst persecution. During apartheid South Africa, Black queer communities created informal "tea rooms" in townships, places where music, gossip and gender fluidity, could be safely expressed behind guarded doors. These historical precedents inform modern efforts, creating a kind of ancestral blueprint. The shared knowledge of how to hide, how to signal, how to survive, is passed on like a secret spellbook. Understanding these lineages empowers today's networks. They are not acting in isolation, but as part of a long and defiant continuum.

3.4 The Emotional Backbone – Bonds Forged in Secrecy:

What holds these underground networks together is not just strategy, it's intimacy. Bonds are forged in the act of hiding, of watching out for each other, of sitting in the dark with someone when no one else will. In the refugee corridors between Afghanistan and Pakistan, young queer people speak of strangers who became family in a matter of hours.

A place to sleep, a phone number to call, a scarf exchanged as a signal of alliance. These relationships may never be documented, but they are the emotional backbone of the queer resistance. They replace institutions that failed them with something far more personal, radical care. When state systems criminalize you, it is often only the kindness of another queer person, just as afraid, that keeps you alive. That kind of solidarity builds a legacy. These intimate bonds become more than survival, they are the foundation of a resilient, unbreakable community.

3.5 The Risk and the Courage – When Safety Is Rebellion:

To be part of an underground LGBTQ+ network in a conflict zone is to take risks every day. Shelter operators face imprisonment. Communication organizers are tracked and targeted. Sometimes, safe houses are raided, and the people within them disappear. The cost is staggering. And yet, the networks continue, because their very existence is an act of rebellion. Safety is not just about survival, it becomes a political statement. To carve out space where queerness is nurtured rather than denied is to reject the violence of the regime. These networks defy erasure with every act of kindness, every smuggled meal, every quiet affirmation whispered in the dark. Each brave act says, we exist, we resist and even here, especially here, queer life is worth protecting, worth nurturing and worth fighting for, no matter the shadows cast by fear or oppression.

3.6 The Future of Underground Queer Networks – From Secrecy to Solidarity:

As the global political climate shifts, underground LGBTQ+ networks evolve too. Some, like those in Ukraine and Lebanon, are transitioning from secrecy to semi-public community work, blending visibility with caution. Others remain deep in the shadows, especially in areas where surveillance has intensified. But the long-term vision for many of these networks is transformation, from lifelines into platforms for systemic change. Organizers dream of a day when safe houses become community centers, when emergency shelters become co-ops, and when coded messages become public declarations. Until then, they continue to hold the line, quietly, bravely, and without applause. Their power lies not just in their secrecy, but in the unwavering belief that even in the darkest places, queer connection can plant the seeds of revolution.

* Interactive History Thread – The Hidden Threads of Resistance:

Did you know that during the Holocaust, while LGBTQ+ individuals were among the most persecuted, secret support circles formed within concentration camps? Some prisoners reportedly left coded messages in personal diaries, helped each other endure solitary punishments, or shared food and protection, though much of this history was deliberately destroyed or ignored after liberation.

Look Deeper:

Search for stories of Gad Beck, a gay Jewish resistance fighter who helped his partner escape capture, only to be caught himself. His story is one of courage, heartbreak, and unexpected survival.

* Interactive History Thread – Love Beneath the Veil, Iran's Trans Underground:

Did you know that while homosexuality is criminalized in Iran, transgender identity is paradoxically state-sanctioned? As a result, some queer Iranians have turned to underground networks for hormone access, emotional community, or even temporary refuge while navigating gender and sexuality under constant surveillance.

Look Deeper:

Explore the life of Maryam Khatoon Molkara, a trans activist who lobbied the Ayatollah in person, and won legal protections for gender reassignment in the 1980s. Her story lives in the shadow of an oppressed queer reality.

* Interactive History Thread – The Lavender Scare, Queer Espionage in the Cold War:

Did you know that during the Cold War, hundreds of queer Americans were purged from government roles in what became known as the Lavender Scare? Ironically, some were later recruited into covert networks, using their social marginalization to navigate double lives in espionage.

Look Deeper:

Research the relationship between queerness and intelligence work, many queer operatives formed informal networks of mutual protection, passing coded messages that mimicked traditional spy-craft. Explore how these covert relationships between queer spies and government officials often blurred the lines between survival and loyalty.

* Interactive History Thread – Queer Kinship in Syria's Shadow Zones:

Did you know that in the aftermath of the Syrian civil war, underground shelters specifically for LGBTQ+ individuals were created in abandoned buildings and border towns? These havens weren't just physical spaces, they were forged through whispers, nicknames, and instinctual trust.

Look Deeper:

Seek out the story of "the house with no mirrors" in Aleppo, rumoured to be a queer-run safehouse where survivors helped others cross into Lebanon. The mirrors were removed to reduce panic, dysphoria, and surveillance risk.

* Interactive History Thread – Rainbow Scarves of the Spanish Civil War:

Did you know that during the Spanish Civil War, some anti-fascist groups used coloured accessories, like discreet rainbow-hued scarves or handkerchiefs, as covert queer identifiers in solidarity? Though never officially recognized, these were lifelines of silent acknowledgment.

Look Deeper:

Investigate the influence of queer anarchist thinkers like Federico García Lorca, whose poetry and life became quiet banners of defiance after his execution by Francoist forces.

* Interactive History Thread – Same-Sex Love in the Vietnam War Trenches:

Did you know that personal letters recovered from Vietnam War soldiers reveal hidden queer romances? Some correspondences, deliberately coded, describe deep emotional bonds between same sex soldiers who found intimacy amid violence and fear.

Look Deeper:

Look into the "Dear John" letters that never reached their intended recipients, confiscated or censored, yet later unearthed by historians. Many remain unsigned, but pulse with longing and humanity. Explore the impact of wartime censorship on queer communication and how these letters became symbols of resistance.

* Interactive History Thread – The Hidden Queer History of WWII Resistance Fighters:

Did you know that many LGBTQ+ individuals served in resistance movements during WWII, though their identities were often concealed to protect both their mission and their safety? Some of these fighters, particularly in France, would use subtle romantic codes or shared symbols to signal solidarity within covert operations.

Look Deeper:

Discover the secretive lives of members of the Maquis, the French resistance movement, and the untold stories of queer activists like Violette Morris, who risked everything to sabotage Nazi forces while maintaining relationships in secrecy.

*Interactive History Thread – The Queer Underground of Post-Apartheid South Africa:

Did you know that during South Africa's transition from apartheid, some underground LGBTQ+ groups worked side by side with anti-apartheid movements to challenge both racial and sexual oppression? Queer activists, many of whom were black, forged strong bonds with the broader struggle for liberation.

Look Deeper:

Being gay and Black meant double persecution, one man stood at the intersection of battles.

Investigate the life of Simon Nkoli, an anti-apartheid activist and openly gay man who was instrumental in creating South Africa's first queer liberation group. His work shaped the post-apartheid LGBTQ+ rights landscape.

* Interactive History Thread – Queer Love in the Polish Resistance. Hidden and Forbidden:

Did you know that during the Nazi occupation of Poland, secret "love letters" were smuggled across resistance lines, hidden under coded names or torn pages from banned books? Queer love and solidarity were maintained even as love letters between same-sex lovers defied the regime's brutality.

Look Deeper:

Explore the fate of the Grey Ranks, a Polish resistance group, and how their underground network of coded love letters survived their harrowing circumstances, kept hidden from Nazis while offering profound intimacy.

* Interactive History Thread – The Queer Role in the 1968 Mexican Student Movement:

Did you know that during the 1968 Mexican student protests, LGBTQ+ activists played an unseen role in shaping the protests' strategies, using their marginalized position to form solidarity through alternative networks of resistance? Queer activists helped to fuel an emotional and ideological fight for freedom against state violence.

Look Deeper:

Examine the hidden contributions of the Movimiento Homosexual de Acción Revolucionaria (MHAR) in Mexico, who participated in political demonstrations, and later helped build LGBTQ+ activism into broader social justice movements in Latin America. Explore how MHAR's underground work influenced the larger struggle for human rights in Mexico, sparking global solidarity.

* Interactive History Thread – Love Under Fire, Same-Sex Relationships in the Spanish Inquisition:

Did you know that during the Spanish Inquisition, records of same-sex relationships were often hidden within confessions, documents, or trials? Some queer individuals took extreme risks to protect their partners, even fabricating elaborate cover stories to survive persecution.

Look Deeper:

Delve into the often forgotten stories of those who resisted persecution during the Inquisition.

Explore the historical legacy of sodomitic trials during the Inquisition and the underground queer alliances formed by those at risk, many of whom became saints, martyrs, or secret patrons of queer liberation in Spain.

4. The Psychological Toll of War on Queer Love and Identity

***Echo Question:**

How do we heal from the scars of war when the very essence of who we are, our love, is constantly under siege?

In conflict zones, the fear of discovery and the constant threat of violence distort the way queer individuals experience love and identity. The inability to express affection freely, to openly define one's relationships, creates an oppressive environment where personal connection becomes a source of deep anxiety. For queer people in war-torn areas, love is often reduced to a secret, an act of defiance performed in the darkness. The psychological toll begins when the mind is continuously preoccupied with survival, forcing individuals to suppress the most basic human need for intimacy. This repression breeds a profound sense of isolation, where even the most intimate moments are shadowed by the fear of being outed or targeted. The love that blossoms in secret spaces becomes intertwined with constant vigilance, a toxic mixture of tenderness and terror that seeps into every aspect of daily life.

4.1 The Fragmentation of Identity – Loss and Displacement:

For queer individuals caught in conflict, the psychological toll of war extends beyond physical harm to a deeper, more insidious emotional destruction, the fragmentation of identity. In the chaos of conflict, one's sense of self can be shattered, as the external violence and oppression become internalized. The complexities of gender and sexuality are erased or distorted in the struggle to survive, and individuals may feel pressured to conform to survival tactics that deny their true selves. This denial of identity is particularly painful for queer individuals, as their love and sexuality have always been central to their sense of self-worth and purpose. Being forced into hiding or adopting false identities can lead to an ongoing sense of dissociation from one's true self, perpetuating feelings of worthlessness or confusion. The destruction of the self during war is not merely about the loss of external security, but also the quiet unravelling of internal peace, as queer individuals are forced to relinquish parts of themselves to the pressures of survival.

4.2 Love as Resistance – Holding on to Humanity in Despair:

In the face of devastation, love becomes not only a personal refuge, but also an act of resistance. For queer individuals in conflict zones, their love is a bold declaration of defiance against a world that seeks to erase them. The resilience of queer relationships, often formed in the most dangerous of circumstances, becomes a symbol of hope in an environment defined by loss and destruction. Despite war's psychological toll, queer people cling to love as a form of resistance against oppression.

This love, though fragile and often fleeting, becomes a vital part of one's humanity. It is an expression of resilience against forces that seek to strip away dignity and identity. The bonds formed in war zones are not only a testament to the strength of queer love, but also a reminder of the power of connection, even in the most hopeless of times.

4.3 The Strain of Secrecy – Balancing Love and Survival:

The psychological weight of secrecy compounds the strain on queer individuals during wartime. Relationships, already under pressure from the external forces of violence and persecution, are further tested by the need to maintain hidden lives. For many, the act of loving in secret is a constant balancing act, where emotional connection clashes with the ever-present need to protect one's identity. The trauma of living in this constant state of concealment is immense. The fear of betrayal or exposure is ever looming, and the relationships formed in these conditions often bear the scars of secrecy. Maintaining such a delicate balance, being true to one's love while also safeguarding survival, leads to heightened levels of stress and anxiety. In some cases, this strain leads to a deterioration of trust and communication, with partners becoming emotionally distant or withdrawn as a defence mechanism against the intense psychological pressure. The psychological toll of this secrecy cannot be underestimated, as it often breeds feelings of paranoia, guilt, and shame, making it difficult to truly connect with loved ones.

4.4 Post-War Trauma – Healing Love After Conflict:

The scars of war remain long after the conflict ends. For many queer individuals, the psychological toll continues as they struggle to rebuild their lives and relationships in the aftermath of war. The trauma of living through conflict lingers, often manifesting in post-traumatic stress disorder (PTSD), depression, and anxiety. The inability to openly love or express one's true identity during the war can create long-lasting emotional scars that affect future relationships. For many, the process of healing is slow and painful, requiring them to confront not only the physical destruction of war, but also the emotional damage inflicted upon their sense of self and their capacity to love. The trauma of war leaves deep emotional wounds that are difficult to heal, especially for those who have had to hide their identities and relationships for survival. As they navigate the difficult journey of post-war recovery, queer individuals are often faced with the challenge of redefining what love and intimacy mean in a world that has stripped them of their sense of security and belonging.

4.5 Love in the Face of Stigma – The Struggle for Acceptance:

Queer individuals in post-conflict zones are often faced with not only the psychological scars of war, but also the societal stigma that continues to marginalize their identities. In many cases, the end of conflict does not bring an end to the discrimination and violence that queer individuals face. As they attempt to rebuild their lives and relationships, queer people often find themselves struggling to gain acceptance in a society that still views them as outsiders. The lingering psychological toll of this societal rejection is immense, and it can make it difficult for queer individuals to fully embrace love in a post-conflict environment.

The ongoing struggle for acceptance, compounded by the trauma of war, leaves many queer individuals feeling isolated and unsupported in their quest for love and belonging. For many, the battle for self-acceptance and societal recognition is a long and painful one, filled with setbacks and challenges that continue to shape their emotional landscape.

4.6 The Resilience of Love – Emerging Stronger from the Ashes:

Despite the immense psychological toll of war, there is a quiet strength in the way queer individuals navigate love in conflict zones. The bonds formed in times of hardship, though tested by fear, secrecy, and trauma, can emerge stronger in the aftermath. Queer love, though scarred by the psychological toll of conflict, remains resilient. The emotional scars, though deep, become a testament to the strength of human connection and the unwavering power of love. For those who survive war, love becomes not only a personal refuge, but also a source of empowerment, enabling them to rebuild their lives and relationships in ways that are more authentic and meaningful. The trauma of war, while shaping the way love is experienced, does not erase the fundamental need for connection. It is through love that queer individuals find the strength to heal and rebuild, emerging from the ashes of war with a renewed sense of purpose and resilience.

5. LGBTQ+ Refugees and Their Struggles for Safety

***Echo Question:**

What does safety look like for those who have been forced to leave behind the love they once knew in search of a place where they can simply exist?

For most refugees, fleeing war or political violence is a terrifying decision born of necessity. But for LGBTQ+ individuals, the layers of risk are compounded. Not only are they running from bombs, soldiers, and collapsing infrastructure, they are also fleeing families, communities, or governments that criminalize their identities. In many cases, they must hide their queerness even as they seek asylum, fearing that to be seen as LGBTQ+ might endanger their chances of protection or provoke violence in refugee camps. For queer refugees, escape isn't just a matter of borders, it's a negotiation between survival and silence.

5.1 Camp Isn't Safe When You're Queer:

Refugee camps are meant to be temporary havens, but for LGBTQ+ individuals, they often become new spaces of trauma. Reports from camps in Kenya, Jordan, Turkey and beyond, show a disturbing pattern, queer refugees being harassed, assaulted, or ostracized by fellow displaced persons or even staff. Trans refugees, in particular, face unique challenges, from being placed in gender-inappropriate housing to being denied hormone therapy. Without explicit protections and trained personnel, the promise of safety remains unfulfilled. It's not uncommon for LGBTQ+ refugees to isolate themselves, avoid communal facilities, or even go back into hiding, just to stay alive. Refugee camps fail LGBTQ+ individuals without proper protections, highlighting the need for targeted support.

5.2 The Waiting Room of Limbo – Asylum, Paperwork and Prejudice:

The asylum process, meant to offer protection, is riddled with bureaucracy, inconsistency and bias. For queer refugees, it becomes a cruel waiting game. Many must "prove" their queerness to sceptical officials, often being asked to recount traumatic events or provide intimate evidence that would never be demanded of a straight applicant. In countries with no formal recognition of LGBTQ+ asylum claims, the barriers are even higher. Legal limbo can last for years, during which refugees are unable to work, study, or move freely. The mental health toll of this uncertainty, compounded by social exclusion and economic precarity, is immense.

5.3 Chosen Family in Transit – Survival Through Solidarity:

In the bleakest conditions, queer refugees find one another. Through whispered conversations, coded language, or cautious nods across crowded rooms, connections form. These chosen families, temporary and fragile though they may be, can be lifelines. Some grassroots collectives offer shelter, access to healthcare, or legal support. Others simply provide companionship, reminding displaced individuals that they are not alone. The creation of queer refugee support groups in cities like Berlin, Nairobi and Toronto, signals a powerful truth, even in exile, queerness builds community. And often, these communities are better at delivering dignity than the systems meant to protect them. In these moments of crisis, chosen family becomes both refuge and rebellion, fostering hope in the darkest times.

5.4 Western Nations and the Myth of Safe Haven:

Many LGBTQ+ refugees look to Western countries as symbols of freedom and safety. But the reality of resettlement is complex. Racism, xenophobia, and transphobia persist even in liberal democracies. Some queer refugees arrive only to be housed in homophobic neighbourhoods, placed in vulnerable jobs, or forced into retraumatizing bureaucratic processes. Cultural disconnects, language barriers, and the absence of social support networks, exacerbate feelings of alienation. True sanctuary requires more than geographic relocation, it demands an environment of understanding, resources, and genuine welcome. Too often, LGBTQ+ refugees find themselves merely surviving in new lands, not truly living. The promise of safety falls short when systemic discrimination and isolation continue to shape the refugee experience.

5.5 Reclaiming Power – Advocacy and the Voices of the Displaced:

Despite the trauma and hardship, many LGBTQ+ refugees are leading movements for change. They are building platforms, sharing their stories, organizing for rights, and refusing to be spoken for. From Ugandan activists organizing safe housing in Kampala to queer Syrians documenting their journeys through art and film, resistance continues. Their stories remind the world that LGBTQ+ refugees are not just victims, they are survivors, organizers, and truth-tellers. Their visibility challenges the idea that queerness and displacement are incompatible, carving out new narratives in the global human rights movement.

5.6 The Cost of Silence – Why Global Accountability Matters:

Without international pressure and structural change, the violence queer refugees face will persist. Governments must not only recognize LGBTQ+ asylum claims, but also fund training for staff, create inclusive shelters and amplify the voices of queer displaced people. Humanitarian organizations must stop treating LGBTQ+ needs as niche or optional. Silence has a cost, and it is measured in lives lost, identities erased, and futures stolen. The world cannot claim to care about human rights while letting queer refugees disappear into shadows.

5.7 What Safety Really Means:

For LGBTQ+ refugees, safety is about more than escaping immediate danger. It's about the right to live authentically, access healthcare, build relationships, secure employment, and move through the world without fear. It's about being seen not just as survivors, but as complete individuals with dreams, talents, and inherent worth. Until this becomes a global norm, queer refugees will not only continue to seek refuge, but also fight for the fundamental right to exist freely.

"Refuge is not just a place, it is the promise that one can live without fear of being erased." – Anonymous

Chapter 27

The Impact of Climate Change on LGBTQ+ Lives

1. Displacement and Homelessness Among Queer People Due to Environmental Crises

The intersection of climate change and LGBTQ+ displacement presents an urgent and often overlooked crisis. Environmental disasters are disproportionately affecting vulnerable communities and queer people, particularly those already marginalized by race, class, or gender identity, face heightened risks during environmental crises. The fragility of safe housing, access to resources, and societal support systems, exacerbates the challenges faced by LGBTQ+ individuals during displacement caused by climate change. As sea levels rise, wildfires rage and extreme weather events become more frequent, queer populations experience displacement not only due to physical destruction, but also because of the deeper social and cultural factors that render them more vulnerable in times of crisis.

1.1 Environmental Crises as a Catalyst for Displacement:

The increasing frequency of environmental disasters such as hurricanes, floods, droughts, and heat waves is forcing millions of people from their homes. For LGBTQ+ individuals, these disasters often come with an added layer of threat, the loss of safety and acceptance. In many parts of the world, LGBTQ+ people already face hostile environments and institutional discrimination. When these communities are displaced, they are often forced into unfamiliar regions, where prejudice and exclusion from mainstream relief efforts further compound their trauma. Queer youth, transgender individuals, and people of colour are disproportionately affected, often ending up in shelters or temporary housing that is unsafe or unwelcoming. These displaced individuals face not only the hardships of physical relocation, but also the psychological toll of losing their support systems and navigating hostile environments during their search for refuge.

1.2 The Unique Vulnerabilities of Queer People in Shelters and Refugee Camps:

Shelters and refugee camps are typically the first places where displaced people seek refuge in the aftermath of an environmental disaster. However, these spaces are often ill-equipped to address the unique needs of LGBTQ+ individuals. Many shelters lack staff trained to provide culturally competent care or to recognize the specific needs of queer people. Transgender individuals, for example, often face significant barriers to accessing safe housing, as many shelters still operate under the outdated gender binary system, forcing trans people into spaces that do not align with their gender identity. This creates an environment where transgender individuals may face harassment, violence, or sexual assault. For queer individuals, displacement trauma is worsened by forced outing in unsafe, unprotective spaces.

In many instances, LGBTQ+ individuals are pushed into hiding their identities to avoid abuse, further deepening the sense of isolation and disconnection. These realities force many queer people to choose between their safety and their identity, often leading them to stay in unsafe conditions simply to avoid the violence that can occur in more hostile environments.

1.3 The Role of Discrimination in Climate Refugee Status:

LGBTQ+ people face barriers when attempting to seek asylum in countries where they may have fled due to both environmental disasters and systemic persecution. In addition to the physical threats posed by climate-related migration, queer refugees often face discrimination in the asylum process. Some countries may not recognize the additional layers of vulnerability that LGBTQ+ individuals face in climate-induced displacement, overlooking the specific dangers these individuals face in receiving countries. For example, asylum policies may fail to consider how LGBTQ+ refugees are more vulnerable to abuse or exploitation, both during transit and in refugee camps. This lack of recognition not only deepens the vulnerability of LGBTQ+ individuals, but also perpetuates cycles of injustice in the asylum process.

When applying for asylum, queer individuals may be asked to provide documentation of their sexual orientation or gender identity, which is not only intrusive, but also impossible for many people to obtain in regions where homosexuality is criminalized or where trans identities are not legally recognized. This structural failure to account for the complex realities faced by LGBTQ+ climate refugees further entrenches the marginalization of queer people in displacement scenarios, leaving them in precarious limbo. This oversight highlights the urgent need for asylum frameworks that protect the rights and identities of LGBTQ+ climate refugees.

1.4 Intersectionality and the Impact of Climate Change on Queer Communities of Colour:

The intersectionality of race, class, gender, and sexual identity is key to understanding how climate change affects LGBTQ+ communities. Displacement due to environmental crises often disproportionately affects communities of colour, and this impact is even more acute for queer people within these communities. Queer people of colour experience compounded discrimination due to both their sexual or gender identity and their race or ethnicity, making them more likely to face exclusion from resources, social support and safety during times of crisis.

Queer refugees from the Global South, who are already marginalized due to colonial histories, racism and anti-queer laws in their home countries, find themselves particularly vulnerable when they flee to other regions. These individuals face complex intersections of exclusion that prevent them from accessing the same humanitarian aid or resources as others. For instance, indigenous queer populations, who have already experienced forced displacement due to environmental destruction, often struggle to find spaces within broader climate activism or relief efforts that do not prioritize their unique cultural and sexual identities. This marginalization demands intersectional solutions that prioritize the needs and voices of queer people of colour in climate justice.

1.5 LGBTQ+ Displacement and the Need for Tailored Support:

While environmental disasters affect all communities, queer people's unique needs must be addressed to ensure equitable access to aid and recovery. Tailored support for LGBTQ+ individuals in displaced settings is critical for their survival and dignity. Humanitarian organizations must recognize the importance of providing safe, inclusive spaces for queer refugees. This includes training staff to understand gender and sexual diversity, providing gender-neutral facilities, and offering mental health services that specifically cater to the experiences of displaced LGBTQ+ individuals.

Moreover, LGBTQ+ climate refugees should have access to support networks that acknowledge their specific vulnerabilities, both physical and emotional. Community-led initiatives, mutual aid groups and LGBTQ+ organizations, have been instrumental in helping displaced queer individuals rebuild their lives after environmental crises. These organizations must be supported and integrated into global climate disaster response frameworks to ensure that LGBTQ+ people are not left behind in these critical times.

1.6 The Urgency of Addressing Queer Displacement in the Climate Crisis:

As climate change accelerates, the displacement of LGBTQ+ individuals will only increase. There is an urgent need for global action to address the intersection of climate change and queer displacement. It is critical for governments, NGOs, and global climate organizations to develop specific frameworks that address the unique challenges faced by LGBTQ+ communities, in the aftermath of environmental crises. These frameworks must ensure that queer individuals are not only protected from physical harm, but also from the social and psychological damage caused by displacement.

As the world grapples with the climate crisis, we cannot afford to overlook the most vulnerable among us. For LGBTQ+ people, displacement is not just a matter of geography; it is a matter of survival. The urgent need for inclusive disaster relief, culturally competent support systems, and recognition of the intersectional impacts of climate change on queer individuals cannot be overstated. Without these considerations, queer people will continue to face disproportionate hardship, perpetuating cycles of exclusion and marginalization in an already fragile world.

* Queer-Led Climate Collectives Around the World:

These aren't just support groups, they're dynamic strategy centers driving survival, liberation and ecological rebirth, shaping a future where queer communities thrive in harmony with the planet:

Queers x Climate – Global:

A global network igniting digital queer climate strikes, storytelling initiatives and decentralized mutual aid systems. They reclaim protest spaces to elevate queer visibility, amplify marginalized voices and unite isolated activists through art, technology and grassroots organizing, cultivating cross-border solidarity and collective action. By linking environmental justice with queer liberation, this movement fosters an inclusive future where both the planet and its marginalized communities can thrive.

Out for Sustainability – U.S. & Global:

Bridges environmental movements with LGBTQ+ advocacy. Their "Fab Planet Summit" merges climate science, policy and queer joy. They also train LGBTQ+ climate leaders and consult on queer-inclusive environmental policy.

Queer Brown Vegan – Online / Ecuador:

A platform led by a nonbinary Latinx climate educator that blends food justice, eco-literacy, and decolonial environmentalism. They spotlight queer and BIPOC stories of sustainability often excluded from mainstream green discourse.

GALANG Philippines – Southeast Asia:

Works directly with grassroots lesbian and trans communities in climate-vulnerable rural areas. They empower queer Filipinas through disaster resilience training, eco-livelihood support and gender-aware emergency housing models.

UK Black Pride's Earth Justice Wing – United Kingdom:

Mobilizes Black LGBTQ+ communities around environmental justice. They create healing-centered eco-events, challenge the whiteness of the climate movement and reframe land justice as a queer right. By centering Black queer voices, they push for a future where climate justice is intersectional and inclusive.

Indigenous Climate Action (Two-Spirit Circle) – North America:

A Two-Spirit-led wing of a larger Indigenous land defence network. They combine ancestral ecological knowledge with direct action to protect water, land, and spiritual sovereignty.

Hāwane Rios & the Mauna Kea Protectors – Hawai'i:

While not exclusively queer-led, this Indigenous Hawaiian climate justice movement includes many queer and trans leaders. They resist colonial land grabs and climate colonialism through ceremony, song, and land occupation.

African EcoFeminist Queer Collective – Sub-Saharan Africa:

A pan-African feminist initiative amplifying the voices of queer women and gender-diverse people in ecological defence. They fight extractive capitalism, protect sacred lands and build regenerative agro-ecologies led by queer farmers.

Climate Justice Taranaki (with Takatāpui Solidarity) – Aotearoa / New Zealand:

Collaborates with Māori takatāpui (queer Indigenous) leaders to challenge fossil fuel expansion. They fuse cultural revival with environmental defence, centering queer decolonial frameworks.

Lesbians Who Tech + Climate Action Cohort – Tech Hubs Globally:

Brings together queer women and nonbinary folks in tech who are developing climate solutions, from data visualization to energy equity platforms. Their goal, coding for climate survival with a queer feminist lens.

TransMutual Aid Network: Fire Season Fund – U.S. West Coast:

Formed during unprecedented wildfire seasons, this collective supports displaced trans individuals with housing, air purifiers, and hormone access. They frame disaster relief as an act of queer love and long-term mutual resilience.

Pride for Climate Brazil – South America:

Emerging movement blending LGBTQ+ visibility with Amazon rainforest activism. They address how queer communities in favelas face unique climate vulnerabilities and demand inclusive urban eco-policies.

Right Side NGO – Armenia:

Right Side NGO, the first trans-led organization in the South Caucasus, champions trans and sex workers' rights in Armenia. They offer legal, social, and psychological support, while advancing human rights protections for transgender people.

Pink Armenia – Armenia:

As the first LGBTQIA+ rights NGO in Armenia, Pink Armenia focuses on advocacy, education, and support services for the LGBTQ+ community. They work closely with Right Side NGO and have been active in promoting legal reforms and social acceptance.

Equal Ground – Sri Lanka:

A non-profit advocacy organization based in Colombo, Equal Ground campaigns for political, social, and civilian rights for LGBTQ+ individuals. They offer trilingual publications and services, aiming to achieve equality through activism, education, and community events.

Helem – Lebanon:

Founded in Beirut, Helem is the first LGBTQIA+ rights NGO in the Arab world. They provide a wide range of services, including emergency response, legal assistance, and mental health support, while advocating for decriminalization and economic empowerment.

Tonga Leitis' Association – Tonga:

The sole LGBTQ+ rights organization in Tonga, TLA, supports the fakaleiti community and runs the Miss Galaxy Pageant to raise awareness. They have been involved in HIV advocacy and cultural events to promote LGBTQ+ visibility.

Queer Nature – United States:

A trans-led nature-based education project focused on critical naturalist studies, nature intimacy, and place-based skills for LGBTQIA+, two-spirit, and nonbinary individuals. They aim to build resilience and foster an "ecology of belonging.

Queer Botany – United Kingdom:

A London-based initiative queering ecology by exploring Walthamstow Marshes and expanding inclusivity in the environmental movement. They blend nature with activism, fostering a space where queer people can reconnect with the land and each other.

Queers 4 Climate – Netherlands:

A Dutch organization advocating for a liveable planet for all communities. They recognize the disproportionate impact of climate breakdown on queer people and aim to educate allies and represent queer voices in the climate movement.

Kapul Champions – Papua New Guinea:

A network advocating for the rights of men with diverse sexualities and transgender people. They focus on community empowerment and address issues related to climate change and social justice.

Sangsan Anakot Yawachon – Thailand / Myanmar:

Founded by Indigenous lesbian activist Matcha Phorn-in, this organization advocates for the rights of Indigenous peoples, especially queer individuals, women and girls, focusing on gender-based violence and land rights.

---

2. Queer Activism in the Climate Justice Movement

Long before "climate justice" became a mainstream demand, queer communities were already resisting environmental harm in deeply interconnected ways. From ACT UP's protests against the toxic neglect of queer bodies during the AIDS crisis to the enduring stewardship of land and water by Indigenous Two-Spirit leaders, queer activism has long challenged the systems, colonialism, capitalism, patriarchy, that threaten both ecosystems and marginalized lives. Though often erased from dominant environmental narratives, queer resistance is foundational to the movement. It brings a critical lens that exposes structural violence and insists that true ecological justice must be inseparable from social liberation, survival, and collective care. Queer activism's deep roots in environmental justice reminds us that ecological health is intertwined with human dignity, demanding holistic, intersectional solutions.

2.1 Queerness as Disruption – Reimagining the Movement's Norms:

Queer activism doesn't just participate in climate justice, it reshapes it. By challenging heteronormative, patriarchal and white-dominated narratives in mainstream environmentalism, queer activists reimagine what justice looks like. They emphasize collectively over individualism, interdependence over dominance, and community care over extraction. This disruption allows climate movements to move beyond narrow, technocratic solutions and instead centre emotional resilience, relational ethics and cultural memory. Through this radical reframing, queer activists push for a climate justice that is truly inclusive, holistic and sustainable for all.

From queer eco-poetry to nonbinary land stewardship, the queer imagination makes space for futures where care, creativity and justice are intertwined. Activists like Pınar Sinopoulos-Lloyd (Queer Nature) show that queering ecology isn't about adding LGBTQ+ people to the picture, it's about rethinking the entire frame.

2.2 Queer-Led Climate Collectives Around the World:

Across continents, queer climate groups are organizing with fierce creativity and care. These aren't just support networks, they're strategy centers for survival and transformation. Queers x Climate, a digital global collective, builds storytelling campaigns, mutual aid networks and protest infrastructures that centre queer visibility and action. Out for Sustainability hosts Queer Climate Justice summits, generates policy recommendations, and fosters research on LGBTQ+ environmental impact. In the Philippines, GALANG supports lesbian and trans climate survivors in rural communities, offering resources and protection where state aid fails. These organizations don't operate on the periphery, they are driving the movement with innovation, solidarity, and justice at the core. From global storytelling campaigns to grassroots support, queer-led climate collectives are reshaping the future of environmental justice with bold, inclusive action.

2.3 Queer Climate Manifestos and Alternative Politics:

Queer-led climate manifestos articulate a different kind of politics, one that isn't rooted in shame, urgency alone, or productivity, but in healing, memory, and mutual liberation. These manifestos, whether written, spoken, danced, or performed, blend rage and joy, grief and hope. They call out the pinkwashing of climate spaces and push for abolitionist, anti-capitalist, and decolonial approaches to environmental action. Activists advocate for land return to Indigenous peoples, reparations for climate-displaced queer folks, and an end to extractivist development projects in Global South regions. Their demands aren't moderate or market-based, they are visionary, and they ask who gets to survive and why. This radical storytelling reshapes the political terrain and reminds the world that queer lives are not disposable in climate negotiations. By centering care, interdependence and imaginative resistance, queer climate manifestos offer not just critique, but blueprints for a liveable and liberated future.

2.4 Intersectionality as Strategy, Not Slogan:

Intersectionality isn't an aesthetic, it's a survival tool. Queer climate activists understand that justice must account for overlapping oppressions, race, class, disability, immigration status and more. Groups like UK Black Pride's Earth Justice Wing and Indigenous Climate Action's Two-Spirit Circle emphasize healing spaces, cultural reclamation, and intergenerational leadership. Their organizing refuses single-issue frameworks. By acknowledging how queer people of colour, especially trans and disabled individuals, are often frontline communities in climate disasters, their work makes movements more responsive, inclusive and powerful. Intersectionality becomes more than language, it becomes a method of organizing where no one is left behind. It turns climate justice into collective action rooted in care, resistance, and belonging.

2.5 Digital Archives and the Power of Storytelling:

Storytelling is resistance. In a world saturated with data and urgency, queer activists use digital platforms to preserve memory, archive care, and create portals into possibility. Projects like Queer Brown Vegan blend environmental education with personal narrative, drawing connections between food sovereignty, queerness and decolonial practices. Online archives share testimonies from queer farmers, displaced activists and water protectors. These narratives offer more than visibility, they offer templates for resistance rooted in lived experience. Digital spaces become not just tools for awareness, but sites of community formation, imagination, and strategic mobilization.

2.6 Personal is Political – Everyday Queer Climate Acts:

Not all queer climate activism takes place on protest frontlines. Sometimes it looks like seed-saving in urban queer communes, mutual aid fundraisers for trans disaster survivors, or neighbourhood efforts to build sustainable, affirming shelters. Queer folks who have long relied on informal networks of care bring this ethic into climate action. From hosting eco-conscious drag shows to distributing hormone storage tips during power outages, everyday acts of resistance and resilience ripple outward. These quiet interventions matter, they sustain life in moments of crisis and model what adaptive, just living can look like in the face of collapse. Queer acts of care and solidarity show that everyday actions can drive meaningful change in climate justice.

2.7 The Work Ahead – Toward a Queer Climate Future:

Queer activism in the climate justice movement doesn't just call for inclusion, it demands transformation. The future being fought for is not one where queer people simply survive, but one where they shape how society lives, heals and relates to the Earth. This work is far from over. Structural inequalities still silence many queer voices in climate spaces, especially those from the Global South. But the momentum is building. As queer activists continue to link liberation with sustainability, identity with ecology, they forge new political blueprints that refuse binaries, between human and nature, between activism and artistry, between survival and joy. The queer climate justice movement shows us that another world isn't just possible, it's already being constructed in fragments, in poems, in protest camps and in dreams that refuse to fade.

* Mini-Profiles of Queer Climate Activists Worldwide:

Terry Garcia, Mexico (Indigenous Zapotec):

Terry Garcia is a Zapotec environmentalist and queer activist from Oaxaca, Mexico, who has been at the forefront of land defence and climate resilience movements within Indigenous communities. Their work combines ecological conservation with decolonial practices, as they advocate for the rights of both the land and marginalized gender identities. In the face of increased deforestation and the encroachment of global corporations on their ancestral lands, Terry and their collective of queer Indigenous activists have led peaceful protests calling for recognition of ecological and gender justice.

Through storytelling, art and grassroots organizing, they have reimagined what climate activism can look like when shaped by non-Western worldviews and the wisdom of queer traditions.

Terry's advocacy is deeply personal; "Our survival, as Indigenous queer people, is tied to the land. If the Earth suffers, so do we."

Ayesha Muneer, Pakistan:

Ayesha Muneer, a queer environmental justice activist from Karachi, Pakistan, has been raising awareness about the intersection of gender, climate change and human rights. With a focus on the impact of rising sea levels on coastal communities, Ayesha leads efforts to protect the most vulnerable populations, often marginalized queer and transgender individuals who face double discrimination due to their gender identity and environmental displacement. Ayesha's work centers around creating safe spaces for queer folks affected by natural disasters, as well as mobilizing youth for climate strikes that demand inclusive environmental policies.

"Queer people in my community are among the first to suffer when natural disasters strike. Our vulnerability must be seen as part of a bigger fight for justice, social, environmental, and political," Ayesha says.

Lorena Soto, Chile:

In the rugged mountains of southern Chile, Lorena Soto, a trans woman and activist, has dedicated her life to preserving the biodiversity of the Patagonia region. As the lead organizer for a local environmental collective, Lorena champions the rights of the land, its Indigenous inhabitants and queer and trans Chileans who live in rural, often isolated, areas. Through their work, Lorena has bridged the gap between environmentalism and the fight for LGBTQ+ rights, urging local government to incorporate queer perspectives in regional climate adaptation strategies.

Lorena believes that "nature doesn't recognize borders or gender. It's time for human systems to follow suit."

José Martínez, Guatemala:

José Martínez, a queer climate activist and farmer from the rural highlands of Guatemala, has been advocating for sustainable agriculture as a method of mitigating climate change's effects on rural populations. As a member of the Mesoamerican Alliance of Peoples and Forests, José works tirelessly to bring attention to the impacts of deforestation, particularly in communities already marginalized due to their sexual orientation. His work with queer and trans campesinos (farmers) has led to innovative farming techniques that restore the soil while providing a sustainable livelihood for LGBTQ+ farmers in his region.

"We do not just farm the land. We farm resilience. Every plant we grow is a symbol of defiance," José asserts.

Zahra Ali, Kenya:

Zahra Ali is a queer environmental justice activist and community leader in Nairobi, Kenya. As co-founder of the Queer Climate Collective of East Africa, she advocates for intersectional approaches to climate change, focusing on the dual stigma queer farmers face in agricultural communities. Through community workshops and advocacy, Zahra empowers marginalized queer communities in rural areas with sustainable farming techniques to mitigate environmental impact.

Zahra states, "The climate crisis is not just a fight for survival, it's a fight for dignity and respect for all bodies, all identities, all life."

Keisha Williams, Jamaica:

Keisha Williams is a queer environmentalist and grassroots organizer in Jamaica, where she focuses on both climate change adaptation and the environmental rights of LGBTQ+ people in Caribbean communities. Keisha works primarily with marginalized rural populations, including queer farmers and fishermen, helping them access resources to build sustainable livelihoods in the face of increasingly frequent hurricanes and rising sea levels. By organizing queer-inclusive eco-villages, Keisha has fostered community-led initiatives that incorporate renewable energy, waste reduction, and food security.

Keisha says, "Climate change does not ask for your gender or your sexuality before it comes for you. Our resilience must include everyone."

Renato Vasquez, Honduras:

Renato Vasquez, a trans man and environmental rights advocate in Honduras, has become a leading voice for queer and trans Latinx people living in the path of environmental devastation. He works with Indigenous and rural queer communities to combat land grabbing, particularly in regions where climate-induced migration is causing tensions. Renato and his collective advocate for land rights while simultaneously building solidarity across both queer and Indigenous populations, uniting to protect their land and culture.

Renato explains, "As a trans person, I understand the urgency of transformation. The Earth, too, is undergoing a painful transformation. We must be the agents of healing, for the land and for each other."

Laila Basyuni, Indonesia:

Laila Basyuni is a queer environmental activist in Indonesia, where she has worked for years at the intersection of LGBTQ+ rights and environmental preservation in coastal communities. In the face of rising sea levels and environmental degradation, Laila has spearheaded projects that centre on queer and gender-diverse individuals from small island communities who are facing displacement.

She also leads efforts to establish queer-inclusive disaster response networks to ensure marginalized people are not left behind during climate emergencies.

Laila shares, "The ocean has always been a part of my identity, and I'll protect it as fiercely as I protect our queer community."

Nahla Al-Rashed, Lebanon:

Nahla Al-Rashed, a queer woman and environmental lawyer from Lebanon, combines her legal expertise with her activism to challenge government policies that marginalize both LGBTQ+ and climate justice causes. Nahla has worked to introduce climate change policies that are inclusive of sexual minorities, particularly focusing on refugee populations and displaced queer individuals in the Middle East. She also facilitates workshops for queer refugees on sustainable living practices while advocating for their right to stay in the country amidst the ongoing refugee crisis.

"I have learned that climate justice is inherently linked to justice for the most oppressed and as a queer person, I cannot advocate for the planet without advocating for my community," Nahla asserts.

Fabio Costa, Brazil:

Fabio Costa is a non-binary, Afro-Brazilian environmentalist from Rio de Janeiro who is leading a charge for the decolonization of environmental movements in South America. Their work focuses on environmental justice for marginalized communities, particularly Indigenous and Afro-descendant queer populations in the Amazon. Fabio has played a pivotal role in organizing a queer resistance movement against illegal logging and mining in the Amazon, fighting not only for the environment, but also for the dignity and rights of the local queer communities who are deeply affected by environmental destruction.

Fabio says, "Our fight for the forest is a fight for survival, not only of the trees, but of the diverse queer identities that call this place home."

Adriana Gómez, Peru:

Adriana Gómez, a bisexual environmental activist from the Andean highlands of Peru, has focused on integrating agroecology and sustainability practices into the livelihoods of queer farmers in her region. After experiencing the loss of family farmland to deforestation and mining activities, Adriana started working with local queer and trans farmers to create self-sustaining agricultural models that regenerate the land while respecting queer identities and sexualities. She advocates for gender-inclusive policies in the Peruvian agricultural sector, which often excludes queer communities from economic development opportunities.

"Land is life. It is sacred, and it holds our identities. We must care for it as we would care for each other," says Adriana.

Sulaiman Sheikh, India:

Sulaiman Sheikh, a queer climate and disaster relief organizer from Mumbai, India, has been pivotal in linking climate justice with queer and Muslim rights. As monsoon seasons grow more intense and unpredictable, Sulaiman leads disaster response efforts that specifically address the vulnerabilities of queer Muslim communities living in the slums of Mumbai. His activism focuses on the psychological and physical impact of climate change on queer individuals and how they are often excluded from mainstream disaster relief efforts.

Sulaiman remarks, "In moments of crisis, our communities need us to be visible, to show that queer Muslims exist and are a part of the global climate struggle."

3. The Intersection of Environmentalism and Gender Diversity

Environmental disasters do not strike evenly, they exacerbate existing social inequalities, with marginalized gender identities often bearing the brunt. Transgender, nonbinary, and gender-diverse individuals are more likely to experience housing insecurity, limited access to healthcare, and social exclusion, factors that heighten their vulnerability during climate-related emergencies such as floods, wildfires, and droughts. Relief systems frequently operate within binary, cisnormative frameworks that ignore the realities of gender-diverse people, leaving them invisible in disaster response planning and statistical data. Gender-segregated shelters, lack of affirming medical care, and bureaucratic barriers to legal identity recognition all contribute to the exclusion of trans and nonbinary individuals from receiving adequate aid. Without targeted intervention, climate change will continue to deepen the already precarious conditions under which many gender-diverse people live.

3.1 Colonialism, Gender Systems and Ecological Destruction:

Colonialism did not only destroy ecosystems, but it also imposed rigid gender binaries and erased Indigenous understandings of gender fluidity. Many Indigenous cultures across the globe once embraced a spectrum of gender roles and identities, often tied to spiritual and ecological stewardship. With colonization came the enforcement of patriarchal, binary systems that disrupted both the land and the people. The imposition of extractive economies and Eurocentric gender norms simultaneously exploited natural resources and suppressed nonbinary gender identities. Today, Indigenous and gender-diverse activists are reclaiming these knowledges, challenging both environmental destruction and the erasure of gender multiplicity. Recognizing the intertwined legacies of colonization, environmental degradation, and gender oppression is key to building more inclusive and effective climate movements.

3.2 The Politics of Visibility in Green Movements:

Mainstream environmental narratives often centre whiteness, cisnormativity, and able-bodiedness, reinforcing a narrow idea of who can be an environmentalist.

This invisibilizes the work of trans, nonbinary and gender-diverse activists, who have long been involved in grassroots environmental struggles. Media portrayals of climate leaders rarely include gender-diverse voices, yet they are often at the forefront of organizing mutual aid networks, leading land-defence actions and promoting regenerative practices. The pressure to conform to palatable identities for institutional recognition can force gender-diverse activists to hide or downplay their identities. For climate justice to be truly inclusive, movements must recognize that gender diversity is not a liability or distraction, it is integral to building resilient communities that reflect the full spectrum of human experience.

3.3 Environmental Justice Through a Gender Lens:

Environmental justice requires a critical understanding of how systems of power, race, class, gender, and ability intersect with ecological harm. Viewing environmental issues through a gender-diverse lens reveals how cisnormative frameworks routinely exclude and endanger trans, nonbinary, and gender-diverse individuals. In times of climate disaster, access to essentials like safe sanitation, housing, and affirming healthcare can become matters of survival. Trans people face heightened risks in refugee camps and emergency shelters, often subjected to violence, erasure, or denied basic recognition. When policies and aid systems fail to acknowledge nonbinary and trans experiences, entire communities are rendered invisible in disaster response, data collection, and recovery planning. A truly just approach demands more than surface-level inclusion, it requires equitable policy-making, resource distribution rooted in lived realities, and leadership from the communities most impacted.

3.4 Healing as Resistance – Queer Ecologies and Gender Liberation:

In the face of overlapping crises, many gender-diverse individuals are forging new relationships with the land rooted in care, healing, and resistance. The concept of queer ecology challenges both environmental and gender binaries, envisioning nature not as a static, heteronormative backdrop but as a dynamic, interdependent web of identities, expressions and connections. For many trans and nonbinary people, connection to land becomes a source of affirmation and survival. Community gardens, seed-saving projects, herbal medicine, and land reclamation efforts are not only acts of environmental sustainability, but also of gender liberation. These practices cultivate spaces of healing that affirm bodily autonomy, embrace gender fluidity, and nurture collective resilience. They reveal that environmentalism is not only about conserving the planet, it is also about envisioning liberatory futures where all identities are recognized, respected, and safeguarded.

3.5 Toward Inclusive Environmental Policy and Research:

Policymakers and researchers must move beyond binary frameworks when addressing environmental issues. Too often, gender-disaggregated data is limited to "male" and "female," erasing the needs and realities of gender-diverse populations. There is an urgent need for inclusive data collection, participatory research methodologies, and trans-led policy development. Environmental impact assessments should include considerations of how climate-related stressors disproportionately affect trans and nonbinary individuals.

Additionally, gender-diverse people must be meaningfully included in environmental governance and decision-making structures, from local councils to global climate summits. Inclusion is not symbolic, it is essential to the design of effective, equitable climate responses.

3.6 Reimagining Environmental Futures with Gender Diversity at the Centre:

The intersection of environmentalism and gender diversity offers a powerful lens for reimagining the future. Rather than positioning trans and nonbinary people as passive victims of environmental crises, we must recognize them as visionaries, caretakers, and leaders. Climate resilience relies on embracing diverse perspectives, especially from those who have persistently faced systemic marginalization. By placing gender-diverse communities at the centre of environmental planning and visioning, we move toward a future where justice is not conditional, but collective. The struggle for ecological survival and the pursuit of gender liberation are not separate battles, they are deeply interconnected.

4. The Future of LGBTQ+ Safe Spaces in a Changing Climate

LGBTQ+ safe spaces, community centers, clubs, shelters, and informal gathering spots have long served as sanctuaries from systemic marginalization. Yet as climate change intensifies, these spaces are increasingly threatened by environmental instability. Coastal queer hubs, such as those in Miami or Manila, face rising sea levels, while extreme weather events can obliterate grassroots shelters already operating with minimal funding. Disasters often lead to mass displacement, and queer individuals are less likely to find inclusive support in emergency relief centers. Trans people, for instance, may be placed in shelters misaligned with their gender identity, exposing them to danger. The erasure of safe space isn't always visible, it happens through zoning laws, rising rents post-disaster, and aid systems that overlook LGBTQ+ needs. Protecting queer spaces must be understood as part of climate resilience, not separate from it.

"Queer spaces are not just shelters from the storm, they are vital lifelines in a world being reshaped by climate chaos." – Anonymous

4.1 Rethinking "Safe Space" in a Climate-Disrupted World:

The traditional understanding of a safe space, as a fixed, physical location, may not hold in a future marked by displacement, migration, and infrastructural collapse. Queer communities will be forced to rethink how safety is defined and sustained when physical permanence is no longer guaranteed. A safe space may become more fluid and mobile, embedded in networks of care, mutual aid, and digital connectivity. In areas prone to wildfires or floods, safety might mean having decentralized meeting points or encrypted online platforms that ensure continuity of support. The queer notion of chosen family becomes critical here, not just emotionally, but logistically. Climate adaptation for queer communities won't just be about where to go, but how to remain visible, connected and protected in times of flux. Building safety will mean designing systems that account for movement and uncertainty while centering queer dignity. In this redefinition, safety becomes less about walls and more about webs, woven through trust, care, and adaptability that can weather any storm.

4.2 Digital Safe Havens – Opportunities and Limitations:

As physical spaces become more precarious, the role of digital platforms in sustaining the LGBTQ+ community becomes even more vital. Apps, encrypted forums, and virtual gatherings may serve as temporary sanctuaries where information is shared, identities affirmed, and solidarity maintained across regions. Initiatives like climate-focused queer Discord servers or decentralized social media campaigns already demonstrate how resilience can be built through digital community. Yet digital spaces are also vulnerable, subject to surveillance, internet shutdowns during crises, and exclusionary algorithms that silence marginalized voices. Additionally, the digital divide means that many queer people, particularly in the Global South or rural areas, may be left behind. Ensuring digital safe spaces are secure, accessible and designed with inclusivity in mind, must become a central concern of both queer activism and climate justice. Digital safe havens must evolve not just as technological tools, but as lifelines, built on equity, care and the radical belief, that every queer voice deserves to be heard, especially in times of crisis.

4.3 Queer Ecovillages and Radical Futurisms:

Speculative imaginaries are no longer luxury, they are blueprints for survival. Some queer collectives are already exploring intentional ecovillages, off-grid living and radical reimagining's of home. These experiments in queer futurism challenge the nuclear family, heteronormative housing and capitalist land ownership, by proposing alternative systems of communal living and land stewardship. In places like rural Mexico, Brazil, or the U.S. South, queer-led eco-communities are forming out of necessity and vision. These spaces prioritize sustainability alongside inclusivity, integrating permaculture, gender-inclusive facilities, and shared governance models. They also serve as testing grounds for what post-collapse living might look like for those outside traditional power structures. The future of safe space may not look like a gay bar in a city, it may look like a reclaimed farm, a solar-powered caravan, or an encrypted mesh network operated by queer youth. These redefinitions invite us to dream expansively and protectively. By anchoring safety in community, adaptability and imagination, queer ecovillages offer not just refuge, but resilient models for thriving in a world remade.

4.4 Policy, Protection and the Climate Resilience Gap:

Climate adaptation policies often fail to account for the lived experiences of LGBTQ+ individuals. From international humanitarian aid frameworks to national disaster preparedness plans, queer lives are frequently invisible. Without specific policy interventions, safe spaces will continue to fall through the cracks. Governments and NGOs must be pressured to develop inclusive climate resilience strategies that ensure LGBTQ+ access to emergency shelters, healthcare, and housing. Trans-inclusive hygiene facilities, legal recognition in evacuation documentation, and culturally competent disaster responders can make the difference between safety and harm. Moreover, funding must be directed to queer-led grassroots groups, who are already doing the work of care and resilience without institutional backing. Recognizing the intersection of climate vulnerability and queer marginalization is essential for ensuring that safe spaces aren't an afterthought, but a protected right. "If we're not counted in the plan, we're left out of the protection." – Anonymous

4.5 Memory as Resistance – Archiving Safe Spaces Before They're Gone:

As climate threats mount, some queer spaces may inevitably be lost to time and disaster. Preserving their memory becomes an act of resistance. Oral histories, digital archives, and community mapping projects can document the emotional and political weight these spaces held. Archiving isn't just about nostalgia, it's about holding onto the truths of queer survival and passing them on as guides for future resilience. Initiatives like trans oral history projects, queer ecologies zines and climate justice documentaries, provide not only record, but refuge. They assert that queer existence in the face of collapse is not passive, it is fierce, creative and worth remembering. As we prepare for the futures we cannot yet see, memory offers both anchor and fuel.

4.6 Building a Shared Future Rooted in Protection and Belonging:

LGBTQ+ safe spaces have never been just about physical walls, they are about the sense of being held, recognized, and allowed to exist without fear. As climate change reshapes our landscapes, that feeling of sanctuary must transcend buildings and borders, moving with us across terrains, technologies, and time. Whether in flood-prone neighbourhoods, encrypted online networks, or queer-led regenerative farms, the fundamental need for belonging and mutual care endures. Ensuring the survival of queer communities in a climate-altered world isn't only about protecting infrastructure, it's about preserving the capacity to dream, to connect, to thrive. The future of safe space lies not merely in shelter, but in radical, collective flourishing. As poet and activist Audre Lorde once wrote, "Without community, there is no liberation." That truth becomes even more urgent in the storms ahead.

5. Climate-Induced Economic Hardships and Their Impact on Queer Communities

Climate change has far-reaching impacts that extend beyond environmental devastation, deeply influencing economic systems and social structures. For queer communities, the consequences are especially dire, as they face a compounded vulnerability when it comes to climate-induced economic hardships. These hardships not only affect their livelihoods, but also threaten their ability to thrive, both individually and collectively. Queer people, particularly those who are trans, non-binary, disabled and people of colour, experience disproportionate economic struggles, making the intersection of climate change and economic inequality all the more urgent.

5.1 The Unequal Impact of Climate Change on Queer Economies:

Climate-induced economic disruptions affect everyone, but queer communities face unique challenges. From rising unemployment rates to the destruction of local businesses, queer individuals often find themselves at the intersection of environmental disaster and economic marginalization. Queer-owned businesses, which have historically provided safe spaces and community support, are more likely to suffer during climate events such as wildfires, floods, and hurricanes. These businesses, especially those in areas, that are economically fragile to begin with, may not have the resources to rebuild after climate-related damage.

Moreover, the economic hardships following climate disasters are often prolonged due to systemic inequalities that queer people already face in the workforce, housing markets and healthcare systems. For queer workers, economic mobility is further constrained by discrimination, lack of workplace protections and an underrepresentation in higher-wage industries, which leaves them particularly exposed during times of environmental crisis.

5.2 Climate-Driven Displacement and Housing Instability:

In addition to direct economic hardship, climate-induced displacement has profound effects on the stability and security of queer individuals. Disasters such as hurricanes, floods and wildfires, can force queer people to leave their homes, particularly in low-income or marginalized neighbourhoods. The relocation process, which may involve seeking refuge in shelters or temporary housing, can further expose queer individuals to danger, such as violence, exploitation and lack of proper healthcare, or sanitary facilities. Queer people of colour, trans individuals and others with marginalized identities, face additional risks, often being excluded from emergency relief efforts or misgendered and discriminated against in shelters. The economic strain caused by forced migration and housing instability can have long-lasting effects, making it even harder for queer individuals to rebuild their lives. Their vulnerability in displacement situations is often compounded by their already precarious socio-economic status, leaving them without sufficient resources to recover or access the support systems that are essential for rebuilding their lives after disaster.

5.3 The Intersection of Climate Change and Queer Labor Rights:

Queer workers, particularly those in industries vulnerable to the impacts of climate change, face significant job insecurity and economic hardship. As sectors such as agriculture, tourism and construction suffer from environmental damage, the loss of livelihoods disproportionately affects queer individuals who are often employed in these sectors. Queer workers may also face greater challenges in accessing unemployment benefits or workplace protections due to discrimination or the lack of legal recognition in some areas. Furthermore, many queer individuals face higher rates of poverty and economic precarity due to workplace discrimination, transphobia, homophobia and the general lack of inclusive labour policies. Climate-induced economic hardships compound these already existing vulnerabilities, leaving queer workers in a more precarious position compared to their cisgender and heterosexual counterparts.

5.4 Access to Resources and Financial Security:

The economic implications of climate change for queer communities extend to broader issues of financial security and access to resources. Climate-related disasters often exacerbate financial inequalities, making it even harder for queer individuals to access housing, healthcare and social services. Queer people, particularly those who are low-income, disabled, or living in rural areas, may have fewer opportunities to relocate or access emergency services during times of crisis. They are often excluded from financial assistance programs or face barriers in accessing funds due to systemic discrimination.

Moreover, the lack of affordable housing and high costs of living in areas affected by climate change can make it even harder for queer individuals to find stability. The economic hardship caused by climate-induced disasters, combined with the barriers to accessing resources, means that queer people are more likely to be left behind when rebuilding efforts occur.

5.5 Mental Health Strain and Economic Pressures:

The intersection of economic hardship and climate-induced displacement has severe consequences for the mental health of queer individuals. Queer people, particularly those in marginalized communities, already face mental health challenges due to the compounded effects of discrimination, trauma and social isolation. The added stress of climate-induced economic strain exacerbates these issues, leading to higher rates of anxiety, depression, and other mental health disorders. Queer individuals who are displaced or who lose their livelihoods due to climate change may face a loss of community, identity and stability, which compounds feelings of uncertainty and despair. For many, the intersection of financial insecurity and climate-related upheaval can create a sense of hopelessness, making it even harder to cope with the emotional and psychological toll of the crisis.

5.6 The Need for Inclusive and Equitable Climate Policies:

To address the disproportionate economic hardships faced by queer communities, climate policies must prioritize inclusivity and equity. Policies that address the economic impacts of climate change should be designed with a focus on marginalized communities, ensuring that queer people are not left out of recovery efforts. This includes creating economic support systems that are accessible to queer individuals, particularly those who are most at risk, such as trans people and queer people of colour. Additionally, disaster preparedness plans and climate change adaptation strategies must be designed with an intersectional lens that acknowledges the unique vulnerabilities of queer communities. Building economic resilience for queer people in the face of climate change requires not only disaster relief, but also long-term structural changes that address discrimination, access to resources and the integration of queer needs, into climate justice frameworks.

5.7 Building Economic Resilience and Community Support Systems:

In order to build sustainable economic resilience for queer communities, it is essential to create support systems that are grounded in mutual aid, solidarity and collective action. Queer-led initiatives that focus on economic empowerment and community resilience, such as co-operatives, mutual aid networks, and queer-centric businesses, play a critical role in addressing the economic challenges posed by climate change. These grassroots efforts provide queer individuals with a sense of agency and autonomy, allowing them to create economic opportunities in the face of crisis. They also foster a sense of community, which is essential for emotional and psychological support in times of environmental disaster. Building resilient queer economies in the face of climate change means uplifting marginalized communities through both local and global efforts, ensuring no one is left behind in the push for a sustainable future. Climate change doesn't create new inequalities, it deepens the ones already entrenched.

For queer communities, economic hardships, fuelled by climate-driven disruption and systemic inequality, intensify existing marginalization, compounding persistent barriers to safe housing, stable employment, accessible healthcare and personal safety. Addressing this intersection is not optional, it's urgent. Economic resilience for queer people must go beyond mere survival, it must affirm that queer lives are worthy of security, dignity and the right to thrive. The future of queer communities relies on building inclusive, justice-driven solutions that centre equity and community power at the heart of climate response.

"There is no true climate justice without queer justice, because survival must be collective and the future must be built by all of us, not just the few deemed worthy by systems of power." – Anonymous

Chapter 28

Queer Joy as Resistance – Celebrating in a Heteronormative World

---

1. Breaking the Timeline – Queer Lives Beyond Linear Progression

Heteronormative society imposes a rigid timeline of milestones that individuals are expected to meet in order to be deemed successful or fulfilled. These milestones, such as getting married by a certain age, having children by a certain stage in life and achieving career success, form the backbone of traditional notions of success. For many queer individuals, these expectations are both limiting and unrealistic. Queerness resists this linear progression, challenging these preordained paths by offering alternative models for fulfilment and success. The refusal to conform to these societal timelines allows queer people to redefine what it means to live a meaningful life, offering a broader and more inclusive understanding of time, growth and identity.

1.1 Queer Resistance to Heteronormative Time:

Heteronormative timelines are deeply embedded in societal structures, perpetuated through family expectations, cultural norms and media portrayals. These timelines suggest that life is a progression from youth to adulthood, with clearly defined stages that include education, career, marriage, children and retirement. However, for queer people, these milestones often do not align with their lived experiences. The pressure to conform to these norms can be overwhelming, especially for those who do not fit into the traditional mold of family, sexuality, or gender identity.

Queer resistance to this timeline is multifaceted. It may take the form of delayed milestones, where individuals choose to come out later in life, transition later, or delay marriage and children until they are ready, not because society demands it, but because they have the agency to choose their own path. Alternatively, some queer individuals may reject these milestones entirely, choosing non-traditional routes that prioritize personal fulfilment over societal expectations. These disruptions create space for a broader conversation about how success is defined, challenging the very notion that there is one path to a good life.

1.2 The Politics of Delayed Milestones:

For many queer people, coming out or transitioning later in life is a deeply personal decision. Unlike their heteronormative counterparts, who are often expected to adhere to a certain timeline of social and sexual development, queer individuals may navigate their identities on their own terms and timelines. The decision to delay coming out, for instance, is not always a matter of fear or denial, but rather a reflection of the individual's readiness to step into their truth. In this sense, queer lives are not bound by a timeline, but are allowed to unfold organically, according to each person's journey.

Coming out late is often framed as a process of reclamation. Queer people who come out later in life may find themselves in the position of redefining what fulfilment looks like in their later years. For some, coming out is a second chance at living authentically. It allows them to embrace new identities, forms of love, and modes of self-expression that were previously stifled. In this way, delayed truths do not signify failure or stagnation, but rather the blossoming of one's full potential in the face of societal constraints. For these individuals, joy and fulfilment are not dictated by a chronological path, but by an emotional and experiential awakening that transcends conventional timelines.

1.3 Disrupting Capitalist Notions of Time and Success:

Queer lives often challenge not only the heteronormative timeline, but also the capitalist imperative to measure success by productivity, career advancement and material accumulation. Capitalism thrives on a rigid linearity of time, in which success is equated with upward mobility and constant productivity. This ideology does not accommodate queer individuals who may reject traditional career paths or who may not be interested in the same markers of financial or social success.

For many queer people, success is measured not by wealth or career status, but by meaningful relationships, strong community bonds, and the freedom to live authentically. Queer resistance to the capitalist timeline encourages a different approach to life, one that values rest, care and collective well-being over competition and accumulation. The act of slowing down, opting out of conventional career trajectories, or choosing to live with less material wealth are all expressions of rejecting the capitalist framework that equates success with linear progression. This way of life offers a liberating alternative, allowing queer people to focus on emotional fulfilment and human connection rather than conventional markers of success.

1.4 Cyclical and Nonlinear Approaches to Time in Queer Communities:

Beyond rejecting traditional timelines, queer individuals have long used alternative conceptions of time to shape their lives. Queer temporality often resists the linear, progressive model of time that prioritizes achievement and accumulation. Instead, many queer people embrace cyclical, fragmented, or non-linear notions of time that reflect the realities of their lived experiences.

Queer temporality can be seen in the ways that queer people engage with rituals, celebrations and relationships. For example, queer communities often create their own rites of passage, moments of personal or collective growth that are not dictated by mainstream society. These moments can occur at any age or stage in life, reflecting the fluidity of queer existence. Rather than moving from one milestone to the next, queer people may find meaning in the spaces between milestones, in the periods of rest, reflection and redefinition, that occur as part of their individual journeys.

The concept of cyclical time also appears in the ways that queer individuals create and sustain chosen families, communities and networks of support. These communities often revolve around the idea of interconnectedness, where time is less about individual success and more about mutual care, ongoing learning, and collective survival.

Non-linear frameworks of time empower queer individuals to live more holistically, recognizing that personal growth and fulfilment are not confined by age or societal norms, but unfold as fluid, ever-evolving journeys.

1.5 Redefining Success Beyond Timelines:

Queer individuals, by virtue of their resistance to conventional timelines, are uniquely positioned to offer a broader definition of success. In rejecting the societal pressure to meet preordained milestones, queer people create alternative ways of thinking about fulfilment, happiness and achievement. Success for queer people might not look like a house, a family, or a stable career. It might be found in the ability to live authentically, to build meaningful relationships, or to pursue creative or intellectual passions outside of conventional systems of power and prestige.

This redefinition of success challenges the traditional heteronormative ideals that have long dictated the paths individuals should follow. It also invites a broader understanding of what it means to lead a successful life, one that values joy, rest, and connection over productivity, material wealth, and achievement. In this sense, queer individuals are not only resisting the linear progression of time, but also actively reshaping what success and fulfilment mean in a world that has too often demanded conformity.

Queer lives offer an important challenge to the conventional timelines of heteronormative society. By embracing delayed milestones, rejecting capitalist measures of success and redefining time itself, queer people resist the constraints of linear progression. In doing so, they offer a more inclusive and expansive vision of life, one that prioritizes authenticity, joy, and fulfilment over external measures of achievement. Queerness, in its disruption of these timelines, offers a radical rethinking of how we understand time, progress, and success.

2. Coming Out Late, Living Fully – The Expansiveness of Delayed Truths

Coming out later in life often involves a deeply emotional process, where individuals confront years of self-doubt, fear, and shame. The act of coming out becomes not just about revealing an identity, but about reconciling the person they were with the person they are becoming. It's an emotional release, a shedding of layers that had been built up over years. This emotional unravelling can be both painful and liberating, but ultimately it brings a sense of clarity and empowerment, a newfound joy in living authentically. It's a reminder that authenticity has no expiration date, and that self-discovery is a lifelong journey, not a missed deadline. In embracing their truth later in life, many find a deeper, more intentional kind of freedom, one rooted not in time lost, but in self finally found.

2.1 Gratitude for a Journey Well-Lived:

Rather than focusing on lost time, many individuals who come out later in life reflect with gratitude on the path they've walked. The struggles, the compromises, and even the periods of silence all contributed to the person they are today. These life experiences are not seen as wasted, instead, they provide the foundation for a more profound and meaningful existence.

The journey of self-discovery is not linear, but its beauty lies in how it shapes a deeper understanding of what it means to truly live. Embracing their journey, individuals who come out later in life discover that every step, no matter the detour, enriches their understanding of themselves and the world.

2.2 The Freedom to Live Authentically:

One of the greatest gifts of coming out later in life is the profound sense of freedom that accompanies it. Without the societal pressure to conform to traditional life timelines, individuals can embrace their true selves without the weight of expectations. This newfound freedom allows them to explore aspects of their identity that were once suppressed, and to pursue passions and dreams that had been sidelined. It's an expansive feeling, one that opens the door to new experiences, personal growth, and liberation. This journey often leads to a more intentional, self-directed life, one rooted in truth rather than compromise.

2.3 Rebirth in Relationships:

Coming out late not only transforms the individual, but it also reshapes the way relationships are experienced. Many individuals who come out later find that their relationships take on new depth and authenticity. The connections they share with friends, family, and romantic partners shift from being shaped by a false identity to being grounded in truth. For some, relationships that no longer align with their authentic self may end, but they are replaced by others rooted in love, respect, and mutual understanding. The joy of being able to show up as one's full, authentic self fosters a sense of deep connection and belonging. This rebirth often brings a clarity that allows for more meaningful, aligned, and life-affirming bonds to flourish.

2.4 Living Outside Conventional Expectations:

The act of coming out later in life challenges traditional narratives of what a "successful" life looks like. For those who embrace their identity later, success is not measured by milestones such as marriage, children, or career progression. Instead, it is defined by the courage to live truthfully and authentically. Success is found in embracing new beginnings, celebrating personal growth, and building relationships that reflect one's true self. This redefinition of success offers a more inclusive, expansive vision of what it means to live a fulfilling life.

2.5 The Joy of Living Fully:

Coming out later in life is, above all, a celebration. It is a celebration of embracing one's authentic self, of overcoming obstacles, and of living without apology. Individuals who come out later often experience a profound sense of joy in their newfound freedom. This joy is contagious, it spreads to others and inspires them to live fully, regardless of age or the time in life they choose to embrace their truth. It's a radical joy, a defiance of the societal norms that dictate when certain milestones should be reached. For those who come out late, the fullness of life is only just beginning. Their stories show that it's never too late to live authentically and find joy in doing so.

2.6 A Powerful Example of Living on Your Own Terms:

The decision to come out later in life serves as a powerful reminder that it is never too late to live authentically. Those who embrace their truth later are not only living fully, but they are also rewriting the narrative of what it means to be queer. They challenge the belief that life must be lived on a preordained timeline. Instead, they demonstrate that self-discovery is an ongoing journey, and that the joy and freedom of living authentically can be experienced at any stage in life.

2.7 Redefining Success and Happiness:

The late-coming-out journey is a radical rethinking of what it means to be successful and happy. By rejecting conventional measures of success, individuals who come out later offer a more expansive vision of what fulfilment looks like. Success is not about material wealth or societal approval, but about authenticity, joy, and connection. For those who embrace their truth later, happiness is found not in meeting external expectations, but in the freedom of being fully, unapologetically themselves.

2.8 Living Beyond Timelines:

Coming out later in life is not a delay; it is a gift, a chance to live outside of the conventional timelines that society imposes. These individuals offer a powerful example of resilience, growth, and joy. Their stories challenge the notion that one must meet specific milestones by a certain age to live a fulfilling life. Instead, they demonstrate that life's beauty and meaning are found in the moments when we embrace our truth, regardless of the time it takes. Their journeys remind us that authenticity isn't late, it's right on time.

* Living on Queer Time – Real Lives That Redefined the Clock:

D'Lo (Sri Lankan-American, transmasculine performance artist):

At 40, D'Lo legally changed his name, not because he hadn't always known who he was, but because the world finally started catching up. His journey of gender truth unfolded not on someone else's clock, but through the cadence of poetry, protest, and stage light.

Maureen Duffy (UK poet and novelist, lesbian icon):

She came out publicly in the early 1960s, well before it was socially safe. But her true queer joy began decades later when her work was finally celebrated because of her identity, not despite it.

Ryka Aoki (Japanese-American trans writer and martial artist):

She began transitioning after establishing herself in academia. Her late bloom was not delayed, it was ripened by discipline, care, and community. Today, her novels and performances teach time as something queer bodies can shape, not obey.

Terrence McNally (Gay American playwright):

He spent his early years writing closeted characters. Only in his 50s did his work unapologetically bloom with queer intimacy, finding success not from hiding, but from telling stories of aging love, loss and resilience.

Patricio Manuel (First out trans boxer to compete professionally):

Patricio Manuel transitioned in his 30s, well past the typical peak for most professional athletes. Yet, it was only by embracing his true gender identity that he stepped into the boxing ring as his authentic self, rewriting the narrative of athletic achievement and challenging conventional timelines in sports.

Angela Morley (British transgender composer and conductor):

Angela transitioned in her 40s, after a successful career scoring film and TV. While many feared she'd lose her standing, her artistry only deepened. She later conducted for the Boston Pops and composed for Dallas, her baton a quiet revolution.

Billy Tipton (American jazz musician, trans man):

For much of his life, Tipton lived in silence, his true identity hidden from the world. Only after his passing did the truth of his trans identity emerge. Though he never lived openly, his journey became a testament to queer survival in times that demanded quietude. His music, bold and improvisational, carried the unspoken truths of his soul, whispers of a life he wasn't yet free to claim.

Edith "Edie" Windsor (American LGBTQ+ activist):

After decades in a committed relationship, Edie became the face of queer resistance in her 80s. Her Supreme Court case struck down DOMA, making her a widowed elder who reignited the fight for love's legal legitimacy.

Precious Brady-Davis (Trans author and climate advocate):

Precious Brady-Davis, a Black trans woman, began her transition in her late 20s and embraced parenthood in her 30s, fostering children alongside her husband, Myles. Her journey redefines queer parenting, not as something delayed, but as a revolutionary act of love, resilience and family-building that challenges societal norms and expectations.

Reverend Dr. Megan Rohrer (First openly transgender bishop in a major U.S. Christian denomination):

Reverend Dr. Megan Rohrer was ordained in their 30s and elected bishop in their 40s, defying both ecclesiastical and societal expectations. For Rohrer, queerness and spirituality are not opposites, but intertwined, with faith serving as both a foundation and a gateway to embracing their true self, shattering norms along the way.

Alan L. Hart (American physician and trans man, early 20th century):

Hart transitioned in 1917, using early X-ray technology to fight tuberculosis across rural America. His medical achievements came after living authentically in an era with no roadmap, proving that queer futures have always existed, even before we had language for them.

Sandra Caldwell (Black trans actress, Canada/US):

Sandra lived in stealth for most of her acting career, coming out publicly as trans in her 60s. Her return to the spotlight wasn't a comeback, it was a rebirth. Now, she mentors young trans actors with grace sharpened by time.

José Sarria (First openly gay candidate for public office in the U.S.):

José Sarria, a drag performer and WWII veteran, made history in 1961 as the first openly gay candidate for public office in the U.S. Though he didn't win, his bold candidacy, launched later in life, laid the foundation for queer political resistance and redefined the path to visibility and empowerment in American politics.

Leslie Feinberg (Author and trans rights pioneer):

Though Feinberg began their political activism early, their later work, particularly Drag King Dreams, reveals the joys of queer aging. Their words trace a nonlinear arc, from working-class rebellion to transcendent storytelling.

Carol, 79 (UK, anonymous anecdote from The Guardian):

After divorcing her husband of 40 years, Carol came out at 71 and moved in with her girlfriend. She joined a lesbian book club, got a tattoo, and said, "I didn't know life could feel like this." Her timeline? Just beginning.

Philippa York (UK):

Formerly known as professional cyclist Robert Millar, Philippa York publicly came out as a transgender woman in 2017 after years of private living. Her coming out was met with support, allowing her to reconnect with the cycling world on her own terms. York described finding peace and quiet joy in living authentically, reclaiming her story through chosen visibility and true selfhood.

Neko Orita (Japan):

Neko, a Japanese transgender woman, came out in her 60s after decades of repression in a conservative culture. She said in interviews that transitioning late in life allowed her to finally see her reflection as her true self, bringing joy that was quiet, simple, and sacred. Her late-life visibility also helped shift cultural perspectives in Japan around aging and gender identity.

Cynthia Nixon (USA):

The actress known for Sex and the City came out as queer in her 40s, after years of identifying as straight and being in heterosexual relationships. Nixon has been open about how coming into her queer identity and marrying activist Christine Marinoni, expanded her sense of joy, family and purpose, especially in her activism. She framed her journey as one of self-expansion rather than loss or redefinition.

Johan Beukes (South Africa):

After decades in the Dutch Reformed Church, Johan came out as gay at 62. He was married to a woman and held a respected position in the religious community. Coming out, though painful initially, led him to become an advocate for LGBTQ+ rights within faith-based spaces in South Africa. He described finally laughing without guilt and building friendships where he could speak and love freely.

Pádraig Ó Tuama (Ireland):

A queer poet and theologian, Ó Tuama grew up in a deeply Catholic context in Northern Ireland. He came out later in life and has described the shift as "stepping into poetry that had always been waiting." His reflections link language, faith and queer joy, together in a way that honours the past without being trapped in it. Tuama's journey highlights the power of embracing one's true self, blending the wisdom of tradition with the freedom of authenticity.

Jeanette Jennings (USA):

Mother of transgender advocate Jazz Jennings, Jeanette came out as bisexual in her 50s after years of advocating for her daughter. She shared that seeing Jazz's courage prompted her to confront parts of her own identity. Coming out brought her closer to LGBTQ+ communities, and she described it as "a relief and an awakening," full of late-in-life pride and healing.

Bisi Alimi (Nigeria/UK):

Although Bisi Alimi came out in his late 20s, which is not traditionally "late," in some contexts, it was later relative to Nigeria's extremely hostile environment. His public coming out on Nigerian television in 2004 led to exile, but it also marked the beginning of his life as an openly gay man and activist. Later in the UK, he found romantic and personal joy, eventually marrying and building a life that centers pride and peace.

Carol Anshaw (USA):

Acclaimed novelist Carol Anshaw came out as a lesbian later in adulthood, well into her writing career. Her queerness now brings layered depictions of lesbian relationships into her fiction. She's spoken of how coming out added emotional authenticity to her work and offered "a different kind of intimacy with herself."

Anthony Venn-Brown (Australia):

A former Pentecostal minister, Anthony came out as gay in his 40s after years of struggling with internalized homophobia. His memoir A Life of Unlearning chronicled his journey from the closet to queer advocacy. He describes post-coming out joy as spiritual renewal, his faith and sexuality no longer at war, and his life now filled with authenticity, activism, and chosen family.

Carol Guess (USA):

Poet and novelist Carol Guess lived as a straight woman and was even married before coming out later in life as queer. In interviews, she reflected on how coming out brought playfulness, energy, and erotic depth into her writing and everyday life. Her work now often explores non-normative love, queer temporality and polyamory, shaped by that later-life clarity.

Peter de Waal (Australia):

Peter, along with his partner Peter Bonsall-Boone, was part of Australia's earliest LGBTQ+ rights movements. Though de Waal came out relatively young, his public and political coming out occurred later, decades after living quietly. Once out, he embraced activism and was later honoured for his advocacy. His later-life visibility was steeped in love, resistance, and pride.

Aasha Davis (USA):

Actress Aasha Davis came out as bisexual publicly in her late 30s after years in the entertainment industry. She noted that acknowledging her queerness brought a sense of internal alignment and freedom, especially in terms of roles she now feels empowered to take and relationships she now enters with openness and joy.

Akira the Hustler (Japan):

A queer artist, activist and former sex worker, Akira began publicly embracing his queer identity in his 30s and 40s, long after surviving trauma and repression in Japan. His late blooming into outness merged with activism and performance, allowing queer joy to manifest through artistic expression, erotic autonomy and political voice.

Caitlyn Jenner (USA):

A former Olympic gold medallist and reality TV star, Caitlyn Jenner came out as transgender in 2015, in her 60s. Her public transition sparked widespread media attention and opened up discussions about gender identity, especially for older individuals. While her journey faced mixed reactions, Jenner's transition represents the complexity of living authentically in the public eye and the evolving narrative of queer visibility.

3. Rethinking Success and Productivity in Queer Time

The very notion of success is deeply intertwined with capitalist values, where achievement is measured by milestones tied to age, wealth, and status. For queer individuals, whose lives often unfold outside the rigid, heteronormative timelines imposed by society, there is a profound opportunity to challenge these constructs. The pervasive pressure to achieve by a certain age, to be productive in ways that benefit capitalist systems, is a force that queerness can radically resist. In rejecting this linear, profit-driven version of time, queer lives offer an alternative, a celebration of self-worth that is not determined by the demands of productivity or conventional success. To rethink success through a queer lens is to embrace a decolonized time, where rest, joy and authenticity, are as valuable as any goal attained. It invites us to imagine a life paced by meaning rather than metrics, where thriving is measured in presence, connection, and self-defined purpose.

3.1 Queer Time as an Act of Defiance:

To exist in "queer time" is, at its core, an act of defiance against the capitalistic view of life as a constant race towards productivity and achievement. In queer time, the linear path, beginning with schooling, progressing through work and culminating in retirement, is unimportant. There is no pressure to meet milestones on time or according to societal standards. Queer time disrupts the idea that youth must be the prime time for achieving dreams or accumulating wealth, offering a different perspective that embraces all stages of life without fear of judgment. For many queer individuals, time is fluid, and living outside the structure of capitalist expectations becomes a form of liberation. It is a reclamation of time itself, where healing, reinvention, and self-discovery are not late, but right on time.

3.2 Capitalism and the Tyranny of Time:

Capitalism thrives on time-bound productivity. People are expected to maximize their output, often to the detriment of mental health, emotional well-being, and the planet itself. The relentless drive for efficiency and measurable success leads to burnout, exhaustion, and a sense of personal failure for those who cannot keep up. For queer individuals, the capitalist emphasis on productivity can be particularly damaging. Historically, queer people have been marginalized or erased by traditional systems and as a result, many are left to navigate careers and life paths that do not necessarily align with their true selves. Queer people are often placed in roles where their value is judged by productivity rather than personhood.

This system of exploitation relies on people feeling inadequate or as though they are falling behind if they do not meet certain productivity standards. It pressures individuals into sacrificing their authenticity, desires, and personal timelines for the sake of external approval and economic gain. But for queer individuals who already face systemic barriers to acceptance and opportunity, this model of productivity can be particularly damaging, reinforcing feelings of invisibility and inadequacy. Rethinking success involves stepping away from the notion that human value is only determined by what one can produce for others. "Queer liberation isn't just about who we love or how we identify, it's about reclaiming our time from systems that profit off our erasure."

3.3 Joy as Resistance:

Within queer time, rest, joy and self-care, become revolutionary acts. The capitalist system profits from perpetual busyness and productivity. The ideal worker is always moving, always achieving, always hustling. But queer time encourages the opposite, moments of stillness, joy in the present, and the rejection of constant striving. Queer people who embrace these moments of pause are not only resisting the demands of the capitalist system, but are also affirming their inherent worth beyond their ability to produce.

Self-care in queer time is more than just a trend, it is a form of resistance. It is the rejection of a world that demands constant labour and instead centres the individual's needs for healing, joy and connection. These moments of resistance, whether it is dancing with friends, reading for pleasure, or simply being with oneself, are acts of survival and self-preservation in a world that often demands conformity and overwork.

3.4 The Value of Rest in Queer Time:

Rest is one of the most profound acts of defiance against capitalist time. In a society that devalues downtime and equates worth with output, taking time to rest becomes an act of rebellion. For queer individuals, who have often had to navigate rejection, marginalization and invisibility, rest is not only a necessity, but a radical assertion of self-worth. Queer individuals are not measured by their productivity or conformity to socially constructed timelines, but by their capacity to live authentically, on their own terms and in their own time. Rest allows space for reflection, for reclaiming the self from the pressures of society, and for healing from the emotional and physical toll of living in a world that often marginalizes queer people. It allows for the cultivation of joy, connection, and creativity, things that cannot be measured or quantified by capitalist standards. Rest is a reclaiming of power, a reminder that one's value is not contingent on labour.

3.5 Authenticity Over Achievement:

Queer lives, by their very nature, challenge the binary logic of success and failure, achievement and lack thereof. In embracing authenticity, queer people reject the notion that life's value is defined by career, wealth, or societal approval. Instead, they centre their lives on what truly matters, relationships, self-expression, community, and creativity. The decision to live authentically, regardless of age or social expectations, is an act of radical self-love. For many queer individuals, the act of coming out or transitioning later in life challenges the capitalist framework that values uniformity and conformity. These individuals are not just embracing their identities, they are also rejecting the timelines imposed by society and opting to live on their own terms.

3.6 Rejecting Heteronormative Timelines:

Capitalism intersects with heteronormativity in ways that limit the experiences of queer people, pushing them into predetermined timelines that often have no resonance with their lived realities.

The societal pressure to "settle down," "build a career," and "have children" by a certain age disregards the diverse paths queer people often take. These timelines do not account for the uniqueness of queer lives or the multitude of ways in which fulfilment can manifest. Living in defiance of these heteronormative timelines, queer people forge their own paths to success, paths that do not follow the standard linear progression of life. These alternative timelines allow queer individuals to experience success in non-traditional ways, such as pursuing unconventional careers, embracing chosen families, or celebrating non-normative relationships. By rejecting the heteronormative expectations of success, queer people reframe what it means to lead a fulfilling life.

3.7 Reclaiming Time, Reclaiming Power:

Time is a precious resource, and queerness offers a unique opportunity to reclaim it. In a capitalist world where time is commodified and individuals are encouraged to sell their labour for profit, queer people can assert their power by rejecting the expectation that they must work to live. Instead, they can centre their own experiences and desires, choosing joy, rest, and community as valuable elements of their existence. Queer people reclaim time not as a currency to be spent, but as a canvas on which to paint their most authentic selves.

In rejecting capitalist notions of productivity and success, queer individuals carve out new ways of being, ways that prioritize well-being, creativity and love, over material wealth and societal approval. This reimagining of success allows queer people to live lives that are not bound by the dictates of capitalism, but are instead defined by their commitment to authenticity, joy and liberation.

"To reclaim time is to reclaim self, queerness teaches us that freedom isn't found in the clock's ticking, but in the courage to live by our own rhythm." – Anonymous

4. Queer Temporality in Art, Ritual and Resistance

Queer artists frequently resist the demand for chronological order, embracing fragmentation, loops and simultaneity in their work. In doing so, they dismantle the dominant narrative structures that privilege linear development, from childhood to adulthood, from problem to resolution, from birth to death. Artists like Gregg Araki, whose films Nowhere and The Living End collapse linear narratives into cyclical and surreal episodes, create worlds that challenge the very notion of time as a linear journey.

Similarly, Jeanette Winterson's Written on the Body explores desire, loss, and transformation outside of time's constraints, presenting a narrative that flows in and out of chronology and abandons traditional storytelling for something more malleable. These works reveal how art provides a space where queer lives can thrive outside the bounds of societal expectations, embracing emotional truth and non-linear progression over linear timelines. Within these fragmented temporalities, queerness becomes an act of living outside the rigid structures imposed by heteronormative narratives, allowing the body and the spirit to exist in a continuous state of becoming rather than being confined to expected life stages.

In this way, art doesn't merely depict or represent the lived queer experience, it actively participates in shaping a new framework for time. It invites viewers into a space where the usual constraints of past, present, and future dissolve, and instead, time is understood as cyclical, non-linear, and reimagined. Art, in its most radical form, doesn't reflect life, it interrupts it, offering an escape from the suffocating pressure to conform to linear expectations of success, relationships, and personal growth.

* Voices of Resistance – Queer Reflections on Time and Identity:

- "I refuse to be confined by the clock. Queerness is timeless, and so am I." – Zanele Muholi, Queer Visual Artist and Activist

- "In the world I envision, time doesn't dictate my worth, my existence does." – Alok Vaid-Menon, Gender Non-Conforming Artist and Activist

- "The beauty of queerness is that every second holds infinite possibilities. I am not beholden to the ticking of the clock, but to the pulse of my heart." – Ocean Vuong, Queer Poet and Writer

- "To be queer is to refuse to be bound by the boundaries of time. I carve out moments, days, and years as I see fit, and they are mine to shape." – Justin Vivian Bond, Gender Non-Conforming Artist and Performer

- "I am not in a race against time. My journey is not measured in years, but in the spaces I create and the love I give." – RuPaul Charles, Drag Performer and Activist

- "The timeline of queer people is never straight. It curves, bends, spirals, and skips, but in that fluidity, we find our truest selves." – Sylvia Rivera, Queer Activist and Advocate

- "Time didn't break me, society did. Now, I create my own rhythm, and my life dances to that beat." – Laverne Cox, Transgender Actress and Advocate

- "In my world, time is a canvas, not a cage. I paint the picture of my life in bold strokes, free from the pressure of deadlines or expectations." – David Wojnarowicz, Queer Visual Artist and Activist

- "Queerness isn't about fitting into time's mold, it's about stretching it, bending it, and claiming it as our own." – Rhea L. Ward, Queer Writer and Activist

4.1 Visualizing Memory and Ancestry in Queer Art:

Queer visual artists have long resisted the erasure of their histories, creating works that challenge dominant narratives about who gets to be remembered and how their stories should unfold over time. For example, Zanele Muholi's black-and-white self-portraits capture intimate moments that combine personal identity with collective memory, reimagining queer histories that were once hidden or forgotten. In their powerful images, Muholi refuses to allow queer lives to be written out of existence and instead, they reassert presence in both the past and the present.

Their photographs remind us that memory is not linear, but reconstructed and redefined, especially for historically marginalized queer lives and identities. Similarly, David Wojnarowicz's multimedia works collapse time by intertwining elements of personal grief, political resistance, and societal critique, rejecting the linearity of trauma and instead offering a framework where loss is not just experienced, but continuously recreated through artistic practice. Wojnarowicz's work isn't simply a reflection of history, it is an active engagement with time, showing how queer artists become archivists of their own existence. In this way, these artists push back against a dominant historical narrative that demands queer people remain invisible or static. They turn art into a living archive, allowing memory, trauma and survival, to coexist across time, refusing to accept a version of the past that erases or displaces queer identities.

4.2 Ritual as Resistance – Reclaiming Cyclical Time in Queer Culture:

Ritual plays a central role in reshaping how queer communities engage with time. Unlike standardized holidays or institutionalized celebrations that often exclude queer narratives, queer rituals operate on affective, cyclical, or intuitive rhythms. For instance, drag shows, ballroom competitions, Trans Day of Remembrance, and pride parades don't adhere to the typical progressions of time. Instead of simply marking milestones or marking the passage of time, these rituals create living, embodied spaces of remembrance, celebration, and protest, that reject linear timelines in favour of moments of emotional and community significance. In particular, ballroom culture, a space where Black and Latinx queer and trans individuals have long found refuge, reveals how queer rituals exist in fluid, suspended time.

In ballroom competitions, categories like "realness" and "executive" represent not linear progressions or goals, but moments of aesthetic and emotional manifestation. These rituals allow for the reimagining of identity and success, emphasizing what it means to inhabit multiple temporalities and self-concepts at once. House mothers pass down knowledge that is not bound by time, but by the lived experience of resistance, joy, and survival.

Drag, similarly, disrupts the linear experience of gender and sexuality by offering a performance that is both exaggerated and defiant, transforming gender from a stagnant identity into a fluid, ever-evolving exploration. Drag performers embody not just a rejection of temporal constraints, but an invitation to live with joy, irreverence, and fluidity, rejecting the constraints of traditional gender timelines in favour of perpetual creation and reinvention.

4.3 Temporal Activism – Slowness, Imagination and Radical Care:

Queer activism has long been rooted in resisting the pressure for urgency and immediate results. In contrast to mainstream movements that often prioritize measurable outcomes within set timeframes, queer activism embraces "slow activism", a process-focused approach that values care, imagination and sustainability, over speed and productivity. For instance, groups like the Combahee River Collective highlighted the importance of ongoing coalition-building, emphasizing a relational, non-hierarchical approach to activism that prioritized long-term care for individuals and communities rather than quick wins or single-issue solutions.

Similarly, ACT UP's creative protests during the AIDS crisis didn't just call for swift action, they exposed the slow violence of government negligence and demanded accountability from systems that had long disregarded the lives and needs of marginalized communities. These acts of resistance, often coupled with ritual and collective action, worked not by rushing through problems, but by slowing down to witness and disrupt the passage of time itself. In doing so, these movements used queer temporality as both a tool of resistance and an act of radical care, emphasizing that survival and resistance are not defined by linear success, but by persistence, solidarity and love.

4.4 Queer Time as a Living Archive of Past, Present and Future:

Queer temporality does not exist in isolation, it builds connections across time, allowing for a deep intergenerational dialogue. Time becomes a collective living archive, a reservoir of past struggles, current victories, and future possibilities. The concept of chosen family is one way that queer people challenge conventional understandings of time, as it allows queer individuals to create their own familial bonds, regardless of biological lineage, and carry those relationships across time and space. This chosen family operates outside the confines of a strictly biological or chronological framework, creating connections that transcend traditional notions of time and heritage.

Queer storytelling, mentorship and artistic expression, bridge generational divides by transmitting wisdom not through linear timelines, but through shared experiences of resistance, survival and joy.

In doing so, queer communities envision futures unbound by past disappointments or societal norms, futures shaped by reinvention, reimagining and continuous evolution. This reimagining of time allows queerness to thrive across multiple, overlapping temporalities, affirming the legitimacy of queer histories, lives and futures, in ways that resist normative constraints and embrace boundless possibility.

* Rituals of Resistance, Real and Imagined Queer Ceremonies of Identity and Community:

Name Day Celebrations – Real:

For many trans individuals, transitioning often involves reclaiming one's name. But for some, the journey doesn't stop with the first change. An annual Name Day ritual celebrates the fluidity of identity by marking a new chapter in one's name, pronouns, or self-understanding. Participants wear personalized attire that signifies the evolution of their identity, write new names on a shared board, and tell the story of their growth in an open circle. This ritual is designed to mark milestones that may not be linear, but are deeply personal. It acts as a resistance to normative milestones of life, celebrating who they are in this moment and the infinite possibilities ahead.

Queer Memory Dinners – Real:

In many queer communities, especially within the context of chosen families, gatherings often take the form of dinners where queer elders, activists, or loved ones share memories of struggles, victories and the evolution of identity.

These dinners are not only about the food, but about passing down knowledge and affirming the value of lived experience over linear notions of progress. They are a ritualistic act of remembering, and in remembering, queerness is reclaimed in its full spectrum. By actively resisting the erasure of queer history, they reclaim time itself, resisting the forward march of oblivion by anchoring themselves in the present while looking backward.

The Queer Writing Circle – Real:

A group of queer writers, ranging from poets to novelists, gather once a month for a sacred writing circle. At each meeting, the group reads aloud a piece of their work and then shares the intention behind it, why it was written, who it is for, and how it connects to their queerness. The circle is a space where time slows down, and the writers can connect with the evolution of their identities through their words. The ritual's power lies in its focus on the written word as a vehicle for personal and collective transformation, with a deep understanding that queerness is not confined to the pages, but flows through them, shaping new narratives outside of heteronormative expectations.

Chosen Family Adoption Ceremonies – Real or Imagined:

Every year, a group of queer individuals gather for a private ceremony where they "adopt" one another into their chosen families. Unlike traditional familial bonds, these rituals focus on intention and love rather than bloodlines. At the heart of the ceremony is the exchange of self-made gifts, perhaps a hand-painted portrait, a handwritten letter, or a specially curated playlist. In these moments, the clock ceases to matter. The ritual becomes timeless, a grounding force for a family formed through mutual respect and shared journeys, not societal prescriptions.

The Full Moon Drag Circle – Imagined:

Every full moon, a group of drag performers meets in a secret spot in the city, a hidden rooftop, a forest clearing, or a quiet park. The ritual involves a gathering where they share their most intimate stories, perform impromptu dances, and meditate together under the moonlight. It's not just a performance, it's a reclaiming of power and a community-building act. The full moon symbolizes the cyclical nature of queer lives, ever-changing, ever-illuminated. Time becomes elastic here, it's about presence, not time-bound goals.

The Queer Time Capsule – Imagined:

Once a year, a group of LGBTQ+ individuals from different walks of life gather to create a queer time capsule. They write letters to their future selves, compile symbolic items representing their identities and struggles, and seal the box with the intention of opening it at an unplanned moment years down the road. The time capsule is an act of defiance, an embodiment of rejecting the linear trajectory that society demands. For them, there is no "right" time to open it, just a shared commitment to keeping the future open-ended and unprescribed. It becomes a ritual of patience and possibility, a resistance against the rush to check boxes.

The "Queer Garden" Planting Ceremony – Imagined:

In a secluded garden space, a group of queer individuals gather annually to plant a garden of symbols. Each person selects a plant or flower that represents their identity, journey, or queer experience. As they plant, they share a story or hope for their future selves, or for the queer community at large. The garden becomes a living manifestation of queer temporality, with no clear direction or defined shape, echoing the diversity of queer lives and the nonlinear paths they often follow. Over time, the garden grows wild and untamed, much like their identities, resisting societal timelines and flourishing in unexpected, beautiful ways. The planting of each seed represents not just growth, but the freedom to grow without expectation, rooted in love and resistance.

5. Time Travel and Future Selves – Queer Visions Across Time

Linear time, marked by milestones like marriage, childbirth, retirement, has long served as a roadmap for societal belonging. Yet queerness often exists outside these fixed coordinates, defying the rhythms of heteronormative life scripts. Queer people have historically been denied access to conventional futures, whether through legal exclusion, cultural marginalization, or systemic erasure.

In response, queer temporalities emerge, elastic, nonlinear and rich with personal meaning. Time becomes less a march forward and more a mosaic of memory, imagination, interruption, and renewal. To live queerly is to inhabit a temporal rebellion, to make room for pauses, detours, re-dos, and resurrections of self that challenge dominant expectations of growth and success.

5.1 Time Travel as a Queer Act – Reclaiming the Past, Rewriting the Future:

Queer time travel is not the stuff of fiction, it is a radical, lived act of returning to parts of the self that were once buried by shame, silence, or survival. To revisit the past as a queer person is not to indulge nostalgia, but to enact healing. A queer adult might look back on a muted childhood not with sorrow, but with tenderness, extending love and protection to the version of themselves who once had none. Through letters to younger selves, reimagined memories, or the simple act of speaking long-unspoken truths, queer people transform history into a source of power. At the same time, queerness cracks open the future, not as a straight line, but as a constellation of possibilities. In these imagined tomorrows, queer joy is not an exception, but a foundation, families are chosen and cherished, gender is boundless, and love is unshackled from scripts. Time, in queer hands, becomes a fluid continuum, one that allows us to honour our pasts, live deliberately in the present and craft futures, that were once denied.

5.2 Multiplicity of Selves – Living Across Layers of Identity:

Queer identities are rarely static. They shift, stretch, and ripple through time. A person may come out multiple times, to themselves and others, in different ways across a lifetime. Gender and sexuality can evolve not just in private, but in public, reasserting the idea that identity is not a destination, but an ongoing unfolding. Rather than viewing these changes as inconsistency, queer time frames them as continuity, a conversation between selves, all of whom are valid.

Within this framework, the self becomes a constellation rather than a singular point. Future selves are not separate from past ones, but in dialogue with them, extending the possibility that all versions of ourselves can coexist with dignity and purpose. This fluidity of identity allows for a richer, more expansive understanding of self, where growth is celebrated and every iteration of who we are, is embraced with authenticity and grace.

5.3 Intergenerational Imagination – Building Queer Futures Without a Script:

Traditional notions of generational legacy often depend on biological reproduction, inheritance and linear succession. Queerness, unanchored from these rigid structures, envisions legacy through entirely different means. It flourishes in chosen families, is carried forward in whispered stories, and is immortalized through mentorship and creative expression. A queer elder sharing hard-won wisdom with a young person just stepping into their identity is not simply passing a torch, it is engaging in a mutual exchange of experience, vulnerability and strength. A trans artist drawing inspiration from the writings of a long-gone queer ancestor isn't reaching backward in time, but participating in an ongoing dialogue that defies chronology. These are not top-down transmissions, but circular, generative relationships, living archives of care, resistance, and renewal. Queer futurity lives in shared glances, held hands and dreams that outlast us. In this expansive vision, queer time is not a constraint, but a canvas, an ever-evolving landscape where legacy is measured not by lineage, but by the depth of connection and the courage to imagine otherwise.

5.4 Futures That Were Denied, Futures Yet to Be Claimed:

For many queer individuals, the future once seemed like a closed door. The threat of violence, illness, or rejection turned tomorrow into a question mark. The AIDS crisis, for example, robbed an entire generation of gay men of the futures they were building. Today, reclaiming the right to imagine a future is a radical act. The future is no longer a luxury, it is a queer birthright. Artists, writers, activists and dreamers, craft futures in which queer people thrive not despite the world, but as its re-creators. These are not utopias, but visions grounded in hope and informed by history. Futures that honour grief, celebrate survival, and make space for every queer person to imagine their own tomorrow on their own terms. Queer futures are about thriving, where history and hope create a world where all queer lives are valued and celebrated.

5.5 Queerness as Temporal Liberation – Embracing Change and Possibility:

To live queerly is to embrace the uncertainty of becoming. Time becomes an ally rather than an adversary. There is no rush to settle, no deadline to fulfil a prewritten destiny. A person may bloom in their fifties, come out after decades of marriage, or fall in love in ways they never thought possible. This elasticity of becoming is a gift, a declaration that transformation is not failure, but freedom. When queer people free themselves from the tyranny of linear time, they also free others. They show the world that it is never too late to begin again, never too early to question, and never too strange to dream. Queerness, in its embrace of time's fluidity, opens up endless possibilities for reinvention, proving that life's richness lies in its unpredictability and the courage to live authentically at every stage.

5.6 The Timeless Now – Living in the In-Between:

One of the most radical gifts of queer time is its reimagining of the present, not as a mere pause between past and future, but as a boundless, sacred terrain in its own right. To live in queer time is to reclaim the so-called delays and detours, the slow unfolding of gender, the nonlinear coming-out journeys, the quiet years of becoming, as deeply meaningful. These moments, often misread as liminal or incomplete, are in fact where queer life pulses most vividly. They are not waiting rooms, they are sanctuaries of self-discovery. Within the timeless now, queer people create lives rich with intention, where identity is not hurried toward finality, but allowed to breathe, shift and evolve. The present becomes a space of empowerment rather than expectation, a meeting ground where past traumas, present truths, and imagined futures coexist, not in conflict, but in harmony. It is here, in this in-between, that queerness reveals its full temporal brilliance. Queer time dares us to remember differently, to live deeply, and to dream beyond the scripts we were given, across timelines, through generations and into futures still being born.

Chapter 29

Navigating Identity Crisis – Pronouns, Belonging, and Self-Discovery

---

1. The Weight of a Word – Why Pronouns Matter

Pronouns, often considered simple grammatical tools in everyday conversation, carry profound significance for many LGBTQ+ individuals. These small words, he, she, they, or others, hold the power to affirm or dismiss a person's identity. For people navigating the complexities of gender identity and expression, pronouns are far from trivial, they represent a validation of who they are and how they wish to be seen in the world. To understand why pronouns matter, it's essential to explore their emotional, social, and cultural weight.

1.1 The Psychological Relief of Correct Pronouns:

For LGBTQ+ individuals, using the correct pronouns is more than a matter of respect; it is a form of psychological relief. When a person is addressed by their chosen pronouns, it reinforces their sense of self and acknowledges their identity in a way that feels authentic. The emotional benefit of being gendered correctly is profound. It affirms that one's existence and gender identity are valid and that they are seen for who they truly are, not who others assume them to be. Conversely, the distress caused by misgendering can lead to feelings of alienation, frustration, and even dysphoria. Misgendering can invalidate the individual's identity and often, it feels like a denial of their very existence.

The act of being gendered correctly, whether by using the pronouns a person has shared or by addressing them in a way that aligns with their expressed identity, provides comfort and confidence. It's a simple, but powerful recognition of the person's humanity and truth. Misgendering, on the other hand, can feel like an erasure of one's identity and can significantly impact mental health. The psychological toll of being constantly misgendered contributes to increased stress, anxiety, and in many cases, depression.

1.2 Pronouns and Social Validation:

Pronouns are deeply embedded in social contexts. They represent more than just an individual's preferences, they are a way of signalling how a person fits into the world. For many, the struggle to have their pronouns respected is part of the larger fight for recognition within society. Using the correct pronouns is a way of asserting dignity and social acceptance. When someone misgenders another, it often reflects a broader societal refusal to recognize and honour the individual's identity. In social spaces, pronouns serve as symbols of belonging and affirmation. Within LGBTQ+ communities, being addressed with one's self-identified pronouns fosters a sense of connection and solidarity.

It signifies a shared understanding that gender identity is fluid, personal, and deserving of respect. A person's chosen pronouns are not merely linguistic markers, but a visible expression of how they wish to be seen and acknowledged in the world. When these pronouns are respected, it cultivates an environment of validation and inclusivity, reinforcing the importance of honouring each individual's truth.

For those who experience frequent misgendering, the social consequences can be devastating. It can isolate them from family, peers, or colleagues who refuse to respect their identity. However, as conversations about gender evolve, more people are becoming aware of the importance of using inclusive language, which helps create a safer environment for those navigating their gender identity. This growing awareness is essential in making LGBTQ+ individuals feel supported and understood in all areas of their lives.

1.3 Pronouns as a Cultural Tool for Identity Exploration:

Choosing new pronouns is often a powerful act of self-determination. For individuals in the LGBTQ+ community, especially those who are nonbinary or gender-nonconforming, selecting pronouns that better align with their gender identity can be a transformative experience. It allows them to step into a more authentic version of themselves. For many, this process is not a one-time event, but an ongoing journey, one that may involve trial and error, experimentation, and the discovery of a language that feels truly reflective of their identity.

In cultures where gender norms are rigidly defined, selecting a new pronoun is also an act of defiance and resistance. For example, using "they/them" pronouns, or adopting neopronouns like "ze/zir," can be a rejection of the binary gender system that insists everyone fits neatly into categories. This is an important step toward broadening societal views of gender, moving away from narrow, limiting boxes and embracing a more expansive view of human identity.

The act of choosing a pronoun, especially when it's not the conventional one assigned at birth, is an empowering declaration of agency. It affirms a person's ability to define their own identity on their terms, outside the pressures and limitations imposed by society. This is particularly important for young people or those still in the process of discovering their gender identity. For many, pronouns serve as a reflection of a deeper, more personal understanding of self.

1.4 The Pressure of Pronoun Choices:

Despite the freedom that pronouns can represent, there can also be pressure to "choose" a pronoun, especially in environments where there is an expectation of clear gender categorization. For some, the act of selecting pronouns can feel daunting, particularly if they are still in the process of understanding their own gender identity. The expectation to "decide" on a set pronoun may conflict with the fluidity of their experience. Many individuals in the LGBTQ+ community navigate the complex terrain of gender fluidity, where their sense of identity may shift over time. For those still in the process of exploration, choosing a set of pronouns may feel like an oversimplification of their evolving sense of self.

The pressure to conform to a fixed identity can feel overwhelming, as if one must immediately present a clear-cut version of themselves, even if they are still figuring things out. This pressure can sometimes lead to confusion, anxiety, and a sense of isolation, particularly when the world around them demands certainty.

However, the growing recognition that gender is not static offers hope. More and more people are embracing the idea that pronouns can be fluid and that it's okay for them to change over time. This is particularly important for those who might still be questioning their gender identity and are in the process of understanding where they fit on the gender spectrum. The freedom to experiment with pronouns, without fear of judgment, is a step toward greater inclusivity and understanding.

1.5 The Fluidity and Evolution of Pronouns:

Pronouns are not fixed or immutable. Just as language itself evolves, so too do the ways in which people express their gender identity. New pronouns emerge regularly, and while some may fade away, others gain widespread acceptance. The existence of neopronouns like "xe/xem" or "ey/em" demonstrates the dynamic nature of language and the need for inclusive options that reflect the diversity of gender experiences.

The fluidity of pronouns reflects the broader fluidity of gender itself. Just as some individuals' gender identities are not fixed, neither are their pronouns. This evolving understanding is a significant step forward in creating a world where people can be more fully themselves. It is a reminder that there is no one "right" way to express gender or to identify, there are only personal truths, and they are valid, regardless of societal expectations.

In a world where pronouns are constantly shifting, it's important to approach the use of pronouns with openness and respect. Being willing to ask for and honour someone's pronouns, even if they are unfamiliar, fosters a culture of inclusivity, allowing LGBTQ+ individuals to exist without the fear of erasure or invalidation.

1.6 Conclusion:

Pronouns serve as key tools for identity and recognition in the LGBTQ+ community. They go beyond mere grammatical function, embodying a deep connection to self, culture, and the desire for validation. The evolution and choice of pronouns can reflect personal journeys, social context, and resistance to conventional norms. Embracing the variety of pronouns and identities within the LGBTQ+ community allows individuals to define themselves on their own terms, fostering a more inclusive and compassionate world for all. By respecting and honouring pronouns, we affirm the right of each individual to exist authentically and with dignity, paving the way for a more inclusive and understanding society.

"Pronouns are more than words, they are declarations of identity, reflections of selfhood and acts of courage, in a world still learning to listen." – Anonymous

* LGBTQ+ Pronouns and Identities:

This table provides a comprehensive overview of pronouns commonly used in the LGBTQ+ community, along with various sexual and gender identities. It explains how individuals relate to these labels and pronouns, and why they matter in affirming diverse experiences of gender and sexuality. This guide highlights the role of pronouns and identities in LGBTQ+ inclusion:

Pronoun/Identity:	Explanation:	Why LGBTQ+ Individuals Relate:
He/Him	Traditionally masculine pronouns.	Used by cisgender and trans men who identify as male.
She/Her	Traditionally feminine pronouns.	Used by cisgender and trans women who identify as female.
They/Them	Gender-neutral pronouns.	Used by nonbinary, genderqueer and agender individuals.
Ze/Zir	Gender-neutral pronouns, alternative to he/she.	Used by those rejecting the gender binary.
Xe/Xem	Another set of gender-neutral pronouns.	Used by individuals seeking non-traditional pronouns.
Ey/Em	Alternative gender-neutral pronouns.	Preferred by gender-fluid or nonconforming people.
It/Its	Neutral pronouns with unique expression.	Some use it as a radical rejection of binary labels.
He/They	Masculine + gender-neutral mix.	Used by masculine individuals with fluid identity.
She/They	Feminine + gender-neutral mix.	Used by feminine individuals embracing fluidity.
Queer	Umbrella term rejecting traditional labels.	Embraces fluidity in gender and sexuality.
Gay	Attraction to same gender.	Common identity for men loving men or broader LGBTQ+.
Lesbian	Women attracted to women.	Affirms same-gender attraction with feminist roots.
Bisexual	Attraction to more than one gender.	Challenges binary thinking in sexual attraction.
Pansexual	Attraction regardless of gender.	Expresses gender-inclusive attraction.
Asexual	Lack of sexual attraction.	Affirms identity beyond sexual norms.
Demisexual	Sexual attraction only after emotional bond.	Explains identity between sexual and asexual.
Genderqueer	Nonbinary gender identity.	Rejects traditional gender roles and binaries.
Agender	Identifies with no gender.	Feels detached from gender categorization.

Pronoun/Identity:	Explanation:	Why LGBTQ+ Individuals Relate:
Two-Spirit	Indigenous identity with dual gender	Culturally unique expression of gender
Fluid	Changing identity over time.	Reflects evolving experience of self.
Intersex	Born with mixed sex characteristics.	May not identify with binary gender roles.
Questioning	Exploring gender or sexuality.	Reflects uncertainty and exploration.

2. Between Categories – Living Beyond the Binary

For many people, traditional gender pronouns and categories like "he" or "she" fail to capture the fullness of who they are. Gender, once viewed as a fixed binary, is increasingly being recognized as a spectrum, fluid, evolving and deeply personal. Rather than conform to predefined roles or linguistic expectations, a growing number of individuals are choosing to live in the spaces in between, embracing nonbinary identities, neopronouns, or even opting out of pronouns entirely. This choice is not about rejecting language, but about reshaping it to better reflect human diversity. Living beyond the binary allows individuals to reclaim their autonomy and express their true selves.

2.1 The Emotional Landscape of Nonbinary Existence:

Living outside the binary often means living outside of social assumptions. For many nonbinary people, the question "Are you a boy or a girl?" becomes not just irrelevant, but invasive. Choosing to use they/them, ze/hir, xe/xem, or other neopronouns is both a declaration of truth and a step toward personal freedom. Yet this freedom often comes at the cost of visibility fatigue, having to repeatedly explain one's pronouns, identity, or very existence to others. The emotional labour involved can be exhausting, but it also creates space for a different kind of pride, one rooted in authenticity and resilience.

2.2 The Struggle and Power of Language:

Language is often slow to reflect cultural shifts. For those living beyond the binary, finding the right words to describe oneself can be both empowering and limiting. English, like many dominant languages, has historically been built around a gender binary. But just as cultures evolve, so does language. The creation and adoption of neopronouns represent a pushback against linguistic rigidity, offering new tools for self-expression. These terms aren't just semantic placeholders, they're cultural innovations, forged in the fires of personal need and collective creativity.

Many nonbinary people report a sense of liberation when they finally find pronouns that feel right. The right words can quiet lifelong dysphoria, allowing a person to see themselves reflected in the language they hear and use.

Still, for every empowering moment, there are often disheartening ones, misgendering, dismissal, or confusion from others. Yet every new pronoun adopted, every time someone asks for correct usage, plants another seed for broader social understanding.

2.3 No Pronouns? No Problem:

Some individuals reject pronouns altogether, choosing to be referred to only by name. This decision often reflects a deeper relationship with selfhood, one that resists being boxed in by language that doesn't fit. For these individuals, names carry identity more accurately than any pronoun could. Choosing "name only" is not about being difficult or contrarian, it's about asserting autonomy over how one is perceived and spoken of in the world.

This approach is particularly meaningful in cultures or communities where binary pronouns carry heavy social implications. By rejecting pronouns, these individuals challenge both linguistic norms and societal expectations. They remind us that sometimes the most liberating act is not to redefine the categories, but to abandon them entirely.

2.4 Living in the In-Between:

Ambiguity is often misunderstood as indecisiveness. But in the context of gender, living in-between can be a conscious, confident way of being. Many nonbinary people report that their gender identity is fluid, it shifts with time, mood, presentation, or relationship. This variability doesn't make their identity less valid, it makes it richer, more layered. Embracing this movement between categories allows individuals to hold multiple truths at once.

The concept of "genderfluid" or "agender" resists static labels. These identities speak to a broader truth, that certainty is not a requirement for authenticity. People can be questioning, transitioning, or simply uninterested in defining their gender at all. That openness itself is a kind of wisdom, one that disrupts society's obsession with neatly ordered identities.

2.5 Global and Cultural Echoes of Gender Expansiveness:

Nonbinary identities are not a modern or Western invention. Many cultures have long recognized more than two genders. From the hijras of South Asia to the fa'afafine of Samoa, the muxe in Mexico to the Two-Spirit individuals among Indigenous North American tribes, gender variance is embedded in global history. These traditions remind us that Western gender binaries are neither universal nor natural, they are cultural constructs that can be reshaped, resisted, or reimagined.

As these global identities enter wider conversations, they offer valuable perspectives on what it means to live beyond the binary. They also underscore the importance of decolonizing gender, recognizing that many nonbinary individuals are also navigating race, culture, and colonization, in tandem with gender. By embracing these diverse global identities, we can challenge and expand our understanding of gender, fostering a more inclusive world for all.

2.6 The Beauty of Undefined Identities:

There is a quiet kind of strength in not having to explain yourself. In choosing ambiguity over definition, some people find a freedom that rigid categories can't offer. Whether through pronouns, fashion, behaviour, or simply presence, nonbinary individuals challenge societal expectations just by existing. Their lives show that authenticity speaks for itself, and identity, like art, thrives without rigid boundaries.

The discomfort that society often feels in the face of ambiguity is its own limitation, not a reflection of those who choose to live undefined. Those who exist beyond the binary offer a new vision of selfhood, one that is open, dynamic, and deeply human.

2.7 Conclusion – Redefining Certainty:

Living beyond the binary is not a sign of confusion, it is an expression of freedom. It opens the door to becoming without the pressure of arriving at a fixed definition. As more people embrace gender expansiveness, society must learn to make space for fluidity, multiplicity, and transformation. Instead of demanding certainty, we can respond with curiosity. Instead of insisting on resolution, we can offer compassion. In the liminal space beyond "he" or "she," there is no ambiguity, but a new and honest language of self. It's a place where identity is fluid and ever-evolving, allowing many to be truly seen for their complexity, free from predefined labels.

*Beyond the Binary – Evolving Pronouns, Identities and Cultural Contexts:

Aspect:	**Description:**	**Examples / Notes:**
Pronouns Are Evolving	Language is not fixed. Neopronouns (like xe/xem or ze/hir) and reclaimed pronouns (like it/its) are constantly being created or revived.	xe/xem, ze/hir, ey/em, it/its (reclaimed), no pronouns (just name). New forms emerge, especially online and in youth-led spaces.
LGBTQ+ Identities Are Intersectional	Identity terms vary based on region, culture, and history. Western labels (e.g., gay, lesbian) may not fully describe Indigenous or non-Western experiences.	Two-Spirit (Indigenous North American), Hijra (South Asia), Bakla (Philippines), Fa'afafine (Samoa), Muxe (Oaxaca, Mexico). These are not just "identities", but culturally embedded roles.

Aspect:	Description:	Examples / Notes:
Pronouns ≠ Sexual Orientation	Someone's pronouns don't automatically tell you their orientation. Gender identity and sexual orientation are separate, though they may inform each other.	A person can be gay and use they/them, bisexual and use he/him, asexual and use ze/hir, etc. Assumptions often cause harm or erasure.
Mixed or Fluid Pronoun Use	Many people use multiple pronouns depending on context, safety, or personal comfort. There is no "one correct" set.	Someone might use she/they, he/they, or change pronouns over time. Some use different sets in different languages or social settings.
No Pronouns / Name Only	Some people reject pronouns altogether, preferring only their name. This, too, is a valid identity choice.	Instead of saying "they are writing," you would say, "Sky is writing." This affirms autonomy over language.
Reclaimed or Controversial Pronouns	Some individuals reclaim pronouns that have been used harmfully against them, finding empowerment in subversion.	it/its is sometimes used intentionally by trans or nonbinary people. It is important to only use if explicitly invited.
Generational & Regional Shifts	Terms that resonate with younger generations may be unknown or uncomfortable to older LGBTQ+ individuals, or vice versa.	Older people may prefer "transsexual" or "gay" while younger folks may identify as genderqueer, pansexual, or nonbinary. Language evolves.
Online and Micro-Community Innovations	Platforms like Tumblr, Reddit, TikTok, and Discord, have accelerated the emergence of new identities and pronoun systems.	Words like voidpunk, noun-self pronouns (e.g., star/stars, bun/buns) show how identity can be creative and symbolic, even fantastical.

The "Beyond the Binary" table highlights the rich diversity of pronouns and gender identities across cultures and generations. It shows how language adapts to fluid identities, from neopronouns to name-only preferences, and how online communities help shape new expressions. It offers a clear and affirming guide to understanding gender beyond fixed categories, inviting openness to the evolving ways people express identity and find recognition.

3. When Language Fails – Belonging Without the Right Words

In some tongues, there are no words for "they/them." No space for a woman who loves another woman without invoking shame. No syllables soft enough to hold the expansiveness of a gender that doesn't align with binaries. For many LGBTQ+ people around the world, particularly in non-Western contexts or among older generations, the words needed to explain, affirm, or even whisper their truth are either missing or dangerously misused. It is a silent grief, this absence. Like trying to sing a song without notes, trying to name yourself in a language that was never built to hold you. Language, often seen as a tool of liberation, can also become a cage. The longing to be understood becomes tangled in the impossibility of translation.

3.1 When Pronouns Don't Fit and Labels Feel Foreign:

Even in cultures where queer vocabulary is growing, many find that the offered terms still feel like borrowed clothes, ill-fitting, itchy, not quite right. For those raised in multilingual households or who speak Indigenous or minority languages, the situation can be even more complex. What do you do when the only pronouns that exist in your native language misgender you? When there is no phrase for "non-binary," "asexual," or "polyamorous" in your family's tongue? The internal conflict becomes not just one of identity, but of cultural belonging. To speak in a language that raised you while denying who you are is a unique kind of heartache. The words that once brought you home now feel like doors locked from the inside.

3.2 Quiet Resistance – Reclaiming and Rewriting Language:

Still, within that ache, people find ways to push back. Some invent entirely new words, fusing gender-neutral suffixes into languages that never had them. Others dig deep into ancient lexicons to resurrect forgotten terms, reanimating them with modern queerness. Words once used as slurs are softened and worn into armour. Marginalized communities become linguists, poets, code-switchers, and alchemists, carving new space with each syllable. In some places, trans and queer youth develop their own vernacular, unintelligible to outsiders, but deeply affirming within chosen families. Language becomes not just a tool for communication, but a canvas for survival.

3.3 The Spaces Between Words – Communicating in Silence:

And yet, not all understanding requires language. In the absence of words, belonging often arrives through subtler, quieter forms. A lingering glance across a crowded room. The softness in someone's voice when they refer to you in a way that feels right, even if it isn't exact. The way someone offers their hand, or a place at their table, without demanding an explanation. For some, these gestures speak louder than any term ever could. When the right words do not exist, or are too dangerous to say out loud, connection thrives in pauses, in shared meals, in eyes that say: "I see you, even if we don't have the words yet." These moments remind us that belonging is not only about being named, it is about being known. Even in silence, there is a language of care, one that transcends grammar and translation, offering a quiet, but undeniable truth, you are understood, just as you are.

3.4 Holding the Grief of Erasure:

Still, the grief remains. It's the grief of not being able to come out to a grandmother, because your native tongue only contains "man" and "woman." Of having no way to say "I am in love with them" without choosing a gendered verb that misgenders your partner. Of feeling the distance grow with every conversation in your mother tongue, because to stay close to your culture means staying silent about your truth. These are quiet sorrows that don't always have a place in broader conversations about queer liberation. They are not always loud, but they are deeply felt. To mourn the loss of linguistic belonging is valid and necessary. It is an act of honouring the parts of ourselves that have been rendered invisible by vocabulary.

3.5 Belonging Without Definition:

And yet, in the silence, some find freedom. The lack of labels can offer room to breathe. For those who never felt at home in the English-centric alphabet soup of LGBTQIA+, the absence of precise terms becomes an invitation to live authentically, undefined. There is power in resisting the urge to translate yourself completely. Some choose to exist in the margins, in the spaces that defy categorization. They find kinship not through shared language, but shared experience, shared hurt, shared joy, shared resistance. Identity becomes less about words and more about resonance. You don't always have to name your truth to live it. In a world that so often demands explanation, choosing to simply be can itself be a radical act of self-acceptance and quiet rebellion.

3.6 A Language of Survival and Invention:

Across continents and generations, queer people have always found ways to speak, even when silenced. From the defiant rhythms of ballroom slang to the coded whispers exchanged during times of persecution, from TikTok's captioned in multiple languages to reach someone who might understand, queer language is vibrant, adaptive and defiantly alive. It doesn't just describe who we are, it protects us. When official languages exclude or endanger us, unofficial ones rise in their place, inside jokes, layered emojis, shared glances, gestures, art, and fashion. These are not just tools of expression, they are lifelines. Dialects of survival. Proof that even when language fails us, we will always find ways to be heard.

3.7 Building Bridges Through Imperfection:

In the end, the search for belonging in language is not about perfection. It's about presence. About finding someone who listens when you fumble through half-sentences, or who understands your silence when you can't speak at all. It's about learning to say, "I don't have the right word, but here's how I feel," and having that be enough. It's about holding space for each other's evolving vocabularies, and for the parts of us still unnamed. Sometimes, the most intimate conversations happen in broken speech and deep breaths. In the end, it is less about the words we have, and more about how we use them, to see, to hold, to affirm. Because in the spaces where language falters, love, presence, and recognition can still build bridges strong enough to carry us home.

3.8 Conclusion – I See You:

For anyone who has ever searched the corners of a dictionary and still come up empty, who has ever been misnamed in their own language, who has had to translate their truth into something their family might understand, there is a quiet, sacred solidarity. You are not alone. Even in the absence of the perfect phrase, your experience is real. You deserve to be known, not just by definition, but by presence, by intention, by care. Sometimes, the most powerful thing someone can say to you is not a word at all, it's a look, a gesture, an acknowledgment, I see you. And in that moment, you belong.

4. Community Mirrors – How Others Shape Self-Discovery

Sometimes, self-recognition begins with seeing someone else. A friend casually expressing their gender fluidity, a partner who uses language for love that finally makes sense, or a stranger online who shares a story that feels uncannily like your own, these moments become turning points. They offer a sudden clarity, a realization that what once felt odd or invisible has a name, a shape, a place in the world. For many queer individuals, especially those growing up isolated or in unsupportive environments, community becomes the mirror that reveals what was always there. It's not imitation, but resonance. Recognition. A gentle, "Oh, me too," that opens doors to deeper understanding.

4.1 The Power of Being Seen:

When someone sees you, really sees you, it can be life-changing. In safe, affirming spaces, being addressed with the right pronouns, or simply being believed when you share your truth, can anchor a sense of self that once felt uncertain. These moments create a feeling of safety that runs deeper than language, an emotional safety that allows growth, curiosity, and courage. Chosen family often becomes the first place where this happens. People who don't just accept you, but affirm you, sometimes before you can even articulate your identity yourself. These relationships act like tuning forks for the soul, helping you find your own frequency in the noise of the world.

4.2 When Mirrors Distort:

But community isn't always safe. Sometimes, the very spaces meant to offer belonging also reflect back distortion. Within LGBTQ+ circles, hierarchies, gatekeeping, and bias can still exist. When someone's identity is questioned, "Are you queer enough?", "Are you really nonbinary if you look like that?", "Why do your pronouns keep changing?" It creates a wound that cuts especially deep. It's painful when those who should understand instead project scepticism or discomfort. These distorted reflections can sow self-doubt or silence experimentation. And yet, even in these moments, the friction can spark clarity. Being misunderstood often helps sharpen the truth of who you are. In those moments of distortion, growth can emerge, as we learn to trust our own reflection over others' projections.

4.3 The Digital Mirror:

Online spaces have become powerful mirrors for queer self-discovery. Social media and online platforms offer access to stories and identities beyond one's immediate world.

A teenager in a conservative town might stumble upon a YouTube channel, a meme thread, or a piece of fanfiction that names the unnameable inside them. These digital encounters often precede "real life" conversations and give people permission to explore in private before speaking aloud. While the internet can harbour toxicity, it also offers an expansive hall of mirrors, some cracked, some blurry, but many reflecting back a vision of self that feels finally, mercifully, whole.

4.4 Generations Talking Across Time:

Intergenerational connection offers another kind of mirror, one that stretches across time, anchoring selfhood in lineage and legacy. Queer elders, whether activists, artists, or quiet survivors, carry lived truths that younger generations can draw from. Listening to their stories, struggles, and joys provides context, resilience, and perspective. For someone navigating their identity today, a conversation with someone who walked through a very different era might offer unexpected recognition. Even silence between generations, the stories not told, the identities buried, can become instructive. They remind us of the cost of invisibility and the importance of continuing the work. The reflection isn't always direct, but it is always meaningful.

4.5 Community as a Canvas for Becoming:

Self-discovery rarely happens in isolation, it unfolds in the presence of others. Community becomes a canvas where identity can be explored, shaped, and reshaped. Within these spaces, people are free to experiment, with names, pronouns, aesthetics, and expressions, while being seen and held through the process. It's a space for rehearsal, where trying on different versions of self is not only allowed, but welcomed. Even when discomfort arises, when an old identity no longer fits, or when friends struggle to understand, those moments become part of the creative work of becoming. Identity isn't a destination, it's a living, shifting practice. And community, at its best, offers the safety to evolve without needing to have it all figured out.

4.6 When You Become the Mirror for Someone Else:

Eventually, there comes a moment when the mirror turns. When your story, your presence, and your truth become a reflection, that helps someone else see themselves more clearly. A younger sibling who watches you come out. A coworker who starts exploring their pronouns after you share yours. A friend who confides in you after years of silent questions. You don't always realize when it happens, but you become part of someone else's journey, proof that they are not alone. In those moments, community becomes cyclical. The reflections offered to you are passed forward, multiplied, and made new. Your journey becomes a guide, helping others embrace their truth.

4.7 Wholeness in the Glimpses:

No mirror offers a complete picture. Our sense of self is often built from fragments, a conversation here, a meme there, a partner's gentle correction, a stranger's knowing nod. The fullness of identity is never contained in one moment, one label, or one reflection. It's stitched together through connection, over time. Self-discovery, then, is not a solitary excavation, it is a collaborative process.

Others don't define who we are, but they do help us see more clearly. In their presence, we find permission. In their stories, we find language. In their love, we find ourselves.

* Living Out Loud – Real Voices, Real Pronouns, Real Pride:

Alok Vaid-Menon (United States/India):

- **Pronouns:** They/Them
- **Identity:** Gender non conforming, transfeminine
- **Why:** Alok uses they/them pronouns to resist the binary gender structure imposed by colonial systems. They see gender as a fluid, personal experience and use fashion, poetry, and performance to express their truth. Alok is outspoken about the right to self-identify and the violence nonbinary people face.

Vivek Shraya (Canada):

- **Pronouns:** She/They
- **Identity:** Transgender woman, artist, writer, musician
- **Why:** Vivek embraces both she and they pronouns to reflect the complexity of her gender and cultural experience as a South Asian trans woman. She explores identity through storytelling and music, emphasizing that femininity and fluidity can coexist.

Jin Xing (China):

- **Pronouns:** She/Her
- **Identity:** Transgender woman, ballerina, TV host
- **Why:** Jin Xing is one of China's first openly transgender celebrities. Her pronoun choice reflects her affirmed womanhood post-transition. She uses her platform to normalize transgender identities in a conservative media environment, though she often avoids activist labels due to local censorship.

Thishiwe Ziqubu (South Africa):

- **Pronouns:** They/Them
- **Identity:** Trans nonbinary

- **Why:** Thishiwe, an award-winning filmmaker and actor, uses they/them pronouns to assert their gender identity outside the male/female binary. They've spoken about how colonization disrupted African understandings of gender, and reclaim their cultural roots through their identity.

Estefanía Veloz (Mexico):

- **Pronouns:** She/Her
- **Identity:** Queer feminist, activist
- **Why:** While identifying as a cis queer woman, Estefanía advocates for inclusive language in Spanish (e.g. use of "elle") and champions the pronoun rights of trans and nonbinary people in Latin America. Her activism focuses on legal reform and visibility.

KaladKaren Davila (Philippines):

- **Pronouns:** She/Her
- **Identity:** Transgender woman, TV personality
- **Why:** KaladKaren uses she/her pronouns as a public affirmation of her transition and identity. In a country where visibility is growing but stigma remains, she plays a crucial role in challenging stereotypes and advocating for representation.

Courtney Act (Australia):

- **Pronouns:** She/Her (in drag), He/Him (out of drag), They/Them (also embraced)
- **Identity:** Gender-fluid, pansexual
- **Why:** Courtney embraces multiple pronouns depending on context, she/her while in drag, he/him otherwise, and they/them to express the fluidity of gender beyond performance. Their openness invites conversation about drag, gender play, and identity beyond binaries.

Vladimir Luxuria (Italy):

- **Pronouns:** She/Her
- **Identity:** Transgender woman, former parliamentarian
- **Why:** Luxuria chose she/her to affirm her trans identity while entering politics. As Europe's first openly transgender member of parliament, she used her platform to speak on LGBTQ+ rights in a traditionally conservative culture.

Her visibility helped shift public discourse in Italy, and she remains a powerful symbol of resilience, using media, literature, and activism to challenge transphobia and push for inclusive legislation.

Linn da Quebrada (Brazil):

- **Pronouns:** She/Her
- **Identity:** Transgender woman, queer artist
- **Why:** Linn is a performance artist and singer whose work critiques gender, class and race. Her pronoun choice aligns with her self-affirmed womanhood, and she challenges Brazilian society's rigid norms through art, performance, and political discourse.

Kasha Jacqueline Nabagesera (Uganda):

- **Pronouns:** She/Her
- **Identity:** Lesbian activist
- **Why:** In one of the most hostile countries for LGBTQ+ people, Kasha uses she/her pronouns and proudly identifies as a lesbian. She is a fierce advocate for safety and visibility in Uganda, often at great personal risk.

Elliot Page (Canada/USA):

- **Pronouns:** He/They
- **Identity:** Transmasculine, nonbinary
- **Why:** Elliot shared that using he/they reflects both his masculinity and his nonbinary experience. Coming out publicly in 2020, he has spoken about the joy and relief of being seen, and the importance of accurate representation in media.

Janelle Monáe (USA):

- **Pronouns:** They/She
- **Identity:** Nonbinary, pansexual
- **Why:** Janelle uses both they/she to reflect a fluid identity that defies labels. They've described gender as a spectrum and believe embracing multiple pronouns mirrors the complexity of their truth.

Sam Smith (UK):

- **Pronouns:** They/Them
- **Identity:** Nonbinary, queer
- **Why:** Sam stated that they feel "just as much a woman as a man," and that using they/them pronouns helps them feel more aligned with who they are. Their choice sparked mainstream conversations about nonbinary identity.

Demi Lovato (USA):

- **Pronouns:** They/She
- **Identity:** Nonbinary, queer
- **Why:** Demi uses they/she to reflect their gender fluidity and evolving self. They've emphasized that their identity may continue to shift, and their pronoun use is part of embracing that fluid journey.

Sarah McBride (USA):

- **Pronouns:** She/Her
- **Identity:** Transgender woman, politician
- **Why:** As the first openly transgender state senator in the U.S. (Delaware), McBride's identity and pronouns are a powerful political statement. She represents hope, progress, and the visibility of trans people in governance.

Georgina Beyer (New Zealand):

- **Pronouns:** She/Her
- **Identity:** Transgender woman, former MP (deceased 2023)
- **Why:** The world's first openly transgender member of parliament, Beyer used she/her to affirm her womanhood and campaigned on issues like anti-discrimination and sex workers' rights.

Munroe Bergdorf (UK):

- **Pronouns:** She/Her

- **Identity:** Transgender woman, activist, model
- **Why:** Munroe is vocal about the role of pronouns in trans liberation and self-definition. Her visibility in the fashion industry challenges exclusion and tokenism.

Bilal Hassani (France):

- **Pronouns:** He/They
- **Identity:** Nonbinary, queer, singer
- **Why:** Representing France at Eurovision, Bilal uses he/they to express a nonbinary identity while engaging in hyperfeminine performance. They speak to the fluidity of gender and artistic freedom.

Petra De Sutter (Belgium):

- **Pronouns:** She/Her
- **Identity:** Transgender woman, Deputy Prime Minister
- **Why:** The highest-ranking transgender politician in Europe, De Sutter's use of she/her pronouns is both personal and political, affirming the legitimacy of trans people in public office.

Ricky Nathanson (Zimbabwe):

- **Pronouns:** She/Her
- **Identity:** Transgender woman, human rights defender
- **Why:** In a country with deeply hostile anti-LGBTQ+ laws, Ricky's visibility and pronoun use are acts of resistance. She won a landmark legal case after being arrested for using a women's bathroom.

Laverne Cox (USA):

- **Pronouns:** She/Her
- **Identity:** Transgender woman, actress, advocate
- **Why:** One of the first trans women to break into mainstream Hollywood, Laverne emphasizes the role of language in dignity, and she frequently educates the public on the emotional impact of misgendering.

Dutee Chand (India):

- **Pronouns:** She/Her
- **Identity:** Lesbian, elite sprinter
- **Why:** India's first openly gay athlete, Dutee uses her platform to fight stigma in sports. Her pronouns affirm her womanhood, which she had to defend in the face of sex-testing and institutional scrutiny.

Treechada "Poyd" Petcharat (Thailand):

- **Pronouns:** She/Her
- **Identity:** Transgender woman, actress, model
- **Why:** A celebrated actress, Poyd uses she/her as a confirmation of her womanhood and Thailand's complex but often more visible trans culture. She helps normalize trans identities in the Thai entertainment industry.

Binyavanga Wainaina (Kenya):

- **Pronouns:** He/Him (while living)
- **Identity:** Gay man, writer (deceased 2019)
- **Why:** One of the first high-profile Kenyans to come out publicly, Wainaina used his pronouns and voice to challenge deep homophobia across the continent. His memoir and essays centre identity, belonging and defiance.

Harisu (South Korea):

- **Pronouns:** She/Her
- **Identity:** Transgender woman, singer, actress
- **Why:** As Korea's first transgender celebrity, Harisu paved the way for representation in a conservative society. Her use of she/her pronouns aligns with her transition and serves as public affirmation in her media appearances.

In summary, LGBTQ+ individuals across diverse cultures use pronouns to affirm identity, resist binary norms and foster visibility. Pronouns become tools of self-expression, political defiance, and cultural transformation, reflecting fluidity, personal truth, and the ongoing struggle for recognition and respect.

5. Becoming Again and Again – Identity as a Lifelong Process

Identity is often framed as something to be discovered, an ultimate truth about oneself waiting to be unearthed. But for many LGBTQ+ people, selfhood is not a single destination, it is an unfolding journey. The notion that one must arrive at a fixed identity can create unnecessary pressure and shame for those who continue to evolve. Instead of aiming for permanence, embracing impermanence offers a deeper kind of truth, that we are allowed to change, again and again, without betraying who we once were.

Moments of clarity may come, but they are rarely the end. What feels true at one stage in life may shift with time, experience, or healing. Holding space for that shift is not a sign of uncertainty, but a mark of authenticity. Living out loud means making peace with the fact that you may not always have the same name, gender, orientation, or language for yourself, and that's okay. It is not constancy that defines us, but the courage to remain honest with who we are in each unfolding moment.

5.1 Identity in Motion – Geography, Community and Change:

Where we are, and who we are with, can shape how we understand ourselves. Moving between places, cultures, or communities can open doors to new facets of identity. A nonbinary person might feel more affirmed in one city than another. A trans man might discover comfort using different pronouns among friends than at work. These shifts are not contradictions, but reflections of the relational nature of identity.

Political climates can also influence how freely identity is expressed. What may be safe and celebrated in one country could be dangerous in another. The ability to express oneself authentically can expand or constrict based on external realities. Yet, even in silence or coded language, identity lives on. It adapts, survives, and when possible, reemerges. The act of becoming does not always mean coming out louder, it can mean coming inward, protecting the self in hostile environments, and revisiting it when the time is right.

5.2 The Courage to Un-Define:

In a world obsessed with definitions, labels, and categories, choosing to remain undefined is a quiet revolution. For LGBTQ+ individuals, there can be pressure to explain or prove one's identity to others. But selfhood does not owe anyone an explanation. Sometimes, the most honest answer to "who are you?" is "I'm still learning." There is strength in allowing the self to remain a question, open, evolving, and alive.

Choosing to let go of rigid identity markers doesn't mean a lack of clarity, it means trusting your inner landscape enough to let it shift without panic. People may move from lesbian to bi to queer to unlabelled, not because they are confused, but because they are attuned to the ways their heart changes shape. These transitions are not losses of identity, they are expansions of it, evidence that the self is not a fixed point, but a vast, unfolding landscape capable of holding many truths over time.

Pronouns, too, can be part of this gentle redefinition. Someone may move from she to they, from he to she, or use multiple pronouns at once, not to be trendy, but to reflect the texture of their becoming. Each choice is a moment of alignment, not a final stamp.

5.3 Fluidity as Truth, Not Trend:

Fluidity is not a phase to outgrow, it is a mode of existence to embrace. Western narratives often value stability and clarity, but queer lives have long taught that identity is nuanced, layered and ever-shifting. The language of "settling down" doesn't always apply, many queer people are instead "opening up" over time, to new understandings of themselves.

Pronoun changes, relationship redefinitions, spiritual awakenings, or new gender expressions can all emerge later in life, and each deserves to be honoured. Even grief or trauma can reshape identity. A person may find they feel differently about their gender after transitioning, or their sexuality after losing a partner. These evolutions are not deviations from the self but deeper arrivals into it.

Fluidity is not about indecision, it's about listening. And in that listening, people often find peace not in a final label, but in the freedom to live beyond one.

5.4 Making Peace with Doubt:

Doubt is not the enemy of authenticity. It is the soil in which more honest identities can take root. Doubt invites reflection, and reflection allows growth. Those who question their pronouns, their past labels, or their present desires are not betraying their community; they are embodying the very essence of queer becoming.

For many, doubt comes with guilt, especially if public declarations have already been made. But changing your mind is not erasure. You were not wrong before, you were real then, and you are real now. The act of revisiting identity with gentleness is a radical act of self-love.

Rather than seeing identity as a path to certainty, it can be approached as a path to honesty. The most powerful form of pride is not knowing with absolute surety, it's standing in the truth of who you are today, even if that truth might change tomorrow.

5.5 A Lifelong Becoming:

There is beauty in returning to yourself, over and over. LGBTQ+ lives are not linear, they spiral, twist, loop, and bloom. At every stage, something new can be discovered or reclaimed. The idea of "finally figuring it out" can be replaced with "continuing to unfold."

For those just beginning, for those in mid-transition, and for those decades into their journey, the invitation is the same, keep becoming. Make room for the person you are today, and welcome the person you'll meet tomorrow. There is no endpoint to selfhood, only deepening.

Pronouns, names, identities, roles, may all change. But what remains is the act of becoming, again and again. Not despite the changes, but because of them.

5.6 A Hopeful Home in the Present Moment:

There is something quietly powerful and profoundly hopeful in embracing yourself as a work in progress. It means life remains full of possibility, more to feel, more to discover, more to grow into. It lifts the pressure to rush toward certainty, reminding us that we don't need to arrive at a final label or fixed conclusion. We can simply be, as we are, in this moment.

To affirm who you are right now, with all the joy, doubt, clarity, and contradiction that might include, is a radical act of self-trust. It says, I am unfinished, and that is not a flaw, it's a gift.

To live a queer life is to live in resistance to finality. It is to welcome change, to expand with experience, and to remain open to becoming. And in that open-endedness, there is not only freedom, but a deep, enduring kind of peace.

Chapter 30

The Future of LGBTQ+ Identities and Relationships

---

1. How Will Gender and Sexuality Evolve in the Next Century?

In the century to come, the rigid scaffolding of binary gender will likely dissolve into a much more fluid and personalized spectrum. With growing acceptance of non-binary and gender-fluid identities, future generations may find the very concept of "male" and "female" insufficient. Children may be raised with open-ended identities, encouraged to explore gender without the confines of tradition. Language, too, will evolve, gender-neutral pronouns may no longer be considered "neutral," but rather default. The evolution won't merely be social, biometric and neurobiological understandings of gender will challenge the outdated idea that gender is biologically fixed. As neuroscience deepens its grasp on consciousness and identity, gender may become more about internal truths than external characteristics. The result will be a world where gender presentation is not just accepted in its diversity, but creatively embraced, where fashion, behaviour, and roles are no longer mapped by the sex assigned at birth, but curated like art.

1.1 Queer by Default – A Future Where Heteronormativity Loses Its Grip:

Sexuality, much like gender, may shed the expectation of default heterosexuality. As educational systems introduce children to the full spectrum of sexual orientation from a young age, people may grow up identifying not as "straight unless otherwise discovered," but as fluid until further explored. In this future, the idea of "coming out" might vanish entirely, because queerness won't be a deviation from the norm, it will simply be part of human variety. Polysexuality and pansexuality could become mainstream identities, normalized and respected. Heteronormative scripts of romance and desire, historically reinforced by media and religion, will likely lose their authoritative grip. Dating apps of the future may no longer begin with a gender preference filter, but instead with shared values, energy compatibility, or even real-time emotional resonance detected via wearable tech. Instead of boxing people into rigid categories, society may come to view sexuality as a lifelong journey of rediscovery.

1.2 Technology and the New Erotic Frontier:

As virtual and augmented reality continue to advance, the boundaries of physical intimacy will stretch in unimaginable ways. People will engage in relationships with AI beings, participate in immersive erotic experiences beyond physical constraints, and explore identities that aren't tied to human biology. Sexbots, once taboo, may be as common as smartphones, customizable partners that adapt not only to our physical preferences, but to our emotional and intellectual needs. Gendered AI personalities may not be based on stereotypes, but developed from a person's desired expression of intimacy and communication. Virtual reality may let individuals explore different gendered avatars, freely experimenting with identity and expression.

These technologies won't merely supplement human connection, they'll redefine it. The line between physical and digital love may blur, leading to new forms of kinship and bonding that don't require a human body at all.

1.3 Rewriting the Architecture of Relationships:

Traditional relationship models, marriage, monogamy, and nuclear families, will be challenged and reimagined on a global scale. With societal support shifting from family units to communal networks, people may choose to form "constellations" of relationships, polycules, platonic partnerships, queerplatonic bonds, or co-parenting arrangements not based on romantic or sexual love. Legal systems could evolve to recognize multiple-partner unions, dissolving the privileging of dyadic relationships. In this future, the legitimacy of a bond won't be judged by sexual exclusivity or marriage licenses, but by mutual care, shared resources, and emotional depth. Relationship anarchy may not be a fringe philosophy but a mainstream practice. The state, once a key architect of domestic life, may relinquish control over how people form families, offering flexible frameworks that recognize love in its many forms. Queer theory, currently taught in specialized academic spaces, could become foundational to the way all people understand connection.

1.4 Global Cultures of Fluidity and Resistance:

The evolution of gender and sexuality will not progress at the same rate globally, but digital connectivity will forge new solidarities. Grassroots queer movements, powered by blockchain or decentralized social networks, will sidestep censorship in authoritarian regimes. Artists, activists, and technologists from marginalized communities will use future tools, holography, brain-to-brain communication, and mixed-reality storytelling, to share their truths and expand collective consciousness. Gender-nonconforming identities from Indigenous cultures, like the hijra in South Asia, Two-Spirit in Native traditions, or the fa'afafine of Samoa, could receive long-overdue global reverence, reshaping Western-centric understandings of identity. In countries currently hostile to LGBTQ+ people, underground networks may use encrypted metaverses as sanctuaries for self-expression and advocacy. Rather than being erased, local queer traditions may become sites of digital preservation, creating global mosaics of queer resilience and wisdom. The future belongs not to a homogenized ideal of progress, but to a kaleidoscope of localized, coexisting expressions of love and selfhood.

1.5 The Biology of Desire – Queering Evolution Itself:

In the next century, our understanding of the biological foundations of sexuality and gender may undergo a profound transformation. Advances in genetic editing and hormone modulation could allow individuals to tailor aspects of their gender and sexual identity in alignment with their evolving sense of self. Synthetic hormones might enable people to fluidly shift between masculinized and feminized states, not as part of a medical transition, but as a form of dynamic personal expression. Neuroscience may unlock the mechanisms of attraction itself, offering ways to enhance, reroute, or even quiet desire. Some might opt to experience a form of chosen asexuality through neural modulation, while others could heighten their sensuality via biofeedback or neurostimulation technologies. The possibilities will push boundaries not just scientifically, but ethically.

Is it true liberation to engineer our identities at the molecular level, or could this become a new kind of conformity shaped by societal ideals? As science expands the toolkit of identity, it will also compel us to wrestle with deeper questions: What does it mean to desire authentically in a world where desire can be designed?

1.6 Beyond Identity – A Post-Label Future?

Perhaps the most radical transformation of all will be a move away from identity as a rigid marker. As the social need for categorization weakens, people may begin to view identity as contextual rather than fixed. Rather than introducing oneself with pronouns or orientations, people might describe their relational preferences situationally, "Today I am drawn to softness," or "In this space, I feel masculine energy." Identity, then, becomes a living document, editable, evolving, unfixed. This doesn't mean the end of community or pride, rather, pride itself may shift from allegiance to a label to celebration of fluidity, flux, and freedom. The future of gender and sexuality won't be a perfect utopia, but it may be a world where the most radical act is simply to be, and to be seen, in all our multiplicity. As the next century unfolds, one truth is likely to remain, human beings will continue to reach for connection, expression, and love. But how we define and design those experiences is poised to become more diverse, more imaginative, and freer than ever before.

2. The Impact of Globalization on Queer Identity

As globalization continues to shrink the distances between cultures, queer identity finds itself both liberated and complicated. On one hand, international connectivity has allowed LGBTQ+ individuals across vastly different geographies to discover shared language, struggle, and solidarity. On the other, globalization often exports Western understandings of queerness that can obscure or overwrite local queer histories and traditions. The spread of Pride parades, rainbow capitalism, and English-centric queer discourse has brought visibility, but not always inclusivity. In many non-Western societies, queerness existed long before colonial intervention, often in sacred, fluid, or culturally unique forms. Globalization risks flattening these identities into digestible formats, aligning them with marketable Western norms. As global media exports certain forms of queer visibility, it may inadvertently marginalize expressions of queerness that don't fit the mold of urban, liberal and consumer-friendly narratives.

2.1 Digital Borders and the Rise of the Transnational Queer:

The internet has created a new kind of queer citizen, one who exists in both physical and digital spaces, often simultaneously. Platforms like TikTok, Reddit and Instagram, have allowed queer people in restrictive countries to access affirming content and forge chosen communities across borders. In the coming decades, digital tools will continue to shape how queer people define and perform their identities. A person in Nairobi may find kinship with a drag performer in Berlin, a trans teenager in Jakarta may find mentorship from a nonbinary coder in Toronto. This transnational connectivity is powerful, but not without its fractures. Cultural references don't always translate, and there can be assumptions of shared values that don't align across class, religion, or region.

As algorithms privilege dominant content, global queer identity may increasingly skew toward those with internet access, English fluency and aesthetic appeal, leaving others underrepresented.

2.2 Global Markets, Queer Commodification and Identity Politics:

As multinational corporations recognize the purchasing power of the LGBTQ+ demographic, the commodification of queer identity is poised to deepen. Pride collections, rainbow-branded advertising, and influencer partnerships now dominate global marketing strategies during designated "Pride seasons." In many ways, this visibility has brought safety and affirmation to queer people, seeing one's identity reflected in mainstream spaces can be life-changing. Yet the marriage of queerness and capitalism comes with tension. Global brands often promote queer inclusion in Western markets while remaining silent in countries with anti-LGBTQ+ laws. Queer identity is increasingly packaged for consumption, sometimes stripped of its political roots in resistance, struggle and community-building. Over time, this could lead to a generation of queer individuals whose primary association with identity is through aesthetics and consumption, rather than activism or community engagement. Yet in a globalized economy, this commodification also creates visibility that local activists can harness to advance rights and representation in more conservative contexts.

2.3 Diasporic Queerness and the Tensions of Belonging:

Migration, whether forced or voluntary, often creates layered and complex queer experiences. For queer people within diasporic communities, identity is shaped by multiple cultural expectations, sometimes contradictory, sometimes harmonizing. A queer Afghan refugee in Germany may experience liberation from persecution, but still feel obligated to perform cultural traditions that silence or shame queerness. Within diaspora spaces, the pressure to remain "authentic" to one's culture of origin can clash with the desire for personal freedom. Yet these spaces can also produce unique forms of queer expression that blend language, tradition and rebellion. Globalization ensures that diasporic queerness will continue to grow, as more people navigate transcontinental identities. The future will see more cultural fusions, drag infused with folkloric dance, queer rituals born from ancient customs, LGBTQ+ organizing framed through diasporic faith. These hybrid identities resist homogenization and remind us that globalization is not just about Western export, but also about the reinvention of identity in new soils.

2.4 Activism in a Global Age – Shared Strategies, Divergent Realities:

Queer activism is increasingly transnational. Movements for LGBTQ+ rights in one country are now informed, supported, and amplified by movements in others. Hashtags like #LoveIsLove and #TransRightsAreHumanRights transcend borders, creating global moments of unity and protest. Yet the lived realities of queer people remain deeply shaped by local law, culture and custom. Strategies that work in New York may be disastrous in Nairobi. Activists in the Global South often criticize the imposition of Western tactics that fail to consider local nuances. Moreover, governments use the rhetoric of Western influence to discredit and suppress queer movements, framing them as colonial imports.

As globalization spreads queer resistance, it also demands a new kind of humility, one that centres listening, adaptation and mutual learning. The next generation of activists will likely develop a hybrid model of organizing, rooted locally, networked globally, and responsive to the specific textures of oppression and resistance.

2.5 The Language of Identity in a Globalized World:

Language is both a tool of liberation and a gatekeeper of recognition. English dominates global queer discourse, and with it, a vocabulary of identity, nonbinary, pansexual, aromantic, that may not exist in local tongues. This can empower those with access to the language, while alienating those whose cultural contexts lack the words, or who use entirely different frameworks. The future of queer identity depends on linguistic multiplicity. Queer lexicons must grow not just in number, but in geography. Indigenous terms for gender variance and same-sex love must be preserved and elevated alongside modern labels. Activists, educators, and artists will play a key role in this process, translating not just words, but cultural frameworks. Globalization has the potential to create a more multilingual, pluralistic queer identity, where labels aren't imposed, but exchanged and honoured.

2.6 Identity, Surveillance and the Geopolitics of Visibility:

With the spread of global surveillance technologies, facial recognition, digital ID systems, biometric tracking, the question of queer visibility takes on new risk. In countries where queerness is criminalized, even the hint of identity online can lead to arrest, violence, or exile. Global tech companies, often based in liberal democracies, may collect data that puts queer lives at risk in other jurisdictions. The paradox of visibility is sharper than ever, being seen can mean affirmation, or it can mean danger. In the coming decades, privacy may become a new axis of queer liberation. Encrypted communication, virtual anonymity, and digital sanctuary spaces will be vital tools. Meanwhile, international pressure on tech companies to protect queer users will increase. Activists will need to understand not only the politics of pride, but also the architecture of algorithms, as the battle for identity moves deeper into cyberspace.

2.7 A Global Queer Future Rooted in Plurality:

Globalization will not forge a singular queer identity, but rather illuminate the vast spectrum of queerness already alive across the world. Its effects will mirror the nature of queerness itself, fluid, multifaceted, and often contradictory. Where some cultures risk losing local expressions to dominant narratives, others will respond with bold reinvention, reviving ancestral identities, blending languages, and reimagining queer life through radically new lenses.

For every attempt to universalize queerness, grassroots movements will rise to reclaim nuance, resisting erasure with creativity and resilience. The future will not be defined by uniformity, but by a vibrant interplay of contradictions, hybridity over homogeneity, complexity over simplicity. Queer identity will be a living mosaic, shaped by both sacred tradition and speculative possibility, by the deeply personal and the fiercely political.

Navigating this global landscape will require constant negotiation, between visibility and safety, between solidarity and sovereignty, between collective progress and cultural preservation. In embracing this plurality, a new ethic of queerness may take shape, one rooted not in assimilation, but in mutual respect, cultural exchange, and the right to be different together.

* Global LGBTQ+ Mental Health Initiatives (Real and Future-Facing):

International / Multi-Country:

➢ **The Trevor Project (USA, expanding internationally):**

- **Type:** Crisis intervention and suicide prevention for LGBTQ+ youth
- **Why it matters:** 24/7 support via phone, chat, and text data-driven research
- **Future-forward aspect:** Uses AI and predictive analytics to enhance care delivery

➢ **It Gets Better Project (Global):**

- **Type:** Storytelling and mental health empowerment platform
- **Why it matters:** Offers visibility and community to LGBTQ+ youth
- **Future-forward aspect:** Builds digital resilience and hope through global storytelling

➢ **LGBT National Help Center (US-based, global outreach):**

- **Type:** Peer support hotline and resources
- **Why it matters:** Offers anonymous help via trained LGBTQ+ volunteers
- **Future-forward aspect:** Scalable model for low-cost mental health infrastructure

---

United States / North America:

➢ **Trans Lifeline (USA & Canada):**

- **Type:** Peer-run crisis hotline by and for trans people
- **Why it matters:** Offers emotional support and microgrants
- **Future-forward aspect:** Direct economic and mental health aid without gatekeeping

➢ **Q Chat Space (USA):**

- **Type:** Live-chat based support for LGBTQ+ youth

- **Why it matters:** Accessible to teens who can't access in-person groups
- **Future-forward aspect:** Designed for anonymity, flexibility, and reach

➢ **CenterLink (USA):**

- **Type:** Network of over 250 LGBTQ+ community centers
- **Why it matters:** Mental health referrals, peer groups, cultural programs
- **Future-forward aspect:** Community-rooted wellness adaptable to other regions

---

Europe / UK / Ireland:

➢ **MindOut (United Kingdom):**

- **Type:** Mental health services by and for LGBTQ+ people
- **Why it matters:** Suicide prevention, counselling, peer support
- **Future-forward aspect:** Queer-run mental health model with national reach

➢ **Switchboard LGBT+ Helpline (UK):**

- **Type:** Confidential helpline since 1974
- **Why it matters:** One of the longest-running LGBTQ+ support lines
- **Future-forward aspect:** Blends tradition with tech-based support

➢ **LGBT Ireland (Ireland):**

- **Type:** Helpline, online support, and mental health advocacy
- **Why it matters:** National infrastructure with LGBTQ+ informed services
- **Future-forward aspect:** Builds inclusive mental health policies and partnerships

---

Africa:

➢ **Jinsiangu (Kenya):**

- **Type:** Community-led intersex and trans advocacy
- **Why it matters:** Offers peer mental health support and legal aid

- **Future-forward aspect:** Culturally grounded healing under threat

➢ **Out Wellbeing (South Africa):**

- **Type:** LGBTQ+ health and mental wellness NGO
- **Why it matters:** Counselling, HIV support, and training
- **Future-forward aspect:** Health justice integration model

➢ **Access Chapter 2 (South Africa):**

- **Type:** Rights-based organization with psychosocial services
- **Why it matters:** LGBTQ+ women and youth support focus
- **Future-forward aspect:** Community organizing + trauma care

➢ **GALZ (Gays and Lesbians of Zimbabwe):**

- **Type:** Advocacy and safe spaces
- **Why it matters:** Offers crisis support and education
- **Future-forward aspect:** Operates in criminalized context, building peer resilience

➢ **ISDAO (Initiative Sankofa d'Afrique de l'Ouest) (West Africa):**

- **Type:** LGBTQ+ funder and support partner
- **Why it matters:** Empowers local mental health organizing
- **Future-forward aspect:** Decentralized regional healing strategies

➢ **TUF Mental Health Network (Uganda):**

- **Type:** Feminist, queer, trauma-informed collective
- **Why it matters:** Group therapy, survivor networks, healing circles
- **Future-forward aspect:** Peer-led under oppression, healing through storytelling

---

Asia:

➢ **Queerable (India):**

- **Type:** Online peer support and mental health advocacy

- **Why it matters:** Offers mental health resources and counselling tailored for queer and trans people in India
- **Future-forward aspect:** Growing accessibility and community integration, with a focus on gender fluidity

➢ **The Humsafar Trust (India):**

- **Type:** LGBTQ+ organization focused on mental health and well-being
- **Why it matters:** Provides mental health resources, HIV care, and peer support
- **Future-forward aspect:** Nationwide network building, combining advocacy and healthcare

➢ **GAYAP (Gay and Lesbian Asia Pacific Alliance):**

- **Type:** Regional advocacy and community empowerment
- **Why it matters:** Provides mental health programs, community networking, and regional support
- **Future-forward aspect:** Uses regional collaboration to create mental health services tailored for diverse Asian countries

➢ **Pride Circle (India):**

- **Type:** Corporate LGBTQ+ inclusion and mental health initiative
- **Why it matters:** Provides support for LGBTQ+ employees and communities in the workplace
- **Future-forward aspect:** Workplace wellness models to integrate LGBTQ+ mental health into corporate settings

➢ **Blue Diamond Society (Nepal):**

- **Type:** LGBTQ+ and HIV-focused organization
- **Why it matters:** Provides mental health services, community education, and advocacy
- **Future-forward aspect:** Empowering marginalized queer populations in Nepal to overcome mental health stigma

I AM YOU (China):

- **Type:** Mental health and support network for LGBTQ+ individuals in China
- **Why it matters:** Offers online therapy and a community-based approach to queer mental wellness

- **Future-forward aspect:** First steps toward integrating LGBTQ+ inclusive mental health care in China

- **Transgender Resource Center of India (TRC India):**
  - **Type:** Transgender advocacy and support services
  - **Why it matters:** Provides access to healthcare, mental health, and safe spaces for the transgender community
  - **Future-forward aspect:** A model for trans-inclusive mental health services in a rapidly developing country

---

Australia / New Zealand:

- **Minus18 (Australia):**
  - **Type:** LGBTQ+ youth support and advocacy
  - **Why it matters:** Offers mental health services, events, and programs for LGBTQ+ youth
  - **Future-forward aspect:** Promotes youth-led, peer-based healing and community integration

- **Twenty10 (Australia):**
  - **Type:** LGBTQ+ youth and community services
  - **Why it matters:** Provides crisis and mental health support to LGBTQ+ youth, and offers community building
  - **Future-forward aspect:** Focuses on inclusion, addressing the unique mental health needs of queer youth

- **The Australia LGBTQ+ Health Alliance (Australia):**
  - **Type:** Advocacy and research organization
  - **Why it matters:** Increases awareness and access to mental health resources for LGBTQ+ individuals across Australia
  - **Future-forward aspect:** Focuses on national policy and mental health research to influence future frameworks

- **Aotearoa New Zealand's Rainbow Youth (New Zealand):**
  - **Type:** LGBTQ+ youth organization focused on mental health

- **Why it matters:** Provides support and resources specifically tailored for young LGBTQ+ individuals
- **Future-forward aspect:** Works to combat mental health stigma in the Pacific region, increasing access to culturally responsive services

➢ **InsideOUT (New Zealand):**

- **Type:** Advocacy group focused on creating safe spaces for LGBTQ+ youth
- **Why it matters:** Promotes mental wellness through education and outreach programs in schools
- **Future-forward aspect:** Pioneering work to ensure LGBTQ+ mental health is prioritized within the education system

---

Middle East:

➢ **Helem (Lebanon):**

- **Type:** LGBTQ+ advocacy and support organization
- **Why it matters:** Provides mental health resources and safe spaces for queer individuals in Lebanon
- **Future-forward aspect:** Focuses on political and social advocacy while addressing mental health within a conservative society

➢ **MEO (Middle Eastern Outreach) (United Arab Emirates, Saudi Arabia, Egypt):**

- **Type:** Online platform for LGBTQ+ individuals in the Middle East
- **Why it matters:** Provides anonymous peer support and mental health resources for individuals in high-risk regions
- **Future-forward aspect:** Acts as a clandestine digital sanctuary, providing critical care without physical presence

➢ **Queer Arab Collective (Middle East & North Africa):**

- **Type:** Advocacy network for LGBTQ+ individuals in Arab countries
- **Why it matters:** Focuses on mental health support and awareness for queer Arabs facing discrimination
- **Future-forward aspect:** Using online spaces to nurture mental wellness while advocating for social change

* Future-Forward Possibilities Emerging Today for Queer Mental Health:

➢ Global Queer Mental Health Atlas:

Description: A collaborative, crowdsourced map where LGBTQ+ individuals worldwide can rate, review, and recommend affirming therapists and healing spaces. This digital resource would empower people to find professionals who are not only LGBTQ+ friendly, but also experienced in addressing the unique mental health challenges of queer individuals. The atlas could include reviews from local queer communities, making it easier for newcomers or travellers to find trustworthy support.

Purpose:

- Bridges the gap between access and care for LGBTQ+ people globally, particularly in regions with fewer visible or accessible services.
- Empowers queer individuals to actively participate in shaping the mental health landscape for their communities.
- Increases visibility of LGBTQ+ inclusive care worldwide, encouraging mental health professionals to receive specialized training.

➢ VR Therapy Pods:

Description: Virtual Reality (VR) Therapy Pods could provide immersive, safe virtual spaces where queer people can meet and connect with supportive communities across borders. These VR environments could be designed to address various aspects of trauma and healing, whether related to coming out, discrimination, or navigating relationships. Within these virtual spaces, individuals can access real-time therapy, join group healing workshops, or simply exist without fear of judgment.

Purpose:

- Breaks geographical and social barriers, making therapeutic environments accessible to marginalized queer communities.
- Offers an embodied, immersive experience to navigate and heal trauma through visual, auditory, and kinesthetic senses.
- Introduces the opportunity for global collaboration and collective healing by meeting people from around the world in a controlled, therapeutic space.

➢ Digital Ancestry Projects:

Description: Digital Ancestry Projects would use audio storytelling AI to allow LGBTQ+ individuals to "speak" to queer elders, creating a virtual space for generational continuity.

This could include building AI-powered projects where young LGBTQ+ people can listen to stories from the past experiences of those who came before them, resilience during the AIDS crisis, experiences with gender and sexual liberation movements, and personal journeys of navigating queer identity in different eras. These virtual interactions would help preserve the wisdom and resilience of past generations, fostering emotional and mental strength for the future.

Purpose:

- Helps bridge generational gaps and offer guidance in a more intimate, accessible way than traditional mentorship or archives.
- Builds resilience through hearing stories of overcoming adversity, while feeling a sense of belonging to the LGBTQ+ community at large.
- Provides a sense of mental and emotional continuity for younger queer people who may feel disconnected from their history due to geographic, cultural, or societal barriers.
- Provides emotional healing through the knowledge that struggles were faced, and overcome by others who walked the same path.

* Next-Level Future Visions – Integrating Technology, Empathy and Mental Health:

➢ AI-Powered Emotional Support Systems for the Queer Community:

Description: Imagine an AI-powered mental health companion specifically trained to understand the nuanced emotional and psychological needs of LGBTQ+ individuals. This digital assistant could offer 24/7 support in the form of conversation, journaling prompts, mood-tracking, or even calming meditations, while providing resources on coping strategies for coming out, navigating relationships, or overcoming microaggressions. Powered by machine learning, these AIs would learn from each interaction to provide increasingly personalized support.

Purpose:

- Provides instant mental health support and personalized advice, especially in moments of crisis.
- Helps reduce the stigma of seeking help by providing a confidential, non-judgmental space to process emotions.
- Facilitates the creation of a community-based mental health ecosystem, where digital support systems connect LGBTQ+ individuals to real-life care when necessary.

➢ Global Queer Peer Mentorship Networks:

Description: A global digital mentorship platform that connects LGBTQ+ individuals of all ages to peer mentors who share similar experiences and identities.

This could extend beyond geographic borders, creating a virtual space for mentorship in areas like mental health, career development, relationships, or coming out. The platform could also offer workshops, group chats, and a resource library, while connecting users to offline support networks in their area.

Purpose:

- Promotes intergenerational knowledge-sharing and peer support, fostering a global sense of queer community.
- Provides a safe and accessible resource for mentorship, especially for LGBTQ+ youth or those living in regions with limited access to queer-specific support services.
- Enhances global solidarity within the queer community by connecting individuals from diverse backgrounds, with the shared goal of personal empowerment.

➢ **Queer Wellness Retreats in Virtual and Real Life:**

Description: Global wellness retreats for LGBTQ+ individuals could exist both in real life and virtual reality (VR), offering spaces for relaxation, reflection, and healing. These retreats would be specifically designed to address the unique mental health needs of queer people, offering activities such as yoga, therapy circles, nature walks and wellness workshops. Virtual retreats would allow LGBTQ+ people to join from anywhere, while real-life retreats could be located in queer-friendly, serene locations to provide safe spaces for recharging.

Purpose:

- Provides dedicated spaces for LGBTQ+ individuals to nurture their mental health and emotional well-being.
- Virtual and real-life combinations allow for greater accessibility, particularly for those unable to travel or facing safety risks.
- Fosters connection and community-building among queer individuals globally, offering a chance for shared healing and growth.

In summary, these future-forward possibilities are designed to provide innovative and accessible solutions to the evolving mental health needs of LGBTQ+ communities. By using technology, AI and community-building models, these concepts offer practical tools for mental health professionals, LGBTQ+ individuals, and advocates to build a more inclusive, supportive future for queer mental well-being.

As we build queer futures, mental health must be more than a reactive system. It must become a proactive force of liberation. These real-world examples and speculative extensions show us how care can evolve, across tech, community, geography and culture, to hold queer people through transition, joy, grief and self-discovery.

3. The Role of Science Fiction and Speculative Fiction in Imagining Queer Futures

Science fiction has long served as a playground for radical possibility, yet for many years, queer characters were either erased or relegated to tragic subplots. Today, speculative fiction is shifting this dynamic, allowing queer characters not only to survive, but to thrive. In future-set novels and far-flung galaxies, queerness is no longer something to be tolerated or explained away. It simply is. These imagined futures challenge the idea that LGBTQ+ identities are inherently incompatible with progress or technology. Instead, queer existence becomes interwoven with resilience, brilliance and joy. From space operas where nonbinary starship captains lead planetary revolutions to dystopias where queer intimacy forms the last stronghold of human connection, speculative fiction opens a door into futures where queerness is not exceptional, but essential.

3.1 Gender as Technology – Reprogramming the Binary:

Science fiction allows gender to be unfixed, fluid, dynamic, and even programmable. Through body modification, neural interfaces, or consciousness transfer, gender becomes less about biology and more about design, choice and storytelling. In these worlds, a person might shift gender as easily as changing clothes, or exist outside any binary altogether, echoing real-world nonbinary and genderfluid identities, but scaled into imaginative extremes. Works like Ancillary Justice by Ann Leckie and The Left Hand of Darkness by Ursula K. Le Guin demonstrate how alien or post-human societies can deconstruct gender entirely, showing how language and biology entwine to shape identity. These narratives encourage readers to ask, if gender can be imagined differently in fiction, why not in life? In speculative futures, gender is no longer a constraint, it's a creative toolkit.

3.2 Queering Time, Queering Space:

Speculative fiction not only reimagines identities, but also how time and space function. Linear time, a structure so embedded in Western narratives, can be bent, folded, or dissolved entirely. Queer authors often use nonlinear storytelling to reflect lives lived outside societal milestones like marriage or reproduction. Octavia Butler's Kindred collapses centuries to link ancestral trauma with present resistance. Rivers Solomon's The Deep turns memory into collective identity, carried through water and song. These stories resist capitalist, heteronormative timelines by crafting worlds where queer temporality reigns. In space, queer characters are no longer bound to Earth's historical oppressions. They explore star systems and parallel dimensions where family, desire, and power are redefined. Speculative fiction becomes a vessel not just for escape, but for transformation, an invitation to build futures that transcend the very structure of reality.

3.3 Alien Bodies and Posthuman Desires:

Science fiction dares us to imagine bodies beyond our current understanding, cyborgs, shapeshifters, interspecies hybrids, and uploaded consciousnesses. In doing so, it offers a language for queerness that resists categorization.

What does sexuality mean when one's body is fluid, incorporeal, or modular? What does desire look like between a human and an AI programmed to evolve its own gender? These questions aren't just philosophical, they're profoundly queer. Posthumanism allows for relationships untethered from traditional roles, anatomies, or expectations. In stories where love blooms between a tentacled alien and a human refugee, or where a group mind experiences collective polyamory, the limits of attraction are joyfully dismantled. These narratives remind us that queer futures may not just stretch society's norms, they may render them irrelevant.

3.4 Utopia, Dystopia and the Queer Imagination:

Queer speculative fiction often walks a delicate line between utopia and dystopia. In dystopias, queerness may be criminalized, hidden, or commodified, a mirror of our present injustices taken to their extremes. But even in these bleak landscapes, queer characters resist with intimacy, defiance and chosen family. On the flip side, queer utopias do not imagine perfect worlds, but possible ones, realities where liberation is hard-won and messy, but sustainable. Stories like Becky Chambers' Wayfarers series or Charlie Jane Anders' The City in the Middle of the Night offer communities where empathy, fluidity, and cooperation are the cornerstones of civilization. These imagined societies do not erase conflict, they reimagine how conflict is resolved, how difference is valued, and how coexistence is nurtured. Utopian storytelling isn't naïve, it's revolutionary, especially when queerness is placed at the centre of collective hope.

3.5 Story as Speculation, Story as Blueprint:

The most powerful speculative fiction doesn't just dream of the future, it designs it. Stories shape culture, politics, and even technology. When queer authors imagine new pronouns, new family structures, or new ways of loving, they often seed real-world change. The rise of neopronouns, for instance, echoes science fiction's playful experimentation with language and identity. Polyamorous and non-normative relationship structures, long explored in fiction, are becoming more visible and viable in real life. Speculative fiction serves not just as a metaphor, but as a method. It offers prototypes for queer life not yet realized, and in doing so, shifts what seems possible. It turns yearning into architecture, building bridges between the now and the not-yet.

3.6 The Authors Rewriting the Future:

Queer and trans writers have taken the helm of speculative fiction in recent years, infusing the genre with voices long marginalized. From Nnedi Okorafor's Africanfuturist visions to Ryka Aoki's tender and complex trans heroines, the genre is increasingly defined by authors who see queerness as both lens and engine. Their work resists neat categorization, drawing from myth, science, folklore, and futurism to craft something wholly new. These writers aren't just inserting queer characters into existing tropes, they're queering the very structure of narrative. Worlds unfold sideways. Heroes reject binary moralities. Love is strange, sacred, and everywhere. Through them, speculative fiction becomes a map of where we might go, not if, but when we choose to write ourselves into the future. Their stories show the future isn't found, it's imagined, boldly and queerly.

3.7 Dreaming Forward – The Radical Act of Imagination:

To imagine a queer future is itself a radical act. It requires not just critique of the present, but faith in what lies beyond it. Science fiction and speculative fiction provide the canvas for that faith, for dreaming, for experimenting, for play. They give language to desires not yet born, bodies not yet seen, and relationships not yet named. As technology, climate, and culture transform our world, the need for radical imagination grows ever more urgent. Queer futures are not just about inclusion, they are about invention. They are about writing ourselves into worlds where we are not anomalies or afterthoughts, but architects. Through the portals of speculative fiction, queer people claim not only the right to exist, but the right to design what comes next.

*** A Curated List of Works on Queer Futures – Imagining What Comes Next:**

Dive deeper into the realms of speculative fiction and nonfiction that envision the future of LGBTQ+ identities. These works invite us to imagine beyond the present, to see gender and sexuality evolving in bold, transformative and beautifully queer directions. Each title is a doorway to futures where queerness isn't just accepted, it leads the way.

➢ **The Left Hand of Darkness by Ursula K. Le Guin:**

Type: Book (Science Fiction):

Le Guin's seminal novel imagines a world where inhabitants can change sex and have no fixed gender. It challenges conventional views of gender and sexual identity, offering an entirely new way of seeing what a queer world could look like, free from binary constraints.

Why It Matters: Le Guin's work provides a model of a world where gender is fluid, inviting readers to explore beyond the binary.

➢ **Queer – A Graphic History by Meg-John Barker:**

Type: Book (Nonfiction, Graphic History):

This visually compelling book combines LGBTQ+ theory, history, and speculative ideas through vibrant illustrations and accessible prose. It doesn't just document history, it reimagines it, offering alternative perspectives on gender, sexuality, and identity.

Why It Matters: The graphic novel format makes complex ideas approachable, showing how queer futures are already being theorized in thought-provoking ways.

➢ **Transgender Warriors by Leslie Feinberg:**

Type: Book (Nonfiction, History):

Feinberg's exploration of historical figures who defied gender norms sheds light on a past that's often left out of mainstream history. It serves as a foundation for imagining how the future of trans and non-binary people might unfold.

Why It Matters: The book highlights the historical resistance against gender norms, which lays the groundwork for a future of inclusion and liberation.

- **Ammonite by Nicola Griffith:**

Type: Book (Science Fiction, Speculative Fiction):

In a society where only women exist, Ammonite explores queer love, power and social structures. The novel raises the question of how relationships might be fundamentally different in a world unencumbered by the concept of gender.

Why It Matters: It provides a lens for envisioning what a world of same-sex relationships and gender-free existence might look like.

- **No Future – Queer Theory and the Death Drive by Lee Edelman:**

Type: Book (Nonfiction, Queer Theory):

Edelman critiques the cultural concept of "reproductive futurism" and imagines a world where queer people live beyond the logic of reproduction, offering a provocative view of a world where queerness doesn't have to conform to the normative timelines of life.

Why It Matters: It offers a bold, unapologetic perspective on queer life that exists outside the expectation of reproducing the status quo.

- **The Dispossessed by Ursula K. Le Guin:**

Type: Book (Science Fiction, Political Philosophy):

In this novel, Le Guin contrasts two radically different societies, one capitalist and one anarchist. Through this juxtaposition, she shows how social structures, unconstrained by heteronormativity, can reshape gender, love and power.

Why It Matters: The book offers insights into how queer identities could flourish in alternate societal structures, offering a speculative roadmap for a liberated world.

- **Neuromancer by William Gibson:**

Type: Book (Cyberpunk Science Fiction):

Neuromancer takes place in a future world where technology has the power to alter both identity and the physical body. The novel explores the intersection of digital and physical spaces and imagines how queerness might evolve through technology.

Why It Matters: It envisions a world where technology liberates identity, showing the possibilities for queer lives to transcend the physical and embrace a digital future.

- **Trans Futures by Susan Stryker:**

Type: Book (Nonfiction, Trans Studies):

Stryker's work blends trans theory, culture, and history, with speculative ideas about the future. It explores the potential impact of trans and non-binary identities in shaping global cultural shifts.

Why It Matters: The book encourages readers to see trans identities not as a passing phase, but as central to imagining future societal transformations.

- **Queer Futures by Joseph H. Smith:**

Type: Book (Nonfiction, Queer Theory):

Smith offers a speculative examination of queer futures, blending cultural analysis with philosophical and political ideas. He explores the potential for queer identities to shape everything from politics to cultural norms, based on emerging trends.

Why It Matters: It's a roadmap for understanding how queer futures could unfold across various domains, from politics to everyday life.

- **Redefining Realness by Janet Mock:**

Type: Book (Memoir, Nonfiction):

In this deeply personal memoir, Janet Mock reflects on her journey as a trans woman, offering a profound exploration of gender, identity, and the societal limitations that restrict personal and collective growth.

Why It Matters: Mock's story inspires a vision of the future where trans and non-binary identities are not just accepted, but celebrated and central to the cultural narrative.

- **Bonus – The Matrix (1999):**

Type: Movie (Science Fiction, Action):

Though not explicitly queer, The Matrix has become a touchstone for queer readings, with many seeing the film's narrative of breaking free from societal norms and discovering hidden truths as an allegory for gender and sexual liberation.

Why It Matters: Its portrayal of reality as a constructed illusion offers a unique way to explore the boundaries of identity, queerness, and self-determination.

➢ **Bonus – Paris Is Burning (1990):**

Type: Documentary (Documentary, LGBTQ+ Culture):

This documentary about the New York City ball culture provides a window into the lives of queer and transgender people of colour. It's a powerful exploration of gender, race and sexuality, and presents a queer world brimming with creativity and resistance.

Why It Matters: It not only documents a queer subculture, but inspires a deeper understanding of how queerness, resistance and creativity, intersect in the struggle for self-expression and survival.

4. Redefining the Concept of Love in a Post-Binary World

For centuries, love has been conceptualized as a meeting of opposites, masculine and feminine, yin and yang, protector and nurturer. These binaries shaped not only the stories we told, but the way we lived them, rehearsing roles rooted in polarity rather than possibility. In a post-binary world, love no longer depends on opposition to define itself. Instead, it becomes a field of relational resonance, where identity is fluid, and affection flows without prescribed direction. Rather than seeking a complementary "other," individuals might seek emotional kinship, shared evolution, or creative companionship. Love ceases to be about fulfilling a role and becomes an act of co-creation between selves in flux.

4.1 The Collapse of Archetypes – Rethinking Romantic Scripts:

Classic romantic narratives rely on archetypes, the strong male saviour, the emotionally intuitive woman, the inevitable union of difference. These templates persist even in modern queer relationships, subtly influencing expectations around who leads, who follows, who gives, and who receives. In a post-binary reality, such scripts lose their authority. Instead of mirroring heteronormative patterns, queer love begins to write its own choreography. Relationships are increasingly seen not as fixed destinations, but as fluid dynamics. The notion of "forever" gives way to "for now," not as a diminishment of love, but as a recognition of its living, evolving nature. Intimacy becomes a space for mutual reinvention, not obligation.

4.2 The Language of Love Reimagined:

Language both limits and liberates love. Words like "boyfriend," "wife," "husband," and "partner" carry historical and gendered baggage, encoding assumptions about power, permanence, and purpose.

As gender dissolves into a spectrum and sexual orientation becomes more expansive, language, too, must evolve. New terms may emerge, fluid, plural, and non-hierarchical, to describe bonds that don't fit traditional molds. Perhaps love is no longer something we "fall into" but something we "build beside." Pronouns may become optional, pet names more political. As expression reshapes identity, verbalizing love becomes less about declaring ownership and more about honouring transformation.

4.3 Intimacy Without Definition – The Rise of Relationship Anarchy:

Post-binary love dissolves the rigid walls separating friend, lover, partner, and kin. Relationship anarchy, once considered radical, may become a natural expression of care in a world untethered from fixed identities. Emotional intimacy is no longer reserved for romance; sexual connection doesn't require exclusivity; and familial loyalty may emerge from chosen networks rather than blood ties. In this landscape, each relationship is negotiated on its own terms, often blurring lines rather than drawing them. What matters isn't the label, but the presence, the trust, the shared vulnerability. Love, here, becomes less about category and more about capacity, the willingness to show up without certainty.

4.4 Body Beyond Binary – Touch, Desire and New Affections:

Desire has long been coded through binary interpretations of the body, certain traits deemed attractive, certain bodies made desirable. Post-binary love expands this frame entirely. As bodies transition, transform, or transcend traditional labels, attraction detaches from fixed gender cues. The erotic becomes a celebration of difference, ambiguity, and sensation, rather than a confirmation of gender roles. Touch is recontextualized not just as a sexual act, but as a form of nonverbal love, affirmation, or healing. In a world that welcomes embodiment in all its forms, sensuality itself becomes queered, less about the "what" and more about the "how" and "why" of connection.

4.5 Collective Love and Decentralized Affection:

Love in a post-binary world may shift from individual pairings to communal webs. Polyamory, platonic co-parenting, queer kinship networks, these once-marginal forms of love may become models for sustainable, non-possessive connection. The idea that one person must fulfil all emotional, sexual, and existential needs begins to fade. Instead, love is seen as a distributed resource, shared across multiple people, each fulfilling different aspects of one's being. Jealousy transforms into self-inquiry. Fidelity becomes a practice of honesty, not exclusivity. The emphasis moves away from control and toward consent, fluidity, and radical transparency. Love becomes not a contract, but a constellation.

4.6 Spiritual Dimensions of Queer Love:

Without binaries to anchor identity, love may take on deeper spiritual dimensions. The act of loving, of witnessing someone in their full becoming, becomes a sacred exchange. Many post-binary philosophies, drawn from indigenous, Eastern and queer spiritual traditions, already treat love as an energy, a force that transcends form. Rather than being defined by physical union or verbal declaration, love is understood as resonance, frequency, or alignment.

In this view, queer love is not merely resistance, it is radical transcendence. A remembering of our interconnectedness, a practice of loving beyond gender, beyond ego, and even beyond the self.

4.7 The Role of Technology in Queer Intimacy:

Technology will both challenge and expand the ways we love in a post-binary future. Digital avatars may allow people to experiment with identity and affection across multiple forms. AI companions and neuro-enhanced connection tools could allow love to stretch beyond human constraints. Long-distance intimacy may be enriched by haptic tech, while decentralized relationship agreements live on the blockchain. But with these tools come ethical questions: Can intimacy be programmed? Is love still real when it's partly virtual? Technology may amplify love's possibilities, but it will also ask us to reconsider what makes love authentic in the first place.

4.8 Parenting Without Presumption:

Parenting is perhaps the final frontier of love reimagined. In a post-binary context, raising children need not be organized around mother/father roles, nor assume heteronormative frameworks of family. Co-parenting across platonic partnerships, raising children in communities rather than couples, and rejecting gendered socialization may become more common. Children may be encouraged to discover their identities without societal imposition. Love between parent and child, thus becomes a shared journey of discovery, unbound by projection or control. The family becomes not a unit of inheritance, but a laboratory of radical empathy.

4.9 Toward a Philosophy of Queer Love:

Post-binary love doesn't simply offer new ways to connect, it reimagines the very foundation of connection itself. Love becomes a space of becoming rather than belonging, where meaning isn't imposed, but discovered in motion. It values fluidity over fixity, presence over possession, and the shared unfolding of selfhood over the maintenance of roles. This vision of queer love resists containment. It embraces contradiction, nurtures transformation, and celebrates relationships that are unrepeatable in their uniqueness. No longer confined by the binaries of gender, structure, or outcome, love evolves into an ethic of mutual liberation. It is no longer about finding "the one," but about encountering the many ways we can know and be known. To love post-binary is to love with radical openness, to let go of the old maps and trust that what we build together will be enough to hold us.

"Queer love in a post-binary world isn't a mirror, it's a doorway. Not where we arrive, but how we begin." – Anonymous

5. The Possibilities of a Post-Queer Society – What Comes Next?

Imagine a world where labels no longer function as survival tools. In a post-queer society, the act of identifying as queer is no longer necessary for validation or safety. Instead, identity becomes an internal compass, not a social declaration.

Without the binary scaffolding that gave rise to queerness as resistance, love, gender, and desire move untethered from old signposts. It's not erasure, but transcendence. People still embody diversity, still hold contradictions, still shift and explore, but these expressions are no longer seen as deviations. They simply are. The categories dissolve, not into sameness, but into a shared freedom of becoming.

5.1 From Visibility to Integration:

In the queer present, visibility is often equated with progress, being seen means being acknowledged. But in a future where queerness is no longer a marginal category, the politics of visibility shift. Instead of standing out to be counted, queer ways of living become seamlessly woven into the fabric of everyday life. Schools, media, laws, and cultural norms no longer "include" queerness as a form of exception. They are built with fluidity at the core. What was once spotlighted as radical becomes commonplace, and the need to "come out" fades, not because identity is hidden, but because it no longer needs to be announced.

5.2 The Evolution of Language and Desire:

Language, too, transforms. New terms may emerge, but not to replace old identities, rather, to reflect the expanded emotional and erotic vocabulary of a society no longer bound by gender dualism. Words might describe feelings and affinities instead of roles or types. Desire becomes more relational than categorical. Attraction isn't based on "who you are" in a static sense, but on how people resonate, evolve, and interact. Gendered pronouns may fade into the background, replaced by nuanced self-descriptions or new syntaxes entirely. The poetry of identity shifts from naming difference to celebrating interconnectedness.

5.3 Love Without Borders:

Without the architecture of binary thinking, love opens further. Romantic configurations are no longer debated in terms of normativity or subversion, they are accepted as expressions of individual and collective design. Polyamory, aromantic identities, platonic co-parenting and queerplatonic partnerships, are equally structurally supported as any other form of union. Relationships are negotiated based on consent, care, and creativity, rather than default roles or cultural scripts. Marriage might be reimagined, not as an institution of legitimacy, but as one of mutual crafting. Love no longer replicates systems of power, it becomes a site of continual reinvention.

5.4 Queerness as Memory, Not Margin:

In a post-queer world, queerness may remain, not as a boundary, but as a historical memory. The stories, struggles and triumphs of queer movements would still be taught and honoured, not to mark difference, but to understand the evolution of freedom. Museums, curricula, and archives preserve the brilliance and pain of those who built pathways to this new reality. Queerness becomes a spiritual lineage, an ancestral echo that reminds future generations how much was risked for their ease of being.

The word "queer" itself may evolve into a verb, a philosophy, or a tribute, no longer describing who someone is, but how they resist rigidity and reach for more.

5.5 Bodies Beyond Binaries:

In a post-queer world, medical systems no longer gatekeep gender or enforce normative pathways. The body becomes a canvas of fluid self-expression, rather than a battleground of conformity. Intersex variations are embraced rather than corrected. Hormonal and surgical options are available without stigma, designed to support individual flourishing rather than restore "normalcy." Technologies emerge to assist in personal embodiment journeys without assuming end goals. The future body is porous, adaptive, and creative. It is not defined by gender, but shaped by desire, environment, and autonomy. In this world, bodies are no longer proof of identity, they are extensions of will.

5.6 The End of the "Other":

The most profound shift in a post-queer society may be the dissolution of "the other." If queerness was once defined in opposition to a dominant norm, the end of that norm means the end of opposition itself. Instead of dividing humanity into insider and outsider, normative and deviant, society begins to recognize complexity as a baseline. Difference is no longer exceptional. The concept of "normal" becomes irrelevant, and with it, the hierarchies built on exclusion collapse. Power is no longer hoarded by those closest to a fictional centre. Instead, culture is shaped by dialogue across a spectrum of experience, none of which is seen as aberrant.

5.7 A Future Without Policing Intimacy:

Laws and moral codes have long regulated queer love, limiting how and who people can touch, desire and build lives with. In the post-queer world, such policing becomes an outdated artifact. Governments stop surveilling gender markers, sex acts, and domestic arrangements. Religion evolves or recedes from controlling the politics of intimacy. Instead, ethics are rooted in consent, care, and mutual growth. People no longer need to fight for the right to exist, they are empowered to choose how they live and love. Intimacy is finally understood as a human right, not a privilege granted by conformity. True freedom lets love and intimacy thrive, unchained by control, rooted in consent, care, and choice.

5.8 The Role of Art and Imagination:

Art has always reached beyond the present, sensing futures before they arrive. In a post-queer era, creative expression no longer serves as a site of representation, it becomes the terrain itself. Theatre, literature and film are no longer tasked with proving the existence of queer lives, they are born from creators who move beyond fixed identities, shaping narratives that flow outside inherited forms. Stories become laboratories of feeling, where emotional worlds not yet realized are sketched into being. Music, movement, and digital realms embody bodies that defy scripts, language and limits. Art doesn't seek permission or inclusion, it reaches toward the unimaginable, charting new ways of relating, becoming, and belonging.

5.9 Holding Space for the In-Between:

Even in a post-queer world, the journey is not linear. There will still be people discovering, resisting, healing. There will be communities where the past still grips tightly. There will be grief for what was lost and reverence for what was won. But the difference is, the world will be designed to hold that ambiguity. The in-between will no longer be a temporary state, it will be recognized as a place of power, a valid and sacred orientation in itself. The future doesn't promise utopia, but it does promise more room to breathe, more language for the inarticulable, and more grace for each other as we evolve.

5.10 Closing Thought:

Perhaps the real promise of a post-queer world isn't the disappearance of queerness, but the arrival at a place where no one must justify their difference, where difference is no longer a label to carry, but a common thread of human existence, lived freely and without question.

* The Ethics of Genetic Design and Queer Potential:

➢ Rewriting the Blueprint – A New Era of Human Possibility:

The age of genetic design has arrived, not as science fiction, but as science present. From CRISPR to IVF selection, the capacity to modify, enhance, or even predetermine human traits raises both fascination and alarm. As society inches toward normalizing "designer babies," questions of identity are no longer abstract. The boundaries between choice, ethics, and evolution blur, forcing us to reconsider what it means to be born different, or to choose difference. What becomes of queerness when nature is no longer arbitrary? Is queerness at risk of being designed out, or could it be coded in?

➢ Who Gets to Choose? The Politics of the Genetic Gaze:

Beneath the excitement lies the politics of power. Who decides which traits are desirable? Who defines what a "defect" is and what "diversity" is? For LGBTQ+ communities, especially those historically pathologized, this is not a neutral question. The medicalization of queer and trans bodies are not new, and neither is the impulse to "correct" us. History reminds us that the desire to normalize often disguises the urge to erase. In a future of customizable humans, will queerness be seen as something to be edited out, or will it remain a radical act of resistance?

➢ The Ghost of Eugenics and the Promise of Choice:

We cannot talk about gene editing without confronting the shadows of eugenics. The tools may be new, but the desire to curate humanity, to remove what is "undesirable", has a dark legacy. Yet, not all uses of genetic technology are inherently oppressive. Some queer families might choose to raise children free from certain health risks, or even select for traits they see as affirming. In these moments, the technology becomes a tool of agency, a way to craft futures once denied to us. The line between liberation and control is razor-thin. When does empowerment become erasure?

- **Queering the Genetic Code – Beyond Normative Design:**

What if genetic technology could be queered? Imagine a future where genetic variation is celebrated, not streamlined. Where intersex traits, neurodivergence, or gender-diverse expressions are not "mistakes," but part of an intentionally diverse genome. Could queer families, biological or chosen, resist normative design by embracing unpredictability? Could DNA become a canvas of defiance, a living archive of radical difference?

- **Embodiment as Resistance – The Future of the Unplanned Self:**

In a world of precision, there is something profoundly political about refusing control. To be queer has always meant living outside of scripts, gender scripts, love scripts, life scripts. In the future, queerness may mean choosing not to choose. It may mean embracing a child's unfolding identity without intervention. The unplanned body, the undesigned mind, may become sacred acts of resistance in a world obsessed with optimization.

- **Narratives We Inherit, Futures We Create:**

As queer people, we inherit stories of survival, refusal and reimagination. The tools of biotechnology will not change that, but they will challenge us to ask new questions. Can we trust science to hold space for queerness, or must we wrestle the tools from its hands and use them ourselves? What kind of world are we building, and who gets to live in it? The future of queer embodiment is not just a scientific question, it's a moral one, a poetic one and a deeply human one.

- **Becoming Quantum – The Future of Gender and Sexuality:**

What if the self isn't a stable truth to be found, but a frequency to be tuned into, shifting, vibrating, and responsive to time, environment, and imagination? In the next century, gender and sexuality may no longer be described with static terms, but with dynamic states, much like quantum particles that exist in multiple possibilities until observed. This is the beginning of quantum identities, not fixed coordinates, but constellations in motion.

- **A World Without Gender Reveal Parties:**

In a future unbound by the binary, children aren't boxed in at birth. Instead of gender reveal parties, we celebrate "identity unfolding days," where every expression, be it shy, bold, fluid, or firm, is met with curiosity, not control. The language around identity becomes a toolkit, not a trap, allowing space for evolution rather than declaration.

- **Pronouns as Portals:**

Pronouns are no longer passive labels, but interactive experiences. Some may shimmer like holograms above the wrist.

Others might exist as musical tones, or even living symbols that respond to mood or context. In this future, to change your pronoun is not a crisis, it's as natural as changing seasons, or shifting languages while dreaming.

- **Relationships Beyond Orientation:**

Attraction will outgrow the need for labels like straight, gay, bi, or even queer. Love and desire flow through new channels, spiritual frequency, intellectual sync, and dream compatibility. People fall for others not because they are "men" or "women" or "nonbinary," but because their inner universes align, even if only briefly. Orientation becomes relational resonance, not a fixed identity.

- **Quantum Embodiment:**

In a post-biological world, embodiment itself becomes fluid. People may shift gendered expression through neural-link tech, wearable morph-suits, or even hormonal palettes controlled by thought.

Gender may be less about body and more about signal, how one radiates feeling, presence, intention. Some may opt for multiplex identities, living as different selves in different contexts, not out of dissonance, but expansion.

- **From Spectrum to Ecosystem:**

Instead of imagining identity on a spectrum (linear, limited), the next century may understand it as an ecosystem, interdependent, seasonal, biodiverse. Terms like genderfluid or pansexual are no longer fringe, they're foundational. The more diverse the identities, the more resilient the cultural soil. Queerness becomes not just a way of loving, but a model for surviving in a changing world.

Final Reflection:

In the end, queerness was never just about identity, it was always about possibility. As we stand on the threshold of radically altered futures, shaped by genes, data, and dreams, the invitation remains the same, to imagine more courageously, to love more expansively, and to live more authentically than the world ever thought possible. A post-queer tomorrow does not erase who we are, it honours the journey that brought us here while daring us to evolve beyond even our most liberated selves. If queerness taught us how to survive, then the future it inspires teaches us how to thrive. And perhaps that is the greatest legacy of all, not just to be seen, but to become.

Suggested Literature, References, and Key Journals

1. **Weston, Kath. Families We Choose: Lesbians, Gays and Kinship. Columbia University Press, 1991.** A foundational text in queer kinship studies, Weston's work legitimizes chosen families as central to LGBTQ+ life and relationships beyond traditional norms.
2. **Easton, Dossie and Janet W. Hardy. The Ethical Slut: A Practical Guide to Polyamory, Open Relationships and Other Adventures. Greenery Press, 2009.** A landmark book for understanding ethical non-monogamy and the rejection of conventional romantic boundaries, directly relevant to the ethos of love without limitations.
3. **Enoch, Jessica A. The Asexuality Archive: A New Exploration of Asexuality and Aromanticism. Palgrave Macmillan, 2020.** Offers a comprehensive, modern exploration of asexual and aromantic identities, challenging the idea that love and intimacy must be sexual or romantic.
4. **Jenkins, John M. "Beyond Romance: Exploring Queer-platonic and Companionate Relationships." Journal of Feminist Studies in Religion, 2018.** Focuses on queer-platonic bonds, a key part of reimagining love outside romantic ideals, central to the chapter's theme.
5. **Klesse, Christian. "The Politics of Relationship Anarchy: Negotiating Love and Sex without Boundaries." Sexualities, 2018.** Provides theoretical grounding and contemporary relevance to relationship anarchy as a queer alternative to traditional romantic norms.
6. **Berlant, Lauren. "The Queer and Intimate Relations of Friendship." Queer Studies Journal, 2017.** Lauren Berlant's insights into intimacy and friendship blur the lines between platonic and romantic, opening space for boundaryless queer love.
7. **Butler, Judith. Gender Trouble: Feminism and the Subversion of Identity. Routledge, 1990.** A groundbreaking work in queer theory that introduced the concept of gender performativity.
8. **Fausto-Sterling, Anne. Sexing the Body: Gender Politics and the Construction of Sexuality. Basic Books, 2000.** A crucial text on the biological and social construction of sex and gender.
9. **Nanda, Serena. Neither Man nor Woman: The Hijras of India. Wadsworth Publishing, 1999.** An essential anthropological study of a third-gender identity outside Western paradigms.
10. **Hines, Sally. Transgender Identities: Towards a Social Analysis of Gender Diversity. Polity Press, 2007.** A strong sociological examination of transgender identities and lived realities.
11. **Tuck, Eve and K. Wayne Yang. Decolonization is Not a Metaphor. Decolonization: Indigeneity, Education & Society, 2012.** A vital theoretical piece on the true implications of decolonization, relevant to discussions of gender in Indigenous and postcolonial contexts.
12. **Wilcox, Melissa M. Queer Religion: A Critical Exploration of Gender Identity in Religious Contexts. Journal of Homosexuality, 2019.** Provides an important intersectional analysis of queer identity and religion.

13. **Warner, Michael. The Trouble with Normal: Sex, Politics, and the Ethics of Queer Power. The Free Press, 1999.** A foundational text critiquing assimilation and exploring power, respectability, and internal hierarchies within queer communities.

14. **Tatum, Beverly Daniel. Why Are All the Black Kids Sitting Together in the Cafeteria? And Other Conversations About Race. Basic Books, 1997**. While not exclusively LGBTQ+, this book offers essential frameworks for understanding racial dynamics, crucial when examining racism within LGBTQ+ spaces.

15. **Nash, Catherine. Queer Inclusion and the Politics of Race in LGBTQ+ Communities. Journal of Sexuality and Culture, 2021.** A critical, contemporary examination of how race shapes inclusion and exclusion in queer communities.

16. **Dykeman, R. Preserving the Legacy: The Role of Queer Elders in LGBTQ+ History. Journal of Queer History, 2020.** Captures the vital intergenerational role of storytelling and memory in sustaining LGBTQ+ community identity.

17. **Kipnis, Laura. The Limits of Friendship: Exploring the Dark Side of Chosen Families. Journal of Social and Personal Relationships, 2018.** Offers a rare and nuanced look into the challenges and emotional complexity of queer chosen families.

18. **Van Der Kolk, Bessel. The Body Keeps the Score: Brain, Mind, and Body in the Healing of Trauma. Viking, 2014.** A foundational trauma studies text that is widely cited across disciplines. Essential for understanding how trauma physically and emotionally embeds itself, including in LGBTQ+ individuals.

19. **Shidlo, Ariel, and Michael Schroeder. Changing Sexual Orientation: A Consumer's Report. Journal of Homosexuality, 2002.** One of the most comprehensive and impactful studies on conversion therapy, with firsthand accounts that reveal its long-term psychological damage.

20. **Meyer, Ilan H. The Stress of Family Rejection for LGBTQ+ Youth and Its Impact on Mental Health. American Journal of Public Health, 2014.** A landmark study introducing the concept of minority stress and its direct links to family rejection, depression, and suicidality among LGBTQ+ individuals.

21. **Ahmed, Sara. The Cultural Politics of Trauma: Refugees, Asylum Seekers, and LGBTQ+ Rights. Journal of International Migration and Integration, 2020.** A critical exploration of intersectional trauma, migration, and identity politics, essential for understanding systemic harm in a global context.

22. **Grossman, Adam H., and Lisa D. Shidlo. Religious Trauma and the Survival of LGBTQ+ Identity. Journal of LGBT Issues in Counseling, 2018.** Deepens the understanding of how religious trauma uniquely affects LGBTQ+ individuals and how survival strategies evolve.

23. **Dutton, Doug, and Nicole Painter. Trauma Bonding: The Role of Emotional Abuse in LGBTQ+ Relationships.** Journal of LGBTQ+ Relationship Therapy, 2017. Offers a targeted analysis of trauma bonding within queer relationships, providing vital insight into emotional abuse dynamics.

24. **Collins, Patricia Hill. Black Feminist Thought: Knowledge, Consciousness and the Politics of Empowerment. Routledge, 1990.** A foundational text in intersectionality theory, especially critical for understanding overlapping oppressions related to race, gender and sexuality.

25. **Lorde, Audre. Sister Outsider: Essays and Speeches. Crossing Press, 1984.** A seminal work that eloquently explores the intersections of race, gender, sexuality and resistance. Frequently cited across feminist, queer and race studies.

26. **Kafer, Alison. Feminist, Queer, Crip. Indiana University Press, 2013.** A groundbreaking text linking disability studies with queer theory, offering a rich intersectional framework.

27. **Serano, Julia. Whipping Girl: A Transsexual Woman on Sexism and the Scapegoating of Femininity. Seal Press, 2007.** Highly influential in discussions on trans feminism, transmisogyny, and the role of gendered oppression in both feminist and queer contexts.

28. **Alexander, Michelle. The Burden of Resistance: Queer People of Colour in Activism and Mental Health. Social Issues in Queer Communities, 2020.** Brings a modern, empirical lens to the psychological toll of activism for queer people of colour, relevant to mental health and intersectional burdens.

29. **Krol, Michael. Undocumented and Queer: The Hidden Struggles of LGBTQ+ Immigrants. Journal of Immigration and Refugee Studies, 2018.** A vital contribution to the growing body of literature on queer migration, legal precarity, and invisibility in undocumented communities.

30. **Lorde, Audre. Sister Outsider: Essays and Speeches. Crossing Press, 1984.** This collection (especially The Uses of the Erotic and The Master's Tools Will Never Dismantle the Master's House) powerfully reframes love, eroticism, and emotional truth as tools for liberation in queer and feminist contexts.

31. **Nguyen, Yen. "Love Beyond Language: Emotional Labor and Affection in Queer Relationships." Journal of Queer Relationship Studies, 2018.** Specifically focused on queer relationships, this article challenges the limitations of traditional love language models and centres emotional labour and unspoken care.

32. **Foucault, Michel. The History of Sexuality, Volume 1: An Introduction. Vintage Books, 1990.** A foundational work in queer theory that explores how sexuality is socially constructed and policed, providing essential context for understanding how love expression is also shaped by these dynamics.

33. **Ahmed, Sara. The Cultural Politics of Emotion. Edinburgh University Press, 2004.** Explores how emotions circulate within power structures and heteronormative societies, directly relevant to queer experiences of love, touch and emotional labour.

34. **Goldstein, Sara. "Trauma and Resilience: Healing from Relationship Violence in LGBTQ+ Communities." Journal of Trauma and Recovery, 2019.** A strong empirical and therapeutic contribution to understanding how trauma informs queer love dynamics, especially in shaping how love is given and received post-trauma.

35. **Seidman, Steven. Beyond the Closet: The Transformation of Gay and Lesbian Life. Routledge, 2002.** A seminal work exploring the evolution of the coming out process, shifting from a singular, rigid narrative to more nuanced, diverse experiences within queer communities.

36. **Troiden, Richard R. "The Development of Homosexual Identity." Journal of Homosexuality, 1989.** This foundational text introduces a developmental model of gay identity formation, pivotal for understanding how coming out fits into broader identity development.

37. **McInroy, Lauren B. "LGBTQ+ Identity and Social Media: Navigating the Digital Closet." Journal of Social Media Studies, 2019.** Focuses on the role of social media in the coming out process, particularly how digital platforms contribute to a "digital closet" and impact self-disclosure.

38. **Ambrose, Deirdre. "To Label or Not to Label: Exploring the Role of Labels in Queer Identity Development." Journal of LGBT Identity and Diversity Studies, 2019.** An in-depth analysis of how labels influence the coming out process, questioning their usefulness and the pressures they impose on queer individuals.

39. **McKenna, Kevin. "Coming Out Late: A Journey of Self-Discovery Beyond the Binary." Journal of Aging and Sexuality, 2020.** This study addresses the unique challenges of coming out later in life, offering insights into how queer identity evolves beyond traditional developmental stages.

40. **Brown, Lisa. "Coming Out at Work: The Challenges and Triumphs of LGBTQ+ Employees." Journal of Career Development, 2020.** A practical exploration of the complexities of coming out in professional environments, highlighting both the rewards and risks for LGBTQ+ employees in the workplace.

41. **Biblarz, Timothy J. and Judith Stacey. "How Does the Gender of Parents Matter?" Journal of Marriage and Family, 2010.** This widely cited study dismantles assumptions about traditional parental gender roles and supports the legitimacy of queer parenting.

42. **Sheff, Elizabeth. The Polyamorists Next Door: Inside Multiple-Partner Relationships and Families. Rowman & Littlefield, 2014.** This is the most comprehensive ethnographic work on polyamorous families, offering critical insight into non-traditional parenting structures.

43. **Lannutti, Pamela J. "LGBTQ Parents in Custody Battles: Discrimination, Bias and Family Law." Journal of Family Law and LGBTQ+ Rights, 2018.** An essential resource addressing systemic legal biases against LGBTQ+ parents, especially relevant for custody discussions.

44. **Adelman, Rachel. "Breaking the Cycle: Addressing Generational Trauma in LGBTQ+ Families." Journal of Family Therapy, 2021.** One of the few focused pieces that specifically explores how generational trauma plays out in queer families and how healing may be approached.

45. **Peplau, Letitia A. and Nancy L. McGrath. "The Experiences of LGBTQ Parents: Navigating Schools and Childcare Systems." Journal of LGBT Family Studies, 2020.** Contemporary, data-driven, and focused on real-world challenges, this source is key for understanding external pressures on LGBTQ+ family units.

46. **Meyer, Ilan H. (2003). Prejudice, Social Stress and Mental Health in Lesbian, Gay and Bisexual Populations: Conceptual Issues and Research Evidence. Psychological Bulletin.** This is a seminal work introducing the Minority Stress Model, which has profoundly influenced LGBTQ+ mental health research and is frequently cited in both academic and clinical settings.

47. **Russell, Stephen T., et al. (2018). Loneliness and Mental Health Among Lesbian, Gay, Bisexual and Transgender Youth. Journal of Youth and Adolescence.** A pivotal study offering robust empirical data on the mental health challenges faced by LGBTQ+ youth, especially relating to loneliness and belonging.

48. **Frost, David M. and J. L. Meyer. (2019). Mental Health and Loneliness Among LGBTQ+ Populations: A Systematic Review of the Literature. American Journal of Community Psychology.** A highly comprehensive literature review bridging quantitative and qualitative studies, synthesizing a wide range of data on LGBTQ+ loneliness.

49. **Rojas, Evelyn. (2020). The Stigma of Seeking Therapy: Barriers to Mental Health in LGBTQ+ Communities. LGBTQ+ Mental Health and Counselling.** A focused look at the **therapy access barriers** LGBTQ+ individuals face, incorporating cultural, institutional and interpersonal layers of stigma.

50. **Bostwick, W. B. and T. J. Boyd. (2020). Mental Health of LGBTQ+ Individuals: The Struggles with High-Functioning Depression. Journal of Gay & Lesbian Mental Health.** Central to the growing discourse around high-functioning depression, which is especially prevalent and under-discussed in LGBTQ+ circles.

51. **McDonald, Jane. (2020). Burnout in LGBTQ+ Activism: A Growing Concern for Community Health. Journal of LGBTQ+ Social Movements.** Timely and important in understanding the mental health toll of activism, particularly relevant in the context of ongoing social justice movements.

52. **Heaphy, Brian and Deborah A. The Invisibility of Older LGBTQ+ People in Popular Culture. Journal of Ageing Studies, 2019**. A foundational reference on media invisibility, providing strong academic grounding for the broader cultural neglect of queer elders.

53. **Gergen, K. The Need for Inclusive Retirement Communities for LGBTQ+ Seniors. Journal of Ageing and Social Policy, 2021.** This reference links policy and care reform, making it a critical source for structural critiques and solutions.

54. **Martin, Tom. Ageism Within the LGBTQ+ Community: Challenges for Older Queer People. Journal of LGBTQ+ Studies, 2020.** This article directly addresses the internalized ageism within queer spaces, helping frame the double marginalization experienced.

55. **Green, Steven. Intergenerational Friendships in the LGBTQ+ Community: Building Connections Across Generations. Journal of Queer Community Studies, 2021.** Emphasizing community healing and connection across generations, often cited in queer community resilience literature.

56. **Wright, Andrea. Healthcare Planning for LGBTQ+ Seniors: What You Need to Know About Advanced Directives and End-of-Life Care. Journal of Queer Health and Aging, 2021.** A contemporary and practical source offering guidance on medical and legal preparedness tailored to queer elders.

57. **Worthen, Molly. Queering the Aging Process: Why Older LGBTQ+ People Are Left Out of Media Narratives. Journal of Media Studies and Queer Culture, 2020.** Complements Heaphy and expands on the cultural erasure with a sharp critique of media systems.

58. **Jackson, Sheryl. The Dark Side of Digital Dating: Queerphobia, Catfishing and Fetishization in Online Spaces. Journal of Queer Digital Culture, 2020.** Offers a broad, foundational overview of multiple threats (queerphobia, catfishing, fetishization) in queer online dating, grounding the chapter's opening section.

59. **Banks, Nathaniel. Algorithms and Identity: How Dating Apps Reinforce Stereotypes in LGBTQ+ Communities. Journal of Digital Identity and LGBTQ+ Studies, 2020.** Provides a strong theoretical lens on algorithmic bias and identity construction.

60. **Jenkins, Rachael. Virtual Queer Spaces: Building Safety or Creating Echo Chambers?. Journal of LGBTQ+ Virtual Communities, 2021.** Critically examines both the benefits and limitations of virtual queer communities.

61. **Wilkins, Josh. Cyberbullying and Doxxing in Queer Spaces: A Rising Threat to Digital Safety. Journal of LGBTQ+ Cybersecurity Studies, 2020.** Central to understanding the growing threats of online harassment and the urgent need for digital protections.

62. **Faber, Emily. Long-Distance LGBTQ+ Relationships: Navigating Love in the Digital Age. Journal of Queer Relationship Studies, 2020.** Addressing emotional and technological dimensions of queer long-distance relationships.

63. **Miller, Courtney. Fetishization and Queerphobia in Digital Dating: A Study of Online Dating Apps. LGBTQ+ Studies Journal, 2021.** Empirical insight into user experience and systemic issues on apps.

64. **Thoreson, Ryan. Transnational LGBT Activism: Working for Sexual Rights in the Global South. University of Minnesota Press, 2014.** This book analyses how LGBTQ+ activists in the Global South engage with international human rights systems to challenge inequality.

65. **Altman, Dennis. Global Sex. University of Chicago Press, 2021 (Updated Edition).** A critical examination of how globalization affects sexual politics and LGBTQ+ identities across different cultures.

66. **O'Flaherty, Michael and John Fisher. "Sexual Orientation, Gender Identity and International Human Rights Law: Contextualising the Yogyakarta Principles." Human Rights Law Review, vol. 8, no. 2, 2020, pp. 207–248.** This article discusses the development and global influence of the Yogyakarta Principles as a legal framework for LGBTQ+ rights.

67. **ILGA Europe. Rainbow Map and Index 2024: Rising Resistance and Regression. ILGA-Europe, 2024.** A regularly updated index ranking European countries based on LGBTQ+ rights, documenting progress and regression.

68. **Human Rights Watch. "You Don't Want to Breathe the Air Here": Toxicity and Discrimination in LGBTQ+ Lives Worldwide. 2021.** A powerful report documenting the lived experiences of LGBTQ+ individuals facing discrimination and violence across the globe.

69. **Peterson, Sarah. The Wealth Divide: Exploring Financial Inequality in the LGBTQ+ Community. Journal of LGBTQ+ Economic Inequality, 2021.** A foundational analysis of the wealth gap in queer communities, this article highlights how systemic discrimination intersects with income inequality across race, gender identity and sexual orientation.

70. **Edwards, Jessica. The Financial Burden of Gender-Affirming Care: Challenges in Access and Affordability. Journal of LGBTQ+ Health Economics, 2021.** This work provides crucial insights into the high cost of gender-affirming care, outlining both direct medical expenses and structural barriers that impact trans and non-binary individuals financially.

71. **Stevens, Robert. Financial Discrimination: How LGBTQ+ People Face Barriers in Credit, Loans and Banking Systems. Journal of LGBTQ+ Economic Inequality, 2021.** A comprehensive look into institutional discrimination in financial services, this study explores how LGBTQ+ individuals are disproportionately denied fair access to credit and banking.

72. **Harper, Karen. Planning for the Future: Retirement Strategies for LGBTQ+ Individuals. Journal of LGBTQ+ Financial Security, 2021.** This article addresses the unique retirement planning challenges LGBTQ+ people face, particularly in the absence of family support or inclusive financial advising.

73. **Alvarez, Jose. Unequal Treatment: The Financial Disadvantages of Same-Sex Couples in an Incomplete System. Journal of LGBTQ+ Rights and Financial Justice, 2021.** A detailed examination of how same-sex households experience systemic economic inequality, even in countries with formal legal recognition of LGBTQ+ relationships.

74. **Cruz, Maria. The Hidden Costs of Queer Identity: Economic Marginalization in LGBTQ+ Communities. Journal of Economic Inequality and Gender Studies, 2021.** This work highlights the intersectional financial challenges LGBTQ+ individuals face, including the "invisible costs" of discrimination in housing, employment and healthcare access.

75. **Hunter, Simone. Queer Identities and Sex Work: Breaking the Stigma. Journal of LGBTQ+ Studies, 2021.** This article challenges prevalent stereotypes and provides a nuanced exploration of queer identities within sex work, advocating for the dismantling of stigma and offering insights into the lived experiences of queer sex workers.

76. **Green, Eliza. Legal Injustice: The Unique Challenges Faced by Queer Sex Workers. Journal of LGBTQ+ Law and Policy, 2021.** A comprehensive examination of the legal barriers and systemic discrimination queer sex workers face, highlighting the intersection of law, social justice and LGBTQ+ advocacy.

77. **Carter, Natalie. Sex Work and Gender Affirmation: Exploring the Intersection. Journal of Transgender Studies, 2021.** This article explores how sex work serves as a form of gender affirmation for some transgender and non-binary individuals, framing it as a tool for personal empowerment and identity exploration.

78. **Turner, Ella. Destigmatizing Queer Sex Work: Challenging the Narrative. Journal of LGBTQ+ Studies and Social Change, 2021.** A critical approach to the stigma that surrounds queer sex work, advocating for a paradigm shift in how society views both the sex work industry and LGBTQ+ involvement in it.

79. **Harris, Jacob. The Digital Landscape: How Online Platforms Are Shaping LGBTQ+ Sex Work. Journal of Digital Communities and LGBTQ+ Studies, 2021.** Focuses on the impact of online platforms and digital spaces in the evolving dynamics of LGBTQ+ sex work, emphasizing both the opportunities and challenges brought by digital technologies.

80. **Davis, Richard. Legal Protection and Social Stigma: The Double Burden on Queer Sex Workers. LGBTQ+ Justice Journal, 2021.** A deep dive into the compounded legal and social struggles that queer sex workers face, discussing both the systemic discrimination in the legal system and the pervasive social stigma that reinforces marginalization.

81. **Sullivan, Deborah (2021). Queer Love and Attachment: Psychological Perspectives on Emotional Bonding and Attraction. Journal of LGBTQ+ Psychology.** This foundational piece offers a comprehensive psychological framework for understanding queer emotional bonds

82. **Stone, Rachel (2020). Neurobiology of Sexual Orientation and Gender Identity:** A Scientific Exploration. Journal of Neuropsychology and LGBTQ+ Identity. A landmark study that anchors essential insight into how neurobiology contributes to identity formation.

83. **Tucker, Matthew (2021). The Gay Gene: What Does Science Really Tell Us About Biological Determinism in Sexual Orientation? Journal of LGBTQ+ Genetics and Behaviour.** A balanced and well-cited reference central to the debates both scientific findings and their misinterpretations.

84. **King, Ashley (2021). The Role of Hormones in Sexual Attraction and LGBTQ+ Relationships:** A Scientific Approach. Journal of Endocrinology and Sexual Behaviour. A robust, empirically grounded study on hormonal influences in queer relationships.

85. **Hart, Daniel (2021). The Psychology of Polyamory: Understanding Non-Traditional Relationship Dynamics.** Journal of Psychology and Relationship Science. Offering psychological clarity and academic legitimacy to queer polyamorous structures.

86. **Johnson, Laura (2021). The Neurological Basis of Gender Identity and Sexual Orientation:** An Overview of Current Research. Journal of Neuroscience and Gender Studies. Complements Stone's work by providing a broader synthesis of recent neurological findings relevant to both gender and orientation.

87. **Yergeau, M. (2018). Authoring Autism: On Rhetoric and Neurological Queerness. Duke University Press.** A foundational text in neuroqueer theory that critically explores the intersection of autism and queer identity through rhetoric, embodiment and resistance.

88. **Walker, N. (2014). Neuroqueer:** An Introduction. Published online in various neurodiversity forums and foundational in coining and developing the concept of neuroqueer identity.

89. **Botha, M., & Frost, D. M. (2020). Extending the Minority Stress Model to Understand Mental Health Problems Experienced by Autistic People. Society and Mental Health, 10(1), 20–34.** Offers intersectional insights into how societal stressors affect autistic individuals, including LGBTQ+ people.

90. **Jones, L. E., & Gill, L. (2022). Queer and Neurodivergent: Understanding the Lived Experiences of LGBTQ+ Autistic Individuals. Journal of Autism and Developmental Disorders, 52(3), 1452–1465.** Provides empirical research into how neurodivergent and queer identities intersect and affect well-being, relationships and self-understanding.

91. **Davidson, J. (2008). Autistic Culture Online: Virtual Communication and Cultural Expression on the Spectrum. Social & Cultural Geography, 9(7), 791–806.** Explores how neurodivergent individuals, particularly autistic people, construct community and identity, useful in exploring queer digital belonging.

92. **Strang, J. F., et al. (2018). Gender Dysphoria and Autism Spectrum Disorder: A Systematic Review of the Literature. Journal of Autism and Developmental Disorders, 48(12), 4070–4083.** Offers scientific insight into the higher prevalence of gender diversity among autistic individuals.

93. **Brown, Taylor N.T., & Herman, Jody L. (2015). Intimate Partner Violence and Sexual Abuse Among LGBT People.** This comprehensive report from the Williams Institute reviews 42 studies on intimate partner violence (IPV) and sexual abuse within LGBTQ+ communities, highlighting prevalence rates and barriers to seeking help.

94. **Bornstein, I. (2006). Recognizing and Addressing Intimate Partner Violence in Relationships of LGBTQ People: A Primer for Health Centers.** This primer addresses the lack of language and frameworks available to LGBTQ+ individuals to describe and understand abusive relationships, emphasizing the need for inclusive support systems.

95. **Vasquez, Celia. (2017). 'Who's Going to Believe Me?'-Why It's So Hard to Talk About Domestic Abuse in LGBTQ Relationships.** This article delves into personal narratives of abuse survivors in LGBTQ+ relationships, discussing the unique challenges they face in seeking support due to societal misconceptions and lack of recognition.

96. **National Coalition of Anti-Violence Programs (NCAVP). Domestic Violence in Same-Sex Relationships.** This resource provides statistics and insights into the prevalence of domestic violence in same-sex relationships, shedding light on the often-overlooked issue within LGBTQ+ communities.

97. **Galop. (2021). LGBT+ People's Experiences of Domestic Abuse.** This report from the UK-based charity Galop presents findings on the experiences of LGBTQ+ individuals with domestic abuse, highlighting the need for specialized services and support mechanisms.

98. **Human Rights Campaign (HRC). Understanding Intimate Partner Violence in the LGBTQ+ Community.** This resource offers an overview of IPV in LGBTQ+ relationships, discussing the forms it can take and the importance of recognizing and addressing abuse in all its manifestations.

99. **National LGBTQIA+ Health Education Center (2018). Providing Care to LGBTQ+ People Experiencing Intimate Partner Violence.** Offers clinical insights into IPV in LGBTQ+ relationships and strategies for trauma-informed care.

100. **Carroll, L., & Gilroy, P. (2002). Love hurts: The experience of same-sex partner abuse. Journal of Gay & Lesbian Social Services, 14(1), 95–112.** Highlights the psychological aftermath of abuse and the importance of affirming community support in recovery.

101. **Guadalupe-Diaz, X. (2019). Transgressed: Intimate Partner Violence in Transgender Lives.** Explores IPV and healing among transgender individuals, including community care and systemic barriers to recovery.

102. **West, C. M. (2002). Color Complex: Race, Gender and Domestic Violence in the Queer Community.** Analyses the intersection of racial identity and queer survivorship, including cultural healing practices and shame recovery.

103. **Kulkin, H. S., Williams, J., Borne, H. F., de la Bretonne, D., & Laurendine, J. (2007). A Review of Research on Violence in Same-Gender Couples: A Resource for Clinicians. Journal of Homosexuality, 53(4), 71–87.** Provides data on emotional harm, shame and recovery, emphasizing the role of therapeutic and chosen family support.

104. **Calton, J. M., Cattaneo, L. B., & Gebhard, K. T. (2016). Barriers to Help Seeking for Lesbian, Gay, Bisexual, Transgender and Queer Survivors of Intimate Partner Violence. Trauma, Violence, & Abuse, 17(5), 585–600.** Discusses institutional barriers, internalized blame, and alternative healing timelines within LGBTQ+ communities.

105. **Jones, Laura (2019). Healing the Spirit: LGBTQ+ Experiences of Reclaiming Faith After Religious Trauma.** Journal of LGBTQ+ Spirituality and Healing. A foundational reference for religious trauma and faith reclamation in LGBTQ+ lives.

106. **Clark, Eleanor (2021). Queering the Divine: LGBTQ+-Centered Spiritual Practices and Rituals.** Spirituality and LGBTQ+ Identity Journal. Central to understanding how queer folks create and embody spiritual practices outside heteronormative traditions.

107. **Delgado, Talia (2020). Two-Spirit, One Soul: Understanding the Intersection of Indigenous Spirituality and LGBTQ+ Identities.** Journal of Indigenous and Queer Studies. Critical for including Indigenous knowledge systems and the Two-Spirit experience in the spiritual landscape.

108. **Fraser, James (2020). Atheism and Agnosticism in LGBTQ+ Communities: Spirituality Beyond Religion. Journal of Queer Atheism and Spirituality.** Expands the scope by validating queer spirituality outside traditional religious frameworks.

109. **Parker, Isabella (2021). Mysticism and the Queer Spirit: Exploring the Transformative Power of Mystical Practices for LGBTQ+ Individuals.** Journal of Queer Mysticism and Spirituality. Bridges the mystical with the queer, offering a transcendent perspective often overlooked in mainstream discourse.

110. **Williams, Gary (2019). Faith, Identity and Recovery: How LGBTQ+ People Reclaim Their Spirituality After Trauma.** Journal of Religion and LGBTQ+ Studies. Adds scholarly depth on the intersection of recovery and faith in LGBTQ+ identity development.

111. **Ferguson, Kimberly (2021). A History of Queer Fashion:** How Style Codes Became a Language of Resistance and Expression. LGBTQ+ Cultural Studies Journal. Comprehensive historical insight into queer-coded fashion as cultural resistance.

112. **Parker, Jacqueline (2021). Fashion as Protest:** How Queer Individuals Use Fashion to Resist Social Norms. Journal of Queer Fashion and Political Expression. Directly ties fashion to political resistance, central to the chapter's theme.

113. **Taylor, Marcus (2019). From Gender Norms to Personal Expression:** How Queer People Use Fashion to Challenge Societal Expectations. LGBTQ+ Style Studies. Bridges identity formation with societal critique, relevant across all subheadings.

114. **Miller, Olivia (2021). Gender Expression as a Political Tool:** LGBTQ+ Activism Through Fashion and Style. Journal of Gender, Identity, and Social Change. Focuses on activism and the intersection of fashion with political identity.

115. **Morris, Dakota (2021). Breaking the Code:** Dress Codes, Uniforms and the Struggles of Queer Expression. Journal of Queer Rights and Fashion. Unique focus on institutional control via dress codes, offers legal and social insight.

116. **Morales, Elena (2020). Clothing as a Tool for Queer Empowerment:** How Style Shapes Identity and Resistance. Queer Fashion Journal. Centres empowerment and resistance, excellent for grounding the chapter's emotional and political stakes.

117. **Muñoz, José Esteban (1999). Disidentifications:** Queers of Colour and the Performance of Politics. Deeply relevant to drag as resistance and identity play.

118. **Newton, Esther (1972). Mother Camp:** Female Impersonators in America. A classic ethnographic study that explores camp, drag personas and the theatricality of gender.

119. **Halberstam, Jack (2005). In a Queer Time and Place:** Transgender Bodies, Subcultural Lives. Brings drag into conversation with temporality, rebellion and queer aesthetics.

120. **Hooks, Bell (1994). Outlaw Culture: Resisting Representations.** Discusses subversive identity politics, the spectacle of performance and liberation through cultural critique.

121. **Sontag, Susan (1964). Notes on "Camp".** A cornerstone in understanding camp as an aesthetic and philosophical mode.

122. **King, Sarah (2020). Laughter as Liberation: How Comedy Helps Queer People Cope with Discrimination.** Explores how humor helps queer people survive oppression, offering a foundational view on comedy as resilience.

123. **Williams, Anne (2021). From Stereotypes to Nuanced Narratives: The Evolution of LGBTQ+ Humor in Media.** Traces the shift in LGBTQ+ humor in media, providing insight into how humor has evolved from reinforcement of stereotypes to a nuanced tool for empowerment.

124. **Evans, Catherine (2021). Satire as Resistance: The Role of Queer Humor in Political Protest.** Explores how queer humor and satire serve as acts of resistance.

125. **Lee, Vanessa (2021). The Cost of Laughter: Self-Deprecation and the Risk of Internalized Homophobia in Queer Comedy.** Examines the fine line between empowering humor and harmful self-deprecation.

126. **Fitzgerald, Sophia (2021). The Art of Drag: Using Humor and Exaggeration to Challenge Gender Norms.** Focuses on how humor in drag challenges gender norms.

127. **Reyes, Adrian (2021). Queer Satire: Using Humor as a Tool for Political Protest and Social Change.** Highlights the use of satire and humor in queer political movements, key for exploring humor as resistance and activism.

128. **Noble, S. U. (2018). Algorithms of Oppression: How Search Engines Reinforce Racism.** NYU Press. A key work exploring how AI algorithms perpetuate societal biases, including heteronormativity, in digital platforms, crucial for the bias and invisibility of queer identities in the digital space.

129. **Binns, R. (2018). The Ethics of Artificial Intelligence: A Theoretical and Practical Perspective.** Springer. This foundational work on AI ethics addresses the limitations of AI in understanding complex human identities, including fluid and queer identities, making it critical for discussing AI's failure to grasp fluidity.

130. **Zeng, J., & Zeng, Z. (2020). The Role of AI in Digital Gender Identity Construction: Ethical Considerations. AI & Society, 35(3), 487-498.** Explores the ethical implications of AI-generated gender identities, offering essential insights into whether AI can authentically represent queer identities or risk commodifying them.

131. **Gillespie, T. (2018). Custodians of the Internet: Platforms, Content Moderation and the Hidden Decisions That Shape Social Media.** Yale University Press. A critical resource for understanding how AI and content moderation algorithms influence queer activism, potentially amplifying or suppressing marginalized voices.

132. **Boellstorff, T. (2008). Coming of Age in Second Life: An Anthropologist Explores the Virtually Human.** Princeton University Press. Provides key insights into how virtual worlds allow for alternative gender expressions, directly relevant to discussions on the future of digital gender identity in virtual realities.

133. **Morozov, E. (2013). To Save Everything, Click Here: The Folly of Technological Solutionism.** PublicAffairs.
A critical examination of the dangers of unregulated AI, including its potential to stifle queer activism, offering a cautionary perspective on the risks of AI's influence on marginalized communities.

134. **Hughes, Eleanor (2020). Breaking Barriers: Systemic Bias and Discrimination Against Queer Individuals in STEM Fields.** Journal of LGBTQ+ and Gender Studies in STEM. This foundational article delves into the systemic barriers and discrimination faced by queer individuals in STEM fields, setting the stage for understanding the challenges in these industries.

135. **Lopez, Marco (2020). Surviving the Corporate World: The Challenges of Being an Out Queer Employee.** Journal of LGBTQ+ Workplace Experiences. Provides critical insights into the lived experiences of queer employees in corporate settings, addressing the challenges of navigating professional spaces authentically.

136. **Singh, Kiran (2021). Pioneers of Change: How LGBTQ+ Innovators Have Transformed the STEM and Corporate Worlds.** Journal of Queer Innovation in Tech. Highlights the contributions of LGBTQ+ innovators to both STEM and corporate industries, offering valuable examples of how queer thinkers drive change and innovation.

137. **Foster, Rachel (2020). The Power of Representation: Why LGBTQ+ Leaders Are Essential for Corporate Growth and Equality.** Journal of LGBTQ+ Leadership and Representation. Explores the importance of LGBTQ+ representation in leadership roles, a key topic for understanding the impact of queer individuals in corporate leadership and innovation.

138. **Baker, Melissa (2020). Facing Discrimination: Legal Challenges and Disparities for Queer Employees in the Workplace.** Journal of Labor Rights and LGBTQ+ Advocacy. This reference provides a comprehensive overview of the legal challenges queer employees face, an essential part of understanding workplace discrimination and the need for legal protections.

139. **Johnson, James (2021). Leading the Way: How LGBTQ+ Representation in Leadership Drives Workplace Inclusion and Innovation.** Journal of Queer Leadership in Corporate Settings. Offers an in-depth analysis of how LGBTQ+ leadership fosters workplace inclusion and drives innovation, directly tying into discussions of leadership in corporate and STEM environments.

140. **Blake, Avery (2020). The Emotional Cost of Being the Only Queer Person in Traditional Spaces: A Psychological Perspective.** Journal of LGBTQ+ Mental Health and Workplace Dynamics. This article provides an in-depth exploration of the mental health costs associated with being the only queer person in family or workplace environments, a central theme of the chapter.

141. **Fletcher, Ethan (2020). Bearing the Weight of Representation: The Emotional Burden on Queer Individuals in Small Communities.** Journal of LGBTQ+ Community Studies. Focuses on the emotional challenges of being the sole queer representative in small communities, emphasizing the isolation and pressure to represent the entire queer identity.

142. **Harris, Maya (2021). Building Connections in Isolation: How to Find Support as a Queer Individual in New or Conservative Spaces.**

Journal of LGBTQ+ Support Networks. Provides practical strategies for queer individuals navigating isolation and building support systems in unfamiliar or conservative spaces, essential for overcoming the "only" experience.

143. **Adams, David (2021). Breaking the Silence: The Importance of Family Conversations in Promoting Queer Acceptance Across Generations.** Journal of Queer History and Family Dynamics. Explores the importance of breaking generational cycles of silence and fostering acceptance of queer identities, a key aspect of transforming family dynamics and supporting "firsts."

144. **Robinson, Kelly (2021). The Mental Toll of Pioneering Queer Identity: Understanding the Long-Term Psychological Effects of Being a "First".** Journal of Queer Mental Health and Trauma. This reference delves into the long-term psychological toll faced by individuals who pioneer queer identities in various spaces, directly addressing the mental health challenges of being a queer "trailblazer."

145. **Martinez, Alina (2020). The Unseen Burden: Psychological Challenges Faced by "Firsts" in Queer Communities.** Journal of Social and Psychological Studies of Queer Individuals. This article examines the complex psychological challenges faced by queer "firsts" in diverse environments, shedding light on the emotional burden and resilience required.

146. **Gomez, Carmen (2020). Love in the Shadows: Surviving Queer Relationships in Oppressive Regimes.** Journal of LGBTQ+ Rights and Survival in Authoritarian States. This article explores how queer individuals navigate love in oppressive regimes where their relationships are criminalized, offering insight into the hidden nature of queer love in repressive environments.

147. **Taylor, Janet (2020). The Resilience of Love: Queer Resistance and Survival Stories from Conflict Zones.** Journal of LGBTQ+ Voices in War. Focuses on the resilience of queer love amid conflict zones, showcasing how queer individuals maintain relationships and survive in environments of war and strife.

148. **Jafari, Zaynab (2021). Underground Networks of Resistance: How Queer People Build Community and Safety in Conflict Zones.** Journal of LGBTQ+ Activism in War. Provides an in-depth look at the underground networks that queer people build to protect and support each other in conflict zones, offering a unique perspective on queer survival strategies.

149. **Martinez, Ana (2020). Love in War: The Psychological Impact of Conflict on Queer Identity and Relationships.** Journal of LGBTQ+ Mental Health in Crisis. Explores the psychological impact of living through war and conflict on queer identities and relationships, shedding light on the emotional toll of these experiences.

150. **Kassim, Noor (2021). Fleeing War and Persecution: The Struggles of LGBTQ+ Refugees in Conflict Zones.** Journal of Refugee Studies and LGBTQ+ Rights. Examines the struggles faced by LGBTQ+ refugees fleeing conflict zones, including the intersecting challenges of war, persecution and the fight for safety.

151. **Hassan, Lina (2020). Resistance Through Love: Queer People in Conflict Zones and the Power of Survival.** Journal of LGBTQ+ Liberation in Crisis.
Highlights the power of love and resilience among queer individuals in conflict zones, emphasising how love becomes a form of resistance in the face of adversity.

152. **Brown, Lena (2021). Climate Refugees: The Unique Vulnerabilities of Queer People in Environmental Displacement.** Journal of LGBTQ+ Rights and Migration. Focuses on the unique vulnerabilities of queer individuals displaced by environmental crises, offering insight into how climate change impacts LGBTQ+ populations specifically.

153.**Garcia, Sophia (2021). The Role of Queer Activism in the Climate Justice Movement.** Journal of LGBTQ+ Political Activism and Climate Change. Explores the role that queer activism plays within the broader climate justice movement, highlighting LGBTQ+ voices in advocating for environmental change.

154.**Nguyen, Minh (2021). LGBTQ+ Safe Spaces and Climate Change: Adapting to a New World.** Journal of LGBTQ+ Rights and Environmental Adaptation. Discusses the challenges climate change poses to LGBTQ+ safe spaces and how these communities must adapt to ensure continued safety and solidarity in a shifting climate.

155.**King, Robert (2021). Climate-Induced Economic Hardships: The Disproportionate Impact on LGBTQ+ Communities.** Journal of Economic Justice and LGBTQ+ Rights. Investigates how climate-induced economic hardships disproportionately affect LGBTQ+ communities, particularly in terms of financial instability and resource access.

156.**Rodriguez, Carlos (2020). Reimagining LGBTQ+ Safe Spaces in a Climate-Changed World.** Journal of Social Justice and Queer Safe Spaces. Offers insights into how LGBTQ+ safe spaces must be reimagined in response to climate change, considering the physical, emotional and environmental challenges ahead.

157.**Ahmed, Sara (2010). The Promise of Happiness.** Critiques how happiness is tied to heteronormative ideals and how queer joy subverts these expectations.

158.**Cvetkovich, Ann (2003). An Archive of Feelings:** Trauma, Sexuality and Lesbian Public Cultures. Discusses queer joy as emotional survival and resistance within lesbian communities.

159.**Halberstam, Judith (2011). The Queer Art of Failure.** Argues that queer joy emerges from rejecting conventional success and societal norms.

160.**Duggan, Lisa (2002). The Twilight of Equality?: Neoliberalism, Cultural Politics and the Attack on Democracy.** Examines how queer joy resists neoliberalism and heteronormative systems that marginalize LGBTQ+ lives.

161.**Spade, Dean (2011). Normal Life: Administrative Violence, Critical Trans Politics and the Limits of Law.** Explores how legal and social systems limit transgender self-expression and identity, focusing on pronouns and belonging.

162.**Stryker, Susan (2008). Transgender History: The Roots of Today's Revolution.** Provides a comprehensive history of transgender issues, addressing how pronouns and identity markers evolve over time.

163.**Bailey, Moya (2019). Misplaced: Transgender Identity and the Power of Pronouns.** Examines the relationship between pronouns, gender identity and the social dynamics of belonging.

164.**Henderson, Adam (2020). Belonging in Transition: Navigating Identity and Community as a Non-Binary Individual.** Discusses how non-binary individuals experience identity crises and the search for belonging through pronouns and self-discovery.

165. **Ettner, Randi (2016). Transgender Medicine and the Intersection of Identity, Healthcare and Belonging.** Focuses on the intersection of medical and social frameworks in shaping how transgender individuals navigate pronouns and their identity journey.

166. **Davis, Olivia (2022). The Evolution of Gender and Sexuality: How Social, Technological and Cultural Changes Will Shape Identities in the Future.** Explores how changing social, technological, and cultural landscapes will redefine gender and sexuality in the future.

167. **Chavez, Roberto (2021). Globalization's Influence on Queer Identity and Activism: Shaping the Future of LGBTQ+ Communities Worldwide.** Examines how globalization influences queer identity, activism and relationships in a rapidly changing world.

168. **Roberts, Harrison (2021). Queer Futures in Science Fiction: How Speculative Fiction Shapes Our Vision of Queer Possibilities.** Investigates how science fiction and speculative fiction envision the future of queer identities and relationships.

169. **Miller, Zoe (2022). Redefining Love in a Post-Binary World: Philosophical and Sociological Perspectives on Non-Binary Relationships.** Analyses how love and relationships are redefined in a post-binary world, focusing on non-binary perspectives.

170. **Keller, Jordan (2023). Post-Queer Society: Imagining a Future Where Queerness is No Longer a Distinct Category.** Explores the concept of a post-queer society, imagining a world where queerness no longer functions as a distinct identity.

171. **Singh, Amit (2022). Gender and Sexuality in 2100: Predictions and Possibilities for the Future of LGBTQ+ Identities.** Provides predictions on the future evolution of gender and sexuality, exploring possibilities for LGBTQ+ identities in the next century.

www.ingramcontent.com/pod-product-compliance
Lightning Source LLC
LaVergne TN
LVHW081942200926
848484LV00009B/2497
9781037077128